The Business Environment

Phil Kelly and Andrew Ashwin

CENGAGE
Learning®

Australia · Brazil · Japan · Korea · Mexico · Singapore · Spain · United Kingdom · United States

**The Business Environment,
1st Edition**
Phil Kelly and Andrew Ashwin

Publishing Director: Linden Harris

Publisher: Andrew Ashwin

Development Editor: Charlotte Green

Production Editor: Alison Cooke

Production Controller: Eyvett Davis

Marketing Manager: Anne Renton

Typesetter: Integra, India

Cover design: Adam Renvoize

For product information and technology assistance,
contact **emea.info@cengage.com.**

For permission to use material from this text or product,
and for permission queries,
email **emea.permissions@cengage.com.**

British Library Cataloguing-in-Publication Data
A catalogue record for this book is available from the British Library.

ISBN: 978-1-4080-3016-5

Cengage Learning EMEA
Cheriton House, North Way, Andover, Hampshire, SP10 5BE
United Kingdom

Cengage Learning products are represented in Canada by Nelson Education Ltd.

For your lifelong learning solutions, visit **www.cengage.co.uk**

Purchase your next print book, e-book or e-chapter at
www.cengagebrain.com

Printed in China by RR Donnelley
1 2 3 4 5 6 7 8 9 10 – 15 14 13

BRIEF CONTENTS

TABLE OF CONTENTS

PART FOUR
Markets 275

PREFACE

ABOUT THIS BOOK

The original plans for this book were made in 2009 and since that time the business world has undergone significant changes. New challenges have arisen along with some familiar old ones that seem to re-occur on a regular, if unpredictable, basis. For students new to Business Environment courses, the challenge facing the authors was to provide an introduction to its different elements and not to assume a great deal of prior knowledge about any aspect of the subject area. Courses in the Business Environment tend to cover a wide range of subject matter which includes features typically found in Business and in Economics degrees. Students must understand not only what business is about but how business activity is affected by the wider environment and how the economic system works within which businesses operate. Many courses in Business Environment will split teaching along particular lines, dealing with the wider business environment through the PESTLE framework but also requiring students to understand how businesses work and how the economy as a whole works.

AIMS OF THE BOOK

This book is an ambitious project. It is ambitious because the subject matter, the Business Environment, is extensive. The authors recognize that students reading this book will have a varied amount of prior knowledge which they bring to the subject. Some of this knowledge will have been gained through following business studies or economics courses at school and college, other knowledge will have been gained through interaction with the business world either through working or through being a consumer. Whilst some of the knowledge gained will have been formal, much knowledge is informal and likely to be taken for granted. Most students know far more about business and the business environment than they either realize or are given credit for. The difference between the prior knowledge brought to a course and a formal course of study of the subject is that the latter seeks to break down what is a complex subject, involving complex processes and relationships, and try and make it understandable.

The book will break down both businesses and their environments into their constituent parts. It will attempt to explain each of these constituent parts but it must always be borne in mind that a business and its environment do not operate as isolated parts like the chapters of a book. There will rarely be times when one factor acts upon a business whilst all others are stable (the principle of ceteris paribus); many different factors act upon an organization at the same time. We will look at these factors as discrete topics (as individual topics in their own right). They will include standard classifications of the factors as political influences, environmental, legal, social, economic, technological, ecological and so on. The business, however, can rarely afford to treat these factors as discrete and must recognize and deal with the way they all interact together.

The way in which businesses recognize and deal with these factors will vary from business to business and so the outcome in each case is also likely to be different. There are rarely any 'right' answers to questions in business so do not expect to either look for them or be able to learn them. Each business situation is different and each business environment impacts to a greater or lesser extent. Your goal, therefore, should be to learn how to think about the subject matter, to understand behaviours and present solutions supported by careful analysis of the key factors which affect the issue you are examining. Others may arrive at different conclusions to the one/s you arrive at – that is fine and perfectly acceptable. Ultimately the success of decision-making is judged by the balance between the costs and benefits arising out of the decision; there will always be some costs and benefits with any decision. For most businesses the challenge is maximizing the benefits and minimizing the costs. This book aims to highlight this approach and recognize the complexity of the business environment.

To gain full benefit from your studies (and make yourself a more marketable individual in the process) it is important that (as a minimum) you learn the content of this book but also look to make connections between the theory in this book and what you see and experience in the outside world. You should look to question what you see, hear and read, to help build a better understanding of the complexities of the subject matter. This might even extend to developing a healthy cynicism of things that go on around you! Such an approach may bring you into conflict with conventional wisdom but may help you arrive at more independent conclusions and develop critical analysis and evaluation skills. The ability to transfer your understanding and deal with unfamiliar situations and contexts is a characteristic of deep learning.

This book also attempts to cover issues from an international perspective. Few business organizations are isolated from the global economy and factors such as the environment, ecology and the economy affect businesses wherever they are and in many different ways. Throughout the book, therefore, we make use of examples and case studies that highlight the international nature of business and the importance of emerging economies.

STRUCTURE AND FORMAT

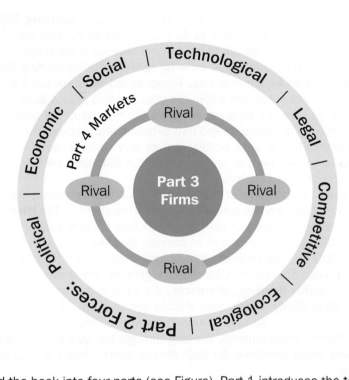

We have divided the book into four parts (see Figure). Part 1 introduces the topic and explains key approaches to help you tackle learning of the subject area. Part 2 covers the PESTLE framework. Some courses may look at this framework after they have covered basic information about how firms operate, others may discuss the framework first. Part 3 looks at how firms operate and Part 4 workings of the markets. Parts 3 and 4 include key theories which must be understood to help make better sense of the PESTLE framework. So, whilst the book is in different sectors the intention is that these parts work together to provide a synergy such that the sum of the parts is greater than the individual sectors. Each chapter is self-contained but helps build understanding when read in conjunction with other chapters – much the same as a lecture programme at university will do.

KEY FEATURES

Each Chapter has a particular format. It starts with a list of **Learning Objectives** to help you understand what you should be able to do having worked through the chapter. A **Mind Map** provides a diagrammatic representation of the content covered in the chapter. Each chapter covers a number of concepts and to help focus on what these are a list of **Key Concepts** is provided. Chapters have **Business in Action** features. These boxed features provide a short case study, highlighting a relevant point contained within the text. There is also a **Business in Debate** feature which profiles a controversial or topical issue relevant to the chapter to help with appreciation that there are no 'right answers' in business and that different perspectives must be taken into account when making decisions. This is also a likely feature of your assessment – you will make judgements and in doing so you will have to provide support. A **Summary** section provides a bulleted list of the key points raised in the chapter.

Revision Questions are provided at the close of each chapter which you should complete to ensure you have understood the key content covered in the chapter. The **Discussion Questions** are designed for progression in terms of your approach and understanding. Your lecturer may use these questions as the basis for a tutorial or seminar following a lecture or you may work through them yourself (or both) to improve your higher order skills. These include the ability to analyze, synthesize and evaluate, to present a balanced argument and arrive at supported judgements. Suggested titles for **Further Reading** (references) are cited in the chapters. These are followed by an **End of Chapter Case Study**. These case studies aim to place the content of the chapter into a context which requires some developed understanding of the issues facing real businesses operating within different environments. Working through the questions linked to the case study will help you prepare more effectively for your assessments. They will also help you to translate theory into practice.

ACKNOWLEDGEMENTS

We would like to thank the Editorial team at Cengage Learning especially Linden Harris, the Publishing Director for her support, encouragement and excellent advice throughout, to Charlotte Green, Development Editor at Cengage who provided fantastic support and dedication to see the book through to publication, Felix Rowe, the Editorial Assistant for his attention to detail and creativity, Lucy Arthy for all the production work and Anne Renton for doing a sterling job as support for Amanda Cheung in the Marketing team.

REVIEWERS

The publisher would like to thank the following academics who supplied feedback on the original proposal and during the writing process:

- Steven McCabe, Birmingham City University
- Steve Millard, Bucks New University
- Sajjad Jasimuddin, Aberystwyth University
- Pat Britten, University of Buckingham
- Jane Harte, University of Aberdeen
- Jan Bamford, London Metropolitan University
- Frank Martin, University of Stirling
- Stuart Challinor, Newcastle University
- Rob Thomas, University of Portsmouth
- Nick Perdikis, Aberystwyth University
- Charles Caplen, Solent University
- Carol Avery, Solent University

The publisher also thanks the various copyright holders for granting permission to reproduce material throughout the text. Every effort has been made to trace all copyright holders, but if anything has been inadvertently overlooked, the Publisher will be pleased to make the necessary arrangements at the first opportunity (please contact the publisher directly).

AUTHORS

Phil Kelly, formerly advisor to Asia's highest paid CEO, worked for over 20 companies in almost as many countries prior to appointment as Senior Lecturer at Liverpool Business School. Having completed his Doctorate in Business Administration, at one of Europe's leading Business Schools, he went on to establish himself in academia, teaching at a range of universities. An experienced lecturer, he has an MA (distinction) in Teaching and Learning in Higher Education, and frequently teaches on a range of business courses. In 2012 Phil's students nominated him for an Amazing Teacher Award. In addition, after being nominated by the Liverpool Business School, he received the University Award for outstanding impact on the student learning experience. Phil has written several books, including *Management: Theory and Practice 7e* with Gerald Cole and *International Business and Management*, both of which were published with Cengage. His books are popular texts on a range of business degree programmes. Phil lives on the Wirral with his wife Rebecca and three sons Toby, Jacob and Ben.

Andrew Ashwin has over twenty years' experience as a teacher and author across all levels of education. His speciality lies within assessment having been a former Chair of Examiners for a major awarding body in the UK for Business and Economics, a Fellow of the Chartered Institute of Educational Assessors and a consultant for regulatory bodies. Andrew has written texts on business and economics across different levels including A-level and undergraduate economics texts and had articles published as a result of his PhD research. This research is looking at assessment and the notion of threshold concepts in economics. He is the Editor of *Teaching Business and Economics*, the journal of the Economics, Business and Enterprise Association (EBEA) and lives in Rutland with his wife, Sue and twin sons Alex and Johnny.

WALK-THROUGH TOUR

Part Openers provide an overview of the book structure and introduce the following chapters.

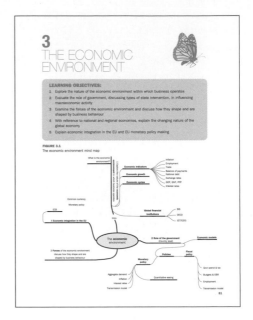

Learning Objectives help you understand what you should be able to do having worked through the chapter. Each chapter covers a number of concepts and to help focus on what these are a list of **Key Concepts** is provided.

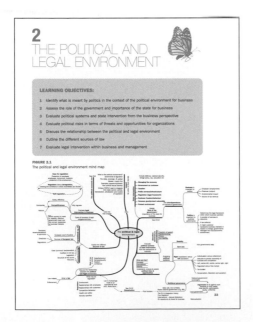

Chapter Mind Map provides a diagrammatic representation of the content covered in the chapter.

Business in Action provides a short case study, highlighting a relevant point contained within the text.

Business in Debate profiles a controversial or topical issue relevant to the chapter to help with appreciation that there are no 'right answers' in business and that different perspectives must be taken into account when making decisions.

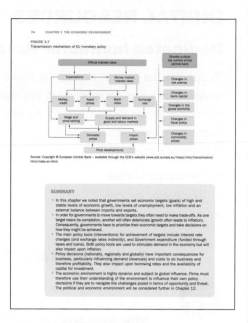

Summary provides a bulleted list of the key points raised in the chapter.

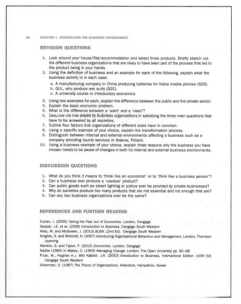

End-of-Chapter Revision provided at the close of each chapter, which you should complete to ensure you have understood the key content covered in the chapter. **Discussion Questions** are designed for progression in terms of your approach and understanding.

Chapter Case Study provided at the end of each chapter, aims to place the content of the chapter into a context which requires some developed understanding of the issues facing real businesses operating within different environments.

DIGITAL RESOURCES

Dedicated Instructor Resources

To discover the dedicated instructor online
support resources accompanying this textbook,
instructors should register here for access:
http://login.cengage.com
Resources include:

- Instructor's Manual
- ExamView Testbank
- PowerPoint slides

Online Student Resources

Instructor access

Instructors can access the online student resources by registering at
http://login.cengage.com or by speaking to their local
Cengage Learning EMEA representative.

Instructor resources

Instructors can use the integrated Engagement Tracker to track students' preparation and
engagement. The tracking tool can be used to monitor progress of the class as a whole, or for
individual students.

Student access

Students can access the online platform using the unique personal access card included in the front
of the book.

Student resources

A range of interactive learning tools tailored to the *The Business Environment* are available on the
online platform, including:

- Interactive eBook
- A range of self-test questions
- Case studies and questions
- Podcasts with tasks and questions
- Games and quizzes
- Glossary
- Links to useful websites
- Flashcards and more

PART ONE
INTRODUCTION

PART ONE
INTRODUCTION

1
INTRODUCING THE BUSINESS ENVIRONMENT

CHAPTER 1 INTRODUCING THE BUSINESS ENVIRONMENT

FIGURE 1.1

Introducing the business environment mind map

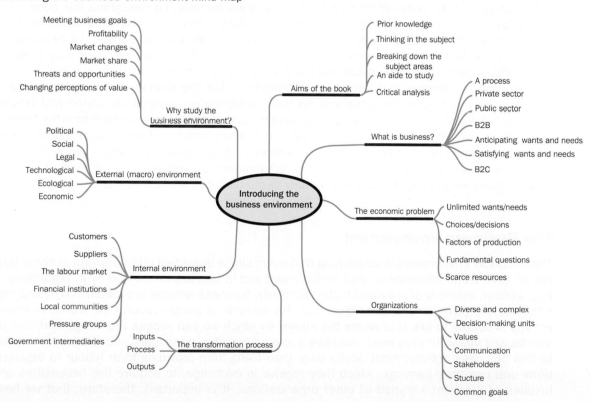

KEY CONCEPTS

Business | Organization | Private sector | Public sector | The transformation process | Public goods | Economic problem | Internal environment | External environment | Opportunity | Threat

INTRODUCTION

This chapter outlines the scope of the book and certain issues that will be explored in more detail in later chapters. It will look at fundamental issues that have to be understood prior to getting involved in deeper study of the business environment – the totality of factors, internal and external, which may influence the organization's achievement of its goals, see Figure 1.1.

Many of you will be reading this book in an attempt to become better, well informed managers. Yet management thinking and action like the firm, organization or business entity does not function in a vacuum; it has to act and react to what happens outside the situation it finds itself in. Factors outside the organization are known as external factors or influences (sometimes referred to as forces or business drivers). These will affect the main internal functions of the business and the business objectives and strategies. The business environment is divided into the external and internal environment. The internal environment consists of all resources and capabilities found within the organization which influence the organization's ability to act (to create outputs). The analysis of the business environment allows the organization and its employees to understand the context within which they operate and strategy is developed and implemented. It is important to note, however, that environments are not static but constantly changing. Thus, understanding the global business environment and its economic, social and political influences is crucial to success in today's international business world. The external environment is complex and its future uncertain yet managers must attempt to make sense of it if they are to identify opportunities and threats and respond appropriately. Through an understanding of the environment the organization can compete and fulfil customer needs more effectively and efficiently. Various models exist to help managers make sense of their environment and will be reviewed throughout this book.

In this chapter we start by asking what business is. We will then introduce a little economics into the discussion to look at the nature of, and how organizations exist to satisfy, the fundamental economic problem that all societies have to answer. We will look at the basic way in which organizations take a variety of inputs and process them into outputs – the transformation process. This process is common to all business organizations but the diverse and complex nature of organizations means that the influences on this transformation process are varied and present significant challenges. These influences can be both internal and external and will form the basis of much of the focus of this book. The internal and external environments facing a business impact on the transformation process and necessitate business making constant changes and decisions. It is for this reason that studying the business environment is important and we shall offer some initial explanations of key reasons why a study of the business environment is of importance.

The Business Environment

The business environment is something that every single individual interacts with in some way. We all have some influence on that environment and in turn are influenced by it, regardless of age, gender, ethnicity or any other factor. Similarly, business entities are influenced by and may influence the environment, see Figure 1.2. For millions of people around the world, business activity is central to life. It provides the means by which we can access the things that help us survive and enjoy our daily lives. We have a role as provider, participant and receiver in relation to this business activity; most adults earn their living from providing their labour to organizations and use their earnings, which they receive in exchange, to acquire the necessities and luxuries of life from a myriad of other organizations. It is important, therefore, that we have

FIGURE 1.2
Business environment influence

Environment

Firm
behaviour

Environment

some understanding of this environment, the various roles we play in it (worker, consumer, producer, owner, customer, etc.) and how it affects our daily lives.

The average daily routine of any human is testament to this interaction. For those in the developed world, the interaction may appear to be mundane and is often taken for granted; journeys to college or work via car or public transport, working in a business organization of some description, selling labour in return for financial remuneration which in turn is used to purchase the goods and services needed to survive and thrive and so on. A large part of the average working person's day is involved with a wide range of business organizations. Food and drink are taken in at regular intervals during the day and we invariably travel to a home which contains a wide variety of goods produced by business organizations and which is also covered by numerous business services such as insurance, banking services and so on. The evening may be spent watching TV produced by an increasing range of business organizations around the world, partaking in some form of entertainment either in the home or outside at specialist providers and entertainment produced by a host of business organizations. At night we clean our teeth using manual or electronic toothbrushes produced by businesses, climb into beds made by others, wrap ourselves in bed covers again produced by businesses and finally switch off the electricity powering the bedroom light that was also produced by a business. The following morning the alarm goes off (probably produced in a factory in the Far East) and we start all over again!

In less developed countries and the emerging world the range of goods and services may be far more limited but a daily routine still exists. For some it may involve long treks to secure vital water supplies in pots that are primarily hand-made or tending to animals and land that may just about, if lucky, provide for the basic needs of life. In emerging economies work may involve long hours for low pay but provide an opportunity to be able to access some additional 'luxuries' that help the family go beyond access to the basics of life. Some in the developing world receive help from agencies either in the form of financial assistance from global institutions, from non-governmental organizations (NGOs) such as the Fairtrade foundation or charities, and others in the form of direct assistance for food and health care which may mean the difference between life and death.

WHAT IS BUSINESS?

Whatever the interaction we have with business organizations it goes without saying that it is essential to have some understanding of what business actually is to provide the foundation for understanding the business environment. A simple definition of business would state that it is a process whereby someone or some organization identifies a good or service (hereafter collectively referred to as 'product') that they can provide and which others are willing to pay for. In general the cost of providing the product has to at least be covered by the price the buyer is willing to pay in order to make the business sustainable.

The decision to provide products might be taken by private individuals with the intention of securing a profit. In some cases it is not possible to provide for needs and wants through private business operations and so the state has to step in to provide for those needs. The extent to which the state can produce products as efficiently and effectively and at what cost is a consideration for those involved in public provision since the stakeholder involvement in such organizations is much wider and more immediate than simply the owners/shareholders.

Private Sector and Public Sector Activity

Most economies, therefore, have two sectors, a private sector and a public sector. The private sector is where business activity is undertaken by organizations which are owned, controlled and financed by private individuals (either individually or as part of groups or other businesses). The private sector is able to produce products that it can charge consumers for the privilege of using. Consumers use these products in different ways to gain some element of satisfaction from their consumption. A crucial point to note, however, is that consumers can prevent others from sharing in that satisfaction if they so choose. An individual buying a cup of coffee in a café in Paris gains the satisfaction from drinking that coffee – a satisfaction that cannot be shared for that same drink by anyone else. An Austrian house owner taking out insurance on a property does not share the benefits of that insurance with any other property owner directly. Goods which share this characteristic are said to be mutually exclusive in consumption – the benefit of their consumption can be restricted to those who paid for them.

Other products are difficult if not impossible to provide in this way. The oft cited examples of street lighting, justice and defence are good examples of such goods. It is difficult to limit the benefits of street lighting, for example, to one person who may choose to pay for it. If a street light is placed directly outside someone's house who is then asked to pay for it, other road users will also benefit – even though they have not had to pay to do so. It would be almost impossible to imagine a situation where individuals would be prepared to pay for national defence – once a defence system is in place everyone benefits regardless of whether they have paid for it or not.

These products are called public goods. They have the characteristics of being non-rival and non-excludable. This means that consumption by one person does not reduce the amount available to another and it is not, therefore, possible to prevent an individual consuming it even though they have not paid for it.

Because of these characteristics, the provision of public goods is made by the state on behalf of everyone. Provision of such products is part of the public sector. The public sector is all business activity which is owned, controlled and financed by the state on behalf of the community as a whole. Different countries place different emphases on the private and public sectors. In the US, the state is responsible for approximately 35 per cent of GDP; in the UK it accounts for around 40 per cent; in Europe it is approximately 47 per cent, in Japan around 37 per cent and in Brazil it is over 40 per cent.[1]

Behind a simple definition of business, however, lies a very complex set of relationships and transactions. These are affected by many factors both internal and external to the business. The behaviour of businesses is influenced to a greater or lesser extent by these factors and as a result we have a myriad of different business models and types that reflect the increasing complexity of life in the 21st century. The definition given above is, therefore, blurred by the way in which business has developed. A business organization is no longer simply one which seeks to engage in business to make profit. The definition of business as a process where a transaction takes place in some form or another is now a more accurate representation of what business does.

[1] http://www.wds.worldbank.org/servlet/WDSContentServer/IW3P/IB/2007/03/20/000020439_20070320092306/Rendered/PDF/365951BR0v2.pdf; and http://129.3.20.41/eps/pe/papers/0507/0507011.pdf

The output produced by a business may be sold to a final consumer (B2C) or to another business organization (B2B). Increasingly the output of business organizations in the developed world is not tangible products but consists of information or knowledge. For example, companies such as Price Waterhouse Cooper (PWC), Excelsoft and Experian all sell knowledge services and information. PWC is a leading firm of accountants providing a range of financial services including auditing, tax and investment advice, analysis and reports and administration and receivership services. Excelsoft are an Indian company specializing in software solutions and Experian provide a range of business services including fraud prevention, debt recovery and collection, payment processing, market research and credit checks.

In addition, the distinction between public and private sector organizations is becoming increasingly blurred as public sector organizations adopt processes and strategies that may have previously been associated with the private sector. The emphasis on generating revenue, keeping costs under control and producing profits (surpluses) is something that has traditionally been associated with the private sector but in the last 20 years the accountability and efficiency of public sector organizations have led to them setting targets (or being set targets), introducing challenging performance goals, appraisal systems and motivational techniques that borrow much from private sector tradition.

THE ECONOMIC PROBLEM

To understand the fundamentals of business, it is necessary to engage in some elementary economics for a moment. The classic definition of economics as given by Lionel Robbins in 1932 is 'the science which studies human behaviour as a relationship between ends and scarce means which have alternative uses'.[2] In his essay, Robbins rejects economics as merely a study of material welfare.

This definition and assumption about what economics is, is important in any discussion of business because business activity is one of the ways in which the relationship between ends and scarce means is resolved. Business is now seen as being more than merely the purveyor of the satisfaction of material welfare (although much business might still be categorized in such a way).

Business is inextricably linked with the fundamental economic problem and the way in which the basic questions of economics are answered. The fundamental problem of economics alluded to by Robbins is the tension between wants and needs on the one hand and the availability of resources to satisfy these needs on the other. These resources are generally classified under the headings of land, labour and capital.

- Land refers to all the natural resources of the earth
- Labour is all the human effort, both mental and physical, in production
- Capital to anything that is not used for its own sake but which contributes to production. Capital is not simply money in economics; it refers to buildings, machines, equipment and so on, that are used to contribute to production.

In relation to wants and needs, these resources are scarce. Humans have a wide range of wants and needs; in some cases these needs will be necessary to sustain life such as food, clothing and shelter. A need might also relate to an individual who has to have certain types of health care treatment in order to survive, such as medication to treat leukaemia or kidney dialysis.

Wants are classed differently. Wants generally refer to things we would like to have rather than things that are essential to life. Wanting to spend a day at Wild Wadi in Dubai might be something that brings great pleasure, as might wanting to go and see the Eiffel Tower, but if we did not have those wants satisfied we would only be marginally worse off.

---

[2]Robbins, L. (1945). *An essay on the nature and significance of economic science (2nd Ed)*. London, Macmillan. Available as a PDF file from http://www.mises.org/books/robbinsessay2.pdf

Over the last few years businesses have found many ways to both create wants and to anticipate and identify wants and have not been slow in meeting these. Products exist which, if looked at carefully, serve very little useful purpose at all yet they are often produced in large quantities and are purchased with enthusiasm. Products such as highlighting pens, decorative desk holders for mobile phones, bracelets, toilet roll dispensers and any amount of merchandise from sports clubs, movies and TV programmes are examples of products that have limited intrinsic value – we could do without most of these products! Millions of homes across the developed world are crammed with products that might contribute to making life slightly easier or to satisfy our demand for entertainment. In purchasing these products we have either been convinced by businesses or have given an indication to businesses that we 'need' such items and businesses have duly supplied them. For the most part, our everyday existence and routine does not depend on these types of products but we 'want' them anyway.

The conclusion to this discussion is that human wants and needs are limitless, infinite. Even billionaires have wants and needs and can find some way to spend their money. The incidence of professional footballers spending tens of thousands of pounds in night clubs on champagne is testament to the fact that whatever our level of wealth we can generally find ways to spend what we have.

The Three Questions Every Economy has to Answer

To produce products, either to satisfy a want or a need, requires resources. Given the almost limitless demand for products around the globe the amount of resources available to meet that demand is simply not enough. That means decisions have to be made about how to use these resources, which have (often) many alternative uses, to meet these needs. In any society (and by extension the world as a whole) there are three basic questions that economics pose:

* What is to be produced?
* How are the products to be produced?
* Who will get what is produced?

The simplicity of these questions belies the important issues that they raise. In a developed economy the question of what is to be produced is normally decided through the workings of the market and through provision by the state. The second question may be determined either by the state allocating funds for the production of the products such as education, justice, defence, health and so on or by businesses constantly looking at ways in which they produce and how their costs behave as a result of the production they carry out. As a general rule business will seek to combine resources used in as efficient a way as possible. If resources can be combined in more efficient ways then business will generally try to do so.

Who gets what is produced is determined by the amount of money that individuals have to be able to exchange for products. A combination of a variety of factors will affect this including the skills that people possess in relation to the demand for that skill, how effectively they work, discrimination, where they work, what they own and inheritance, amongst others. Individuals use their incomes to be able to buy the things they want and need; the more income an individual has the greater the amount of wants and needs they can satisfy.

In less developed economies the questions remain but may be answered in different ways. What is produced may be determined by the desire for survival more than anything else. Production may be focused on the provision of the basics for life – food, clothing and shelter. How products are produced may be constrained significantly by the lack of capital available and much production may be dominated by manual labour. Who gets what is produced may not depend as much on income levels as how successful crop harvest and animal husbandry is. Large swathes of land in some countries yield very little by way of food crops and the people who live in these places barely eke out a living.

ORGANIZATIONS

Whilst individuals are heavily involved in each of these questions it is collections of individuals who are responsible for much of the production and consumption that goes on every day around the world. We refer to these collections of individuals as organizations. Knights and Wilmott (2007) define organizations as:

> A concept used by both practitioners (e.g. managers) and analysts (e.g. academics) to make meaningful and also to organize, the activities and interactions of people who are conceived to be doing organizational work such as being engaged in creating, developing and distributing products or services[3]

This definition helps to broaden the scope of a common perception of an organization in a business context of being simply a 'firm'. Instead it incorporates organizations that not only operate in the private sector but also those that operate in the public sector. The diversity of organizations and the extent to which they touch all our lives needs to be borne in mind throughout any study of the business environment. The complexity of organizations means we have to find ways of breaking them down in order to better understand how they work.

In breaking them down we can identify systems, processes, relationships, groups, teams, individuals, leadership and management processes and styles, rules and regulations, functional groups and departments and many other features. The way that business organizations combined all these features to work in the past and the present is no guide to whether they will operate in a similar way in the future. For example, the principle of open source software development has been adopted by a company producing a hydrogen powered car called the Reversible. We might, in addition, seek to categorize business organizations by size, scale, type of product, type of market, ownership, finance, labour force, legal status and so on.

Organizations provide the answers to the questions that characterize the economic problem that is faced by every society in some way or another. They make decisions about what to produce and how to produce and these decisions play a large part in determining who gets what is produced. These organizations, however, vary in the way they operate and in the aims and objectives they have in carrying out business activity. Some exist to carry out business activity to generate profit, others want to make profits but use those profits in different ways than return them to the owners of the business. Such organizations are referred to as social enterprises. Others are set up by governments in order to provide products that might not be available otherwise or to monitor and regulate the activities of other businesses. Whilst business organizations operate to satisfy wants and needs the reasons for doing so may be very different, therefore.

Most business organizations share a range of other common features:

* The individuals within them have common/shared goals
* They have a structure in which individuals have different roles and functions – often shared between a group of individuals
* The organization tends to have particular values
* It has decision-making structures
* It has ways of disseminating and communicating information and decision-making
* There are a variety of stakeholders who have an interest in the organization and how it operates
* These stakeholders are affected by decisions made by the organization and the operations of the business. In addition, they have an influence on the way the organization operates.

THE TRANSFORMATION PROCESS

Business organizations have another thing in common, the way they operate. Business organizations take various resources and use them to produce products that satisfy a need – they are involved in transformation. The resources they use are referred to as inputs and the products that

---

[3]Knights, D and Wilmott, H. (2007). *Introducing Organizational Behaviour and Management*. London, Cengage.

FIGURE 1.3

The transformation process

Organizations take various inputs – generically classed as land, labour and capital, combine them to produce goods and services which are the outputs of the transformation process. These outputs are sold to other organizations and individuals.

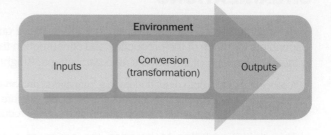

result from the transformation are called outputs. Whatever the type of business organization, this activity is carried out in some form or another. In some cases the activity is relatively simple and in others highly complex, see Figure 1.3.

The transformation process aims to produce products that generate sufficient revenue to enable resources to be replenished so that further transformation can be carried out. This relies to a large extent on the organization adding value during the transformation process so that the price consumers or customers are prepared to pay is greater than the cost of the bought in inputs and the payment for the risk of organizing these inputs.

Such a principle is increasingly applied not only to private sector activity but also to that in the public sector. Some private sector organizations such as social enterprises and charities may use the profit or surplus generated by the process in a different way to that of other private sector organizations and some public sector organizations may look to manage the transformation process to at least cover the costs involved of production.

BUSINESS IN ACTION

The Transformation Process at Intel

Intel is a business organization that produces computer processors – computer chips – that are found in millions of computers and devices that use computers to operate, across the globe. Intel is based in California but has plants and offices in many different countries including Costa Rica, the United States, Ireland, Israel, China, Malaysia and the Philippines. The 18 manufacturing plants that it has across the world have an interesting thing in common – they are all identical. Intel calls it *Copy Exactly!* Every building configuration, every process, every piece of equipment in every plant is exactly the same. What this means is that if any sort of disruption is caused to production in one plant, production can be switched to another easily. If demand for a particular product rises and production bottlenecks occur additional capacity can be brought on line easily ensuring that delivery from multiple production sites can be utilized to meet customer needs. It also means that if a process is improved at its development site then that process can be copied directly to every other plant thus increasing productivity and efficiency. Quality

and reliability of its products can be assured throughout its manufacturing plants

Chip manufacture is highly complex and relies on sterile conditions. Intel plants are amongst the cleanest places on the planet. A minute speck of dust or dirt can cause manufacture and thousands of dollars of production time and product to be wasted. Work carried out at its development site is copied exactly to its manufacturing sites. Each plant is encouraged to work towards a constant improvement in its operations. Intel states that it gives the responsibility and authority to local plants to:

- Identify and record problems and corrective actions
- Initiate and provide solutions and improvements
- Verify implementation of solutions
- Control nonconforming products until deficiencies are corrected
- Initiate actions to prevent nonconformities
- Share information and best-known methods across the geographically-dispersed organizations

Source: Compiled from content on http://www.intel.com/technology/manufacturing/index.htm?iid=subhdr+tech_mfg. Reproduced with permission

The basic transformation process, however, is influenced by a range of factors. These factors are constantly changing not only in their nature but in their relative importance in the process. Some of these factors arise from within the organization itself such as human relationships and personnel changes, the availability and use of finance, the relationship with suppliers and customers and so on. Other factors affect the process which is largely out of the control of the business itself such as legal, economic and social change.

The production of a computer chip for a processor that is used in a Dell computer is highly complex as described by Yossi Sheffi in his book 'The Resilient Enterprise'[4]. Sheffi shows how production starts with outsourced manufacture of silicon in Japan, the resulting wafers are flown back to the United States to be processed in plants in Arizona and Oregon, flown back to assembly and test operations centres in Malaysia, sent back to Arizona and the finished products shipped to factories in Texas, Ireland, Brazil, Malaysia, Taiwan and China where they are installed in computers being manufactured in those locations. From there the chips will make their way to hundreds of different countries, housed in computers bought by customers of those countries.

Such a complex manufacturing and distribution process involves and is affected by internal and external business environments.

INTERNAL AND EXTERNAL BUSINESS ENVIRONMENTS

Businesses therefore, have to operate both in an internal environment and an external one, see Figure 1.4. These two environments are not mutually exclusive and issues that affect the internal environment not only affect decision-making on issues that the business takes internally but also these decisions will feedback to effects on the external environment. Other businesses will also be affected by these decisions and in turn make their own internal and external decisions based on these changes. The result is that business behaviour is affected by the complex web of these decisions. The effects and affects act to create a dynamic business environment in which multiple factors influence decision-making and behaviour.

FIGURE 1.4

The transformation process with internal and external factors

Figure 1.4 represents the various pressures acting on organizations from both within and without. Internal factors influence the transformation process such as the type and motivation of employees, and the aims of owners and managers, whilst external factors heavily influence that same process.

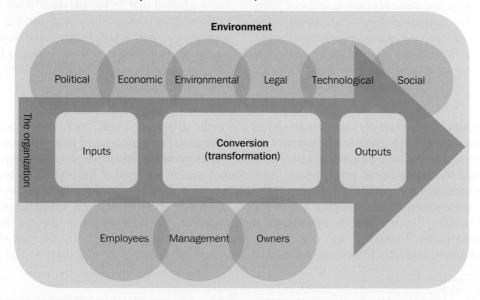

---

[4]Sheffi, Y. (2007). *The Resilient Enterprise: overcoming vulnerability for competitive advantage*. Cambridge, Massachusetts, MIT Press.

BUSINESS IN DEBATE

Controlling the Environment

The role of business has been under increasing scrutiny in recent years. The responsibility of businesses has extended far further than simply to those who own them. It is now widely acknowledged that businesses do need to take account of wider stakeholder groups and individuals in decision-making and behaviour. Whilst business has some control over its own actions, increasingly those actions may be frustrated or compromised by the way in which business is now carried out.

Business does not operate within a vacuum, it has to operate in an environment where there are laws and regulations as well as external economic, technical, social, and political pressures. Many large businesses are global operators and have to adapt their business practice to take account of different cultures and different laws in the countries they operate in. The perception of a business is often seen from that of a developed country but in reality many businesses operate in countries where different cultural norms and rules exist which may not be understood in other parts of the world which deal with these businesses.

The clothing retailer, Primark, for example, uses suppliers to provide the range of clothing that it sells, many of these items are manufactured in factories and backstreet producers in countries where poverty is a way of life to many. Some would argue that Primark and others like it, help to provide investment into these countries which the countries use to improve living standards. From a developed world perspective paying workers 5 cents an hour is exploitation; others might point out that 5 cents per hour is better than nothing and may mean the difference between feeding a family

and starvation. In the UK in 2008 a BBC investigation into factories in southern India found children employed making garments for companies sub-contracted to Primark. The BBC informed Primark who announced that it had broken its relationship with three suppliers in southern India. The company said that only a tiny fraction (0.04 per cent) of the goods affected were sourced from these factories and that the actions by the suppliers in instituting home working and employing child labour was not sanctioned or condoned by Primark. The company also announced that it would set up meetings with its suppliers to 'reinforce the stringent trading standards it expects and to emphasize that it will not tolerate this type of sub-contracting'. It also said that it was appointing a non-governmental organization (NGO) to 'act as its eyes and ears on the ground' and to report any unauthorized sub-contracting by its suppliers. This raises the issue of whether any multi-national company can fully control its external business environment.

In Malaysia one of the problems facing business is corruption. A prominent human rights campaigner and lawyer, Tunku Abdul Aziz, wrote a blog for Malaysia Today[5] lamenting the corruption in Malaysia. Aziz noted how the country has an excellent legal framework, rules regulations and procedures but that this was being constrained by the prevalence of corruption. The view that corruption is a malaise in the country is also supported by reports from the World Bank. Studies by that institution suggested that standards in four out of six categories of good governance had fallen since 2003 in a report published in 2009.[6] Aziz suggested that 'In the globalized world in which we operate with its own set of demanding rules of engagement, with emphasis on transparency and accountability, we have to learn quickly to be adaptable or we will be marginalized'.[7]

Inputs come from and are influenced by the external environment. They enter a business and become part of the internal environment of the business. Once processed they are then sold into a different but related external environment. The environment, therefore, can be seen as all the factors that have some effect, direct and indirect and in increasing degrees of importance and significance, on the ability of the organization to carry out its operations effectively. In order to try and understand these complex environments we break them down into individual areas under the heading 'immediate or operational environments', sometimes also referred to as micro environments. These include customers, suppliers, competitors, the labour market, financial institutions, local communities, pressure groups and government intermediaries. The other main

---

[5]https://mt.m2day.org/2008/content/view/23926/84/
[6]Governance Matters VIII: Aggregate and Individual Governance Indicators, 1996-2008 http://papers.ssrn.com/sol3/papers.cfm?abstract_id= 1424591www.themalaysianinsider.com/index.php/malaysia/30914-world-bank-says-malaysias-governance-worsened-in-last-five-years
[7]http://mt.m2day.org/2008/content/view/24235/84/

area is the general contextual environment sometimes referred to as the macro environment. This includes political, social, legal, economic, technological and ecological environments.

These two examples highlight some of the issues that face businesses in operating in a global business environment, but many of the same operational and external issues exist for businesses which simply operate at a more local, regional or national level. Part of the problem is in placing some value on the different perspectives that exist. Did Primark respond in the way it did because it was genuinely concerned about the fact that its operational procedures had been broken? To what extent do Primark's customers know or care about where the clothes they buy come from provided the price is right? What do those who work for suppliers for developed world businesses think or know about their 'plight'? Can governments ever be effective enough in policing the activities of business organizations to ensure that they operate to internationally recognized standards (whatever that means)? Is the fact that corruption still exists in countries like Malaysia testament to the fact that no matter how effective the external legal framework, political and social pressures will often circumvent this environment. Is corruption simply another form of business enterprise? Are we ever right to view an issue from our own perspective?

WHY STUDY THE BUSINESS ENVIRONMENT?

Business organizations must constantly monitor both internal and external environments to adjust the transformation process to ensure that it meets the aims and objectives laid down by the business and customer needs. These aims and objectives will relate to both the organization's internal and external stakeholders, see Figure 1.5.

Failure to study the business environment can mean that the organization experiences a decline either in its profitability or in its effectiveness and meeting needs which may be the case with organizations in the public sector. For example, In August 2009, the broadcaster ITV sold the social

FIGURE 1.5

Internal and external stakeholders of a business

An organization's internal stakeholders are those which are directly associated with the business – its employees, managers and owners while the external stakeholders are indirectly affected by the business such as suppliers, customers, the local community, government and the environment.

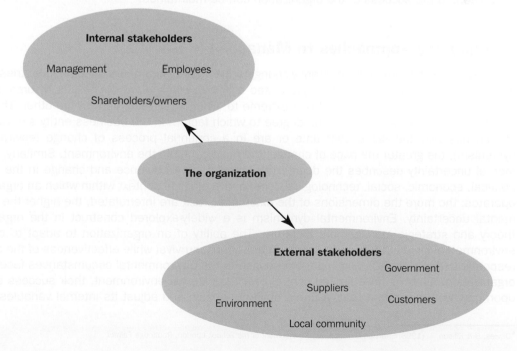

networking site Friends Reunited to a publisher, D C Thomson, for £25 million. In December 2005 ITV paid £175 million for it; the fall in value of the asset was largely seen as due to the fact that its revenue model, based on fees, was outdated, it had served its purpose and had been superseded by other more sophisticated social networking sites that better met the needs of customers.

Failure to monitor and understand the business environment can lead to loss of market share, loss of first mover advantage, reputation, sales and profits. The business world is full of examples where the changing environment has led to the failure or loss of many organizations including the high street value store Woolworths in the UK. The changes in media and news access through the Internet and the availability of free newspapers have affected a number of established titles such as the *Boston Globe* and the *Tucson Citizen* in the US and the *London Evening Standard* in the UK and *Ora gia Spor,* in Greece. In 2009, Rupert Murdoch announced that the News International Group planned to charge users for accessing its news services amidst headlines that the era of 'free' news had come to an end.

The changing business environment also provides opportunities; emerging markets in China, India, Brazil and Eastern Europe are providing new opportunities for existing and new businesses. Part of the skill in spotting opportunities is to have an understanding of how the changing environment affects perceptions of value. What consumers see as value added today is not likely to be the same as perceptions in 5, 10 and 20 years' time. Business organizations may do well to indulge in some 'futures thinking'. Futures thinking is not a wish list or an attempt to predict the future, but is an attempt to think through possible trends and directions in the future, and allows an organization to put itself on the boundary between stability and instability.[8] Such thinking may enable the business to attempt to identify areas which may warrant investment but also to identify where growth is declining and where products with potential might need a helping hand.

Market analysts invariably look ahead rather than dwell on the present or the past. Past performance is no indicator or guarantee of future performance. The skill in assessing the possibilities and potential of the future is aided by informed judgement and risk assessment as well as being able to critically analyze and evaluate issues, situations and topics. Organizations will not only search for opportunity but will also seek to identify threats – circumstances with the potential to cause loss or harm and may hinder goal achievement – within the external and internal environment.

Both for the organization and for the student, therefore, the skills required and the importance of studying the business environment are in being able to anticipate and identify changes that impact on a business organization and be able to see how individual changes in the environment are interrelated and are interdependent. In having such an understanding decision-making can be improved and the success of the organization can be maintained.

Contingency Approaches to Management

The business environment is constantly changing. Yet the environments of some industries change more than others. Emery and Trist presented a typology describing four kinds of organizational environment from placid (static) at one extreme to dynamic and turbulent at the other. The static-dynamic dimension is viewed as the degree to which factors in the business entity's environment remain basically the same over time or are in a continual process of change (environmental dynamism); the greater the pace of change, the more dynamic the environment. Similarly, environmental uncertainty describes the degree of unpredictable turbulence and change in the external political, economic, social, technological, legal and ecological context within which an organization operates; the more the dimensions of the external context are interrelated, the higher the environmental uncertainty. Environmental dynamism is a widely-explored construct in the organization theory and strategic management literature. The ability of an organization to adapt to changing environmental circumstances is a key to organizational survival while effectiveness of the adaptive response is dependent on aligning the response to the environmental circumstances faced by the organization. As firms have limited control over the external environment, their success depends upon how well they adapt to it. A firm's ability to design and adjust its internal variables to take

[8]Davies, B & Ellison, L. (1998) *Strategic Direction and Development of the School.* London, Routledge Falmer

advantage of opportunities offered by the external environment, and its ability to control threats posed by the same environment, help determine its success.

Having briefly considered both the external (macro and micro) and internal business environment we now further explore the relationship, drawing on contingency theory, between the two. Managers study the environment to enable their organizations to be more effective and efficient. There are many ways for managers to organize the firm and many strategies to follow. However, there is no single best way of doing things and there is widespread acceptance that the best way to organize is based upon (contingent) the situation. Strategic 'fit' (alignment) is about matching the internal (resources, capabilities and transformational activities) with the needs and demands of the external environment. If the external environment is constantly changing, then the internal environment needs to be flexible. Contingency theories have been applied to strategy, structure, culture, leadership, management styles and capabilities. Environmental determinism is a contingency perspective which claims that internal organizational responses are wholly or mainly shaped, influenced or determined by external environmental factors. Nadler (1980) discussed different ways of thinking and the views held about organizations, starting with systems views where organizations are seen as 'composed of interdependent parts' where 'change in one element of the system will result in changes in other parts of the system'. Nadler points out that 'often changes in the environment necessitate organizational change. For example, factors related to competition, technology, or regulation, shift and thus necessitate changes in organizational strategy'. Nadler argues that incongruent organizations are ineffective organizations. The contingency approach to management (also called the situational approach) assumes there is no universal answer to many organizational problems because organizations, people, the environment and situations vary and change over time. Thus, the right thing to do depends on a complex variety of critical environmental and internal contingencies. That is why you need to study the business environment in the chapters that follow.

SUMMARY

- In this chapter we have outlined the business environment, reviewed what business actually is and its relationship to the basic economic problem. The world has wants and needs that are infinite but the fact that we have scarce resources means that decisions have to be made about how these resources are used to answer the basic questions all societies have to answer. Business organizations are at the heart of this decision-making.

- Business organizations are varied in size and complexity. In order to understand them more easily we categorize them in different ways according to size, ownership, control, method of finance and location, amongst others. One of the key ways in which businesses are categorized is into public and private sector.

- The aims and objectives of businesses in both sectors differ but in essence they are all doing the same thing – taking in inputs and doing some sort of processing of these inputs to varying degrees to produce outputs. The outputs are designed to satisfy consumer needs. The consumer might be the final user or might be other business organizations.

- The transformation process is affected by many influences that exist both internal and external. Internal factors cover customers, operational issues, suppliers and resources whereas external factors include many which businesses do not have direct control over, including economic, technological, political and social factors.

- Businesses need to be aware of these changing factors to be able to maintain their position in markets, to take advantage of new opportunities and to improve the effectiveness and efficiency of their decision-making.

- The contingency approach to management (also called the situational approach) assumes there is no universal answer to many organizational problems because organizations, people, the environment and situations vary and change over time. Thus, the right thing to do depends on a complex variety of critical environmental and internal contingencies. Incongruent organizations are ineffective organizations.

REVISION QUESTIONS

1. Look around your house/flat/accommodation and select three products. Briefly sketch out the different business organizations that are likely to have been part of the process that led to the product being in your hands.
2. Using the definition of business and an example for each of the following, explain what the business activity is in each case:
   a. A manufacturing company in China producing batteries for Nokia mobile phones (B2B).
   b. GUL, who produce wet suits (B2C).
   c. A university course in introductory economics
3. Using two examples for each, explain the difference between the public and the private sector.
4. Explain the basic economic problem.
5. What is the difference between a 'want' and a 'need'?
6. Describe the role played by business organizations in satisfying the three main questions that have to be answered by all societies.
7. Outline four factors that organizations of different sizes have in common.
8. Using a specific example of your choice, explain the transformation process.
9. Distinguish between internal and external environments affecting a business such as a company providing tourist services in Krakow, Poland.
10. Using a business example of your choice, explain three reasons why the business you have chosen needs to be aware of changes in both its internal and external business environments.

DISCUSSION QUESTIONS

1. What do you think it means to 'think like an economist' or to 'think like a business person'?
2. Can a business ever produce a 'useless' product?
3. Can public goods such as street lighting or justice ever be provided by private businesses?
4. Why do societies produce too many products that are not essential and not enough that are?
5. Can any two business organizations ever be the same?

REFERENCES AND FURTHER READING

Curran, J. (2000) *Taking the Fear out of Economics*. London, Cengage

Gaspar, J.E. *et al.* (2006) *Introduction to Business.* Cengage South Western

Kelly, M. and McGowen, J. (2010) *BUSN.* (2nd Ed). Cengage South Western

Knights, D. and Willmott, H. (2007) *Introducing Organizational Behaviour and Management*. London, Thomson Learning

Mankiw, G. and Taylor, P. (2010) *Economics*. London, Cengage

Nadler (1980) in Mabey, C. (1993) *Managing Change.* London: The Open University pp. 85–98

Pride, W., Hughes R.J. and Kapoor, J.R. (2010) *Introduction to Business, International Edition.* (10th Ed) Cengage South Western

Silverman, D. (1987) *The Theory of Organizations.* Aldershot, Hampshire, Gower

GLOSSARY

Business A process whereby someone or some organization identifies a product that they can provide and which others are willing to pay for

Economic problem Scarcity, requiring the allocation of resources between competing wants or needs; the need to minimize resource use and the need to ensure equitable distribution

External environment Environmental forces, such as political, economic, social, technological, ecological, legal or competitive, that operate in the world outside the organization

Internal environment Anything which is internal to an organization, that is, within its boundary, including resources, structures and culture

Opportunities Occur where the external environment offers business the possibility of meeting or exceeding its targets

Organization A concept used by both practitioners (e.g. managers) and analysts (e.g. academics) to make meaningful and also to organize, the activities and interactions of people who are conceived to be doing organizational work such as being engaged in creating, developing and distributing products or services

Private sector Business activity organized, owned and controlled by private individuals

Public goods Goods which cannot be provided by the market because it is not possible to exclude those who do not pay for the goods from benefiting from them

Public sector Business activity organized, owned and controlled by the state on behalf of the public at large

The transformation process The process of taking factor inputs and transforming them into outputs for consumption by other organizations and individuals

Threat Circumstances with the potential to cause loss or harm and may hinder goal achievement

CHAPTER CASE STUDY

Most of Us are Broke ... Literally
America's Biggest Economic Problem?

By MARSHALL AUERBACK

My bills are all due and the baby needs shoes and I'm busted
Cotton is down to a quarter a pound, but I'm busted
I got a cow that went dry and a hen that won't lay
A big stack of bills that gets bigger each day
The county's gonna haul my belongings away cause I'm busted.

– Ray Charles

Almost half of US homeowners with a mortgage are likely to owe more than their properties are worth before the housing recession ends, Deutsche Bank AG estimates. The percentage of 'underwater' loans may rise to 48 per cent, or 25 million homes, as prices drop through the first quarter of 2011, Karen Weaver and Ying Shen, analysts in New York at Deutsche Bank, wrote in a report published August 6.

In December 2006, only a few months after the peak of the housing bull market, the total value of US residential property stood at $21.9 trillion. Prices have dropped by 31 per cent since the end of 2006, so the estimated value today is about $15 trillion; however, the mortgage debt remains more or less unchanged and stands at $10.6 trillion. In other words, whereas debt-to-equity in the US housing market was 48 per cent as recently as in December 2006, it is now 70 per cent and will rise to 80 per cent once house prices have mean-reverted.

Although painful, a rise in debt-to-equity of that magnitude would actually be manageable if it were not for the fact that income and wealth in the US is extremely skewed. The top 1 per cent of income earners in the US account for more than 20 per cent of national income while the median household has seen no improvement in income for the past ten years. Within the median household sector itself, then, there is still a tremendous financial vulnerability which has not been addressed at all by the Obama administration. Home ownership in the US is far greater than in most modern economies. Equity ownership is also high. The bursting of the real estate and equity bubbles has destroyed the wealth of the US middle class to a devastating degree. And it is with this middle class that the high private indebtedness lies. If there is going to be a further financial crisis in the US it is probably going to be focused on the household sector. If balance sheet recession dynamics are going to depress aggregate demand through wealth destruction and debt repayment, it is probably household sector demand where this will surface.

Almost one-third of all US households have no mortgage. If you adjust for that, the 70–80 per cent debt-to-equity ratio suddenly becomes a major challenge because it means that the two-thirds who do have a mortgage already face a debt-to-equity ratio in excess of 100 per cent. Even worse, once the mean reversion has run its course, two-thirds of US households will be facing a debt-to-equity ratio of 120–125 per cent on average. US consumers are effectively broke.

Obviously, households have assets and liabilities other than property and mortgages. But it's clear that the US consumer has been repeatedly on the losing end of the serial 'bubblelization' of the American economy. The collapse of the dot.com bubble and the more recent plunge in real estate means that the great majority of US households are more financially stressed now than at any time since the Great Depression. And yet policy has been largely directed toward 'solving' the 'problems' of the financial sector (where much of the country's existing wealth is concentrated), and only minimal efforts have been applied to solve the debt problems of households and non-financial businesses.

As the DB Securities report illustrates, households' ability to spend is a function of three factors – cash flow (which again is driven mainly by income, mortgage rates and tax), credit (bank lending) and homeowner equity (property prices). Now, with negative equity against their main asset, with even more pressure on income as a result of the recession and with virtually no savings to cushion the pain, the majority of US households have no choice but to cut back drastically on their consumption. And with the US consumer being forced to pull back, the global recovery story turns very pale indeed in the absence of sustained fiscal stimulus WHICH PUTS THE FOCUS ON AGGREGATE DEMAND, NOT BANK BALANCE SHEETS, as I have repeatedly argued.

The US economy is today crushed by massive household indebtedness. Maintenance of the status quo is not a solution. Administration proposals to relieve debt burdens by encouraging lenders to renegotiate mortgages have failed miserably. Personal income is falling at a terrifying rate. Already 6.5 million have lost their jobs – with June, alone, adding a half million job losses. The administration's promise that the stimulus package will create 3.5 million jobs over the next two years is unsatisfying in the face of the challenges faced. And yet we are told to 'be patient'.

We need federal government spending programs to provide jobs and incomes that will restore the creditworthiness of borrowers and the profitability of for-profit firms. We need a package of policies to relieve households of intolerable debt burdens. In addition, given that the current crisis was fuelled in part by a housing boom, we need to find a way to deal with the oversupply of houses that is devastating for communities left with vacancies that drive down real estate values while increasing social costs. And we've got to rein in the born-again deficit hawks who, having got their fill from the government's fiscal trough, have all of a sudden become preoccupied with 'paying for' additional spending through tax hikes or spending cuts elsewhere.

If home prices revert to their mean the average mortgage indebted American homeowner will have a deeply negative home equity. Given the paltry liquid wealth and 401K holdings (pension plans), most of such households may have no net worth at all. Under current US law widespread negative home equity could lead to mass debt repudiation as opposed to debt paydown, which could lead to an ever growing number of foreclosures which in turn could further weaker house prices. Because so much of the broad US middle class will have their personal net worth decimated, it might lead to a social and political crisis of sorts. Such a crisis could materialize sooner and more abruptly than is now appreciated in Washington. The brief populist anger felt in the wake of the AIG bonus payouts might be child's play compared to what is in store in the future.

Marshall Auerback is a market analyst and commentator. He is a brainstruster for the Franklin and Eleanor Roosevelt Institute. He can be reached at MAuer1959@aol.com

Source: http://www.counterpunch.org/auerback08112009.html

Reproduced with permission. With thanks to Marshall Auerback – Director of Pinetree Capital and a Fellow for the Economists for Peace and Security.

Questions

* What is the economic problem that is the focus of the article?
* Businesses providing mortgages and real estate agents are two businesses involved in the housing market. Analyze the impact on each of them of the changes in the business environment in 2008–2009.
* How might an economy 'deal with the oversupply of houses that is devastating for communities left with vacancies that drive down real estate values while increasing social costs'?
* Analyze why 'households' ability to spend is a function of three factors – cash flow (which again is driven mainly by income, mortgage rates and tax), credit (bank lending) and homeowner equity (property prices)'.
* How does this case study highlight the importance of business organizations and individuals being aware of the business environment?

PART TWO
THE
ENVIRONMENTS

The external environment is complex and its future uncertain yet managers must attempt to make sense of it if they are to identify opportunities and threats and respond appropriately. One of the first challenges is to recognise the multiplicity of factors within the external business environment and the second is to decompose it into manageable parts. Environmental variables are factors that affect the organization, but are beyond the direct or positive control of the organization. The external environment may be divided into layers. The macro environment is the wider environment of social, legal, economic, political and technological influences (forces). These are explained in Chapters 2-5. The macro environment contains the more general factors likely to affect organizations in a similar manner whereas, at the industry level, the factors are of more particular concern to a specific set of organizations. The micro environment is the immediate (industry) environment including customers, competitors, suppliers and distributors. These factors are considered within Chapter 6. One of the main factors affecting most organizations is the degree of competition faced. Greater influence is likely to come from the actions of competitors and the behaviour of customers or prospects. Markets change rapidly through the entrance of new competitors, technologies, legislation and evolving customer needs. Finally, we discuss the sustainable environment in Chapter 7.

Making sense of the macro environment poses a significant challenge. However, the diagnostic framework presented in this part of the book will help break the macro environment down into more manageable components which can then be investigated. PESTEL (see also PEST, SLEPT, STEP and PESTLE) analysis is a common technique for analyzing the general external environment of an organization in terms of the political, economic, socio-cultural, technological, environmental and legal aspects.

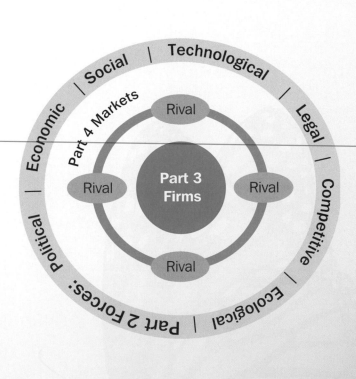

2
THE POLITICAL AND LEGAL ENVIRONMENT

FIGURE 2.1

The political and legal environment mind map

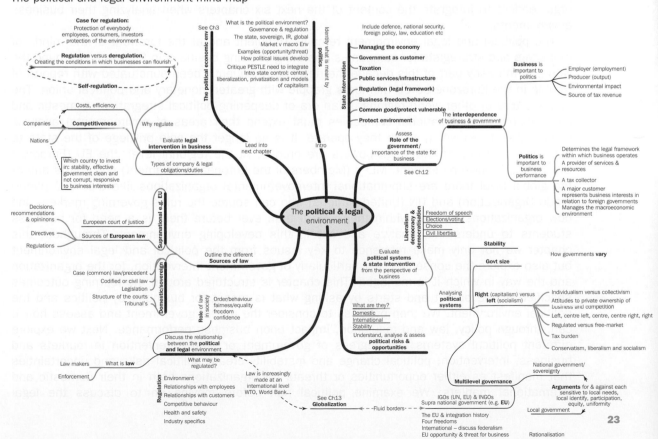

23

KEY CONCEPTS

Capitalism | Common good | Free market | Government | Law | Legal system | Liberalism | Political environment | Political system | State | Supranational governance

INTRODUCTION

In the opening chapter we outlined the internal and external business environment. A useful framework used to analyze the external environment decomposes that environment into factors such as Political, Economic, Social, Technological, Legal and Environmental – PESTLE, see Figure 2.1. These are factors of the wider/macro environment as opposed to the specific market for an industry or company under analysis. We noted that organizations do not operate or do business in a vacuum. There are laws and regulations, political and other pressures or forces which influence business decision-making and conduct (behaviour). Organizations are influenced by these forces and must therefore adapt or seek to sway such forces. Environmental forces impact upon the goals of the organization and how it achieves them. Forces are generally considered during the formulation of strategy but will also have an impact on management, tactics and operations. Organizations vary in attempts to manage themselves and may consider such forces proactively or reactively. However, whilst attention to the PESTLE factors can guide analysis and subsequent action, the framework is not without criticism. Some scholars and critics argue that the framework forces organizations to focus on the factors in compartments i.e. individually and separately. However, the factors are strongly related and should also be considered together. For example there are strong links between the political and economic environment, the political and legal environment, the political and social environment, the social and economic environment, legal and environmental issues, social and legal issues, etc. In structuring this part of the book we have discussed the political and legal environment together and this is followed by consideration of the economic environment in the following chapter. However, we urge readers to integrate the content of the next six chapters when analyzing their business environments.

The political and legal environment remains turbulent and at the forefront of the minds of managers and strategists for companies operating or doing business in Europe and around the world. In the early part of this decade the news has frequently been punctuated with reports of trouble in the Eurozone as EU members grapple with greater monetary and political union. The same is true of other world regions. In an era of deepening political integration, domestic and international or multinational companies must extend their areas of environmental analysis beyond the states within which they operate. It is no longer the sole privilege of the state to set policy and law as sovereign powers are eroded. At the regional level, the EU (European Union) has its own parliament, MEPs (Members of the European Parliament) and courts and at the global level there are supranational intergovernmental organizations like the WTO (World Trade Organization) and UN (United Nations) who can source the rules governing markets and how organizations operate within them. More than ever before there is a need for business students to understand, analyze and act in this developing environment. Throughout this chapter we not only make reference to key issues from the political and legal environment but also explore the consequences, particularly of government intervention, for the organization and the way in which it is managed. This chapter is structured around the learning outcomes specified at the outset and starts by asking what is meant for business by politics and the political environment. We then progress to consider the role of government and assess how it can, through policy, law and regulation, impact upon business performance. Next we explore different political systems and degrees of government or state intervention in markets and business. Intervention, political change and instability create political risks and uncertainties that manifest as either opportunities or threats for organizations both in their domestic and international markets. We examine political risk before moving on to discuss the legal environment and its relationship with the political climate. We consider what may be regulated, through law, by the state or supranational governance such as the EU and then consider, more broadly, the role of law in society. Considering the law in a little more detail, we identify the different sources of law and then evaluate legal intervention in business. In particular we contemplate the impact upon competitiveness and how compliance with laws and regulations may impact upon organizational efficiency and costs.

WHAT IS MEANT BY POLITICS IN THE CONTEXT OF THE POLITICAL ENVIRONMENT FOR BUSINESS?

Whilst there is no single definition of politics, it may be regarded as the activity concerned with determining the *rules* under which we live in society – the activities associated with the governance of a country or area. Under the general umbrella of 'rules' we might include laws, directives and principles (regulation). Politics is about the competing views regarding the kind of society within which we wish to live. Who then has the power and authority to govern and control the conduct of people and organizations within a society? The highest form or source of authority is the sovereignty. Sovereignty is the quality of having supreme, independent authority over a geographic area and is evidenced in the power to rule and make law. Sovereignty is based on the concept of the **state** – the set of institutions having the legal power to make decisions in matters of government over a specific geographical area and over the population living there. The state has a ruling government which has sovereignty over its domestic affairs. States reject any foreign interference but may work closely together to ensure peace and mutual prosperity. The political environment is that part of the macro environment concerned with impending and potential legislation (to include policy and rules) and how it may affect a particular organization.

THE ROLE OF THE GOVERNMENT AND THE IMPORTANCE OF THE STATE FOR BUSINESS

In the previous section we introduced the concept of the state and government. The, government refers to structures and processes by which laws are made and administered; it also refers to the particular office holders at any given time. We consider and evaluate different types of government in the next section but for now focus on the general role of government and its importance for organizations and business. The main role for government in democratic countries is the pursuit of good for society as a whole – the common good. More specific roles might include:

* managing the economy
* protecting the vulnerable
* protecting the environment
* providing public services (e.g. health) and infrastructure (e.g. transportation)
* defence and national security
* education
* foreign policy
* ensuring employment and the distribution of income

Such roles are achieved through the passing of laws, creation of policy and allocation of funds (budgets). In doing this, the government has a role to collect taxes and may act as both provider and customer in society. As a customer the government may procure goods and services from private companies. A review of the aforementioned roles reveals that not only is politics important for business but business is also important for politics – they are interdependent.

BUSINESS IN ACTION

Employment and Government Intervention

The global recession of 2008 is considered a key cause of unemployment in many countries worldwide. Indeed unemployment rates continued to rise in 2012. The UK's unemployment rate, at 8.4 per cent (April 2012), was the highest for 17 years but the latest forecast from the Office for Budget Responsibility (OBR) shows it will rise further to 8.7 per cent. Similarly, the number of registered job seekers in Spain hit a new high in March (2012), the government declared, adding to its economic problems as it tries to reduce the public deficit with a tough 2012 budget.[1] In Spain, 'The government expects the jobless rate – already the highest in the industrialized world – to hit 24.3 per cent this year as the economy continues to reel from the collapse of a labour-intensive property boom in 2008'. Governments face conflicting goals as on the one hand they seek to control spending, resulting in job cuts in the public sector, whilst, on the other hand trying to ensure employment through investment.

To fight unemployment, the Prime Minister of Spain's Conservative government passed a labour reform package, making it cheaper and easier for companies to lay people off and cut wages unilaterally. The government argued that the reform – hotly contested by unions – will spur job creation in the long term as it will make Spanish labour competitive even though unemployment will rise in the short term. Discussing unemployment trends,

Kayte Lawton, Institute for Public Policy Research (IPPR) senior research fellow, said:[2] 'it is short-sighted of the Government not to do more to get people back into jobs'. She said the [UK] Government's new £1bn Youth Contract, which pledges wage subsidies for more than 100 000 young people and came into force this month, was a 'good first step' but warned people who have been out of work for a year or longer face being 'scarred' by the experience and without help, may never work again. Lansley[3] suggests 'One of the deepest economic and social problems facing the UK has been surging youth unemployment. More than a million 16- to 24-year-olds are without a job … Government attempts to tackle this problem have been hopelessly inadequate.' He argues that 'Only action on a much bigger scale by business can make a significant dent in what is fast becoming a disaster for this generation of the young.' Commenting on the significant cash reserves of many large companies, he states, 'Since 2008, there has been much talk, not least among business figures themselves, about the need for a more responsible capitalism. If this talk is to be translated into action, there are few better places to start than putting these reserves to good use by attempting to break the scourge of youth unemployment.'

Source: (1) AFP (2012), 'Unemployment in Spain hits record high of 4.7 million, adds to deficit woe', *The Sunday Times of Malta* online Sunday, April 8, 2012; (2) Peacock, L (2012), 'Unemployment to rise as 100 000 lose job before summer', *The Telegraph* (online) 9th April 2012); (3) Lansley, S (2012), 'The solution to youth unemployment lies in the coffers of big business', guardian.co.uk, Monday 2 April 2012

Politics is important for business, impacting upon what business is done, how and where it is done. It may impact upon pricing, standards, relationships and ultimately efficiency and cost and therefore performance. Through its effect on markets, the government can exert influence on competitiveness. The government can set and vary tax rates and collect money from organizations and their employees and determine the legal framework within which business operates (discussed towards the end of this chapter). In many cases such interventions might manifest as threats to the organization, increasing costs and eroding profits (political risk). However, governmental action can also be a source of opportunity for organizations either by representing business interests in relation to foreign governments, through the provision of services and resources or through trade, when the government may act as a customer of products and services from private companies. Whilst many arguments have been proposed in support of state intervention in business (to protect the workings of the free market etc.) there are a number of reasons why state intervention in business is difficult. Firstly, it is often difficult to measure the impact of government policy upon business activity thus making justification difficult; secondly, changes to government often result in policy changes and different approaches to intervention and thirdly, the business community may not welcome intervention, resisting government efforts to control their environments.

Organizations and their business are important to politics and the government for several reasons. Organizations are employers and therefore provide employment opportunities in different parts of the country. Not only do they influence income distribution but also play a role in the collection of tax revenues. As producers, organizations create outputs that can benefit society, supplying to meet demand. However, as producers they may use up natural resources and may need to import goods and services, affecting economic variables such as the balance of payments and Gross Domestic Product (GDP). Finally, in the process of production, their activities might have a negative impact upon the environment and society, through pollutants and work practices. Chapter 12 revisits the role of government in greater detail but for now we turn our attention to political systems and evaluation of how governments vary. Since not all governments are the same, typically varying in terms of size and degree of intervention, business performance may be correlated with the type of political system and government in place.

POLITICAL SYSTEMS AND STATE INTERVENTION FROM THE PERSPECTIVE OF BUSINESS

In the next section we introduce differing political ideologies and examine and evaluate aspects of the political system and its impact upon commercial organizations and business. Differing types of government formed by differing political parties contribute to an ever-changing political environment in democratic societies. At the general level, a system can be defined as a collection of interrelated components working together towards a collective goal. The political system refers to the structures and processes used by a nation state to govern (rule). A unitary state is a state, like the UK, in which power is concentrated at the centre, as opposed to a federal state in which power is shared between different levels of government. The political ideology is the associated set of doctrines or beliefs that form the basis of the political system. The political system is widely regarded as the most important determinant of the business and social environment of a country. Whilst there are many types of political system, at a general level, the most favoured is based on democracy; a system in which political power is in the hands of the people: 'rule by the people'. Democratic states are characterized by freedom of speech, choices of political ideology and associated party, regular elections and voting. Members of the public can vote and seek to elect their representatives. A further political system that may run hand-in-hand with democracy is capitalism. This is the ('right-wing ') political system in which private (as opposed to governmental) capital and wealth is the predominant means of producing and distributing goods. At the other end of this continuum is socialism – a 'left-wing' political ideology, involving a critique of capitalism and support for state regulation and/or control of business (advocating substantial public involvement, through government ownership, in the means of production and distribution). Socialists favour greater regulation. Regulation is government intervention. It is a political as well as an economic instrument (see next chapter).

Political pluralism is a participatory type of government in which the politics of the country are defined by the needs and wants of many. Political pluralism is a government of the people, by the people and for the people. This is similar to the government of the United States of America. In politics, pluralism is often considered by supporters of modern democracy to be in the interests of its citizens. In democratic politics, pluralism (multiple) is a guiding principle which permits the peaceful coexistence of different interests, convictions and lifestyles. Proponents of pluralism argue the negotiation process is the best way to achieve the common good. A politically pluralistic society develops a tolerance for divergent thinking. This means that all ideas and beliefs of the people are valid. In political science, it is the view that in liberal democracies, power is (or should be) dispersed amongst a variety of economic and ideological pressure groups and is not (or should not be) held by a single elite or group of elites. Pluralism assumes that diversity is beneficial to society and the disparate functional or cultural groups of which society is composed – including religious groups, trade unions, professional organizations and ethnic minorities – should be autonomous. At the beginning of this section we noted that political ideologies form the basis of the political system. A common political ideology is liberalism – a political or social philosophy believing in or allowing more personal freedom and a development towards a fairer sharing of wealth and power within society, civil liberties and individual rights, and non-violent modification of institutions to permit continued individual and social progress.

Earlier we discussed regulation. Government regulation has been in existence for many centuries. Regulation, whether it originates from the state or a supranational organization (to be discussed later), is a broad subject that in some cases may have general application, across business as a whole, but in many cases will often be specific to particular industries and products. There are many examples of regulation as intervention. Regulations may be used to set and control pricing, a minimum wage, working hours and other employment practices, ensuring equal opportunity, providing consistency, controlling the number of market participants through the award of licences, etc., ensuring product safety, protecting the environment (controlling pollutants), establishing standards, specifying industry boundaries and even limiting ownership of companies.

When analyzing political systems it is sometimes useful to imagine a spectrum from left (socialism) through to the right (capitalism); though life is rarely this simple. Using a continuum as a framework for analysis suggests the presence of a centre and we might also make use of categories such as centre-left or centre-right. English politics has been characterized by the presence of three dominant political parties: Conservative, Labour and Liberal. Historically, Conservatives were viewed on the right of the spectrum, Labour on the left and Liberal somewhere near the centre. More recently the main parties have undergone changes to their political ideologies with Labour and Conservative taking positions closer to the centre. Conservatism refers to a political philosophy or attitude which seeks to maintain the existing or traditional order. The Conservative Party is a centre-right political party that adheres to the philosophies of conservatism whereas the Labour Party is a centre-left democratic socialist party in the United Kingdom.

It is interesting to contrast the 'right' with the 'left' as they may lead to differing threats and opportunities for organizations and business. The first point and difference worthy of note relates to both the size of government and degree of intervention. By definition, we expect left-wing ideologies (favouring government ownership) to manifest as larger sized governments, intervening more in the activities of business. Not only is the 'left' associated with state control, it tends to be associated with increased taxation (to fund a larger government, greater public spending and an enhanced welfare state), collectivism and centralized planning and control. Such ideologies seek to empower trade unions and may seek to change a business from private to state ownership or control (nationalization). The 'right' on the other hand are more likely to embrace a smaller government, less intervention and a reduction in public spending. Consequently they favour a free market (a market that is free of government regulation or intervention), individualism, privatization and deregulation. In practice, supporters of the free market advocate minimum government. As has been discussed already, such variations will impact upon business costs, practices, performance and ultimately profitability.

Whilst it remains important to consider specific governments within particular countries, current political trends seem, especially in Europe, to be moving away from exclusive state and sovereign control to a model of multilevel governance. Under such a model, governance takes place on a number of spatial scales – national, subnational and supranational. In the case of the latter, there is a level of political authority above the nation-state e.g. the European Union (EU). The EU is a regional grouping of European countries which evolved from trade agreements to deeper economic integration. As an authoritative and empowered source of regulation, domestic and multinational organizations must be aware of the political and legal issues this supranational organization brings to the political environment. In the subsequent paragraphs of this section we outline briefly the history of integration in Europe, discuss the four freedoms pursued by the EU member states and evaluate potential opportunities and threats for organizations and business. Later in this chapter we revisit the EU as a source of law impacting upon multinational companies and domestic organizations.

Doing business in the EU (Regional, international, economic and political integration)

As the world's largest trading economy, the EU presents an important environment for doing business. The European Union (EU) is an economic and political union of 27 member states which are located primarily in Europe. The historical roots of the EU lie in the Second World War. Europeans were determined to prevent repeated broad scale death and destruction. Soon after the war, Europe was split into East and West as the 40-year-long Cold War began. West European nations created the Council of Europe in 1949. In the intervening years the EU has grown in size and power by the addition of members and policy areas to its remit. The *Maastricht Treaty* established the European Union under its current name in 1993. The last amendment to the constitutional basis of the EU, the *Treaty of Lisbon*, came into force in 2009. The EU member countries have transferred some of their law-making authority (see later in this chapter) to the EU in certain policy areas. In other areas, policy-making is shared between the EU and national governments. Politically, the EU operates through a hybrid system of supranational independent institutions and intergovernmentally-made decisions negotiated by the member states. EU policies aim to ensure the free movement of people, goods, services, and capital. Legislation is passed concerning judicial and home affairs, and to maintain common policies on trade. The EU's GDP – output of goods and services – is now bigger than that of the US: GDP (€12 268 387 million 2010). With just 7 per cent of the world's population, the EU's trade with the rest of the world accounts for around 20 per cent of global exports and imports. The EU is the world's biggest exporter and the second-biggest importer. The United States is the EU's most important trading partner, followed by China.

FYI

The Institutions of the EU

The key institutions of the EU are discussed on the European Union web site (europa.eu). The *European Council* defines the general political direction and priorities of the European Union. It became an institution with the entry into force of the Treaty of Lisbon. The EU's decision-making process in general and the co-decision procedure in particular involve three main institutions:

European Parliament, which represents the EU's citizens and is directly elected by them;

Council of the European Union, which represents the individual member states; and the

European Commission, which seeks to uphold the interests of the Union as a whole.

This 'institutional triangle' produces the policies and laws which apply throughout the EU. In principle the Commission proposes new laws, but it is the Parliament and Council that adopt them. The Commission and the member states then implement them, and the Commission ensures the laws are properly taken on board. Other institutions have a vital part to play, for example; the *Court of Justice* upholds the rule of

European law (see also the *European Central Bank* which is responsible for European monetary policy). Each is briefly described below. The powers and responsibilities of these institutions are defined in the Treaties, which are the foundation of all EU activity. They also determine the rules and procedures the EU institutions must follow. The Treaties are agreed by the Presidents and/or Prime Ministers of all the EU countries, and ratified by their parliaments.

The **European Council** began informally in 1974 as a forum for discussion between EU leaders. It rapidly developed into the body determining goals and priorities for the bloc. Acquiring formal status in 1992, in 2009 it became one of the EU's 7 official institutions. Its role is twofold – setting the EU's general political direction and priorities, and dealing with complex or sensitive issues which cannot be resolved at a lower level of intergovernmental cooperation. Though influential in setting the EU political agenda, it has no power to pass laws. The European Council brings together the heads of state or government of every EU country, the Commission President and the European Council President, who chairs the meetings. The EU's High Representative for Foreign Affairs and Security Policy also takes part. The European Council decides, by consensus, except if the

(continued)

Treaties provide otherwise. In some cases, it adopts decisions by unanimity or by qualified majority, depending upon what the Treaty provides for.

The **European Parliament** members (MEPs), directly elected by EU voters every five years, represent the people. Parliament is one of the EU's main law-making institutions, along with the Council. It has three main roles: debating and passing European laws, with the Council; scrutinizing other EU institutions, particularly the Commission, to ensure they are working democratically; and debating and adopting the EU's budget, with the Council. In many areas, such as consumer protection and the environment, Parliament works together with the Council (representing national governments) to decide upon the content of EU laws and officially adopt them. This process is called 'co-decision'. Under the Lisbon Treaty, the range of policies covered by co-decision has increased, giving Parliament more power to influence the content of laws in areas including agriculture, energy policy, immigration and EU funds. Parliament must also give its permission for other important decisions, such as allowing new countries to join the EU.

The **Council of the European Union** is where national ministers from each EU country meet to adopt laws and coordinate policies. The Council and Parliament have shared authority regarding the adoption of new EU laws proposed by the Commission. In addition, the Council coordinates the broad economic policies of EU member countries; develops the EU's foreign and defence policies and coordinates cooperation between courts and police forces of member countries.

The **European Commission** is one of the main institutions of the European Union. It represents and upholds the interests of the EU as a whole, drafts proposals for new European laws and manages the day-to-day business of implementing EU policies and spending EU funds.

The **Court of Justice** interprets EU law to ensure it is applied uniformly in all EU countries. It also settles legal disputes between EU governments and EU institutions. Individuals, companies or organizations may also bring cases before the Court if they consider their rights to have been infringed by an EU institution.

Source: Adapted from http://ec.europa.eu © European Union, 1995–2011. Reproduced with permission.

Ever since the Second World War, the European integration process has always hesitated between two opinions or two approaches (Somers 2010:p52). Certain states favour federalism (e.g. Germany) whilst others favour intergovernmentalism (e.g. The UK). The Federalists support greater political integration whilst the intergovernmentalists promote economic without political integration. In the intergovernmental approach there is no sharing of sovereignty. In the European Union, the Council of Ministers is an example of a purely intergovernmental body whilst the Commission, the European Parliament and the European Court of Justice represent the supranational mode of decision-making.

The central component in European integration from a business point of view is the single market, with its 'four freedoms': the free movement of goods, services, capital and people. The free movement of goods and services overcomes trade barriers (tariffs, quotas and border controls), encouraging export. The free movement of capital increases competition in the banking sector but also enables investment by citizens and businesses throughout the EU. The introduction of a common currency removes or reduces exchange-rate risk in support of this. And finally, the free movement of people increases the likelihood of domestic organizations employing foreigners leading to a multicultural workforce but also impacting upon the availability of talented human resources and cost. Somers (2010:p20) discusses the European business environment and doing business in the EU. He notes that 'today, more than half the new rules and regulations come from Brussels. European citizens are free to travel and settle in other EU countries and find jobs there. About 40 per cent of all products sold in the EU are obliged to satisfy EU norms concerning, for instance, health, safety and the environment … The majority of EU citizens – more than 300 million – use the same currency: the euro … European integration is shaping a new business environment … The present-day EU offers great potential for the development of new markets, the expansion of sales or imports, the relocation of production facilities, outsourcing, the recruitment of foreign employees and external financing.' He stresses the implications for competition, suggesting that it will become more competitive in home (domestic) markets due to the appearance of foreign companies. Competitors may have access to cheaper inputs and resources from elsewhere in the EU and they may have relocated part of their production to low-cost environments (see value chain fragmentation – Kelly 2009:p23).

The main *advantages* of European integration for commercial organizations include a significant reduction in transaction costs, the elimination of currency risks, lower borrowing costs due to more efficient financial markets and lower administration costs. For consumers that should mean increased choice and greater price and market transparency. In many cases, businesses will pass on the efficiency savings in the form of reduced product and service prices. Clearly, there will also be disadvantages for business. The main *disadvantage* being increased competition and rivalry. The changing competitive landscape can be analyzed with Porter's five competitive forces framework (to be discussed in Chapter 10). Aside from rivalry, Porter discusses the threat of new entrants and new products or services. Since European integration should lower the cost of doing business in the EU we should expect an increased threat of new entrants in many industries. Porter also discusses the bargaining power of both suppliers and customers. The Internet represents a significant technology, altering the bargaining power of customers in particular. Customers can compare, with ease, the pricing of competing company products and services, selecting their preferred supplier, regardless of where they are located within the EU.

We have promoted the EU as an example of regional integration. Analysis of the history of the EU reveals a trend towards greater integration, starting from loose economic integration through to more formal economic integration and eventually not just a common market but economic union. However, more recently this has extended to include political union and steps towards political integration. At the same time we have witnessed the EU undergoing a series of enlargements as additional countries seek membership. Within Europe there has been concerted effort to remove barriers in order to realize integration. Physical barriers have been removed – (the movement of goods and people-eliminating customs, goods inspections and removing restrictions on the entry of people); and fiscal barriers have been reduced through the development of a common set of policies for all member states (harmonization). Fiscal harmonization pertains to tax policy, government fiscal policy and subsidization, see the next chapter.

Whilst the EU has the necessary economic force to make many of the rules influencing world trade, it remains a *regional* supranational government. Worldwide surges in regional trade agreements have continued unabated since the early 1990s. They include The European Union, the North American Free Trade Agreement, the Association of Southeast Asian Nations, the South Asian Association for Regional Cooperation, the Common Market of the South (MERCOSUR), and the Australia-New Zealand Closer Economic Relations Agreement. In the next section we consider global governance and supranational organizations such as the UN and WTO. We also examine integration on a worldwide scale and the global removal of barriers between countries.

Doing business globally (Global, international, economic and political integration)

The EU is not the only supranational organization of which European companies must be aware. The need to be aware of world politics is emphasised by Haynes *et al.* (2010:p698) who argue, 'there seems little doubt that governments have become less and less able fully to control events in their states in the face of globalization'. In the next paragraph we outline briefly the meaning of globalization and then discuss further supranational and intergovernmental organizations and their influence on business organizations.

Globalization concerns growth and integration to a global or worldwide scale and the growing interdependency between nations and organizations through international trade (Kelly 2009). Institutional globalization is typified through organizations such as the International Monetary Fund (IMF), World Bank and World Trade Organization (WTO) which seek to make markets more flexible and demolish international trade barriers. Scholars also discuss the concept of political globalization and the relationship between the power of markets and multinational organizations versus the nation state. As a result of globalization, the international organization faces the global–local dilemma. This relates to the extent to which products and services may be standardized across national boundaries or need to be adapted to meet the requirements of specific national markets. Consequently, globalization is considered to impact upon the political environment of the domestic organization. It can also lead organizations to invest in or set up operations in other countries around the world. Thus, a company may offer its goods and services solely in its domestic market or wider in a global market. Clearly there is more opportunity associated with the latter but not all organizations become multinational. The gradual process of taking organizational activities into other countries is termed Internationalization. International organizations must take account of the local political environment in which they choose to operate as well as their own domestic environment. Globalization and the challenges posed by global problems encourage governments to pursue greater forms of supranational governance including that offered by regional bodies such as the EU and global bodies like the WTO.

Intergovernmental organizations include the UN, Interpol, NATO, OPEC, NAFTA, the EU and the WTO. Such organizations vary according to whether they have a global (UN/WTO) or regional purpose (EU, Commonwealth, and NATO). Organizations such as the World Trade Organization (WTO), established in 1995 to free up and harmonize international trading standards, have supranational powers to punish member states who violate WTO treaties. A selection of inter-governmental organizations are considered next before we consider the political risks associated with undertaking business in different regions.

Two key financial intergovernmental organizations operating globally are the World Bank and the International Monetary Fund (IMF). The World Bank is a vital source of financial and technical assistance to developing countries around the world. Established in 1944 and headquartered in

---

FYI

The World Trade Organization (WTO)

The World Trade Organization (WTO) deals with the global rules of trade between nations. It is the only global international organization dealing with the rules of trade between nations. Essentially, the WTO is the organization to which member governments turn when seeking to resolve trade problems faced between each other. Its main function is to ensure that trade flows as smoothly, predictably and freely as possible (liberalizing trade). The WTO is run by its member governments. All major decisions are made by the membership as a whole, either by ministers (who meet at least once every two years) or by their ambassadors or delegates (who meet regularly in Geneva). Decisions are normally taken by consensus. In this respect, the WTO is different from some other international organizations such as the *World Bank* and *International Monetary Fund*. In the WTO, power is not delegated to a board of directors or the organization's head. At its heart are the WTO agreements, negotiated and signed by the bulk of the world's trading nations and ratified in their parliaments. The goal is to help producers of goods and services, exporters, and importers conduct their business. Established in 1995 and located in Geneva, Switzerland the WTO was created by the Uruguay Round negotiations (1986–94). Over 150 countries belong to the WTO whose functions include:

- Administering *WTO trade agreements*
- Forum for trade negotiations
- Handling trade disputes
- Monitoring national trade policies

The **WTO agreements** are lengthy and complex because they are legal texts covering a wide range of activities. However, a number of simple, fundamental principles are common throughout all of these documents. These principles are the foundation of the multilateral trading system. The trading system should be without discrimination – a country should not discriminate between its trading partners (giving them equally 'most-favoured-nation' or MFN status); and it should not discriminate between its own and foreign products, services or nationals (giving them 'national treatment'); freer – barriers coming down through negotiation; predictable – foreign companies, investors and governments should be confident that trade barriers (including tariffs and non-tariff barriers) should not be raised arbitrarily; tariff rates and market-opening commitments are 'bound' in the WTO; more competitive – discouraging 'unfair' practices such as export subsidies and dumping products at below cost to gain market share; and more beneficial for less developed countries – giving them more time to adjust, greater flexibility, and special privileges. The WTO agreements cover goods, services and intellectual property and:

- spell out the principles of liberalization, and the permitted exceptions
- include individual country commitments to lower customs tariffs and other trade barriers, and to open and keep open services markets
- set procedures for settling disputes
- prescribe special treatment for developing countries
- require governments to make their trade policies transparent by notifying the WTO about laws in force and measures adopted, and through regular reports by the secretariat on the trade policies of countries

These agreements are often called the WTO's trade rules, and the WTO is often described as 'rule-based', a system based on rules. It is important to remember that the rules are actually agreements negotiated by governments. The economic case for an open trading system based on multilaterally-agreed rules is simple enough and rests largely on commercial common sense. It is also supported by evidence: the experience of world trade and economic growth since the Second World War. The data shows a definite statistical link between freer trade and economic growth. Economic theory points to strong reasons for the link. All countries, including the poorest, have assets – human, industrial, natural, financial – which they can employ to produce goods and services for their domestic markets or to compete overseas. Economics tells us that we can benefit when these goods and services are traded. The principle of 'comparative advantage' says that countries prosper first by taking advantage of their assets in order to concentrate on what they can produce best, and then by trading these products for products that other countries produce best. In other words, liberal trade policies – policies that allow the unrestricted flow of goods and services – sharpen competition, motivate innovation and breed success. For a discussion on such theories see Kelly (2009: Chapter 1).

Disputes in the WTO are essentially about broken promises. WTO members have agreed that if they believe fellow-members are violating trade rules, they will use the multilateral system of settling disputes instead of taking unilateral action. That means abiding by the agreed procedures, and respecting judgements. A dispute arises when one country adopts a trade policy measure or takes action that one or more fellow-WTO members considers to be breaking the WTO agreements, or to be a failure to live up to obligations. Although much of the procedure does resemble a court or tribunal, the preferred solution is for the countries concerned to discuss their problems and settle the dispute by themselves. The first stage is therefore consultations between the governments concerned, and even when the case has progressed to other stages, consultation and mediation are still always possible. Settling disputes is the responsibility of the Dispute Settlement Body (the General Council in another guise), which consists of all WTO members. The Dispute Settlement Body has sole authority to establish 'panels' of experts to consider the case, and accept or reject panel findings or the results of an appeal. It monitors implementation of the rulings and recommendations, and has power to authorize retaliation for a country's non-compliance with a ruling. In cases of non-compliance the Dispute Settlement Body encourages swift correction of the fault. If non-compliance continues, the WTO invokes a penalty (trade sanctions are the conventional form of penalty typically imposed).

Source: Material adapted from the World Trade Organization. Reproduced with permission.

Washington, D.C. it has more than 10 000 employees in 100 offices worldwide. It operates like a cooperative, with its 187 member countries as shareholders. The shareholders are represented by a Board of Governors, who are the ultimate policy makers. Generally governors are ministers of finance or ministers of development from the member countries. They meet once a year at annual meetings of the Boards of Governors of the World Bank Group and the International Monetary Fund. The World Bank's two closely affiliated entities – the International Bank for Reconstruction and Development (IBRD) and the International Development Association (IDA) – provide low or no interest loans (credits) and grants to countries with unfavourable or no access to international credit markets. The International Monetary Fund (IMF) is an organization of 187 countries, working to foster global monetary cooperation, secure financial stability, facilitate international trade, promote high employment and sustainable economic growth, and reduce poverty around the world.

The IMF has played a part in shaping the global economy since the end of World War II. The IMF's fundamental mission is to ensure stability in the international system.

The final Intergovernmental Organization (IGO) to be considered here is the United Nations (UN), an international organization founded in 1945 after the Second World War by 51 countries committed to maintaining international peace and security, developing friendly relations amongst nations and promoting social progress, better living standards and human rights. The work of the UN reaches every corner of the globe. Although best known for peacekeeping, peace building, conflict prevention and humanitarian assistance, there are many other ways the UN affects our lives and makes the world a better place. The organization works on a broad range of fundamental issues, from sustainable development, environment and refugee protection, disaster relief, counter terrorism, disarmament and non-proliferation, to promoting democracy, human rights, gender equality and the advancement of women, governance, economic and social development and international health, expanding food production, and more, in order to achieve its goals and coordinate efforts for a safer world for this and future generations. The UN has four main purposes:

* To keep peace throughout the world;
* To develop friendly relations among nations;
* To help nations work together to improve the lives of poor people, to conquer hunger, disease and illiteracy, and to encourage respect for each other's rights and freedoms; and
* To be a centre for harmonizing the actions of nations to achieve these goals.

A more detailed account of globalization will be provided later in Chapter 13.

POLITICAL RISKS IN TERMS OF THREATS AND OPPORTUNITIES FOR ORGANIZATIONS

All of the institutions mentioned thus far can influence the political environment for business. Political risk is the term used to describe the likelihood that political forces will cause dire changes in a country's business environment that will have an adverse affect on the profit and other goals of a particular organization. The chance of politically-induced events having an adverse affect on the profit and other goals of a business organization are considered downside risks (threats) whereas events that may benefit the business organization are upside risks (opportunities). In this section we consider political risk in more detail before moving on to discuss the legal environment.

When there are market imperfections, government intervention could improve efficiency. According to Kelly (2009:47), governments can grant access to markets and rescind such permission at any time. Governments formulate policy towards international trade and vary in the degree to which they may intervene in order to protect or help their domestic organizations competing at home or abroad. The policies adopted by individual countries affect the size and profitability of markets and may create unfair competition; acts of government create winners and losers in the marketplace. However, political behaviour can be a source of efficiency and market power, particularly in international contexts. All organizations, to some extent, are exposed to political risk and forces – it is intrinsic to business. Within countries, it is the political ideology that may direct the actions of society. Earlier we noted that the political system may be described in a number of ways, typically on a continuum between democracy and totalitarianism. Systems exist on a continuum where power is centralized (with the government) at one extreme and decentralized at the other. A totalitarian regime is characterized by the centralization of power, an imposed authority (typically supported through a powerful military). Even within democracies, different beliefs exist. At the country and regional level, a by-product of democracy is often a frequent change of government and consequently some degree of instability. When undertaking business the organization will adapt to meet the demands of the local political system. For example, the law may be considered more vague or non-existent in totalitarian nations. In such countries, more emphasis may be placed on how individual bureaucrats interpret the law, making business dealings more risky. Political risk arises from a variety of sources such as an unstable political system, policy change, conflict, poor political leadership or poor relations with other countries. Managers must be aware of how political risk can affect their organization and trade. In some cases, certain political risks will affect all organizations operating in or trading with a particular country whilst, in other cases, a particular industry or small group may be threatened. There are many types of political and associated risk such as security risks, corruption, civil protest and economic sanctions. There are a variety of consequences (business impacts) arising from such risk. Conflict, terrorism and kidnapping may disrupt business operations and revenue generation; local content requirements impact upon labour cost and quality of outputs and profits may be affected in the event of asset seizure (see confiscation, expropriation or nationalization).

Managing political risk helps in two fundamental ways. Firstly, it protects new and existing global investments and operations by helping management anticipate the business risk implications of political change or instability. Prepared and aware, management are more likely to be able to exit markets in danger of growing too unstable. Where short-term instability does not dampen the appetite to pursue long-term opportunity, management can implement risk mitigation and operational oversight to control against shocks. Secondly, monitoring political risk within target regions or across continents can help management hone in on political developments which reveal new opportunities. An understanding of how political issues develop can assist with management. Typically, issues develop over time as does the impact on the organization and business. First of all an issue has to be identified (e.g. the safety of a particular product or service). This may then lead to the formation of interest groups, who, through pressure, may lobby government for the creation of legislation to protect people and/or property. Law-making is then followed by administration and enforcement. As issues progress through the stages, the impact upon business and organizations tends to increase. Furthermore, management discretion over how to deal with such issues tends to decrease over time.

Throughout this chapter, so far, we have discussed the political environment in terms of sovereign, regional and global systems of intervention in markets and the activities of organizations operating within them. We noted that governments rule in order to create a desirable society for members. One key aspect of government is law, an area we focus upon next at the national and supranational level.

THE RELATIONSHIP BETWEEN THE POLITICAL AND LEGAL ENVIRONMENT: SOURCES OF LAW AND LAW MAKING

The system of rules that regulate behaviour and the processes by which the laws of a country are enforced and through which redress of grievances is obtained is termed the legal system. The laws and the impact of the legal system on business, together with the general nature of the relationship between government and business, may be collectively described as the Legal and Political Conditions. Earlier we discussed the role of the state or government and noted that such roles are achieved through the passing of **laws**, creation of policy and allocation of funds (budgets). For the remainder of this chapter we turn our attention and focus on the legal environment. We will consider the role of law in society and in particular the way the law impacts upon business activity. We start by asking what is the law and then take a brief look at the infrastructure of the law such as the court system and different sources from which the law is derived. We also consider how law is drafted at both the country, using the UK as an example, and EU level. Many aspects of life may be regulated through the law and similar controls. For example, governments may seek to pass laws to help protect the environment, manage relationships between employer and employee, manage relationships between suppliers and their customers, and manage competitive behaviour within industries. Generally the role of the law in society is to create order and predictability, ensure freedom, fairness and equality and in the case of business, to enhance confidence amongst investors, partners, suppliers and customers.

We have already defined the law in terms of rules emanating from authorities within a state. Such rules (laws) may be categorized as civil or criminal law and in the case of business there are a group of rules that may be classified as employment (labour) law. Civil law refers to a body of rules that delineate private rights and remedies, and govern disputes between individuals in such areas as contracts and property; distinct from criminal law. Other types of law include torts, public law and trusts. Laws are vital to society in every country and in Britain there are three main varieties of law at work – Statute Laws, Common Law and European Laws. *Statute Laws* are laws made by Parliament. Statute Laws can be made either directly, through the passing of Acts of Parliament, or indirectly, through the creation of Statutory Instruments (see The Working Time Regulations 1998 discussed later) that contain rules and regulations. England also has a body of law known as the Common Law which has developed over centuries from judgements given in courts. The *Common Law* has been extremely important in the development of the English legal system. Common Law works through the system of precedent. If a judge makes a decision in a case then other judges will typically follow the example set and give a similar verdict in cases involving similar facts. If the decision of the first judge is later overruled by a higher court, then subsequent judges follow the decision of the higher court instead. The judge who makes the first decision effectively makes law since this ruling will be followed in the future. Finally, as a member of the EU, Britain has agreed to be subject to European Community Laws. *European Laws* have direct effect within the legal systems of the countries that make up the European Union and actually override national laws in many cases (as the business in debate section will reveal).

Correspondingly, there are different courts of law for administering the rules. A court, a duly instituted part of the government that administers justice, hears cases and makes decisions based on statutes or the common law. In the UK, the county court deals with civil cases. County courts can deal with a wide range of cases, such as consumer disputes, for example, faulty goods or services, discrimination cases, and employment problems. Magistrate courts deal with criminal and some civil cases. The Crown Court deals with the more serious criminal offences tried by judge and jury. Certain matters are covered by European law, and cases may now be referred to the European Court of Justice (ECJ), based in Luxembourg. This may happen if European legislation has not been implemented properly by a national government, if there is confusion over its interpretation, or if it has been ignored. A case must first be pursued through the **national legal system**, but the national court can (and in some cases must) refer an issue to the ECJ for guidance (a ruling). The case is then sent back to the national court to make a decision based on the ruling of the ECJ. The Court of Justice interprets EU law to make sure it is applied in the same way in all EU countries. It also settles legal disputes between EU governments and EU institutions. Individuals, companies or organizations can also bring cases before the Court if they feel their rights have been infringed by an EU institution.

The EU is based on the rule of law. This means that everything that it does is derived from treaties. The ECJ may be regarded as a good example of a **supranational legal order** and the primary sources of EU law include the Treaty on European Union (TEU) (signed in Maastricht on 7 February 1992) and the Treaty on the Functioning of the European Union (TFEU). The Treaty on European Union (TEU) represented a new stage in European integration since it opened the way to political integration. The Treaty of Lisbon, amended the two fundamental treaties – the TEU and the TFEU. The Treaty of Lisbon made changes to the organization and jurisdiction of the ECJ. This was extended to the law of the European Union, unless the Treaties provided otherwise. Thus, the Court of Justice acquired general jurisdiction to give preliminary rulings in the area of freedom, security and justice.

Passing legislation in the EU

EU law is divided into 'primary' and 'secondary' legislation. The treaties (primary legislation) are the basis or ground rules for all EU action. Secondary legislation – which includes regulations, directives and decisions – are derived from the principles and objectives set out in the treaties. The EU's standard decision-making procedure is known as 'codecision' (the 'ordinary legislative procedure'). This means that the directly elected European Parliament must approve EU legislation together with the Council (the governments of the 27 EU countries). The Treaty of Lisbon increased the number of policy areas where 'codecision' is used.

Drafting EU law – Before the Commission proposes new initiatives it assesses the potential economic, social and environmental consequences these initiatives may have. It does this by preparing 'Impact assessments' which set out the advantages and disadvantages of possible policy options. The Commission also consults interested parties such as non-governmental organizations, local authorities and representatives of industry and civil society. Groups of experts give advice on technical issues. In this way, the Commission ensures that legislative proposals correspond to the needs of those most concerned and avoids unnecessary red tape. National parliaments can express their reservations formally if they feel issues would be better dealt with at national rather than EU level.

Review and adoption – The European Parliament and the Council review proposals by the Commission and propose amendments. If the Council and the Parliament cannot agree upon amendments, a second reading takes place. In the second reading, the Parliament and Council can again propose amendments. Parliament has the power to block the proposed legislation if it cannot agree with the Council. If the two institutions agree on amendments, the proposed legislation can be adopted. If they cannot agree, a conciliation committee will attempt a solution. Both the Council and the Parliament can block the legislative proposal at this final reading. The aforementioned EU law making process is summarized in Figure 2.2.

As was highlighted earlier, the EU is based on the rule of law. This means that every action taken by the EU is founded on treaties approved voluntarily and democratically by all EU member countries. For example, if a policy area is not cited in a treaty, the Commission cannot propose a law in that area. A treaty is a binding agreement between EU member countries. It sets out EU objectives, rules for EU institutions, how decisions are made and the relationship between the EU and its member countries. Under the treaties, EU institutions can adopt legislation, which the member countries then implement. The main treaties are: Lisbon (2009) – to make the EU more democratic, more efficient and better able to address global problems, such as climate change, with one voice; Amsterdam (1999) – to reform the EU institutions in preparation for the arrival of future member countries; Maastricht (1993) – to prepare for European Monetary Union and introduce elements of a political union (citizenship, common foreign and internal affairs policy); Single European Act (1986) – to reform the institutions in preparation for Portugal and Spain's membership and speed up decision-making in preparation for the single market and Rome – (1958) – to set up the European Economic Community (EEC).

Passing legislation in the UK

There are similarities between the EU and UK law making processes. Within the UK, a draft piece of legislation is called a Bill and when this is passed by Parliament it becomes an Act and part of statute law. Bills pass through a number of stages before becoming legislation. In many cases there will be a period of consultation before a bill is drafted. At this stage, interested parties both within and outside government may be consulted and their views on any proposals sought. Following consultation, the government may publish either a green paper (a proposal without any commitment to action) outlining various options or a more definitive White Paper. Following a process of consultation, the sponsoring department will send drafting instructions to expert lawyers working for the government responsible for writing legislation. These instructions will describe what the bill should do but not the detail of how this is achieved. Legislation drafts must minimize the possibility of legal challenge and embed the bill with existing UK, EU and delegated legislation. A finished bill must then be approved or scrutinized by the sponsoring entity. The bill is then submitted and ready for introduction. A notice appears on the *order paper* (a daily publication in the Westminster system of government which lists the business of Parliament for that day's sitting) for the relevant first reading. This is more a formality as no debating or voting occurs. On the day of the first reading, the sponsoring MP submits the title of the Bill and a list of supporters. This is then read out and a date scheduled for the second reading. In the second reading a debate on the general principles of the bill is followed by a vote. If successful it then passes to the committee

FIGURE 2.2

EU codecision flow chart

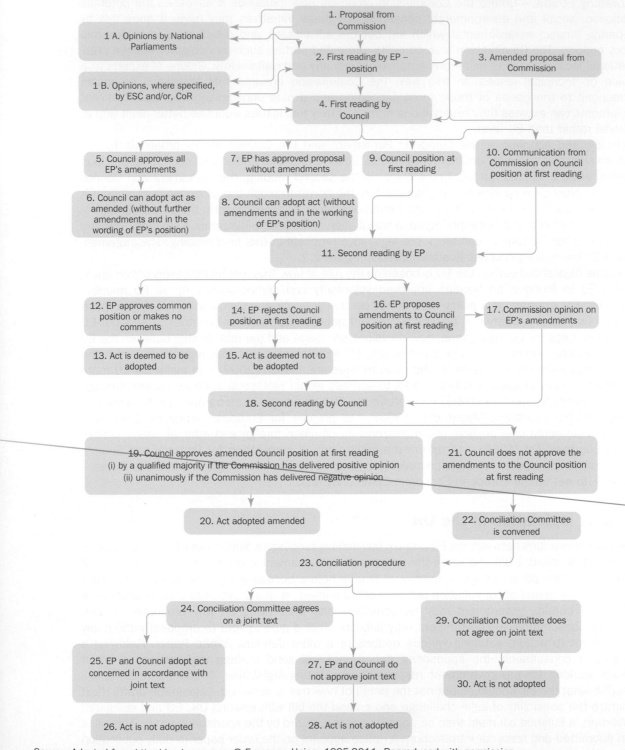

Source: Adapted from http://ec/europa.eu © European Union, 1995-2011. Reproduced with permission.

stage where each clause of the bill is considered and amendments may be made; in the third reading MPs debate the final text of the bill, leading to a vote. The bill is then sent to the other House (to the Lords, if it originated in the Commons; to the Commons, if it is a Lords bill), which may amend it. The Commons may reject a bill from the Lords outright; the Lords may amend a bill from the Commons but, if they reject it, the Commons may force it through without the Lords' consent in the following Session of Parliament. In the UK there is still a presumption that Parliament is sovereign, however it is recognized that Acts of Parliament are no longer sovereign but can be overruled if they are incompatible with European Laws. European Law can overturn such Acts because the European Communities Act 1972 agreed that UK law should not wish to conflict with European Law. The European Communities Act 1972 (c. 68) is an Act of the Parliament of the United Kingdom, providing for the incorporation of European Community law into domestic law.

LEGAL INTERVENTION IN BUSINESS AND MANAGEMENT

Having just discussed how legislation is made, once implemented, it may impact upon the conduct of business and management within organizations. There are several different types of commercial organization; each with its own legal structure. The most common types include limited companies, sole traders, partnerships and cooperatives. For a detailed description see Chapter 8 and Cole and Kelly (2011). There are different legal implications associated with the company type. When a limited company is formed, it is said to have become 'incorporated', i.e. endowed with a separate body, or person. The corporation so formed is treated in English law as a separate entity, independent of its members/owners. The corporation, or 'company', as it is generally called, is capable of owning property, employing people, making contracts and of suing or being sued. The key feature of a 'limited' company is that, if it fails, it can only require its members (shareholders) to meet its debts up to the limit of the nominal value of their shares. The principle of legally limiting the financial liabilities of persons investing in business ventures was introduced by Parliament in the 1850s to encourage the wealthy to give financial support to the inventors, engineers and others who were at the forefront of Britain's Industrial Revolution. Without the protection of *limited liability*, investors could find themselves stripped of their home and other personal assets in order to meet debts arising from failure of the company in which they had invested their money.

Once formed, many of the 'rules' of business and management are influenced by legislation. Since the turn of the twentieth century, in the UK for example, various Company Acts have laid down the principles and procedures to be followed in the conduct of business organizations. Such legislation intended to minimize the risk to suppliers and customers as well as to shareholders, and to a lesser extent employees, arising from gross mismanagement of, or deliberate restriction of information about, a company. Legislation was consolidated into one Principal Act – the Companies Act, 1985 – as amended by the Companies Act, 1989. The Companies Act 2006 superseded the Companies Act 1985. The implementation of the Companies Act 2006 was fully completed in 2009. The Act provides a comprehensive code of company law for the United Kingdom, and made changes to almost every aspect of the law in relation to companies. The Act codifies certain existing common law principles, such as those relating to the duties of directors and introduces various new provisions for private and public companies but otherwise amends or restates almost all of the Companies Act 1985.

Aside from the aforementioned general business legislation, companies must also be aware of employment (labour) law and industry-specific legislation. For example, in Telecomms there is the Telecommunications Act 1984 for the UK. In 1984 British Telecom's monopoly of the telecommunication industry came to an end as the country went through privatization. This brought about significant changes in the telecoms industry, opening opportunity to many competing companies running telecommunication services in the UK. In 2002, the European Union brought in new directives. These changes were implemented in 2003 to push competitiveness within the industry and increase consistent practice throughout Europe.

For markets to operate efficiently, participating entities must be confident that the terms of their exchanges will be fulfilled. They may rely upon trust, honesty and the reputations of suppliers and customers. In such an environment, disputes are resolved to mutual satisfaction without the intervention of a third party and may take the form of customer services and refund policies. Alternatively, an exchange (trade) may be supported by a contract specifying mutual obligations.

Laws may be established, providing protection to those involved and thus enhancing confidence in the market. Not only may the law play a role in ensuring the effective functioning of markets but it may be used to establish property rights, protect intellectual property (through patents, copyright, trademarks). Consequently, many argue the law is an important institution for improving the efficiency of markets.

Legal intervention into business affairs can impact upon the competitiveness of an organization. Compliance with regulatory frameworks may increase the costs of doing business and may decrease efficiency, thus impacting upon profitability. Many countries seek to encourage foreign direct investment and the establishment of operations in the country as this can impact upon employment, income distribution, tax revenues and GDP. The extent of legal intervention and the nature of political risk can impact upon the competitiveness of nations as well as organizations. Investors and multinational companies will seek out opportunity but will only be prepared to tolerate a certain level of political risk (see earlier discussion). When deciding which country in which to invest they may take account of stability, exchange-rate fluctuations, effective government (clean and not corrupt), and the responsiveness to business interests.

So far we have discussed the role of the law with regard to a company's relationships with its customers, suppliers, and investors. We have also considered the role of the law within an industry. In this final section we consider the organization's relationships with employees and the role of *employment law*. Specifically we consider the subject of employment law in the regulation of the relationship between employer and worker (Sargeant and Lewis 2010). Sargeant and Lewis suggest that the sources of this regulation are diverse and include government legislation, EU treaties and legislation (typically in the form of directives), court decisions (including employment tribunals), decisions of international courts, especially the European Court of Justice and the European Court of Human Rights and codes of practice. The authors note the scope of EU activities has grown in recent years. Employment law is typically found in areas such as contracts of employment, termination of employment, discrimination in the workplace, time and pay, parental and maternity rights, business restructuring, collective bargaining, industrial action and trade unions.

For example, in the UK, the Contracts of Employment Act 1963 required employers to give each employee a written statement outlining certain particulars of employee terms of service. This act subsequently amended and now contained in the Employment Rights Act (ERA) 1996, preceded an

BUSINESS IN DEBATE

Regulating the employment relationship – Modernizing labour law

The Working Time Regulations

EU intervention in National Employment (Labour) Law: Who decides – the EU or the Sovereign State?

In 1990 the Commission tabled the proposal for the Working Time Directive (WTD) as a 'health and safety' measure, amid UK opposition. The proposal was introduced under the EU's social legislation, but was eventually tabled by the European Commission under the health and safety articles of the Treaty of Rome (then Article 118a). Making it a matter of health and safety means that the proposal is subject to majority voting, effectively meaning that the UK

could not block it. This was perceived as a way for the Commission and the other member states to circumvent British opposition. In other policy areas Britain would have a veto, because a unanimous vote is required. The UK had opted out of social legislation under the Maastricht Treaty, (Open Europe 2009). In 1992, the Conservative leader of government in the UK (John Major) reportedly said that unnecessary interference with working practices is bad for business. Measures in the proposed working time directive would hurt British industry and destroy jobs. The UK was outvoted 11 to 1 in Council negotiations and the proposal was adopted in 1993. However, in 1993 the United Kingdom won an opt-out clause allowing it not to apply the maximum 48-hour working week where workers agree to work longer.

EU Law (2003/88/EC): The WTD 2003/88/EC is a European Union Directive, which creates the right for EU workers to a minimum number of holidays each year, paid breaks, and rest of at least 11 hours in any 24 hours; restricts excessive night work; and makes a default right to work no more than 48 hours per week. Excessive working time being a major cause of stress, depression and illness, the purpose of the Directive is to protect people's health and safety. Like all European Union directives, this is an instrument which requires member states to enact its provisions in national legislation. The core rules of the Working Time Directive are also contained in the EU Charter of Fundamental Rights, which provides at Article 31(2) that: 'Every worker has a right to limitation of maximum working hours, to daily and weekly rest periods and to an annual period of paid leave.' The Court of Justice, moreover, has repeatedly held that the Directive's requirements on maximum working time, paid annual leave and minimum rest periods 'constitute rules of Community social law of particular importance, from which every worker must benefit'.

The UK strongly opposed any attempt to tell people they could no longer work the hours they wanted. Following the vote, the UK (then Conservative) Government threatened to contest the Directive. The Government challenged its validity, questioning the commission's jurisdiction in the matter (not a matter of health and safety) and in 1994 brought the matter before the ECJ in an attempt to change the legal base of the WTD, from health and safety to the so-called Social Chapter. In 2006, the ECJ ruled against the UK Government. Following the ruling, Prime Minister John Major pledged to reverse the ECJ verdict and a Conservative Cabinet Minister voiced concern about the Government constantly losing cases (that go against national interest) in the European Court. Whilst the Conservative government opposed the WTD, Labour was in favour of more regulation as were the UK trade unions (the TUC General Secretary, called the ruling great news). Business representatives (the CBI), on the other hand, said it was legislation at its worst.

The WTD came into force in the UK in 1998, after the UK Government failed to block the proposal in the EU's Council of Ministers. Although the directive applies to all member states, in the UK, it is possible to opt out of the 48-hour working week and work longer hours (The 'opt-out' under Article 22(1) of the Directive presently allows Member States to provide that a worker may agree with his or her employer to work hours which exceed the 48-hour limit, subject to

certain protective conditions). However, it is not possible to opt out of the other requirements. The (incumbent) Labour Government transposed the Directive into UK law via the Working Time Regulations 1998 – which included the right for individuals to voluntarily opt out from the 48-hour maximum working week. The Working Time Regulations (1998), amended, with effect from 1 August 2003, implement the European Working Time Directive into GB law. Within the UK, the Health and Safety Executive (HSE) is responsible for the enforcement of the maximum weekly working time limit and certain other aspects of the law.

GB Law: STATUTORY INSTRUMENTS 1998 No. 1833 TERMS AND CONDITIONS OF EMPLOYMENT, The Working Time Regulations 1998, Made 30th July 1998 - Laid before Parliament 30th July 1998 and Coming into force1st October 1998.

The Secretary of State, being a Minister designated for the purposes of section 2(2) of the European Communities Act 1972(1) in relation to measures relating to the organization of working time and measures relating to the employment of children and young persons, in exercise of the powers conferred on him by that provision hereby makes the following Regulations (cited as the Working Time Regulations 1998) and extend to Great Britain only.

Maximum weekly working time: 4.(1) Subject to regulation 5, a worker's working time, including overtime, in any reference period which is applicable in his case shall not exceed an average of 48 hours for each seven days. (2) An employer shall take all reasonable steps, in keeping with the need to protect the health and safety of workers, to ensure that the limit specified in paragraph (1) is complied with in the case of each worker employed by him in relation to whom it applies. (3) Subject to paragraphs (4) and (5) and any agreement under regulation 23(b), the reference periods which apply in the case of a worker are – (a) where a relevant agreement provides for the application of this regulation in relation to successive periods of 17 weeks, each such period, or (b) in any other case, any period of 17 weeks in the course of his employment. For the purposes of this regulation, a worker's average working time for each seven days during a reference period shall be determined according to the formula: $(A+B)/C$ where – A is the aggregate number of hours comprised in the worker's working time during the course of the reference period; B is the aggregate number of hours comprised in

(continued)

his working time during the course of the period beginning immediately after the end of the reference period and ending when the number of days in that subsequent period on which he has worked equals the number of excluded days during the reference period; and C is the number of weeks in the reference period. 5. – (1) The limit specified in regulation 4(1) shall not apply in relation to a worker who has agreed with his employer in writing that it should not apply in his case, provided that the employer complies with the requirements of paragraph (4). (2) An agreement for the purposes of paragraph (1) – (a) may either relate to a specified period or apply indefinitely; and (b) subject to any provision in the agreement for a different period of notice, shall be terminable by the worker by giving not less than seven days' notice to his employer in writing. (3) Where an agreement for the purposes of paragraph (1) makes provision for the termination of the agreement after a period of notice, the notice period provided for shall not exceed three months. (4) The requirements referred to in paragraph (1) are that the employer – (a) maintains up-to-date records which – (i) identify each of the workers whom he employs who has agreed that the limit specified in regulation 4(1) should not apply in his case; (ii) set out any terms on which the worker agreed that the limit should not apply; and (iii) specify the number of hours worked by him for the employer during each reference period since the agreement came into effect (excluding any period which ended more than two years before the most recent entry in the records); (b) permits any inspector appointed by the Health and Safety Executive or any other authority which is responsible under regulation 28 for the enforcement of these Regulations to inspect those records on request; and (c) provides any such inspector with such information as he may request regarding any case in which a worker has agreed that the limit specified in regulation 4(1) should not apply in his case.

UK Employer's obligations (simplified): For most workers, the law specifies the maximum number of hours they can work in an average week. The law applies to nearly all businesses. Workers can agree to work beyond the 48-hour weekly limit but must not be forced to work more than 48 hours on average over a 17 week period. Agreement to work beyond the 48-hour weekly limit must be in writing and signed by the worker ('opt-out' agreement). Employers must keep records to demonstrate that weekly limits (regulations) are complied with and must monitor those workers close to the 48-hour weekly limit. There is also a need to keep an up-to-date list of workers who have agreed to work more than 48 hours a week on average.

Developments: Some articles of the 1993 WTD were due to be reviewed after ten years. The Commission, in September 2004, proposed to amend the directive. The European Parliament voted at first reading in May 2005. In parallel, after three years of deadlock, the Council reached an agreement in June 2008. The EP Committee on Employment and Social Affairs voted at second reading on 5 November 2008 and restated its first-reading position, notably on the two controversial points: opt-outs and on-call time. In the debate on Monday (15 December), MEPs were divided as to the continuation of the opt-out. In December 2008, the European Parliament (opposing the Council) voted to end the UK's opt-out from the EU's 48-hour week. However, because the WTD is subject to what is called 'co-decision', the European Parliament and the Council of Ministers have to agree on the proposal before it can become law. MEPs stated that there must be no exceptions to the 48-hours maximum working time calculated over a (revised) reference period of 12 months and say the opt-out must end three years after adoption of the directive. Most MEPs felt that an annualization of the reference period for calculating weekly working hours would allow a sufficiently flexible organization of working time (a matter that had been suggested in 2005). MEPs adopted the amendment on the abolition of the opt-out 36 months after the entry into force of (revised) Directive with 421 votes in favour 273 against and 11 abstentions. This then led to formal 'conciliation' talks beginning between the EP and the Council. The European Commission is currently reviewing Directive 2003/88/EC, by means of a two-stage consultation of the social partners at EU level and a detailed impact assessment. In December 2010, the Commission adopted a second-stage consultation paper asking workers' and employers' representatives for their views on possible changes to the Directive.

The Working Time Directive is reviewed In a communication from the Commission to the European Parliament, the Council, the European Economic and Social committee and the committee of the regions (Brussels, 21.12.2010 COM(2010) 801 final). The Commission argue the Working Time Directive forms a cornerstone of Social Europe by ensuring minimum protection for all workers against excessive working hours and disregard of minimum rest periods. Over the last few years, however, the effectiveness of EU working time legislation has been questioned on several grounds. Some of its provisions have lagged behind rapid changes in working patterns, making the Directive less helpful for responding to employee and business needs. Moreover, difficulties in implementing some of its provisions or Court of Justice rulings have led to legal uncertainty or even slippage in compliance as regards some important aspects. Hence the urgent need for a review of the Directive, which the Commission is determined to conduct in accordance with the principles of Smarter Regulation. The aim of this Communication is to seek the views of the social partners at EU level, in accordance with Article 154(3) of the Treaty on the Functioning of the European Union (TFEU), on the content of envisaged action at EU level to amend the Working Time Directive.

Source: Open Europe (2009), 'TIME'S UP! The case against the EU's 48 hour working week', www.openeurope.org.uk/research/wtdoptout2.pdf. Reproduced with thanks to Open Europe.

EC directive on the issue. Council Directive 91/533/EEC of 14 October 1991 presents rules on an employer's obligation to inform employees of the conditions applicable to the contract or employment relationship. It stipulates the fundamental points to be communicated respectively in the case of domestic workers and expatriate workers. It also specifies the authorized means of information and the periods within which information must be provided. Employers must provide employees with the following fundamental information: title, grade, nature or category of work or brief job specification; date of commencement of contract or employment relationship; amount of paid leave or procedures for allocating and determining such leave; employee's normal working hours; and periods of notice to be observed by the employer and the employee should their contract or employment relationship be terminated.

There are a number of ways in which a contract of employment can be brought to an end. In some cases, the employee may view this to be done unfairly and may be protected through common or statute law. In some cases, the employer may terminate the contract by dismissal and this may occasionally be a wrongful dismissal. The statutory concept of unfair dismissal was first introduced in the Industrial Relations Act 1971 and the right to claim is now contained in ERA 1996. More recently, in addition to statutory legislation, a code of practice has also been developed for disciplinary and grievance procedures within the workplace. Following the Dispute Resolution Review (DRR), the Government changed the way we deal with problems at work. As of 6 April 2009, as part of the DRR, the Advisory, Conciliation and Arbitration Service (ACAS) has revised its Code of Practice on disciplinary and grievance procedures and produced a new Code. ACAS aim to improve organizations and working life through better employment relations. The Code is issued under section 199 of the Trade Union and Labour Relations (Consolidation) Act 1992 and was laid before both Houses of Parliament on 9 December 2008. It came into effect by order of the Secretary of State on 6 April 2009 and replaces the Code issued in 2004. A failure to follow the Code does not, in itself, make a person or organization liable to proceedings. However, employment tribunals will take the Code into account when considering relevant cases.

Applying for employment and once employed, people may enjoy the protection from discrimination afforded by the Equality Act 2010. Council directive 2000/78/EC (see also Council directive 2000/43) established a general framework for equal treatment in employment and occupation. With regard to time and pay, the discussion about the regulation of a person's working time encapsulated the arguments about the degree to which governments should intervene in the employment relationship and the extent to which such regulation should originate with the EU (Sargeant and Lewis 2010). The British government argued that such matters were an issue of **subsidiarity** (the principle of subsidiarity is defined in Article 5 of the Treaty establishing the European Community. It is intended to ensure that decisions are taken as closely as possible to the citizen and that constant checks are made as to whether action at Community level is justified in the light of the possibilities available at national, regional or local level. Specifically, it is the principle whereby the Union does not take action – except in the areas which fall within its exclusive competence – unless it is more effective than action taken at national, regional or local level) and should be settled within member states rather than by the community. The Council argued that the justification for the working time directive was a health and safety one and that the community had confidence in this field. In the event, the UK finally transposed the directive into law.

SUMMARY

- Throughout this chapter we have discussed political and legal systems and their impact upon organizations, the way they work and the business they undertake.
- We have focused on governance (multilevel) and rules that regulate markets, industry competitive forces and business relationships with employees, customers, suppliers, investors and the public at large.
- We noted the trend towards supranational governance and that regional intergovernmental organizations have become empowered not only through economic but greater political integration. Companies must no longer restrict their environmental analysis to national issues but must look further afield if they are to manage political risk, seek out opportunity and minimize threat.
- At the world level of analysis, globalization has led to greater harmonization and the erosion of country boundaries in the pursuit of liberalization. Additionally, at the regional level (see for example the EU) the free movement of goods, services, capital and people is having a profound impact upon organizations, where they locate operations, their strategies and business practices.
- Through globalization and internationalization organizations, on the one hand, become more exposed to a greater number of political and legal systems, often increasing costs and competition whilst, on the other hand, they are able to grow their markets, access lower cost facilities and the workforce of other countries.
- The nature of democracies ensures that, through regular elections and political choice, the political and legal environment remains incredibly dynamic and turbulent, necessitating the organization to appraise constantly the flurry of new rules governing behaviour within its environment.
- We have summarized in Figure 2.3 this complex environment and build upon it in the next chapter during discussion of the closely-related economic environment.

REVISION QUESTIONS

1. If British workers are permitted by their own elected government to work more than 48 hours per week, then why should it matter to other EU Member States? Do we need a directive on working time? Also, evaluate whether EU Citizens have a right not to work in excess of 48 hours a week on average.
2. Critically evaluate, highlighting advantages and disadvantages, the WTD from the perspective of a variety of EU and UK stakeholders.
3. What is meant by politics in the context of the political environment for business?
4. What is the role of the government in business?
5. How can political and state intervention impact upon business? Your answer should make reference to threats and opportunities for organizations.
6. How can political intervention at the level of the EU impact upon business? You should discuss the main advantages and disadvantages of European integration.
7. In what ways are the political and legal environments related?
8. Why must managers be aware of how political risk can affect their organization and trade?
9. Outline the different sources of law.
10. Evaluate legal intervention within business and management.

FIGURE 2.3

The business political and legal environment: a model of interdependency-layers of influence

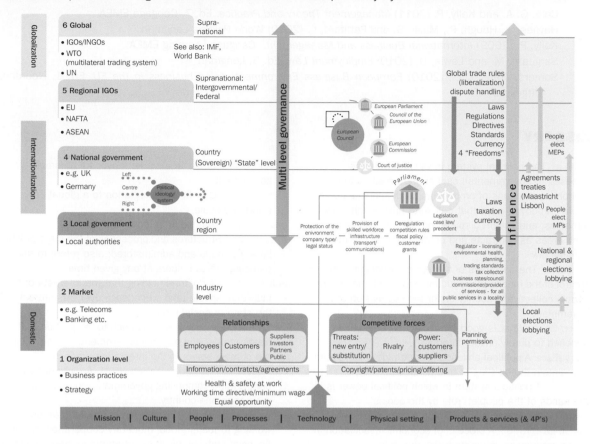

DISCUSSION QUESTIONS

First, you should re-read the 'Business in Debate: Regulating the employment relationship – Modernizing labour law' section. The debate on the organization of working time is complex. Discuss in groups, or write an essay individually on the following:

1. If British workers are permitted by their own elected government to work more than 48 hours per week, then why should it matter to other EU Member States? Do we need a directive on working time? Can the WTD be ignored?

2. How is compliance with WTD measured? How do you believe compliance with WTD should be measured?

3. Debate whether EU Citizens have the right not to work more than 48 hours a week on average.

4. Critically evaluate, highlighting advantages and disadvantages, of the WTD (version 2003/88/EC and then proposed revisions, focusing on the 48-hour rule and the opt out) from the perspective of a variety of EU and UK stakeholders such as the employee and Trade Union (EU and UK), the UK Government (Conservative v Labour), the Employer (public/private), the EP, and other Member States (consider a role play debate).

5. Outline the type of working time rules that would be needed at EU level to cope with the economic, social, technological and demographic realities of the 21st century.

REFERENCES AND FURTHER READING

Cole, G. A. and Kelly, P. (2011) *Management Theory and Practice.* Ed. 7, Cengage EMEA

Haynes, J., Hough, P., Malik, S. and Pettiford, L. (2010) *World Politics.* Longman

Kelly, P. (2009) *International Business and Management.* Cengage Learning EMEA

Sargeant, M. and Lewis, D. (2010) *Employment Law.* Ed. 5, Longman

Somers, Frans J. L., (2010) *European Business Environment: doing business in the EU.* Ed. 1. Noordhoff Uitgevers

GLOSSARY

Capitalism The political system in which private (as opposed to governmental) capital and wealth is the predominant means of producing and distributing goods

Civil Law A body of rules that delineate private rights and remedies, and govern disputes between individuals in such areas as contracts and property; distinct from criminal law

Collectivism The principles or system of ownership and control of the means of production and distribution by the people collectively, usually under the supervision of a government

Common Good What is good for society as a whole, as opposed to purely private interests

Conservatism A political philosophy or attitude which seeks to maintain the existing or traditional order

Democracy A political system in which political power is in the hands of the people: 'rule by the people'

Downside Risk Risk associated with loss or harm only

European integration A process of economic association in which progressive integration requires policy harmonization and institutional changes rather than merely the removal of trade barriers

European Union (EU) Regional grouping of European countries which evolved from trade agreements to deeper economic integration

Federalism A system of government in which power is divided between a national (federal) government and various regional governments; a union of states under a central government distinct from that of the separate states, who retain certain individual powers under the central government

Federal State A state in which power is shared constitutionally between the centre and localities (as opposed to a unitary state)

Five Competitive Forces Together these determine competition in an industry or market: rivalry amongst existing like-for-like players; the threat of new entrants; the threat of substitute solutions; the bargaining power of buyers; and the bargaining power of suppliers

Freedom A key political principle referring to the ability of individuals to decide for themselves how to live their own lives, often linked with arguments in favour of the 'free market'

Free market In a strict sense refers to a market that is free of government regulation or intervention. In practice supporters of the free market advocate minimum government

Globalization Growth and integration to a global or worldwide scale

Governance Exercise of authority and control

Government Structures and processes of the state by which laws are made and administered; also refers to the particular office holders at any given time

Individualism A doctrine holding that the interests of the individual should take precedence over the interests of the state or social group

Intergovernmentalism An approach to integration that treats states, and national governments in particular, as the primary actors in the integration process

Intergovernmental Organization (IGO) An international organization comprising government representatives of more than one country

International Monetary Fund (IMF) An organization, working to foster global monetary cooperation, secure financial stability, facilitate international trade, promote high employment and sustainable economic growth and reduce poverty around the world

Legal and Political Conditions The laws and the legal system's impact on business, together with the general nature of the relationship between government and business

Legal System System of rules that regulate behaviour and the processes by which the laws of a country are enforced and through which redress of grievances is obtained

Liberalism A political philosophy allowing more personal freedom and a development towards a fairer sharing of wealth and power within society, civil liberties and individual rights, and nonviolent modification of institutions to permit continued individual and social progress

Multi-level Governance Governance takes place on a number of spatial scales – national, sub-national, supranational

Nationalization Changing something from private to state ownership or control

Pluralism A model or theory which emphasizes the dispersal and fragmentation of political influence among a large number of groups and interests in society

Policy A guiding principle designed to influence decisions, actions, etc.

Politics The activities associated with the governance of a country or area

Political Environment That part of the macro environment concerned with impending and potential legislation and how it may affect a particular organization

Political Ideology A set of doctrines or beliefs that form the basis of a political system

Political Risk The likelihood that political forces will cause dire changes in a country's business environment that will adversely affect the profit and other goals of a particular organization

Political System Structures and processes by which a nation state is governed

Regulation A rule (principle, law or directive) made and maintained by an authority designed to control or govern conduct

Socialism A left-wing political ideology, involving a critique of capitalism and support for state regulation and/or control of business (advocating substantial public involvement, through government ownership, in the means of production and distribution)

Sovereignty A term referring to the highest form or source of authority, e.g. parliamentary sovereignty

Supranational Governance A level of political authority above the nation-state e.g. the EU

Unitary State A state, like the UK, in which power is concentrated at the centre, as opposed to a federal state in which power is shared between different levels of government

United Nations (UN) An international organization committed to maintaining international peace and security, developing friendly relations among nations and promoting social progress, better living standards and human rights

Upside Risk The opposite to downside risk, typically emphasising benefits and rewards (generally beyond expectations)

Welfare State Refers to the growth of state expenditure on a range of public services such as education, health, housing, social services and income support

World Bank International institution providing financial and technical help to developing countries

World Trade Organization (WTO) An international organization that deals with the rules of trade among member countries

CHAPTER CASE STUDY

EU Postal Policy – Liberalizing Postal Services: creating a single market (opening the market to competition)

Plans to open up postal services to competition across the EU by 2011/13 – eliminating postal service monopolies

The postal sector is an important business area in Member States of the European Union. The national postal operator is one of the largest employers in most countries and the postal service is offered in every part of the EU, allowing almost every citizen relative ease of access to the postal network. In addition, the postal sector is of major economic importance. Postal services are a key element of the so called network industries (energy, transport and telecommunications) opened to competition in the 1990s in accordance with Treaty provisions providing for the free movement of products and services. Prior to the 1997 Directive, postal services were often fragmented across the EU. Ownership was usually lodged in public corporations and while some services within the sector were open to competition, others were not (letter mail). At the same time, the sector as a whole was operating at a loss whilst much of its infrastructure required modernization and renewed investment. The sector is of vital importance for commercial users and consumers alike and is considered a service of general economic interest (SGEI). The postal markets are dynamic and quickly evolving (influenced by markets of communication, advertising and electronic commerce). Overall in the EU, postal services are estimated (2002) to handle 135 billion items per year, reflecting a turnover of about € 90 billion or about 1 per cent of Community GDP. About two-thirds of this turnover is generated by mail services. The remainder is generated by parcels and express services which are already open to competing operators. Around 5.2 million people are employed in postal services in the EU. The objective of the EU postal policy is to accomplish the Single Market for postal services and ensure a high quality universal postal service. Objectives are pursued by opening up the sector to competition in a gradual and controlled way, on the basis of the regulatory frameworks of the EC. The improvement of quality of service, in particular in terms of delivery performance and convenient access, are fundamental aspects of policy.

Efforts towards reforming the postal market began in the early 1990s, as part of the push to create a European single market. The aim was to open national monopolies to competition in order to make postal services cheaper, faster, more efficient and more innovative – similar to what was done in the telecom and energy sectors; harmonize performance across member states; and improve the quality of cross-border services. The EU postal services directives (97/67/EC of 1997, as amended by Directive 2002/39/EC of 2002), have established a regulatory framework for universal service, and progressively reduced the monopoly **reserved area**. The two directives succeeded in opening up a number of postal services, including the delivery of parcels and express services, but stopped short of imposing competition for the delivery of letters weighing less than 50g. Current operators were entitled to retain this so-called 'reserved area' – which represents more than 70 per cent of all letter post in the EU and around 60 per cent of all revenues from postal services – in order to maintain their role of 'universal service provider' (USP). However, on 18 October 2006, Internal Market Commissioner Charlie McCreevy confirmed, in his proposal for a third Postal Services Directive, the Commission's intention to eliminate all remaining obstacles to a single postal market. By 2008, five Member States had already liberalized their postal service markets, including items under 50g. They were: (1) Sweden (1993), whose incumbent operator Posten AB is in charge of universal service, (2) Finland (1994), whose 'Posti' services are provided by Itella Corporation, (3) the UK (from 2006), whose state-owned operator is the Royal Mail, (4) Germany (from 2008), where Deutsche Post is a listed company, in which the German state is no longer the majority shareholder and (5) the Netherlands (from 2008), where three postal service firms – Sandd, Selekt Mail and TNT Post – share the market). Opening up postal service markets to competition does not necessarily entail privatizing current operators. For example, the UK's Royal Mail operates in a fully liberalized market, but is 100 per cent state owned. By contrast, the Dutch operator TNT, although until recently a monopoly supplier of some services, is privately owned. In 2008, the majority of member state postal service suppliers were state owned.

The proposed third directive maintained the obligations on Member States to ensure a high-quality **universal service** comprising at least one delivery and collection five days a week for every EU citizen. The obligation to ensure affordability of postal services was maintained, as was the possibility for Member States to impose a uniform tariff for single piece tariff items such as consumer mail. Other measures within the proposal included control of fair competition. In a fully competitive environment, Member States must conduct the delicate exercise of providing sufficient freedom to universal service providers to adapt to competition and at the same time, ensure adequate monitoring of the behaviour of the likely dominant operator in order to safeguard effective competition. At a second reading in Parliament (2008) it was suggested the deadline for market opening would be set for 31 December 2010 (2012 in some cases). Full market opening should mean national operators will no longer have a monopoly on mail. The European Regulator Group for Postal Services (ERGP) was established by the EC in 2010, to advise and assist the Commission on postal service matters. The ERGP advise and assist the Commission in consolidating the internal market for postal services. The role of the ERGP is to facilitate consultation, coordination and cooperation between the independent national regulatory authorities in the Member States, and between those authorities and the Commission. Additionally, the EU (through the Commission) has, since 1993, promoted and supported the process of technical standardization within the postal sector. Postal standardization is focused in two areas: Harmonization of technical methods within the universal service, in particular for external measurement of quality of service performance; and Facilitation of interoperability of postal industry stakeholders along the postal value chain. In a Speech on the new Postal Directive in October 2008, Charlie McCreevy (the European Commissioner for Internal Market and Services from 2004–2010) stated: 'Postal reform's key objective is a high quality, highly efficient, innovative and sustainable postal sector, adapted to meet the needs of users in the 21st century. Market opening is not an end in itself. It is the means through which we pursue the objectives of reform.'

In seeking change through increased liberalization, the EU rather than disrupting the sector, has tried reconciling the interests of a number of key stakeholders – national postal operators, the

KEY CONCEPTS

Reserved Area: This is the segment of postal services which is reserved to those postal operators (which may be either public or private) providing universal services within national boundaries. In practice, this means that letter mail/parcel under certain weight and cost limits can only be handled by those operators who are bound by universal service obligations described above. The rationale behind the reserved area is that it is an appropriate form of compensation for taking on the uneconomic burden of universal service, when this burden has been shown to exist. The size of the reserved area is progressively reduced and might not be retained in the context of a fully liberalized sector. In line with the target date set out in the current Directive, the new Commission proposal confirms the final step in this long reform process and recommends the removal of remaining reserved areas in all Member States.

Universal Service: Universal implies something which is available or accessible everywhere and to everyone and on the same conditions. In practice, this means relatively easy access to certain postal services, the most common being letter and parcel post. In other words, citizens/businesses located in rural areas should enjoy broadly the same or at least comparable access to that available to their urban counterparts. Within the postal sector, universal service involves the permanent and obligatory provision of a service at sufficient points within a national boundary in order to take account of the needs of users. Such services must also meet specified quality targets and be available at affordable prices.

current postal operators, 'would be' new entrants and users/consumers and to strike the right balance between increasing competition and the reduction of existing monopolies. Rules on access (to postal services) for users, quality of service standards and pricing levels are all designed to ensure that citizens and businesses get value for money whilst at the same time providing postal operators with a stable environment and the opportunity to invest in new products and services. The European Communities and their Member States believe that citizens and businesses world-wide need efficient, reliable and good quality postal/courier services at affordable prices. From a global perspective, the EU aims to update and improve international rules to ensure fair trade and to harness globalization and promote greater trade with WTO member countries. The EU is ready to subscribe internationally to basic pro-competition principles (which already exist in the EU), provided that others are ready to do the same. At the end of the Uruguay round, only a few WTO Members (about 40) undertook commitments in the postal/courier sector. When looking at these commitments, it seems that Members wanted to ensure their existing monopoly situation. Since then, much progress has been made towards the continuing liberalization of the postal/courier sector.

Source: Adapted from http://ec.europa.eu/internal_market/post/news/index_en.htm © European Union, 1995-2012. Reproduced with permission.

Questions

- Reform process: why does the EU phase in major changes – why does change take so long (more than a decade with postal service liberalization)?

- Why does the postal market need liberalizing – who wins and who loses as a result?

- Postal services are dynamic and face a serious threat (but also opportunity) from new technology – discuss.

- Citizens continue to be significant users of postal services and their interests are being protected in a number of different ways. Identify/suggest how this might be accomplished.

- How might member state policies and national regulator decisions about their respective country's postal service conflict with the policy goals of the EU? How can/should the EU assure compliance with their obligations?

- Why do so many states own a significant share of the dominant postal service in their country? Does privatization bring any benefits to the country?

- The pace of competitive entry has been slower than originally anticipated and national postal operators have retained their dominant positions in markets open to competition. Identify and propose ways to dismantle remaining market barriers.

- A level playing field is a pre-condition for a truly open and competitive market. Evaluate the use of the 'reserved area' as a policy tool to manage phased liberalization of the postal sector.

- To what extent should the national government/EU interfere in the market/industry? What is their role?

- Prices for consumer letter mail have generally increased in recent years. Prices for business users (which generate three quarters of mail volumes) have decreased overall. What is the present state of the postal services market in the EU? Analyze competition, company ownership (in terms of the state) and the extent of regulation by the EU and member states. Is the EU achieving its goal (in terms of creating a Single Market for postal services and ensuring a high quality universal postal service? Has the quality of service improved, in particular in terms of delivery performance and convenient access)?

- Overall, have EU postal customers, both business and consumers, benefited from liberalization?

3
THE ECONOMIC ENVIRONMENT

FIGURE 3.1

The economic environment mind map

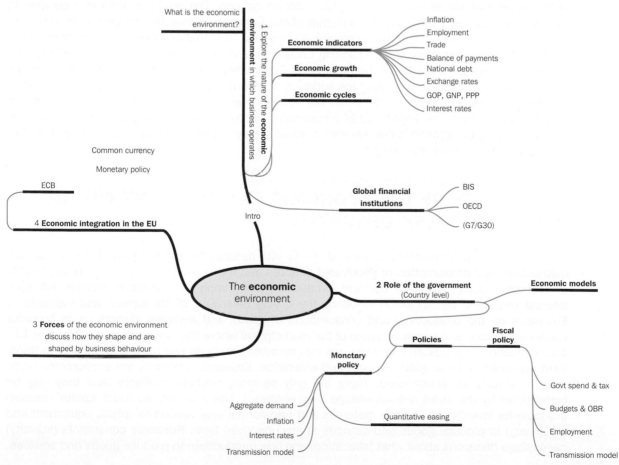

KEY CONCEPTS

Economic environment | Economic system | Free market economy | Gross domestic product (GDP) | Macroeconomic policy | Monetary policy

INTRODUCTION

An understanding of the national, regional and global economic environment is essential for business managers primarily because of changes to demand and supply, interest, exchange and inflation rates, pricing, borrowing rates and investment opportunities, costs, competition, employment rates and export opportunities, see Figure 3.1. Such changes manifest themselves in terms of business revenues, costs and profit margins. In the past decade we have witnessed fluctuations in such an environment that can bankrupt business or fuel its growth (see the global financial crisis of 2008). Adopting a business perspective, this chapter examines issues relating to the economy. We start by asking: What is the economic environment and consider the indicators used to evaluate and compare such environments. We then consider the important issues and concepts associated with business cycles (and international/global business cycles) when seeking to understand economies. After this introductory session we consider the attempts of national governments to manage and influence their economies. Targets and the outcomes of policy decisions utilize the economic indicators introduced in the first section. Two key macroeconomic policy areas of fiscal and monetary policy are then investigated and models presented to explain the effect of policy decisions on economic variables and activity. In the third section we pay particular attention to the interplay between business and the economy, as mediated by government policy. In this section we explore the business consequences of fiscal and monetary policy. Finally, we take a brief look at EU monetary policy as an example of economic integration across nations. The reader is then in a position to contrast the sovereign UK approach with that of the Euro zone. Once this chapter is studied, the reader should be better placed to appreciate and respond to actual or expected future government budgets (taxation and government spending decisions), and interest rate changes (to include consequential exchange and inflation rate changes). Governments, influenced by their specific ideologies, play an active role in managing the economy and so this chapter will build upon the previous chapter. Similarly, decisions made within the economic environment will impact upon the social environment, through its impact upon employment, income and spending and the sustainable environment, as the economic environment is about supply. Supply is about production and production makes use of world resources.

THE NATURE OF THE ECONOMIC ENVIRONMENT WITHIN WHICH BUSINESS OPERATES

Economics is a social science, concerned chiefly with description and analysis of the production, distribution, and consumption of goods and services and the economic environment is the totality of economic factors, such as demand, productivity and supply, employment, income, inflation, interest rates and wealth which influence the *buying behaviour* of consumers and institutions. Emphasis on the productivity and consumption of goods and services, directs us to consider issues of demand and supply and also of the marketplace where this will happen (see Chapter 11). The production of goods and services requires resources such as raw materials; labour, to transform raw materials into goods; capital and enterprise. *Economic problems* are encountered when such resources are constrained. There are only so many workers available (and they may be constrained by the skills and knowledge they possess). There is only so much capital (money) available for investment and raw materials and transformational resources (plant, equipment and machinery) to produce goods and services at any one given time. Resource constraints (scarcity) necessitate decisions about what (allocation) and how (production) to produce goods and services.

In some cases such decisions may be made by the government, whilst, in other cases, such decisions may be made by the consumer and producers collectively (remember from the previous chapter, a capitalistic economy is an economy that relies chiefly on market forces to allocate goods and resources and to determine prices). Consequently, in a capitalist economy, businesses will produce the goods and services, for which resources are available, in the quantities and at the price that consumers want and are prepared to pay, whilst providing the company with a profit margin. In a competitive market, commercial organizations must do this efficiently, offering value for money, or consumers will simply switch to a different supplier. Consequently, the concept of efficiency is typically associated with economics and the challenges of the economic environment. In many cases this will mean ensuring that the average cost of each item produced is minimized (productive efficiency).

Economic Indicators

An economic indicator is simply any economic statistic, such as Gross Domestic Product (GDP), the unemployment rate, or the inflation rate. Variables like these can indicate how well the economy is performing and how well the economy is going to perform in the future. In the previous paragraph we set out to identify what constitutes the economic environment. This environment varies according to the country or region within which a particular organization may be operating. Economies may be evaluated in a number of ways, using a number of performance indicators:

- Gross Domestic Product (GDP) – is a measure of a country's overall economic output. GDP measures aggregate economic activity, encompassing every sector of the economy – the total value of all goods and services produced by a country in one year, i.e. the total monetary value of all goods and services produced domestically by a country. GDP growth is widely followed as the primary indicator of the strength of economic activity.

- Gross National Product (GNP) – is an economic statistic which includes GDP plus any income earned by residents from their overseas investments, minus income earned within the domestic economy by overseas residents, i.e. it is the total domestic and foreign added value claimed by residents of a state; the wealth of a country. Its total income divided by its total population.

- Balance Of Payments (BOP) – is a system of recording all of a country's economic transactions with the rest of the world over a period of one year; the difference between the payments made to and the receipts from foreign nations in a given period (the summation of imports and exports made between one country and the other countries with which it trades) – a favourable balance of payments exists when more payments are coming in than going out.

- Employment rate – the percentage of the working age population who are currently employed. See also the unemployment rate, the percentage of the work force currently unemployed. If unemployment figures are up, it indicates a lack of expansion within the economy. The employment rate is an important indicator of the state of the wider economy. It is a lagging indicator; that is, following a recession, the employment rate tends not to grow to any significant degree until the rest of the economy has recovered.

We listed economic indicators above but it is the changes in their values over time that help us understand the economy and how it is changing. Economic growth is growth in the level of national income, typically measured as the percentage change in real GDP. This means the change in GDP after inflation has been taken into account.

Inflation – may be defined as a persistent rise in the general price level or an increase in the average of all prices of goods and services over a period of time (an opposite term is Deflation – decline in prices in an economy, associated with recession and falling demand). Inflation is closely related to interest and exchange rates. There are a number of ways in which inflation can be measured, such as changes in the Retail Prices Index (RPI). The Consumer Prices Index (CPI) and the RPI are the two main measures of consumer inflation in the UK. The RPI measures the changing prices from one month to another in a representative 'basket' of commodities bought by the 'average' consumer. Inflation concerns the value of money and impacts upon the spending power of consumers and businesses. It also has external consequences, making domestically produced goods more expensive and less competitive on world markets. When inflation rises, imported goods become cheaper, resulting in greater demand for goods that are not produced in the home country. This will then impact upon the balance of payments.

- **Consumer Prices Index** – a consumer prices index (CPI) measures changes in the price level of consumer goods and services purchased by households; it is also called the Harmonized Index of Consumer Prices (HICP). Since December 2003 the UK Government has used the CPI as its main measure of inflation in the economy rather than the Retail Prices Index (RPI)

- **Interest rate** – the price paid for the use of borrowed money – the rate at which interest is paid by a borrower for the use of money borrowed from a lender. When interest rates rise, consumers spend less, causing retail sales to slow. Interest rate changes impact upon the value of a currency, reflected in the exchange rates.

- **Exchange rate** – the price of one national currency in terms of another (the value of one currency for the purpose of conversion to another; the rate at which one currency is converted into another)

National debt – the total debt accumulated by a central government's borrowings over the years; the national debt is measured in billions of pounds (£bn). The debt ratio is a measure of how much the government has borrowed – it is the national debt as a percentage of GDP. The higher this percentage, the more significant is the debt to the economy. The debt ratio is important because the higher the debt ratio, the higher the interest payments the government has to make. Consequently the government no longer has available money for the provision of other public services. See also the Public Sector Net Cash Requirement (PSNCR) previously termed the PSBR – the public sector borrowing requirement. This measures the amount the government needs to borrow to meet all its expenditure commitments. Governments frequently spend more than they are earning in tax revenue, and so are forced to borrow to fill the gap.

The aforementioned indicators may be used as economic targets and measurable outcomes of macroeconomic policy discussed later in this chapter. However, when evaluating or pursuing economic growth, analysts and policy makers must recognize it tends to follow a cyclical pattern. There may be boom periods when economic growth is faster, but these may well be followed later by periods of economic slow-down. This pattern is known as the trade cycle or business cycle. One application of economic indicators is the study of business cycles, a concept we consider next.

Business cycles

Business (economic) cycles are fluctuations in the economy (economic activity/production) that follow the general pattern of expansion and prosperity (boom), downturn, recession, depression and recovery. A business cycle can last from a year to more than a decade. However, there is no regularity in the timing of such cycles. Thus, a business cycle occurs due to the fluctuations an economy experiences over time, resulting from changes in economic growth. The cycle is shown in Figure 3.2. Within the overall cycle are mini cycles. For example, when the economy is expanding, increased sales (demand) leads to increased production and supply which then necessitates an increase in employment and as a result, incomes rise. This cycle leads to more growth and a repeat of the cycle. The opposite is true of a downturn. When consumers, businesses or governments have less to spend, sales and demand decrease. This is followed by reduced production and supply which leads to redundancies, shorter working hours and consequently, income. People then have less to spend and thus begins a vicious downward cycle. Consequently certain economic indicators (GDP, employment rates, and disposable income or interest and exchange rates) decline or rise together. It is important to recognize how such cycles may spread across industries and country borders. If a particular industry faces downturn, the result is that the companies and workers directly affected will have less to spend on the outputs of other industries and in this way,

FIGURE 3.2
Business cycle

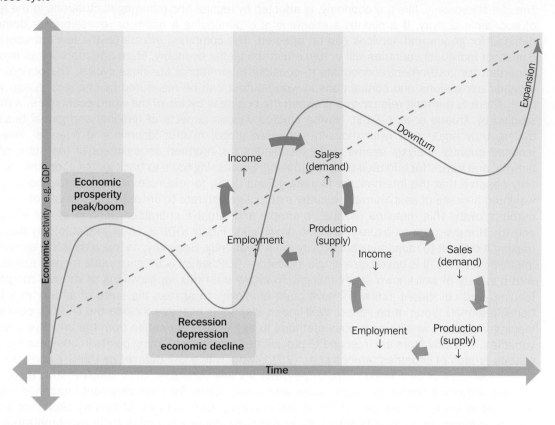

the downturn (or upturn) spreads. Not only does it spread across industries within a country but also across countries, a matter we explore later.

Business cycles are an integral part of all free market economies. Governments monitor such cycles and associated indicators in order to manage the economy. If it is known where the economy is heading, fiscal or monetary policy tools (see later) can be applied to change the course of the economy. Cycles may be measured using GDP, which typically varies over time. In the previous section we discussed growth, demand and inflation. Growth is about economic expansion and eventually leads to higher prices and rising inflation rates. Governments then act to reduce inflationary pressures, leading to recession. Governments do this through various macroeconomic policies but recognize that economics is a somewhat imprecise field, especially when it relates to dealing with business cycles. Economic indicators such as GDP and the inflation rate are trailing indicators. They tell us a good deal about the economy, but importantly they tell us where the economy is at or has been, but not where it is going. Knowing current economic conditions is useful information for economists, but knowing where the economy is going is critical. Later in this chapter we explore how economic policy makers interpret and react to business cycles. Two of the most important macroeconomic variables identified in the previous section include the real growth rate of GDP and inflation. Tracking such variables helps policy makers in their goals to maintain a constant rate of real GDP growth (e.g. 3 per cent), a satisfactory employment rate and acceptable level of inflation (e.g. 2 per cent).

The OECD Business Cycle Clock has been designed to better visualize business cycles – fluctuations of economic activity around their long term potential level – and how some key economic indicators interact with the business cycle.
Try it out at http://stats.oecd.org/mei/bcc/default.html

The Global Economy and International Business Cycles

The global economy, like any economy, is affected by regular and recurring fluctuations in the levels of economic activity. If a country's economy is experiencing a boom or recession, its domestic demand for goods and services can be affected. The combined effects on the level of economic activity of individual countries will in turn affect the global economy. More and more it has become important for government economists to consider International business cycles. The periodic and irregular expansions and contractions in world output can be measured by changes in real world GDP. There is a strong relationship between the business cycles of the world economies, a matter studied by Aruoba *et al.* (2011). Having studied various aspects of national and global business cycles, they argue that (with radically enhanced global macroeconomic and financial linkages) isolated country analysis seems highly insufficient for informed assessment of the state of real activity, and hence for informed decision making. Discussing tools to track global economic activity, they observe that the International Monetary Fund (IMF), for example, uses a simple country size weighted average of each member country's output growth rate to arrive at its estimate of the world output growth. This measure provides a simple and intuitive characterization of global economic activity. However, the measure has some drawbacks. Firstly, GDP is often available only quarterly, making it difficult to monitor global activity more frequently. Secondly, as much as it is a simple and intuitive measure, it is based on a single indicator – GDP, which is a rather crude measure of activity with a variety of well-known shortcomings. To improve on this, applications of various composite, leading, and coincident indicators have been employed to assess the state of activity in a (functional/regional) group of countries. Well-known examples of these include the OECD's composite leading indicators which use various methods to aggregate information from the underlying activity variables. The indicators are intended to provide early signals of turning points in business cycles of various groups of countries. Aruoba *et al.* (2011) work with a G-7 dataset as the G-7 is responsible for 50 per cent of real world output. They use six key variables: GDP, employment, disposable income, industrial production, retail sales and initial claims for unemployment insurance – which are used to study the direction of the global economy. Comparisons of country economic activity provide evidence of a global business cycle and cross-country business cycle synchronization.

Globalization is often associated with increased international trade and financial linkages and consequently the synchronization of international business cycles (see also globalization of markets). International trade linkages generate both demand and supply-side spillovers across countries, which can increase the degree of business cycle synchronization. For example, on the demand side, an investment or consumption boom in one country can generate increased demand for imports, boosting economies abroad. On the supply-side, lower prices from foreign producers makes imported inputs cheaper. Through these types of spillover effects, stronger international trade linkages can result in more highly correlated business cycles across countries (business cycle comovement), Aruoba *et al.* (2011:p4). From a financial perspective, if consumers from different countries have a significant fraction of their investments in a particular stock market, then a decline in that stock market could induce a simultaneous decline in the demand for consumption and investment goods in these countries because of its impact upon domestic wealth. Increased financial integration and developments in communication technologies lead to faster dissemination of news shocks in financial markets. This could have a positive impact on the degree of business cycle synchronization. For example, good news about the future of an economy is likely to increase demand. Shocks associated with news, which are rapidly transmitted in global financial markets, could lead to a higher degree of interdependence across economic activity in different countries. Consequently, Gross World Product (GWP) tends to go through upswings, booms, downswings and troughs just like the business cycles in a particular country. Business cycles, whether global or country specific, include recessions. There have been many recessions and each is unique, triggered by a different set of factors. The Global Financial Crisis (GFC) is an example of how events in a region of the world can impact on the international business cycle. In the next paragraph we explore the last global recession in more detail.

The 2008–09 recession represents the longest and deepest recession in Germany, Italy, the UK and Japan. The GFC began in 2007 with a financial crisis in the US housing market. Many financial institutions lent money, to high credit risk ('subprime') consumers for house purchases, which the borrowers could not repay. Yet lenders made commission and fees from lending the money whilst the risks were taken by the actual providers of the capital and funds for lending. At first, when interest rates were high, the lenders were happy to lend the money. Everyone seemed to win. However, in late 2007 the number of house buyers unable to pay their loans increased rapidly. This affected the mortgage lending market and very quickly lenders stopped advancing loans for house purchases. Consequently house prices started to fall (as very new buyers entered the market). Financial institutions began to make losses which led to panic as people withdrew their funds from financial institutions. A number of big investment banks then failed. Lehmann Brothers, one of the largest investment banks, became bankrupt. In a short time the credit markets (where businesses borrow to fund investment and business expansion) seized up and it was difficult to borrow funds. Business could not borrow to fund investment or working capital. As many businesses had also borrowed heavily, with large debts they also began to fail and unemployment rose swiftly. This rise in unemployment caused more and more consumers and mortgage holders to default on their mortgages, leading to bankruptcy, a reduction in spending and demand and more 'subprime' mortgage losses. This impacted upon financial institutions around the world. The subsequent downturn in the US economy, coupled with the worldwide 'credit squeeze', created the Global Financial Crisis (GFC) and the global recession, dubbed the 'great recession'.

The 'Great Recession of 2008–09' (OECD 2011) is considered by many economists to be the worst financial crisis since the Great Depression of the 1930s. It resulted in the collapse of large financial institutions, the bailout of banks by national governments, and downturns in stock markets around the world. It contributed to the failure of key businesses, declines in consumer wealth, and a significant decline in economic activity, leading to a severe global economic recession in 2008. The Great Recession affected the entire world economy, with higher detriment in some countries than others.

A recession is a period of reduced economic activity. Specifically it is the contraction phase of a business cycle (see earlier), with two or more consecutive quarters of negative GDP growth. The aforementioned global recession resulted in a sharp drop in international trade, rising unemployment and slumping commodity prices. Fiscal and monetary policies (discussed later) were significantly eased to stem the recession and financial risks. The financial phase of the crisis led to emergency interventions in many national financial systems. As the crisis developed into genuine recession in many major economies, economic stimulus intended to revive economic growth became the most common policy tool. Having implemented rescue plans for the banking system, major developed and emerging countries announced plans to relieve their economies. In particular, economic stimulus plans were announced in China, the United States, and the European Union. Bailouts of failing or threatened businesses were carried out or discussed in many countries and regions. In August 2008, the Office for National Statistics reported that the UK economy had reached a standstill, with 0 per cent growth, during the second quarter of that year. Statistics for the third quarter of the year showed the first contraction in the national economy for 16 years. The UK government said the economy was feeling the effects of global pressures such as high commodity prices and the continuing credit squeeze. The Bank of England Governor warned the UK economy was set for a difficult and painful period due to a combination of high inflation and rapidly slowing growth. Inflation, at 4.4 per cent, was well above the 2 per cent target rate, making it more difficult for the Bank to cut interest rates to spur the economy. With further contraction in the final quarter of 2008, the recession was officially declared in January 2009. In October 2009, it was reported that the British economy had contracted for six successive quarters – the longest run of contraction since quarterly figures were first recorded in 1955. The end of the recession was declared in January 2010, when the economy was reported to have grown by 0.1 per cent in the final quarter of 2009. However, fears of a double-dip recession were sparked in January 2011 when it was reported that the economy had contracted by 0.5 per cent during the final quarter of 2010, following a full year of growth, although this was largely blamed on the severe weather which affected the nation in late November and almost all of December. The IMF stated, in September 2010, that the financial crisis would not end without a major decrease in unemployment as hundreds of millions of people were unemployed worldwide. The IMF urged governments to expand social safety nets and to generate job creation despite the pressure to cut spending. Governments were also urged to invest in skills training for the unemployed and even governments of countries like Greece, with major debt risk, were encouraged to first focus on long-term economic recovery through job creation. Most political responses to the economic and financial crisis have been taken, as outlined above, by individual nations. Some coordination took place at the European level, but the need to cooperate at the global level has led leaders to activate the G-20 major economies entity.

Economic Power and Global Financial Institutions

As a consequence of global cycles and recession, governments from around the world have sought to improve management of the global economic environment. This has meant new collaborations, new regulations, new institutions and shifts in economic power or developments to the roles and responsibilities of certain global financial institutions. In the final quarter of 2008, the financial crisis saw the G-20 group of major economies assume a new significance as a focus of economic and financial crisis management. Various institutions such as the World Bank, WTO and IMF were discussed in the previous chapter and they play an important role in global macroeconomics. In this section we consider three further institution types: Government Groups such as the G-6, G-7, G-8, G-20, the Bank for International Settlements and the OECD.

Inter Government Groups

The concept of a forum for the world's major industrialized democracies emerged following the 1973 oil crisis. In 1974, a series of meetings, an informal gathering of senior financial officials from the US, the UK, West Germany, Japan and France, took place in the library of the White House. In 1975, the French President invited the heads of government from West Germany, Italy, Japan, the United Kingdom and the United States to a summit. The six leaders agreed to an annual meeting, organized under a rotating presidency, forming the Group of Six (G-6). The following year, Canada was invited to join, creating the G-7 – an economic and political group. The G-7 may be contrasted with the E-7 – a group of seven countries with emerging economies. The E-7 are predicted to have larger economies than the G-7 countries by 2050. This group includes China, India, Brazil, Mexico, Russia, Indonesia and Turkey. There are other similar groups also defined by the countries that are members. The G-8 includes the G-7 and Russia. The G-8 deliberately lacks an administrative structure like those in place for international organizations such as the UN or the World Bank and does not have a permanent secretariat or offices for its members. The presidency of the group rotates annually amongst member countries and the country holding the presidency is responsible for planning and hosting a series of ministerial-level meetings, leading up to a mid-year summit attended by the heads of government. Typically they discuss issues of mutual or global concern.

Earlier we introduced the G-20. The Group is composed of the 20 Finance Ministers and Central Bank Governors from 20 major economies: 19 countries plus the EU, which is represented by the President of the European Council and by the European Central Bank. Collectively, the G-20 economies comprise more than 80 per cent of global GDP and world trade (including EU intra-trade) and two-thirds of the world population. The G-20 was proposed by former Canadian Finance Minister Paul Martin for cooperation and consultation on matters pertaining to the international financial system. Collectively they discuss policy issues designed to promote international financial stability, and seek to address issues that go beyond the responsibilities of any one organization.

The OECD

The Organization for European Economic Cooperation (OEEC) was established after the Second World War, in 1947. By making individual governments recognize the interdependence of their economies, it paved the way for a new era of cooperation. In 1960 Canada and the US joined the OEEC, creating the opportunity to influence economic environments and promote cooperation on a global stage. Thus, the Organization for Economic Co-operation and Development (OECD) was formed the following year. Other countries joined in, starting with Japan in 1964. Today, 34 OECD member countries worldwide regularly turn to one another to identify, discuss, analyze and promote policies to solve problems related to the economy. The US has seen its national wealth almost triple in the five decades since the OECD was created, calculated in terms of gross domestic product per head of population. Other OECD countries have seen similar and in some cases even more remarkable progress. Previously minor players such as China, India and Brazil have emerged as new economic giants. Most of the countries that formed part of the former Soviet bloc have either joined the OECD or adopted its standards and principles to achieve common goals. Russia is negotiating to become a member of the OECD, and there are close relations with Brazil, China, India, Indonesia and South Africa.

The Bank for International Settlements (BIS)

Established in 1930, the BIS is the world's oldest international financial organization. As an institution it serves central banks in their pursuit of monetary and financial stability and acts as a bank for central banks. As its customers are central banks and international organizations, the BIS does not accept deposits from, or provide financial services to, private individuals or corporate entities. Since 1930, central bank cooperation at the BIS has taken place through regular meetings in Basel of central bank Governors and experts from central banks and other agencies. In support of this cooperation, the Bank has developed its own research in financial and monetary economics and makes an important contribution to the collection, compilation and dissemination of economic and financial statistics. In the 1970s and 1980s the focus was on managing cross-border capital flows following the oil crises and the international debt crisis. The 1970s crisis also brought to the fore the issue of regulatory supervision of internationally active banks, resulting in the 1988 Basel Capital Accord and its 'Basel II' revision of 2001–06 (recommendations on banking laws and regulations). More recently, the issue of financial stability in the wake of economic integration and globalization, as highlighted by the 1997 Asian crisis, has received much attention. Apart from fostering monetary policy cooperation, the BIS has always performed 'traditional' banking functions for the central bank community. Finally, the BIS has also provided or organized emergency financing to support the international monetary system when needed.

In this section we have discussed what constitutes the economic environment, economic indicators and business cycles – focusing on the global economic environment, integration and the recent global financial crisis. In the next section we take a closer look at how individual governments manage their economic environment. As an example, we focus on the UK, its economic environment and the role of Government and will later consider economic integration from the regional perspective of Europe.

THE ROLE OF GOVERNMENT IN INFLUENCING MACROECONOMIC ACTIVITY AT THE COUNTRY LEVEL

Whilst governments recognize a need to create an economic environment that allows businesses to operate efficiently, they differ in their views of how to go about it. Different perspectives may be analyzed in terms of the degree of intervention (see previous chapter) in the running of the market. At one extreme there is the free market whilst at the other end there is the interventionist view. In this section we examine the role of government in influencing macroeconomic activity and will consider the UK as an example. We saw from Osborne's arguments (Osborne is the shadow chancellor for the UK – see the business in debate section below) for a 'New Economic Model' that his (centre-right) Government favoured a degree of intervention though this intervention may be less than that favoured by the' left' such as a Labour government. Before considering specific interventions it is worth noting that, for most Governments, the main economic targets (goals) are:

* A high and stable level of economic growth
* Low level of unemployment
* Low inflation
* Balance between imports and exports

BUSINESS IN DEBATE

A 'New' Economic Model for the UK

Prior to the 2010 UK general election, the Shadow Chancellor set out[1] the Conservative vision for a new *economic model*. He argued Britain had been failed by the economic policy framework of the last decade – the debt-fuelled model of growth the (Labour) Government had pursued was unsustainable, and that we needed to move from an economy built on debt to an economy where we save and invest for the future. To revive the economy, the UK had to deal with its debts. Economic policy makers in Britain faced a number of challenges. A period of recession had recently passed, but the return to growth was proving too slow. According to the Shadow Chancellor the UK public finances were the worst they had ever been for many years. With the largest budget deficit in the developed world; UK national income per person had actually declined. The Shadow Chancellor suggested a need to head in a completely new direction – from an economic model based on unsustainable private and public debt to a new model of economic growth rooted in investment, savings and higher exports.

New policies and institutions were proposed

The Shadow Chancellor's new model had three components:

1 **Macroeconomic and financial policy** seeking to contain credit cycles as well as target price stability;

2 **Fiscal policy** with an independent Office for Budget Responsibility; and

3 **Supply side** policies.

Managing debt

The Shadow Chancellor argued that the lack of a credible plan to deal with the deficit had pushed up market interest rates, undermined the monetary stimulus supporting the economy, exhausted the confidence of investors and consumers and caused the credit rating agencies to threaten downgrading the UK unless urgent action was taken. He believed that a loss of market confidence could force intense tax rises and severe spending cuts. He was not alone in his thoughts on debt. The former Chief Economist of

the International Monetary Fund warned[2] high levels of government debt around the world remain the most likely trigger of the next economic downturn. UK banks had become more leveraged (debt financed) than American banks, and households had become more indebted than any other major economy in history. In the aftermath of the crisis, the UK public debt had risen more rapidly than any other major economy. Research suggests that once debt reaches more than about 90 per cent of GDP, the risk of a large negative impact on long term growth becomes highly significant. The Shadow Chancellor feared the UK was forecast to break through 90 per cent of GDP in two years time. Baseline projections produced by the Bank for International Settlements (BIS) showed the scale of the adjustment needed to avoid that risk. Once the costs of an ageing population were accounted for, they calculated that UK debt would rise to 200 per cent of GDP in just ten years without significant adjustments – that would be higher than any other country except Japan. Interest payments on that debt would rise above 10 per cent of GDP within ten years and to almost 30 per cent in 30 years – the highest of all the countries analyzed including Greece and Ireland. The BIS argued, 'persistently high levels of public debt will drive down capital accumulation, productivity growth and long-term growth potential'[3]. For an economy like the UK, with such high levels of private debt, increases in market interest rates would be particularly devastating to the prospects of a private sector recovery. The Shadow Chancellor discussed[1] the idea of a new system of financial regulation, with the Bank of England controlling the overall level of debt in the economy. Given unsustainable increases in debt cause devastating financial crises, the Shadow Chancellor remained concerned about credit cycles like business cycles.

Monetary policy

The Shadow Chancellor also argued that monetary policy should be the main tool of short term macroeconomic management, whilst fiscal policy (see next para) should be set for the medium term. He declared he would keep the inflation targeting framework and maintain arrangements and protocols for making decisions around quantitative easing.

Fiscal policy

There was broad agreement amongst economists concerning the need for more independent scrutiny of fiscal policy. At the time there was growing support for the concept of fiscal councils (which exist in Sweden, Denmark and the Netherlands) that could bring to bear on governments' independent and forward-looking scrutiny. A fiscal council has the power to hold politicians to account for the fiscal implications of their tax and spending plans. The Conservatives therefore planned to create an Office for Budget Responsibility (OBR), accountable to Parliament, and responsible for publishing independent fiscal forecasts at least twice a year, around the time of the Budget, leading to a transparent national balance sheet.

Tackling budget deficit

The Shadow Chancellor[1] noted disagreements within the economics profession over how quickly the record budget deficit should be tackled. He believed there was recognition that the scale of the deficit and the rapid increase in the national debt could not be overlooked, and that public expenditure would have to be cut. There was also general agreement that Britain needed a more credible medium term plan to deal with the deficit, as both the IMF and the OECD had argued. Disagreements remained, based on details of the timing and pace of deficit reduction. Whilst some economists cautioned against early action, the Shadow Chancellor, took a different view. The argument to delay action assumes that when private demand is weak, swift reduction of government spending risks damaging recovery. However, some believe that this does not consider the importance of expectations and confidence. Uncertainty over the future paths of tax rates and government spending can play an important role in behaviour: consumer spending and business investment. For the Conservatives, a credible fiscal consolidation plan could have a positive impact through greater certainty and confidence about the future. They held the belief that businesses could expand, safer in the knowledge that an out of control budget would not lead to ever

higher taxes. Consumers could spend, safer in the knowledge that mortgage rates would remain lower for longer. Where markets start to lose confidence in a country and interest rates are driven up, recovery is undermined and the inevitable spending cuts are subsequently deeper and more savage than would have been necessary to maintain market confidence in the first place. So that is why the Shadow Chancellor advocated an early start – in order to bring confidence to the economy, establish credibility with markets, and to ensure spending cuts were well targeted.

Growth

The UK also needed a programme of supply side reform. All evidence suggested that Britain's trend rate of growth had declined over the last decade. The Shadow Chancellor[1] also sought to answer the key question of: from where might the growth emerge? He advocated the need for a higher savings rate, more business investment, and rising net exports.

The Shadow Chancellor recognized that delivering the new economic model would not be easy. He concluded Britain could not run away from its problems and would have to deal with its debts in order to restore to health the UK economy. The Shadow Chancellor argued an economy built on debt was living on borrowed time. His ambition was nothing less than a new economic model for Britain – from an economy built on debt to an economy which saves and invests for the future.

Source: (1) www.conservatives.com/News/Speeches/2010/02/George_Osborne_Mais_Lecture_-_A_New_Economic_Model.aspx (2) Quinn J (2009), 'Debt levels risk another crisis', www.telegraph.co.uk/finance/g20-summit/6228450/Debt-levels-risk-another-crisis.html; (3) Cecchetti S G, Mohanty M S and Zampolli F (2010), The future of public debt: prospects and implications, Working Papers No 300, March 2010 accessible at http://www.bis.org/publ/work300.htm

In order for governments to move towards targets they often need to make trade-offs. As one target nears achievement, another will often deteriorate (growth often leads to inflation). Consequently, governments must make decisions, firstly about which targets are a priority at that moment and secondly about how these targets can be achieved. The main policy tools (interventions) to achieve targets include Interest rate changes (and exchange rates indirectly), and government expenditure (funded through taxes and loans). Both policy tools are used to stimulate *demand* in the economy. With total annual government spending at almost 0.75 Trillion (£700 Billion in 2012, i.e. £700 000 000 000) demand can be significantly impacted upon and the

BUSINESS IN ACTION

Morocco aids drought-stricken farmers

In 2012 the Moroccan agricultural season was troubled due to cold weather earlier in the year and then the onset of a drought. Farming in the kingdom provides the main source of income for 80 per cent of the rural population and 14–20 per cent of the country's GDP, according to figures from the finance ministry. The Moroccan Government took action to help farmers suffering from the drought. Prime Minister Abdelilah Benkirane stated that

it is the government's duty to help the agriculture sector, as he explained that the government decided to safeguard a key component of the Moroccan economy. The government made plans to implement a 1.53 billion dirham programme for the affected areas. The government will waive customs duty on imported barley, implement a livestock assistance programme, supply seed, boost subsidies granted for certified seeds and ensure that insured farmers whose crops and legumes have been harmed are compensated for their losses.

Source: http://magharebia.com/cocoon/awi/xhtml1/ en_GB/features/awi/features/2012/04/12/feature-03

importance of government expenditure to the economy is very clear. Government spending is set out in the annual budget discussed later. Changes in the government's spending policies will have a major impact on the economy. Spending raises demand and demand is met through increased production (growth), which itself increases employment and the disposable income of workers. They then have more money to spend on goods and services, further increasing demand (refer back to Figure 3.2). However, if demand exceeds supply, prices may rise, thus causing inflation. This may then be controlled through interest rate changes but this intervention can have a negative consequence in the form of increased exports and a weaker balance of payments. As we stated, as one target nears achievement, another often deteriorates.

Decisions about interest rates and spending manifest from two important (sister) policy areas used to influence the economy: monetary and fiscal. At the beginning of this chapter we introduced the concept of the business cycle; modern economic thought is characterized by the use of both fiscal and monetary policies to counteract and smooth out the business cycle. Monetary policy focuses on interest rates whilst fiscal policy makes use of taxation and government expenditure to attain targets. Each of these will be discussed in this section. The outcomes of policy and expenditure changes include economic growth, inflation, unemployment (an economic waste), the debt ratio, and PSNCR. In the Mais lecture, Osborne stated that economic theory and evidence both suggest that the macroeconomic policy combination most likely to encourage recovery was tight fiscal policy, supportive monetary policy and countercyclical financial regulation. Osborne discussed monetary policy, arguing that monetary policy should be the main tool of short term macroeconomic management whilst fiscal policy should be set for the medium term. We consider fiscal policy next and then turn to monetary policy, before moving on to consider the impact upon business.

Fiscal Policy

In this section we turn our attention to fiscal policy – measures that alter the level and composition of government expenditure and taxation in order to manage the economy. The main changes to fiscal policy are announced in the Budget, usually in March (set by the Chancellor each year – for the fiscal year which runs April to April in the UK). This is where the Government adjusts its level of spending to influence a nation's economy. Changes in the level and composition of taxation and government spending can impact upon the level of economic activity. Governments spend money in a broad spectrum of areas, from defence and law enforcement to education, healthcare, and welfare benefits. This expenditure can be funded in a number of different ways such as tax revenues, borrowing or printing money, reserves and the proceeds of sales. Governments vary in the extent of their borrowing, spending and taxation policies. In some cases they may spend more

BUSINESS IN ACTION

Budget 2011 – the economy

The Chancellor's Budget of 2011 announced borrowing, inflation and growth figures for the UK economy as a whole. Public sector net borrowing stood at £146 billion in 2011. It was forecast as: £122 billion in 2012, falling each subsequent year to £29 billion in 2015–16. The UK's national debt, as a share of national income, was forecast to be 60 per cent in 2011, before peaking at 71 per cent, and then starting to fall – reaching 69 per cent by the end of the period. The independent Office of Budget Responsibility predicted inflation to remain between 4 and 5 per cent for most of 2011, before dropping to 2.5 per cent in 2012 and then to 2 per cent. The Chancellor wrote to the Governor of the Bank of England to confirm that the inflation target for the Monetary Policy Committee would remain at 2 per cent, as measured by the Consumer Prices Index. The Chancellor estimated growth in the UK economy for the coming five years to be: 1.7 per cent in 2011, and between 2–3 per cent in the subsequent years to 2015. The independent Office of Budget Responsibility's judgement is that the government is on track to eliminate the structural current deficit and place debt on a downward path by the end of the Parliament in 2015. The government's economic policy objective is to achieve strong, sustainable and balanced growth that is more evenly shared across the country and between industries. The Chancellor stated that this requires the economy to be rebalanced towards exports and private sector investment. Budget measures designed to support private sector investment, enterprise and innovation included: a reduction in the main rate of corporation tax by two per cent; an increased rate of R&D tax credits for small and medium-sized enterprises and creation of 21 new Enterprise Zones, to focus growth in specific parts of the UK.

than they collect in taxes, whilst in other cases they may spend less. When the government runs a budget deficit, funds will need to come from public borrowing (the issue of government bonds) or overseas borrowing. Governments use fiscal policy to influence the level of aggregate demand (total spending by consumers, businesses and the Government) in the economy, in an effort to achieve economic objectives of price stability, full employment, and economic growth. Increasing government spending and decreasing tax rates are methods used to stimulate aggregate demand. This can be used in times of recession or low economic activity as an essential tool for building the framework for strong economic growth and working towards full employment. In theory, resulting deficits would be paid for by an expanded economy during the boom that would follow (refer back to business cycles).

Traditionally fiscal policy has been seen as an instrument of demand management (see Figure 3.3). Fiscal policy is typically based on the theories of the British economist, John Maynard Keynes. Also known as Keynesian economics, this theory states that governments can influence macroeconomic productivity levels by increasing or decreasing tax levels and public spending. This influence, in turn, impacts upon inflation, increases employment and maintains the value of money. The Keynesian school argues that fiscal policy can have powerful effects on aggregate demand, output and employment when the economy is operating well below full capacity (national output), and where there is a need to provide a demand-stimulus to the economy. Keynesians believe there is an important and influential role for the government to make active use of fiscal policy measures to manage the level of aggregate demand. Others argue more for the role of monetary policy (see next section), believing it to be more effective in controlling demand and inflationary pressure.

How then does a change in fiscal policy feed through the economy to affect variables such as aggregate demand, national output, prices and employment? We have depicted the transmission mechanism (the way policy spreads – chain of events – throughout the economy) for fiscal policy in Figure 3.3. The process starts with the budget, which is followed by Government spending and taxation. Each will be discussed below.

FIGURE 3.3
Fiscal policy

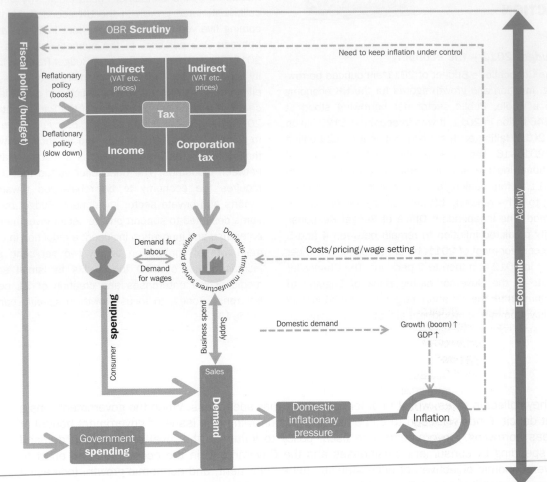

Government Spending and Taxation

Her Majesty's Treasury (commonly known as HM Treasury) is the United Kingdom's economics and finance ministry. The Chancellor has overall responsibility for the work of the Treasury which concentrates on the core business of finance and economics. In 1997 monetary policy was transferred to the Bank of England, while the Treasury retained control of fiscal policy. The year 2001 marked a major reform in government finances managed by the Treasury. Traditional cash accounting for income and expenditure was replaced by 'resource accounting and budgeting' which introduced commercial-style budgets and accounts in government. In 2008, the Treasury had to come to terms with the largest banking crisis (refer back to the global economy section) for several decades. Ministers and officials worked to nationalize British banks and to protect the fragile economy. Now that the Treasury has emerged from recession, the department is focusing on rebuilding the UK economy and reforming regulation to reduce the chance of another downturn in the future.

In times of recession or a general downturn in economic activity a government may decrease taxation, thus giving consumers more spending money (resulting in increased demand) and may increase government spending in the form of buying services from the market (such as building roads, hospitals or schools, etc.) – see reflationary policy. Government (or public) spending each year takes up almost half of GDP. This creates jobs and wages that are in turn pushed into the economy. In the meantime, overall unemployment levels (see later paragraph in this section) will fall. However, continued action of this type may eventually result in higher inflation. A key challenge for Government is deciding upon the degree of intervention in the economy. For the most part, it is accepted that a degree of government involvement is necessary to sustain a vibrant economy. Much of the first decade in the new millennium witnessed a fiscal stimulus to the UK economy, through substantial increases in government spending on transport, and in particular on health and education.

Government spending results in cash flowing out of government. Revenue flows into the government's accounts from taxation. There are many different kinds of taxation. Direct taxation is levied on income, wealth and profit. Direct taxes include income tax, national insurance contributions, capital gains tax and corporation tax. Indirect taxes are taxes on spending – such as excise duties on fuel, cigarettes and alcohol and Value Added Tax (VAT) on many different goods and services. By far the biggest source of income for the government is income tax. As part of their reflationary policy, the Government may decide to lower indirect taxes which will lower the prices of the taxed goods and encourage demand. Instead, or additionally, they could lower direct taxes. For example they may reduce the lower, basic or higher rates of tax and/or increase the level of personal allowances. This raises disposable income (people's take-home pay) and consequently encourages more spending. Whether lowering direct or indirect taxes, the level of demand should rise and encourage economic growth. Should demand exceed capacity and inflation follow, the Government might attempt to slow down the economy – typically by doing the opposite to that suggested above.

Fiscal policy usually acts on the level of demand in the economy and the deflationary and reflationary policies are often known as demand-side policies. However, it is also possible for fiscal policy to act on the level of supply (increasing the capacity of the economy to produce). Changes to fiscal policy can affect the supply-side capacity of the economy and therefore contribute to long term economic growth. The need for supply side policies was emphasized by Osborne in his Mais lecture. The effects tend to be longer term in nature. Cuts in income tax might be used to improve incentives for people to seek work actively. Lower rates of corporation tax and other business taxes might be used as a policy to stimulate a higher level of business investment and attract inward investment from overseas. Government capital spending on the national infrastructure can lower distribution costs for business and make more efficient use of the labour force – an enhanced transport infrastructure is seen by many business organizations as absolutely essential if the UK is to remain competitive within the European and global economy. Furthermore, Government spending might be used to fund an expansion in the rate of new small business start-ups; tax credits and other tax allowances could be used to encourage an increase in private business sector research and development – designed to improve the international competitiveness of domestic businesses and contribute to a faster pace of innovation and invention. Higher government spending on education and training is designed to boost the human capital of the workforce. However, despite argued benefits of government spending, not everyone agrees this is the best course of action. Recall discussions in the previous chapter where we noted free market economists are normally sceptical of the effects of government spending in improving the supply-side of the economy. They argue that lower taxation and tight control of government spending and borrowing is required to allow the private sector of the economy to flourish.

Earlier we identified the Budget as the major financial and economic report compiled each year by the Chancellor of the Exchequer. Chancellors use the Budget statement to update Parliament and the nation on the state of the economy, on the public finances and on progress against the Government's economic objectives. They can review and change tax rates, and make announcements on how taxpayers' money will be spent in the coming years. Other announcements often made in the Budget include how the government plans to encourage economic growth, create jobs or protect the environment. The Office for Budget Responsibility (OBR) was formed in May 2010 to make an independent assessment of the public finances and the economy, the public sector balance sheet and the long term sustainability of the public finances. The establishment of the OBR marks a step change in the transparency and openness of economic and fiscal policy making. It is one of a growing number of official independent fiscal watchdogs around the world. The OBR produces forecasts for the economy and public finances, see the Economic and Fiscal Outlook

BUSINESS IN ACTION

OBR EFO March 2011

The key economic developments since the November 2010 Outlook have been an unexpected fall in UK GDP in the final quarter of 2010, a rise in world oil prices, and higher-than-expected UK inflation. The labour market has performed much as expected, with unemployment rising, after registering significant falls in the middle of last year. This data has, on average, prompted external forecasters to reduce their estimates of economic growth in 2010 and 2011. The average external forecasts for CPI and RPI inflation have risen significantly, again reflecting recent data. The OBR has endorsed all but one of the costings for the tax and spending measures outlined in the 2011 Budget as reasonable central estimates, although there are significant uncertainties around a number of them. Reporting on the economic outlook, the report states that higher-than-expected inflation is likely to squeeze household disposable income in the coming months and thereby weaken consumer spending growth. Below-trend growth will increase the amount of spare capacity in the economy this year, with the output gap then beginning to close in 2012 (GDP is expected to be lower).

Source: Office for Budget Responsibility: Economic and fiscal outlook, Presented to Parliament by the Economic Secretary to the Treasury by Command of Her Majesty March 2011, © Crown copyright 2011

(EFO). Additionally they judge progress towards the Government's fiscal targets and assess the long-term sustainability of the public finances. The OBR also scrutinizes the Treasury's costing of Budget measures – during the run-up to Budgets and other policy statements; the OBR subject the Government's draft costings of tax and spending measures to detailed challenge and scrutiny. An extract from the March 2011 EFO is provided above.

Despite expectations, policy and planning, actual inflation did exceed 5 per cent toward the end of 2011.

Employment

Earlier we recognized unemployment as an outcome of macroeconomic policy and indicator of economic activity. Not only are the unemployed not working, and therefore not contributing to the economy, but they will also be claiming benefits and costing the government money. The aim should therefore be to keep unemployment as low as possible. In all countries, a strong and sustainable economic recovery is more likely if workers have the skills that employers require and are employed in jobs which make good use of their skills, (OECD 2011). Discussing the 'world of work' the OECD ask what does working life in the 21st century look like – and what are the social and economic consequences of a world where, for millions, no job and no immediate prospect of one marks the transition to adulthood? They suggest that work is an important aspect of our lives and without it our economies and societies could not function. The OECD also ask, 'What can be done for jobless youth, and for the many millions of others without work at a time of high public debt and reduced public spending?' noting there is no magic solution to these problems, but that better unemployment policies can limit the damage and help to deliver improved lives. At the launch in Paris, 15 September 2011 of the OECD Employment Outlook 2011, Angel Gurría, OECD Secretary-General argued that tackling high and persistent unemployment, improving job opportunities and ensuring adequate social safety nets should be at the top of the political agenda. He also suggested that 'of all the facets of this crisis, from sovereign debt to banking, high unemployment is the elephant in the room. This is the human face of the crisis, the most visible manifestation of the challenge we face to restore sustained growth.' In support, he argued the crisis had affected unemployment in different OECD countries. In particular, some countries have contained the rise in unemployment, or even reduced unemployment, through timely investments in labour market policies. 'In other words, policies and institutions matter' he declared. How should governments respond to this difficult labour market situation and prevent a persistent rise in unemployment? 'First and foremost, they must ensure that they have in place a credible medium-term

FIGURE 3.4

Unemployment levels

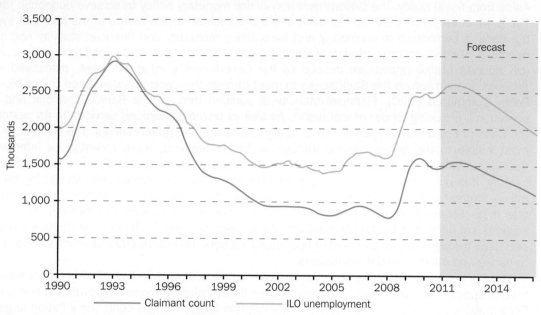

Source: The OBR Economic and fiscal outlook, Outturn data ONS, forecast produced by the OBR (March 2011), p72
Unemployment levels 2011 – © Crown copyright

strategy of fiscal consolidation. This is important for unwinding large increases in public debt, rebuilding confidence and ultimately renewing the basis for sustained growth. At the same time, in those countries where the labour market remains sluggish and economic growth has weakened, further measures may be required to stimulate job creation where there is room for fiscal man-oeuvre.' Renewed job creation is essential for bringing down unemployment and long-term unemployment. Net hiring subsidies which support companies deciding to expand their workforce can be a cost-effective way to boost job creation in the short-run. Other policies include job-search assistance, hiring subsidies and remedial assistance. In a number of countries, there is also a need to expand opportunities for 'study and work' programmes, such as apprenticeships and other dual vocational education and training programmes. Additionally, policies must be implemented to overcome the long-term failure to give all youth a better start in the labour market. This requires improving early childhood education and development and ensuring young people do not drop out of school. It also means achieving a better match between the skills young people acquire at school and those skills needed in the labour market. Barriers to the employment of youth also need to be removed. These may include overly-high labour costs of hiring unskilled youth, as well as hiring and firing rules that relegate youth to dead-end temporary jobs. Interestingly, the OECD recognize that 'there are no quick fixes here and governments will face difficult trade-offs in managing the constraints imposed by fiscal consolidation with the need for additional measures to kick-start job creation while bolstering social safety nets for the vulnerable'.

The OBR Economic and fiscal outlook, March 2011, suggests employment will rise by 2015 (from 29 to 30 Million). This will be accompanied by an increase in average earnings and reduction in unemployment rate (see Figure 3.4). Consequently, the number of claimants and output gap will also fall and GDP will increase. Between 2010 and 2015 the OBR expect total employment to increase by around 900 000. This comprises an increase in market sector employment of around 1.3 million, partly offset by a reduction in general government employment of around 400 000 between 2010–11 and 2015–16. Total weekly hours worked are expected to fall back slightly over the course of 2011, consistent with below trend growth. Beyond 2011, total hours are forecast to rise as employment growth picks up, offsetting a fall in average hours worked. The OBR expect average hours worked to revert to a gradual trend decline over the medium term.

Monetary policy

Aside from fiscal policy, the Government may utilize monetary policy to achieve economic targets. The Bank of England is the central bank of the UK. Located at the centre of the financial system, the Bank is committed to promoting and maintaining monetary and financial stability and consequently a healthy economy. Monetary stability means stable prices and confidence in the currency (UK pound). Stable prices are defined by the Government's inflation target, discussed in the previous section, which the Bank seeks to meet through the decisions delegated to the Monetary Policy Committee (MPC). Financial stability is pursued through the Bank's financial and other operations, including lender of last resort. As well as providing banking services to its customers, the Bank of England manages the UK's foreign exchange and gold reserves. The Bank is perhaps most visible to the general public through its banknotes and, more recently, its interest rate decisions. Whilst it has been responsible for the issue of banknotes in England and Wales for a century, it is only since 1997 that the Bank has held statutory responsibility for setting the UK's official interest rate. Interest rate decisions are taken by the MPC which has to judge what interest rate is necessary to meet a target for overall inflation in the economy (remember, the inflation target is set each year by the Chancellor of the Exchequer). The Bank implements its interest rate decisions through its financial market operations – it sets the interest rate at which the Bank lends to banks and other financial institutions.

The Bank's monetary policy objective is to deliver price stability – low inflation – and, subject to that, to support the Government's economic objectives, including those for growth and employment. Price stability is defined by the Government's inflation target of 2 per cent. The inflation target of 2 per cent is expressed in terms of an annual rate of inflation, based on the Consumer Prices Index (CPI). If the target is missed by more than one percentage point on either side, the Governor of the Bank must write an open letter to the Chancellor explaining the reasons why inflation has increased or fallen to such an extent and what the Bank proposes to do to ensure inflation returns to the agreed target. The remit recognizes the role of price stability in achieving economic stability more generally, and in providing the right conditions for sustainable growth in output and employment. The Bank aims to meet the inflation target by setting an interest rate. The MPC's aim is to set interest rates so that inflation can be brought back to target within a reasonable time period without creating undue instability in the economy. The level of interest rate is decided by the MPC which consists of nine members – five from the Bank of England and four external members, appointed by the Chancellor. It is chaired by the Governor of the Bank of England. Each member of the MPC has expertise in the field of economics and monetary policy. The MPC meets monthly and decisions are taken by a vote of the Committee on a one-person, one-vote basis. The interest rate decision is announced at 12 noon on the second day. Throughout 2011, the MPC agreed to maintain the rate at 0.5 per cent. Interestingly, two members frequently voted for an increase in the rate but this was against the majority and was therefore not implemented.

When the Bank of England changes the official interest rate it is attempting to influence the overall level of expenditure (spending and therefore demand) in the economy. When the amount of money spent grows more quickly than the volume of output produced, inflation is the result. Thus, changes in interest rates are used to control inflation, see Figure 3.5. The Bank of England sets an interest rate at which it lends to financial institutions. This interest rate then affects the whole range of interest rates set by commercial banks, building societies and other institutions for their own savers and borrowers. It also tends to affect the price of financial assets, such as bonds and shares, and the exchange rate, which affect consumer and business demand. Lowering or raising interest rates affects spending in the economy. When interest rates are reduced, saving is less attractive and borrowing more attractive, which stimulates spending. Lower interest rates can affect consumer and company cash flow – a fall in interest rates reduces the income from savings and the interest payments due on loans. Borrowers tend to spend more of any extra money they have, so the net effect of lower interest rates through this cash flow channel is to encourage higher spending in aggregate. The opposite occurs when interest rates are increased. Furthermore, lower interest rates can lift the prices of assets such as shares and houses. Higher house prices enable existing home owners to extend their mortgages in order to finance higher consumption. Higher

FIGURE 3.5

Monetary policy in action (adapted from 'the transmission mechanism of monetary policy')

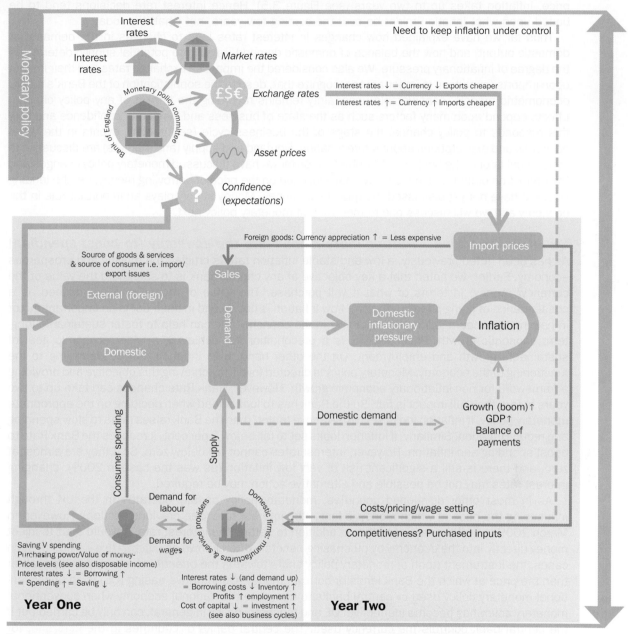

Source: Adapted from "The transmission mechanism of monetary policy" © Bank of England (2011)

share prices raise household wealth and can increase public willingness to spend. Changes in interest rates can also affect the exchange rate. An unexpected rise in the UK interest rate, relative to overseas, provides investors with a higher return on UK assets relative to their foreign-currency equivalents, tending to make sterling assets more attractive. Consequently, the value of sterling should rise, reducing the price of imports, and demand for UK goods and services abroad. Changes in spending (demand) drive an increase in manufacturing (supply) and, in turn, employment (number of employees, wages, hours of work, etc.). The impact on output and wages feeds through to producers' costs and prices, and eventually consumer prices. Some of these influences can work more quickly than others and there tend to be time lags before changes in interest rates affect spending and saving decisions, and longer still before they affect consumer prices. Whilst only an estimate, the maximum effect on output is estimated to take up to one year and on consumer price, inflation takes up to two years (see Figure 3.5). Hence interest rate decisions tend to be based upon what inflation might be over the coming few years, not what it is today.

Thus far we have explained how changes in interest rates lead to changes in the demand for domestic output, and how the balance of domestic demand, relative to potential supply, determines the degree of inflationary pressure. We also considered the impact on exchange rates and their impact upon imports/exports. It is important to recognize that, despite the sophistication of the Bank's macro econometric models, considerable uncertainty remains regarding the impact of any policy change. Effects depend upon many factors such as the state of business and consumer confidence and how this responds to policy change, the stage of the business cycle (see earlier), events in the world economy, and expectations about future inflation. Demand and supply (and markets) are discussed in more detail later in the book (see Chapter 11). So far we have discussed monetary policy changes and their effect on output and inflation. We have focused on the price of borrowing money, i.e. the lending rate, but have not yet discussed the quantity of money. Money supply plays an important role in the economy and we will discuss one further 'tool' of monetary policy next.

Quantitative easing – Putting more money into the economy (to boost spending)

As has been noted previously, a low and stable inflation rate is crucial to a thriving and prosperous economy. Earlier, we noted that a key objective of any central bank is to safeguard the value of the currency (money) in terms of what it will purchase. The value of money may be reduced as a consequence of rising prices (inflation). Low inflation is not an end in itself but is an important factor in helping to encourage long-term stability in the economy and can help to foster sustainable long-term economic growth. Price stability is a precondition for achieving a wider economic goal of sustainable growth and employment. On the other hand, high inflation can be damaging to the functioning of the economy. Monetary policy is directed towards achieving this objective and providing a framework for non-inflationary economic growth. However, Bank Rate changes can take up to two years before their full impact is felt. So the Bank has to look ahead when deciding on the appropriate monetary policy. If inflation looks set to rise above target, then the Bank raises rates to slow spending and reduce inflation. Similarly, if inflation looks set to fall below 2 per cent, it reduces the Bank Rate to boost spending and inflation. However, interest rates cannot fall below zero. So if they are almost at zero, and there is still a significant risk of very low inflation (as was the case in 2009), changing interest rates may not be possible and alternative action may be required.

As in most other developed countries, monetary policy usually operates in the UK through influencing the price at which money is lent – the interest rate (see previous section). However, in March 2009 the MPC announced that in addition to setting the interest rate, it would start to inject money directly into the economy by purchasing assets – often known as quantitative easing. In such cases, the instrument (tool) of monetary policy shifts towards the *quantity* of money provided rather than the price at which the Bank lends or borrows money. Quantitative easing (QE) is an unconventional monetary policy used by central banks to stimulate the national economy when conventional monetary policy has become ineffective. QE and monetary policy in general, can only be carried out if the central bank controls the currency used. The central banks of countries in the Eurozone, for example, cannot unilaterally expand their money supply, and thus cannot employ QE. They must instead rely on the European Central Bank (ECB) to set monetary policy (discussed in the final part of this chapter). However, quantitative easing may cause higher inflation than desired if the amount of easing required is overestimated, and too much money is created – an increase in money supply has an inflationary effect. In addition, increasing the money supply tends to depreciate a country's exchange rate versus other currencies. Thus too much money circulating in the economy is likely to result in too much inflation. But if the economy weakens sharply, as it did in the final months of 2008, the problem is different. There is a risk of too little money circulating, not too much.

The MPC's decision to inject money directly into the economy did not involve printing more banknotes. Instead, the Bank bought assets from private sector institutions – such as insurance companies, pension funds, banks or non-financial firms – and credited the seller's bank account. So the seller had more money in their bank account, while their bank held a corresponding claim against the Bank of England (known as reserves). The end result is more money out in the wider economy. QE should make it cheaper and easier for companies and households to borrow than it would otherwise have been. A key goal of QE is to make credit cheaper and more widely available. Together, large cuts in the Bank Rate and QE provide the economy with a substantial boost, and reduce the risks of inflation falling below the 2 per cent target. Just as the Bank takes the steps necessary to contain the risks of below-target inflation, it also acts if it believes inflation looks set to rise above 2 per cent. Under these circumstances, the MPC can put downward pressure on spending and inflation by raising the Bank Rate and removing the extra money by selling assets it previously purchased. Economic conditions can and do shift rapidly. The job of the MPC is to navigate through these changes and to take the steps necessary to keep inflation as close to the 2 per cent target as practical. By delivering low and stable inflation, the Bank of England will play its part in fostering the climate of stability that is essential to the UK economy. It is important to recognize that the economy (environment) is continually changing and that the aim of monetary policy is to return the economy to some equilibrium.

In summary, governments use the two policy areas (monetary and fiscal) in various combinations in an effort to direct a country's economic goals and manage economic activity. In the next section we take a closer look at the implications for business.

ECONOMIC ENVIRONMENT FORCES INTERACTING WITH BUSINESS BEHAVIOUR

Throughout the previous sections on fiscal and monetary (macroeconomic) policy we observed how government decisions influenced the economic environment. The influence and intervention of Government and related institutions may present themselves as challenges, forces, threats and opportunities to the firm. Firms combine capital, labour and purchased inputs and transform them (production) into goods or services that can be sold to gain revenue and hopefully profit (supply side issues). As was discussed in the previous section, economic forces (particularly in the form of demand influenced by monetary policy and taxation – influenced by fiscal policy) can impact upon company borrowing (cost and availability of capital) and investment decisions, costs, pricing, competitiveness and outputs. Similarly, company activity in terms of output, pricing and employment (and wage payments) can impact upon GDP and inflation within an economy, i.e. the relationship is two way, with mutual influence occurring. In this section we take a closer look at the impact of economic forces and associated policies on the firm.

Whilst firms may be affected in different ways (dependent upon whether they are large or small, domestic or international, are cash rich, etc.) an increase in interest rate will affect borrowing, making it more costly. Increased costs erode profit margins unless efficiency gains are made or output prices increased. As a consequence, investment may be reduced if earning opportunities are reduced. Furthermore, it becomes more costly to hold stock and inventories are reduced or just-in-time (JIT) strategies adopted. A reduction in supply may stifle ability to meet demand – when it arises. Where increased interest rates stifle demand and consumer spending, output will be reduced and the firm will require less labour, either in the form of hours worked or number of employees. We might describe such impacts as a contraction of activity as opposed to the expansion and boom associated with interest rate reductions (refer back to Figure 3.2).

Exchange rate changes (see Exchange rate volatility) also have an important impact on many firms. Impacts depend upon whether the firm is producing in the UK, where they are purchasing inputs from and to whom they are selling outputs. As was mentioned in the previous chapter, globalization and regionalization encourages internationalization and the fragmentation of value chains. Firms must examine their primary activities and decide where to locate them worldwide. In the case where the firm is producing in the UK, its costs may be met with sterling. However, it may face competition from a firm whose costs may be met with other currencies. When the domestic currency, in this case sterling (UK pound) appreciates in the foreign exchange market, the competitive position of the UK firm worsens.

FIGURE 3.6
Favourable business impacts of macroeconomic policy

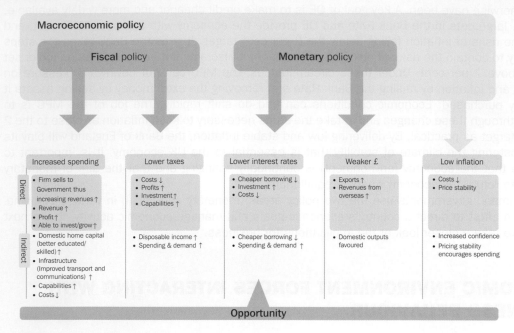

We have summarized the major business impacts (from macroeconomic policy) in Figure 3.6. The figure shows favourable changes and their impacts in terms of business opportunity. Direct and indirect benefits are shown. Of course the opportunities would turn to threats and challenges should the policies be reversed, i.e. decreased government spending, higher taxes and interest rates would all limit business revenues and profits.

At the beginning of this chapter we discussed the Global Economy and International Business Cycles and concluded that not only government policy but events around the world can impact upon the domestic and global economy, resulting in threats and opportunities for business. In the final section of this chapter we will continue to consider the forces that shape business but will focus on the EU and consider how it shapes macroeconomic policy. This will have implications for businesses and consumers both within and outside the EU. When reading the next section EU macroeconomic policy, institutions and infrastructure should be contrasted with that of the UK (as discussed earlier in the chapter).

ECONOMIC POLICY IN THE EU

Earlier in the chapter we discussed the role of government and the Central Bank in influencing macroeconomic activity through monetary and fiscal policy. Within a single market and major trading bloc like the EU (see previous chapter), many politicians and economists believe it makes good sense to coordinate national economic policies. This enables the EU to act rapidly and coherently when faced with economic challenges. The framework for cooperation on economic policy is the economic and monetary union (EMU) – a monetary union in Europe which succeeded the European Monetary System. This union began to take effect in 1990, over a series of three steps. The first step abolished individual member exchange rate control, the second step established the European Central Bank (ECB) and the third step created the Euro as the common currency. This cooperation enables the EU to react to global economic and financial challenges in a coordinated way. In this section we outline briefly, EU monetary policy. At the heart of monetary policy in the UK is the Bank of England. This final section introduces us to the ECB, which is at the heart of European monetary policy.

The ECB was established in 1998 and employs around 1350 people from all 27 EU countries. It has been responsible for conducting monetary policy for the euro area since 1999. The euro area came into being when responsibility for monetary policy was transferred from the national central banks of 11 EU Member States to the ECB. The legal basis for the single monetary policy is the Treaty establishing the European Community and the Statute of the European System of Central Banks and of the European Central Bank. To join the euro area, countries had to fulfil the convergence criteria, as will other EU Member States prior to adopting the euro. The criteria set out the economic and legal preconditions for countries to participate successfully in Economic and Monetary Union. The ECB is the central bank for Europe's single currency, the euro. Today, the single currency is used by more than 60 per cent of EU citizens in an area that stretches from Cyprus to Ireland and from Portugal to Finland (2011). Many have argued the benefits of the euro. The single currency has benefits such as: the cost of changing money when travelling or doing business within the euro area has disappeared; the cost of making cross-border payments has, in most cases, either disappeared or been reduced significantly; and consumers and businesses may compare prices more readily, which stimulates competition.

The ECB's main task is to maintain the euro's purchasing power and thus price stability in the euro area. Maintaining price stability is the key provision of the monetary policy chapter of the Treaty on the Functioning of the European Union. According to the ECB, a large number of economic studies suggest that monetary policy will contribute most to improving economic prospects and raising the living standards of citizens by maintaining price stability in a lasting way. Although the Maastricht Treaty clearly established maintaining price stability as the primary objective of the ECB, it did not define what was meant by 'price stability'. With this in mind, in October 1998 the Governing Council of the ECB announced a quantitative definition of price stability: 'a year-on-year increase in the Harmonized Index of Consumer Prices (HICP) for the euro area of below 2 per cent'. The Council also specified that price stability 'is to be maintained over the medium term'. Indeed, the Governing Council aims to maintain inflation rates at levels below, but close to, 2 per cent over the medium term.

As defined earlier in the chapter, monetary policy strategy is a coherent and structured description of how monetary policy decisions (typically about interest rates) will be made in order to achieve the objective of the central bank. Like the UK, the main task of the ECB, as the heart of the Eurosystem, is the conduct of monetary policy in the euro area, with the aim to maintain price stability. The ECB and the national central banks of all EU countries form a group called the European System of Central Banks (ESCB). The process through which monetary policy decisions affect the economy in general, and the price level in particular, is termed the 'transmission mechanism of monetary policy' (see Figure 3.7). We explored the UK transmission mechanism of monetary policy in Figure 3.5. Whilst it is difficult to predict the precise effect of monetary policy actions on the economy and price level, the transmission mechanism helps us gain insight into the cause and effect of monetary policy decisions. The ECB sets key interest rates at levels designed to keep euro area inflation below 2 per cent in the medium term. It also manages the EU's foreign exchange reserves and can intervene in foreign exchange markets to influence the exchange rate of the euro. By setting short-term interest rates, monetary policy influences the economy, and ultimately price levels. Like the Bank of England, the central bank provides funds to the banking system and charges interest. Given its monopoly power over the issuing of money, the central bank can be sole determinant of this interest rate. The change in the official interest rate affects money-market interest rates directly and indirectly via lending and deposit rates, which are set by banks for their customers. Changes in interest rates affect saving and investment decisions of households and firms. For example, everything else being equal, higher interest rates makes it less attractive to take out loans for financing consumption or investment. Interest rate changes also have effects on the supply of credit. For example, higher interest rates increase the risk of borrowers being unable to pay back their loans. Banks may cut back on the amount of funds they lend to households and firms. This may also reduce the consumption and investment by households and firms respectively. Changes in consumption and investment will change the level of domestic demand for goods and services relative to domestic supply. When demand exceeds supply, upward price pressure is likely to occur. In addition, changes in aggregate demand may translate into tighter or looser conditions in labour and intermediate product markets. This in turn can affect price and wage-setting in the respective market.

FIGURE 3.7

Transmission mechanism of EU monetary policy

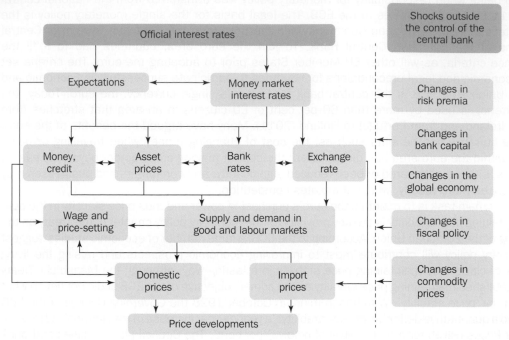

Source: Copyright © European Central Bank – available through the ECB's website (www.ecb.europa.eu/mopo/intro/transmission/html/index.en.html)

SUMMARY

- In this chapter we noted that governments set economic targets (goals) of high and stable levels of economic growth, low levels of unemployment, low inflation and an external balance between imports and exports.
- In order for governments to move towards targets they often need to make trade-offs. As one target nears its completion, another will often deteriorate (growth often leads to inflation). Consequently, governments have to prioritize their economic targets and take decisions on how they might be achieved.
- The main policy tools (interventions) for achievement of targets include interest rate changes (and exchange rates indirectly), and Government expenditure (funded through taxes and loans). Both policy tools are used to stimulate demand in the economy but will also impact upon inflation.
- Policy decisions (nationally, regionally and globally) have important consequences for business, particularly influencing demand (revenues) and costs to do business and therefore profitability. They also impact upon borrowing rates and the availability of capital for investment.
- The economic environment is highly dynamic and subject to global influence. Firms must therefore use their understanding of the environment to influence their own policy decisions if they are to navigate the challenges posed in terms of opportunity and threat. The political and economic environment will be considered further in Chapter 12.

REVISION QUESTIONS

1. Evaluate Osborne's 'New' economic model and argue whether or not it is working – was he right to reduce government spending so much, so quickly? What alternatives might have been considered?

2. Towards the end of 2011, UK inflation exceeded 5 per cent, despite a target of 2 per cent. You are going to attend the next MPC meeting. What do you think the committee should discuss and what recommendations might you make?

3. List and explain five important initiatives or policy areas the Government could consider to stimulate and grow the supply side of the UK economy?

4. Imagine the economy is sluggish and in need of stimulation. Critically evaluate a reflationary policy initiative to reduce taxation – would you recommend cuts to direct or indirect taxes? Explain your answer from the perspective of the Chancellor, business and then consumers.

5. The present Government has targets to increase employment/decrease unemployment rates. Advise the Government on how it might meet this goal.

6. Consider whether the UK should participate in Economic and Monetary Union and further integrate within the EU. In your answer you should present arguments for and against and consider the potential impact upon UK business.

7. Evaluate the role of the UK (or any other country) government, discussing types of state intervention, in influencing macroeconomic activity.

8. With reference to national and regional economies, explain the changing nature of the global economy.

9. Explain economic integration in the EU and EU monetary policy making.

10. Identify and explain the indicators that may be used to either evaluate how well the economy is performing or how well the economy is going to perform in the future.

DISCUSSION QUESTIONS

1. The OECD Business Cycle Clock has been designed to better visualize business cycles – fluctuations of economic activity around their long term potential level – and how some key economic indicators interact with the business cycle. Try it out at http://stats.oecd.org/mei/bcc/default.html

2. Re-read 'A "New" Economic Model for the UK'. In what ways does the new economic model reflect a conservative ideology (evaluate and contrast the new model with the old).

3. Read the section about fiscal and monetary policy and then read this speech again. What would your fiscal policy have been if you were the Chancellor at this time?

4. Osborne emphasizes the need for supply side reform – what does this mean and what initiatives might he consider to accomplish this goal?

5. How important are expectations and confidence? Osborne believes uncertainty over the future paths of tax rates and government spending does play an important role in behaviour: consumer spending and business investment. Does a credible fiscal consolidation plan have to make a positive impact through greater certainty and confidence about the future? If so why?

REFERENCES AND FURTHER READING

Aruoba, S. B., Diebold, F. X., Kose, A. and Terrones, M. E. (2011) 'Globalization, the Business Cycle, and Macroeconomic Monitoring – IMF Working Paper WP/11/25', International Monetary Fund available at www.imf.org/external/pubs/ft/wp/2011/wp1125.pdf

OECD (2011) *OECD Employment Outlook 2011.* OECD Publishing

Office for Budget Responsibility (2011) 'Office for Budget Responsibility: Economic and fiscal outlook – March 2011', Crown copyright – The Stationery Office Limited

GLOSSARY

Balance Of Payments The difference between the payments made to and the receipts from foreign nations in a given period

Budget Deficit A financial situation that occurs when an entity has more money going out than coming in

Business (economic) Cycle Fluctuations in the economy (economic expansion and contraction) that follow the general pattern of prosperity (boom), recession, depression and recovery – economy-wide fluctuations in production or economic activity over several months or years

Consumer Price Index Consumer price index (CPI) - index which tracks the percentage rise or fall in prices (for retail goods and other items), with reference to a specific starting point in time.

Deflation Decline in prices in an economy, associated with recession and falling demand

Deflationary Policy A macroeconomic (government) policy used to reduce aggregate demand in the economy typically by raising taxes and reducing spending. Typically used when there is a significant increase in inflation necessitating an action to dampen the rate of economic activity. Deflationary policies may either be a deflationary fiscal policy or a deflationary monetary policy

Economics A social science concerned chiefly with description and analysis of the production, distribution, and consumption of goods and services

Economic Environment The totality of economic factors, such as employment, income, inflation, interest rates, productivity, and wealth, that influence the buying behaviour of consumers and institutions

Economic Growth The process of increasing productive capacity

Economic Integration The elimination of tariff and nontariff barriers to the flow of goods, services, and factors of production between a group of nations, or different parts of the same nation

Efficiency Doing things right

Employment rate the percentage of the working age population who are currently employed

Eurozone EU member states which are members of the European Monetary Union (EMU). Members of the EU having the euro as their currency

Exchange Rate The price of one national currency in terms of another (the value of one currency for the purpose of conversion to another/ the rate at which one currency is converted into another)

Exchange Rate Volatility A measure of the fluctuations in an exchange rate. It can be measured on an hourly, daily, or annual basis

Fiscal Consolidation A policy aimed at reducing government deficits and debt accumulation

Fiscal Policy Measures that alter the level and composition of government expenditure and taxation

Fiscal Stimulus An increase in government expenditure or reduction in taxation used to boost aggregate demand during a recession

Free Market In a strict sense refers to a market that is free of government regulation or intervention. In practice supporters of the free market advocate minimum government

Global Economy An integrated world economy with unrestricted and free movement of goods, services and labour transnationally

Globalization Of Markets Moving away from an economic system in which national markets are distinct entities, isolated by trade barriers and barriers of distance, time, and culture, and toward a system in which national markets are merging into one global market

Gross Domestic Product (GDP) The total value of all goods and services produced by a country in one year

Gross National Product (GNP) Total domestic and foreign added value claimed by residents of a state

Inflation A rise in the general price level or an increase in the average of all prices of goods and services over a period of time

Interest Rate The price paid for the use of borrowed money

Macroeconomics/microeconomics Macroeconomics is the study of the economy in terms of the broad aggregates of employment, inflation, economic growth, trade, and the balance of payments as well as levels of inequality. Microeconomics is the study of individual product and resource markets

Macroeconomic Policy Is action by policymakers to improve aspects of the performance of the whole economy

Market A system of voluntary exchange, created by the relationship between buyers and sellers

Monetary Policy Attempts by the authorities to influence monetary variables such as money supply, interest rates, exchange rates

National Debt The total debt accumulated by a central government's borrowings over the years

Price Stability Price level stability refers to the concept that price levels are stable enough so that people do not feel forced to take inflation into account when making economic decisions

Quantitative Easing The introduction of new money into the money supply by a central bank

Reflationary Policy Fiscal policy aimed at boosting the level of economic activity, usually through inflationary means such as public spending or reduction in the taxation level

Single Market The single, common or internal market of the EU involves the abolition of obstacles to trade among members. It embraces the four freedoms covering the movement of goods, people, capital and services

Supply-side Policies Government policies designed to increase productivity and the productive potential of an economy

Unemployment rate The percentage of the work force that is unemployed

CHAPTER CASE STUDY

Government Debt: Italy and Greece owe more than they earn...

Europe is in the grip of tough austerity measures - some of the deepest public sector cuts for a generation

Throughout the 2012 financial crisis, Europe witnessed many high profile protests as citizens of debt stricken countries objected publicly and sometimes violently to the austerity measures imposed by their national governments; austerity policies were prescribed by the European Union and other lenders leading to deep public sector cuts and further discontent. To make matters worse, the crippling debts had to be repaid at a time when many countries were experiencing little if any growth. This led to a spiralling downward of market and public confidence. Countries and their banks found it hard or even impossible to borrow in international markets. Greece, Ireland and Portugal had all received substantial bailouts from the EU and International Monetary Fund (IMF). The crisis widened. Spain was also seen as vulnerable and by mid-2012 there were headlines about how to save Spain. Whilst Greek opinion waivered over whether to stay in the eurozone, economists suggested that Greek politics may determine the euro's short-term future, but it was Spain that posed the single currency's most difficult problem. Like Greece and others, Spain was caught in an increasingly desperate spiral of deepening recession, sinking banks and mounting borrowing costs. Throughout 2012, such countries continued with national plans to resurrect their economies. However, the crisis escalated beyond the country level and the euro faced 'disintegration', the European Commission warned.

During the financial crisis, many national economies have looked to their government and foreign lenders for financial support, which has led, in most cases, to growing national debt. Sovereign debt problems (Debt crisis is the general term for an increase of massive public debt relative to tax revenues) continue to be a major public policy issue.

Government debt (public/national debt) is the debt owed by a central government, see Figure 3.8. Countries, through their Governments, usually borrow by issuing government bonds and bills (bank notes). Poorer countries may borrow directly from a supranational organization (e.g. the World Bank) or international financial institutions. Since tax is a significant source of government income, government debt is an indirect taxpayer debt. Debt is a key concern since repayment and interest payments can often place significant demands upon governments and individuals.

Using a debt to GDP ratio is one of the most accepted measures of assessing a nation's debt. The report by Eurostat, the statistical office of the European Union, showed that the ratio of government debt to GDP increased from 74.4 per cent in 2009 to 80.0 per cent in 2010 across all 27 member states.

The European sovereign debt crisis (ESDC) is an ongoing financial crisis that has made it difficult or impossible for some countries in the euro area to re-finance their government debt without the assistance of third parties. From late 2009, fears of a sovereign debt crisis developed amongst investors as a result of the rising government debt levels around the world, together with a wave of downgrading of government debt in some European states. Concerns intensified in 2010, leading Europe's finance ministers to approve a rescue package worth €750 billion, aimed at ensuring financial stability across Europe by creating the European Financial Stability Facility (EFSF). Later, the Eurozone leaders agreed on more measures designed to prevent the collapse of member economies. To restore confidence in Europe, EU leaders also agreed to create a common fiscal union. Whilst sovereign debt has risen substantially in only a few Eurozone countries, it has become a perceived problem for the area as a whole. The three countries most affected, Greece, Ireland and Portugal, account collectively for six per cent of the Eurozone's gross domestic product (GDP).

FIGURE 3.8

General government consolidated gross debt, in percentage of GDP. Main EU economies.

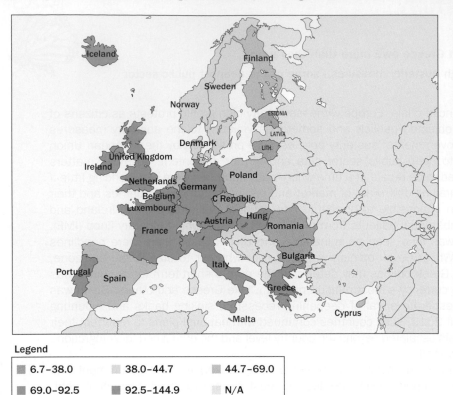

EU (27 countries)	80.1
Belgium	96.2
Bulgaria	16.3
Czech Republic	37.6
Denmark	43.7
Germany	83.2
Estonia	6.7
Ireland	92.5
Greece	144.9
Spain	61
France	82.3
Italy	118.4
Cyprus	61.5
Latvia	44.7
Lithuania	38
Luxembourg	19.1
Hungary	81.3
Malta	69
Netherlands	62.9
Austria	71.8
Poland	54.9
Portugal	93.3
Romania	31
Slovenia	38.8
Slovakia	41
Finland	48.3
Sweden	39.7
United Kingdom	79.9
Iceland	92.9
Norway	44

Legend

■ 6.7–38.0	▨ 38.0–44.7	■ 44.7–69.0
■ 69.0–92.5	■ 92.5–144.9	▨ N/A

Source: EUROSTAT. © European Unoin. 1995–2012. Reproduced with permission.

Questions

- In early 2010, there was renewed anxiety about excessive national debt. How does this impact upon investor decision making? What are the secondary consequences of investor actions?
- How have government measures (to stem the crisis) contributed to social unrest?
- How risky is it for investors/banks to lend to Eurozone countries? What are the risks to lenders when the borrower is a country?
- Research, identify and discuss the factors that may have caused the European sovereign debt crisis. Do you think high debt levels alone explain the crisis?
- In 1992, members of the EU signed the Maastricht Treaty, under which they pledged to limit their deficit spending and debt levels. For example, in theory, one of the criteria of admission to the EU's Euro currency is that a country's debt should not exceed 60 per cent of that country's GDP. However, a number of member states, including Greece and Italy, saw their deficit and debt levels rise. Research how and why this happened.
- Could Eurozone members simply 'print money' in order to pay creditors and ease their risk of default? What would be the consequences of printing money?
- Towards the end of 2011 S&P placed its long-term sovereign ratings on 15 members of the Eurozone on 'CreditWatch' with negative implications; why was this done?
- Slow GDP growth rates correspond to slower growth in tax revenues, increasing deficits and debt levels. Consequently, a number of people have suggested Europe's core problem [is] a lack of growth. What then must crisis-hit countries do to improve their situation?

4
THE SOCIAL AND DEMOGRAPHIC ENVIRONMENT

LEARNING OBJECTIVES:

1   Analyze the interplay of environmental forces from the perspective of social factors

2   Analyze demographic trends and the implications for business

3   Explain how migration brings about changes to social forces

4   Discuss the importance of diversity and multiculturalism in society, the market and workplace

5   Recognize the need for organizations to alter their policies, strategies, products, services and practices in response to social forces

FIGURE 4.1

The social and demographic environment (mind map)

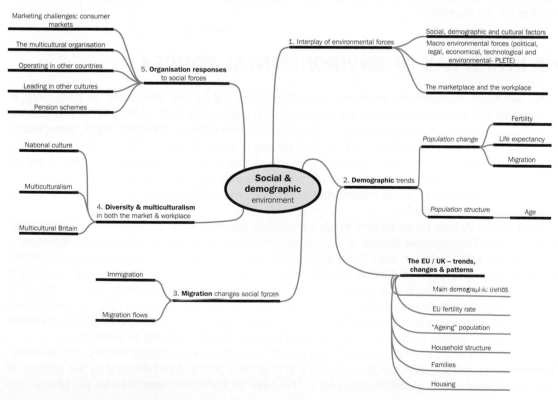

KEY CONCEPTS

Culture | Demographics | Diversity | Socio-cultural environment

INTRODUCTION

The social or socio-cultural factors in the macro environment typically include social values, attitudes and beliefs, demographic trends, lifestyle preferences and skills availability (Socio-cultural environment, see Figure 4.1). In the first section of this chapter we recognize that social forces do not exist in a vacuum, they interact with other environmental forces. Social forces can explain the behaviour of consumers, investors and other stakeholders in the market or workplace. In the marketplace this manifests as demand for products and services. However, we note that not all consumers are the same and use customer segments to group together similar customers. This enables organizations to target and serve the needs of specific groups. For example, segments may be defined in terms of age, gender, nationality or disposable income and needs. Having explained the interplay of environmental forces from a social perspective, we then analyze demographic trends, focusing on the EU in particular. Population structure and changes are considered and evaluated in terms of implications for business; whilst arguably a good thing, we consider the problems associated with the trend of people living longer. Problems associated with caring for a growing number of dependents (ageing population) places greater demand on a shrinking workforce. Additional issues such as low fertility rates and population replenishment are discussed, alongside migration. Whereas migration is used to grow the working population it introduces diversity and creates a multicultural society and workplace. Associated challenges are then considered. We start by explaining what is meant by national culture and how citizens of different countries may hold different values and beliefs thus impacting upon their behaviour in the market and workplace. Next we consider the benefits and costs for organizations finding themselves managing a diverse and multicultural workforce. Finally, we position the social forces in terms of threats and opportunities for business. In particular we consider key challenges for the marketing and HR departments; the former focusing on demand and the latter on the workforce.

THE INTERPLAY OF ENVIRONMENTAL FORCES

So far, we have analyzed environmental forces whilst emphasizing one force in particular. In keeping with this approach, this chapter considers social forces (social, demographic and cultural factors) and their relationships with other macro environmental forces (political, legal, economical, technological and environmental – PLETE) and business through the mediating concepts of the marketplace and the workplace. Figure 4.2 presents a model of such relationships which will be discussed in the following paragraphs. Having presented a holistic overview of the social forces as determinants of behaviour in the market and workplace, we will then move on to consider various social factors in more detail.

Social forces include those factors which can explain the behaviour of consumers in the market and workplace. They typically include demographics, individual and cultural differences. Migration is often included since this can lead to changes in the social environment, impacting upon national culture, increasing diversity and introducing the concept of multiculturalism. Demographics concerns the distribution of individuals in a society in terms of age, gender, marital status, income, ethnicity, and other personal attributes which may determine their buying patterns. Culture, at the national level, refers to shared ways of thinking and behaving (uniformity) in a society and migration concerns the movement of people across national borders from one country (culture) to another.

The aforementioned social factors are influenced by other environmental forces. For example, migration is dependent upon the government's immigration policy, itself swayed by the actions of other governments (see globalization) and in the case of European countries by EC policy. The

FIGURE 4.2
Social forces dependency model

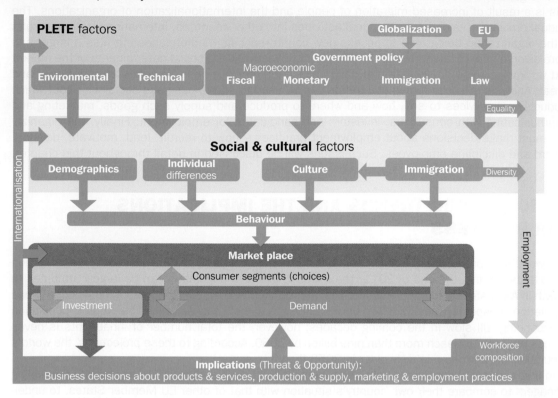

implications of migration policy for business are then influenced by legal forces in terms of the law. Various equality laws seek to outlaw discriminatory practices (see Equality of outcome). Immigration impacts upon culture, making the society more heterogeneous and multicultural; immigrants bring their values, traditions and cultural practices which may then alter the cultural characteristics of the host country. Later in this chapter we suggest that national culture is typically defined in terms of the common values within a particular society. Values help direct consumer behaviour, impacting upon matters such as perceptions of quality, loyalty and trust. For many nations, immigration is a process that is continually changing social forces. There is considerable interplay between government macroeconomic policy and demographics. As demographics change, see for example the ageing population, fiscal and monetary policy are likely to change. As the population ages, a government is more likely to allocate more of its spending on welfare for pensioners. This increase in spending occurs at a time when income from taxation may be reducing, thus the relationship is interdependent. Demographics are also associated with technical forces in so much as the youth of today are more likely to engage with recent technological products and innovations. There is also a relationship between environmental forces and the way people think and behave as consumers. Responsible and ethical consumers will be influenced by environmental challenges such as global warming, the depletion of non-sustainable resources and the needs of future generations.

Demographical variation (see also Demographic diversity), individual and cultural differences associated with the way we think and see (perceive) the world impact upon consumer behaviour in the marketplace. Consumers sharing similar characteristics are often grouped together to form segments. These groups tend to behave in a similar manner and represent opportunity for business. This opportunity can and does vary in size and is related to the size of the segment. Segments have different levels of disposable income and make choices related to their specific needs when demanding products and services from business. However, consumers may also be investors and in a similar fashion, social and cultural factors can be used to explain investment choices. The implications for business do not rest with the marketplace. Domestic and international organizations alike are witnessing increased diversity and multiculturalism in the workplace. This is a result of increased migration of people and the internationalization of organizations. The gradual process of taking organizational activities into other countries, internationalization, results in the organization being able to access new country-specific marketplaces but also a larger and more diverse pool of talent from which to recruit. Collectively, the social determinants of the market and workplace raise challenges and have implications for business, in terms of opportunity and threat. Analysis of social forces and trends can be used to inform business decisions about which products and services to sell, how and where to produce and supply such goods, marketing and communicating with consumers, investors and candidates for employment. Finally, the organization must make decisions about employment practices – how to recruit, lead, motivate, develop, reward and discipline employees. Such issues will be discussed in detail throughout this chapter.

DEMOGRAPHIC TRENDS AND THE IMPLICATIONS FOR BUSINESS

The world's population more than doubled between 1960 and 2010, exceeding seven billion inhabitants towards the end of 2011. The increase in global population can be largely attributed to growth in Asia, Africa and Latin America. The latest United Nations (UN) population projections (world population prospects: the 2008 revision) suggest that the pace at which the world's population is expanding will slow in the coming decades; however, the total number of inhabitants is nevertheless projected to reach more than nine billion by 2050. According to these projections, the world's population will also be relatively older in 2050 than it is now.

In this section, demographic data about population change and structure are provided, enabling managers to compare their own country's situation with that of other EU Member States, to understand the specific characteristics of their country and, possibly, to identify other countries that could provide business opportunities. The three drivers of *population change* considered here are *fertility*, *life expectancy* and *migration* (the subject of the next section of this chapter). In this section we will also consider *population structure* by age. Most of the data in this chapter is derived either directly or indirectly from Eurostat's database. To obtain the most up to date statistics it is advised that you access this database. A URL is supplied at the end of this chapter for this purpose. Eurostat provides information for a wide range of demographic data. Data on population includes breakdown by various characteristics, such as age and gender. Eurostat produces national level population projections every three years. These projections are 'what-if' scenarios that aim to provide information about the likely future size and age structure of the population, based on assumptions of future trends in fertility, life expectancy and migration; the latest projection exercise was EUROPOP2010, Population Projections 2010-based. Eurostat's population projections are used by the EC to analyze the impact of ageing populations on public spending. Increased social expenditure related to population ageing, in the form of pensions, healthcare and institutional or private healthcare is likely to result in a higher burden for working age populations. A number of important policies, notably in social and economic fields, use demographic data for planning actions, monitoring and evaluating programmes – for example, population ageing and its likely effects on the sustainability of public finance and welfare provisions, or the economic and social impact of demographic change. Toward the end of this and subsequent sections we will consider the business implications of demographic trends. Such data is of particular use to strategists, marketers and HRM professionals. First we consider the main demographic trends and patterns for the EU, with a particular focus on the UK.

The EU and the UK – Population Trends, Changes and Patterns

According to the European Commission (2011) the EU population has now exceeded 500 million (see Figure 4.3); this is approximately 7 per cent of the world's population (7 billion). The EC, in their Demography report 2010 note 'The EU's demographic picture has become clearer: (population)

FIGURE 4.3

EU population trend

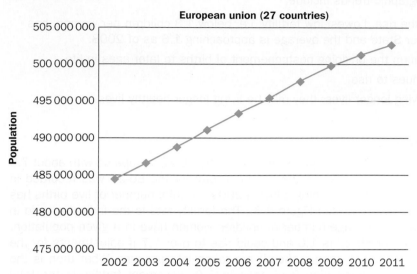

Source: EUROSTAT. © European Union, 1995–2012. Reproduced with permission.

FIGURE 4.4

Population as a percentage of EU-27 population

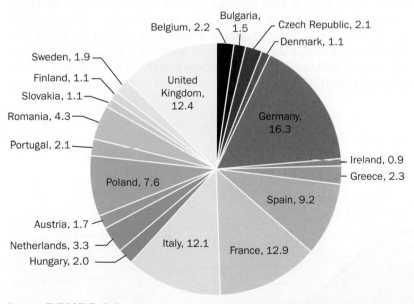

Source: EUROSTAT. © European Union, 1995–2012. Reproduced with permission.

growth is fuelled mainly by immigration, whereas the population is becoming older and more diverse.' Gradual but nonetheless major changes are affecting the population of Europe. Two main positive trends are emerging: a slight increase in *fertility* and greater *life expectancy*.

The EU population is dispersed throughout the 27 member countries to differing degrees as shown in Figure 4.4. From the diagram we can see that Germany, the UK, France, Italy and Spain account for over 60 per cent of the EU population.

Main Demographic Trends

The EU-27 is undergoing major demographic changes. These changes are slow, but they are very significant. The main demographic trends include:

* Fertility is slightly on the rise. Lowest-low fertility, i.e. below 1.3 children per woman, has ended in every Member State and the average is approaching 1.6 as of 2008.
* Fertility indicators confirm the on-going postponement of births to later ages in life.
* Life expectancy continues to rise.
* Not only are people living longer lives; they may be living longer healthy lives.

Population change – EU Fertility rate

In 2010, around 5.4 million (5 358 716) children were born in the EU-27, compared with about 7.5 million at the beginning of the 1960s. The highest annual total for the EU-27 was recorded in 1964, with 7.7 million live births. After reaching a low in 2002 the total number of live births has been growing again, albeit moderately, (see Figure 4.5). The fertility rate is the indicator used in population studies to assess the average number of children women have in a given population. The most recent fertility figure for EU-27 is 1.6 and could rise to over 1.7 if adjustments for the postponement of births (the so-called 'tempo effect') are taken into account. What then is the fertility rate required to prevent a population from shrinking? Replacement fertility is the total fertility rate (TFR) at which new-born girls would have an average of exactly one daughter over their lifetimes. In more familiar terms, women have just enough babies to replace themselves. If there were no mortality in the female population until the end of the childbearing years (generally taken as 44 or 49, though some exceptions exist) then the replacement level of TFR would be very close to 2.0 (actually slightly higher because of the excess of male over female births in human populations). However, the replacement level is also affected by mortality, especially childhood mortality. The replacement fertility rate is roughly 2.1 births per woman for most industrialized countries. Thus a replacement ratio of 2.1 would be required to maintain the size of the EU; a rate below this (as is the case in 2010) would contribute to population shrinkage. However a possible increase in fertility might be expected as EU Member States become wealthier. A systematic review of European fertility rates concluded that European fertility rates do not seem to decrease

FIGURE 4.5

Number of live births in EU-27, 1980–2010

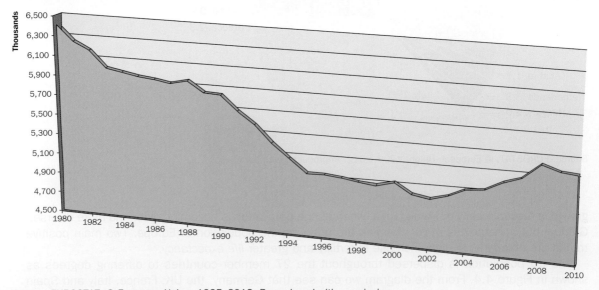

Source: EUROSTAT. © European Union, 1995–2012. Reproduced with permission.

significantly by availability of contraception. It identified significant factors for low fertility rates, to include instability of modern partnerships and value changes; however, government policies that provide benefits (cash) to families for pregnancy and child support only have a small effect on total fertility rate. The modest increase in EU fertility results from somewhat new family building patterns: countries with fewer marriages, more cohabitation, more divorces and an older average age of women at childbirth tend to have higher fertility rates. Changing social perceptions of the role of marriage and greater fragility of relationships have resulted in more extramarital births, including to single parents. Over the past 30 years, total fertility rates in the EU-27 Member States have been converging. Despite this, there remain significant differences. For example, compared with the EU 27 mean of 1.6 (2009), some countries were as low as 1.3 whilst others were closer to the replacement rate: such as the UK (1.96) and France (1.98). Over the past 30 years, the timing of births has also changed significantly: in 2009 the mean age of women at childbirth had been postponed – on average EU mothers tended to have children aged 30. In 2009 the difference between the highest and the lowest mean age at childbirth was 4.6 years.

Population structure by age – An 'ageing' population

Low fertility rates represent one variable, another being a decline in the number of deaths (see death rate) – an increase in life expectancy. Life expectancy at birth has risen rapidly in the last century due to a number of important factors, including reductions in infant mortality, rising living standards, improved lifestyles and better education, as well as advances in healthcare and medicine. Over the past 50 years, life expectancy at birth has increased by about 10 years for both men and women in the EU-27. Further gains will be achieved mostly from the reduction in mortality at older ages. In 2009, the median (middle) age of the population was 40.6, and it is projected to reach 47.9 years by 2060. The EUROPOP2008 projections prepared by Eurostat and presented in the previous Demography Report indicate that by 2014 the working age population (20–64) will start to shrink, as the large baby-boom cohorts born immediately after World War II are now entering their sixties and retiring. The number of people aged 60 and above in the EU is now rising by more than two million every year, roughly twice the rate observed until about three years ago. The working population is also ageing, as the proportion of older workers in employment increases compared with the cohorts made up of younger workers. In 2008 life expectancy for the EU-27 was 76.4 for men and 82.4 for women. A British male is expected to live, on average (2009) to approximately 79 years, whilst his female counterpart should reach 82, see Figure 4.6.

Whilst life expectancy is rising in all Member States, there are still major differences between and within countries. In some cases, improvements in education and standards of living have contributed to longer life expectancy, suggesting that it could be extended further in future. Life

FIGURE 4.6

Life expectancy (UK trend)

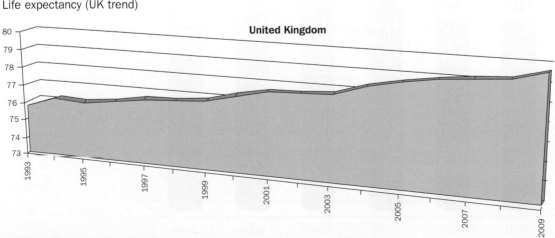

expectancy in the EU-27 is generally higher than in most other regions of the world. Significant differences in life expectancy at birth are nevertheless observed between the EU Member States. The gradual increase in life expectancy is one of the contributing factors to the ageing of the EU-27's population – alongside the low levels of fertility sustained for decades.

Population structure and ageing

The impact of demographic ageing within the European Union (EU) is expected to be of significance in the coming decades. Consistently low birth rates and higher life expectancy will change the shape of the EU-27's age profile (see Figure 4.7); perhaps the most important change will be the marked shift towards a much older population. The population of the EU-27 is growing, whilst the age structure of the population is becoming older. Consequently, the proportion of people of working age in the EU-27 is shrinking whilst the relative number of those retired is expanding (see Figure 4.8). The share of older persons in the total population will increase in the coming decades, as a greater proportion of the post-war baby boom generation reaches retirement. This will lead to an increased burden on those of working age to meet the costs (reflected in Government spending) of caring for the ageing population.

Young people (0 to 14 years old) made up 16 per cent of the EU-27's population in 2010, whilst persons considered to be of working age (15 to 64 years old) accounted for 67 per cent of the population, and older persons (65 or more years old) had a <18 per cent share. Age dependency ratios may be used to study the level of support of the young and/or older persons by the working age population; these ratios are expressed in terms of the relative size of young and/or older populations relative to the working age population. The old age dependency ratio for the EU-27 was approximately 26 per cent in 2010. As such, there were around four persons of working age for every person aged 65 or over in the EU-27. The combination of young and old age dependency ratios provides the total age dependency ratio, which in 2010 was almost 50 per cent in the EU-27, indicating that there were about two working age persons for every dependent person. *Population ageing* is a long-term trend which began several decades ago in the EU. This ageing is visible in the

FIGURE 4.7

EU Population (millions) by age groups

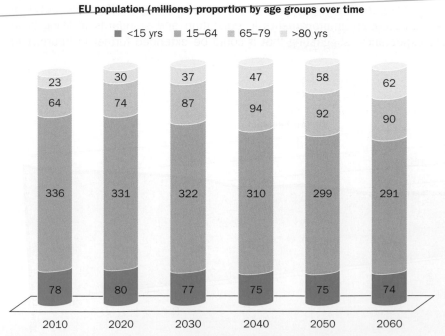

Source: EUROSTAT. © European Union, 1995–2012. Reproduced with permission.

FIGURE 4.8

EU population (per cent) by age groups

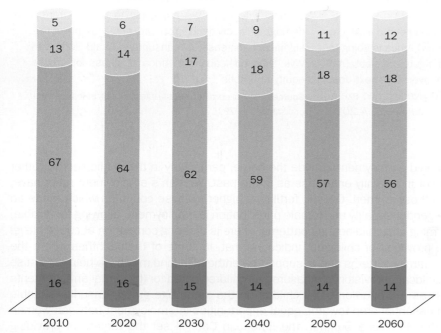

EU population (%) by age groups over time

■ <15 yrs   ■ 15–64   ■ 65–79   ■ >80 yrs

Source: EUROSTAT. © European Union, 1995–2012. Reproduced with permission.

development of the age structure of the population and is reflected in an increasing share of older persons at the same time as a declining share of working age persons in the total population. Eurostat's Population Projections 2010-based (EUROPOP2010), with projected populations from 2011 to 2060, show that population ageing is likely to affect all EU Member States. According to this scenario, the EU's population will be slightly higher in 2060, whilst the age structure of the population will be much older than it is now. The population of working age is expected to decline steadily, whilst elderly people will likely account for an increasing share of the population – those aged 65 years or over will account for almost 30.0 per cent of the EU's population by 2060 (17.4 per cent in 2010). Another aspect of population ageing is the progressive ageing of the older population itself, as the relative importance of the oldest people is growing at a faster pace than any other age segment of the EU's population. The share of those aged 80 years or above in the EU-27's population is projected to almost triple by 2060. As a result of the population movement between age groups, the EU's old age dependency ratio is projected to more than double from 25.9 per cent in 2010 to 52.6 per cent by 2060. The total age dependency ratio (calculated as the ratio of dependent people, young and old, over the population aged 15 to 64 years old) is projected to rise from 49.3 per cent in 2010 to 77.9 per cent by 2060.

Families

In their attempt to capture and track changing family forms and composition, demographers most often refer to the family nucleus and to private household units. The number of marriages is decreasing and the number of divorces is increasing, although these trends may be due in part to the ageing of the population. In addition, more and more children are born to unmarried women, and the countries with the highest extramarital birth rates are often also those with the highest fertility rates. Arguably one of the most important trends of the past 50 years affecting family life has been the marked increase in female employment rates. Since the 1960s, more women have become economically

BUSINESS IN ACTION

Focus on Africa – Population to double in 40 years

'In 1900 there were only 110 million people in Africa, now there are over a billion. In 2050 Africa is going to have 2 billion.' The latest UN figures project that Africa's population will double over the next four decades to almost two billion. To give just one example, 46 per cent of Zambians are below 15. A 2010 study by the McKinsey Global Institute projected the number of African households with discretionary income earning over $5000 would rise to 128 million by 2020 from 85 million. Africa's demographic profile could make it a dream for retailers if spending power continues to rise. 'We are going to benefit from a demographic dividend. You are going to have this significant increase in consumers', said John van Wyk, who co-heads the Africa business of private equity firm Actis.

Source: www.iol.co.za/business/international/africa-dividend-or-disaster-1.1279117

active and have entered paid employment outside the home, particularly in the public sector, rather than working on the land or in a family enterprise as in the past. Women's employment rates have, thereby, moved closer to those of men. Overall, fertility is higher in those countries which made an earlier transition to more gender equality and female participation in employment, allowing for flexible, less traditional family-forming and child-bearing patterns. There is a strong correlation at country level between fertility and the provision of childcare, indicating that, in some of the countries where the transition to more diverse family patterns and to support parenthood in kind may have helped to raise their fertility levels. The childcare provision is measured as children cared for (by formal arrangements other than by the family) as a proportion of all children in the same age group. Ensuring suitable childcare provision is an essential step towards equal opportunities in employment between women and men. In 2002, at the Barcelona Summit, the European Council set the targets of providing childcare, by 2010, to at least 33 per cent of children under three years of age. Studies have revealed considerable differences both in public policy as well as in cultural approach as regards informal support within families. Within the EU the traditional stereotype of poorer families having several children seems to have given way to a resumption of pre-industrial revolution patterns whereby better-off families tend to have more children. Nevertheless, at the other end of the income range, there is a persistent association between poverty and number of children.

Household structure is constantly changing. As the population ages, more people live in smaller households, increasingly consisting of a single person. At the same time, many young adults, especially men, delay leaving the parental home to found their own household. Average family and household size has been declining since the 1960s. The decline in household size continued between 2005 and 2009 and For EU-27, average household size fell from 2.5 members to 2.4. Many reasons have been provided to explain the changes observed in family and household size over the past half century. The ageing of Europe's population led to a decline in the proportion of young people, automatically resulting in fewer new candidates for marriage and family building. At the same time, changing value systems contributed to lower fertility rates and an increase in the number of childless couples. The majority of households with children in the EU comprise two adults, almost always living as a couple. Single-parents households are relatively common in Estonia and the United Kingdom (both above 20 per cent). In the United Kingdom and Ireland, 8 per cent and 6 per cent respectively of young women aged 15–24 are single parents. Between 2005 and 2009, young adults in their twenties seemed to be leaving the family home a little earlier, whereas young adults over 30 were remaining somewhat longer with their parents. The proportion of young adults (aged 25–29) living with their parent(s) varies from 15 per cent or less in France, the Netherlands and Finland to 55 per cent or more in some EU countries. It exceeds 50 per cent in 16 Member States. Cultural aspects or different lifestyle arrangements, which are difficult to assess, may help to explain differences between countries. Changes in the housing and labour markets (for instance, lack of job security), or the conditions under which young people pursue their education are considered typical explanations. However, a large number of young people live with their parents even if they are employed.

BUSINESS IN ACTION

Focus on the UK: Integrated Household Survey April 2010 to March 2011

The Integrated Household Survey (IHS) is the largest social survey ever produced by the UK Office for National Statistics (ONS). The survey covers a number of themes including health, education, migration, housing and employment. In terms of Religion, the IHS data showed that 69 per cent of people in Great Britain stated that they had a religious affiliation with Christianity; 4 per cent of people stated that they had a religious affiliation with being a Muslim and 23 per cent stated that they had no religious affiliation. Turning to Ethnicity, 89 per cent of people in the UK identified themselves as belonging to the White ethnic group; 5 per cent identified themselves Asian or Asian British; 3 per cent identified themselves Black or Black British and 3 per cent identified themselves in another ethnic group (Mixed, Chinese or Other Ethnic Group).

Housing

According to the EU (2011), in 2008, 41.8 per cent of the EU-27 population lived in flats, 34.1 per cent in detached houses and 22.6 per cent in semi-detached houses. Just over one quarter of the EU-27 population lived in an owner-occupied home for which there was an outstanding loan or mortgage, whilst close to half of the population lived in an owner-occupied home without a loan or mortgage. As such, a total of nearly three quarters (73.6 per cent) of the population lived in owner-occupied dwellings, whilst approximately 25 per cent lived in rented or in reduced-rent or free accommodation. One of the key dimensions in assessing the quality of housing conditions is the availability of sufficient space in the dwelling. The overcrowding rate describes the share of people living in a dwelling considered as overcrowded. Based on the number of rooms available to the household, this indicator depends upon the household's size, as well as its members' ages and family situation. Almost one in five (18.2 per cent) of the EU-27 population lived in overcrowded dwellings in 2008.

In this section we have focused on demographic data about population change and structure. The drivers of *population change* considered were *fertility and life expectancy*. We also considered *population structure* by age. In the next section we will also focus on demographic data about population change but consider *migration* in particular. Having explained migration, in the next section we discuss the importance of diversity and multiculturalism in both the market and workplace and finish Chapter 4 with recognition of the need for organizations to alter their policies, strategies, products, services and practices in response to the social forces outlined.

HOW MIGRATION BRINGS ABOUT CHANGES TO SOCIAL FORCES

Migration is the main driver of population growth in most of the EU-27 Member States and plays a significant role in the population dynamics of European societies; in recent years, the increase in the population of the EU-27 Member States has mainly been due to high net migration rates. Migratory movements are making the EU's population more diverse and creating new challenges and opportunities for European societies. In many EU-27 Member States, immigration is not only increasing the total population, but also bringing in a much younger population. Migration is influenced by a blend of economic, political and social factors within a migrant's home (push factors) or destination country (pull factors). The relative economic prosperity and political stability of the EU are thought to exert a sizeable pull effect on immigrants. In destination countries, international migration may be used as a solution to labour market shortages. However, international migration alone is unlikely to reverse the ongoing trend of population shrinkage and ageing discussed in the previous section. Eurostat define Immigration as the action by which a person establishes his or her usual residence in the territory of a Member State for a period that is, or is expected to be, of at least 12 months, having previously been usually resident in another Member

State or a third country; and Emigration is the action by which a person, having previously been usually resident in the territory of a Member State, ceases to have his or her usual residence in that Member State for a period that is, or is expected to be, of at least 12 months. Eurostat make various migration Indicators available: Immigration/Emigration flow into/out of the reporting country during the reference year by sex, age (group), citizenship, country of birth, or country of previous/next residence of migrants.

Migration flows

EU citizens are becoming more mobile. The first decade of the 21st century has seen large waves of migration both within the EU and from outside it. The highest inflow in that decade appears to have peaked in 2007. During 2009, about three million people immigrated into one of the EU Member States with at least 1.9 million emigrants reported to have left an EU Member State (includes international flows within the EU – between different Member States). Just over half of the total immigrants to EU Member States, in other words 1.6 million people, were previously residing outside the EU. Figures reveal a substantial decline in immigration in 2009 as compared with 2008. The country that reported the largest number of immigrants in 2009 was the United Kingdom (566 000), followed by Spain (499 000) and Italy (443 000). Almost half of all immigrants to EU Member States were recorded in these three countries. There has been a growing trend in UK immigration for the past ten years as can be seen from Figure 4.9. However, The UK also reported the highest number of emigrants in 2009 (368 000). Most EU Member States reported more immigration than emigration in 2009.

In 2009, in the UK, the number of immigrants accounted for almost ten in 1000 of the domestic population, i.e. around 1 per cent, see Figure 4.10. The UK is thus one of the top 10 EU destinations for immigrants, relative to the size of the population (the EU Member States' average is six immigrants per 1000 inhabitants). The country that recorded the highest number of immigrants in 2009 was Luxembourg with 31 immigrants per 1000 inhabitants. Immigrants to a Member State include both nationals and non-nationals (people who are not citizens of the destination country). The nationals include former emigrants returning 'home' and citizens born abroad who are immigrating for the first time. Eighteen per cent of all immigrants, into the EU Member States in 2009 were nationals. The share of non-nationals among immigrants to EU Member States in 2009 was 81 per cent. More than half of them (61 per cent) were citizens of non-EU countries and the rest (39 per cent) were citizens of other EU Member States. There were almost an equal number of men and women amongst the immigrants, with the median age of immigrants typically considerably less than the median age of the EU population (41 yrs.).

FIGURE 4.9

UK immigration trend

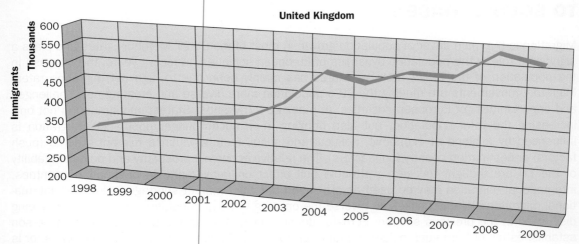

Source: EUROSTAT. © European Union, 1995–2012. Reproduced with permission.

FIGURE 4.10

Immigrants (per 1000 inhabitants) in 2009

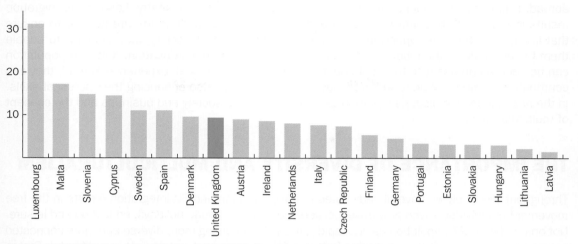

Source: EUROSTAT. © European Union, 1995–2012. Reproduced with permission.

The total number of non EU citizens resident in the EU, on 1 January 2010, was 20.2 million. The largest proportion (36.5 per cent) were citizens of a European country outside of the EU-27, a total of 7.2 million people; among these more than half were citizens of Turkey, Albania or Ukraine. The second biggest group was from Africa (25.2 per cent), followed by Asia (20.9 per cent), and the Americas (16.4 per cent). The citizenship structure of the population of non-nationals living in the EU varies greatly between Member States; it is influenced by factors such as labour migration, historical links between origin and destination countries, and established networks in destination countries.

Migration, especially from non-EU countries, could provide a (temporary) relief from population ageing; since most people migrate primarily as young adults (aged 25-34). As young cohorts of foreigners feed progressively into the older national cohorts, the total population is rejuvenated and diversity increases. Migration flows impact upon the size and structure of the population. Unprecedented levels of immigration both from third countries and within the EU-27 (intra-EU mobility) over the past decade have substantially increased the proportion of EU-27 inhabitants who do not live in their own native country or culture. There are an increasing number of European citizens who seek opportunities across national borders for study, work, and life experience, resulting in different forms of international connectedness across national borders. The EC, in their Demography report 2010 noted 'The EU's demographic picture has become clearer: growth is fuelled mainly by immigration'. In its October 2006 Communication entitled 'The Demographic Future of Europe – from Challenge to Opportunity', the Commission presented its views on the demographic challenges the EU was facing and on options for tackling them. The Communication expressed confidence in Europe's ability to cope with demographic change and an ageing population in particular, but also stressed the need to act in five key policy areas: demographic renewal, employment, productivity, integration of migrants and sustainable public finances. Every year over two million people immigrate into the EU. As a result, migration accounts for a significant proportion of the EU's population growth, (European Commission 2011). As most migrants are relatively young and have arrived quite recently, they contribute to the size of the EU-27 labour force. In the future, the labour force will increasingly include people with a migration background. By 2060, persons of all nationalities with at least one foreign-born parent are expected to account for close to a third of the EU-27 population. An even larger percentage of the workforce will be of foreign descent.

Alongside traditional migration and mobility, new forms of mobility are taking place. People are moving abroad for shorter periods, mainly to other Member States, to seek work, pursue their education or other life opportunities. These mobile people tend to be well-educated young adults, towards the higher end of the occupational scale. Increasingly, this form of mobility is based on personal preferences and life choices, and not only on economic opportunities. The Eurobarometer survey also indicates that around one in five of the EU-27 respondents has either worked or studied in another country at some point, lived with a partner from another country or owns a property abroad. Half of these respondents have ties to other countries by ancestry. Large-scale migration results in the mixing of cultures. These trends imply that additional efforts are needed to ensure that immigrants have the opportunity to integrate into their host society and, crucially, to enable them to contribute to the labour market by making full use of their education. A mobile population can be seen as an asset to the host countries. As more people seek experience abroad, they can contribute to a more efficient and productive economy, whilst also enhancing their personal skills. In the next section we discuss the importance of diversity to society and business and the concept of multiculturalism.

THE IMPORTANCE OF DIVERSITY AND MULTICULTURALISM

Throughout this book we have already noted that globalization and EU integration results in the free movement of individuals who now travel between countries for work, holidays, education and leisure. Not only is the EU-27 population ageing rapidly; it is also becoming more diverse and more connected across borders. As the flow of migration from non-EU countries and mobility between Member States has intensified, a growing proportion of the working-age population (15 per cent in 2008) was either born abroad or has at least one parent who was born abroad. Consequently both the marketplace and workplace are becoming more diverse; particularly from a national culture perspective. Kelly (2009) presents an enlightening discussion of diversity and culture and the implications for the market and workplace. There are many definitions for Diversity. It has been described as the heterogeneity of attitudes, perspectives and backgrounds amongst group members; valuing, respecting, and appreciating the differences (such as age, culture, education, ethnicity, experience, gender, race, religion, and sexual orientation, amongst others) that make people unique or more simply as all the ways in which we differ. Cultural diversity is taken to mean the representation, in one social system, of people with different group affiliations of cultural significance. The term 'cultural diversity' is used interchangeably with racial diversity. Because race has been cited as the most frequently selected component of diversity by Human Resource (HR) Managers and CEOs, and because past findings validate race as a dimension of cultural diversity, few would argue that it is not a major dimension of diversity.

Moving abroad, or having a foreign partner/spouse, creates strong links with other countries. There are also other, less direct ways in which people develop connections across borders. Some take up jobs in other countries whilst continuing to live in their own. In many such cases, they live near a border. Cross-border commuting is relatively common amongst the closely-linked countries in the centre-north of the EU (France, Germany and, especially, Belgium, Luxembourg and the Netherlands). Other people feel attached to the culture of another country. They speak the language, follow its news, and spend holidays there regularly. There are about one million cross-border workers within the EU, representing 0.4 per cent of the working population. They reside in one EU Member State and work in another. About five times as many people (roughly 1 per cent of EU's resident nationals) declare that they have been cross-border workers at some time during their life. Many have either relatives or close friends abroad, or close friends of foreign origin in their own country. This leads to an increase in cultural connections across borders. There are therefore various cultural links with other countries. One important indicator of cultural ties is fluency in at least one other language. Almost one third of EU citizens say that they are able to hold a conversation in another language. Furthermore, about 22 per cent of EU nationals regularly spend their holidays in one particular country abroad. According to a Eurobarometer survey, some 4 per cent of EU nationals received medical treatment in another EU Member State in 2007. Many found themselves in need of medical attention during short visits abroad. Health care abroad is now facilitated by the Cross Border Healthcare Directive, adopted in 2011. In the following paragraphs we will first explore the concept of national culture before discussing the meaning of multiculturalism. Having defined and explained these key concepts we will be well placed to discuss the business implications of demographics and the related issue of multiculturalism as experienced in both the society and workplace.

National Culture

The starting point in comparing different national cultures and predicting a citizen's likely thinking and behaviour, concerns how to define culture and the cultural dimensions to study. A dimension in this sense is an aspect, property or feature of culture; sometimes this may be measurable in some defined way. There is no standard definition of culture and no universal set of cultural dimensions (values at the national culture level). There are potentially many ways that cultures can be different. Different cultural dimensions were first presented by the Dutchman Geert Hofstede – who studied how values in the workplace are influenced by national culture. He analyzed a large database of employee values scores collected by IBM between 1967 and 1973, covering more than 70 countries, from which he first used only 40 and later extended the analysis to 50 countries and three regions. From the initial results, and later additions, Hofstede developed a model that identifies five primary dimensions to assist in differentiating national (country) cultures: Power Distance PD (related to the problem of inequality), Uncertainty Avoidance UA (related to the problem of dealing with the unknown and unfamiliar), Individualism–Collectivism IND (related to the problem of interpersonal ties) and Masculinity–Femininity MAS (related to emotional gender roles). Later he added the fifth dimension: Long versus Short-Term Orientation (related to deferment of gratification). Despite arguments suggesting some aspects of culture cannot be measured or compared, or that the differences between countries is diminishing, the study and its findings have been widely embraced and continue to be used by many when seeking to explain or predict the collective behaviour of a nations' citizens. Using a country response (surveying many citizens and calculating a mean country score) to various questions, Hofstede computes a country score along each dimension (typically between 0 and 100). The score may then be used to indicate a low or high position on the scale and then infer likely behaviours of citizens. For example, Hofstede reported UK scores as follows: IND (89), PD (35), UA (35) and MAS (66) i.e. they score low on UA, suggesting a tolerance for ambiguity and uncertainty; low on PD, suggesting that in organizations UK employees are more likely to challenge-the-boss; and high on Individualism. Consequently citizens typically emphasize autonomy, self-respect and independence and individual achievement is highly valued. In contrast we may take a country such as the Philippines with scores similar to the UK on UA and MAS but at the opposite end of the scale for IND and PD. A low score for the IND dimension (32) indicates a collectivist culture where people from birth onwards are integrated into strong, cohesive in-groups, often extended families which continue protecting them in exchange for unquestioning loyalty. Members of collectivist cultures are more likely to favour group decision making, value harmony and will engage in face-saving behaviours. Hofstede records a high PD score of (94) for the Philippines. Societies high on PD tend to expect obedience towards superiors and clearly distinguish between those with status and power and those without it. In countries with a high power score (Discipline), superiors are supposed to initiate contact and subordinates will follow command, without question (rule orientation). Organizations in such countries tend to be bureaucratic, having tall hierarchies, with consequences of slower decision-making.

The cultural dimensions proposed by Hofstede, defined in more detail in Table 4.1, can be used, in conjunction with other information, to evaluate cultural differences and therefore predict consumer or employee behaviour. However, caution must be applied when generalizing from samples and taking such a quantitative approach. The reality is that all people within a country and between countries have similarities and differences. Hofstede's thesis is that citizens from the same country will, on average, share a common position on each dimension's scale. Specific country scores can be found in Cole and Kelly (2011:p168 or Kelly 2009:p54). Since the landmark work of Hofstede there have been a number of similar studies – see for example project Globe (Javidan and House 2001).

Generally, it is advisable to consider culture as a broad concept that cannot simply be reduced to a small number of dimensions. Differences in societies arise through education, religion, language and social systems, inculcating values and meanings that become shared by the country's people. Differences may also arise as a result of the country's location, physical environment, geography and climate. The environment is a source of challenge shared by inhabitants who develop similar coping behaviours. Having discussed what national culture means we can now consider societies (countries) containing significant groups of people from different countries that have migrated.

TABLE 4.1

Dimension	Consequences
Power distance (PD)	Societies that are high on PD tend to expect obedience towards superiors and clearly distinguish between those with status and power and those without it. In countries with a high power score (Discipline), superiors are supposed to initiate contact and subordinates will follow command, without question (rule orientation). Organizations in such countries tend to be bureaucratic, tall hierarchies with consequences of slower decision-making. In low PD countries, an employee is more likely to challenge-the-boss. A belief or attitude such as 'The boss knows best' may result in negative behaviour such as not speaking out about problems. High PD cultures are like military machines whilst in lower PD cultures, employees of organizations are more likely to think like owners.
Uncertainty avoidance (UA)	Societies that are high on uncertainty avoidance have a stronger tendency toward orderliness and consistency, structured lifestyles, clear specification of social expectations, and rules and laws to cover situations. In contrast, the people of countries where there is strong tolerance of ambiguity and uncertainty are used to less structure in their lives and are not as concerned about following rules and procedures. Hofstede lists characteristics of high uncertainty avoidance such as fear of failure, less risk-taking, a belief in expertise, a preference for clear requirements and instructions, and orientation to rules, and lower readiness to compromise.
Individualism (IND)	On the individualist side we find societies in which the ties between individuals are loose: everyone is expected to look after themselves and their immediate family. On the collectivist side, people from birth onwards are integrated into strong, cohesive in-groups, often extended families which continue protecting them in exchange for unquestioning loyalty. Members of collectivist cultures are more likely to favour group decision making, value harmony and will engage in face-saving behaviours; members of individualist cultures emphasize autonomy, self-respect and independence. Individual achievement is highly valued in individualistic cultures.
Masculinity (MAS)	Countries with the least gender-differentiated practices tend to accord women a higher status and a stronger role in decision-making. They have a higher percentage of women participating in the labour force and more women in positions of authority. Men and women in these cultures tend to have similar levels of education. In contrast, countries reported to have high degrees of gender differentiation tend to accord men higher social status and have relatively few women in positions of authority.
Future orientation	Countries with a strong future orientation, such as Singapore, Switzerland, and the Netherlands, are associated with a higher propensity to save for the future and longer thinking and decision-making time frames. Countries with weak future orientation, such as Russia, Argentina, and Italy, are associated with shorter thinking and planning horizons and greater emphasis on instant gratification.

Multiculturalism

Earlier we discussed migration and in the previous paragraphs considered culture at the country level. It is worth noting that immigrants often want to maintain a close attachment to their country of origin, but these linkages tend to weaken over time. Changing patterns of migration and mobility in Europe are making national sentiments and feelings about belonging to a particular nation more diffuse and complex. Increased immigration and the general free movement of people across borders results in more heterogeneous populations – a country's population will have proportions of people from other national cultures residing there. Multiculturalism is a concept that can be applied at the level of a society or an organization (or any type of group). We will first discuss multiculturalism at the country/society level before considering the organization and the workforce. Multiculturalism describes a phenomenon, trend or the characteristics of a society which has or is moving toward many different ethnic or national cultures mingling and coexisting freely. Taken literally, it refers to the existence of several different cultures (rather than one national culture) significantly represented within a country. However, we should note that, in any given country, there may be an acceptance or promotion of multiple ethnic cultures existing side-by-side or a belief that such cultures should, eventually, assimilate the values and beliefs of the host country. In this sense we might also consider it to be an ideology that favours and deliberately fosters the presence of many cultures in society, each with equal rights – a doctrine asserting the value of different cultures coexisting within single society. As an example we will consider the UK as a multicultural society.

Multicultural Britain

According to the ONS (2011) for England and Wales, new population estimates by ethnic group indicate the population belonging to other groups (non-white British) has risen by around 2.5 million to 9.1 million over the period between 2001 and 2009; the majority White British group has stayed the same size over the period. With the White British group static in size, overall population growth averaging 0.6 per cent per year is the result of growth of the Non-'White British' grouping (that is, all ethnic groups other than White British). This overall growth of the Non-'White British' part of the population encompasses a range of different patterns of growth for individual ethnic groups, see Figure 4.11.

FIGURE 4.11

Population growth within different ethnic groups: England and Wales: 2001–2009

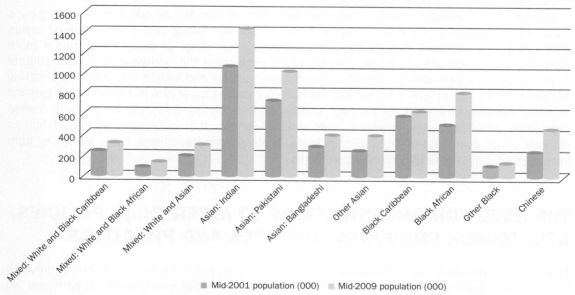

■ Mid-2001 population (000)   ■ Mid-2009 population (000)

Source: Adapted from data from the Office for National Statistics licensed under the Open Government Licence v.1.0.

The BBC (2004) asked, 'So what exactly is multiculturalism'? BBC News Online asked a range of thinkers for a short definition. Professor Sir Bernard Crick, Chair of the 'Life in the UK' report which led to the new citizenship tests, sees no incompatibility between multiculturalism and Britishness. Britishness must be part of multiculturalism. In a previous report he said: 'Who are we British? For a long time the UK has been a multicultural state composed of England, Northern Ireland, Scotland and Wales, and also a multicultural society... made up of a diverse range of cultures and identities, and one that emphasizes the need for a continuous process of mutual engagement and learning about each other with respect, understanding and tolerance.' In other words, dual identities have been common, even before large scale immigration. He further wrote: 'To be British means that we respect the laws, the parliamentary and democratic political structures, traditional values of mutual tolerance, respect for equal rights...' but Britishness does not mean a single culture. Integration is the co-existence of communities and unimpeded movement between them, it is not assimilation. Britishness is a strong concept but not all embracing. Ruth Lea argues there is another way to define multiculturalism which she would call diversity, where people have their own cultural beliefs and they happily coexist – but there is a common thread of Britishness or whatever you want to call it, to hold society together. Lord Parekh, Professor of Political Philosophy, argues multiculturalism is sometimes taken to mean that different cultural communities should live their own ways of life in a self-contained manner. This is not its only meaning and in fact it has long been obsolete. Multiculturalism basically means that no culture is perfect or represents the best life and that it can therefore benefit from a critical dialogue with other cultures. In this sense multiculturalism requires that all cultures should be open, self-critical, and interactive in their relations with each other. However, more recently (2011) David Cameron, UK Prime Minister, has criticized 'state multiculturalism'. At a conference in Munich, he argued the UK needed a stronger national identity.

The term multiculturalism can also be used to describe a market or workplace. In the organizational studies context, it is another term for cultural differentiation or the existence of subcultures within an organization. Thus, the multicultural organization is an organization that contains many different cultural groups and values diversity. As organizations internationalize their operations it is likely that the frequency with which employees will interact with people from different countries will increase. Further, through migration, domestic populations are becoming more diverse, suggesting that domestic organizations will also need to learn how to manage more heterogeneous and multicultural workgroups than they have managed previously. Immigration, changing demographics, globalization, increased international business and technology impact upon today's workforce which is older, more racially diverse, and more female, more varied. The 21st century workplace typically has a diverse (heterogeneous) workforce.

Proponents of diversity maintain that different opinions provided by culturally diverse groups make for better-quality decisions. Heterogeneity in decision-making and problem-solving styles produces better decisions through the operation of a wider range of perspectives and a more thorough critical analysis of issues. Orlando (2000) examined the performance impact cultural diversity has on organizations; benefits include skills transfer and insight and cultural sensitivity pertinent to reaching different market segments as companies enter new markets or their existing markets change and develop. Furthermore, cultural diversity can provide organizations with diverse experience and knowledge. However, research has shown that although diversity in human resources may contribute to the quality of ideas, it also creates additional costs stemming from increased coordination and control requirements.

THE NEED FOR ORGANIZATIONS TO ALTER THEIR POLICIES, STRATEGIES, PRODUCTS, SERVICES AND PRACTICES

This section considers the implications of the social environment for business. In the previous sections we have identified forces within the organization's social environment. In particular we analyzed demographic changes (population changes, the ageing population, migration changes and changes to the proportions of ethnic groups within a society – population structure), cultural changes in the way that members of the population think and behave and changes resulting from increased migration. All of these changes create a dynamic social environment from which customers, investors, employees and stakeholders of the organization will emerge. Such changes may manifest as opportunities or threats to the organization's established strategies, products and services, policies and practices. Globalization opens many opportunities for business, but it also creates major challenges. An important challenge is the understanding and appreciation of cultural values, practices, and subtleties at home and in different parts of the world. To be successful in dealing with people from other cultures, managers need knowledge about cultural differences and similarities amongst countries. They also need to understand the implications of the differences and the skills required to act and decide appropriately and in a culturally-sensitive way. The implications for business were discussed in the previous two chapters when we noted the importance of the EU economy. The Commission's Europe 2020 Strategy has identified concern about population ageing, together with globalization, climate change, competitiveness and macro-economic imbalances, as one of the key challenges the European Union must overcome. The impact of demographic ageing within the EU is likely to be of major significance in the coming decades. Consistently low fertility levels and higher life expectancy will transform the shape of the EU-27's age pyramid. The most important change is likely to be the marked transition towards a much older population. In the final paragraphs of this chapter we will outline a selection of key social environmental challenges and implications for the firm. First we will examine challenges from a marketing perspective, considering the market and its groups of customers (segments) which may be targeted with the supply of products or services. Next we consider challenges associated with managing a diverse and multicultural workforce, a consequence of globalization and migration. Next we will evaluate the challenges of working in other countries and the implications for how the human resources of the multinational organization may be managed, debating whether workers can be managed using the same HR practices worldwide. We will also discuss implications for leadership in different countries and cultures before considering a special challenge associated with the ageing population: pensions. This is an issue for Government and organizations alike. Responses to the needs of an ageing population include changes to retirement ages, pension contributions and taxation; all of which impact upon the firm.

Marketing Challenges: Consumer markets (Demand)

The demographic profile of a given country, coupled with an understanding of cultural values (how people think and behave) may be of use to the marketing department when seeking to segment and understand markets. A market segment is a group of customers who have similar needs that are different from customer needs in other parts of the market. Segments should be distinct, accessible and profitable. The organization must decide which segments to serve, i.e. determine its target markets. Marketers must communicate with consumers within the target market segment through the transmission of persuasive information about goods, services or an idea. Marketing communication aims to raise product visibility and awareness and, at the same time, differentiate the company's products and services from its competitors. Direct marketing may be used to focus marketing communications on specific segments and targeted customers. Specific goals may include niche-focus on a small part of a segment where customers' special needs can be met through a strongly differentiated product offering. In summary, segmentation is the process of grouping customers in heterogeneous markets into smaller, more similar or homogeneous segments – customers are aggregated into groups with similar needs and buying characteristics. Utilizing the concept of segmentation and positioning, marketing strategy can be defined as a means that identifies the target markets towards which activities are to be directed, types of competitive advantages to be developed and exploited. The purpose of market segmentation is to leverage scarce resources: to ensure that the elements of the marketing mix (product, promotion, price and place/ distribution decisions) are designed to meet particular needs of different customers. Market segmentation is related to product differentiation, i.e. companies adapt to different offerings and variations of offerings to satisfy segments.

There are a number of ways to segment the market. All of the diversity and population or cultural variables discussed so far can be used as a basis for segmentation. From a cultural standpoint, many studies have sought to link Hofstede's cultural dimensions with particular customer behaviours. For example, high levels of uncertainty avoidance have been associated with loyalty to existing domestic retailers. On the other hand, the more individualistic the culture, the less loyalty there is likely to be. Gender is also considered to be associated with loyalty; men being more loyal to domestic retailers. Cultural differences have also been shown to impact upon new product adoption. Many organizations use knowledge of country cultural values when determining how to communicate with consumers of that country. For example, the use of role models or authority figures may be more successful in marketing communications with high-power distance cultures. In countries that avoid uncertainty, marketers will typically seek to demonstrate products in use, making use of opinion leaders to explain the merits of a product. It may also be beneficial to provide free samples, offer guarantees, after sales services and tolerant refund policies to such segments.

Returning to demographic profiles, the Marketing Department is likely to use age cohorts to identify similar groups (segments) within the population. Of course knowledge of fertility, population, migration and mortality rates can all be of use in defining the overall market size. But as has been discussed already, marketers are likely to focus on subgroups with similar characteristics. Younger people are more likely to make greater use of the Internet, mobile telecommunications, social networking applications, etc. and will therefore be more likely to use information technology to communicate both nationally and internationally. Similarly, younger people are more likely to study abroad and embrace multiculturalism. It is the youth who formed the bulk of the immigrants discussed earlier in this chapter. Consequently (without wishing to generalize too much), electronic communications, commerce and business are more likely to appeal to younger generations whilst the traditional marketing media may have greater impact on older generations. What is important to note with demographic profiles, is the extent of change to the age structures within the population as this will lead to changes in the nation's social forces and changes to the needs of the population and size of different market segments. This dynamic situation results in the shrinkage of some segments (markets) and the enlargement of others. This will have implications for supply and demand and therefore the design of products and services, value propositions and marketing strategies alike. In summary, if we conclude that each age cohort has unique preferences and consumption patterns, it will be necessary to target the firm's production and marketing at specific age cohorts. Analysis of the numbers in each age cohort can enable managers to predict the future numbers of such groups, thereby guiding future planning and decision-making (refer back to Figure 4.8).

The Multicultural Organization

As society becomes more multicultural, so too does the workforce, both domestically and internationally. A competitive edge can be gained by optimizing the people resource of the organization. A critical challenge for senior management today is to turn cultural diversity into a differentiating advantage in an increasingly competitive global marketplace. Human resource executives must create a clear, compelling business case for diversity, linked to the company's strategic business objectives. Business reasons for managing diversity include: Cost savings – higher turnover costs (dissatisfied employees leaving the company), higher absenteeism rates and possible lawsuits on sexual, race and age discrimination. Winning the competition for talent, companies must attract, retain and promote excellent employees from different demographic groups. Companies cited as the best places to work for women and minorities have reported an increased inflow of applications (better recruitment opportunities). Companies who appreciate their workforce should reflect their consumer base, benefit financially from improved marketplace understanding. Research shows that heterogeneous (diverse) teams produce more innovative solutions to problems. A diverse workforce, with established customer relationships is an example of a difficult to imitate resource that can confer a sustainable competitive advantage for the firm. There are, however, a number of counterarguments that may be presented, suggesting that diversity may actually be counterproductive for the firm. Diverse groups require more effort to integrate, coordinate and control. Minority members of groups may feel alienated and pushed out. Diversity integration requires a long-term commitment and the payback is often not as tangible or predictable as, for instance, investing in new product development.

Operating in other countries: MNCs and business practice adaptation

In the previous paragraph we discussed the management of diversity within the domestic (heterogeneous) workforce. However, when an organization pursues an international strategy it will have employees located in a variety of countries worldwide, thus creating new challenges. In such cases, the MNC may be viewed more like a collection of self-contained cultures, i.e. a situation where the workforce has many separate cultures but each is relatively independent (homogenous). Organizations may consider the challenges of the domestic social environment or those challenges in the social environments of other countries in which they may operate, i.e. a new challenge of considering multiple social environments is presented. When operating internationally, an organization must decide whether or not to adopt a global or multidomestic strategy. In the case of the former, all countries are treated essentially the same. In such cases, the organization will adopt standard approaches to its worldwide operations. In the case of the latter, the organization will treat each country as being fundamentally different and will recognize a need to operate differently (locally) in each country. However, reality is not so simple. Organizations must make such decisions (a global standard or local approach) in each of its main functional areas (marketing, IT, finance and accounting, etc.) and product or service offerings.

An organization is a social system consisting of subsystems of resources, interrelated by various management policies, practices and techniques which interact with variables in the environmental suprasystem to achieve a set of goals or objectives. From an international organizational perspective it is important to recognize that legal, economic and sociocultural factors exist within each country. Consequently, the environment of the international organization is more diverse and complex. Not all factors will influence the organization's industry and the analyst must identify the more important factors, understand the implications and then act accordingly – typically adapting the strategy, structure, practices, systems, culture, products and services of the organization. Differences in culture (fit) may necessitate changes to business practices, management styles, products and services. We need to determine whether management practices are culture-bound or culture-free – 'can management policy developed within the culture of the multinational's home country be transferred elsewhere?'

Whilst some organizations may act in the belief that there may be a universal best set of practices for every organization, others argue there may actually be no one best set of practices. When considering the management of human resources (HR) in different countries, in some cases the headquartered HR function may develop HR practices for subsidiary use. In other cases subsidiaries will be autonomous, developing their own practices but in line with the overarching philosophy/policy framework. Decisions regarding whether to standardize globally or act locally will affect the choice of appropriate HR practices, whether to inherit them from the parent company, adapt or create them locally. Transferring practices (diffusion) enables the beneficial transfer of knowledge and expertise (competencies and capabilities) across parts of the multinational company. Practices originate and become established in a given legal, institutional, political and cultural context. To some extent, they are dependent on this context and cannot operate as effectively in a different environment. The extent of this dependence varies from one area of HRM to another; in other words the diffusion ability of some practices is higher than that of others. Managers at the headquarters of the multinational may seek to operate a practice in a number of countries that might be prevented from doing so by the legal, institutional and cultural constraints of the country to which the practice is directed. The country of origin, the way the multinational is structured, the way in which it established its foreign subsidiaries and the nature of production, integration or either may constrain or facilitate the transfer of practices across borders. The major objective of International Human Resource Management (IHRM) regarding internal operations is being responsive to and effective in the local environment. To facilitate local adaptation and fit, the subsidiary or local unit may staff the HR function with host-country nationals. In fact, this is one of the positions that MNEs seem to insist upon filling with a host-country national. Questions concerning which HR practices to use are heavily influenced by culture. Cultural factors, discussed earlier, can include aspects of the local culture, economy, legal system, religious beliefs and education. The cultural imperative is important in IHRM because of its impact upon acceptable, legitimate and feasible practices and behaviours; acceptable in terms of 'can we pay workers different rates, and thereby differentiate them, according to performance?'; legitimate in terms of 'are there any legal statutes prohibiting us from not paying workers overtime for work on Saturday and Sunday?'; feasible in terms of 'while the society is hierarchical, authoritarian and paternalistic, can we empower the workforce to make workplace decisions in order to facilitate our quality strategy?' Culture determines the way in which an organization treats its human resources. This is reflected in their practices.

As an example, staffing (recruitment and selection) is a major practice that MNEs have used to help coordinate and control their far-flung global operations. Traditionally MNEs have sent Parent Country Nationals (PCN – the employee's nationality is the same as the organization's) or expatriates abroad to ensure that the policies and procedures of the home office were being carried out to the letter within foreign operations. As costs became prohibitive and career issues made these assignments less attractive, MNEs turned to TCNs (Third Country Nationals – the employee's nationality is neither that of the organization nor that of the location of the subsidiary) and HCNs (Host Country Nationals – the employee's nationality is the same as the location of the subsidiary) to satisfy international staffing needs. Approaches to recruitment vary worldwide. Variance may be determined by culture, law, government policy and other factors. Such factors may require a specific approach. In some cases a country may require an organization to recruit locally, requiring permission to hire PCNs or TCNs. In choosing the right candidate, a balance between internal corporate consistency and sensitivity to local labour practices is a key goal. Different cultures emphasize different attributes in the selection process, dependent upon whether they use achievement or ascriptive criteria. When determining a hiring decision, people in an achievement-oriented country consider skills, knowledge, and talents. In an ascriptive culture, age, gender, and family background are important. An organization selects someone whose personal characteristics fit the job. Good recruitment practices ensure the best candidates are identified for the job, resulting in decreased staff turnover and costs.

Leading In Other Cultures

Other than HR specialists, leaders and managers must be culturally aware when working with employees of different cultural backgrounds. Organizational leadership is the ability of an individual to influence, motivate, and enable others to contribute towards the effectiveness and success of the organizations of which they are members. Leaders in the international organization must be capable of identifying global opportunities and have a good appreciation of company strengths and weaknesses and the resources and capabilities to seize such opportunities. As with the domestic leader, the international leader must inspire and influence people anywhere in the world. Leadership is required within every organization around the world, however culture must be considered when contemplating the different theories of leadership. Being a participative leader is more important in some countries as opposed to others. Once again, Hofstede's cultural dimensions provide a useful framework or model to study leader-subordinate relationships. Subordinates from high power distance countries are more likely to favour autocratic leadership whilst employees of lower power distance countries are more likely to prefer a consultative or participatory leadership style. An inappropriate style can be counterproductive in certain cultures. Leaders who are required to interact with a diverse set of followers, or who work in a foreign environment, need to recognize that notions of what constitutes ideal leadership may vary culturally. Followers who categorize a manager as a typical leader are likely to allow him/her to exert leadership influence on them. If leadership concepts differ as a function of cultural differences, they can constrain the influence of foreign managers: in other words, the more leadership concepts differ between managers and subordinates or colleagues, the less influence will be exerted.

Pension Schemes – Workplace pensions are changing

Earlier, we recognized changes in the dependency ratio, see Table 4.2 below. An increase in the number of dependents (particularly from the ageing/nonworking part of the population) coupled with a decrease in the size of the workforce is likely to result in a number of changes. In the previous chapter we discussed government spending and taxation. The cost of pensions and health care for the elderly is likely to increase. These costs will need to be met either through increased taxation of firms and employees or through borrowing. The changing nature of the composition/structure of the population alters the demand for various types of goods and services creating new business opportunities and requiring new types of market segmentation. Population ageing is likely to reduce growth (see previous chapter). Whilst the aforementioned paragraphs have considered implications in terms of supply and demand, the ageing popula- tion is also having other, more secondary impact upon the workforce. People are living longer lives and this means they need to plan and save for their later years. Millions of people are not saving enough to have the income they are likely to want in retirement. Life expectancy in the UK is increasing and, at the same time, people are contributing less towards their pensions. In the UK, the Department for Work and Pensions (DWP) recognize a need to address these challenges. The workplace pension reforms they are introducing from 2012 will help to address the issues that prevent people from saving into a pension. A workplace pension is a way of saving for retirement, arranged via the employer and is termed: 'company pension', 'occupational pension' or 'work's pension'. Pension challenges can be met by employees and employers (saving more) and the government. In the UK the government has introduced new laws designed to help millions of people save more for their retirement. Starting from 2012 there will be a requirement for every employer to enrol workers automati- cally into a workplace pension scheme. The pension scheme must be a qualifying scheme, meaning it must meet certain government standards. This is the first time that employers have been required by law to contribute to their workers' pensions. A key consequence of this will be the need for employers to contribute to all employees' pensions.

In 2010 the UK Government announced three significant pension policy reviews: the increase in state pension age to 66; automatic enrolment into workplace pensions; and of public sector pensions. The proposals set out in the Pensions Bill 2011 help ensure a pensions system that is fair and financially sustainable. The proposed regulatory changes build on the reforms introduced by the Pensions Acts 2007 and 2008, designed to respond to shifts in demographic, social and economic contexts since the Acts and to refine existing legislation. Under legislation introduced by the Pensions Act 1995, women's state pension age is to be equalized with men's, rising from 60 in 2010 to 65 by 2020. Following this, both women's and men's state pension age is to rise to 66 by 2026 under the Pensions Act 2007. It is then to rise to 67 by 2036, and to 68 by 2046. Since then, official projections of average life expectancy have been revised upwards. Life expectancy projections (made in 2009) indicate that men and women reaching 66 in 2026 are expected to live, on average, at least one-and-a-half years longer than was thought at the time the Pensions Act 2007 was legis- lated. Further, the UK economy is recovering from the longest and deepest recession since official records began in 1955. In response to these challenges, in June 2010 the Government issued a Call for Evidence on the timing of the increase in state pension age to 66. This was followed in November 2010 by the publication of a White Paper outlining the Government's response, and decision to bring forward the increase to 66. The Pensions Bill 2011 proposes an amendment to the timetable for the increase to 66, so that state pension age increases from 65 to 66 between 2018 and 2020. The increase in state pension age to 66 must be applied to both men and women, to comply with the EU Directive that requires equal treatment of men and women in social security matters. To enable the increase to 66 to be implemented from 2018, the Bill also proposes an amendment to the timetable for equalizing women's state pension age with men's so that women's state pension age rises more quickly from 2016 to reach 65 by 2018. This change to the timetable for increasing state pension age will affect approximately five million men and women in Great Britain, of whom approximately four-and-a-half

BUSINESS IN DEBATE

Demography Report 2010

The UK's fertility rate is above the EU average and it is assumed this will persist. Life expectancy is close to the EU average. These trends, combined with a significant level of immigration, will lead to a growing population and a much more favourable evolution of the old-age dependency ratio than for the EU as a whole. The UK population is projected to grow by 20 per cent by 2050. Many children younger than 17 (17 per cent), especially those with single parents, live in jobless households. The debt to GDP ratio is now above 80 per cent, constraining policies. EU (2011)

The gap between male and female employment rates is smaller than for the EU as a whole, but, at 11 percen-tage points, there is scope for further progress. The gender pay gap is particularly large and many women only work part-time. An improvement in the situation may require better availability of childcare. Improved female employment might also reduce the risk of poverty for households with children. Employment rates of older workers are high, even for people in their 60s. Government initiatives are focused on increasing labour market participation by reforming the incapacity benefit policy and expanding the initiatives to guide people back to work - around half the potential customers are over 50. There is also a focus on skills enhancement – particularly in pre- and in-work support. Public debt is comparatively low; the expected ageing-related increase in public social protection expenditure is slightly above the increase for the EU as a whole. EU (2011)

Source: http://ec.europa.eu © European Union, 1995-2012. Reproduced with permission.

TABLE 4.2

UK demographic trends	2000	2009	2030	2050
Population (thousands)	58,785	62,008	69,224	74,506
Total fertility rate	1.64	1.96	1.84	1.84
Old age dependency ratio (65 or over / 15–64 yrs. old) (%)	24.3	24.5	33.2	38
Average exit age from the labour market, women (years)		62		
Average exit age from the labour market, men (years)		64.1		
University graduates aged 20–29 (per 1000 of the pop. of that age)	66.4	82.4		
Non-nationals in the population (%)		6.8		
General government consolidated gross debt (% of GDP)	41	68.2		
Public expenditure on pensions (% of GDP)	14.8	11.5		

Source: http://ec.europa.eu © European Union, 1995–2012. Reproduced with permission.

million will increase their state pension age, against the legislated timetable, of a year or less. The measure will deliver significant net savings to Government. The Pensions Act 2008 introduced a series of private pension reforms to enable and encourage individuals to save more for retirement, building on the foundation of the State Pension. The 2008 Act was followed by the Workplace Pension Reform Regulations of 2010. These reforms focused on the use of auto-enrolment into workplace pension schemes, from which an individual would need to actively opt-out, to build private saving. This was combined with a minimum employer contribution, and the creation of a pension scheme – now known as the National Employment Savings Trust (NEST) – that could be used by any employer.

SUMMARY

- Social forces are dynamic, shaped by political, economic, legal and technological forces in particular and by globalization, manifesting in migration trends. Similarly, an organization's internationalization strategy will bring it into 'new' and country specific social forces as it seeks to fragment its value chain, establishing operations and selling in foreign places.
- Social forces, particularly in terms of demographics (population changes in structure) and culture are of particular importance to the marketing and HR functions due to their impact upon demand and diversity.
- For HRM, diversity brings costs and benefits: costs in terms of coordination and control, integration needs, and benefits in terms of creativity and enhanced market understanding.
- In the case of marketing, an understanding of demographics and culture has much to offer, enabling segmentation and enhanced understanding of demand and customer needs.
- However, there are broader issues arising from population changes. The ageing population and shrinking workforce in many EU countries places a burden on governments, employers and employees who must fund care for the older dependents in society.
- Finally, managing the international organization requires the company to determine how to operate in the context of different and multiple environments. This raises the question of international strategy. A company may pursue standardization of its products, services and practices (a global approach) or may seek to create or adapt such products, services and practices for the local environment (a multidomestic approach).

REVISION QUESTIONS

1. Analyze the interplay of environmental forces from the perspective of social factors in the UK. In your answer you should discuss the following: (a) the impact of demographic trends, now and over the next 20 years, on Government spending, taxation and employee/employer pension contributions; (b) whether immigration into the UK is beneficial for the UK (population, Government or employers) and (c) how an understanding of demographic trends and migration can be used to inform fiscal policy decisions.
2. Analyze EU demographic trends and the implications for UK business. In your answer you should explain and evaluate why population ageing and shifts in population structure may present particular challenges and problems for government and business.
3. Explain how migration brings about changes to social forces in the UK.
4. Discuss the importance of diversity and multiculturalism in UK markets and the workplace.
5. Write a brief essay constructing the business case in favour of diversity (to include multiculturalism) within a UK organization. Consider three types of organization in the essay: (a) a domestic mobile phone company, (b) an international bank and (c) a steel manufacturer.
6. As a UK citizen and manager in a UK MNC you have been asked to prepare for an assignment in Thailand: Hofstede scores – IND (20), PD (64), UA (64) and MAS (34). With reference to Hofstede's cultural dimensions, compare the two countries and make predictions about how management may be similar or different in the Thai subsidiary.
7. Discuss the need for a UK organization to alter its policies, strategies, products, services or practices when conducting business in (a) another EU country or (b) a country in Asia e.g. Malaysia or the Philippines.
8. Explain how household structure is constantly changing and discuss the implications for business in terms of opportunity, threat and working practices.
9. Identify and explain one framework used to compare national cultures.
10. Explain what is meant by 'Uncertainty Avoidance' (with reference to Hofstede) and discuss how a spcoety's tolerance of ambiguity might be reflected in its practices both at work and generally.

DISCUSSION QUESTIONS

1. What does 'Britishness' mean to you?
2. Do you think that, within the UK, different cultural communities live their own ways of life in a self-contained manner OR that such communities are generally open, self-critical, and interactive in their relations with each other?
3. Do you think David Cameron, is correct and the UK needs a stronger national identity? Explain your answer.
4. How significant is the EU's demographic time bomb? In your discussions you should make reference to other regions of the world.
5. Discuss the future impact of demographic ageing within the European Union (EU) – what would you advise (a) Governments and (b) businesses do to prepare?

REFERENCES AND FURTHER READING

Cole, G. A. and Kelly, P. (2011) 'Management Theory and Practice', Ed. 7., Cengage EMEA

European Commission (2011) 'Demography report 2010 – Older, more numerous and diverse Europeans', Luxembourg: Publications Office of the European Union

Hofstede, G. (1984) *Cultures Consequences – abridged,* Sage

Javidan, M. and House, R. (2001) 'Cultural Acumen for the Global Manager: Lessons from Project GLOBE', *Organizational Dynamics,* Spring2001, Vol. 29 Issue 4, 289–305

Kelly, P. P. (2009) *International Business and Management,* Cengage Learning EMEA

Orlando, R. (2000) 'Racial Diversity, Business Strategy, And Firm Performance: A Resource-Based View', *Academy of Management Journal,* Vol. 43, No. 2, 164–177

GLOSSARY

Ageing Population An increase in the average age of the population

Age Structure Structure of the population in terms of the proportions in each age band

Birth Rate The number of births per 1000 of the population

Culture Shared ways of thinking and behaving (Uniformity)

Death Rate The ratio of deaths to the population of a particular area during a particular period of time, usually calculated as the number of deaths per one thousand people per year

Demographics The distribution of individuals in a society in terms of age, sex, marital status, income, ethnicity, and other personal attributes that may determine their buying patterns

Demographic Diversity A measure of the variation within a group determined by properties of the group members such as age, gender, culture, ethnicity and language

Diversity All the ways in which we differ

Equality Of Outcome Equality between people measured in terms of outcomes such as income and wealth

Fertility Rate Indicator used in population studies to assess the average number of children women have in a given population

Inequality Being unequal. Not being allowed the same rights or opportunities as everyone else in the community. Differences between people or groups in terms of power, status, and/or access to resources

Individualism versus Collectivism Theory focusing on the relationship between the individual and his or her fellows. In individualistic societies, the ties between individuals are loose and individual achievement is highly valued. In societies where collectivism is emphasized, ties between individuals are tight, people are born into collectives, such as extended families, and everyone is supposed to look after the interests of his or her collective

Masculinity versus Femininity Theory of the relationship between gender and work roles. In masculine cultures, sex roles are sharply differentiated and traditional 'masculine values' such as achievement and the effective exercise of power determine cultural ideals. In feminine cultures, sex roles are less sharply distinguished, and little differentiation is made between men and women in the same job

Multiculturalism A phenomenon, trend or the characteristics of a society which has or is moving toward many different ethnic or national cultures mingling and coexisting freely. Taken literally, it refers to the existence of several different cultures (rather than one national culture) significantly represented within a country. Also considered to be an ideology that favours and deliberately fosters the presence of many cultures in society, each with equal rights – a doctrine asserting the value of different cultures coexisting within single society

Multicultural Organization An organization that contains many different cultural groups and values diversity

Overcrowding Rate The overcrowding rate is defined as the percentage of the population living in an **overcrowded household** (a household is overcrowded if the household does not have at its disposal a minimum number of rooms equal to: one room for the household; one room per couple in the household; one room for each single person aged 18 or more; one room per pair of single people of the same gender between 12 and 17 years of age; one room for each single person between 12 and 17 years of age and not included in the previous category; one room per pair of children under 12 years of age)

Power Distance (PD) The extent to which the less powerful members of institutions and organizations within a country expect and accept that power is distributed unequally

Socio-cultural Environment The common behavioural influences of stakeholders on organizations

Stakeholders Individuals or groups who depend on the organization to fulfil their own goals and on whom, in turn, the organization depends

Uncertainty Avoidance (UA) The extent to which the members of a culture feel threatened by uncertain or unknown situations

CHAPTER CASE STUDY

Japan's demographic time bomb:

How do a shrinking proportion of workers cope with the expanding costs of social welfare for the elderly?

Demographic time bomb: a predicted shortage of school-leavers and consequently of available workers, caused by an earlier drop in the birth rate, resulting in an older workforce

'Few countries face the demographic time bomb that Japan does' (Zwi 2012). In an editorial for the *Japan Times*, it was written that a population trend estimate announced on Jan. 30 by the health and welfare ministry's National Institute of Population and Social Security Research shows that in 2060, Japan's population will fall to about 30 per cent below the current level, whilst people aged 65 or older will account for 40 per cent of the population (from 23 per cent in 2010). 'It is imperative that the government take effective measures.' People will also live longer than now. The average life expectancy will rise from 86 years in 2011 to 91 years in 2060 for women and from 80 years to 84 years for men during the same period. Nursing care and medical services will become increasingly important. The total fertility rate is forecast to be 1.35 in 2060. This is well below the 2.07 needed to maintain a stable population. The working population – those between the ages of 15 and 64 – is expected to be 44 million in 2060, or 51 per cent of the total population, compared with 64 per cent in 2010. The burden of social welfare costs falls on the shoulders of this group.

Many have commented on Japan's population crisis. The BBC's Philippa Fogarty looked at what the demographic changes mean for Asia's economic giant (2007). She declared that Japan is about to experience demographic change on an unprecedented scale. The birth rate has been falling steeply for half a century and the population shrinking. Japan has the world's highest proportion of elderly people. Across Japan, people know this demographic shift constitutes an enormous challenge. It is an issue that 'will not only have an impact on economic, industrial and social security issues, but … is intertwined with the very existence and viability of Japan as a country,' the Policy Council for Declining Fertility wrote in a report last year.

These problems are not unique to Japan. South Korea and Taiwan both have lower birth rates. Italy, Greece and Germany have all suffered, whilst several Eastern European countries are facing population decline.

Sources: Zwi, P (2012), 'Japan's demographic timebomb', Posted on February 15, 2012 Clime – www.clime.com.au/blog/japans-demographic-timebomb/; Editorial, 'Japan's population time bomb' Wednesday, Feb. 8, 2012, the Japan Times online – www.japantimes.co.jp/text/ed20120208a1.html; Fogarty, P. (2007), 'Japan eyes demographic time bomb', BBC online http://news.bbc.co.uk/1/hi/7084749.stm; http://epp.eurostat.ec.europa.eu/portal/page/portal/statistics/themes

Questions

- What can the Government do to increase the labour force?
- Should the Government change its immigration policy?
- What are the economic consequences of an ageing society?
- How will the demographic time bomb impact upon pension provision?
- Demographic changes are not sudden; the trends have been obvious for many years. Successive administrations have taken steps to boost the birth rate and introduce financial reforms to meet rising costs, but the problems remain. What can the Government do to increase fertility rates?
- In 2009 Japan's ambassador to Thailand Kyoji Komachai wrote in the *Bangkok Post* on how 'Thailand needs to prepare now for an ageing society' – The present demographic situation of Thailand resembles that of Japan in the mid-80s. What advice would you give to the Thai Government?
- Identify business opportunities as more Japanese citizens retire, with considerable savings and personal financial assets.

5
THE TECHNOLOGICAL ENVIRONMENT

FIGURE 5.1

The technological environment mind map

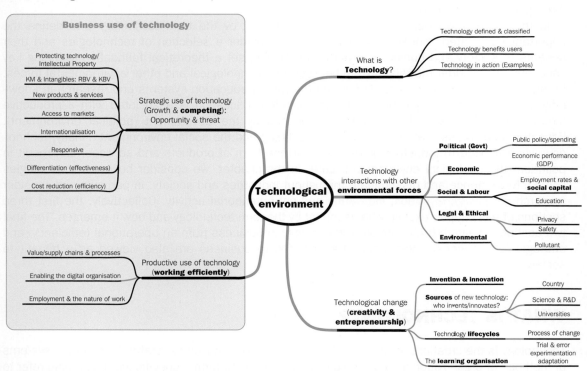

Note: On the mind map – Knowledge Management (KM), Resource Based View (RBV) and Knowledge Based View (KBV)

KEY CONCEPTS

Creativity | Entrepreneurship | Information technology | Innovation | Invention | Productivity | Research and experimental development (R&D) | Technology | Technology management (TM)

INTRODUCTION

Technology is a broad concept that literally means the application of science, especially to industrial or commercial objectives; for most people technology represents electronic or digital products and systems (such as communication devices, machines, computers, robots, etc. see Figure 5.1). It is a factor that features in all aspects of the business environment – external and internal. Technological change may result in new ways of behaving both at work and at home and can raise productivity, improve and change the way we communicate and impact upon mechanisms of trade, affecting how we buy and sell goods and services. Aside from impacting upon business practice itself, new technology may also feature within products and services. The application of new technologies in any of these areas can result in new opportunities and threats for business. Technological developments often bring about direct substitutes for end-products; catalyse societal changes that affect life styles and shopping patterns; spawn environments that lift constraints; alter cost structures, and create substitutes for industrial processes. Technology may be transferred from outside the organization or from within. For example, international organizations, the multinational in particular, may transfer to their subsidiaries the benefits of technologies developed in-house (intra organizational transfer). Technology may also be transferred externally through franchises, licences, and joint ventures or from university and other forms of research. Different technologies impact upon work in different ways, changing the nature of work and therefore may impact upon the organization and structuring of work. The relationship between technology and work is captured in a theory known as technological determinism. Technological determinism is a contingency theory arguing that technology determines aspects of organizational structure, i.e. it should be possible to predict aspects of organizational structure from knowledge of the organization's technology.

In this chapter we begin by asking what is meant by the term *technology* and define the important associated concepts. Additionally, we consider a selection of technologies and their benefits to society and business in particular. Having set a theoretical foundation, defining key concepts, we consider the relationship between the technological and other environmental forces. In this section we focus on knowledge and the role of education systems and research in knowledge and technology acquisition and dissemination. Education is associated with a productive 'knowledge' economy and is therefore influenced by the Government (political environment). Education is also associated with personal wellbeing and the social environment. Finally, technology, when applied to industrial processes or in the form of products and services, can result in pollution (the ecological environment). Later in the chapter, we consider how new technologies come into existence and disseminate throughout industries and society. In particular we consider research, creativity, invention, innovation and entrepreneurial activity. Collectively, the first three sections of this chapter explain what is meant by the term technology and how it emerges. The final two sections evaluate the adoption of technology in business from an operational (efficiency) and strategic (effectiveness) standpoint. The benefits to business are also viewed as a benefit to society.

WHAT IS TECHNOLOGY?

Technology is the creation, usage, and knowledge of tools, machines, crafts, techniques, systems or methods of organization in order to solve a problem or perform a specific job. It can also refer to the collection of such tools, machinery, and procedures. From a business standpoint, organizations

BUSINESS IN ACTION

Lab126 (part of the Amazon group) and the Kindle

Amazon.com is a multinational electronic commerce Fortune 500 company and the world's largest online retailer, offering the 'Earth's biggest selection'. Founded in 1994, and online since 1995, it started as an online bookstore, but soon diversified. Amazon.com and other sellers offer millions of unique new, refurbished and used items in categories such as Books; Movies, Music & Games; Digital Downloads; Electronics & Computers; Home & Garden; Toys, Kids & Baby; Grocery; Apparel, Shoes & Jewellery; Health & Beauty; Sports & Outdoors; and Tools, Auto & Industrial. The company seeks to be 'Earth's most customer-centric company', where customers can find and discover anything they might want to buy online, and endeavours to offer its customers the lowest possible prices. Released in November, 2007, the Amazon Kindle is an e-book reader, developed by Amazon.com subsidiary Lab126 (a small California-based subsidiary responsible for developing easy-to-use, highly integrated consumer products to serve Amazon customers) which utilizes wireless connectivity to enable users to shop for, download, browse and read e-books, newspapers, magazines, blogs and other digital media. The Kindle hardware devices use an E Ink electronic paper display that shows up to 16 shades of grey, minimizes power use and simulates reading on paper. Lab126 develop and design wireless electronic reading devices that embrace the traditional book's simplicity, utility, and experience. Their devices offer capabilities that are only possible through digital technology and wireless connectivity. Starting with Kindle, the technology developed by Lab126 enables users to think of a book, newspaper or blog and begin reading it in less than a minute. The company designs and engineers tightly integrated products that bring together cutting edge hardware and powerful software to make an unmatched user experience.

Amazon published a press release Nov 28, 2011 about the Kindle family – the $79 Kindle, $99 Kindle Touch, $149 Kindle Touch 3G and the $199 Kindle Fire – which are available at www.amazon.com/kindle and at over 16 000 retail locations throughout the US. Kindle Fire is the bestselling item on Amazon.com and offers more than 18 million movies, TV shows, songs, books, magazines, apps. and games as well as free storage of Amazon digital content in the Amazon Cloud, Whispersync for books and movies, a light design which is easy to hold with one hand, a vibrant, colour touch screen, a powerful dual-core processor and Amazon Silk – Amazon's new revolutionary web browser that accelerates the power of the mobile device by using the computing speed and power of the Amazon Web Services cloud – all for only $199. Kindle is now small and light enough to fit easily in a pocket and be carried everywhere, yet it still features the same 6-inch, advanced electronic ink display that reads like real paper, even in bright sunlight. Kindle Touch and Kindle Touch 3G feature an easy-to-use touch screen that makes it easier than ever to turn pages, search, shop and take notes. Certain models offer audio capabilities, such as text-to-speech, extra-long battery life and hold thousands of books. Kindle's free 3G connection means never hunting or paying for a Wi-Fi hotspot – simply download and read books anytime, anywhere in over 100 countries around the world. With an Amazon Prime membership, all of the new Kindles offer access to the new Kindle Owners' Lending Library. Kindle owners can now borrow thousands of books for free, as frequently as a book a month, with no due dates. In 2010, Amazon remained the undisputed leader in the e-reader category, accounting for almost 60 per cent of e-readers shipped. According to an IDC study from March 2011, sales for all e-book readers worldwide reached 12.8 million in 2010; almost half of them were Kindle models.

Source: Best Black Friday Ever for Kindle Family: Kindle Sales Increase 4X Over Last Year, 28th November 2011. Accessed at: http://phx.corporate-ir.net/phoenix.zhtml?c=176060&p=irol-newsArticle&ID=1633690&highlight=

may manufacture technological products for sale, or may use technology to undertake work. In the case of the latter, it is the machinery, equipment, processes, work layout, methods, systems and procedures in carrying out the work of the organization and converting inputs to outputs. There are many types of technology, such as information and communications technology (ICT). Information technology is the hardware and software used to store, retrieve, and manipulate information and Information technology (IT) infrastructure refers to the computer hardware, software, data and

FIGURE 5.2
Technology benefits users

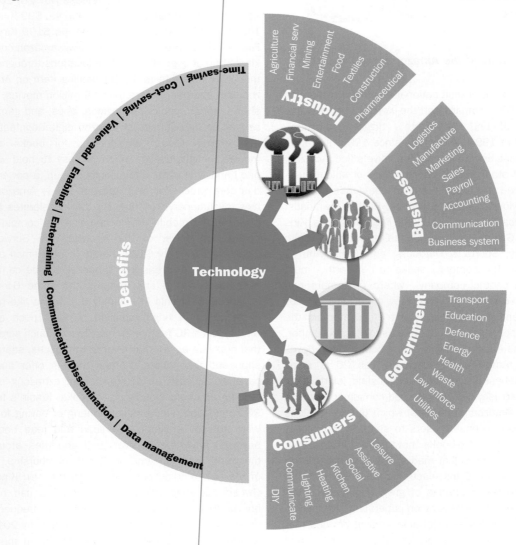

storage technology, and networks providing a platform of shared information technology resources for the organization. The technological environment refers to those forces that affect the technology used by the organization and which can create new products, new markets, and new opportunities. Specific examples of technologies are provided subsequently.

It is important to recognize that some technologies may be proprietary technology, i.e. secret or patented technology that give incumbent firms important advantages over potential entrants. It is also important to recognize technology convergence – the combining of several technologies into a single device, such as mobile phone, digital camera and web browser (or Kindle!). An outline of the key benefits, technology users and typical applications is shown in Figure 5.2. Technologies, such as those outlined above, may be used by industry, governments, consumers and specific businesses to save time and money, add value to outputs, enable communication and collaboration, transport resources and entertain people. Technology use is often of a general nature or may be industry or business specific. The business benefits of technology are evaluated in detail in the second half of this chapter (sections 4 and 5). Prior to evaluating the benefits in detail, we will now consider the interrelationships between environmental forces from the technological perspective and then consider how new technologies are created and associated knowledge shared.

Ten specific technologies include: (1) Internet Technologies – The Internet and its technologies are used to build interconnected enterprises and global networks, like intranets and extranets that form information superhighways to support enterprise collaboration, electronic commerce, and internal business applications; (2) Process technologies – the tools (equipment, machines and other devices) used in operations that transform materials, information or customers; (3) Product technology – the embedded technology within a product or service, as distinct from process technology; (4) Self-service technologies (SST) – Technological tools enabling customers to produce services for themselves without assistance from firm employees; (5) Communications technology – Technology relevant to communications, ie. the Internet, satellite communications, mobile telephony, digital television (see also Storage technology – Physical media and software governing the storage and organization of data for use in an information system and Wireless Technologies – Using radio or infrared transmissions to link devices in a local area network); (6) Automating technology – Replacement of the actions of the human body by the machine; (7) Biotechnology – The use of biological systems or living organisms to make or modify products or processes; (8) Coordination and control technology – aids to managing dependencies amongst agents within a business process, also provides automated support for the most routinized component processes; (9) Flexible manufacturing technologies – Manufacturing technologies designed to improve job scheduling, reduce setup time, and improve quality control; and (10) Social technology – the methods which order the behaviour and relationships of people in systematic, purposive ways through structures of co-ordination, control, motivation and reward.

TECHNOLOGY: INTERACTIONS WITH OTHER ENVIRONMENTAL FORCES

Social, political, economic, environmental and technological forces are tightly intertwined. As are legal forces when considering patents, intellectual property and laws associated with goods and services. Having considered what constitutes technology and the meaning of the technological environment, we will consider how technological forces interact with the other forces in the external environment before considering how new technologies emerge and then how they may be exploited by entrepreneurial organizations. Technology comes from science, research and the problem solving activities of organizations. Technology creation and diffusion are strongly linked with knowledge and knowledge with education and research. Since its early days, the OECD has emphasized the role of education and human capital (human competencies) in driving economic and social development, (OECD 2011). Governments must determine, through policy, the extent of funding for the country's education systems and associated scientific research (typically at universities); they may also influence the numbers and types of people who progress to higher education. Educational attainment is a commonly used proxy for the stock of *human capital* – that is, the skills available in the population and the labour force. Following a decline in demand for manual labour and for basic cognitive skills that can be replicated by computers, recent trends show sharp increases in the demand for complex communication and advanced analytical skills. These trends generally favour a more educated labour force, and the demand for education is thus increasing at a rapid pace in many countries. Tertiary attainment levels have increased considerably over the past 30 years. On average, across OECD countries, 37 per cent of 25–34 year-olds have completed tertiary (university level) education, compared with 22 per cent of 55–64 year-olds. Japan and Korea, together with Canada and the Russian Federation, have the highest proportion of young adults with a tertiary education. Over 50 per cent of young adults in these countries have attained a tertiary education. Tertiary graduation rates indicate a country's capacity to produce workers with advanced, specialized knowledge and skills. Graduation rates are influenced by both the degree of access to these programmes and the demand for higher skills in the labour market. Figure 5.3 presents data on enrolment in tertiary education for the 18–34 year-olds (per cent of the total population), 1999–2009 in specific countries.

FIGURE 5.3

Enrolment in tertiary education for the 18–34 year-olds (per cent of the total population), 1999–2009.

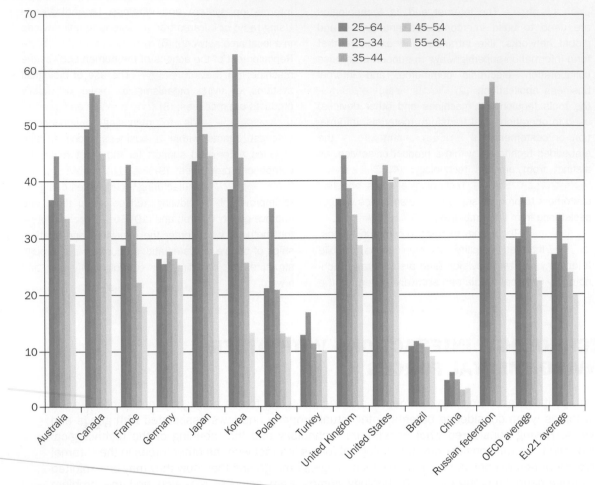

Source: EUROSTAT. © European Union, 1995–2012. Reproduced with permission.

A knowledge economy (economic activity involving industries or services in which technological and other advanced forms of knowledge are an important resource) is dependent upon a constant stream of well-educated graduates who can disseminate state-of-the-art knowledge and understand how to build upon it. According to the OECD (2011) Education at a glance report, across the EU, governments have to work with shrinking public budgets whilst designing policies to make educa- tion more effective and responsive to growing demand. Governments must formulate effective policies to enhance individual social and economic prospects. More education does not only benefit individuals but the general public too. In the UK, the public benefit generated by tertiary graduates through higher income tax and social contributions, far outweigh the public costs. As a result, the UK taxpayer gains USD 95 000 per man and USD 79 000 per woman with a tertiary qualification, the 7th highest net return for man among the 25 OECD countries with available data. The gross earnings premium is substantial for individuals with both an upper secondary and tertiary education. After direct and indirect costs are taken into account, the earnings and employment benefits that accrue over the working life of a man with an upper secondary education amount to a net present value (NPV) of USD 151 000 – the highest value after that observed in the United States. The private NPV that accrues to a man with a tertiary education is USD 208 000, close to the OECD average of USD 175 000. The UK has slightly higher labour costs than other OECD countries, on average, and these increase substantially with educational attainment, making workers with more qualifications comparatively expensive. Labour costs for a 25–64 year-old

BUSINESS IN DEBATE

UK's graduation rates fall to below average – OECD

UK plummets from third to fifteenth place in OECD University listing, behind Slovakia and Czech Republic

In 2000, the UK had the third-highest graduation rate among OECD countries, with 37 per cent of young people obtaining a degree compared with an average of 28 per cent (Williams 2010). By 2008 the UK had fallen to fifteenth place (35 per cent compared with an average of 38 per cent) with a higher proportion of young people now obtaining a degree in Slovakia, Poland and the Czech Republic, and behind countries including Iceland, Portugal and Ireland. The UK also lagged behind competitors in public investment in higher education. A strict cap on student numbers in 2010 left tens of thousands without a place at university. The HE sector in 2010, faced cuts of more than £1bn with the UK level of public investment in higher education at 0.7 per cent of GDP, below the OECD average of 1 per cent and behind countries such as the US, Canada, Sweden, Germany, Poland and Slovenia. The OECD said governments had to aim for world-class quality in their education systems to ensure long-term economic growth. Not only is there a benefit associated with growth. Placing public resources into university education also pays off, through the extra tax revenue it generates. The OECD calculated that on average, a man with a degree would earn almost £77 500 more in income taxes and social contributions over his working life than one with only a school-level education. Furthermore, the OECD argued that, 'Labour market demand for highly qualified workers has grown significantly and countries with high graduation rates, at the tertiary level, are also those most likely to develop or maintain a highly skilled labour force.' Closer to home, the vice-chancellors' body, Universities UK (UUK), questioned how long the country's higher education system could maintain its world-class position in the field given its comparative 'under-investment' and the National Union of Students (NUS) said the UK was being outpaced by countries who had recognized the importance of funding colleges, universities and students to produce a highly skilled workforce.

Source Zwi, P. (2012), 'Japan's demographic timebomb', Posted on February 15, 2012 Clime -www.clime.com.au/blog/japans-demographic-timebomb/ ; Editorial, 'Japan's population time bomb' Wednesday, Feb. 8, 2012, the Japan Times online - www.japantimes.co.jp/text/ed20120208a1.html; Fogarty, P. (2007), 'Japan eyes demographic time bomb', BBC online http://news.bbc.co.uk/1/hi/7084749.stm

worker without an upper secondary diploma amount to USD 40 000; for a worker with an upper secondary degree, they average USD 54 000; and for a worker with a tertiary degree, they average USD 81 000. A UK employer can expect to pay an additional USD 23 000 per year for a 45–54 year-old tertiary graduate with work experience compared with a 25–34 year-old recent graduate. Whilst factors other than potential earnings can spur migration flows, particularly for those with higher education, economic considerations are likely to become more influential as labour markets become more global. In 2008, UK spending on educational institutions as a share of GDP remained at 5.7 per cent (below the OECD average of 5.9 per cent).

Countries differ in their approach to funding tertiary education. Policy decisions on tuition fees charged by educational institutions affect both the cost of tertiary education to students and the resources available to tertiary institutions. Subsidies to students and their families also serve as a way for governments to encourage participation in education – particularly amongst low-income students – by covering part of the cost of education and related expenses. Among the EU21 countries for which data are available, only public institutions in Italy, the Netherlands, Portugal and the United Kingdom charge annual tuition fees of more than USD 1200 per full-time national student.

The OECD (2011) explores the incentives of investing in education. In all OECD countries, individuals with a tertiary-level degree have a greater chance of being employed than those without such a degree. Higher education improves job prospects in general and the likelihood of remaining employed in times of economic hardship. The net public return on an investment in tertiary education is USD 91 000 for men – almost three times the amount of public investment. The economic benefits of education flow not only to individuals but also to society, in the additional taxes individuals pay once they enter the labour market. There is growing interest in looking beyond the traditional economic measures of individual success, such as income, employment and GDP per capita, towards non-economic aspects of well-being and social progress, such as life satisfaction, civic engagement and health. According to the OECD, adults aged 25 to 64 with higher levels of educational attainment are, on average, more satisfied with life, engaged in society and likely to report that they are in good health, even after accounting for differences in gender, age and income.

In 2008, OECD countries spent 6.1 per cent of their collective GDP on educational institutions. Expenditure on educational institutions is an investment that can help foster economic growth, enhance productivity, contribute to personal and social development, and reduce social inequality. Relative to GDP, expenditure on educational institutions indicates the priority a country gives to education. The proportion of a country's total financial resources devoted to education is the result of choices made by governments, enterprises and individual students and their families. Given that expenditure on education largely derives from public budgets, it is closely scrutinized by governments, particularly at times when governments are being urged to cut spending. Tertiary education accounts for nearly one-third of the combined OECD expenditure on educational institutions, or 1.9 per cent of the combined GDP. On average, OECD countries devote 12.9 per cent of total public expenditure to education. Public expenditure on education, as a percentage of total public expenditure, indicates the extent to which governments prioritize education in relation to other areas of investment, such as healthcare, social security, defence and security. Faced with an economic downturn and shrinking budgets, governments need to invest in the fields of education that respond to labour-market needs. Different fields include: health and welfare, social sciences, business and law, humanities, arts and education, engineering, manufacturing and construction, science, and agriculture. OECD countries' economies and labour markets depend upon a sufficient supply of well-educated workers. Indicators related to labour-market outcomes by educational attainment show how well the supply of skills matches demand.

Aside from investing directly into education, the Government can invest in research – much of this research being undertaken by universities (tertiary education institutions). Gross domestic expenditure on research and development (GERD) is total intramural (within an institution) expenditure on research and development performed on the national territory during a given period. Scientific research and technological development more particularly, are crucial to a well-functioning society (European Commission 2000). More and more, activities undertaken in this domain are for the express purpose of meeting a social demand and satisfying social needs, especially in connection with the evolution of work and the emergence of new ways of life and activities. Authors of the UNESCO Science Report 2010 believe the global recession is likely to have had a severe impact on investment in knowledge across the globe. R&D budgets, especially, tend to be vulnerable to cutbacks in times of crisis. Patents and publications will in turn be affected by the drop in R&D expenditure but this will probably occur in the longer run and affect scientific output less directly, owing to pipeline effects that smother sharp fluctuations. As for trends in education of the labour force, this sector tends to be less affected by short-term distortions. As for the world's largest R&D-intensive firms, circumstantial evidence for 2009 reveals that the majority of the big R&D spenders in the USA cut their R&D expenditure by 5–25 per cent that year.

There are additional relationships between technological and social forces. In the previous chapter we discussed immigration. Interestingly, several studies have linked immigration with entrepreneurial activity. Such studies suggest immigrants are more likely to be risk-takers, have more experience of at least two social systems and are therefore able to draw upon a richer set of experiences. Similarly, studies have established a relationship between a country's national culture and risk-taking, creativity and entrepreneurial activity. Furthermore, technology may enable or replace human labour, thus impacting upon employment and unemployment rates. In the previous three chapters we emphasized the importance of employment to the government, economy and society. Technology can impact upon the quality of working life, work–life balance and flexibility, changing the way we go about work, where and how work is undertaken. Such matters are explored in more detail later in this chapter.

TECHNOLOGICAL CHANGE: CREATIVITY AND ENTREPRENEURSHIP

In previous paragraphs we defined *technology*. In this section we define the key concepts associated with technology acquisition and diffusion. Science is often considered hand-in-hand with technology. Science and technology (S&T) are bound together through their relationship with knowledge. In the case of science, such knowledge is created through research and experimentation. Basic research is the search for knowledge. Applied research is the search for solutions to practical problems using this knowledge. In some cases, research is undertaken by universities and governments and in other cases by commercial organizations seeking to profit from the solutions to practical problems they create. Producers must create new products and services and businesses must create profitable ways of delivering them (work processes and technologies) to the market place. In turn, some of the procured products and services may themselves enable other businesses, governments and consumers to work and operate in a more effective and efficient manner. In this sense, creativity refers to the phenomenon whereby something new is created which has some kind of value. Creativity concerns the use of imaginative thought, leading to new ways of seeing things and may result in innovative solutions to a problem or the initiation of change. An output of creativity may be new technology. Indeed, technology will often be used in the process of creativity and creating. Whilst creativity is a broad term, Invention is a term used to describe the *creation* of a new technology and is typically followed by Innovation which seeks to create value out of new technologies. Innovation is the spread and diffusion of technology into society and organizations. From a business perspective, the aforementioned key concepts are encapsulated in entrepreneurship which can be defined as the process of creating value by bringing together a unique package of resources (and technologies) to exploit an opportunity. Corporate entrepreneurship can broadly be defined as entrepreneurship within an existing organization. Corporate entrepreneurship includes all an organization's innovation, renewal and venturing efforts.

Ultimately, much of research, science and technology manifests as goods, supplied through business to solve everyday living problems, and provide entertainment. However, it is clear that goods take time to permeate society and do so to greater or lesser degrees. The Technology adoption lifecycle model describes the adoption or acceptance of a new product or innovation, according to the demographic and psychological characteristics of defined adopter groups. The process of adoption over time is typically illustrated as a classical normal distribution curve (though this may not reflect reality). The model indicates that the first group of people to use a new product/technology are called 'innovators', followed by 'early adopters'. Next come the early and late majority, and the last group to eventually adopt a product are called 'laggards'. Similarly, from a supplier perspective, the Technology maturity lifecycle can be broken down into five distinct stages/categories: (1) 'Bleeding edge' – any technology that shows high potential but has yet to demonstrate its value or settle down into any kind of consensus; (2) 'Leading edge' – a technology that has proven itself in the marketplace but is still new enough that it may be difficult to find knowledgeable personnel to implement or support it; (3) 'State of the art' – when people generally agree that a particular technology is the right solution; (4) 'Dated' – continues to be useful and used by some, but a replacement leading edge technology is readily available; and (5) 'Obsolete' – has been superseded by state-of-the-art technology, may be maintained but no longer implemented.

Much of our discussion so far has focused on knowledge appropriation which typically manifests as patents and then saleable goods. However, the technological environment is also about knowledge *diffusion*. Technological diffusion refers to the spreading of new technologies within and between economies. Communication technologies and behaviours impact upon diffusion. For example, the UNESCO Science Report (2010) comments upon the number of Internet users – a variable used to gauge whether easier access to information and knowledge has provided opportunities for a more rapid diffusion of S&T. UNESCO find that the BRIC (Brazil, Russia, India and China) and numerous developing countries are quickly catching up to the USA, Japan and major European countries on this indicator. This shows the crucial importance of the emergence of digital communications like the Internet on the world distribution of S&T and, more broadly, knowledge generation. The rapid diffusion of Internet in the South is one of the most promising new trends of this Millennium, as it is likely to bring about a greater convergence in access to S&T over time. A similar concept to diffusion is Technology transfer – a process of acquiring technology from another country, especially in manufacturing; whereby skilled workers in the host country are able to learn from the technology of the foreign investor. Globalization has had a significant impact upon technology transfer.

Sources of new technology: who invents and who innovates?

Basic research is carried out in various institutional frameworks: universities, research institutes, companies and consortia of each. In this section we first introduce a global perspective before taking a more detailed European perspective on science and technology – invention and innovation.

A Global Perspective On Science And Technology

Science and technology is one of the main drivers of economic growth – discussed in Chapter 3. It is therefore of interest to Governments (and regional powers such as the EU) and commercial entities alike. Such interest can be seen from the growing number of researchers; there were over seven million worldwide researchers in 2007, up from 5.8 million in 2002. The world devoted 1.7 per cent of GDP to R&D (Research and Development) in 2007. In monetary terms this translates into USD 1146 billion. UNESCO Institute for Statistics (UIS) regularly report on Global Investments in R&D. The UIS collects science and technology data from more than 200 countries and territories through its biennial research and experimental development survey and partnerships with other statistical organizations (see the UIS Data Centre http://stats.uis.unesco.org). Their data can be used to present a worldwide snapshot of R&D expenditure. The most commonly used indicator,

FIGURE 5.4

Where are R&D investments made?

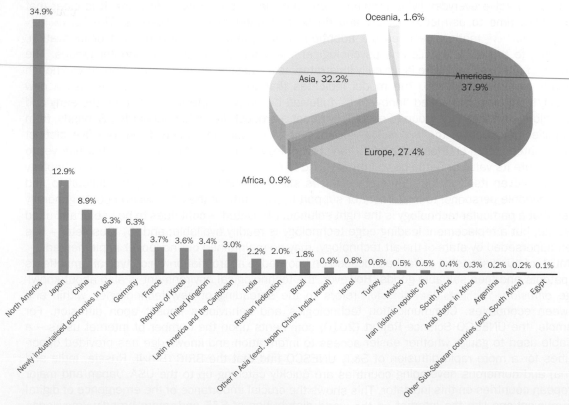

Source: UNESCO Institute for Statistics (UIS) Reproduced with permission.

monitoring resources devoted to worldwide R&D, is gross domestic expenditure on R&D (GERD). The information presented in Figure 5.4 illustrates global and regional trends in the allocation of R&D resources. The figure shows distribution of world R&D expenditure (2007) by main regions/countries in terms of GERD. A significant proportion of world R&D takes place in just a small number of countries. For example, over 80 per cent of world R&D Expenditure (GERD) in 2007 was made by the following countries: North America, Japan, China, Germany, France, Republic of Korea, United Kingdom and India. There are significant variations between countries and regions. In developing countries (those in the process of becoming industrialized), there were 502 researchers compared with 3656 researchers per million inhabitants in developed countries (2007). The number of researchers (also used as a measure of R&D activity) in developing countries jumped from 1.8 million to 2.7 million in five years (2002–2007) whilst the number of researchers in developed countries increased from 4.0 to 4.5 million. In the drive to strengthen knowledge-based societies, policymakers are looking to ensure their countries have an adequate supply of researchers.

The current status of science around the world is discussed in the UNESCO Science Report 2010. It shows, in particular, whilst the disparities between countries and regions remain huge, the proliferation of digital information and communication technologies is increasingly modifying the global picture. By making codified information accessible worldwide, it is having a dramatic effect on the creation, accumulation and dissemination of knowledge, whilst at the same time providing specialized platforms for networking by scientific communities operating at a global level. Irina Bokova, Director-General of UNESCO notes that the distribution of research and development (R&D) efforts between 'North and South' has changed, with the emergence of new players in the global economy. A bipolar world in which science and technology (S&T) were dominated by the Triad (the three developed markets of Japan, North America and Western Europe) is gradually giving way to a multipolar world, with an increasing number of public and private research hubs spreading across North and South. Early and more recent newcomers to the S&T arena, including the Republic of Korea, Brazil, China or India, are creating a more competitive global environment by developing their capacities in the industrial, scientific and technological spheres. One consequence is greater competition between countries to attract scientific personnel from abroad and to retain or recall their best researchers and graduates living abroad. Bokova argues that those developing countries showing the most rapid progression in recent years are the ones that have adopted policies to promote science, technology and innovation. China is on the verge of overtaking both the USA and the EU in terms of sheer numbers of researchers.

In the UNESCO Science Report 2010, Hugo Hollanders and Luc Soete take a closer look at some of the broad trends that have characterized the past decade and discuss the growing role of knowledge in the global economy. They refer to a 'growth spurt' (historically unique period of rapid global economic growth from 1996 to 2007) arguing it to have been driven by new digital technologies. It was brought to a sudden and somewhat brutal halt by the global economic recession discussed in Chapter 3. They suggest cheap and easy access to new digital technologies such as broadband, Internet and mobile phones accelerated the diffusion of best-practice technologies. Citing the work of Zanatta and Queiroz (2007), they believe it is the trends in business investment in R&D which best illustrate the rapid geographical changes taking place worldwide in privately funded R&D centres. Increasingly, multinational companies are decentralizing their research activities to parts of both the developed and developing worlds within a strategy to take on R&D at the global level. For multinationals, this strategy reduces labour costs and gives companies easier access to markets, local human capital and knowledge, as well as to host country natural resources. The favoured destinations are the so-called Asian 'tigers', the 'old' newly industrialized countries in Asia, and, secondly, Brazil, India and China. However, this is no longer a one-way traffic: firms from emerging economies are now also buying up large firms in developed countries and thereby acquiring the firms' knowledge capital overnight.

A European Perspective On Science And Technology

In pursuit of growth and prosperity, the EU has a vested interest in S&T and R&D. The European Parliament has, for many years, looked increasingly at the problem of what shape to give to the Union's research effort. The role of the EU in R&D has been defined in the various treaties which have successively shaped the EU over the past 50 years. The European Council has stressed, on several occasions in recent years, the importance of sustained research and technological development for growth and employment. The creation of a European Research Area (ERA) was proposed by the European Commission in its communication 'Towards a European Research Area' of January 2000. The authors of the communication (European Commission 2000) argued that the present will be the century of science and technology. More than ever, investing in research and technological development offers the most promise for the future. However, at the time, they painted a negative picture stating, 'The situation concerning research (in Europe) is worrying. Without concerted action to rectify this, the current trend could lead to a loss of growth and competitiveness in an increasingly global economy. The leeway to be made up on the other technological powers in the world will grow still further. And Europe might not successfully achieve the transition to a knowledge-based economy.' They noted, in 2000, that the average research effort in the Union (the differences being significant from one country to another) was only 1.8 per cent of Europe's GDP, as against 2.8 per cent in the United States and 2.9 per cent in Japan – a gap that seemed to be on the increase. In terms of employment, researchers accounted for only 2.5 in every thousand of the industrial workforce in Europe (2000), as against 6.7 in the United States and six in Japan. However, research and technology accounts for 25 to 50 per cent of economic growth and has a strong influence on competitiveness and employment and the quality of life of Europeans. It was further noted that if technological progress creates the jobs of tomorrow, it is research which creates the jobs for the day after tomorrow. The current trends in research could therefore have a negative influence on the development of employment in Europe in the years ahead. Despite Europe investing less and less of its richness in progress in knowledge it 'produces a third of the world's scientific knowledge' (European Commission 2000:p5). The Commission concluded it was time for an in-depth debate to define a policy approach in order to reinvigorate research in Europe.

In recognition of entry into the knowledge-based society, the Commission (2000) called for better investment in knowledge, arguing economic and social development would depend essentially on knowledge in its different forms, on the production, acquisition and use of knowledge. Additionally they called for more public research, 'the product of a creativity which must not disappear in the Europe of the 21st century'. Discussing private investment, they noted the private sector finances more than half and carries out two thirds of Europe's research and technological development activities. Private investment in research and development in Europe, which had dipped, has picked up again in recent years. Investment by international and multinational concerns in Europe has maintained at a high level and even increased. Because of the globalization of the economy, together with the industrial and technological alliances, mergers and acquisitions that are growing in every sector, these companies are building research and development strategies on an international scale. For some of the private sector, research is thus increasingly at European and even world level. That said, the global increase in expenditure on research and development in the private sector is less than it has been amongst its main competitors in the United States and Asia. This is mainly due to the somewhat limited research effort of medium sized businesses and small enterprises. In Europe the latter are made up essentially of companies that do or could use technology and whose future depends on the development of their technological capacities. But only a limited number of small businesses are exploiting the potential of high technology, and the creation of companies commercializing the results of research and development is still on the low side in Europe (European Commission 2000:p6).

The (Lisbon) Treaty provides the European Union with a legal basis for measures to support European cooperation in research and technological development. However, the principal reference framework for research activities in Europe was, at the time, national. The Commission believed that fragmentation, isolation and compartmentalization of national research efforts and systems and the disparity of regulatory and administrative systems only serve to compound the impact of lower global investment in knowledge. In short, they recognized a need for a real (integrated) European research policy. The Commission, in its communication (2000), proposed the creation of a European research area (ERA) which should: create a common approach to the needs and means of financing large research facilities in Europe; and develop closer relations between the various organizations of scientific and technological cooperation in Europe – bringing together the scientific communities, companies and researchers of Western and Eastern Europe. The objective for creating ERA was endorsed by the EU shortly afterwards, at the March 2000 Lisbon European Council.

The EU Research Framework Programmes (FPs) were explicitly designed to support the creation of ERA. With a budget of EUR 53.2 billion, the seventh framework programme of the European Community for research, technological development and demonstration activities (FP7) is the EU's main instrument for research funding, running from 2007 to 2013. FP7 is also designed to meet European needs concerning employment, competitiveness and quality of life. The EU has established a number of organizations to form and contribute to the ERA. The Community Research and Development Information Service (CORDIS), is an information space devoted to European Research and Development (R&D) activities and technology transfer. CORDIS is the primary repository for EU-funded R & D projects covering a myriad of science, technology, and research-related fields and topics. The main aims of CORDIS are: to facilitate participation in European research and take-up activities; to improve exploitation of research results, with an emphasis on sectors crucial to Europe's competitiveness; and to promote the diffusion of knowledge, fostering the technology take-up to enterprises and the societal acceptance of new technology. New initiatives launched in conjunction with FP7, such as the European Research Council, will have an important impact upon the European research landscape. Peter Tindemans wrote in the UNESCO Science Report (2010:p147) on the EU, saying: The European Institute of Technology should also play a substantial role in creating world-class 'knowledge and innovation communities'. He discusses the Lisbon Strategy, and that subsequently heads of state and government had agreed each EU country would, by 2010, strive to devote 3 per cent of GDP to expenditure on research and development (GERD), with the private sector expected to contribute two-thirds of this effort. This target was not met. Tindemans suggests that, despite the fact that co-ordination between national programmes has always been part of European rhetoric, it is now being admitted that mechanisms to bring about co-ordination have not worked well.

Throughout this chapter we emphasized the importance of education systems to society and technology. Aside from integrating research efforts, the EU has undertaken to integrate and harmonize education systems, particularly at the tertiary level. Amongst EU initiatives worthy of further note is the *Bologna Process*. The Bologna Process aims to create a European Higher Education Area (EHEA). The three priorities of the Bologna Process are: the introduction of the three-cycle system (bachelor's, master's and doctorate); quality assurance; and the recognition of qualifications and periods of study across Europe. For the EU, the Bologna Process is part of a broader effort to drive a 'Europe of knowledge'. The EHEA seeks to ensure more comparable, compatible and coherent systems of higher education in Europe. For the first decade of the twenty first century, the efforts of the Bologna Process members were targeted at creating the European Higher Education Area. The next decade will be aimed at consolidating the EHEA. In many respects, the Bologna Process has been revolutionary for cooperation in European higher education.

The Commission is now preparing the launch of a new initiative to create an 'Innovation union' as part of the Europe 2020 strategy. Europe 2020 proposes mutually reinforcing priorities which include the need to develop an economy based upon knowledge and innovation. The EU needs to define where it wants to be by 2020. To this end, the Commission (2010) proposed several EU headline targets which included a 3 per cent investment of the EU's GDP in R&D. The Commission proposed that EU goals be translated into national targets. The Commission suggested several flagship initiatives such as: (1) the 'Innovation Union' to improve framework conditions and access to finance for research and innovation in order to ensure that innovative ideas can be turned into products and services that create growth and jobs; and (2) 'A digital agenda for Europe' to speed up the roll-out of high-speed Internet and reap the benefits of a digital single market for households and firms. Commenting on the recent economic crisis, the Commission (2010) believe the steady gains in economic growth and job creation witnessed over the last decade have been wiped out – GDP fell by 4 per cent in 2009, industrial production returned to the levels of the 1990s and 23 million people – or 10 per cent of the active population – are now unemployed. The crisis has been a huge shock for millions of citizens and it has exposed some fundamental weaknesses of the EU economy. Moving out of the crisis is the immediate challenge for the EU. However, even before the crisis, there were many areas where Europe was not progressing fast enough relative to the rest of the world. Europe's average growth rate had been structurally lower than that of its main economic partners, largely due to a productivity gap that has widened over the last decade. Much of this is due to differences in business structures, combined with lower levels of investment in R&D and innovation, insufficient use of information and communications technologies, reluctance in some parts of EU societies to embrace innovation, barriers to market access and a less dynamic business environment. The Commission argue that Europe has many strengths and can count on the talent and creativity of its people. Focusing on a vision for where the EU should be in 2020, they emphasize a need to strengthen knowledge and innovation as drivers of future growth. This requires improving the quality of education, strengthening research performance, promoting innovation and knowledge transfer throughout the Union, making full use of information and communication technologies and ensuring that innovative ideas can be translated into new products and services that create growth, quality jobs and help address European and global societal challenges. However, to succeed, this must be combined with entrepreneurship, finance, and a focus on user needs and market opportunities (European Commission 2010:p10). In summary and moving forward, the Commission believes Europe must act to increase innovation, education, training and lifelong learning.

The Learning Organization

So far we have focused on the role of Governments in research, science and technology. We have noted the contribution of commercial organizations to R&D and will take a more detailed look at the productive use of technology and the strategic use of technology later in the chapter. Prior to this, in this final part we will discuss how organizations create, acquire, and transfer knowledge as a transformational resource and 'ingredient' of their outputs. Not all organizations are adept at this and scholars identify a learning organization as one skilled at creating, acquiring, and transferring knowledge, and at modifying its behaviour to reflect new knowledge, technologies and insights; the organization has developed the continuous capacity to adapt and change, typically through experimentation, trial and error. Organizational culture is closely associated with the concept of the learning organization. Scholars typically identify values, attitudes, beliefs and behaviours that can either promote or discourage experimentation and change. Whereas the learning organization emphasizes the creation of new knowledge and technologies in order to adapt continuously to the changing environment, knowledge management infrastructure is used to transfer and enable knowledge diffusion throughout the organization. Infrastructure design is dependent upon the type of knowledge most valued by the organization (e.g. tacit versus explicit). Typical aspects of the organizational infrastructure (internal environment) include the use of Internet technologies (intranets), databases and software applications on the ICT side and make use of softer, HR networks (communities of practice, interest groups and informal networks). For a more detailed discussion of knowledge management, see Kelly (2009: Chapter 12). The learning organization seeks to create new knowledge continuously in order to maintain competitive advantage; a matter discussed in the next two sections.

THE INTERNAL TECHNOLOGICAL ENVIRONMENT: THE PRODUCTIVE USE OF TECHNOLOGY, DEVELOPING STRENGTHS

The preceding sections have emphasized the acquisition of knowledge and development of technologies in the broader external environment. In this section we consider how technology is used in the day-to-day activities of the business organization (internal environment). Having analyzed various indicators of global S&T (R&D) activity, UNESCO (2010:p25) conclude that the increase in the stock of 'world knowledge', as epitomized by new digital technologies and discoveries in life sciences or nanotechnologies, is creating fantastic opportunities for emerging (and developed) nations to attain higher levels of social welfare and productivity. Throughout operations and the primary value adding activities of the firm, there is an emphasis on efficiency. This section will not only consider the application and management of technology to enable efficient working (and productive capacity) but will also consider implications for the changing nature of work. Technology management (TM) is the management of technological capabilities to shape and accomplish the strategic and operational objectives of an organization. Having considered the operational aspects in this section, we turn to the strategic objectives of an organization in the next section.

Producing products and services requires the business to plan, organize, coordinate, control and undertake work activities. Technologies are used to conduct (replacing people) or enable people to complete such work activities both physically and mentally. During the industrial revolution, machines typically replaced the physical activities of people and were sometimes applied to boring and repetitive work. In many cases, low-paid manual work is more easily automated. However it is much more difficult to substitute technology for people in jobs that require more complex problem-solving abilities. During the information revolution, technology, primarily through information systems and communications, sought to replace particular thinking-tasks whilst assisting people with other work. Examples of the application of technology to work are shown in the diagram (Figure 5.5) below.

The important technologies for the workplace are shown on the left hand side of Figure 5.5. Such technologies include tools, equipment, plant, factories and other buildings, robotics, ways of working, and computer-based information systems and communications. Some of the technologies will have been procured from other businesses or acquired from research activity, whilst others may have been created in-house. Technologies are applied to work tasks such as those shown in the centre of the figure. In each case the technology may help with manual labour, cognitive (thinking) tasks or may support transactions and the flow of information between business entities. As was discussed previously, productivity is concerned with the output from a production process. Businesses typically

FIGURE 5.5

Technology and work

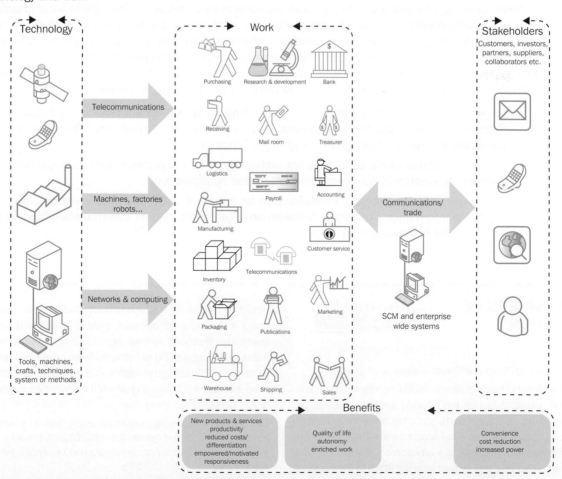

Source: Adapted from P. Kelly (2009) International Business, Cengage Learning, p56. Reproduced with permission.

want to produce more output with less cost in order to become more efficient. In this way, technology can reduce labour costs or enable workers to achieve more than they could if acting without the technology. The benefits are shown at the bottom of the figure. Benefits may be accrued by the business, customer, investors, employees and other stakeholders.

In recent years technology has primarily been directed at integrating and making supply chains more efficient. The supply chain is all of the activities (by manufacturers and retailers collectively) related to the acceptance of an order from a customer and its fulfilment. In its extended format it also includes connections with suppliers, customers and other business partners. Whereas the supply chain may include several organizations and entities, the value chain is that set of activities, completed by a single organization which contribute to bringing a product or service to the point whereby it can be sold to a customer – the sequence of activities that a firm undertakes to create value (see Chapter 10). Both frameworks can be used to analyze where technologies can be deployed and utilized for business benefit. The value chain presents a tool to decompose organizations into their parts and then focus attention on specific activities. Business process maps and flow charts can be used in a similar, more detailed, way. Understanding how organizations use technology is therefore based on an analysis of how the organization adds value. Value is essentially what something is worth, the amount customers are willing to pay for a product or service (goods). Added-Value is the difference between the amount customers are willing to pay for a product minus the cost of inputs and transformational activities used to create that product or service (offering). There are three main factors influencing the value equation: input costs (supply-side), transformation costs and the amount the buyer is willing to pay for products or services on the demand side (based on perceived product benefits) relative to competing products. Whilst the value chain dominated thinking in the 1980s, in the 1990s companies (like Dell and Amazon) turned their focus towards the supply chain. Such companies recognized the benefits (see next section) of being efficient whilst being more responsive to customers. The 1990s were characterized by developments in Internet, database and communication technologies, enabling such companies to integrate business processes and enable the flow of information throughout the supply chain; they enabled e-business and e-commerce activity and created the digital organization. Key supply chain technologies include enterprise systems (ERP and CRM, EC and EB) typically integrated with warehouse management and flexible manufacturing systems.

- A Digital organization is an organization where nearly all significant business processes and relationships with customers, suppliers, and employees are digitally enabled and key corporate assets are managed through digital means.

- E-business (EB) is about using Internet technologies as the platform for internal business operations, electronic commerce and enterprise collaboration.

- E-commerce (EC) is generally considered to be a subset of EB and is all electronically mediated information exchanges between an organization and its external stakeholders (see sell-side and buy side e-commerce).

BUSINESS IN ACTION

South African National Roads and e-tolls

The South African National Roads Agency Limited (Sanral), plans to launch the e-tolling system – Sanral has been urging road users to 'get e-tag ready' by getting an e-tag, registering an e-toll account and fitting the e-tag to the inside of the vehicle's windscreen. Registered Gauteng road users who have an e-tag fitted to their vehicle would be eligible for all the discounts available to e-tag users including a 31 per cent e-tag discount and frequent user discount. Further, special arrangements for fleets and groups of 50 or more vehicles have been put in place for obtaining the tags and registering an e-toll account. About 2.5-million transactions were expected at highway gantries every day.

Source: www.engineeringnews.co.za/article/business-organizations-call-for-delay-of-gauteng-e-tolls-2012-04-17; www.engineeringnews.co.za/article/over-200-000-gauteng-e-toll-accounts-registered-2012-01-11

Employment and the nature of work

In addition to the intended benefits discussed in previous paragraphs, there are often unintended side effects associated with the introduction of new technologies to the workplace. Working conditions, health and safety, demand for labour, quality of life, employee loyalty and job satisfaction may be affected. Technology changes the way businesses work and operate, making it possible to accomplish more work more quickly. It has been argued that some jobs (work tasks) have been eliminated as a result of technology (replacement) whilst in some cases it has created jobs. Similarly, it has been argued that technology can deskill work whilst others have argued that it increases demand on people at work. Thus there seem to be both positive and negative effects of technology, depending upon the perspective taken. Evaluating the impacts and benefits of technology requires a multiple stakeholder perspective, as many entities, including the environment, may be affected. Technological determinism is the argument that technology can be used to explain internal aspects of the organization. An understanding of the changing nature of work is important as this will influence the need for labour, desirable skills, knowledge and competencies. Earlier in this chapter we noted the role of education to the economy and suggested that governments need to invest in the fields of education that respond to labour-market needs. Thus there are complex relationships between technology, work, society and government. In the remainder of this section we explore, in more detail, the relationship between technology and the changing nature of work, before discussing the strategic importance of technology to business.

- Technology and job numbers: Technology, particularly in the form of machines and robotics, may well reduce the need for labour in the production (and supporting) processes. It can be used to do the repetitive mundane jobs, 24 hours a day, seven days-a-week eliminating boredom and mistakes through tiredness or concentration difficulties. However, whilst it might be argued that technology has reduced employment in some industries and business activities, it has spawned new opportunities in other areas. In particular, where technology gives consumers more time, these consumers can focus on leisure and, as a consequence, the entertainment and leisure industry has grown. Likewise, we have observed growth in employment in computer, electronics and telecommunications sectors.

- Enabling: Aside from impacting upon the need for human resources, technology can be used to enable people in their work activities. The marketing function can create richer communications, providing product information to prospects. This information can be delivered to virtually anybody anywhere at very low cost. The technology can be used to create a dialogue and may lead to a sale. In the sales department, technology can be used to process the resulting customer order and trigger activities automatically in other departments such as the warehouse. Within production, we already recognized the role of technology through computer-aided manufacture. Further applications include computer-aided design. Technology empowers all activities within the organization, no matter what the size.

- Enrich work: In many cases, technology has been used to enrich work, empowering people and enabling group work. Consequently, not only does technology impact upon the number of jobs but also job content and the way in which work is undertaken.

- Autonomous team working: is a process whereby management gives formal groups the right to make decisions on how their work is performed on a group basis, without reference to management. Collaborative Work Management Tools can help groups work together. Such tools include software that helps people accomplish or manage joint work activities.

- Structural implications: In the previous paragraph we noted how technology may reduce the number of operational jobs within an organization. Advances in communication and information systems technologies have also caused a reduction in the number of middle management jobs. In many instances, middle managerial roles were established in order to act as a communication link between more senior and junior managers. Intranet and associated collaborative technologies have replaced much of this role. Information systems can empower employees enabling them to take on additional responsibilities normally associated with higher levels in the organization. The removal of management layers causes structural changes within the organization design. Technological change, in conjunction with broader political and economic change led to the delayering and downsizing of organizations throughout the 1990s.

- Flexible working arrangements: technology can be used to provide flexibility on patterns of work in the organization, including part-time work and flexitime. Overcoming both time and distance problems it may enable home and teleworking – a situation whereby the main place of work is the employee's home (full-time) or the employee works either completely, or for a percentage of time, from his/her home or somewhere other than the company base; moving the work to the workers instead of moving the workers to work. Also referred to as telecommuting, telework allows employees to work at an alternative location and communicate using computers, phones or other electronic devices; is the process of enabling work to be conducted from any place, at any time, through the use of telecommunications links; developments in computing and telecommunications have made such options more viable. Tele or home-working may benefit the organization in many ways. The organization requires less office space, thus reducing building and utility costs; the employee may be more motivated through flexibility and autonomy, and may witnesses a reduction in their personal work-related costs (transportation to and from work and possibly childcare). Such workers may be more time-rich, possibly saving several hours per week in travel time (improving the quality of life). Such time savings may be shared to benefit both employer and employee alike. Furthermore, the organization requires less supervisory control and employees typically report increased efficiency and productivity due to less distraction. There are however downsides as home workers or teleworkers often feel isolated and may not share the typical attitudes, assumptions and beliefs developed through the organizational culture.

- Quality of working life: refers to an individual's overall assessment of satisfaction with their job, working conditions, pay, colleagues and management style, organization culture, work–life balance, and training, development and career opportunities. Work–life balance is the allocation of time and commitment between work and personal life, which reflects the personal needs of the employee.

- Employee stress: One major downside often associated with technology implementation is employee stress. Work associated stress-related illnesses can lead to avoidable absences which can impact upon performance. Cole and Kelly (2011) define stress as the adverse psychological and physical reactions that occur in individuals as a result of their being unable to cope with the demands being made on them; it is a form of strain provoked in response to the situational demands which typically occur in jobs with high demand. Respondents of a Health and Safety Executive (2000) survey who considered themselves to be stressed at work, cited the following work characteristics as being associated with stress: working long hours, having to work rapidly, high skill level required, taking the initiative, not being given enough information, high workload, responsibility, frequent interruptions over time, being treated unfairly, no respect from others and inadequate support. Essentially, the results confirm the importance of perceptions of the physical work environment, working hours, job demand and discretion and social support at work in determining reported stress levels.

Finally, but extremely important, is the impact of technology on the natural environment – pollution. The sustainable environment and challenges associated with pollution and the by-products of technology utilization are considered in Chapter 7. The ecological environment is concerned with the use of natural resources (inputs), pollution (outputs), global warming and similar issues. In recent times there has been considerable concern about the effects of pollution (greenhouse gases and acid rain) and the depletion of natural resources (rain forests and the ozone layer). Carbon dioxide emissions from industry and the CFCs from their products have contributed to global warming and a myriad of secondary consequences. Such environmental problems result from economic activity. The production and consumption of goods and services can generate spill over effects, impacting upon the wider population and not just producers and consumers.

Organizations and their industries vary in the extent of environmental damage they cause. Whereas agriculture, mining and chemicals are likely to have a high impact, tourism, packaging and electronics a moderate impact, areas such as advertising, education and government will have a lower impact. Not only do we observe variation in the impact but also in the responses available to organizations. In some cases the organization may simply comply (minimal response) with regulations; in other cases the organization will go further, taking a positive and proactive stance towards environmental issues (green organizations).

STRATEGIC USE OF TECHNOLOGY: OPPORTUNITY AND THREAT

In order to generate profit, a business must generate revenue through sales and then profit by making goods and services at a cost below the price at which they are sold. In the previous section we evaluated the role of technology in terms of business operations – the work undertaken by employers. The emphasis was on reducing costs which then increased the profit margin. Technology also determines and enables strategy: what the organization should do (purpose) and how it should be done. In particular it impacts upon organizational ability to compete and win business. Changes in the external environment and the intensity of competition create threats and opportunities that can motivate creativity, innovation and entrepreneurial activity within organizations. When technology is used to differentiate products and add more value or reduce costs, it enables the business to increase revenues through sales, to seize opportunities. In this sense, we can evaluate technology's role in increasing the performance of the business.

Performance relates to organizational purpose (mission); reflects achievements relative to the resources used by the organization (how well the organization manages its resources) and must be considered within the environment in which the organization does its work (adaptability). Organizational performance must integrate the concepts of 'effectiveness' and 'efficiency'. That is, the organization must be able to meet its goals (effectiveness) and do so with an acceptable outlay of resources (efficiency). The organization must be able to develop and implement strategies which will ensure performance over extended periods of time. The performance of organizations can be considered in three broad areas: performance in activities which support the mission (effectiveness), performance in relation to the resources available (efficiency), and performance in relation to long-term viability or sustainability (ongoing relevance). However, it is worth remembering that organizational performance is a broad construct and may include productivity (quantity and effort), employee satisfaction (the extent to which workers are satisfied with their work and conditions), client or customer satisfaction and quality dimensions.

The external environment is a source of opportunity and threat. The internal environment can be viewed in terms of strengths and weaknesses when compared with industry competitors. Opportunities may be present in the organization's present strategic group, the value system, other strategic groups, in substitute industries, new market segments and for complementary products and services. The organization's strengths and weaknesses, opportunities and threats (SWOT) are typically analyzed during the strategy formulation process. The organization may be considered a success when the objectives or goals of the organization and its evaluators are fulfilled. One generic objective for the organization is the pursuit of sustainable superior performance; superior means greater than the performance of comparable organizations, such as competitors, and sustainable means the continuance of such superior performance over a long period. There are many ways by which the organization can achieve superior performance such as through posses sion of sustainable competitive advantage. The main task for managers would then be to find strategies to create, renew, and maintain competitive advantage. For this reason, the literature has mainly focused on competitive advantage as the dependent variable for organizational performance and we discuss this later in more detail. Superior performance is often conceived in terms of abnormal profits and is about the organization outperforming its industry.

Competitive advantage is an advantage over a competitor, such as lower cost, a better product or quicker deliveries. More specifically, it is the achievement, through differentiation, of superior performance in relation to rivals, to create distinctive product appeal or brand identity; through providing customer value and achieving the lowest delivered cost; or by focusing on narrowly scoped product categories or market niches in order to be viewed as a leading specialist. Porter and Millar (1985), in their landmark article, evaluate how IT can provide a competitive advantage. They also discuss its role in shaping the forces that govern the extent of competition within an industry (see five forces). Technology can both remove and create barriers to entry within an industry. For example, imagine the cost of establishing a mobile telephone network that must comply with a variety of industry, country and global standards. Many organizations and investors could not afford the start-up costs. On the other hand, consider how Internet technologies and e-commerce have lowered barriers to entry for many traditional businesses such as retailing. It is now relatively inexpensive to set up a book or music store for example. Similarly, technology can increase the threat of product substitution as has been seen in the entertainment industry – MP3s replacing CDs replacing records and cassettes, DVDs replacing videos. The ease with which products can be substituted, coupled with the extent to which technology may reduce barriers to entering an industry is likely to have an impact upon the extent of rivalry and competition within an industry. As the number of rivals increases so too does the significance of the bargaining power of customers and suppliers within the industry. Internet technologies, through search and price comparison engines, enable consumers to identify effortlessly a broad range of potential suppliers and then compare product features and costs in order to determine the best deal for themselves. This has the effect of increasing their bargaining power and in many cases increasing rivalry and price competition within the industry. Thus, whilst technology may bring about efficiency gains for the company (reducing transaction, logistics and manufacturing costs), revenues and margins may be eroded through reductions in market share and price.

Operational effectiveness and strategy are both essential to superior performance but they work in very different ways (Porter 1996). A company can outperform rivals in the long run, only if it can establish a difference that can then be preserved. It must deliver greater value to customers or create comparable value at a lower cost, or do both. Delivering greater value allows a company to charge higher prices and greater efficiency results in lower costs. Ultimately, all differences between companies in cost or price derive from the hundreds of activities required to create, produce, sell, and deliver their products or services (refer back to the value chain). Cost is incurred by performing activities, and cost advantage arises from performing particular activities more efficiently than competitors. Similarly, differentiation arises from both the choice of activities and how they are performed. Activities, then, are the basic units of competitive advantage, argues Porter (1996). Overall advantage or disadvantage results from all a company's activities. Decomposing the organization into its core activities and processes is also useful when analyzing the organization. Decisions can then be made about where such activities will take place and who and what resources and technology will be required to complete the activity.

Operational effectiveness (and efficiency) is about performing similar activities better (through operational improvements) than rivals perform them. Improvements can be made in productivity, quality, or speed. Technology can be used to change how organizations perform activities in order to eliminate inefficiencies, improve customer satisfaction, and achieve best practice. Some companies are able to maximize their resources better than others because they eliminate wasted effort, employ more advanced technology, motivate employees better, or have greater insight into managing particular activities or sets of activities. Operational effectiveness refers to any number of practices that allow a company to better utilize its resources, resulting in differences in profitability among competitors because relative cost positions and levels of differentiation are directly affected. However, few companies have competed successfully on the basis of operational effectiveness over an extended period. One important reason for this is the speedy dissemination of best practices (technology diffusion). Competitors can quickly imitate management techniques, new technologies, input improvements, and superior ways of meeting customers' needs. The most generic solutions – those that can be used in multiple settings – diffuse most rapidly. The more benchmarking companies do, the more they look alike. The more that rivals outsource activities, often to the same or similar companies, the more generic those activities become. When rivals invest in the same technologies or best practices, the resulting major productivity gains are captured by customers and equipment suppliers, not retained in superior profitability. As rivals imitate one another's improvements in quality, cycle times, or supplier partnerships, strategies converge to the point where no one can win. Competition based on operational effectiveness alone is mutually destructive, halted only by limiting competition (to be discussed further in the next chapter). This may lead to the simple approach, to buy up rivals. In such a case, the remaining companies in an industry are those which outlasted others, not companies with real advantage.

Competitive strategy is about being different and strategic positioning means performing activities which differ from rivals or performing similar activities in different ways (Porter 1996). Strategy is the creation of a unique and valuable position, involving a different set of activities. The essence of strategic positioning is to choose activities that are different from rivals. Positioning can be based on: producing a subset of an industry's products or services (variety); serving most or all the needs of a particular group of customers (targeting a segment of customers) or segmenting customers who are accessible in different ways. Although their needs are similar to those of other customers, the best configuration of activities to reach them is different (access-based positioning). Access can be a function of customer geography or customer scale or of anything that requires a different set of activities to reach customers in the best way. Whatever the basis – variety, needs, access, or some combination of the three – positioning requires a tailored set of activities because it is always a function of differences on the supply side; that is, of differences in activities.

Scholars and practitioners alike strive continuously to perfect our knowledge of what makes some organizations perform better than others. Looking at organizations in terms of their resources has a long tradition in economics; however, analysis is typically confined to categories such as labour, capital and land. Strategists view organizations as a broader set of resources which can lead to high profits. They view a resource as anything which could be thought of as a strength or weakness of a given organization. More formally, an organization's resources at a given time could be defined as those (tangible and intangible) assets which are tied semi-permanently to the organization. Examples of resources are: brand names, in-house knowledge of technology, employment of skilled personnel, trade contacts, machinery, efficient procedures, capital, etc. The resource based view (RBV) theory is the perspective on strategy stressing the importance of capabilities (sometimes known as core competencies) in determining sustainable competitive advantage. The fundamental principle of the RBV is that the basis for competitive advantage of an organization lies primarily in the application of the bundle of valuable resources at its disposal. The bundle of resources, under certain conditions, can assist the organization, sustaining above average returns. Such resources must be valuable and must enable the achievement of goals. Which resources matter? Resources within the RBV are generally broken down into two fundamental categories: 1) tangible resources and 2) intangible resources. Tangible resources include those factors containing an accounting value as recorded in the organization's balance sheet. Intangible resources, on the other hand, include those factors that are non-physical (or non-financial) in nature and are rarely, if at all, included in the organization's balance sheet. Intangible resources can be defined as either assets or capabilities. If the intangible resource is something that the organization 'has', it is an asset. If the intangible resource is something the organization 'does', it is a capability. Thus, resource constructs may be conceptualized as: 1) tangible resources which include: a) financial assets and b) physical assets; 2) intangible resources - assets which include: a) intellectual property assets b) organizational assets and c) reputational assets; and 3) intangible resources that are capabilities. The central proposition of the RBV is that not all resources are of equal importance in contributing to organizational performance. The resource-based literature describes resources in terms of their value, rareness, inimitability and non-substitutability (VRIN).

Aside from determining *how* to compete in terms of technology driven efficiencies and product differentiation, companies must decide *where* to compete as part of their strategy. In previous chapters we defined Internationalization as the gradual process of taking organizational activities into other countries. A company may offer its goods and services solely in its domestic market or wider in a global market. Clearly there is more opportunity associated with the latter but not all organizations become multinational. Technology can be used to grow and enter markets. E-Commerce, for example, enables companies to reach out across country borders and therefore grow market potential. Technology can also be used to coordinate and control subsidiaries across geographical and time barriers, thus enabling fragmentation of the value chain. Markets were discussed in previous chapters and in more detail in Chapter 11. Firms can use technology to enter new and existing markets and gain access to customers. They can also use technology to lock customers into their sales channels. Market growth is the change over time in the demand for goods or services. There are, however, other types of growth that may form the basis of a strategic goal. Diversified growth is growth that occurs when new products are developed to be sold in new markets. Economic growth is the process of increasing productive capacity. Profit growth describes the percentage increase in net profits over time.

Protecting technology/Intellectual property

Throughout this chapter we have advocated the benefits of technology to business and the economy and recognized that, in some cases, the source of technology is the business itself. A company's technology, either used within transformational processes or manifest in its products and services, can be so important to company performance that additional resources are committed to ensure its protection. Intellectual property (IP) is a generic term used to describe designs, ideas and inventions. In general, intellectual property covers technology patents, trademarks, designs and copyright. Related to this are Intellectual property rights (IPR); this is an umbrella term for various legal entitlements that attach to certain names, written and recorded media, and inventions. At a micro level, the organization's technology and intellectual property may be copied or stolen. Text, pictures, video, music or anything else can now be produced on a desktop PC almost infinitely at next to zero cost. Illegal downloads and pirated products erode the revenues for business and therefore make it more difficult for them to recover venture capital. Furthermore, the organization's technology assets may be threatened, particularly those relating to its information systems and IT. Such technologies may be confronted with viruses, denial of service attacks or hacked and accessed without authority. In many cases, organizations are critically dependent upon such technology and such attacks pose threats to business.

SUMMARY

- Throughout this chapter we have emphasized technology as an application of knowledge in the workplace and throughout society.
- Businesses use technologies to compete and create products and services for the marketplace.
- Recognizing the application of knowledge, we explained how knowledge is created within society, through scientific research. This research can take place in institutions such as universities or in the research and development departments of commercial organizations.
- We also recognized, with particular reference to the learning organization, that entrepreneurial activity, creativity and innovation can occur in any part of the organization and its supply chain.
- Ultimately, new technologies are applied to improve organizational performance, society and the lives of people worldwide.
- Technology is inextricably linked with competition, the attainment of goals and the other forces within both the external and internal environment. Aspects of the competitive environment will be considered in more detail in the next chapter.

REVISION QUESTIONS

1. Explain why entrepreneurial activity is so vital in a dynamic environment. In your answer you should make reference to one of the following industries: Telecomms, Pharmaceuticals or Banking.

2. Discuss the links between government policy, the economy, technology, productivity and growth.

3. Evaluate the importance of technology as a source of competitive advantage and discuss the impact of technology upon the competitive forces of an industry.

4. Evaluate the impact of technology on jobs and work from the perspective of the employer and employee.

5. Evaluate the importance of investment in tertiary education and research for the economy and social well-being.

6. Amazon seeks to be 'Earth's most customer-centric company', where customers can find and discover anything they might want to buy online, and endeavours to offer its customers the lowest possible prices. Suggest how Amazon might use technology to achieve such goals.

7. Why do you think that Amazon uses 16 000 retail locations throughout the United States in addition to its online presence?

8. Consider the specific technologies outlined throughout this chapter – which do you think are utilized at Amazon? Next, from the perspective of Amazon, place the list in rank order, explaining your choices.

9. What might be the effect of (relatively) reduced graduation rates within the UK? How might it impact upon the economy, taking into account the different graduation rates in other countries?

10. Compare and contrast the purchasing of a physical book in a physical store with an e-book on an e-reader. Evaluate the impact of this technology on business. Consider impacts upon (a) the traditional book publishing industry, (b) libraries and (c) traditional book sales (retail)?

DISCUSSION QUESTIONS

1. Is there a case for the Government to change its policy on the level of investment (say as a proportion of GDP) in Education (HE in particular)? What are the incentives to invest in education?

2. How might reduced graduation rates impact upon the technical and then the economic environment?
   Consider the Business in Action topic at the start of the chapter. Technology has disrupted every industry. Consider e-book readers and discuss the following:

3. Does the Kindle impact upon the environment, if so how? How do you think Amazon is able to price the Kindle so low? Do you believe that they offer value for money?

4. What type of skills, knowledge and competencies do you think Lab126 look for in an employee? How do you think Lab126 set about designing new products?

5. How does the internet technology-enabled Amazon online business model impact upon the traditional book industry?

REFERENCES AND FURTHER READING

Cetindamar, D., Phaal, R. and Probert, D. (2010) *Technology Management – Activities and Tools,* Palgrave Macmillan

Cole, G A. and Kelly, P. (2011), *Management: Theory and Practice*, Ed 7, Cengage EMEA.

European Commission, (2000) 'Communication from the Commission to the Council, the European Parliament, the Economic and Social Committee and the Committee of the Regions – Towards a European Research Area', Commission of the European Communities Brussels, 18.1.2000 COM(2000) 6 final

European Commission, (2010) 'EUROPE 2020 A strategy for smart, sustainable and inclusive growth', Brussels, 3.3.2010 COM(2010) 2020

Garvin, D. (1993) 'Building a Learning Organization', *Harvard Business Review,* July–August 1993, 78–91

Health and Safety Executive, (2000), 'The scale of occupational stress: the Bristol stress and health at work study', Health and safety executive-Crown copyright - available for dowload from http://www.isma.org.uk/wp-content/uploads/crr00265.pdf

Kelly, P. P. (2009) *International Business and Management,* Cengage Learning EMEA

OECD (2011) 'Education at a Glance 2011: OECD Indicators', OECD Publishing. Http://dx.doi.org/10.1787/eag–2011–en

Porter, M. E. and Millar, V. E. (1985) 'How information gives you a competitive advantage', *Harvard Business Review,* July–August 63, 149–174

Porter, M. E. (1996) 'What Is Strategy?', *Harvard Business Review,* Vol. 74 Issue 6, 61–78

UNESCO (2010) 'UNESCO Science Report 2010', United Nations Educational, Paris Scientific and Cultural Organization, Paris

Williams, R. (2010) 'UK's graduation rates fall to below average – OECD', *The Guardian* – guardian.co.uk, Tuesday 7 September 2010

Zanatta, M. and Queiroz, S. (2007) The role of national policies in the attraction and promotion of MNEs' R&D activities in developing countries. *International Review of Applied Economics*, 21(3), 419–435

GLOSSARY

Automating Technology Replacement of the actions of the human body by the machine

Biotechnology The use of biological systems or living organisms to make or modify products or processes

Coordination Technology An aid to managing dependencies among the agents within a business process, and provides automated support for the most routinized component processes

Corporate Entrepreneurship Can broadly be defined as entrepreneurship within an existing organization. Employees, perhaps engaged in a special project within a larger firm, are encouraged to behave as entrepreneurs, with the resources and capabilities of the firm to draw upon. Corporate entrepreneurship includes all an organization's innovation, renewal and venturing efforts

Creativity The application of imaginative thought which may lead to new ways of seeing things and result in innovative solutions to a problem or the initiation of change

CRM Customer relationship management (CRM) uses technology-enhanced customer interaction to shape appropriate marketing offers designed to nurture ongoing relationships with individual customers within an organisation's target markets

Digital Organization An organization where nearly all significant business processes and relationships with customers, suppliers and employees are digitally enabled and key corporate assets are managed through digital means

E-business Using Internet technologies as the platform for internal business operations, electronic commerce and enterprise collaboration

E-commerce All electronically mediated information exchanges between an organization and its external stakeholders (see sell-side and buy side e-commerce)

Entrepreneurship Entrepreneurship can be defined as the process of creating value by bringing together a unique package of resources to exploit an opportunity

ERP Enterprise Resource Planning (ERP) refers to a complex software package commonly used to implement an enterprise information system.

Flexible Manufacturing Technologies Manufacturing technologies designed to improve job scheduling, reduce setup time and improve quality control

Gross Domestic Expenditure On R&D (GERD) Gross domestic expenditure on research and development (GERD) is total intramural (within an institution) expenditure on research and development performed on the national territory during a given period

Information and Communication Technology (ICT) A phrase used to describe a range of technologies for gathering, storing, retrieving, processing, analysing, and transmitting information - often used as an alternative term for information technology (IT) but is a more specific term that stresses the role of integrated telecommunications with computing hardware and software

Information Technology The hardware and software that are used to store, retrieve, and manipulate information

Information Technology (IT) Infrastructure Computer hardware, software, data and storage technology, and networks providing a platform of shared information technology resources for the organization

Innovation Creating value out of new ideas, new products, new services or new ways of doing things

Internet Technologies The Internet and its technologies are being used to build interconnected enterprises and global networks, like intranets and extranets that form information superhighways to support enterprise collaboration, electronic commerce, and internal business applications

Invention The creation of a new technology

Learning Organization An organization skilled at creating, acquiring, and transferring knowledge, and at modifying its behaviour to reflect new knowledge, technologies and insights; the organization has developed the continuous capacity to adapt and change, typically through experimentation

Productivity Economic measure of efficiency that summarizes the value of outputs relative to the value of inputs used to create them

Process Technologies The tools (equipment, machines and other devices) used in operations that transform materials, information or customers

Product Technology The embedded technology within a product or service, as distinct from process technology

Research And Experimental Development (R&D) Creative work undertaken on a systematic basis in order to increase the stock of knowledge, including knowledge of man, culture and society, and the use of this stock of knowledge to devise new applications. The term R&D covers three activities: basic research, applied research and experimental development

Self-service Technologies (SST) Technological tools that enable customers to produce services for themselves without assistance from firm employees

Social Technology The methods which order the behaviour and relationships of people in systematic, purposive ways through structures of co-ordination, control, motivation and reward

Supply Chain All of the activities related to the acceptance of an order from a customer and its fulfilment. In its extended format, it also includes connections with suppliers, customers and other business partners

Sustainable Competitive Advantage An advantage over a competitor, such as lower cost, a better product or quicker deliveries that is not easily imitated

Technology Technology is the creation, usage, and knowledge of tools, machines, crafts, techniques, systems or methods of organization in order to solve a problem or perform a specific job. It can also refer to the collection of such tools, machinery, and procedures. From a business standpoint, organizations may manufacture technological products for sale, or may use technology to undertake work. In the case of the latter, it is the machinery, equipment, processes, work layout, methods, systems and procedures in carrying out the work of the organization and converting inputs to outputs

Technology Adoption Lifecycle Model Describes the adoption or acceptance of a new product or innovation, according to the demographic and psychological characteristics of defined adopter groups. The process of adoption over time is typically illustrated as a classical normal distribution curve (though this may not reflect reality). The model indicates that the first group of people to use a new product/technology are called 'innovators', followed by 'early adopters'.Next come the early and late majority, and the last group to eventually adopt a product are called 'laggards'.

Technology Convergence The combining of several technologies into a single device, such as mobile phone, digital camera and web browser

Technological Determinism The argument that technology can be used to explain internal aspects of the organization

Technological Diffusion The spreading of new technologies within and between economies

Technological Environment Those forces that affect the technology used by the organization and which can create new products, new markets, and new opportunities

Technology Management (TM) Is the management of technological capabilities to shape and accomplish the strategic and operational objectives of an organization

Technology Maturity Lifecycle Similar to the product or technology adoption lifecycle, the technological maturity lifecycle can be broken down into five distinct stages/categories: (1) 'Bleeding edge' – any technology that shows high potential but hasn't demonstrated its value or settled down into any kind of consensus; (2) 'Leading edge' – a technology that has proven itself in the marketplace but is still new enough that it may be difficult to find knowledgeable personnel to implement or support it; (3) 'State of the art' – when people generally agrees that a particular technology is the right solution; (4) 'Dated' – continues to be useful and used by some, but a replacement leading edge technology is readily available; and (5) 'Obsolete'– has been superseded by state-of-the-art technology, may be maintained but no longer implemented

Technology Transfer Process of acquiring technology from another country, especially in manufacturing, whereby skilled workers in the host country are able to learn from the technology of the foreign investor

Value Chain That set of activities that must be accomplished to bring a product or service from raw materials to the point that it can be sold to a final customer

CHAPTER CASE STUDY

Asian Brickmaking: Business opportunity in Vietnam for cleaner brick kilns

Reporter David Markiewicz (2012) wrote about a new company with a mission 'to clean up brickmaking operations across Asia by using a simple, low-cost technology'. Rural industries in developing nations often burn waste biomass, a dirty process emitting carbon dioxide and other pollutants. Brick kilns are one of the main offenders, and Vietnam is cracking down on the industry. Mekong Green Tech developed a **gasifier** to cut emissions; it can be used with existing kilns.

Growth in terms of the economy and/or population of certain Asian countries, coupled with urbanization, has resulted in increased demand for residential, commercial, industrial and public buildings. Solid fired clay bricks are among the most widely used building materials in a number of countries. The building boom of the 1990s created a huge increase in demand for bricks, which continues in the present day.

Bricks and Brickmaking

A strong building material, used throughout history, the brick is a block, or a single unit of a ceramic material used in masonry construction, usually stacked together, or laid using various kinds of mortar to hold the bricks together and make a permanent structure. Bricks are typically produced in common or standard sizes, in bulk quantities. They are made from a variety of materials including clay. Bricks are the preferred building material in many tropical countries (such as Vietnam) since there is little timber but many wood-eating insects.

Jensen and Peppard (2004) analyzed the rural (small scale) brickmaking industry in Vietnam and explored traditional brickmaking technology – an industry that employs a large number of people. They argue that, in many important respects, the brickmaking industry is an ideal rural industry for the largely agricultural population of Vietnam. However, because of environmental concerns and technological advances in both agriculture and industry, traditional brickmaking in Vietnam is also confronted with real threats to its survival over the next ten years. In the Red River delta region of northern Vietnam, there are many factories that make bricks in a traditional way. Jensen and Peppard (2004) use the term 'traditional' to characterize the process of making bricks with very few machines, in kilns made of brick, and using coal as the firing medium. The bricks produced are sold to households for their own construction needs and also to retailers to be used in the construction of buildings throughout the delta region. Thus, whilst the technology involved in this type of brickmaking is old and processes are done by hand, both the structure of firms in the industry and use of its products place the industry in the formal sector of the economy. Factory owners sign contracts with the local communes allowing them access to lands where clay is found. The owners then build one or more kilns on the land rented, using ready-made bricks as the principal construction material. Approximately two kilns are built in each factory. The division of labour associated with brick production is characterized by four principal tasks: (1) shaping and cutting of uncooked ('green') bricks from raw clay and the stacking of those bricks in rows where they are left to air-dry; (2) 'fuel bricks' are produced from crushed coal, mud and water (they may also make use of biomass such as wood and rice husk). (3) Once dry, uncooked bricks must be carried into the kilns; and (4) people load the furnace by building up layers of an interspersed mix of clay bricks and coal fuel bricks. The kiln is lit and the bricks fired (Jensen and Peppard 2004).

Bricks are fired to a temperature of 700–1100 °C, requiring a large amount of fuel for the firing operation. Brick kilns consume millions of tonnes of coal (and biomass) per year, thus making them significant industrial consumers of coal. This gives rise to environmental concerns (see Chapter 7). Combustion of coal and other biomass fuels in brick kilns results in the emissions of carbon, sulphur dioxide, oxides of nitrogen, carbon dioxide and carbon monoxide. The emission of these pollutants has an adverse effect on workers' health and vegetation around the kilns. Many factories are located either in the middle of rice fields or in close proximity to them, and may be closed for as much as a month at a time to prevent crop damage caused by the combination of heat and smoke from the kilns. Environmental regulations related to brick factory operations are typically enacted at the level of the local communes. Apart from the environmental concerns, the industry faces other challenges, including: a shortage of workers, increases in fuel cost and limited availability of good quality coal, good quality clay in some regions and an inability of brick makers to adopt technologies to utilize alternate raw materials. There is a need for brick making technologies that offer improved energy utilization and emissions and cleaner brick production. In 2001, the Vietnamese government, with an aim to improve air quality, issued a regulation to prohibit traditional brick making kilns by 2010 (Decision 115/2001/ QD-TTg of the Prime Minister). Objectives of the regulation included reorganizing production of hand-made building materials which cause environmental pollution; elimination of production of clay bricks baked by manual kilns; and continual improvement of technologies and stabilization of the production of existing brick tunnel kilns. The growing interest in black carbon (commonly known as soot) as one of the significant contributors to global warming, after carbon dioxide, has brought international attention to identify its sources and find ways to curb black carbon emissions.

How then can small brick factories, using traditional kilns, adopt cleaner technologies and improve efficiency without causing rural unemployment? Many have turned to gasification technologies for a solution.

Mekong Green Tech & the gasifier

In Asia, brickmaking is a massive industry. Approximately one trillion bricks are produced yearly. In southern Vietnam, brickmaking is particularly concentrated with over ten thousand kilns in the region; the majority use rice husk as fuel. The Vietnamese government has long tried to clean up the industry and kilns are being shut down due to high pollution. Most solutions require expensive infrastructure change. Mekong Green Tech simply 'replace the fire' with a vastly more efficient combustion process, retrofitting existing kilns. The business recently won first prize in Georgia Tech's Ideas to SERVE Competition for innovative business concepts that can help society or the environment.

Source: http://mekonggreentech.com. Reproduced with permission.

Gasification technology: to gasify simply means to turn into gas. Gasification is most simply thought of as incomplete combustion. It is burning solid fuels like wood or coal without enough air to complete combustion, so the output gas still has combustion potential. The unburned gas is then piped away to burn elsewhere as needed. Several types of gasifier are currently available for commercial use. Gasification is a process converting carbonaceous materials such as coal, into a gas, then burned as a fuel. In the gasifier, rice husk is processed to generate a combustible gas mixture. The combustible gas mixture is then conveyed through filter systems to remove dust, tar and other by-products for a cleaner, combustible gas. This is then delivered to a burner used in the kiln for the firing process.

Vietnam is one of many countries using brick kilns. India is the second largest producer of clay fired bricks, accounting for more than 10 per cent of global production. India is estimated to have more than 100 000 brick kilns, producing billions of bricks, employing about ten million workers and consuming about 25 million tons of coal annually. India's brick sector is also characterized by traditional firing technologies, environmental pollution and a reliance on manual labour. The sector is dominated by small-scale brick kilns with limited financial, technical and managerial capacity.

Sources: Markiewicz, D. (2012), 'Georgia Tech students see business opportunity in Vietnam, cleaner brick kilns', Atlanta Business News (online) Wednesday, April 11, 2012 – http://www.ajc.com/business/georgia-tech-students-see-1413722.html; Jensen, R. and Peppard, D. (2004), 'The Traditional Brickmaking Industry and the Rural Economy of Vietnam', *Journal of Asian and African Studies* June 2004 vol. 39 no. 3 193–207; Maithel, S. et al (2012), 'Brick Kilns Performance Assessment: A Roadmap for Cleaner Brick Production in India', www.catf.us/resources/publications/files/Brick_Kilns_Performance_Assessment.pdf

Questions

- List a range of other products that may require heat in the manufacturing process? Discuss the disadvantages of inefficient combustion.
- What are the advantages of commercializing a low-cost gasifier technology?
- Is it feasible to replicate and diffuse this technology in other countries? How would you enable such technology transfer?
- Is it feasible to replicate and diffuse this technology in other industries?
- Discuss this case in relation to (1) the political environment and (2) the sustainable environment, considering the influence of a variety of stakeholders on the industry and its applied technologies
- Discuss this case from a competitive environment perspective – what competitive advantages might be derived from adoption of the 'new' technologies highlighted?

6
THE COMPETITIVE ENVIRONMENT

FIGURE 6.1

The competitive environment mind map

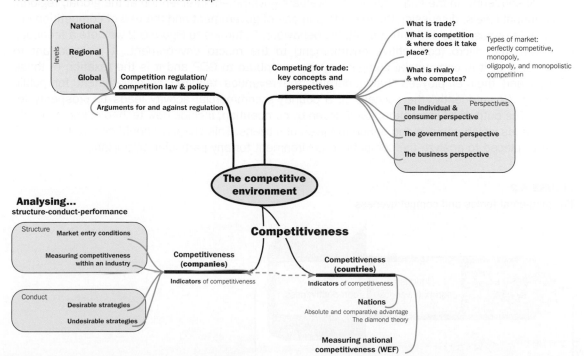

KEY CONCEPTS

Competition | Competitive advantage | Competitive environment | Competitive factors | Competitiveness | Five competitive forces | Internal environment | Rivalry

INTRODUCTION

Recently we have witnessed significant developments in the *competitive environment,* influenced by changes in demand, the forces of *globalization, government intervention, deregulation* and significant shifts in the *bargaining power* of consumers – brought about by Internet technology in particular. Generally, and as a consequence, we have observed increased rivalry and competitiveness from nations and individual firms. Industries and markets are in a state of continuous flux, fuelled by a constant barrage of merger and acquisition activity, coupled with new market entrants impacting upon market concentration and consequently competitive strategies (see also competitive factors). Yet the nature of competition within specific industries varies considerably and is dependent upon a range of factors such as demand, the nature of the product and service and degree of differentiation, the extent of rivalry, the ease with which new firms can enter a market and the relative bargaining power of suppliers and customers. Consequently, the competitive context varies from industry to industry and over the course of time. Managers must analyze the competitive environment if they are to make quality business decisions – particularly of the strategic nature, seize opportunity and act on threats. See Figure 6.1.

In this chapter we describe the competitive environment and implications for future organizational profitability and performance. The structure of this chapter, in relation to the rest of the book, is outlined in Figure 6.2. Previous chapters have described the macro environment, focusing on the PESTLE factors. These forces shape the competitive environment. Beginning with an explanation of key concepts, we then focus on competitiveness. In the next section we consider the competitiveness of nations and then later consider the competitiveness of firms. In both sections we introduce relevant theory and frameworks for analysis. Familiarity is required with the role of government and regulatory authorities in the market, plus an appreciation of the need for and methods of intervention. Consequently, in the final section, we evaluate government intervention at the global, regional and national levels, discussing the role and purpose of government and the use of competition law to regulate undesirable and anti-competitive behaviour. Returning to Figure 6.2 we note a feedback loop from the micro (competitive environment) to the macro environment. It is important to recognize that it is commercial companies who contribute to GDP and it is the taxation of these entities and their employees that generates the revenues required by government for public spending. Consequently, the success of a country's commercial activity leads to prosperity for society. The outputs of innovation, itself driven by competition, include new technologies, products and services which improve and enrich the lives of citizens. This chapter should ensure the reader is better placed to analyze the competitive environment for any particular organization.

FIGURE 6.2

Environmental forces and competitiveness

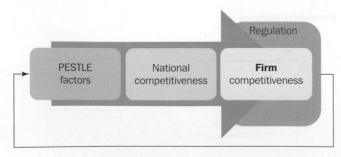

COMPETING FOR TRADE: KEY CONCEPTS AND PERSPECTIVES

In this section we define the key concepts associated with the competitive environment. First we consider related concepts associated with trade, then markets, followed by competition. The action of buying and selling goods and services is known as trade. Organizations provide goods and services to others and in some cases goods and services are exchanged for money, which generates revenue for the organization. Organizations with profit goals will consider potential market size and the potential for revenue, typically competing for trade through selling. Globalization and a growing population have driven an increase in trade both internationally and nationally. Increased trade produces increased competition. Competition in this sense means rivalry. Competition also refers to those companies (the 'competition') marketing products which are similar to, or can be substituted for, a given business's products in the same geographic area. The part of a company's external environment that consists of other firms (rivals) trying to win customers and the 'rules' and determinants of competition in the same market/industry segment is termed the Competitive environment. The competitive environment is often considered a micro environment; the immediate environment including customers, competitors, suppliers and distributors in which the organization is situated. Indeed, microeconomics is the study of economic activity at the level of individuals and firms. A key component of the competitive (micro) environment is competition and competitor behaviour is described in terms of rivalry. Rivalry is the act of competing – a quest to secure an advantage over another. Competitiveness, when applied to an organization, is the ability to compete effectively against rivals; when applied to a country, it is the ability to create an environment which is conducive to good economic and business performance.

Factors influencing the level of competition

There are many *factors* influencing the *level of competition* such as the attractiveness of the market, demand, the nature of the product or service, the number and concentration of firms in the market, market entry conditions, government intervention, regulation and law. Such factors are explored throughout this chapter. In this section we outline a number of generic factors, providing, in isolation, a brief explanation for each. In subsequent sections we discuss them in more detail.

- Industry growth rates when an industry is growing slowly, competition will be more intense. The only way an organization can expand is by taking market share from competitors.
- The nature of the product or service goods may take the form of commodities (supplied without differentiation – each competitor's output is essentially the same product, i.e. homogenous) or may vary in the extent of their differentiation. The level of competition is increased with degrees of differentiation. When goods are undifferentiated they tend to be priced the same, reducing the power of producers to compete.
- Market entry (and exit) conditions there is considerable variation in the significance of barriers to entry to a particular industry. In some cases the barriers will be deliberately erected to prevent new entrants, whilst in other cases the barriers may be innocently erected. Deliberate barriers may be erected through capital requirements, access to distribution channels, investment in R&D, new technologies and standards; innocent barriers may exist due to economies of scale, learning, specialization and experience curves. The influence of barriers will have an impact upon the threat of entry and therefore concentration rates.
- Number of firms and concentration the level of competition increases as the number of competitors increases. Consequently, if there is just one organization in the market (monopolist) then there is no competition. As the number of organizations in the market increases, the ability of organizations to protect their profits declines. Two methods used to determine concentration ratios and the competitiveness of industries are described below.

Market concentration measures the distribution of market power by market share. There are a number of methods to measure concentration. Such methods are used by the competition analyst, whether they are working in the marketing strategy department of the firm or in some government regulatory body. The first method we consider is the concentration ratio (CR) – the number of firms in an industry accounting for total sales. A high concentration ratio implies a relatively small number of firms account for a majority of the total sales of the industry.

BUSINESS IN ACTION

Method 1 – the market concentration ratio

The n-firm concentration ratio is the market share of the n largest firms in an industry; it can be expressed as:

$CRm = s1 + s2 + \cdots + sm$ where si is the market share and m defines the ith firm

Such measures are used by regulatory bodies like the OFT (see later) when analyzing industries to determine whether mergers should be allowed (because of potential adverse impacts on competition). Analysis will typically consider 3–5 firms. Concentration ratios, especially the four-firm concentration ratio, are designed to measure industry concentration, and by inference, the degree of market control. For example, consider the number of firms offering ferry services in the Irish Sea. Ferry operators (freight and passenger services) active on the Irish Sea include: Stena, DFDS, Seatruck, P&O, Irish Ferries and Fastnet. Freight ferry service volume-based market shares for the northern corridor are dominated by Stena, DFDS, Seatruck and P&O. If market shares were (32, 26, 10, 32) respectively, then the concentration ration of the three largest firms would be CR3 90. Concentration ratios range from 0 to 100 per cent. At the lower end (No concentration) the largest firms in the industry would not have any significant market share (perfect competition), i.e. competition that is EXTREMELY competitive, whilst at the other end, 100 per cent means an extremely concentrated oligopoly (Total concentration). Generally, below 50 per cent is low, 50–80 is medium and >80, high. Thus, in our example above, we might describe the Irish Sea ferry market as highly concentrated from oligopoly toward monopoly.

Mahajan (2005) provides detailed information and statistics produced by the Office for National Statistics (ONS) covering UK concentration ratios. Concentration ratios can also provide information regarding industry competitiveness and the scope for economies of scale. Such ratios provide estimates of the extent to which the largest firms contribute to activity in an industry. In the report, Mahajan shows that in the UK, there are wide variations between the CRs across industry groups and, for certain industries, between time periods. Some industries include many small businesses, some of which are run by the self-employed, and these industries have low CRs. Examples of these industries are Construction or Furniture manufacture. In the UK, there are a number of industries where a few, very large, businesses have dominated their respective industries for several years, and these industries have high CRs. Some of these industries have many of the characteristics of oligopolies. Examples of these industries include Tobacco products, Air transport, Banking and finance and Gas distribution. Aside from the entry of new competitors, CRs are typically changed through mergers and acquisitions. For example, in the banking and finance industry, large mergers and takeovers have increased the ratios of the industry. Examples of which include: Barclays and Woolwich; Banco Santander and Abbey; Halifax and Bank of Scotland; HSBC and Midland, etc. Utilities, transport, telecommunications, services and infrastructure have undergone subsequent mergers and takeovers, generating a rise in their respective industry's concentration ratios.

Whilst simple to apply, the definition of the concentration ratio does not use the market shares of all the firms in the industry and does not provide the distribution of firm size. It also does not provide much detail about the competitiveness of the industry. The concentration ratios merely provide an indication of the oligopolistic nature of an industry and indicate the degree of competition. The Herfindahl index (method 2 below) provides a more complete picture of industry concentration than does the concentration ratio.

Method 2 – Herfindahl–Hirschman Index (HHI)

HHI is a measure of the size of firms in relation to the industry and an indicator of the amount of competition amongst them. The index involves taking the market share of the respective market competitors, squaring it, and adding them together:

$H = \sum_{i=1}^{N} S_i^2$ Where S_i is the market share of firm i in the market, and N is the number of firms

Example: Contrast ferry operators in the Irish sea with those in the North Sea. Hypothetically, in both cases the six largest operators could account for 90 per cent of the market: Irish Sea: All six firms have 15 per cent each, and in the North Sea: One firm has 80 per cent while the five others share 2 per cent each. Assume that the remaining 10 per cent of output is divided amongst ten equally sized operators. The six-firm concentration ratio would equal 90 per cent for both the Irish Sea case and the North Sea case. But the first case would promote significant competition, where the second case approaches monopoly. The Herfindahl index for these two states of affairs makes the lack of competition in the second case patently clear: Irish Sea: Herfindahl index = $6 * 0.15^2 + 10 * 0.01^2 = 0.136$ (13.6 per cent) – A HHI index below 0.15 indicates an unconcentrated index – indicating a competitive industry with no dominant players; whilst in the North Sea example, the Herfindahl index = $0.80^2 + 5 * 0.02^2 + 10 * 0.01^2 = 0.643$ (64.3 per cent) – A HHI index above 0.25 indicates high concentration.

Activity: try out the worksheet for the calculation of the HHI statistic under various scenarios commonly considered during merger reviews at http://www.unclaw.com/chin/teaching/antitrust/herfindahl.htm

Source: Markiewicz, D. (2012), 'Georgia Tech students see business opportunity in Vietnam, cleaner brick kilns', Atlanta Business News (online) Wednesday, April 11, 2012 - http://www.ajc.com/business/georgia-tech-students-see-1413722.html; Jensen, R. and Peppard, D. (2004), 'The Traditional Brickmaking Industry and the Rural Economy of Vietnam', Journal of Asian and African Studies June 2004 vol. 39 no. 3 193-207; Maithel, S. et al (2012), 'Brick Kilns Performance Assessment: A Roadmap for Cleaner Brick Production in India', www.catf.us/resources/publications/files/Brick_Kilns_Performance_Assessment.pdf

Neoclassical Competition spectrum

In order to understand competition there is a need for an awareness of the classification of markets and an appreciation of how competition within markets differs. Companies compete within markets and industries. This creates the context of where competition takes place. Thus the type of market defines the context. Several market types can be distinguished:

- **Perfectly competitive** – a market structure with many sellers, homogeneous products, free entry and exit, and where buyers and sellers have perfect knowledge of market conditions.

- **Monopolistic competition** – market structure of an industry in which there are many firms and freedom of entry and exit but in which each firm has a product somewhat differentiated from the others, giving it some control over its price.

- **Oligopoly** – a market structure that exists when a few sellers control the supply of a large proportion of a product. Because of the small number of competitors each organization has to consider how its actions will affect the decisions of its rivals (i.e. they are interdependent). This is particularly important with regard to pricing decisions. Consequently, competitors in such an industry will often compete through differentiation. Examples might include: the small number of banks who dominate the UK banking sector; the four companies (Tesco, Sainsbury's, Asda and Morrisons) share of the grocery market or the energy utility companies.

- **Monopoly** – there is a lack of competition and the industry is dominated by one firm of the market for particular goods or services, enabling the firm to determine price and supply and make abnormal profits. Such firms enjoy a protected position and economies of scale advantages. In many cases they are state controlled or recently privatized. Prior to deregulation many state owned utility companies were monopolies.

Competition

The market or competitive structure of an industry relates to the degree of competition firms in the industry experience. It is often depicted as a scale with very high levels of competition at one extreme (referred to as perfect competition) through to no competition at the other (monopoly). In reality most firms operate within these extremes and the lines between one form of competition and another are blurred. However, it is useful to think of four main competitive structures around which to model the behaviour of firms. We can then observe how an individual firm behaves and assess the extent to which that behaviour is congruent to the competitive structure it operates in and if it deviates from this modelled behaviour, why. We will deal with the major characteristics of each of these structures in turn.

Perfect Competition

There are a number of assumptions about the model of perfect competition, as the name 'perfect' would suggest. It is assumed that there are a large number of firms in the industry so much so that each has very little power over the market. Consumers are also assumed to have perfect knowledge of the market; in other words they know information about each firm in the market, the product offering and so on. This implies that firms are not in a position to be able to gain any short term advantages because customers would know about any such changes and be able to adjust their consumption decisions accordingly. In addition, it is assumed that the product they produce is homogenous, in other words, there is little or no difference in the product produced by one firm compared to another. This assumption is a fundamental characteristic of highly competitive markets. As a result, no individual firm can exercise any influence over the market and so each firm is a price taker – they have to accept the price determined in the market for the good as a whole. Perfect competition is characterized by freedom of entry and exit – it is, therefore, easy for any firm to enter the industry. If one firm, for some reason, was able to gain some short-term benefit which generated abnormal profit, new firms would enter to take advantage of the abnormal profit. The supply in the industry would increase and price would fall to a point where every firm was making normal profit.

Perfect competition does not exist in its purest form with all these assumptions in the business world. There are, however, a number of industries where some of these assumptions have some relevance. For example, if we take the dairy industry, the milk produced by cows does differ in terms of protein content and how rich it is; it can also be differentiated by being sold as full fat, semi-skimmed and skimmed. But to the average consumer one litre of milk is pretty much identical to another. There are around three quarter of a million dairy farmers in the industry in Europe. Each farmer produces a very small proportion of the total milk sales, estimated at around 135 billion litres a year. As a result, no individual farmer can adjust his or her output to have any influence on the market as a whole, which firms in other markets where they account for a large proportion of total sales may be in a position to do. Equally, there is very little any individual farmer can do to differentiate his/her product, even if some attempt is made to brand the product. In the long run all farmers in the industry make normal profit and entry and exit is relatively easy. There has been a significant fall in the number of dairy farmers across the EU in the last five years as highlighted by Figure 6.3.

FIGURE 6.3

EU dairy producer numbers, 2005–2009.

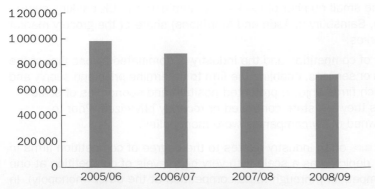

Source: © European Union, 1995–2011. Reproduced with permission.

In part this highlights the fact that where there are very high levels of concentration and little opportunity for firms to exercise any power in the market, profit levels tend to be relatively small in comparison with firms who can exercise market power. However, high levels of competition do not have to be synonymous with low profits; much will depend on the extent of the homogeneity of the product produced and the extent to which an individual producer can gain competitive advantage through lowering cost, especially in the supply chain.

Imperfect or Monopolistic Competition

This is exactly what firms in imperfect or monopolistic competition may be able to do. This competitive structure is also characterized by a relatively large number of firms but in this case the crucial difference is that the firm is able to exercise some power over the product to differentiate it in some way from its rivals. This is where the term 'monopolistic' comes from. Each firm is able to exploit a little monopoly on its own product. This will vary according to the type of business. Typical examples of firms operating in imperfectly competitive market structures include restaurants, conference organizers, plumbers, decorators, builders, solicitors, garden centres, coach hire, funeral directors, landscapers, tailors, fabric manufacturers and environmental consultants. Firms operating in these markets are likely to have many hundreds if not thousands of rivals but there are likely to be reasons why these firms are able to find some way of differentiating their offering from their rivals. This is what gives them some small element of monopoly power.

The opportunity for firms to differentiate their product in some way means that the characteristic of homogeneity outlined in perfect competition does not hold. Products cease to be perfect substitutes, therefore, and firms can find ways of making their product appear different in some way to that of their rivals. If successful, the firm can build up degrees of customer loyalty and possibly charge prices above those that might exist in perfect competition. This means the firm can have some control over the market and is not a price taker. The extent to which firms are able to influence the market will be dependent on the degree to which they can differentiate their product and whether they are able to persuade a sufficient number of customers to buy into this differentiation.

In monopolistic competition this may not always be possible. For example, a solicitor may decide to specialize in employment law and offer a specialism and expertise in this area of law. This may give it an advantage over rival solicitors who may offer a range of legal services without specializing in any one but there would be little to prevent any other solicitor from seeing the potential benefits of tapping into this market and developing a similar expertise. It may take some time for them to do so and this will have an effect on the extent to which a firm can maintain an advantage over its rivals before it is copied.

A restaurant may develop a particular offering based on organic produce and while it may gain a short-term advantage there would be little to stop any other restaurant from copying the idea. Entry and exit into and from the industry is relatively easy in monopolistic competition, therefore, and so abnormal profits tend to be competed away in the long-run unless the differentiation is distinctive and defensible. In the long-run firms in imperfect competition are likely to make normal profit unless they can retain the competitive advantage they build up.

In perfect competition we assumed that consumers had perfect knowledge of the market. In monopolistic or imperfect competition this assumption does not hold. As a result the market may become localized with consumers having knowledge of firms in their locality but not of possible competitors further afield. For example, an individual may require a firm to build an extension to their house; they look for building firms in their locality but there may be firms hundreds of miles away that offer a far better quality service at lower prices. It is unlikely that the individual will contact or even know of all builders in the country (or even outside) who could do the work and so knowledge of the market as a whole is fragmented. Firms may be aware of this and be able to exploit the local monopoly that exists.

The development of online sales via the Internet has affected some firms in that customers now have access to more information than may have been the case before the web. Review sites, the development of online retailers, blogs, comparison websites and so on do mean that customers have more opportunity of finding out about products, services and prices before making purchasing decisions and so increases the degree of knowledge in the market. Firms have to take this into consideration and adjust their offering to maintain a competitive edge. For example, some smaller hotels may have held some degree of local monopoly power; customers looking for hotel accommodation may have looked up hotels via a telephone directory such as Yellow Pages or Yellobook Europe. On booking the hotel the customer has little knowledge of the type of accommodation s/he will experience. With review sites such as TripAdvisor available via the Internet, potential customers can check the experience of others at the hotel prior to booking and make a more informed decision as a result. If a hotel gets a series of negative reviews it may find its bookings falling and as a result have to make changes to the way it operates to maintain competitiveness.

Many smaller firms have found that their market has been eroded by the existence of online retailers. The reason is often due to the fact that online retailers can offer wider choice, lower prices because they do not have expensive real estate to maintain, more convenience but also more information. Customers searching for books, for example, can relatively easily find not only new books at competitive prices but also second hand books, often at considerably lower prices. The transaction costs associated with online retailing are significantly lowered due to the increase in the information which consumers have at their fingertips and this has changed the way many businesses have to operate and has also led to the closure of a large number of businesses such as independent bookshops and music retailers.

Oligopoly

Oligopoly refers to competition amongst the few. In this competitive structure there might be a large number of firms but sales in the industry are dominated by a relatively small number of large firms. The proportion of firms accounting for total sales is referred to as the concentration ratio. A five firm concentration ratio of 78 per cent means that the top five firms in the industry account for 78 per cent of the total sales in that industry; a four firm concentration ratio of 84 per cent means that the top four firms account for 84 per cent of total sales and so on.

An oligopolistic market structure has a number of particular characteristics which may be present. Firms in an oligopoly may produce products which are relatively homogenous or be capable of some differentiation. Because of this it has been observed that prices in an oligopolistic market structure are relatively stable compared to other forms of imperfect competition and instead firms compete through various types of non-price competition such as branding, generating brand loyalty, promotions, advertising, management of the supply chain and emphasizing distinguishing features of its product or service.

Where firms perceive that their product offering is homogenous there is a high degree of substitutability between products in the industry. In addition, firms in an oligopoly are highly interdependent – they are very aware that the actions they take will be responded to by others and vice versa. If a firm considers changing its price (or takes any other action to gain some competitive edge) then it has to consider what its rivals will do.

Where products are relatively homogenous, there is little or no incentive to raise price because firms believe that their rivals **will not** follow suit. An increase in price will result in a loss of market share if this is the case because the demand curve facing the firm at prices higher than the prevailing price will be relatively elastic. If the firm raised its price by (say 5 per cent) customers would switch to buying from rivals and demand would fall by more than 5 per cent. This would reduce total revenue and thus not be a tactic worth pursuing.

If the firm contemplated reducing its price to gain market share, if it believed its rivals **would** follow suit then it might enter into a price war. If it lowered its price by 5 per cent its rivals would immediately do the same so the portion of its demand curve would be highly inelastic at prices below the prevailing price. Any benefit from reducing price would quickly disappear as rivals also reduced their prices and so total revenue would again fall. If the assumptions behind this model work in practice then the oligopolist faces a kinked demand curve and prices in the market will remain relatively stable or rigid. The theory of the kinked demand curve was developed by Paul Sweezy in 1939. It may help explain price rigidity in oligopolistic markets but one criticism of the theory is that it does not explain how firms set prices in the first instance.

If price competition is not an option for firms in this type of market structure then there may be a significant emphasis placed on developing the brand and seeking to create brand loyalty amongst customers. If a firm is able to do these things then it is better able to withstand competitive pressures from rivals. The fact that many larger organizations spend large sums of money on building brand awareness may be testament to the importance of this as a strategy in oligopolistic markets.

There are, of course, other ways in which firms might be able to improve their competitive position in relation to rivals and that is through collusion. In Europe collusion is illegal but the practice does go on and is often difficult to discover or prove (hence such agreements are often referred to as 'tacit collusion'). Collusion occurs where firms agree to fix prices, limit supply, divide up markets, arrange distribution agreements and share information. The incentive for rival firms is that they can gain some mutual benefit from collusive behaviour that leads to an improved outcome compared to a situation where such cooperation is not evident. For customers, such behaviour can mean higher prices, more limited choice and poorer quality service than might be the case if more competitive conditions prevailed.

The dominance of a relatively small number of large firms does mean that barriers to entry in oligopolistic markets are high; new firms are free to enter the industry but may find it very difficult to compete with established brands that have spent large sums of money over long periods of time to

BUSINESS IN ACTION

Anti-trust Behaviour

The European Commission has fined 17 producers of prestressing steel a total of €518 470 750 for operating a cartel that lasted 18 years until 2002 and covered all but three of the then European Union Member States. During 18 years, the companies fixed individual quotas and prices, allocated clients and exchanged sensitive commercial information. In addition, they monitored price, client and quota arrangements through a system of national co-ordinators and bilateral contacts. The first pan-European cartel meetings were held in Zurich, Switzerland, hence the 'Club Zurich' name it was initially referred to. Later it became 'Club Europe'. But there were also two regional branches, in Italy ('Club Italia') and in Spain/Portugal ('Club España'). The different branches were interconnected by overlapping territory, membership and common goals. The companies involved usually met in the margin of official trade meetings in hotels all over Europe. The Commission has evidence of over 550 cartel meetings.

The Commission decision concludes that the producers violated the European Union's ban on cartels and restrictive business practices. Prestressing steel comprises long, curled steel wires used with concrete in construction sites to make foundations, balconies or bridges. This is the fourth cartel decision since the

beginning of February bringing the total amount of anti-trust fines imposed so far in 2010 to € 1493 million.

'It is amazing how such a significant number of companies abused nearly the entire European construction market for such a long time and for such a vital product. This was almost as if they were acting in a planned economy,' said Joaquín Almunia, Commission Vice-President in charge of Competition, adding: 'the Commission will have no sympathy for cartelists; recidivists will be fined more and inability-to-pay claims will be accepted only when it is clear the fine would send a company into bankruptcy, which is rare even in the current difficult times.'

The following table lists the total maximum amounts that each group has to pay. Within each group there may be individual companies that are each liable for part or the total amount. In total, there are 36 companies concerned.

In setting the fines, the Commission takes into account the sales of the companies involved in the market concerned in the last year prior to the end of the cartel (2001), the very serious nature of the infringement, the geographic scope of the cartel and its long duration. The Commission increased the fines for ArcelorMittal Fontaine and ArcelorMittal Wire France by 60 per cent because they had already been fined twice for cartels in the steel sector. Saarstahl was also previously fined in the steel beams cartel, but received full immunity in the present cartel because it was the first to come forward with information under the Commission's 2002 Leniency Notice.

	Fine (€)	Includes reduction (%) under the Leniency Notice and for co-operation outside the Leniency Notice
1. ArcelorMittal (L, F, B, I)	276 480 000	20%
2. Emesa/Galycas/ArcelorMittal (España) (ES, L)	40 800 000	5% (Em/Gal)/20% (AM)/ 35% (AM es)
3. GlobalSteelWire/Tycsa (ES)	54 389 000	
4. Proderac (ES)	482 250	
5. Companhia Previdente/Socitrel (P)	12 590 000	
6. Fapricela (P)	8 874 000	
7. Nedri/HIT Groep (NL)	6 934 000	25% (Nedri)
8. WDI/Pampus (DE)	56 050 000	5%
9. DWK/Saarstahl (DE)	0	100%
10. voestalpine Austria Draht (AT)	22 000 000	
11. Rautaruukki/Ovako (FI/SE)	4 700 000	
12. Italcables/Antonini (I)	2 386 000	50%
13. Redaelli (I)	6 341 000	
14. CB Trafilati Acciai (I)	2 552 500	
15. I.T.A.S. (I)	843 000	
16. Ori Martin/Siderurgica Latina Martin (I)	19 800 000	
17. Emme Holding (I)	3 249 000	
TOTAL	518 470 750	

The Commission recognized the more limited participation of Proderac and Emme Holding by reducing their fine by 5 per cent.

Because of the very long duration of the cartel, the fines on several companies would have exceeded the legal maximum of 10 per cent of the 2009 turnover, and was therefore reduced to this level.

In addition, the Commission granted reductions of fines for cooperation under the 2002 Leniency Notice to Italcables/Antonini (50 per cent), Nedri (25 per cent), Emesa and Galycas (5 per cent), ArcelorMittal and its subsidiaries (20 per cent) and WDI/Pampus (5 per cent). The fine for ArcelorMittal España was reduced by 15 per cent for its co-operation outside the Leniency Notice. Redaelli and SLM did not meet the requirements for co-operation and therefore received no reduction of the fine.

Finally, the Commission accepted three inability-to-pay applications and granted reductions of respectively 25 per cent, 50 per cent and 75 per cent of the fine that would otherwise have been imposed.

Source: http://ec.europa.eu © European Union, 1995-2012. Reproduced with permission.

build up brand loyalty. To persuade customers to switch to new products is difficult in such circumstances and new firms may not have the financial muscle to be able to advertise and promote their products and gain market penetration.

Monopoly

The term 'monopoly' strictly means 'one producer' but the term is used fairly liberally in relation to competitive market structures. In a situation where there is only one producer in the industry, consumers have no choice about who to buy from. In this case it may be that there is a very good reason why only one producer is operating. This is a situation where a natural monopoly exists. In a natural monopoly, one firm is able to produce all the output at a cost which is lower than if there were more competitive conditions in the market. This is because the product requires significant capital to be able to operate efficiently and more than one producer would be increasingly inefficient. Examples include the utilities, gas, water and electricity. In these cases, it would be a waste of resources if several firms all provided distribution networks, all would have to operate on a smaller scale and so would not be able to gain the advantages of economies of scale. As a result, consumers might end up paying higher prices as well as having to put up with the externalities which come from having duplicate networks. Whilst a pure monopoly (where there is only one producer) implies that there are no substitutes, in practice this is rarely the case. If we are talking about utilities, for example, it might be thought that if there was only one gas supplier that consumers would have no choice at all but a substitute for gas might be electricity or oil which could also be used for cooking and heating.

The essence of monopoly, therefore, is control; the ability of a firm to exercise some control over the market in terms of pricing or setting supply. Because such control can arise in markets where a firm is not the only producer, it is appropriate to refer to degrees of monopoly power. The more control a firm has over the market the more monopoly power it has. This is why competition authorities will investigate acquisitions where firms gain in excess of 25 per cent market share. At this level of operation, a firm may well be able to exercise some degree of control over the market and thus exercise monopoly power.

The result of such monopoly power might include situations where customers pay higher prices, face more limited choices and receive a quality of product or service that is not as high as under more competitive conditions. However, whilst firms who are able to exercise monopoly power are viewed as bringing disadvantages to consumers, there are some benefits that arise from firms having monopoly power. See Figure 6.4.

Firstly, if a firm enjoys some monopoly power today, this does not mean that this power will continue tomorrow. Many firms will be mindful of the competitive pressures that exist and appreciate that if they stand still and ignore the needs of customers then others will eventually take over. There is still an incentive for firms with monopoly power to innovate, to focus on quality, value for money and take into account customer needs. Monopoly power is not synonymous with exploitation of the customer (or any other stakeholder).

In addition, there are certain types of firms where some element of monopoly power is essential to the development of new products and the provision of high quality services. Some firms provide specialist services or products to particular industries. One example of such specialist services are cranes to the petrochemical industry. Maintaining oil rigs, refineries and so on requires specialist knowledge and equipment and there might only be a very small number of firms with such knowledge and skills. The assumption that such firms would seek to exploit their monopoly power may not be the case in reality.

Firms in the pharmaceutical industry have to invest huge sums of money in research and development often over many years before the product comes to market and begins generating streams of income. The products they are developing are often at the leading edge of research and technology and there are considerable risks associated with the

FIGURE 6.4

Jenny knew that in order to have a Monopoly on the train set... she would have to either suppress her competition or attempt a merger.

Source: Patrick Currier (Media Select International)

development of these products. It is also the case that the benefits to the eventual customers of such products could be significant and even life-saving. In order to encourage such firms to undertake these risks there has to be some guarantee that the returns they will eventually make outweigh the costs associated. The granting of monopoly rights to production through patents and licences which create barriers to entry is essential in providing the incentive for firms to develop these new products.

Perspectives on competition

Whilst there are many stakeholders who can offer a perspective on competition, the three important perspectives considered here include those of the consumer, government and business. The consumer typically wants value, choice and convenience. Understanding what customers value is encapsulated within critical success factors – product features particularly valued by customers, hence, where the organization must outrival competition. From a business perspective, the goal of competitiveness is to increase sales and prosper. Competitiveness drives efficiency, differentiation, focus and the search for advantage. The government, on the other hand, must support business, ensuring competitiveness drives the prosperity of the nation and its people. Government must foster a climate that drives innovation, choice and price reduction. Consequently, as will be seen at the end of this chapter, government typically prohibits agreements that result in the prevention, restriction or distortion of competition.

STRUCTURE

↓

CONDUCT

↓

PERFORMANCE

The **traditional microeconomic view** of competition emphasizes the role of market structures in the market economy. This view is based on the *structure-conduct-performance* (SCP) paradigm. *Market structure* is described in terms of the number of firms operating, their concentration, entry conditions, level of vertical integration and diversification. The *conduct* or behaviour of firms is described in terms of a firm's goals, pricing and output decisions, degree of cooperation and interdependence, etc. A firm's *performance* is evaluated in terms of output, growth, profitability, employment and efficiency. The paradigm postulates a causal relationship between structure of a market, the conduct or behaviour of firms, and the performance of firms in the market. The SCP paradigm submits that a monopolistic market structure will lead to high prices, excess profit, and inefficiency in the use of resources, whilst a competitive market structure will lead to lower prices, normal profit and the efficient use of resources. The paradigm has influenced views on competition and helped focus attention on key areas.

COMPETITIVENESS (NATIONS)

Government plays a significant role in competition, particularly when home firms must compete with foreign firms either at home or abroad. Government actively encourages exports as a means to generate wealth for the nation. Historically, government actively discouraged imports, viewing this as wealth lost to other countries. In the previous section we outlined the meaning of trade. At the country level, theories of international trade seek to explain why trade occurs and how it can benefit the different parties to an exchange. Throughout history governments have actively intervened in international trade to maintain a trade surplus. This was achieved by banning or restricting (through tariffs or quotas) imports and subsidizing domestic producers whilst encouraging exports. In the 18th and early 19th century the theories of absolute and comparative advantage emerged.

Absolute advantage describes the ability of a country to produce goods more efficiently than any other country. A country with an absolute advantage can produce a greater output of goods or services than other countries, using the same amount or fewer resources. Under this theory, a country should concentrate on producing the goods in which it holds an absolute advantage. It can then trade with other countries to obtain the goods it needs but does not produce. Whilst this theory shows the gains from international trade, it raises the problem of what a country should do when it does not hold an absolute advantage in the production of any product. English economist, David Ricardo developed the theory of comparative advantage which suggests that trade is still beneficial even if one country is less efficient in the production of two goods, as long as it is less inefficient in the production of one of the goods. This theory states that a country specializes in producing the goods that it can produce more efficiently than any other goods. The absolute and comparative advantage theories, focusing on the productivity of the production process for a particular good, remained popular until the 20th century but were problematic in their main focus on labour as opposed to other resource types and their lack of consideration of transportation costs and transportation problems.

In economic theory, a country has a comparative advantage over another in the production of a good if it can produce it at a lower opportunity cost – this is the benefit, profit, or value of something that must be given up to acquire or achieve something else. Since every resource (land, money, time, etc.) can be set to alternative uses, every action, choice, or decision has an associated opportunity cost. That means it has to give up less labour and resources in other goods in order to produce it. Comparative advantage describes a situation in which a country, individual, company or region can produce a good at a lower opportunity cost than that of a competitor; the concept provides a fundamental insight into international economics. Comparative advantage is also a theory suggesting that specialization by countries can increase worldwide production. Comparative advantage results from different endowments of the factors of production (capital, land, labour) entrepreneurial skill, power resources, technology, etc. It therefore follows that free trade is beneficial to all countries, because each can gain if they specialize according to comparative advantage. Multinational organizations have the opportunity to benefit from the comparative advantage of different countries, be they technology driven or factor abundance driven, to reduce the total costs of production, particularly through the ever more popular method of fragmentation (slicing up the value chain) in which different parts (activities) of the production process are located in different countries.

Early in the 20th century an international trade theory emerged which focused attention on a country's resources. The **factor proportions** (Heckscher-Ohlin) theory is a trade theory suggesting that countries produce and export goods that require resources (factors) which are abundant and import goods that require resources in short supply. Whereas earlier theories focused on productivity, the factor proportions theory suggests a country specializes in producing and exporting goods using the factors of production that are most abundant and thus cheapest. Input resources (factors) include labour, land and capital equipment. Thus, a country with cheaper labour will specialize in products that require labour and a country with plenty of land will specialize in creating products that require land. However, studies examining trade flows between countries have not supported the factor proportions theory (FPT) despite its conceptual appeal.

Later, during the 1970s and 1980s the 'new trade theory' was proposed to explain trade patterns. This theory again emphasizes (like the comparative advantage theory) productivity, suggesting there are gains to be made from specialization and increasing economies of scale. Furthermore, those entities first to market may create barriers to entry. Later, in 1990, Michael Porter proposed a theory, 'national competitive advantage' (see competitiveness (national)), to explain why certain countries are leaders in the production of certain products. This theory emphasized the need for organizations to be both dynamic and innovative. Porter identified four elements, present to varying degrees in every country, that form the basis of national competitiveness, (1. factor conditions, 2. firm strategy, structure and rivalry, 3. demand conditions and 4. related and supporting industries) –referred to as the 'Porter Diamond'. The factor conditions element draws on factor proportions theory and is used to explain which products a country will produce and export. Factors include labour and natural resources but extend to skill levels, the technological infrastructure and country educational systems and research and development capabilities. Porter argues that sophisticated buyers in the home market are also important to national competitive advantage in a product area (demand conditions) as such buyers drive companies to develop products and services which satisfy their needs. Furthermore, a country industry characterized by high degrees of competition and rivalry will help those companies compete against imports and develop a presence in foreign markets. The framework/theory can be used both to analyze a firm's ability to function in a national market, as well as analyze the ability of a national market to compete in an international market.

Whereas mercantilism (an economic philosophy advocating that countries should simultaneously encourage exports and discourage imports) encouraged protectionism, later theories favoured free trade; free trade is simply trade in the absence of barriers. Over the past 50 years, through a variety of treaties and agreements, countries have set out to encourage free trade collectively. Many argue that the erection of barriers to competition results in less competitive organizations and industries, greater job losses and lower standards of living than would be the case under free trade. Thus far we have explained international trade according to access to resources and other advantages. There are challenges associated with trade across country borders. For example, the existence of distance-related barriers to trade. Whilst some studies do not consider location to be important, others find distance to be very important, i.e. the position of a country relative to other countries determines its market potential. The gravity model of international trade flows looks more closely at the link between distance and trade. Large countries with a common language and sharing a common border are more likely to trade with one another whilst landlocked countries and those with cultural differences are less likely to trade with one another. Furthermore the presence of transportation costs and other trade barriers impact upon international trade flows.

We have recognized that industries and firms from particular countries may be better placed to compete globally and at home because of factor conditions, firm strategy, structure and rivalry, demand conditions and related and supporting industries. Their respective country context may be a source of advantage but how can this be measured – how can we analyze countries to determine national competitiveness?

Global Competitiveness Index

The World Economic Forum (WEF) is an independent international organization committed to improving the state of the world by engaging business, political, academic and other leaders of society to shape global, regional and industry agendas. The World Economic Forum publishes a comprehensive series of reports which examine, in detail, the broad range of global issues it seeks to address with stakeholders as part of its mission of improving the state of the world. One of its most popular reports is the Global Competitiveness Report. The Global Competitiveness Report remains the most respected assessment of *national competitiveness*, providing a useful portrait of a nation's economic environment and its ability to achieve sustained levels of prosperity and growth (WEF 2011: p75). The report's competitiveness ranking is based on the Global Competitiveness Index (GCI), developed for the WEF and launched in 2005. Since its introduction in 2005, the GCI has been used by an increasing number of countries and institutions to benchmark national competitiveness. The GCI comprises 12 categories – the pillars of competitiveness – which together provide a comprehensive picture of a country's competitiveness landscape. The pillars are listed and described in Table 6.1. The rankings are calculated from both publicly available data and the Executive Opinion Survey, a comprehensive annual survey conducted by the Forum with its network of partner institutes. The survey is designed to capture a broad range of factors affecting an economy's business climate. The report contributes to the understanding of the key factors determining economic growth, helps to explain why some countries are more successful than others in raising income levels and opportunities for their respective populations, and offers policymakers and business leaders an important tool in the formulation of improved economic policies and institutional reforms. The report benchmarks the many factors underpinning national competitiveness.

WEF (2011: p4) define *competitiveness* as the set of institutions, policies and factors that determine the productivity level of a country. The level of productivity, in turn, sets the level of prosperity that can be earned by an economy. The productivity level also determines the rates of return obtained by investments in an economy, which in turn are the fundamental drivers of its growth rates. In other words, a more competitive economy is one that is likely to grow faster over time. The concept of competitiveness thus involves static and dynamic components: although the productivity of a country determines its ability to sustain a high level of income, it is also one of the central determinants of its returns to investment, which is one of the key factors explaining an economy's growth potential. There are many determinants driving productivity and competitiveness. Many are captured as indicators used to measure the GCI's twelve pillars.

Whilst all of the pillars described will matter, to a certain extent, for all economies, it is clear the pillars will affect different economies in different ways: In line with the economic theory of **stages of development**, the GCI assumes that, in the first stage, the economy is factor-driven and countries compete, based on their factor endowments – primarily unskilled labour and natural resources. As a country becomes more competitive, productivity will increase and wages will rise alongside

TABLE 6.1   The 12 pillars of (national) competitiveness

Basic requirements	Institutions	The institutional environment (which should be sound and fair) is determined by the legal and administrative framework within which individuals, firms, and governments interact to generate wealth. Government attitudes toward markets and freedoms and the efficiency of its operations are also very important: excessive bureaucracy and red tape, overregulation, corruption, dishonesty in dealing with public contracts, lack of transparency and trustworthiness, and political dependence of the judicial system impose significant economic costs to businesses and slow the process of economic development.	for factor-driven economies
	Infrastructure	Extensive and efficient infrastructure is critical for ensuring the effective functioning of the economy – developed infrastructure reduces the effect of distance between regions, integrating the national market and connecting it at low cost to markets in other countries. A well-developed transport and communications infrastructure network is a prerequisite for the access of less-developed communities to core economic activities and services. Effective modes of transport enable entrepreneurs to get their goods and services to market in a secure and timely manner and facilitate the movement of workers to the most suitable jobs. Economies also depend on electricity supplies that are free of interruptions and shortages so that businesses and factories can work unimpeded. A solid and extensive telecommunications network allows for a rapid and free flow of information, which increases overall economic efficiency by helping to ensure that businesses can communicate and decisions are made by taking into account all available relevant information.	
	Macroeconomic environment	The economy cannot grow in a sustainable manner unless the macro environment is stable. The government cannot provide services efficiently if it has to make high-interest payments on its past debts. Running fiscal deficits limits the government's future ability to react to business cycles. Firms cannot operate efficiently when inflation rates are out of hand.	
	Health & primary education	A healthy workforce is vital to a country's competitiveness and productivity. Investment in the provision of health services is thus critical. Basic education increases the efficiency of each individual worker. Lack of basic education can therefore become a constraint on business development, with firms finding it difficult to move up the value chain by producing more sophisticated or value-intensive products.	

Efficiency enhancers	Higher Ed. / training	This pillar measures secondary and tertiary enrolment rates as well as the quality of education as evaluated by the business community. Quality higher education and training is crucial for economies that want to move up the value chain beyond simple production processes and products.
	Goods market efficiency	Healthy market competition, both domestic and foreign, is important in driving market efficiency and thus business productivity by ensuring that the most efficient firms, producing foods requires a minimum of impediments to business activity through government intervention. Market efficiency also depends on demand conditions such as customer orientation and buyer sophistication. This can create an important competitive advantage, as it forces companies to be more innovative and customer oriented and thus imposes the discipline necessary for efficiency to be achieved in the market.
	Labour market efficiency	Efficient labour markets must ensure a clear relationship between worker incentives and their efforts to promote meritocracy at the workplace, and they must provide equity in the business environment between women and men. Taken together these factors have a positive effect on worker performance and the attractiveness of the country for talent.
	Financial market development	Economies require sophisticated financial markets that can make capital available for private-sector investment from such sources as loans from a sound banking sector, well-regulated securities exchanges, venture capital, and other financial products. In order to fulfil all those function, the banking sector needs to be trustworthy and transparent, and financial markets need appropriate regulation to protect investors and other actors in the economy.
	Technological readiness	This pillar measures the agility with which an economy adopts existing technologies to enhance the productivity of its industries, with specific emphasis on its capacity to fully leverage information and communication technologies (ICT) in daily activities and production processes for increased efficiency and competitiveness.
	Market size	Market size affects productivity – large markets allow firms to exploit economies of scale.
Innovation factors	Business sophistication	Business sophistication concerns two elements that are intricately linked: the quality of a country's overall business networks and supporting industries, as measured by the quantity and quality of local suppliers and the extent of their interaction, is important for a variety of reasons. When companies and suppliers from a particular sector are interconnected in geographically proximate groups, called dusters, efficiency is heightened, greater opportunities for innovation in processes and products are created, and barriers to entry for new firms are reduced. Individual firms' advanced operations and strategies (branding, marketing, distribution, advanced production processes, and the production of unique and sophisticated products) spill over into the economy and lead to sophisticated and modern business processes across the country's business sectors.
	Innovation	Progression requires an environment that is conducive to innovative activity, supported by both the public and the private sectors. In particular, it means sufficient investment in research and development (R&D), especially by the private sector, the presence of high-quality scientific research institutions; extensive collaboration in research between universities and industry; and the protection of intellectual property.

↑ for Efficiency-driven economies

↑ for Innovation economies

Pillars are not independent – they reinforce each other, and a weakness in one area often has a negative impact on other areas.

Source: © 2011 the World Economic Forum. Reproduced with thanks to the World Economic Forum.

BUSINESS IN DEBATE

UK GCI

The United Kingdom (10th) benefits from clear strengths such as the efficiency of its labour market (7th), in sharp contrast to the rigidity of those of many other European countries and continues to have sophisticated (8th) and innovative (13th) businesses that are highly adept at harnessing the latest technologies for productivity improvements and operating in a very large market (it is ranked 6th for market size). All these characteristics are important for spurring productivity enhancements. On the other hand, although improved since last year, the country's macroeconomic environment (85th) represents the greatest drag on its competitiveness, with a double-digit fiscal deficit in 2010 (placing the country 138th) that must be restrained to provide a more sustainable economic footing moving into the future. The situation is made worse by the mounting public debt (77 per cent of GDP in 2010, 120th) and a comparatively low national savings rate (12.3 per cent of GDP in 2010, 119th).

Respondents were asked to select the five most problematic factors for doing business in their country (the UK) and to rank them. Respondents ranked tax rates as the most problematic factor in the UK, followed by access to financing, inefficient government bureaucracy, tax regulations and Inflation (2011, p360). These were similar to the US though US respondents considered inefficient government bureaucracy more problematic than access to financing.

Source: © 2011 the World Economic Forum. Reproduced with thanks to the World Economic Forum.

FIGURE 6.5
UK Global Competitiveness Index

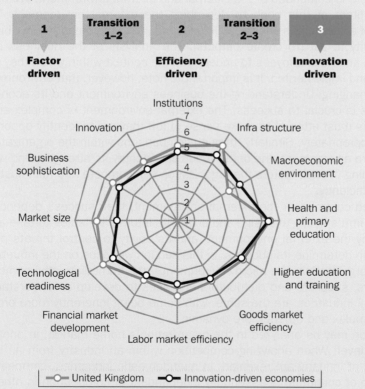

Source: © 2011 the World Economic Forum. Reproduced with thanks to the World Economic Forum.

advancing development. Countries will then move into the efficiency-driven stage of development, when they must begin to develop more efficient production processes and increase product quality. Finally, as countries move into the innovation-driven stage, wages will have risen to such an extent that they are able to sustain those higher wages and the associated standard of living only if their businesses are able to compete with new and unique products. At this stage, companies must compete by producing new and different goods, using the most sophisticated production processes (pillar 11) and by innovating new ones (pillar 12).

The top ten competitive countries for 2011/12 remain dominated by European countries, such as Switzerland, Sweden, Finland, Denmark, Germany, the UK and the Netherlands. A summary of the UK GCI profile is shown below.

In summary, we have outlined the country factors that may impact upon the competitiveness of a nation. We discussed factor conditions, firm strategy, structure and rivalry, demand conditions and related and supporting industries. With reference to WEF (2011) we then defined competitiveness as the set of institutions, policies, and factors determining a country's level of productivity. The level of productivity, in turn, sets the level of prosperity that can be earned by an economy. Finally we presented an analytical framework (the GCI) to benchmark countries. However, whilst this helps us understand why some countries seem more prosperous than others, we must remember that it is firms who compete with each other, not countries. The actions of governments, country resources and infrastructure can enable firms but they must still compete with each other. Consequently, in the next section we turn our attention to the competitive conduct of firms.

COMPETITIVENESS (FIRMS)

The business environment is comprised of the external and internal environment. We have devoted the previous four chapters of this book to describing the external environment. The internal environment consists of all resources and capabilities found within the organization which influence the organization's ability to act (to create outputs). The analysis of the business environment allows the organization and its employees to understand the context within which they operate and strategy is developed and implemented. It is important to note, however, that environments are not static but constantly changing. Understanding the business environment and its economic, social and political influences is crucial to success. The external environment is complex and its future uncertain, yet managers must attempt to make sense of it if they are to identify opportunities and threats and respond appropriately. Similarly, through comparisons within the organization and with competitors in the micro environment, the organization can identify its strengths and weaknesses. Through an understanding of such factors the organization can compete and fulfil customer needs more effectively and efficiently.

As firms have limited control over the external environment, their success depends upon how well they adapt to it. A firm's ability to design and adjust its internal variables to take advantage of opportunities offered by the external environment, and its ability to control threats posed by the same environment, help determine its success. In this section we focus on the influences (forces) that are closer to the organization, the micro-environment – the immediate environment including customers, competitors, suppliers and distributors and seek to develop an understanding of the industry context. Not all industries are the same, with some being inherently more profitable than others, some more complex and others more dynamic.

Firm-level competition may be analyzed in the organization's home market, in another specific country or at a global level. When analyzing competition within an industry from an international perspective, two types of industry are revealed. In multidomestic industries, competition in each country (or small group of countries) is essentially independent of competition in other countries, i.e. there is a particular industry present in many countries but competition occurs on a country-by-country basis. The international industry becomes a collection of domestic industries – hence the term multidomestic. At the other end of the spectrum are global industries. A global industry is an industry in which a firm's competitive position in one country is significantly influenced by its position in other countries. In such cases rivals compete against each other on a truly worldwide basis (Porter 1986). As a part of environmental analysis, the organization should seek to identify, as precisely as possible, the market within which it is operating. Scholars and practitioners alike strive continuously to perfect their knowledge of what makes some organizations perform better than others. A matter we investigate next.

Competitive advantage (External focus)

In order to win business from competitors and grow market share, companies must distinguish themselves from rivals, they must develop advantages that enable them to compete. We discussed competitive advantage in the final section of the previous chapter. When analyzing the competitive environment, the firm must understand both how it seeks to compete and how its rivals will compete. Whilst a PESTLE analysis would help make sense of the macro business environment it would not provide the detailed understanding needed to compete in the industry. Consequently, in this section we consider tools such as the five forces framework to enable a more detailed understanding of the business environment at the industry and specific firm level.

Porter's five forces framework (Competitive forces model – Five competitive forces), see Figure 6.6, can help in identifying the sources of competition in an industry. An organization must confront (1) rivalry of competitors within its industry, (2) threat of new entrants, (3) threat of substitutes, (4) the bargaining power of customers and (5) the bargaining power of suppliers – together these *determine* competition in an industry or market. This framework is used to determine the competitive intensity and therefore attractiveness (the overall industry profitability) of a market. Average industry profitability is influenced by both potential and existing competitors. Assessing industry attractiveness includes an analysis of entry barriers such as the scale of investment required, the cost and time to establish a brand name and differentiated products. Analysis extends to consideration of substitution threats which may be affected by switching costs. An 'unattractive' industry is one where the combination of forces act to drive down overall profitability. They consist of those forces close to a company which affect its ability to serve customers and make a profit. The ultimate *profit potential of an industry* is governed by the collective strength of the five forces; organizations in certain industries typically earn high profits whilst organizations in other industries may earn relatively low profits; the weaker the forces collectively, however, the greater the opportunity for better performance. Some scholars believe the corporate strategist's goal is to find a position in the industry where his or her company can best defend itself against these forces or can influence them in its favour (positioning). The organization must probe below the surface and analyze each force. For example, what makes the industry vulnerable to entry by new competitors (who steal market share and reduce opportunity) and what determines the

FIGURE 6.6
Competitive forces

bargaining power of suppliers or customers (who may increase costs or reduce margins)? Knowledge of these underlying sources is used by the organization to inform action. New entrants to an industry bring new capacity, the desire to gain market share, and often considerable resources. However, they may face barriers to entry such as economies of scale, capital requirements, the need for access to distribution channels and political limitations. The threat of entry changes, as these conditions change. Suppliers can exert bargaining power on participants in an industry by raising prices or reducing the quality of purchased goods and services. Powerful suppliers can thereby squeeze profitability out of an industry. A company can improve its strategic posture by finding suppliers or buyers who possess the least power to influence it adversely. Rivalry amongst existing competitors takes the familiar form of jockeying for position – using tactics like price competition, product introduction, and advertising. Intense rivalry is related to the presence of a number of factors: competitors are numerous or are roughly equal in size and power; industry growth is slow; the product or service lacks differentiation or switching costs; fixed costs are high or the product is perishable and exit barriers are high.

The five forces framework focuses an industry's potential for profit. Next we must determine how such profit is shared between the different organizations competing in that industry. To do this we must identify the key success factors – who the customers are and what their needs are, and how they choose between competing offerings. We must understand what customers want and what the organization must do in order to survive competition. Competitive analysis involves the systematic collection and analysis of public information about rivals (competitive intelligence) in order to predict and determine future rival behaviour. Strategic analysis should not be restricted to the present actions of competitors. The organization should also think through future competitive behaviour – competitors do not stand still. Forecasting what they may do in the future enables the organization to contemplate moves that maintain or enhance their competitive position.

McGahan (2000) argues that improved corporate performance hinges on understanding how industries evolve and that the main framework currently in use for this purpose is the product life cycle model. The Product-Life-Cycle (PLC) framework is based on the idea that industries move through periods of emergence, shake-out, maturity and decline. McGahan believes that rigorous analysis of industry evolution is necessary to anticipate when different kinds of opportunities are likely to emerge over time. Analyzing industry evolution can generate compelling insights into emerging opportunities, which may reveal critical weaknesses in the old approaches of organizations. The first analytical step involves taking a snapshot of the current environment.

The industry life cycle is used to describe change within an industry, see Figure 6.7. Producers introduce their offerings as the industry emerges, however, sales are initially small and products less well-known. New industries tend to begin in high income countries. It takes time for the customer base to grow until saturation is reached (maturity stage) whereupon any demand is wholly for replacement. Finally the industry enters decline as it is challenged by new industries and customer needs change. The different stages of the industry life cycle place differing demands on organizations. Changes in demand growth and technology over the cycle have implications for industry structure, competition, and the sources of competitive advantage. Creativity and

FIGURE 6.7
Industry life cycle

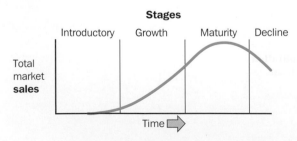

innovation in the form of product development are responsible for the birth of the industry. With time comes a greater emphasis on process innovation. In the introduction phase, products may be of a poorer quality and more costly to produce. Low demand necessitates short production runs and the use of more specialized distribution channels. As demand grows in other countries, they are serviced initially by exports. Customers tend to be high income early adopters, probably located in advanced countries. At this stage there may be few competitors. There is increased demand in the growth phase, placing pressure on production processes and often leading to capacity shortages. Geographical scope is likely to increase as customers are likely to emerge in more places, yet with the increased demand comes increased competition. Competitors will seek to develop their brand and will design the product with quality and manufacture in mind. Competitors start to consider standardization and process innovation. Once the industry reaches the maturity stage, customers are more knowledgeable and have increased bargaining power. This may result in organizations lowering prices, particularly if the product becomes commoditized. Consequently organizations tend to differentiate through branding and other tactics. Repeat buying is likely, forcing organizations to focus on customer relationship management. Increased competition is likely to result in overcapacity and a focus on price is likely to result in the selection of different manufacturing processes that emphasize longer production runs or flexibility. The value chain is more likely to be fragmented, with aspects of production located in developing countries (international migration of production). Mature industries tend to be more stable and efficiency goals are likely to be met through bureaucracy. Efficiency is achieved through standardized routines and tight control. Finally as the industry enters decline, differentiation and innovation become unprofitable and increased overcapacity is observed. This may result in the pursuit of cost reduction strategies and price based competition (price wars), thus the intensity and nature of competition changes during the course of the industry life cycle; rivalry increases with time, as do the number of competitors and there is a shift to price-based competition. Rivalry is accompanied by a reduction in margin. Competitive advantage, from an internal perspective, will be considered further in Chapter 10.

Throughout this section we have discussed the competitive behaviour of the firm, in the context of country competitiveness. Such behaviour is influenced by regulation in the form of laws and rules and systems of governance at the national, regional and global level. Each will be explained in the final section.

REGULATION: COMPETITION LAW

Competition is viewed by the authorities as a process of rivalry between suppliers (i.e. firms) seeking to win customer business over time by offering them a better deal. Rivalry may take various forms. Firms may seek to undercut each other on price, produce more output, outperform each other by reducing costs, improving quality, enhancing productivity or increasing innovation to create new or improved products or markets. For customers, rivalry can therefore have many beneficial effects, for instance by driving down prices, by increasing output and by improving quality and variety. However, competition places firms under constant pressure to offer the best possible range of goods at the best possible prices because if they do not, consumers can buy elsewhere. Consequently, sometimes companies try to limit competition. Some firms attempt to distort free competition and adopt anti-competitive behaviour to impose their own rules on the market. Firms carrying out similar activities may come to arrangements with each other to control prices or to divide up the market among themselves. A firm that holds a dominant position in a market may also abuse this position and exclude its competitors from the market.

Competition law (known in the United States as antitrust law), is law that promotes or maintains market competition by regulating anti-competitive conduct by companies. See Table 6.2. Competition law has three main elements: (1) prohibiting agreements or practices that restrict free trading and competition between business e.g. cartels; (2) banning abusive behaviour by a firm dominating a market, or anti-competitive practices that tend to lead to

TABLE 6.2   Prohibited anti-competitive practices

Anti-competitive agreements	Agreements likely to be prohibited include those which: fix the prices to be charged for goods or services, limit production, carve up markets and discriminate between customers (charge different prices or impose different terms where there is no difference in what is being supplied). Such agreements prevent, restrict or distort competition.
Cartels	Cartels are the most serious form of anti-competitive agreement. They are agreements between businesses not to compete with each other.
Abuse of a dominant market position	A dominant market position occurs when a business is able to behave independently of competitive pressures, such as other competitors in that market. Conduct which may be considered an abuse by a business in a dominant position includes: charging excessively high prices, limiting production, refusing to supply an existing long standing customer without good reason, charging different prices to different customers where there is no difference in what is being supplied, and making a contract conditional on factors that have nothing to do with the subject of the contract

such a dominant position (predatory pricing, tying, refusal to deal); and (3) supervising the mergers and acquisitions of large corporations, including some joint ventures. Mergers refer to all types of arrangements that may give rise to two or more enterprises ceasing to be distinct. Transactions that are considered to threaten the competitive process can be prohibited altogether, or approved subject to 'remedies'. Important objectives of such laws and regulations include protecting the interests of consumers (consumer welfare) and ensuring that entrepreneurs have an opportunity to compete. Furthermore, aside from stimulating competition through regulation of company behaviour, as was seen in Chapter 2 and earlier in this chapter, government intervention can play a role in promoting innovation and entrepreneurship, thereby enhancing the competitive advantage of nations. Competition policy is about making sure that companies compete with each other on an equal footing – on the basis of their products and prices – with no unfair advantages. In the final part of this chapter we will explore competition policy at the national, regional and global level.

National regulation: UK competition law

The political and legal environment and the legislative process were introduced in Chapter 2. In this section we consider competition law in the UK, specifically as an example of national regulation and intervention. UK competition law is affected by both British and European elements (considered in the next section). The Competition Act 1998 (CA98) and the Enterprise Act 2002 are the most important statutes for cases with a purely national dimension. However, if the effect of a business' conduct would reach across borders, the European Union has competence to deal with the problems, and exclusively EU law would apply. Like all competition law, UK competition law has three main tasks, outlined in the introduction to this section. The Office of Fair Trading (OFT) and the Competition Commission (CC) are the two primary regulatory bodies for competition law enforcement. The OFT has a wide range of powers to investigate businesses suspected of breaching these laws and can take enforcement action. Businesses who break the law can be fined up to 10 per cent of their worldwide turnover. In addition, individuals found to be involved in cartels can be fined and imprisoned for up to five years and directors of companies who breach the prohibitions can be disqualified for up to 15 years. Competition law is closely connected with law on deregulation of access to markets, state aids and subsidies, the privatization of state-owned assets and the establishment of independent sector regulators. Specific 'watchdog' agencies such as Ofgem, Ofcom and Ofwat are charged with overseeing how operation of those specific markets work. The OFT and the Competition Commission's work is confined to the rest.

In the UK anti-competitive behaviour is prohibited in two main ways: firstly, anti-competitive agreements (e.g. cartels) between businesses are prohibited by Chapter I of the Competition Act 1998 (CA98) and Article 81 of the EC Treaty and secondly, abuse of a dominant position in a market is prohibited by Chapter II of CA98 and Article 82 of the EC Treaty. The laws contained in the CA98 and Articles 81 and 82 of the EC Treaty are similar but not the same: the CA98 prohibits anti-competitive behaviour affecting trade in the UK. Articles 81 and 82 prohibit anti-competitive behaviour affecting trade in the EU. The Enterprise Act 2002 is an Act of the UK Parliament which made major changes to UK competition law with respect to mergers. The provisions of the Act are complementary to those of the Competition Act 1998, which remains in force. The Act amends the existing framework for control of UK mergers and acquisitions; decisions on merger control will, in general, be taken by the OFT. Mergers will be assessed against a pure competition test – generally, mergers will be prohibited, or remedies required, if they would result in a substantial lessening of competition in a UK market. The OFT may investigate mergers which meet either the 'turnover test' or the 'share of supply test'. The turnover test is met if the target company has a UK turnover exceeding £70 million. The share of supply test is met if the merging parties will together supply at least 25 per cent of goods or services of a particular description, either in the UK as a whole or in a substantial part of it. This test is only met if the share of supply increases as a result of the merger.

Theories of harm are drawn up by the authorities to provide the framework for assessing the effects of a merger and whether or not it could lead to a 'substantial lessening of competition' (SLC) – reduction of the beneficial effects of rivalry, creating an 'adverse effect' for consumers. They describe possible changes arising from the merger, any impact on rivalry and expected harm to customers as compared with the situation likely to arise without the merger (referred to as the *counterfactual*). The authorities seek to understand the commercial rationale for the transaction from the perspective of each of the parties concerned. In formulating theories of harm, the authorities consider how rivalry might be affected. In considering the SLC test, the authorities conduct their analysis under a variety of headings such as market definition; measures of con-centration; efficiencies; entry and expansion; and countervailing buyer power. The authorities identify the market within which the merger may give rise to an SLC (the relevant market). There are normally two dimensions to the definition of the relevant market: a product dimension and a geographic dimension. Markets may also be defined by reference to customer group or temporal factors. The relevant product market is a set of products that customers consider to be close substitutes, for example in terms of utility, brand or quality. The relevant geographic market may be local, regional, national or wider. Imports may be taken into account as well as UK products. As part of their assessment of the effects of a merger on competition, the authorities may use market share and measures of concentration, assessed on the relevant market. Market share of firms in the market, both in absolute terms and relative to each other, can give an indication of the potential extent of a firm's market power. The combined market share of the merger firms, when compared with their respective pre-merger market share, can provide an indication of the change in market power resulting from a merger. A straightforward count of the firms in a market is a basic measure of concentration. Concentration ratios (see the opening section of this chapter) measure the aggregate market share of a small number (three or four generally) of the leading firms in a market (e.g. the three-firm concentration ratio, or C3, shows the proportion of the market supplied by the three leading firms). As was noted earlier in this chapter, the ratios are absolute in value and take no account of differences in the relative size of the firms which make up the leading group. Thus the Herfindahl-Hirschman Index (HHI) measure of market concentration may be used. The absolute level of the HHI post-merger can provide an indication of the change in market structure resulting from the merger. In relation to market share, previous OFT decisions for mergers in markets where products are undifferentiated suggest that combined market share of less than 40 per cent will not often give the OFT cause for concern. In relation to the number of firms, previous

BUSINESS IN ACTION

Television LCD screen cartel

In 2001–06, Asian producers of LCD screens formed a cartel, agreeing prices and exchanging sensitive information on large screens for TV and computer applications. The six producers involved were: Samsung Electronics and LG Display (Korea), AU Optronics, Chimei InnoLux Corporation, Chunghwa Picture Tubes and HannStar Display Corporation (Taiwan). The cartel had a direct impact upon European consumers, as most LCD TVs, computer monitors and notebooks come from Asia. The Commission fined the companies €649m. Samsung received full immunity for reporting the cartel and providing valuable evidence. The other companies faced reduced fines due to their cooperation.

Source: http://ec.europa.eu/competition/consumers/ how/index_en.html © European Union, 1995-2012. Reproduced with permission.

OFT decisions in mergers involving retailers suggest that the OFT has not usually been concerned about mergers that reduce the number of firms in the market from five to four (or above).

Regional regulation and the EU

EU competition policy ensures competition is not distorted in the internal market by guaranteeing that similar rules apply to all the companies operating within in it. In the previous section we pointed to key EU regulations associated with competition law (Articles 81 and 82 of the Treaty of Amsterdam – see also Articles 101 and 102 TFEU). The European Commission ensures the correct application of EU competition rules. To preserve well-functioning product markets, authorities like the Commission must prevent or correct anti-competitive behaviour. The Commission monitors:

* agreements between companies that restrict competition
* abuse of a dominant position
* mergers
* efforts to open markets up to competition (liberalization)
* financial support (state aid) for companies from EU governments
* cooperation with national competition authorities in EU countries

The European Commission brings cases in a wide variety of different sectors of industrial activity, affecting many products often used by consumers. In some instances, these cases may cover products directly used by consumers, whilst in others the cases may relate to products or materials further up the supply chain. The Court of Justice is the main European judicial body ensuring uniform interpretation and application of competition law across the EU.

The final section offers a brief outline of the present state of International Competition Policy, considering the work of key international institutions such as the WTO, OECD and UN.

International Competition Policy and the WTO

The protection of international competition is governed by international competition agreements. The WTO was introduced in Chapter 2 when we discussed 'doing business globally'. In that section we noted the WTO It is a key global organization, dealing with the rules of trade between nations. At its heart are the WTO agreements, negotiated and signed by the bulk of the world's trading nations and ratified in their parliaments. The goal is to help producers of goods and services, exporters and importers conduct their business. At the WTO the Interaction between Trade and Competition Policy is one of the so-called 'new issues'. At the 1996 Ministerial Conference in Singapore the ministers

BUSINESS IN ACTION

The antitrust case against Microsoft Corporation

Microsoft refused to share certain (interoperability) information with rival vendors that would allow other products to interact with its own products, and later charged unreasonable prices for the information it was ordered to share; whilst also forcing customers to purchase its Windows Media Player product by 'tying' it to Windows. These are crucial issues. For example, many of the recent benefits technology has brought to the economy and lifestyles are made possible by interoperability (the ability of different products and services to work together). Companies who undermine interoperability hurt hundreds of millions of computer users across the EU. Likewise, if there was a company with a monopoly in toothbrushes customers would not want to be forced to buy toothpaste from the same company. This type of problem is why the Commission did not want computer users to be deprived of choice with regard to media players. In its 2004 finding the Commission ordered Microsoft to address these issues. Microsoft contested these findings and continued to stifle innovation until October 2007, by overcharging other companies for the essential information they needed to offer interoperable software products to computer users around the world. In September 2007, Microsoft lost their appeal against the Commission's case. The Commission's initial decision and the later non-compliance by Microsoft led to record fines of €1.677 billion. Since this, Microsoft has released more extensive interoperability information and has moved from insisting on charging between 2.98 per cent and 3.87 per cent of a licensee's product revenues for relevant interoperability information, to a flat fee of €10 000 and an optional worldwide patent licence for just 0.4 per cent of licensees' product revenues. Furthermore, Microsoft sells a version of its flagship operating system without Windows Media Player.

Source: http://ec.europa.eu © European Union, 1995–2012. Reproduced with permission.

decided to establish two working groups to look at how trade relates to competition policies. The Working Group on the Interaction between Trade and Competition Policy (WGTCP) was set up to study various aspects of this issue, with the participation of all WTO Members. At the WTO Ministerial Conference in Doha (2001), Ministers 'recognized the case for a multilateral framework to enhance the contribution of competition policy to international trade and development, and the need for enhanced technical assistance and capacity-building in this area'. However, at the Ministerial Conference in Cancun (2003), no consensus could be reached on modalities for negotiations in this area, although ministers 'reaffirmed all their Doha Declarations and Decisions and recommitted themselves to working to implement them fully and faithfully'; members failed to reach a consensus on the content of possible rules, mostly due to the objections of developing countries. Later, the WTO General Council decided the issue of competition policy 'will not form part of the Work Programme set out in that Declaration and therefore no work towards negotiations on any of these issues will take place within the WTO during the Doha Round'. The Working Group is currently inactive. Even though competition policy was deleted from the Doha agenda, anti-competitive practices continue to attract attention. The growth of cartels and boom (until the 2008 financial crisis) in cross-border mergers and acquisitions (M&As) raised concerns about possible negative impacts. Whilst developed countries generally enforce competition policies at the national level, many developing countries do not. What is more, cross-border practices often escape the scope of national governments (except possibly EU and US authorities). Therefore, several international institutions – the Organization for Economic Cooperation and Development (OECD), the International Competition Network (ICN), the United Nations Conference on Trade and Development (UNCTAD), and the WTO – actively discuss the creation of international frameworks to shape competition policy. Although WTO negotiations on an international competition regime have stalled, some countries have addressed competition policy issues in their bilateral or regional agreements. Despite this, many remain convinced of the need for a multilateral agreement on competition policy.

SUMMARY

- Throughout this book we have focused on the analysis of environmental factors (forces) that may determine organizational decisions, particularly those of a competitive nature. We started out by considering macro environmental forces (PESTLE) and, throughout this chapter, have developed an understanding of the micro (competitive) environment.
- From a competitive perspective we have introduced the concept of advantage at the firm and national levels, and recognized the need for such advantages to be sustainable if the organization is to deliver superior long term performance.
- The competitive forces framework was introduced to analyze industry structure, and the Resource-based perspectives also introduced direct consideration to the internal environment.
- Teece, Pisano and Shuen (1997) argued that winners in the global marketplace are organizations who can demonstrate timely responsiveness and rapid and flexible product innovation, coupled with the management capability to coordinate and redeploy internal and external competencies effectively. They advance the argument that the competitive advantage of organizations lies with its managerial and organizational processes (the way things are done), shaped by its specific asset position (resources to hand), and the available paths (strategic alternatives). Readers of this chapter should now be better placed to analyze competition using a variety of theoretical approaches, frameworks, tools and techniques.

REVISION QUESTIONS

1. Define (in your own words) the key concepts associated with the competitive environment (i.e. Competition| Competitive Advantage| Competitive Environment| Competitive Factors| Competitiveness| Five Competitive Forces| Internal Environment |Micro Environment |Rivalry).
2. Discuss the consumer, government and business perspectives on competition and evaluate potential sources of conflict.
3. List and describe the factors influencing the level of competition.
4. Evaluate the contribution of the structure-conduct-performance (SCP) paradigm to theories of business competition.
5. Contrast two methods used to measure concentration.
6. List and describe factors used for analysing the competitiveness of nations.
7. Explain the Porter's five forces framework (Competitive forces model) and the industry life cycle, evaluating their use in the analysis of firm competitiveness.
8. Explain how analysis of a firm's internal environment enriches our understanding of firm competitiveness.
9. Discuss the role and purpose of competition policy and law at the national, regional and global level.
10. Identify methods used for the classification of markets and explain how competition within markets differs.

DISCUSSION QUESTIONS

1. Activity: try out the worksheet for the calculation of the HHI statistic under various scenarios commonly considered during merger reviews at http://www.unclaw.com/chin/teaching/antitrust/herfindahl.htm Discuss the application of the HHI when analyzing industries to determine whether mergers should be allowed (because of potential adverse impacts on competition).
2. How useful is the Global Competitiveness Index (GCI), developed by the WEF?

3. Select an industry and identify a number of rivals operating within it. Discuss the application of the Competitive forces model and evaluate its usefulness in helping companies understand how to compete.

4. Discuss how an understanding of the industry life cycle may be used to help companies focus their competitive strategies.

5. Select an industry and then discuss how companies may compete within it – which, if any, strategy seems to dominate?

REFERENCES AND FURTHER READING

Brakeman, L., Garretsen, H., Marrewijk, C. and Witteloostuijn, A. (2006) *Nations and Firms in the Global Economy*, Cambridge

Garelli, S. (2006) *Top Class Competitors: How Nations, Firms and Individuals Succeed in the New World of Competitiveness*, Wiley

Mahajan, S. (2005) 'Input–Output: Concentration ratios for businesses by industry in 2003 – Economic Trends 624 November 2005', Office for National Statistics

McGahan, A. (2000) 'How Industries Evolve', *Business Strategy Review,* Autumn 2000, Vol. 11 Issue 3, 1–16

Porter, M. E. (1986) 'Changing Patterns of International Competition', *California Management Review,* Winter 86, Vol. 28 Issue 2, 9–41

Sambamurthy, V., Bharadwaj, A. and Grover, V. (2003) 'Shaping Agility Through Digital Options: Reconceptualizing The Role Of Information Technology In Contemporary Firms', *MIS Quarterly,* Jun 2003, Vol. 27 Issue 2, 237–263

Teece, D. J., Pisano, G. and Shuen, A. (1997) 'Dynamic Capabilities and Strategic Management', *Strategic Management Journal*, Vol. 18, No. 7. (Aug., 1997), 509–533

Wernerfelt, B. (1984) 'A Resource-based View of the Firm', *Strategic Management Journal,* Apr-Jun 84, Vol. 5 Issue 2, 171–180

World Economic Forum, (2011) 'The Global Competitiveness Report 2011–2012', World Economic Forum, Switzerland Geneva, Switzerland

GLOSSARY

Acquisition Acquisition is where strategies are developed by taking over ownership of another organization

Benchmark A process of systematically comparing your own organizational structure, processes and performance against those of best practice organizations, to achieve sustainable business excellence

Business Environment The totality of factors, internal and external, which may influence the organization's achievement of its goals

Competition Those companies marketing products that are similar to, or can be substituted for, a given business's products in the same geographic area

Competencies Capabilities fundamental to the organization's strategy and performance – the basis of a competitive advantage and something that an organization can do distinctively well

Competitiveness When applied to an organization, the ability to compete effectively against rivals; when applied to a country, the ability to create an environment which is conducive to good economic and business performance

Competitive Advantage Used interchangeably with 'distinctive competence' to mean relative superiority in skills and resources

Competitive Disadvantage A firm generates less economic value than rival firms

Competitive Environment The part of a company's external environment that consists of other firms (rivals) trying to win customers and the 'rules' and determinants of competition in the same market/ industry

Competitive Factors The factors such as delivery time, product or service specification, price, etc. that define customers' requirements

Competitiveness (national) The set of institutions, policies, and factors that determine the level of productivity of a country

competitive structure competitive structure is a description of the current state of a product's market indicating the number of competitors, their relative strength, level of demand and supply, and ease of entry into the market

concentration ratio The number of firms in an industry who account for total sales. A high concentration ratio implies a relatively small number of firms account for a majority of the total sales of the industry.

Consumer The user of a product, service, or other form of offering

Critical Success Factors (CSFs) Product features that are particularly valued by customers, hence, where the organization must outrival competition

Differentiation A strategy of gaining competitive advantage by providing a product (or service) of the same cost and quality as a competitor, but with some additional attribute(s) that makes it different from the competition

Five Competitive Forces Together these determine competition in an industry or market: rivalry amongst existing like-for-like players; the threat of new entrants; the threat of substitute solutions; the bargaining power of buyers; and the bargaining power of suppliers

Industry Comprises all those firms who are competing directly with each other – a group of firms producing the same principal product or service

Industry Life Cycle A theory linking the intensity of competition in a particular market with the time since the breakthrough innovation that made that market possible

Internal Environment Anything which is internal to an organization, that is, within its boundary, including resources, structures and culture

Market A system of voluntary exchange, created by the relationship between buyers and sellers

New Entrants Firms that have either recently begun operations in an industry or that threaten to begin operations in an industry soon

Rivalry The act of competing – a quest to secure an advantage over another

Trade The action of buying and selling goods and services

CHAPTER CASE STUDY

OFT refers Irish Sea ferries merger to the Competition Commission

Stena AB, a private company registered in Sweden, is the parent company of Stena Line. Stena Line is one of the world's largest ferry operators with northern Europe's most extensive route network – a ferry operator that transports both passengers and freight. The company argues that in the shipping industry it pays to be big and thus be able to benefit from economies of scale. Launching new routes and acquiring other companies increases growth, but in order to maintain or improve profitability, Stena Line has to continue to plan and use its fleet of vessels effectively. The company has 19 ferry routes in Scandinavia and around the United Kingdom, connections between eight countries, 35 vessels and 5700 employees. During 2010, 15 million passengers travelled with Stena Line. The company also transported 3.2 million vehicles and 1.6 million freight units. Stena Line has a route-based organization with business areas made up of three geographical markets: Scandinavia, Irish Sea and North Sea.

A competitor, DFDS, also operates a similar sized sea-based freight and passenger transport network in Northern Europe. Until 2011, it ran four routes on the Irish Sea: from Heysham to Belfast or Dublin, and from Liverpool to Belfast or Dublin. Like Stena, DFDS Seaways also has an extensive route network on the North Sea.

Other ferry operators active on the Irish Sea include: Seatruck, which focuses on unaccompanied freight services, operating routes from Heysham to Warrenpoint, Larne and Dublin, and from Liverpool to Dublin; P&O, which operates routes from Cairnryan and Troon to Larne, and Liverpool–Dublin; Irish Ferries, which operates Holyhead–Dublin and Rosslare–Pembroke; and Fastnet, which operates a route between Swansea and Cork.

Ferry operators on the Irish Sea have experienced tough economic conditions over recent years. Following a period of rapid economic expansion, the UK and Irish economies have contracted. Simultaneously, ferry capacity has expanded, and continues to expand as ships ordered (particularly by Seatruck) during the boom are delivered during the aftermath of the recession.

In 2010 it was announced that DFDS sold to Stena Line its DFDS Seaways Irish Sea Ferries Limited, including two routes in the northern part of the Irish Sea. The sale covers the routes between Belfast and Birkenhead (Liverpool), and Belfast–Heysham. The sale and purchase agreement (SPA) between the parties did not include two routes retained by DFDS in the Irish Sea: Liverpool–Dublin and Heysham–Dublin. As a result of the acquisition, Stena took over two of the routes that DFDS had been operating: Liverpool–Belfast, and Heysham–Belfast. Following the acquisition, DFDS closed the two other routes (Liverpool–Dublin and Heysham–Dublin). The primary concern expressed by freight customers' results from the **loss of rivalry** between two of the three ferry operators active in the diagonal corridor.

The map shows ferry services across the Irish Sea in 2010 prior to the merger, prior to the closure of Stena's Fleetwood–Larne route and prior to the announced closure of DFDS's Heysham–Dublin and Liverpool–Dublin routes. The shaded area shows the routes most relevant to the merger i.e. those between Northwest England and Northern Ireland in what is known as the 'diagonal corridor'. See Figure 6.8.

Freight and passenger ferry services in the Irish Sea constitute separate markets because of their different demand characteristics. Freight services may cater for either accompanied freight (where the freight is accompanied by a dedicated driver) or unaccompanied freight (where the haulier leaves the trailer at a dock depot, the ferry operator loads, transports and unloads it and the haulier arranges collection from the destination port).

The location of ports, relative to the origin and destination of the goods and any depots, is accepted to be the key factor affecting customers' choice of routes. However, other important factors include the availability of timely crossings, the reliability of the crossings, road and ferry costs, the

FIGURE 6.8

Irish Sea Operators

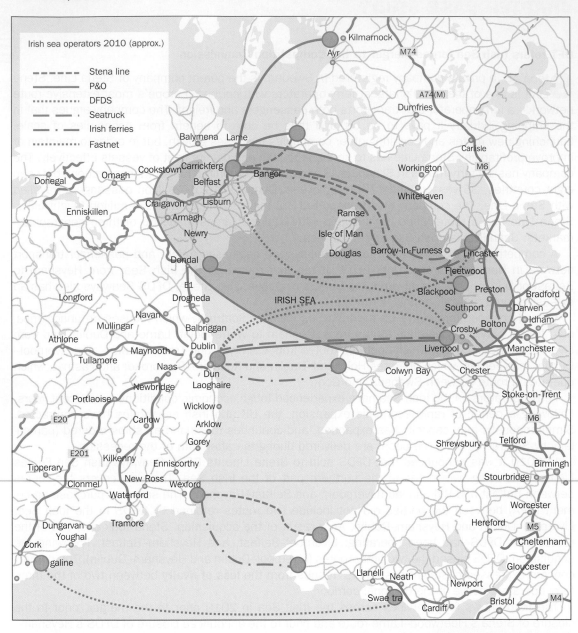

operational relationship between the customer and the ferry company, and drivers' facilities. These factors suggested at least some willingness by customers to substitute between ports.

The acquisition by Stena of the Liverpool–Belfast and Heysham–Belfast routes was completed in 2010. The next day Stena announced that it was closing its competing Fleetwood–Larne route. Prior to its closure, Stena's Fleetwood–Larne service was competing head-to-head with the routes Stena had now acquired and customers had been benefiting from that competition. In assessing the acquisition, the OFT considered whether Stena would have exited the Fleetwood–Larne route regardless of the merger. If so, then the closure and not the merger may be the reason for the loss of any competition between the parties. However the evidence available to the OFT was not compelling enough to dismiss its concerns that the closure of the route may have been influenced by the merger. For this reason, in its assessment, the OFT examined the acquisition as if Stena's

Fleetwood–Larne service had continued to operate. The OFT concluded that the acquisition created a realistic prospect of a substantial lessening of competition (SLC) in the supply of ferry services for freight from the North West of England to Northern Ireland. The main competition concern arises as a result of the reduction from three to two ferry freight operators in the diagonal routes, a market which was already highly concentrated. The estimated combined market of the merged company post-merger is 70–80 per cent, with a share of over 90 per cent for accompanied freight traffic, giving rise to substantial competition concerns. The presence of the remaining competitor (Seatruck) may not be sufficient to constrain price increases resulting from this merger. Consequently, the OFT believed the merger could result in a substantial lessening of competition. The OFT has therefore referred the merger to the Competition Commission for a more detailed investigation.

In 2011, the OFT referred Stena's completed acquisition of two Irish Sea ferry services to the CC.

Source: www.oft.gov.uk/news-and-updates/press/2011/13-11 - press release 8 February 2011. Reproduced with permission.

Questions

- Identify and discuss how ferry operators benefit from economies of scale
- Identify and discuss why customers might be concerned by a loss of rivalry
- The OFT has a duty to refer to the Competition Commission if the OFT believes that it is or may be the case that a relevant merger situation has been created (the Enterprise Act 2002); and the creation of that situation has resulted or may be expected to result in a substantial lessening of competition within any market or markets in the United Kingdom for goods or services.

Do you think the merger would result in a substantial lessening of competition? How might you determine this? Now read Part 2 of the case.

Part 2:

Later in 2011, the CC published its report on the acquisition by Stena. The CC terms of reference required it to decide whether a relevant merger situation had been created and, if so, whether the creation of that situation resulted or may be expected to result in a substantial lessening of competition (SLC) within any market or markets in the UK for goods and services.

A key initial question was the CC view of what would have happened absent the acquisition, i.e. the counterfactual. Stena's closure of Fleetwood–Larne happened at almost the same time as the acquisition. The CC found that the two events were linked as Stena's decisions about the acquisition and the closure were taken by the same people at the same times, and it was part of Stena's strategy to transfer its business from Fleetwood to Liverpool.

However, the CC examined closely whether Stena would have shut Fleetwood–Larne in any event, and decided, based on a comprehensive review of the evidence that it would.

The CC investigated the ways in which the acquisition might have led to a substantial lessening of competition; their principal concern related to loss of competition between routes that would have been controlled by different companies had the acquisition not proceeded. Compared with the CC counterfactual, under which Stena would have exited the diagonal corridor leaving two competitors DFDS and Seatruck, they found that the acquisition had not led to a substantial lessening of competition within the diagonal corridor.

The CC was also concerned that the acquisition may have reduced competition between routes previously operated by DFDS and Stena within a broader geographic area, since in the counterfactual DFDS would have operated diagonal routes whilst Stena operated on the northern and central corridors. The acquisition brings these routes under the control of a single company, Stena. To assess this, the CC considered firstly, the degree of competition between the relevant routes in different corridors, and secondly, the degree of competition Stena would face in each corridor following the acquisition. Taking the evidence as a whole, the CC did not find that the acquisition had led, or was likely to lead, to a substantial lessening of competition by reduction in competition across a broader geographic area in the provision of freight services.

At the outset of this inquiry, the CC identified theories of harm in their Issues Statement. The first theory of harm was that the acquisition removed competition between Stena and DFDS that would otherwise have constrained their behaviour. The second theory of harm was that the acquisition may have removed potential competition. The CC focused initially on the effect on competitive constraints on routes within the diagonal corridor, since Stena had taken over DFDS's Belfast routes, removing rivalry between two (Stena and DFDS) of the three operators (Stena, DFDS and Seatruck) active in the diagonal corridor before the acquisition. However, since the CC found that Stena would not be present in the diagonal corridor in the counterfactual, there was no reduction in the number of competitors within the diagonal corridor as a result of the acquisition and so the CC were satisfied that the acquisition had not removed actual competition in the diagonal corridor.

In conclusion, the CC did not consider that the evidence supported the view that Stena would be able to raise prices and/or worsen services as a result of the acquisition. In particular, the loss in competition across corridors appeared modest and it was felt Stena would continue to face substantial competition in each of the three corridors in which it operates, for the business of large and small hauliers of both accompanied and unaccompanied freight from existing operators. The CC did not find an SLC with regard to the supply of freight services or to the supply of passenger services and that the acquisition had resulted or may be expected to result in an SLC within any market in the UK for goods or services.

Further questions

- Use the Neoclassical Competition spectrum and classify the Irish sea ferry market(s)
- Discuss the Irish sea ferry market using Porter's five forces framework
- Discuss the Irish sea ferry market using the Industry life cycle

7

THE SUSTAINABLE ENVIRONMENT

FIGURE 7.1

The sustainable environment mind map

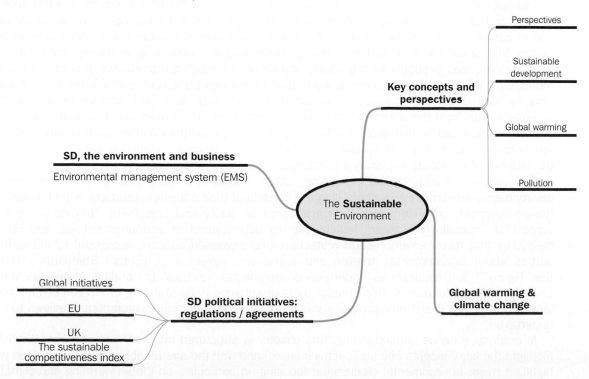

KEY CONCEPTS

Climate Change | Corporate Social Responsibility (CSR) | Ecological Environment | Environment | Environmental Aspect | Environmental Impact | Environmental Management System (EMS) | Stakeholder | Sustainable Development

INTRODUCTION

'Earth is the only place in the universe known to sustain life. Yet human activities are progressively reducing the planet's life-supporting capacity at a time when rising human numbers and consumption are making increasingly heavy demands on it. The combined destructive impacts of a poor majority struggling to stay alive and an affluent minority consuming most of the world's resources are undermining the very means by which all people can survive and flourish (IUCN world conservation strategy 1980).' This was a poignant call for action in the world conservation strategy, but what then has happened since? In answer to the question, many argue not enough. Roll forward three decades and the year 2007 marked a new and disturbing global realization. The world learnt that year that climate change was human-made, definitely happening, and that the collective global effort so far to keep greenhouse gases to a 'safe' level was grossly insufficient (UNFCCC 2012). The world has warmed by an average of 0.76°C since pre-industrial times and the temperature rise is accelerating, according to the 2007 Fourth Assessment Report (AR4) from the Intergovernmental Panel on Climate Change (IPCC). Sea levels rose almost twice as fast between 1993 and 2003 as during the previous three decades. Man-made emissions of greenhouse gases are causing these changes. Without action to limit future emissions, the global average temperature is likely to increase further by 1.8° to 4°C this century, and in the worst case scenario, by as much as 6.4°C, the AR4 projects (European Commission 2009). To ensure the world is on track to reduce global emissions by 2050 to at least half the 1990 levels, the IPCC's AR4 shows that collectively, developed countries need to cut their emissions by 2020 to 25-40 per cent below 1990 levels and by 2050 to 80–95 per cent below 1990 levels.

The natural environment, a significant part of the context of the firm, presents threats, opportunities and challenges for organizations; such challenges derive from global warming, the depletion of natural resources and pollution. The natural environment creates the challenges faced by people that drive the demand for certain products and services. It is a starting point for the resources required to supply such products and services through the production process. Through moral, ethical and regulatory concerns the natural environment is a source of influence on the way work is carried out and business transacted. Considerable past and present environmental damage stems from the effects of economic development. The environment is also a place to deposit waste, unwanted products and by-products (such as pollutants) of production. Man and the firm is both influenced by and influences the natural world. Understanding how each may influence the other is of significant importance to the business practitioner.

Organizations of all kinds are increasingly concerned with achieving and demonstrating sound environmental performance by controlling the impacts of their activities, products and services on the environment, consistent with their environmental policy and objectives. They do so in the context of increasingly stringent legislation, the development of economic policies and other measures that foster environmental protection, and increased concern expressed by interested parties about environmental matters and sustainable development (British Standards 2010). See Figure 7.1. Organizations undertake environmental 'reviews' or 'audits' to assess their environmental performance. This chapter aims to enhance understanding of environmental challenges and issues whilst also providing the knowledge that will help environmental reviews to be undertaken.

In order to enhance understanding, this chapter is structured into four key sections. We first highlight the key concepts and perspectives associated with the sustainable environment. Next we highlight major environmental challenges, focusing, in particular, on global warming and climate change. Then we consider global, EU (regional) and UK (national) responses to such challenges and finally, responses at the level of the firm.

KEY CONCEPTS AND PERSPECTIVES

We may start by asking what is meant by the term the ecological environment or simply the 'environment'. At a basic level it is the natural world; the surroundings or conditions within which a person, animal, or plant lives or operates. It is a part of the context in which business operates – it is capable of exerting influence on and may be affected by the activity of the firm. Any change to the environment, whether adverse or beneficial, wholly or partially resulting from an organization's products, services or activities is termed an environmental impact. Sources of environmental impact are shown in Figure 7.2.

Perspectives

Fundamentally, we may view the ecological environment from three basic perspectives: (1) a source of threat or challenge; (2) a resource – something to tap into and (3) a place to deposit the unwanted by-products (and side-effects) of production. Adopting a more values-based approach, people may view the environment from one of two perspectives: (a) something for humans to exploit or (b) a living thing of which humans form a part. The former has its roots in classical economics and will see environmental problems and pollution as 'side-effects' (externalities) of the production process. This approach has often been labelled a short-sighted approach when exploiting natural resources. The latter is a more contemporary perspective, aligned with sustainable development and may be associated with the green movement and the world conservation strategy. This latter perspective is

FIGURE 7.2
Sources of environmental impact

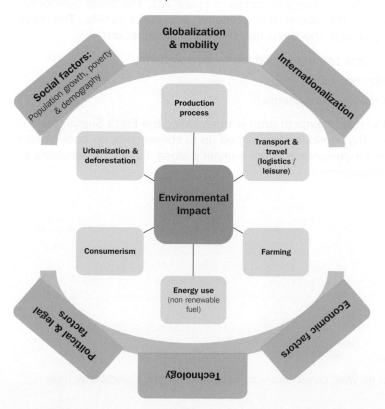

borne out of growing populations placing increasing demands upon natural resources, the depletion of and new threats to those resources. According to the IUCN (1980) humanity's relationship with the biosphere (the thin covering of the planet that contains and sustains life) will continue to deteriorate until a new international economic order is achieved, a new environmental ethic adopted, human populations stabilize, and sustainable modes of development become the rule rather than the exception. Amongst the prerequisites for sustainable development is the conservation of living resources. Man has come to realize that his actions can bring about significant detrimental changes to the ecological environment. The first perspective is a selfish one that has little regard for the needs of future generations.

Sustainable development

The concept of sustainable development (SD) was introduced in the World Conservation Strategy (IUCN 1980) and had its roots in the concept of a sustainable society and in the management of renewable resources. The authors of the strategy argued that 'Human beings, in their quest for economic development and enjoyment of the riches of nature, must come to terms with the reality of resource limitation and the carrying capacities of ecosystems, and must take account of the needs of future generations. This is the message of conservation. For if the object of development is to provide for social and economic welfare, the object of conservation is to ensure Earth's capacity to sustain development and to support all life.' The term sustainable development came to prominence through the United Nations Brundtland Commission. The Commission's 1987 report, 'Our Common Future' defined sustainable development as 'development which meets the needs of the present without compromising the ability of future generations to meet their own needs'. SD was adopted by the WCED in 1987 and by the Rio Conference in 1992 as a process of change in which the exploitation of resources, the direction of investments, the orientation of technological development, and institutional change are all in harmony and enhance both current and future potential to meet human needs and aspirations. SD integrates the political, social, economic and environmental dimensions.

The symbol of the World Conservation Strategy is shown in figure 7.3. The circle symbolizes the biosphere – the thin covering of the planet that contains and sustains life. The three interlocking, overlapping arrows symbolize the three objectives of conservation:

- maintenance of essential ecological processes and life-support systems;
- preservation of genetic diversity; and
- sustainable utilization of species and ecosystems.

Sustainable development was the main theme of what is often called the Earth Summit held in Rio de Janeiro in 1992. It was here that world leaders signed up to conventions on both climate change and biodiversity. They issued a declaration at the summit's close, listing 27 principles on the environment and sustainable development.

FIGURE 7.3
World conservation strategy symbol

Source: © IUCN-UNEP-WWF. With thanks to the WWF, United Nations Environmental Project and International Union for Conservation Nature.

Global warming and Greenhouse gases (GHG)

According to United Nations Framework Convention on Climate Change (UNFCCC 2012), Greenhouse gases occur naturally and are essential to the survival of humans and millions of other living things, through keeping some of the sun's warmth from reflecting back into space and making Earth liveable. But it is a matter of scale. A century and a half of industrialization, including clear-felling forests and certain farming methods, has driven up quantities of greenhouse gases in the atmosphere. As populations, economies and standards of living grow, so do the cumulative level of GHG emissions.

Pollution

Pollution is the release of harmful substances from a source through air, soil or water. The production and consumption of goods and services can generate spill over effects impacting upon the wider population and not just producers and consumers. However, many organizations do not consider fully the wider social costs of their business activities. When shareholder returns are the primary goal, the organization may be less likely to spend revenue (decreasing margin) in taking action to curtail environmental damage. Furthermore organizations may be reluctant to pass on to consumers the costs of such initiatives which may result in a need to raise prices and become less competitive. Industrial waste from production processes can also impact upon other companies and individuals – not just nature. In short, there may be negative consequences of economic activity and in some cases the organization responsible may not be motivated to put right any harm caused. Environmental aspects may be associated with emissions to air, releases to water, releases to land, use of raw materials and natural resources, use of energy, energy emitted, e.g. heat, radiation, vibration, waste and by-products, and physical attributes, e.g. size, shape, colour, appearance. Organizations are also encouraged to consider goods and services used by themselves and those related to products and services that they provide. The prevention of pollution involves the use of processes, practices, techniques, materials, products, services or energy to avoid, reduce or control (separately or in combination) the creation, emission or discharge of any type of pollutant or waste, in order to reduce adverse environmental impacts. Prevention of pollution can include source reduction or elimination, process, product or service changes, efficient use of resources, material and energy substitution, reuse, recovery, recycling, reclamation and treatment. We explore global warming in more detail next. This will act as a foundation for discussion about the role of governments and the impact of the ecological environment, sometimes mediated by regulation, on the firm and its internal environment.

GLOBAL WARMING AND CLIMATE CHANGE

In a statement by the Chairman of the IPCC at the COP-17 Plenary, Durban, South Africa, Rajendra Pachauri (2011) argued that global weather – and climate-related disaster losses reported over the last few decades reflect mainly monetized direct damages to assets, and are unequally distributed. Since 1980 estimates of annual losses have ranged from a few billion to above 200 billion USD (in 2010) with the highest value for 2005 (the year of Hurricane Katrina). Loss estimates are lower bound estimates because many impacts, such as loss of human lives, cultural heritage and ecosystem services, are difficult to value and monetize, and thus they are poorly reflected in estimates of losses. Models project substantial warming in temperature extremes by the end of the 21st century. It is certain that increases in the frequency and magnitude of warm daily temperature extremes and decreases in cold extremes will occur in the 21st century on a global scale. Based on specific emissions scenarios, a 1-in-20 year hottest day is likely to become a 1-in-2 year event by the end of the 21st century in most regions. Heavy rainfalls associated with tropical cyclones are likely to increase with continued warming. At the same time droughts will intensify in the 21st century in some seasons and areas due to reduced precipitation and/or increased evapotranspiration. The very likely contribution of mean sea level rise to increased extreme coastal high water levels, coupled with the likely increase in tropical cyclone maximum wind speed, is a specific issue for tropical small island states. In the case of mountain areas there is high confidence that changes in heat waves, glacial retreat and/or permafrost degradation will affect high mountain phenomena such as slope instabilities, movements of mass and glacial lake outburst floods.

An integrated view of climate change is presented within the IPCC's Fourth Assessment Report (AR4). Such a view incorporates observed changes in climate and their effects on natural and human systems, the causes of the observed changes, projections of future climate change and related impacts under different scenarios. It discusses adaptation and mitigation options over the next few decades and their interactions with sustainable development. A schematic framework representing anthropogenic drivers (alterations in the environment due to the presence or activities of humans), impacts of and responses to climate change, and their linkages, is shown in Figure 7.4.

In 2010, governments agreed that emissions need to be reduced so that global temperature increases are limited to below 2 °C. So far, most developed countries have announced mid-term target reductions for 2020, but most targets are far short of the IPCC range of a 25–40 per cent

FIGURE 7.4
Anthropogenic drivers, impacts of and responses to climate change, and their linkages

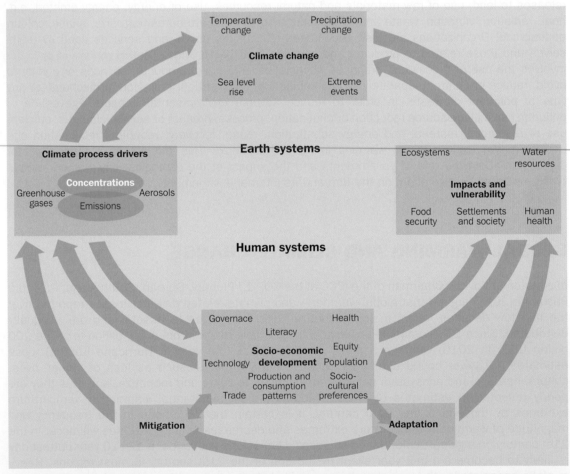

Source: Climate Change 2007: Synthesis Report. Contribution of Working Groups I, II and III to the Fourth Assessment Report of the Intergovernmental Panel on Climate Change, Figure I.1. IPCC, Geneva, Switzerland.

Each part of the framework is explained briefly below:

- **Climate change** Warming of the climate system is indisputable, as is now evident from observations of increases in global average air and ocean temperatures, widespread melting of snow and ice and rising global average sea level

- **Causes of change ('Climate process drivers')** Climate change may be associated with both natural and anthropogenic factors (drivers). Most of the observed increase in global average temperatures since the mid-20th century is very likely due to the observed increase in anthropogenic GHG concentrations. Human activities result in emissions of four long-lived GHGs: Carbon dioxide, methane, nitrous oxide and halocarbons (a group of gases containing fluorine, chlorine or bromine). Atmospheric concentrations of GHGs increase when emissions are larger than removal processes. Carbon dioxide (CO_2) is the most important anthropogenic GHG. Its annual emissions have grown significantly between 1970 and 2004. Growth has come from energy supply, transport and industry in particular. The observed widespread warming of the atmosphere and ocean, together with ice mass loss, support the conclusion it is extremely unlikely that global climate change in the past 50 years can be explained without external forcing and very likely that it is not due to known natural causes alone.

- **Impacts and vulnerability** *Ecosystems*: Approximately 20 to 30 per cent of plant and animal species assessed so far are likely to be at increased risk of extinction if increases in global average temperature exceed 1.5 to 2.5°C *Food*: Crop productivity is projected to increase slightly at mid- to high latitudes for local mean temperature increases of up to 1 to 3°C depending on the crop, and then decrease beyond that in some regions. At lower latitudes, especially in seasonally dry and tropical regions, crop productivity is projected to decrease for even small local temperature increases (1 to 2°C), which would increase the risk of hunger *Coasts*: Coasts are projected to be exposed to increasing risks, including coastal erosion,

due to climate change and sea level rise. *Industry, settlements and society*: The most vulnerable industries, settlements and societies are generally those in coastal and river flood plains, those whose economies are closely linked with climate-sensitive resources and those in areas prone to extreme weather events, especially where rapid urbanization is occurring *Health*: The health status of millions of people is projected to be affected through, for example, increases in malnutrition; increased deaths, diseases and injury due to extreme weather events; increased burden of diarrhoeal diseases; increased frequency of cardio-respiratory diseases due to higher concentrations of ground-level ozone in urban areas related to climate change; and the altered spatial distribution of some infectious diseases *Water*: Climate change is expected to exacerbate current stresses on water resources from population growth and economic and land-use change, including urbanization.

- **Climate change and its impacts in the near and long term under different scenarios** There is high agreement and much evidence that with current climate change mitigation policies and related sustainable development practices, global GHG emissions will continue to grow over the next few decades. Continued GHG emissions at or above current rates would cause further warming and induce many changes in the global climate system during the 21st century that would be larger than those observed during the 20th century.

- **Adaptation and mitigation (What we can do)** The two primary responses to climate change are *mitigation* – cutting down on greenhouse gas emissions – and *adaptation* – acknowledging the changes and implementing systems to increase our resilience (see adaptation to climate change). Societies can respond to climate change by adapting to its impacts and by reducing GHG emissions (mitigation), thereby reducing the rate and magnitude of change. The capacity to adapt and mitigate is dependent on socio-economic and environmental circumstances and the availability of information and technology. A wide array of adaptation options are available, but more extensive adaptation than occurs currently is required to reduce vulnerability to climate change. There is also high agreement and medium evidence that changes in lifestyle and behaviour patterns can contribute to climate change mitigation. Policies that provide a real or implicit price of carbon could create incentives for producers and consumers to invest significantly in low-GHG products, technologies and processes. There is high agreement and much evidence that notable achievements of the UNFCCC and its Kyoto Protocol are the establishment of a global response to the climate change problem, stimulation of an array of national policies, the creation of an international carbon market and the establishment of new institutional mechanisms to provide the foundation for future mitigation efforts.

reduction below 1990 levels by 2020, which would be necessary to limit temperature increase to 2°C. Mitigation initiatives seek to avoid emissions. Measures include reducing demand for emissions-intensive goods and services, boosting efficiency gains and increasing the use of low-carbon technologies and renewable energy. Another way to mitigate the impacts of climate change is by enhancing 'sinks' – reservoirs that absorb CO_2, such as forests or peat bogs. Leaving existing forests intact and planting new trees are two examples of how this can be achieved. However, in parallel, governments seek to adapt to climate change. Adaptation (dealing with climate impacts) concerns the adoption of policies and practices to prepare for the effects of climate change, accepting that complete avoidance is now impossible. Next we explore government policy in more detail.

BUSINESS IN DEBATE

Do you believe in climate change?

Covering the presidential candidate's campaign in the US, Olga Bonfligio reported[1] 'Climate Change Denial'. She notes promises by both major political parties three years ago to do something about climate change have gone by the wayside. 'Today's Republican presidential candidates have, in fact, gone further in the opposite direction, rejecting evidence that humans are responsible for (or principle contributors towards) the warming of the earth.' Numerous scientists and academics have discussed the phenomenon of 'climate change denial' to understand what is preventing people from tackling climate change as a political priority despite scientists writing thousands of peer-reviewed papers and reports concluding that climate change is real and caused, or at least accelerated, by human activity.

Recent studies show that public acceptance of the scientific evidence for man-made climate change has decreased. The scientific evidence that humanity is having an effect on the climate is overwhelming and increasing every year. Yet public perception of this is confused. A Cardiff/Ipsos Mori study on public perceptions of climate change, published in 2010, identifies a number of possible contributory factors: the move from being a science issue to a political issue may have introduced more distrust. Vicky Pope, senior scientist at the Met Office, is one of many who have raised the issue of the way that science can be misused. In some cases scare stories in the media have over-hyped climate change and she thinks we are paying the price for this now with a reaction the other way. She was concerned then that science was not always presented objectively by the media and interested parties (even sometimes scientists themselves) in important areas, like climate change.[2] Which brings her to the question, should you believe in climate change?

Source: (1) Bonfligio, O. (2012), 'Presidential Candidates and the Sociology of 'Climate Change Denial', The Blog, TheHuffingtonPost.com, Posted: 04/ 4/2012; and (2) Pope, V. (2012), 'Do you believe in climate change? That's not a question you should be asking – it's a matter of empirical evidence, not belief', guardian.co.uk, Friday 23 March 2012

SD POLITICAL INITIATIVES: REGULATIONS AND AGREEMENTS

Two features characterize our time (IUCN 1980):

> The first is the limitless capacity of human beings for building and creation, matched by equally great powers of destruction and annihilation. The escalating needs of soaring numbers have often driven people to take a short-sighted approach when exploiting natural resources. The toll of this approach has now become glaringly apparent: a long list of hazards and disasters, including soil erosion, desertification, loss of cropland, pollution, deforestation, ecosystem degradation and destruction, and extinction of species and varieties. This situation underlines the need for conservation, comprising the ecologically sound management of productive systems and the maintenance of their viability and versatility. The second is the global interrelatedness of actions, with its corollary of global responsibility. This in turn gives rise to the need for global strategies both for development and for conservation of nature and natural resources.

Source: With thanks to the WWF, United Nations Enivromental Project and International Union for Conservation Nature.

The international community addresses the former through a variety of initiatives outlined in this section. The World Conservation Strategy provided both an intellectual framework and practical guidance for the conservation actions necessary. It called for global coordinated efforts, backed by will and determination, for concerted action at national and international levels, and for global solidarity to implement its programmes. Within the strategy it was argued that development and conservation are equally necessary for our survival and for the discharge of our responsibilities as trustees of natural resources for generations to come. However, many people believe that the global community and particular countries have not done enough to act on the environmental issues raised so far in this chapter. When Rajendra Pachauri (2011) accepted the Nobel Peace Prize on behalf of the IPCC he asked the rhetorical question, 'Will those responsible for decisions in the field of climate change at the global level listen to the voice of science and knowledge, which is now loud and clear?' He argues that we need to keep in mind two profound statements from Nelson Mandela: 'Education is the most powerful weapon which you can use to change the world', and 'We know what needs to be done – all that is missing is the will to do it'. In this section we will consider global, regional and national initiatives to manage global warming and related environmental challenges. From a national and regional perspective we ask what the UK and then what the EU is doing but first start with an outline of global initiatives.

Global initiatives

The United Nations Framework Convention on Climate Change (UNFCCC) was established in 1994 and has near-universal membership. The ultimate objective of the Convention is to stabilize greenhouse gas concentrations 'at a level that would prevent dangerous anthropogenic (human induced) interference with the climate system'. It states that 'such a level should be achieved within a time-frame sufficient to allow ecosystems to adapt naturally to climate change, to ensure that food production is not threatened, and to enable economic development to proceed in a sustainable manner'; we know what constitutes 'dangerous anthropogenic interference' from the IPCC's 4th Assessment Report. The idea is that, as the source of most past and current greenhouse gas emissions, industrialized countries are expected to do the most to cut emissions on home ground. They are called Annex I countries and belong to the Organization for Economic Cooperation and Development (OECD). Industrialized nations agree under the Convention to support climate change activities in developing countries by providing financial support for action on climate change above and beyond any financial assistance they already provide to these countries. A system of grants and loans has been implemented through the Convention and is managed by the Global Environment Facility. Industrialized countries also agree to share technology with less-advanced nations. Industrialized countries (Annex I) must report regularly on their climate change

Kyoto Protocol (KP)

The Kyoto Protocol was adopted in Kyoto, Japan, in 1997. However, a complex ratification process meant it did not enter into force until 2005. In short, the Kyoto Protocol is what 'operationalizes' the Convention. It commits industrialized countries to stabilize greenhouse gas emissions, based on the principles of the Convention. The Convention itself only encourages countries to do so. KP, as it is referred to in short, sets binding emission reduction targets for 37 industrialized countries and the European community. Overall, these targets amount to an average five per cent emission reduction compared with 1990 levels over the five-year period 2008 to 2012. KP was structured on the principles of the Convention. It only binds developed countries because it recognizes they are largely responsible for the current high levels of GHG emissions in the atmosphere, which are the result of more than 150 years of industrial activity. KP places a heavier burden on developed nations under its central principle: that of 'common but differentiated responsibility'.

policies and measures, including issues governed by the Kyoto Protocol (for countries which have ratified it). They must also submit an annual inventory of their greenhouse gas emissions, including data for their base year (1990) and all the years since.

There have been a number of conferences and agreements since Kyoto. The World Summit on Sustainable Development (WSSD) took place in Johannesburg in 2002. The summit delivered three outcomes: a political declaration, the Johannesburg Plan of Implementation and the establishment of numerous partnership initiatives. Key commitments covered sustainable consumption and production, water and sanitation, and energy. The outcomes complemented the Millennium Development Goals, reinforce Doha and Monterrey agreements and set challenging global goals and targets on accessing water, sanitation and modern energy services; increasing energy efficiency and use of renewable energy; sustainable fisheries and forests; reducing biodiversity loss on land and in our oceans; chemicals management; and decoupling environmental degradation from economic growth – that is, achieving sustainable patterns of consumption and production. The Bali Road Map was adopted at the 13th Conference of the Parties and the 3rd Meeting of the Parties in December 2007 in Bali. Later, in Cancun, Mexico, at the 2010 United Nations Climate Change Conference, the Cancun Agreements were created and celebrated as an achievement for the international community. They form the basis for the largest collective world effort to reduce emissions, in a mutually accountable way, with national plans captured formally at international level under the banner of the UNFCCC. The Copenhagen Climate Change Conference raised climate change policy to the highest political level. Close to 115 world leaders attended the high-level event, making it one of the largest gatherings of world leaders ever outside UN headquarters in New York. COP 15 (Fifteenth session of the Conference of the Parties)/CMP 5 (Fifth session of the Conference of the Parties serving as the meeting of the Parties to the Kyoto Protocol) was a crucial event in the negotiating process. It advanced significantly the negotiations on the infrastructure needed for effective global climate change cooperation, including improvements to the Clean Development Mechanism of the Kyoto Protocol. It produced the **Copenhagen Accord**, which expressed a clear political intent to constrain carbon and respond to climate change, in both the short and long term. The Copenhagen Accord embraced several key elements on which there was strong convergence of the views of governments. One such element included the long-term goal of limiting the maximum global average temperature increase to no more than 2 degrees Celsius above pre-industrial levels, subject to a review in 2015. There was, however, no agreement on how to achieve this in practical terms.

The European Commission (2009) refer to a global challenge that requires global action. They believe the Kyoto Protocol was a vital first step. It required developed countries to commence emission reductions and has instigated a set of international rules, market-based mechanisms and funds for addressing climate change. However, climate change is a global problem, and only global action can bring it under control, argues the EC. They believe that a global agreement, covering all major emitters, is needed for the period after 2012, when the emission targets set by the Kyoto

Protocol for developed countries expired. It is suggested that a new agreement will need to be far more ambitious in order to keep global warming below 2°C compared with the pre-industrial temperature. Most of the technologies required to achieve deep reductions in emissions exist already or are well on the way to becoming operational. In the next section we take a closer look at what the EU is doing to make development sustainable. In particular we outline the EU's SD strategy.

What is the EU doing about climate change and SD?

Climate change is no longer a distant threat, it's here now and it's speeding up (European Commission 2008: p11). Europeans are feeling the effects of global warming: droughts, floods, heat waves and forest fires are all becoming more frequent. Such changes are largely the result of billions of tonnes of carbon dioxide (CO_2) released daily into the atmosphere from burning coal, oil and natural gas. These fossil fuels provide us with the energy needed to run cars, heat homes and light up offices. However, as a consequence of excessive use of fossil fuels our environment is, and will continue to suffer, as will our economy and society. The 2006 Stern Review projected that, in the long term, climate change could cut global gross domestic product (GDP) each year by between 5 per cent and as much as 20 per cent or more if it is not brought under control by cutting greenhouse gas emissions (GHGs). The European Commission's analysis shows the investment needed to achieve a low-carbon economy would cost only around 0.5 per cent of world GDP between 2013 and 2030. The growing evidence of the cost of climate change points to one simple conclusion: 'we cannot afford to do nothing' (European Commission 2009: p7). Combating climate change is a key priority for the EU. Europe is working hard to cut its greenhouse gas emissions substantially whilst encouraging other nations and regions to do likewise. At the same time, the EU is developing a strategy for adapting to the impacts of climate change which can no longer be prevented. The challenge is a complex one argues the EC. Today our main energy sources are finite reserves of fossil fuels which take millions years to replenish. There is a danger that at current consumption levels these reserves will expire. What is more, the International Energy Agency forecasts a 60 per cent rise in energy needs between 2000 and 2030. With no one miracle energy source, the only solution lies in increasing efficiency and finding alternatives, whilst making full use of renewable sources. To identify and develop targeted means of mitigation, the EU formed a European Climate Change Programme in 2000. This programme devises ways in which the EU can reduce its own emissions which account for 14 per cent of global emissions. It identified numerous areas, which together can reduce Europe's emissions by up to 16 per cent compared with 1990 figures. Its major achievement has been the Greenhouse Gas Emissions Trading Scheme which began in 2005. This is the largest multi-country, multi-sector emissions trading scheme in the world. It helps countries reach their CO_2 obligations under the 1997 Kyoto Protocol agreement by teaming up an over-producing country with one that is under its Kyoto limit. The over producer then pays for the right to use the spare capacity of the other country concerned: in the end, both emit no more than the amount agreed upon.

Sustainable development is a fundamental and overarching objective of the EU, enshrined in Treaty. The EU SD strategy was launched by the European Council in Gothenburg in 2001 and aims for continuous improvement of the quality of life for current and future generations. In January 2004 the EU implemented its Environment Technology Action Plan (ETAP). Examples of environmental technologies include recycling systems for waste water in industrial processes, energy efficient car engines and soil improvement techniques. ETAP focuses on creating alternative ways of production with less environmental impact. In February 2005 the European Commission audited progress made and came to the conclusion that the situation was deteriorating. In an attempt to halt the destructive trends leading to exploitation of natural resources and environmental degradation, the EU Council adopted a revised strategy in June 2006. The 2006 EU Sustainable Development Strategy (EU SDS) describes how the EU will more effectively meet the challenge of SD. The overall aim is to achieve a continuous improvement in the quality of life of citizens through sustainable communities that manage and use resources efficiently and unleash the ecological and social innovation potential of the economy, so as to ensure prosperity, environmental protection and social cohesion. However, it is widely recognized that SD will not be brought about by policies alone: it must be adopted by society at large, as a principle guiding the many choices each citizen makes every day…this requires profound changes in thinking and in consumption and production patterns. The strategy sets overall objectives and concrete actions for seven key priority challenges:

* Climate change and clean energy
* Sustainable transport
* Sustainable consumption and production
* Conservation and management of natural resources
* Public health
* Social inclusion, demography and migration
* Global poverty and sustainable development challenges

The first long-term specific objective of the strategy is to limit climate change and its effects by meeting commitments under the Kyoto Protocol and under the framework of the European Strategy on Climate Change. Energy efficiency, renewable energy and transport are the subject of particular efforts. At the European Council on the 9th March 2007, leaders agreed on a comprehensive package of measures, establishing a new integrated climate change and energy policy, (European Commission 2008). This would exceed all previous commitments. Its targets include: reducing greenhouse gas emissions in the EU by 20 per cent; improving energy efficiency by 20 per cent; raising the share of renewable energy to 20 per cent and increasing the level of biofuels in transport fuel to 10 per cent by 2020. A set of measures under the Ecodesign Directive is being developed to ensure that cost-effective improvements are made to the most energy-hungry products. Minimum energy efficiency requirements will be combined with clearer labelling for these products. It is estimated that improvements to central heating boilers and water heaters alone could lead to 3 per cent less overall emissions by 2020 (compared with 2004). Through the Energy Taxation Directive, the EU will seek to discourage pollutant behaviour and reward positive behaviour in terms of energy savings and environmentally friendly activities. Transport is another sector with great potential for mitigating climate change and a number of legislative proposals are being examined. These include: increasing the proportion of biofuels used in transport; decreasing the carbon intensity of fuel, and restoring balance between different modes of transport. Renewable energy is also under examination as a way to further increase sustainable energy sources. Through water power, solar energy, biofuels, biomass and geothermal energy, the EU aims to guarantee that 20 per cent of its overall energy mix derives from renewable energy sources by 2020. Biofuels figure highly in this mix and are to supply 10 per cent of petrol and diesel needs in the EU by 2020.

Limiting the adverse effects of transport and reducing regional disparities is another long-term objective, which requires the EU to do more to develop transport that is environmentally friendly and conducive to health. The strategy envisages, amongst other measures, infrastructure charging (the EU has created a framework to encourage Member States to use taxation and transport infrastructure charging in the most effective and fair manner in order to promote the 'user pays' principle, important to maintain and develop the trans-European infrastructure network, and the 'polluter pays' principle, as enshrined in the treaties), and promotion of alternatives to road transport and vehicles which produce less pollution and use less energy. To promote more sustainable modes of production and consumption, the link between economic growth and environmental degradation needs to be broken and attention paid to how much ecosystems can tolerate. With this aim in view, the EU must, amongst other things, promote green public procurement, define environmental and social performance targets for products in cooperation with stakeholders, expand the distribution of environmental innovations and environmental technologies and produce information about and appropriate labelling of products and services.

Consumption and production and the smarter use of resources are key themes for EU SD. From disposable cameras to electrical goods that are cheaper to replace than repair, throwing things away is part of everyday life; the way we consume and produce these products and services are the main source of the pressures we place upon the environment. These pressures continue to increase as world population continues to grow. How we make and buy goods must change. By 2050, with current trends, the global energy demand could double as populations rise and developing countries expand their economies. Products and services need to be urgently developed that use fewer resources, to prevent needless waste of resources and to consume more responsibly. Achieving sustainable consumption and production involves changing the way we produce (discussed later in this chapter), buy and throw away. The EU SDS, which complements the Lisbon Strategy, should be a catalyst for policy makers and public opinion, to change society's behaviour. It is based on the guiding principles which include involvement of citizens, involvement of businesses and social partners, policy coherence and governance, policy integration, use of best available knowledge, the precautionary principle and the polluter-pays principle. The Knowledge Society must be the driving force behind sustainable development. Special efforts are required in education and training to attract the greatest number of participants, in order to bring about a change in behaviour and give the public the necessary skills to meet the objectives laid down in the strategy. Financial and economic instruments are another way to engender a market that offers less polluting products and services and to change consumer behaviour. Prices therefore need to reflect actual environmental and social costs, whereas fiscal measures should be applied to energy and resource consumption and/or pollution.

Evaluating progress towards the agreed goals is an integral part of the SDS and monitoring reports are published by Eurostat every two years. The evaluation of progress since 2000, based on the headline indicators, shows a rather mixed picture. There have been favourable changes for indicators of Greenhouse gas emissions and Consumption of renewables (since 2006) but moderately unfavourable changes for the indicators such as Energy consumption of transport relative to GDP. Overall, changes in sustainable consumption and production since 2000 show some success but also failure. The consumption of materials continues to rise, though aspects of waste management are improving. There has been a decrease in atmospheric emissions and final energy consumption decreased in 2009. However, the number of cars on the roads continues to rise, see Figure 7.4; between 2000 and 2009 the number of passenger cars per 1000 inhabitants in the EU increased significantly from 423 in 2000 to 473 in 2009. In 2009, at country level, the number of passenger cars per 1000 inhabitants ranged from 197 in Romania to 678 in Luxembourg. There was more than one car for every two inhabitants in Germany, Italy, Cyprus, Lithuania, Luxembourg, Malta, Austria and Finland. See Figure 7.5. On a positive note, there was an increase in the number of EU based organizations certified with an environmental management system. EMSs are discussed later in this chapter. The European Union (EU) Eco-management and audit scheme, abbreviated as EMAS, is a management tool for companies and other organizations to evaluate, report and improve their environmental performance. Since 2001, EMAS has been open to all economic sectors, including public and private services. The scheme was further strengthened by the integration of the ISO 14001 international standard, which focuses on environmental management and aims to help organizations establish or improve an environmental management system, to minimize harmful effects on the environment resulting from their activities, and continually improve their environmental performance. There have been substantial reductions in the emissions of important air pollutants (contributing to acidification, eutrophication and ground-level ozone – emissions of sulphur oxides, nitrogen oxides, and ammonia declined substantially), and there has been progress related to production patterns regarding the ecological dimension of corporate social responsibility and towards more environmentally friendly agricultural practices.

Overall, the changes since 2000 concerning sustainable transport present a rather unfavourable picture. Neither freight nor passenger transport has shown any shift towards modes with lower environmental impacts (rail, maritime and inland waterways). There have been substantial decreases in the average CO_2 emissions of new cars. Between 2000 and 2009 greenhouse gas emissions from transport (excluding international aviation and maritime) grew in the EU. Transport (even when excluding international aviation and maritime) is an important emitter of greenhouse gases (GHGs), responsible for a share which has grown from 14 per cent of total EU emissions in 1990 to 20 per cent in 2008. It is the only major source category currently producing considerably more greenhouse gas emissions than in 1990. In the EU-15 the average CO_2 emissions of new

FIGURE 7.5

Motorization rate, 1991–2009 (Source: Eurostat)

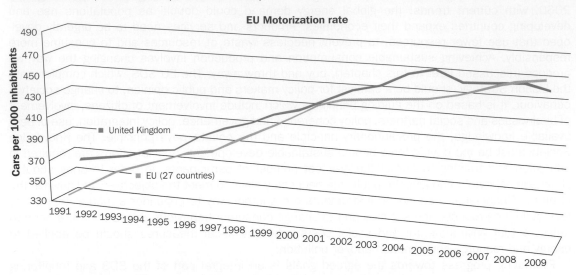

Source: http://ec.europa.eu © European Union, 1995-2012. Reproduced with permission.

passenger cars per km decreased by 3.0 grams per year between 2000 and 2009, reaching 145.2 grams in 2009. The current progress rate is sufficient for reaching the recently set target of 130 grams by 2015. Improved engine efficiency, e.g. fuel-saving technologies, due to efforts of car makers, accounted for the most recent reduction. On the other hand, these reductions could not compensate for the increase of total emissions from road transport due to increased traffic. With demand-oriented incentives, member states can additionally speed up the reduction of average CO_2 emissions of new cars. Such incentives have already been implemented in some countries and include scrappage incentives, extra taxes on cars with high CO_2 emissions or purchase grants for low emission vehicles such as hybrids.

Between 2000 and 2009 EU-27 greenhouse gas emissions declined. This reduction places the EU below the target path towards a reduction of 20 per cent below 1990 levels by 2020. EU-27 greenhouse gas emissions were 17.4 per cent below 1990 levels in 2009. The reductions achieved between 2000 and 2008 result from more efficient use of energy and also reflect a switch to fuels with lower carbon content. An increase in renewable energy consumption and the economic recession are the main factors behind the stark reduction in greenhouse gas emissions in the EU in 2009. Even with the average rate of decline between 2000 and 2009 the EU is not yet on track to meet its long term commitment to reduce greenhouse gas emissions by 80–95 per cent by 2050 compared with 1990. In 2009, among the largest emitters, Germany (20 per cent share of total EU-27 emissions), the United Kingdom (12 per cent) and France (11 per cent) decreased their emissions by 25 per cent, 27 per cent and 10 per cent respectively compared with the base year; whilst Italy (11 per cent of the total) increased them by 5 per cent. Between 1990 and 2009, EU-15 greenhouse gas emissions declined by 12.7 per cent, positioning the group as well on track towards the 8 per cent reduction target for 2008–2012 as set in the Kyoto Protocol.

The share of renewable energy in gross final energy consumption was 10.3 per cent in the EU-27 in 2008; the remaining 89.7 per cent was covered through the use of conventional fuels such as natural gas or oil products. In 2008, renewable electricity comprised electricity from hydro (60 per cent), wind (21 per cent), biomass (17 per cent), geothermal energy (1 per cent) and solar energy (1 per cent). The transport sector, accounting for one third of final energy consumption; 95 per cent of transport consumption is covered by petroleum products, mainly petrol and diesel for land transport. The use of biogasoline and biodiesel, practically all blended with fossil petrol and diesel, increased significantly since 2004.

BUSINESS IN ACTION

Sustainable and responsible business – Ecodesign

Directive 2005/32/EC of the European Parliament and of the Council established a framework for the setting of ecodesign requirements for energy-using products. Ecodesign is a new concept, aimed at reducing energy consumption by products such as household electrical appliances. Information concerning product environmental performance and energy efficiency must be visible, if possible, on the product itself, thus allowing consumers to compare before purchasing. The Ecodesign Directive provides with consistent EU-wide rules for improving the environmental performance of energy related products (ERPs) through ecodesign. It prevents disparate national legislation on the environmental performance of these products from becoming obstacles to the intra-EU trade. This should benefit both business and consumers, by enhancing product quality and environmental protection and by facilitating free movement of goods across the EU. Energy related products (the use of which has an impact on energy consumption) account for a large proportion of the energy consumption in the EU and include: Energy-using products (EUPs), which use, generate, transfer or measure energy (electricity, gas, fossil fuel), such as boilers, computers, televisions, transformers, industrial fans, industrial furnaces, etc. and other energy related products (ERPs) which do not use energy but have an impact on energy and can therefore contribute to saving energy, such as windows, insulation material, shower heads, taps etc. Apart from the user's behaviour, there are two complementary ways of reducing the energy consumed by products: labelling to raise consumer awareness of the real energy use in order to influence buying decisions (such as labelling schemes for domestic appliances), and energy efficiency requirements imposed upon products from the early stage of the design phase.

FIGURE 7.6
Energy certificate image

Source: Media Select International. Reproduced with permission.

The EU Sustainable Development Strategy's (EU SDS) overall objective relating to natural resources is to improve management and avoid overexploitation of natural resources, recognizing the value of ecosystem services. On the one hand, there has been continued progress in the designation of protected areas and in water quality, and the harvesting of wood from forests remains sustainable. On the other hand, marine fish stocks remain under threat and built-up land continues to increase at the expense of areas of semi natural land. Despite temporary improvements in 2002 and 2005, 23.9 per cent of total fish catches in 2009 were from stocks outside safe biological limits, and catches of all categories of non-industrial fish considerably exceeded sustainable levels of exploitation. During the period from 2000 to 2006 artificial surfaces as a whole grew in the EU. Built-up land is continuously encroaching on farmland and semi-natural land. If natural areas and ecosystems become too small, they might cease to deliver their services, such as the provision of clean air and water, water retention and carbon intake.

In the paragraphs above we have outlined the key components of the EU SDS. In particular we highlighted objectives in the areas of clean energy, sustainable transport, sustainable consumption and production and the conservation and management of natural resources. Such objectives must be accomplished through action of member states who must devise national strategies and review progress accomplished. Thus, EU SD strategy informs national SD strategy. In the next section we review one example, the UK, of such a national strategy before considering business strategies (influenced by EU and national strategies and regulations).

What is the UK doing about climate change and SD?

Not only has the UK been influenced by global bodies, it remains tied to EU policy. Environmental policy is one of the most important and far-reaching areas of EU legislation. The EU is the leading authority in this area with up to 80 per cent of UK legislation on environmental affairs estimated to derive from the EU. Towards Sustainability, the fifth Environmental Action Programme of the European Union, was adopted in 1992. The Programme sought to integrate environmental concerns with other policy areas in order to achieve sustainable development. Changes to the Treaty of Rome, agreed in the Treaty of Amsterdam, gave sustainable development a much greater prominence in Europe, by making it a requirement for environmental protection concerns to be integrated with EU policies. In 1999, the UK government outlined how it proposed to deliver sustainable development in 'A Better Quality of Life'. See Figure 7.7. This strategy set out the framework for action to deliver SD in the UK; a vision of simultaneously delivering economic, social and environmental outcomes. A better quality of life aimed to provide a national focus from which local and regional action could follow. The Government recognized that it could not do the job alone and needed to work together, forging partnerships with business, local authorities and voluntary groups. In the foreword, then Prime Minister, The Rt Hon Tony Blair, argued the last hundred years have seen a massive increase in the wealth of the UK and the well-being of its people; but focusing solely on economic growth risks ignoring the impact – both good and bad – on people and on the environment. In this publication the Government suggest that at the heart of SD is the simple idea of ensuring a better quality of life for everyone, now and for generations to come. However, they note that although the idea is simple, the task is substantial. It means meeting four objectives at the same time, in the UK and the world as a whole:

* social progress which recognizes the needs of everyone;
* effective protection of the environment;
* prudent use of natural resources; and
* maintenance of high and stable levels of economic growth and employment.

FIGURE 7.7
UK guiding principles for sustainable development

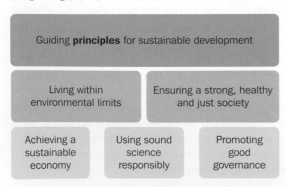

The UK's strategy was also influenced by the 'Earth Summit' in Rio de Janeiro (1992) discussed earlier. At this event it was recommended that all countries should produce national SD strategies. The UK was one of the first to do so, in early 1994. In 1997 the Labour Government committed itself to prepare a new strategy. Many of the policies in the resultant 1999 strategy were shaped by decisions at European level. Through the strategy, the Government recognised that we live in an increasingly interdependent world – 'Sustainable development in the UK cannot be considered in isolation from sustainable development elsewhere'. The UK's international priorities on sustainable development have principally been framed by the Millennium Development Goals, the Doha Development Agenda of the World Trade Organization, the Monterrey Consensus on Financing for Development and the Plan of Implementation of the 2002 World Summit on Sustainable Development (WSSD). 2005 saw the publication of Securing the Future, a revised UK Government strategy for sustainable development. More recently (2011) the UK government published 'Mainstreaming sustainable development'. This document reaffirmed UK government commitment to SD. For the present Government 'this means making the necessary decisions now to realize our vision of stimulating economic growth and tackling the deficit, maximizing wellbeing and protecting our environment, without negatively impacting on the ability of future generations to do the same.' This coalition Government states that it believes in going beyond the short term, with eyes fixed firmly on a long term horizon shift in relation to the UK economy, society and the environment.

Until March 2011, the sustainable development commission held government to account to ensure the needs of society, the economy and the environment were properly balanced in all UK decisions taken and policies implemented. Since then, the Government has set the goal of living within environmental limits and a just society. This will be achieved by means of a sustainable economy, good governance, and sound science. The government has formulated guiding principles for SD.

This set of shared principles forms the basis for sustainable development in the UK and devolved administrations. Sustainable policy must respect all five of these principles, though some policies, whilst underpinned by all five, will place more emphasis upon certain principles than others. A complete package, outlining the Government's vision for sustainable development and measures to support it is documented in 'Mainstreaming sustainable development – The Government's vision and what this means in practice', Department for Environment, Food and Rural Affairs, February 2011.

The Sustainable Competitiveness Index (SCI)

In the previous chapter we introduced the GCI which aims to capture the complexity of the concept of national competitiveness. Later in the report (2011: p51) the WEF discuss the long term view and developing a framework for assessing sustainable competitiveness. The goal of this work is to

---

Living within environmental limits – Respecting the limits of the planet's environment, resources and biodiversity – to improve our environment and ensure the natural resources needed for life are unimpaired and remain so for future generations

Ensuring a Strong, Healthy and Just Society – Meeting the diverse needs of all people in existing and future communities, promoting personal wellbeing, social cohesion and inclusion and creating equal opportunity for all

Achieving a Sustainable Economy – Building a strong, stable and sustainable economy which provides prosperity and opportunities for all, and in which environmental and social costs fall on those who impose them (polluter pays), and efficient resource use is incentivized

Using sound science responsibly – Ensuring policy is developed and implemented on the basis of strong scientific evidence, whilst taking into account scientific uncertainty (through the precautionary principle) as well as public attitudes and values

Promoting good governance – Actively promoting effective, participative systems of governance in all levels of society – engaging people's creativity, energy, and diversity

provide diagnostic tools which indicate the areas of strength upon which economies can build as well as the challenges that must be overcome in order to increase national competitiveness. As may be noted from discussions thus far, the literature on sustainability and its measurement is vast and growing rapidly. Over recent decades several efforts have been made to devise methods to capture the concept of sustainability. One such effort is triple bottom line accounting, which emerged in the 1980s in an attempt to expand the traditional reporting framework to take into account environmental and social performance as well as financial or economic performance. In addition, some progress has been made towards measuring many of the environmental aspects of sustainability. The World Economic Forum believes the relationship between *competitiveness* and *sustainability* is crucial. Given the importance of the longer-term economic performance of countries and the emergence of many factors now recognized as having a bearing on it, the Forum has embarked on an effort to integrate the concept of sustainability more fully and more explicitly into its competitiveness work. In overlaying a sustainability perspective with the GCI approach, it becomes apparent that some drivers do not matter significantly in the shorter term – and are therefore not accounted for in the GCI – but are nevertheless important over the longer term and therefore essential from a sustainability perspective. In this light, it is necessary to integrate concepts that correct for situations that might have no negative impact on productivity, or might even enhance it in the short term, but that are not sustainable or are even detrimental in the longer run.

In their 2011/12 report the authors lay out preliminary thinking about a new index – The Sustainable Competitiveness Index (SCI). This proposed index reflects the fact that some components of sustainability affect national productivity in the longer run but are not important in the short term. Sustainable competitiveness is defined by the WEF as the set of institutions, policies, and factors that determine the level of productivity of a country whilst ensuring the ability of future generations to meet their own needs. In other words, the SCI accounts for the elements required to make competitiveness sustainable over the longer run, in economic, social and environmental terms. Specifically, this new Index maintains almost all of the elements already captured by the GCI, which are important over both the shorter as well as the longer term (e.g., governance, education and health, infrastructure, the functioning of markets, innovation), but it also integrates a number of additional concepts of particular importance in the longer term (e.g., demographics, social cohesion and environmental stewardship). The resulting broader index provides a deeper understanding of the drivers of longer-term sustainable competitiveness whilst retaining the time series data of the forum's well-established GCI. In this way, the GCI can be seen as presenting a short- to medium-term view of the future, whilst the SCI presents the longer-term view, looking 20 years ahead. It makes it possible to compare and contrast those countries that are preparing well not only for a short- to medium-term future, but also for the longer term. The structure of the SCI is presented in Table 7.1.

Table 7.1 shows all of the 12 pillars of the GCI, as described earlier, which have been retained in the SCI, but reorganized into a framework of five sub-indexes that makes it possible to highlight the new elements that are critical over the longer term. The five sub-indexes are human capital, market conditions, technology and innovation, policy environment and enabling conditions, and the physical environment. To this reorganized framework the WEF have added a number of entirely new categories (new pillars) that capture areas important over the longer term: social cohesion, environmental policy, resource efficiency, management of renewable resources, and environmental degradation. High-quality **human capital** is a critical driver of productivity over the shorter as well as the longer term. Today's globalizing economy requires countries to nurture pools of healthy and well-educated workers who are able to adapt rapidly to their changing environment and the evolving needs of the production system. A key feature of human capital over the longer term that is not part of the GCI is that of changing demographics. On the one hand, some countries – particularly in the developing world – have young populations with the potential to contribute to productivity and to support the non-working population, most notably those who have retired from the workforce, for years to come. On the other hand, a number of advanced economies – including Japan and several European countries – are characterized by aging populations and relatively low fertility rates, which means they are facing significant increases in the median age of their populations over the coming

TABLE 7.1   The Sustainable Competitiveness Index framework

Human capital	Market conditions	Technology & innovation	Policy environment & enabling conditions	Physical environment
• Health and primary education • Higher education and training • Social cohesion	• Labour market efficiency • Financial market development • Market size • Goods market efficiency	• Technological readiness • Business sophistication • Innovation	• Institutions • Infrastructure • Macroeconomic environment • Environmental policy	• Resource efficiency • Management of renewable resources • Environmental degradation

Source: © 2011 The World Economic Forum. Reproduced with thanks to the World Economic Forum.

decades. An aging population may translate into lower worker productivity, a smaller economically active percentage of the population, and higher age-related costs (such as retirement benefits and healthcare needs). Such a demographic development represents a significant vulnerability to national competitiveness. Additionally, in order to retain a socially cohesive society, a population that is increasingly growing older may require a greater focus on the needs, expectations and rights of the elderly. An excessively young population also increases costs by raising the dependency ratio. Further, **social cohesion** is recognized as another critical factor in ensuring the proper functioning of the economy and the optimal allocation of resources. Social cohesion can be defined as 'the capacity of a society to ensure the well-being of all its members, minimizing disparities and avoiding marginalization'. Indeed, unequal societies are vulnerable to instability over the longer term, as they foster discontent among those excluded from the benefits of the social and economic progress enjoyed by some. Sustainable competitiveness thus requires a focus both on economic performance and on social development and cohesion.

A new pillar on **environmental policy** has been added, with four new indicators measuring the extent to which economies have instituted the types of policies necessary to protect the environment from degradation. In this pillar WEF measure the stringency of the government's environmental regulations in each country as well as the extent to which they are actually enforced. A high-quality and well-managed **physical environment** is critical for sustainable competitiveness through three key channels. Firstly, the efficient use of energy and other resources lowers costs and boosts productivity directly by virtue of making better use of inputs. Secondly, the efficient management of renewable resources (such as wood or fish that can be replenished naturally with the passage of time) ensures the extraction and use of resources today, such as water and forests, is not at the expense of the ability to use such inputs fully in the future. Thirdly, a high-quality natural environment supports a healthy workforce, avoiding damaging effects on human capital (such as illness and lower human capital productivity) brought about by pollution and other environmental degradation. Environmental degradation can also reduce the productivity of sectors directly such as agriculture, which in turn lowers output and the ability for a country to meet the food needs of the population.

WEF acknowledge there are several concepts they have not been able to capture because of lack of data, or because the relationship between the factor and sustainable competitiveness is not yet clearly established. In this light, it is important to see the work presented as the first step in a process. WEF will update and refine its thinking and methodology over time, integrating feedback and the latest research on an on-going basis.

SD, THE ENVIRONMENT AND BUSINESS

We saw from the previous section (the UK government guiding principles) a need to maintain a strong and sustainable economy which provides prosperity but within environmental limits. In their SD strategy of 1999, the UK government highlighted that, as the economy grows, consumers will have more money to spend. Economic growth of around 2¼ per cent – the average over the past 30 years – would mean that, by 2050, real incomes in the UK would be around three times their 1999 levels. If that increased spending power is to be compatible with SD, then: the products we purchase must be more efficient than they currently are in terms of the resources they use throughout their lifetime; and businesses will need to meet consumer demands with new kinds of goods and services which have a low environmental impact. In their SD vision of 2011 the UK government recognizes that the three 'pillars' of the economy, society and the environment are interconnected. In this final section we consider SD issues within the context of the firm and in particular its operations. The natural environment, with associated SD issues, presents challenges in the form of opportunities and threats to the firm. Organizations have a responsibility to seek out initiatives to reduce their own environmental impact and that of their products or services and may also look to develop products and services to help others with their environmental responsibilities.

Being more environmentally friendly and responsible often causes the organization to incur a cost and it is this that acts as a disincentive to action. In some cases, organizations may be less inclined to incur such costs when faced (see previous chapter) with less environmentally conscious competitors. The pressure for the organization to act in the interests of the ecological environment may come from customers, the Government, other stakeholders or from within the organization itself. The organization may voluntarily set goals and standards for environmentally responsible behaviour. Alternatively, companies may be encouraged to act more responsibly through the activities and influence of government in the form of taxes, fines, grants, regulation and legislation (see previous section). The tax mechanism can be used to impose extra costs on both producers and consumers (polluter pays). The effect of the tax is to increase the cost of production and reduce the output of pollutants. Grants can be used as an incentive to reduce pollution, waste and emissions and encourage environmentally friendly behaviour. Regulations can be used in a variety of ways such as to prohibit certain activities (abstraction or disposal), to set minimum and maximum limits for the abstraction of particular natural resources and discharge of pollutants and prescribe appropriate technology and activities. Environmental standards, regulations and penalties can create barriers to entry (see Porter's five forces), facilitate the search for substitute inputs and may spawn new business opportunities. Furthermore, in the future, organizations based in heavily regulated countries (early movers) may be in position to gain competitive advantage over organizations operating under less regulation. Not only may such companies gain from positive consumer perceptions, they may also accumulate experience. In some cases regulation will occur at the national level whilst in other cases environmental issues are being tackled on a regional and global scale (see for example the United Nations or European Union).

Yet many now argue that the aforementioned approach typically reflects the classical economic approach and that we need a more values based approach from the firm. When the firm values the environment as a living thing of which people are a part and recognizes that their actions leave a legacy for descendants, the firm is likely to act voluntarily in a manner associated with sustainable development. Thus, in some cases the organization may simply comply (minimal response) with regulations; in other cases the organization will go further, taking a positive and proactive stance towards environmental issues. Those organizations that see regulation as a constraint may simply pursue avoidance strategies, choosing to locate in less regulated, developing countries in order to escape tougher environmental legislation. However, there is a danger that consumers and other stakeholders consider this to be an example of the organization trying to avoid their environmental responsibilities. Many companies subscribe to self-regulation schemes and make information available to the public, principally by an environmental policy statement, together with clear targets and goals needed to meet the policy. Environmental issues are becoming increasingly important in consumer buying decisions. Consumers may avoid products that cause environmental damage or unnecessary waste or use scarce resources or resources likely, through their depletion, to impact upon other animals. In some cases the customer may be prepared to pay a higher price or seek out those organizations which they believe to be ethical.

There have been growing calls from organizations in the UK and elsewhere for clear, practical guidance to support the cost-efficient and effective integration of SD principles into business as usual, both for commercial and non-commercial private and public organizations (British Standards 2006). It is a considerable challenge to embed a systematic approach to SD into an organization's practices, given the breadth and complexity of the vision it represents, and the evolving understanding of what it really means and implies for planning and daily behaviour. British Standard 8900 starts by identifying the possible benefits and desirable outcomes of managing sustainable development. The approach throughout is to provide a framework for embedding SD management in everyday decision-making and is necessarily challenging, provoking and continually evolving. Society's expectations of both public and private sector organizations continue to expand and deepen. The concept of SD provides a framework for responding to a significant number of these expectations. For the purpose of this standard, sustainable development is taken to mean: an enduring, balanced approach to economic activity, environmental responsibility and social progress.

The long-term success of any organization will depend on the integration of economic, environmental and social performance into all aspects of operation. Thus, a coherent and comprehensive approach is needed to weigh and address the opportunities, pressures and constraints of operating in the modern world. Just like the UK government's approach to SD, discussed in the previous section, an organization's management of SD should be based on a set of principles and values with which decision-making and behaviour need to be consistent. Principles should be informed by an organization's values and should also relate to commonly held ethical norms. The principles that an organization identifies for itself would normally include inclusivity, integrity, stewardship and transparency, (British Standards 2006). In determining such principles, the organization may ask questions such as: (1) **Inclusivity** – How do you identify those who could affect or be affected by your decisions and actions? (2) **Integrity** – How do you demonstrate that your decisions and actions are unbiased, and comply with relevant rights, legal obligations and regulations? (3) **Stewardship** – In any activity will the use of resources and their consequent impact be considered and monitored? And (4) **Transparency** – How do you make certain that relevant and reliable information is available in an accessible and comparable way?

In the next part, BS 8900 provides guidance on implementing SD in practice. Firstly, at a strategic level the organization should clarify and communicate the primary *purpose* of the organization, referring to sustainable development. Management's commitment is integral to the success of any SD programme. Management should promote the *values* which express the types of behaviour they want the organization to become known for and develop a culture in which SD issues are fully incorporated within organizational activities. The purpose, vision and values of the organization with respect to SD should be reflected in its operations at all levels – embed SD into planning and management processes. At an operational and day-to-day level, the organization should identify and manage its sustainable development issues. The main mechanism should be through stakeholder engagement; stakeholders having opportunities to express views and organizations accounting for their decisions. For all organizations the issues associated with SD present both opportunities for innovation and development as well as potential risks. In order to maximize opportunities and minimize risks, an assessment should be undertaken which identifies potential issues and impacts, positive and negative, direct and indirect, and analyses key risks and opportunities (in terms of impact and likelihood) to establish their significance; the assessment enables actions to be prioritized and resources allocated to maximize opportunities and minimize risks, to achieve organizational SD objectives. For the principles of SD to be converted into practice the organization requires appropriate resources and a range of competencies. Finally, to achieve SD objectives and measure progress in a way which enhances transparency, the organization should identify performance indicators and establish processes to review progress against SD objectives (this approach is similar to that described for EU SDS earlier).

Environmental management system (EMS)

Recently, organizations have implemented EMS to help them attain their sustainability goals. In the following paragraphs we identify what constitutes an EMS, the standard requirements to create such a system and finally consider the role and adoption of EMS standards worldwide. An environmental management system (EMS) is a management approach which enables an organization to identify, monitor and control its environmental aspects. An EMS is part of the overall management system that includes organizational structure, planning activities, responsibilities, practices, procedures, processes and resources for developing, implementing, achieving, reviewing and maintaining the policy for environmental protection. International Standards covering environmental management are intended to provide organizations with the elements of an effective environmental management system (EMS) that can be integrated with other management requirements and help organizations achieve environmental and economic goals. ISO 14001 was first published in 1996 and specifies the actual requirements for an environmental management system. It applies to those environmental aspects over which the organization has control and upon which it can be expected to have an influence. ISO 14001:2004 gives the generic requirements for an environmental management system. The underlying philosophy is that whatever the organizational activity, the requirements of an effective EMS are the same. This has the effect of establishing a common reference for communicating about environmental management issues between organizations and their customers, regulators, the public and other stakeholders. ISO 14001:2004 is a tool used to provide assurance to management that it is in control of the organizational processes and activities having an impact on the environment and assure employees they are working for an environmentally responsible organization. See Figure 7.8.

The ISO 14001:2004 (British Standards 2010) *requirements* for an environmental management system, in brief, are that: the organization shall (1) establish, document, implement, maintain and continually improve an environmental management system; and (2) define the organization's environmental policy. From a planning perspective (3) establish, implement and maintain a procedure(s) a) to identify the environmental aspects of its activities, products and services and b) to determine those aspects that have or can have significant impact(s) on the

FIGURE 7.8
Legal and other requirements

environment. Furthermore, (4) establish, implement and maintain a procedure(s) to identify and have access to the applicable legal requirements (see Figure 7.8); (5) establish, implement and maintain documented environmental objectives and targets and establish, implement and maintain a programme(s) for achieving its objectives and targets. In order to do this, management shall ensure the availability of resources essential to establish, implement, maintain and improve the environmental management system. Finally, the organization shall establish, implement and maintain a procedure(s) to monitor and measure, on a regular basis, the key characteristics of its operations that can have a significant environmental impact.

In the previous paragraph we noted a need to establish a programme for achieving SD goals. Every business will have different initiatives for reducing the impact of its operations. Reducing the impact of business services and products benefits the environment and society, but also has the potential to benefit businesses themselves, through efficiency savings, reduced risk from climate change and resource constraints, improving reputation and opening new market opportunities. Examples of more sustainable business practice include:

Sustainable procurement: buying goods and services sustainably

Energy efficiency: the CRC Energy Efficiency Scheme is a mandatory energy efficiency scheme aimed at improving energy efficiency and cutting emissions in large public and private sector organizations

Resource efficiency and waste reduction: using natural resources in the most effective way and as many times as possible

Sustainable travel: teleconferencing can reduce business travel; incentive schemes can encourage employees to use alternative forms of transport

Sustainable logistics: more efficient distribution can reduce environmental impact and deliver significant cost savings

Sustainable strategy and decision making: leadership is essential to achieve sustainability in any organization

Consideration should be given to aspects related to the organizational activities, products and services, such as:

- design and development,
- manufacturing processes,
- packaging and transportation,
- environmental performance and practices of contractors and suppliers,
- waste management,
- extraction and distribution of raw materials and natural resources,
- distribution, use and end-of-life of products, and
- wildlife and biodiversity.

BUSINESS IN ACTION

Saudi Arabia has enormous potential to develop renewable energy and energy efficiency to become a global leader

The Kingdom in its pursuit to lessen dependence on oil for power generation is considering the development of alternative energy sources. Saudi Arabia is looking at various alternatives for energy resources that can help boost the country's power generation and to meet rising electricity demand. Solar energy is being increasingly seen as a likely solution that can meet this jump in power demand.

Source: http://arabnews.com/economy/article613901.ece

FIGURE 7.9

Influencing SD in firms

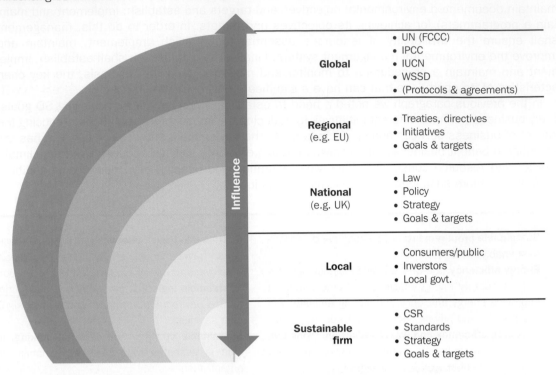

The ISO Survey of Certifications, for 2010, underlines the global market relevance of ISO's management system standards. ISO 14001:2004 retains its global relevance for organizations wishing to operate in an environmentally sustainable manner. Up to the end of December 2010, more than 250 000 ISO 14001:2004 certificates had been issued in 155 countries and economies, a growth of 12 per cent; ten years previously a total of less than 25 000 certificates had been issued worldwide. China, Japan and Spain are the leading three countries for the total number of certificates, whilst China, the United Kingdom and Spain are the leading three for annual growth. Certification of conformity is not a requirement of the ISO standards themselves, which can be implemented without certification for the benefits that they help user organizations to achieve for themselves and for their customers. Nevertheless, many thousands of organizations have chosen certification because of the perception that an independent confirmation of conformity adds value. The standard is more popular within the Far East and Europe, where 90 per cent of certificates are issued. It is less popular in North America which accounted for fewer certificates than Africa. See Figure 7.9.

SUMMARY

- Businesses have a major role to play in helping protect and enhance the environment, in line with wider goals of sustainable development. As depicted in Figure 7.2, human and earth systems are interdependent. Firms are a key part of the human system and cause changes to the world's resources and system. Earth systems shape the demand of humans creating opportunities for business to supply products and services that meet such demand.

- Whilst benefiting people in the short term, business activities also lead to long term problems in the form of global warming and the depletion of resources needed by future generations.
- Global warming and sustainable development arguments shape the actions of the firm, necessitating responsible behaviour. Short termism and profit goals can work against this if not regulated by government, other stakeholders or the firm itself.
- There is undoubtedly a consensus on the need for SD action throughout the world by business and consumers but the will to act today for the needs of the future may not always be at the forefront of daily business or consumer decision making. Consequently, collective actions may take the form of mitigation – for those motivated to sustain today's world proactively – or adaptation, for those who believe we will do too little too late to preserve it.

REVISION QUESTIONS

1. List and briefly discuss sources of environmental impact.
2. Explain why Global Warming and Climate Change are major concerns for governments, businesses and consumers.
3. Describe key global, EU and UK initiatives to address significant environmental challenges.
4. Evaluate the role of business in causing, preventing and helping to manage environmental impact.
5. Understand the meaning and significance of sustainable development in relation to business.
6. Outline the Environmental Management System (EMS) approach which enables an organization to identify, monitor and control its environmental aspects.
7. Assess how the EU implements its SD strategy, providing examples to support your answer.
8. Evaluate the seven key priority challenges reflected in the EU SDS and suggest which is most important from a business perspective.
9. Evaluate how the SCI may help countries attain their longer-term economic performance goals.
10. Discuss the 2006 EU Sustainable Development Strategy commenting on its overall aims. In your answer you should list the key priority challenges.

DISCUSSION QUESTIONS

1. Is the EU doing enough about climate change and SD?
2. Should the government be responsible for taxing carbon emissions?
3. Do developing nations have the same responsibility to limit their emissions as developed countries do?
4. Do you believe everything scientists/politicians say about climate change?
5. With such robust scientific consensus that global warming is real and is largely due to human activities, why is there so much confusion and controversy?

REFERENCES AND FURTHER READING

British Standards (2006) 'BS 8900:2006 Guidance for managing sustainable development', BSI

British Standards (2010) 'BS EN ISO 14001:2004 Environmental management systems – Requirements with guidance for use', BSI

European Commission (2009) 'EU action against climate change – Leading global action to 2020 and beyond', European Commission: Luxembourg: Office for Official Publications of the European Communities

European Commission (2011) 'Communication from the Commission to the European Parliament, The Council, the European Economic and Social Committee and the Committee of the Regions A Roadmap for moving to a competitive low carbon economy in 2050', European Commission /* COM/2011/0112 final */

European Commission (2008) 'A Sustainable Future In Our Hands – A Guide to the EU's Sustainable Development Strategy', European Communities – Luxembourg: Office for Official Publications of the European Communities

European Union (2011) 'Climate Change – KEY TERMS', European Union, General Secretariat of the Council Directorate-General

European Union (2011) 'Climate change', MARCH 2011 European Union, ec.europa.eu/clima/publications/docs/factsheet-climate-change_en.pdf

IPCC (2007) 'Climate Change 2007: Synthesis Report. Contribution of Working Groups I, II and III to the Fourth Assessment Report of the Intergovernmental Panel on Climate Change [Core Writing Team, Pachauri, R.K and Reisinger, A. (eds.)]', IPCC, Geneva, Switzerland, 104 pp.

IUCN (1980) 'The World Conservation Strategy: living resource conservation for sustainable development', Gland, Switzerland, IUCN/UNEP/WWF

Pachauri, R. (2011) 'Statement by R K Pachauri, Chairman of the Intergovernmental Panel on Climate Change, Wednesday 30th November 2011 Durban, South Africa', IPCC, available from www.ipcc.ch/docs/COP17/IPCC_chair_speech_COP_17.pdf

UNFCCC (2012), 'Feeling the Heat: Climate Science and the Basis of the Convention', http://unfccc.int/essential_background/the_science/items/6064.php

GLOSSARY

Adaptation to Climate Change The process of preparing to cope with living in a changing climate, e.g. Increased rainfall, higher temperatures, scarce water or more frequent storms

Climate Change A change of climate which is attributed directly or indirectly to human activity that alters the composition of the global atmosphere and which is in addition to natural climate variability observed over comparable time periods

Climate Change Mitigation Action to reduce the net amount of greenhouse gases released into the atmosphere, and thus helps to slow down the process of climate change resulting from human activities

Corporate Social Responsibility (CSR) The responsibility of an organization for the economic, social, ethical and environmental impacts of its activities

Ecodesign The integration of environmental aspects into product design with the aim of improving the environmental performance of the energy-using product throughout its life cycle

Ecological Environment The natural world; the surroundings or conditions in which a person, animal, or plant lives or operates. It is a part of the context in which business operates – it is capable of exerting influence on and may be affected by the activity of the firm

Emissions Trading A market-based approach to achieving environmental objectives that allows those reducing e.g. greenhouse gas emissions below what is required to use or trade the excess reductions to offset emissions at another source inside or outside the country

Emissions Trading Scheme (EU ETS) Company-level 'cap-and-trade' system of allowances for emitting carbon dioxide and other greenhouse gases, launched by the EU at the beginning of 2005

Environment Surroundings in which an organization operates, including air, water, land, natural resources, flora, fauna, humans and their interrelation

Environmental Aspect Element of an organization's activities or products or services that can interact with the environment

Environmental Impact Any change to the environment, whether adverse or beneficial, wholly or partially resulting from an organization's products, services or activities

Environmental Management System (EMS) Part of an organization's management system used to develop and implement its environmental policy and manage its environmental aspects (element of an organization's activities or products or services that can interact with the environment) Or a management approach which enables an organization to identify, monitor and control its environmental aspects. An EMS is part of the overall management system that includes organizational structure, planning activities, responsibilities, practices, procedures, processes and resources for developing, implementing, achieving, reviewing and maintaining the policy for environmental protection

Environmental Policy Overall intentions and direction of an organization related to its environmental performance as formally expressed by top management. The environmental policy provides a framework for action and for the setting of environmental objectives and environmental targets

Externalities By-products of activities that affect the well-being of people or damage the environment, where those impacts are not reflected in market prices

Greenhouse Gas (GHG) A gas, such as water vapour, carbon dioxide, methane, chlorofluorocarbons (CFCs) and hydro chlorofluorocarbons (HCFCs) that absorbs and re-emits infrared radiation, warming the Earth's surface and contributing to climate change

Green Movement The trend arising from society's concern about pollution, waste disposal, manufacturing processes and the greenhouse effect

Kyoto Protocol An international agreement, linked to the United Nations Framework Convention on Climate Change, which commits industrialized countries to reducing greenhouse gas emissions

Low-carbon Technology Technology which results in reduced emissions of carbon dioxide compared with conventional technology

Policies Procedures developed and implemented by government(s) regarding the goal of mitigating climate change through the use of technologies and measures

Prevention Of Pollution Use of processes, practices, techniques, materials, products, services or energy to avoid, reduce or control (separately or in combination) the creation, emission or discharge of any type of pollutant or waste, in order to reduce adverse environmental impacts

Scenario A plausible description of how the future may develop, based on a coherent and internally consistent set of assumptions about key relationships and driving forces (e.g. rate of technology changes, prices). Note that scenarios are neither predictions nor forecasts

Sink Any process, activity or mechanism which removes a greenhouse gas, an aerosol or a precursor of a greenhouse gas from the atmosphere

Sustainability The ability of productive activities to continue without harm to the ecological system

Sustainable Development Is development that meets the needs of the present without compromising the ability of future generations to meet their own needs

CHAPTER CASE STUDY

Focus on the EU: turning strategy into action

Here we use two case studies to show how the EU assures SD strategy results in the action needed to attain goals. Both studies consider the EU SD objective of Sustainable Consumption and Production.

In the first case EU legislation established a voluntary ecolabel award scheme, intended to promote products with a reduced environmental impact during their entire life cycle and to provide consumers with accurate, non-deceptive, science-based information on the environmental impact of products; this results in a burden on business, should they wish to seek accreditation.

In the second case we consider legislation targeted more at consumers but also at suppliers. We consider EU regulations to improve the energy efficiency of household lamps and of office, street and industrial lighting products.

Both cases can be used to explore political intervention, through SDS, and the impact on business in terms of opportunity and threat.

1. Celebrating 20 Years of the EU Ecolabel!

Enabling consumers to make more environmentally sustainable choices in their everyday lives
The Ecolabel (see Figure 7.10) is backed by all EU Governments: Regulation (EC) No 1980/2000 (later replaced by (EC) No 66/2010 on the EU Ecolabel) established a voluntary ecolabel award scheme intended to promote products with a reduced environmental impact during their entire life cycle and to provide consumers with accurate, non-deceptive, science-based information on the environmental impact of products. The EU Ecolabel scheme is part of the sustainable

FIGURE 7.10
Ecolabel symbol www.ecolabel.eu

Source: With thanks to the European Commission EU Ecolabel scheme for use of their logo.

consumption and production policy of the Community, which aims to reduce the negative impact of consumption and production on the environment, health, climate and natural resources. The scheme is intended to promote those products which have a high level of environmental performance through the use of the EU Ecolabel. To this effect, it is appropriate to require that the criteria with which products must comply in order to bear the EU Ecolabel be based on the best environmental performance achieved by products on the Community market. Criteria should be simple to understand and to use, be market-oriented and limited to the most significant environmental impacts of products during their whole life cycle.

The EU Ecolabel is the premier European award for products and services which meet the highest environmental standards. It is a rapidly growing brand – starting with just two, Dishwashers and Washing Machines, the scheme now has many more product groups. However, instigation and implementation of the label has not been without its problems. In the early days, consumers and manufacturers alike could not see the benefits of an EU Ecolabel. As the methodology for criteria development was strengthened and the criteria themselves became more stringent, companies began to see how obtaining the EU Ecolabel could set them apart from competitors. Whilst some EU countries like Denmark, Italy and France, took a keen interest in the scheme early on, in other Member States the EU Ecolabel had a slow start. Many producers wanting to sell their products across Europe have realized the benefits the European Ecolabel brings… The voluntary nature of the scheme means that it does not create barriers to trade. On the contrary – many producers find it gives them a competitive advantage. Established in 1992 to encourage businesses to market products and services which are kinder to the environment, products and services awarded the Ecolabel carry the flower logo, allowing consumers to identify them easily. Today the EU Ecolabel covers a wide range of products and services, with further groups being added. Product groups include cleaning products, appliances, paper products, textile and home and garden products, lubricants and services such as tourist accommodation. Whilst the logo may be simple, the environmental criteria supporting it are tough, and only the very best products, which are kindest to the environment, are entitled to carry the EU Ecolabel. What is more, this is a label that consumers can genuinely trust. The criteria are agreed at European level, following broad consultation with experts, and the label itself is only awarded after verification that the product meets these high environmental and performance standards. Ecolabel criteria are not based on one single factor, but on studies which analyze the impact of the product or service on the environment throughout its life-cycle, starting from raw material extraction in the pre-production stage, through to production, distribution and disposal. Since 1992, the number of companies receiving the label has increased year after year. At the end of 2010, more than 1150 EU Ecolabel licences were awarded, see Figure 7.11. Italy and France have the greatest number of EU Ecolabel holders; they are followed by Spain and Germany.

Aside from influencing consumer purchase decisions, the EU Ecolabel makes green procurement easy – Green Public Procurement (GPP) is a process whereby public authorities seek to procure goods, services and works with a reduced environmental impact throughout their life cycle when compared with goods, services and works with the same primary function that would otherwise be procured. There are many examples of the benefits to the EU and global SD goals. According to a study by Lexmark, each European employee prints an average of 30 paper pages per day. Choosing EU Eco labelled paper guarantees paper coming from recycled fibres or sustainably managed forests. The energy consumption of an EU Eco labelled television during standby mode is half that of a standard TV. EU Eco labelled products can be an important part of the solution to global warming as they must use less energy, both in production and in use, and must be easily disposable. In the second case we explore a specific example of ecolabel application – the light bulb. First we discuss minimum legal requirements and then voluntary SD targets.

2. Household lighting is becoming greener as the EU sets higher energy efficiency standards

Introduced 130 years ago, conventional incandescent light bulbs convert only around 5–10 per cent of the energy they use into light; the rest is given off as heat. They are far more wasteful than newer devices like compact fluorescents and low-energy halogens or emerging products such as

FIGURE 7.11
Evolution of the total number of licences from 1992 to 2010

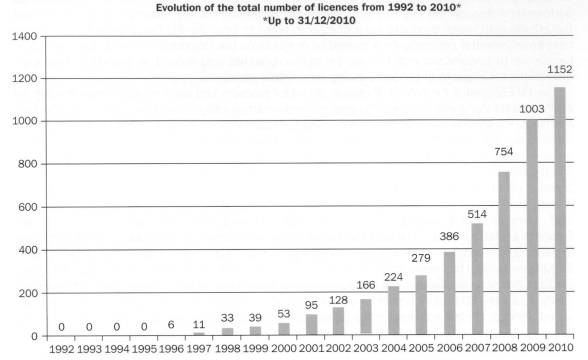

Source: European Comission 2009 © European Union, 1995-2012. Reproduced with permission.

light-emitting diodes. The EU endorsed energy efficient light bulbs by banning 100w incandescent light bulbs in 2009. The Commission adopted two ecodesign regulations to improve the energy efficiency of household lamps and of office, street and industrial lighting products, see Figure 7.12. The restrictions will be introduced as 'implementing measures' under the energy-using products (EuP) directive.

The two regulations specified energy efficiency requirements with a saving close to 80 TWh by 2020 (roughly the electricity consumption of Belgium, or of 23 million European households, or the equivalent of the yearly output of 20 power stations of 500 megawatts) and will lead to a reduction of about 32 million tons of CO_2 emission per year. Inefficient incandescent light bulbs must progressively be replaced by improved alternatives by the end of 2012. As a result of these regulations, 11 billion euros are expected to be saved and re-injected every year into the European economy. By switching to more energy efficient lighting products, European households can save energy and contribute towards reaching the EU's climate protection targets. Under the new rules, manufacturers and importers can no longer sell clear incandescent light bulbs of 100 watts or above in the EU.

However, some suppliers have gone further still and criteria for the Ecolabel for light bulbs have been established. The logo on light bulbs informs: the product has a life span of between five and nine years (10 000 hours), i.e. ten times longer than incandescent light bulbs; It will consume five times less electricity than an incandescent light bulb; It will not flicker when switched on; It contains very little mercury; It uses at least 65 per cent recycled packaging and It is guaranteed to light at 70 per cent or 90 per cent after 10 000 hours, depending upon type of bulb (see 2011/331/EU: Commission Decision of 6 June 2011 on establishing the ecological criteria for the award of the EU Ecolabel for light sources).

Acknowledgements: With thanks to the European Commission EU Ecolabel scheme for use of their logo.

FIGURE 7.12

Energy saving vs energy consumption

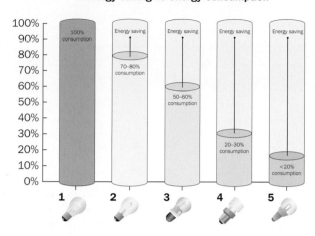

1: Conventional incandescent bulbs
2: Improved incandescent bulbs
   (class C of energy label, halogen lamp with xenon gas filing)
3: Improved incandescent bulbs
   (class B of the energy label, halogen lamp with infrared coating)
4: Compact fluorescent lamps (CFLs)
5: Light-emitting diodes (LEDs)

Source: http://ec.europa.eu © European Union, 1995-2012. Reproduced with permission.

Questions

- Do we need an EU Ecolabel award scheme?
- Discuss ways producers can show their environmental commitment.
- Identify possible advantages, for small and medium sized companies who seek accreditation under the Ecolabel award scheme.
- Should the EC adopt ecodesign regulations or is this a policy area best left to sovereign Governments?
- Discuss how the EU Ecolabel may influence consumer purchase decisions
- Identify additional (Government and Company led) initiatives that may help influence consumer (SD) purchase decisions

PART THREE
FIRMS

Having investigated the factors and analytical tools used in the external environment we now turn our attention to the *internal* environment of the organization. However, as you will see, the internal environment is partly understood with reference to the external environment. The internal environment consists of all resources and capabilities found within the organization which influence the organization's ability to act (to create outputs). There are three chapters in this part of the book:

Chapter 8: The Concept of the Firm

Chapter 9: Inside the Firm

Chapter 10: The Behaviour of Firms

Aside from an awareness of the external environment, managers must also know the internal business environment – managers need to understand the strengths and weaknesses of their organizations. They must also make decisions in the context of their external environment, shaping internal arrangement to align with the situation faced. As was highlighted in chapter 1, there is a need for the internal environment to be congruent with the external environment if the organization is to be effective. There are several favoured ways to analyze the internal environment such as the resource or skills audit, value chain analysis and comparative methods such as competitor intelligence, benchmarking and internal comparisons. We will examine the aims of the firm; strategy and structure, costs and sources of advantage and power, competences and performance.

Studying the internal and external environments in Parts 2 and 3 will ensure you are well placed to learn, through markets, how they interact, as outlined in the final part (4) of this book.

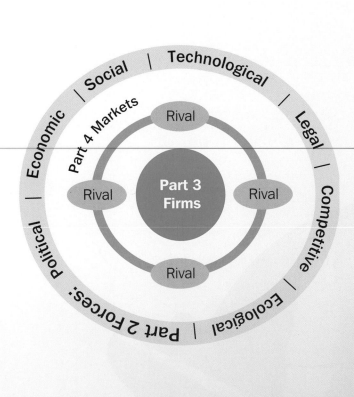

8
THE CONCEPT OF
THE FIRM

FIGURE 8.1
The concept of the firm mind map

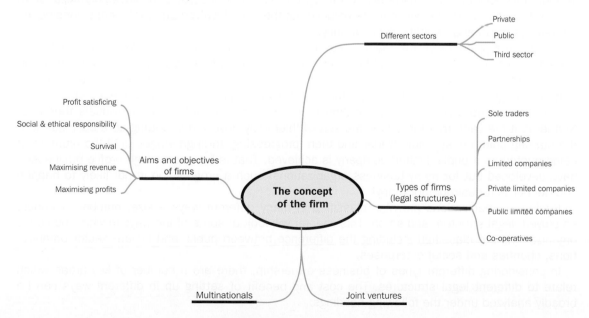

KEY CONCEPTS

Limited liability | Partnership | Public limited company (PLC) | Sole trader | Unlimited liability

INTRODUCTION

In Part 2 we introduced the PESTLE factors and discussed the competitive environment. Such factors affect organizations in different ways. There are different types of organization and each is subject to particular legal obligations and constraints; they will have differing tax regimes and may serve society in different ways. Similarly, an organization may pursue different fundamental goals and objectives (they may emphasize profit maximization or social responsibility for example) which may make aspects of the external environment more or less relevant. See Figure 8.1. In short, there is a relationship between aspects of the internal (type of firm and goals pursued) and external environment. Contingency theories (first discussed at the end of Chapter 1) emphasize this relationship suggesting that one should 'fit' with the other. Thus, knowledge of the internal environment is needed when seeking to analyze the relevant aspects of the external environment. Consequently, an understanding of firm types and goals is important for the business student seeking to analyze the external business environment. Reading this chapter will help you attain selected aspects of this requisite knowledge. There are other aspects of the internal environment to consider. These will be considered in the remaining chapters that make up this third part of the book.

There are many different types of business organization. One of the first decisions any individual or business has to consider is what type of business organization to set up. The decision may be dependent on a variety of factors including the nature of the business activity, the aims and objectives of the individuals behind the business, the access to finance, the degree of control required to be exercised over the business and so on.

In addition to being classified according to ownership, businesses are also classified according to the main markets they serve. Business to Business (B2B) organizations are primarily set up to sell to other businesses whereas business to customer (or consumer) (B2C) organizations sell to the final consumer.

There are a range of options in terms of what type of business organization to set up. As with any decision, there are advantages and disadvantages, costs and benefits and pros and cons. It is important to remember that there is never a 'right' answer to what type of business organization to set up. The decision-maker will have to balance out the risks involved and that means considering the relative costs and benefits, etc. carefully.

This chapter will look at the main types of business organization and consider the costs and benefits involved. These costs and benefits have to be considered against a background of the aims and objectives that those setting up the business organization have. It must be remembered that even large businesses will set up other business enterprises as separate legal entities. The decision to set up a business organization is not one that is confined to individuals therefore. Neither is it the case that there is some sort of 'hierarchy' involved in setting up a business with the starting point being a sole trader and then 'progressing' through stages until the ultimate of being quoted as a public limited company is achieved. That is how some high profile businesses have developed but for many business organizations, such a progression in not likely to happen and neither is it desirable for many!

Business organizations are also classified in many different ways – size, number of people employed, legal structure and so on. This chapter will look at some of the ways in which business organizations are classified including the difference between public and private sector organizations, charities and social enterprises.

In considering different types of business ownership, there are a number of key areas which relate to different legal structures. The cost and benefit of setting up in different ways can be broadly analyzed under the following headings:

- Tax liability and rules
- Extent of the liability of investors in the business
- The degree of risk taken by the owners/investors
- The degree of control of owners/investors
- The extent to which the set up requires formal structures
- Continuity of existence in the event of the death of owners/investors
- The cost of set-up

PRIVATE AND PUBLIC SECTOR ORGANIZATIONS

Chapter 1 provided an outline of the difference between the public and the private sector. Essentially the difference rests on the control, ownership and finance of organizations in these sectors. There have been increasing moves in the UK in recent years to expand the cooperation between the government, the public sector and the private sector in the form of public-private partnerships (PPPs). The principle behind PPPs is that the private sector can bring expertise, financial know-how, skills and productivity to the provision of public sector activities which will provide better value for money for taxpayers and improvements in public services.

Public sector organizations

Public sector organizations are owned, financed and controlled by institutions of the state on behalf of the public at large. They are funded primarily by taxpayers although many of them also raise money through selling products or service, for example, through the requirement to make a contribution to prescriptions for medicinal drugs or payments of fees for planning applications, official documents such as passports or driving licences and pest control. In different countries, responsibility for certain activities is split between national, regional and local government. In the UK, for example, county councils have overall responsibility for provision of education and the emergency services whilst district and parish councils oversee things such as parks and open spaces, planning issues, street lighting and refuse disposal. National government will take responsibility for the armed forces, overall education policy, trade and industry, prisons, health policy and so on. In Germany there are three main levels of responsibility, the Federal Government (Bund), regional government (Länder) and local authorities (Gemeinden). In South Africa, there are a number of areas covered by the public sector including the arts and culture, education, environment and tourism, justice, rural development and land reform, home affairs and social development.

The common feature of most public sector provision, regardless of country, is in the provision of merit goods and public goods. Public goods were outlined in Chapter 1 (see page 6); the state has to step in to provide these goods and services because it would be difficult if not impossible for any market mechanism to provide them. Merit goods are those goods and services which it is considered important to provide and which could also be provided by the private sector but which may not be consumed at the levels deemed desirable if solely provided by the market. Examples of merit goods include health and education provision.

Private sector organizations

The private sector contains a range of business organizations from small one-person businesses to massive multinational corporate enterprises. The essential characteristic of the private sector is that organizations are owned, controlled and financed by private individuals and are generally run for some specific purpose such as making profit or to promote a specific cause or policy.

The Department of Business, Enterprise and Regulatory Reform (BERR) published data in 2009 which shows that there were around 3.0 million sole proprietorships in the UK at the start of 2009, 444 000 partnerships and 1.3 million companies. Together these organizations employ millions of people as highlighted in Table 8.1.

TABLE 8.1 UK Private Sector

	Number				Per cent		
	Enterprises	Employment (/ 1 000)	Employees (/ 1 000)	Turnover (/ € million)	Enterprises	Employment	Employees
All enterprises	4 783 285	23 128	19 055	2 994 978	100.0	100.0	100.0
All employers	1 237 565	19 239	18 532	2 763 280	25.9	83.2	97.3
With no employees [1]	3 545 720	3 888	523	231 698	74.1	16.8	2.7
1	192 055	438	192	31 323	4.0	1.9	1.0
2-4	617 130	1 868	1 612	210 984	12.9	8.1	8.5
5-9	223 585	1 551	1 454	177 975	4.7	6.7	7.6
10-19	116 645	1 612	1 561	190 499	2.4	7.0	8.2
20-49	55 415	1 720	1 687	251 897	1.2	7.4	8.9
50-99	17 105	1 189	1 182	171 373	0.4	5.1	6.2
100-199	7 985	1 113	1 108	164 183	0.2	4.8	5.8
200-249	1 620	363	361	70 893	0.0	1.6	1.9
250-499	3 070	1 061	1 058	269 371	0.1	4.6	5.6
500 or more	2 955	8 325	8 316	1 224 781	0.1	36.0	43.6

Source: Small and Medium-sized Enterprise Statistics for the UK and Regions' publication (SME). Available at: http://stats.berr.gov.uk/ed/sme/
[1] comprises sole proprietorships and partnerships comprising only the self-employed owner-manager(s), and companies comprising of only one employee director.

The next section will outline the main types of business organization in the private sector. Whilst there are individual differences in the legislation relating to these types of organization in different countries there are a number of essential similarities as described below.

TYPES OF FIRMS

Sole Traders

A sole trader is the simplest and most common form of business organization in existence in the world today. Millions of people set themselves up in business with little or no formal procedures being carried out. In some countries such business activity may be in the form of a painter and decorator, a corner shop newsagent, a window cleaner, chimney sweep, plumber, landscape garden designer, builder, farmer, musician and so on. In less developed countries, individuals may 'be in business' selling shells, trinkets and souvenirs, newspapers by the side of the road, a shoe-shine facility, making clay bricks, acting as a tourist guide or golf caddy, etc.

Setting up as a sole trader is popular primarily because it is so simple. If an individual has a business idea that they think will work there is nothing to stop them from starting their business immediately and beginning to trade. As the name implies, a sole trader or sole proprietor is the owner of the business. Many sole traders employ other people but these people are not owners of the business. An important principle of a sole trader (or sole proprietorship) is the fact that there is no legal difference between the owner and the business. Dave Moss and his chimney sweep business, is one and the same thing as far as the law is concerned. What this means is that if any legal action was taken against the 'business' then Dave, as the owner, would be responsible for answering that action. For example, if an accident occurred during the sweeping of a chimney which was the result of negligence on Dave's part, then the customer might choose to sue Dave for damages. Dave would be personally responsible for the payment of those damages if the action was upheld in court.

The principle of no legal separation between the owner and the business also has implications for taxation and where profit or loss is made. The sole trader is classed as being self employed and is responsible for the payment of national taxes such as income tax and National Insurance Contributions (NICs) in the UK, for example. For a sole trader it is important, therefore, that accurate records are kept of all income and payments in relation to the business to enable them to complete accurate tax returns. Failure to do so can result in the presentation of tax demands that can seriously affect the ability of the business to be able to continue.

Equally, if the business makes any profit (which for this type of business is classed as the same as the individual's income) then it is the owner who is able to benefit solely from those profits. S/he keeps all the profit as his or her own. However, the reverse is also the case. One of the main disadvantages of being a sole trader is that the owner has unlimited liability. This means that the owner is personally responsible and liable for all the debts of the business. If a sole trader had to cease trading then any debts owed to creditors, such as suppliers, landlords, the tax authorities and so on, are the personal responsibility of the owner. In some cases this can mean that a sole trader has to sell personal assets to raise the funds to settle these debts. If this means having to sell the house, car, prized antique or any other personal possession, then this has to be done.

Ultimately if the sole trader cannot settle these debts then they are declared bankrupt. Note that whilst the term 'bankrupt' is often used in a generic way to describe any business failure, in legal terms it has a specific meaning. An individual can become bankrupt, a business becomes insolvent. The lack of legal separation between business and owner as a sole trader means that if the 'business' fails the sole proprietor can declare bankruptcy.

Unlimited liability is the biggest risk facing a sole trader. It is important, however, to think about it in exactly this way – as a risk. Risk is defined as the chance or possibility of reward, loss, harm, or damage; it may have an upside (benefit to the organization) or downside (negative occurrence).

For a sole trader the risk is that if the business does not succeed (and many do not) then there is a chance that they could lose everything. However, the perception of this risk is important. For a chimney sweep like Dave Moss, the risk involved in setting up in that line of business might be small. The cost of setting up the business is limited – he does not need any expensive office space, the basic equipment needed – brushes, ladders and vacuum cleaner – are not expensive, a vehicle will be needed for transport and apart from fuel costs, insurance and depreciation, the set up and running costs are limited in comparison to an individual setting up a plant hire operation, for example. Assume Mike is setting up this type of business. In this case the set up costs are likely to be significant. The business will need extensive premises, the initial capital outlay on a wide range of equipment can be high, maintenance and insurance costs will be much higher than for Dave, several transport vehicles will be needed to transport hired equipment to customers and a number of employees might be needed to help run the business. The set up and running costs, therefore, are likely to be significantly higher. Assume that the set up costs for Dave were €8000 whereas the set up costs for the plant hire business were €125 000. Both Dave and Mike might have borrowed the money from a bank to set themselves up; however, if both businesses failed then Dave risks having to meet his liability to the bank to pay back the €8000; for Mike the situation is much worse, he risks having to find a way of paying back €125 000, which may involve him having to sell his house in order to fund the debt. Dave may have to sell his van and personal car and whilst that is inconvenient it is not as serious a situation as that faced by Mike.

Any decision to set up as a sole trader, therefore, may have to balance out the likelihood of risk against the extent of the risk faced. For example, the risk of failure might be estimated by an individual at being 1 : 4 after four years. The potential loss incurred might total €100 000. The possible benefit might be estimated in terms of forecast profits of a total of €80 000 after four years. Given these 'odds' should the sole trader go ahead? There is no right answer to this question. There is a 25 per cent chance that the individual could lose €100 000 after four years but a 75 per cent chance that profits of €80 000 could be realized after the same period of time. This risk-reward ratio has to be considered by the individual and a judgement made about whether the reward is worth the risk involved. Some individuals are risk averse and may feel that the prospect of the possible losses and the chance of it happening is too great; others may be more risk seeking and feel that the chance of success (as measured by the forecast profit) is worth taking since the prospect of loss is relatively small (at 25 per cent). However, these same individuals' judgements might change if the odds of failure were higher (say 50 per cent) or that the chance of generating €80 000 in profits was only estimated at 20 per cent.

For many people considering setting up as a sole trader, the key issues to consider are the likelihood of the business not succeeding in relation to the extent of the loss that could be incurred as a result. The figures for survival rates of new businesses are notoriously difficult to identify with any certainty, partly because many small businesses are sole traders and do not have to submit accounts. This means the data is not recorded and so it is often difficult to be precise. However, estimates put the failure rates for new businesses at between 75 per cent and 90 per cent in the first ten years. In many cases the reasons for the failure of sole traders is not that the business itself is inherently 'bad' but because of problems with cash flow.

Failure rates for businesses do depend to an extent on the type of business. The following represents an estimate of failure rates in different industries recorded in 2007. Whilst the precise proportions may have changed since then, the data does give an overall picture of variations in failure rates.

Manufacturing – 11 per cent
Marketing services – 8.9 per cent
Personal services (includes hairdressers, beauticians) – 8.1 per cent
Private hire transport – 7.5 per cent
Retail – 6.9 per cent
IT services – 6.3 per cent
Financial services – 6.3 per cent

Printing – 5.6 per cent
Building & construction – 5 per cent
Media & Entertainment – 2.5 per cent
Recruitment and other professional services – 2.1 per cent[1]

Source: With thanks to UHY Hacker Young LLP Charted Accountants. Stats available at: http://www.smallbusiness.co.uk/homepage/news/254967/failure-rates-for-uk-business.html

Sole traders are likely to be represented more in some of these sectors than others, for example, in personal services and building and construction, but they do highlight the potential risks in setting up different businesses.

One of the problems facing sole traders is that there are weaknesses in fundamental underlying business understanding. Planning, sources of finance, cash-flow forecasting and management and often simply the capacity to be able to manage time effectively, as well as many competing skills required, are not given due weight and consideration. Setting up a restaurant because you are interested in and very good at cooking is one thing; managing and running a successful restaurant, which is about far more than simply food, is another matter. The pressure on sole traders to take full responsibility for every aspect of the business can be draining and whilst the promise of being able to enjoy all the profits will motivate many to continue to work hard at their business, many find the expected profits do not materialize in the way they expected.

Despite the potential risks involved, setting up as a sole trader is still extremely popular as a form of business organization. One of the main reasons is its simplicity. The individual has to register with tax authorities as being self employed and a self-assessment tax form completed each year for submission. The individual may have to gain various legal permissions to trade, depending on the type of business and of course has to adhere to the law of the land. Licences may be required to set up as a care home, for example, if food or alcohol is being produced and sold and so on. Sole traders have a considerable degree of internal control over their business and can be flexible in response to changes. The business can also be 'juggled' to balance out the competing demands facing the individual since all decision-making is in the hands of the owner.

Partnerships

A partnership is a business organization that consists of two or more people. In many respects it has similarities with a sole proprietorship in that it is relatively simple to set up. A partnership has unlimited liability and so has no legal status separating the partners from the business. Individuals considering entering a partnership would normally draw up some sort of partnership agreement which clarified roles, responsibilities and liabilities. If, for example, five people entered a partnership but one put in 50 per cent of the capital of the business then the agreement might state that this individual would be entitled to 50 per cent of the profits generated by the business.

As is the case for a sole trader, partners have to register as self employed with the tax authorities but in addition to individual returns the partnership as a whole has to submit a self assessment form. Income tax and NICs will have to be paid on profits. Given that a partnership is not a legal entity, if one of the partners dies or wishes to leave then the partnership must be dissolved.

Limited Liability Partnerships

In recent years, changes to company law in the UK have permitted the setting up of limited liability partnerships (LLPs). There are similarities to a traditional partnership but in addition similarities to the setting up of limited companies. However, non-profit making charities cannot form a LLP. The main reason for setting up a LLP is that the partners (of which there must be at least two) can limit their liability to the debts of the business. In an LLP the business is responsible for the debts of the

[1]Source: http://www.smallbusiness.co.uk/homepage/news/254967/failure-rates-for-uk-business.thtml

business rather than the individual partners. In the UK contact needs to be made with Companies House and an incorporation form completed. There is a small charge for this. The rights and responsibilities of each partner are laid out in a Deed of Partnership and one of the partners is identified as the contact with Companies House. This person would be responsible for the preparation of accounts and acting on behalf of the LLP in any legal negotiations.

The Deed of Partnership is a legally binding agreement which will include the personal details of the partners, how much capital each has put into the business, details of how the partnership would be terminated if one of the partners left or died as well as the roles and responsibilities of each partner. The designate partner must also contact the tax authorities to file a Partnership Statement along with the LLP's tax return which provides details of how any profits made in the business have been divided up amongst the partners.

An LLP must have at least two designated members. A designated member has the same duties in an LLP as a member but in addition is responsible for appointing auditors, signing and delivering accounts, notifying the Registrar of Companies of changes to the business, such as change of address or name, preparing other documents that the Registrar of Companies may require and acting on behalf of the business if it is wound up.

An LLP can choose its own name but there are certain restrictions over this. Using the same name as a company already registered would not be allowed nor would a name which implies that the business is a government agency, is deemed offensive or where its use would constitute some sort of criminal offence. For example, names which use the words Authority, European, Charter, Registered, Association, Benevolent, Trade Union, Trust, Foundation, National and British might have to have approval from the Secretary of State. The reason being that the use of these and other words may mislead the public into thinking the business is something it is not.

There are also regulations relating to where the name of the LLP should appear. For example, the name must appear on all business letters sent by the LLP, all notices and official publications, invoices, receipts, credit notes, cheques or other documents that have come from the business.

Private Limited Companies

Private limited company status is an important and popular form of business organization because it confers the benefits of limited liability on owners. A private limited company (abbreviated to Ltd) is a distinct legal entity. This means that the business is the entity that can sue or be sued rather than any of the individuals that may own the business. It is this legal status that makes a Ltd company attractive. If the business fails then the owners risk losing the money they have invested into the company. However, creditors cannot seek to claim recovery of what they are owed by forcing owners to sell their personal possessions to settle these debts. This is an advantage to the company owner but not to the company who may be dealing with it. This is why some smaller limited companies have greater problems accessing credit and supply agreements compared to non-limited companies.

A limited company can issue shares as a means of raising capital, however, these shares cannot be sold to, or traded by, the public. There are normally two or more people involved as shareholders although there are cases of single member companies, limited by shares or guarantee, consisting of one member. Such cases usually arise when a limited company is reduced to one member due to the death of a shareholder or some other circumstance. Single member companies have to adhere to certain regulations given that the business could have some continuity, for example, it might be subject to acquisition by another business. As such it needs to have records of decisions taken and hold general meetings with notes made on any decisions taken even if the only person attending is the single member.

There are three types of private limited company:

• **Private company limited by shares**

The business is owned by shareholders whose liability is limited to the amount they have agreed to invest in the business. If a member holds 10 000 shares with a nominal value of £1 each then

this is termed 'unpaid share capital'. If the business has to close then the shareholder risks losing all or part of this sum. If the business closed but was able to pay back £2000 to the shareholder from the remaining assets of the business then the amount unpaid that the owner would be liable for would be £8000. However, the shareholder would not be liable for any of the debts of the company in excess of the £10 000 they have originally invested.

• Private company limited by guarantee

This type of company is used in cases such as social enterprises, sports associations and non-governmental organizations (NGOs) where the members, who are referred to as guarantors and not shareholders, wish to specify the liability they have to the business. In this case the business does not have share capital and so guarantors do not contribute to the capital of the business and do not, as a consequence, purchase shares. The members agree to a nominal sum, which may be £1, in the event of the business being wound up.

It should be noted that there are in existence some companies limited by guarantee with share capital but these were formed prior to 1981. Legislation at that time prevented such companies from being formed.

• Private unlimited company

A private unlimited company is one in which members may contribute share capital and be shareholders or guarantors the difference being that the liability of the members is unlimited. The trade-off for this lack of protection is that the amount of information that the members have to disclose is less than the other types of limited company.

The rules surrounding Ltd companies in the UK have changed in recent years as a result of the Companies Act 2006. Much of the change relates to the documentation that has to be submitted and the way in which the company is organized and run. Two key documents are (1) the Memorandum of Association – a document which specifies basic details of the business and (2) the Articles of Association – that detail the rules for the running and regulation of the company's internal affairs.

Public Limited Companies (PLCs)

Public Limited Company status tends to be associated with larger business organizations (although not exclusively). PLCs have to follow clear guidelines and regulations as well as the legislation. The main reason for this is the way that these organizations are financed. PLCs are able to sell shares to members of the general public and as such safeguards have to be put in place to protect members of the public who do choose to invest in these organizations.

In the UK, PLCs cannot commence trading until they have fulfilled a number of requirements and received a Trading Certificate from Companies House. To get this the company has to have a minimum allotted share capital of £50 000 or £65 000 in either pounds or euro but not a mixture. PLCs are subject to many of the same rules as private companies in respect of the number of members (at least two) and to have at least two company directors one of whom must be a human. In addition a PLC must have a company secretary who must meet certain qualifications and experience criteria, for example by having served as a secretary of a public company for three years out of five prior to appointment, be a member of a chartered accountant organization or other similar recognized body, be a barrister, advocate or solicitor or deemed to have sufficient experience and qualities to be capable of carrying out the role.

There are a number of provisions in the 2006 Act outlined above that do not apply to PLCs. For example, these organizations have to submit accounts within 6 months of its accounting reference period to Companies House and failure to meet such a deadline incurs a penalty charge.

The major benefit of setting up a PLC is that the access to capital is much wider than in other forms of business organization because a PLC can issue shares to the public. These shares can be freely traded through a stock exchange. If it needs additional capital, adverts can be placed inviting the public to take up more of its shares.

Flotation

It is possible for a private limited company by shares to be able to convert to PLC status. This is referred to as flotation. It has to go through a number of processes to do so including having members pass a special resolution, amending the memorandum and articles of association to suit, submitting up-to-date financial documents such as the balance sheet and a copy of a report and statement by the company's auditors and other documentation relating to the assets of the business and the valuation of its shares. If the company was a private unlimited company then it also has to state that a resolution has been passed confirming the fact that members will now have limited liability and the amount of share capital to be raised.

A public limited company can also revert back to being a private limited company. Again there are statutory requirements to go through this procedure including passing of resolutions showing the agreement of members. A number of firms do this through management buyouts where the directors of the business, who may also be shareholders, buyout the remaining shareholders and re-register with Companies House as a private limited company. In some cases the managers concerned will raise the finance to buyout shareholders through borrowing funds and this is referred to as a 'leveraged buyout'.

Business Organization Outside the UK

In other countries, the principles of limited liability are similarly enshrined in law. In Germany, owners of a business are called Gesellschafter (members) and the wording after a business name GmbH (Gesellschaft mit beschränkter Haftung) signifies that these members have limited liability. Such companies must have a minimum starting capital of €25 000 and are run by a managing director who acts on behalf of the company unless the business employs more than 500 workers. In this case the company has to be run by a supervisory board (Aufsichtsrat).

German company law has a number of features that increase bureaucracy. For example, stock issues, share transfer or any changes to articles of association have to involve the services of a specialist lawyer called a notary which can increase both the time taken and the cost. In addition, members can place significant limitations on the actions of directors through the issuance of bonding orders to which they must adhere.

Table 8.2 below shows the number of steps entrepreneurs have to go through to set up a business and the time taken in different European countries. Included are the number of steps entrepreneurs can expect to go through to launch, the time it takes on average, and the cost and minimum capital required as a percentage of gross national income (GNI) per capita.

It can be seen that procedures in Germany can be more time consuming than in other European countries, with the exception of Spain where the procedures are clearly even more onerous.

Other forms of business organization in Germany include the Aktiengesellschaft (AG). This used to be the more popular type of business organization but was replaced by the GmbH primarily because of the complexity of the AG. The AG consists of a supervisory board controlled by shareholders and possibly employees, who provide the overall policy for the company which is managed

TABLE 8.2

Indicator	Germany	Denmark	Spain	Iceland	UK	OECD Average
Procedures (number)	9	4	10	5	6	5.7
Time (days)	18	6	47	5	13	13.0
Cost (% of income per capita)	4.7	0.9	15.0	3.0	0.7	4.7

Source: http://www.doingbusiness.org

on a day-to-day basis by a management board. The activities and remuneration of the management board is largely determined by the supervisory board that also have the power to remove members of the management board. This form of business organization does have similarities with structures in other countries such as the Aktiebolag (AB) in Sweden, the Societate pe Actiuni (SA) in Romania and Aktieselskab (AS) in Denmark.

There are also a number of countries who use the suffix SA after the company name. These are similar to public limited companies in the UK. The initials SA stand for Société Anonyme which translates in English to 'anonymous society'. The wide variation in the detail of company law throughout the European Union and the different regulatory structures under which countries operate can present problems to companies either operating in different European countries or who are seeking to consolidate through acquisition. As a result, Europe-wide legislation has been passed to help companies overcome some of these difficulties.

The Council Regulation on the Statute for a European Company of the EU became law in 2001 and applied to all EU states in 2004. It allows for companies to become a Societas Europaea (SE) and also enables the setting up of European Co-operative Societies. An SE can be set up in four main ways; through conversion from a national company, through the creation of a subsidiary to the main company, by acquisition of companies originating from different EU nations or through the creation of a joint-venture between companies from different European nations. The SE must have a minimum share capital to the value of €120 000 and have a registered office in a location where it carries out its main administration – its headquarters, in other words. The running of the SE combines elements of the single-tier administrative board system with the two-tier system outlined in the AG above. The management board are appointed by the supervisory board and carries out the day-to-day operations of the company. No member can be on the supervisory and management board. If running as a single-tier company, the administrative board runs the business.

Regardless of the system, each of these boards has responsibilities for authorizing different actions including raising finance, acquisitions or disposal of assets, the signing of large scale contracts relating to supply or performance and certain investment projects. As with PLCs, an annual statement of accounts must be drawn up and made public. The SE is liable for tax in relation to wherever the administrative offices are located.

Co-operatives

The International Co-operative Alliance is an organization that represents co-operative organization around the world. It defines a co-operative as:

> '… an autonomous association of persons united voluntarily to meet their common economic, social, and cultural needs and aspirations through a jointly-owned and democratically-controlled enterprise' It adds: 'Ranging from small-scale to multi-million dollar businesses across the globe, co-operatives employ more than 100 million women and men and have more than 800 million individual members'.

(Source: With thanks to ICA http://www.2012.coop/en/what-co-op/co-operative-identity-values-principles)

From this definition and additional information, it is clear that co-operatives are a significant force in the way in which businesses are organized. The roots of this type of organization go back to the North West of the UK in 1844 when workers in the cotton mills of Rochdale formed the Rochdale Equitable Pioneers Society. The basic idea was to try and find a way to gain some benefits of economies of scale by pooling their resources together to bulk purchase basic foodstuffs such as sugar, butter, flour and oatmeal. In so doing they aimed to get lower prices on these goods and then share the benefits between the members. Members had an equal say in the running of the co-operative and shared in any profits that were made. The success of the so-called Rochdale Pioneers has led to the expansion of the movement around the world. Whilst the modern co-operative movement has adapted to changing times the basic principles have been retained. Co-operatives have close philosophical ties with the social enterprise movement (see below).

There have been a number of different types of co-operative organization relating to wholesale, retail, manufacturing, employee, banking and savings and agricultural and fishing activities amongst other things. Whilst these activities vary, the basis of the movement is similar.

A number of key principles underpin every co-operative movement. These include:

* Equality of opportunity for anyone to be a member of the organization regardless of gender, race, religion, etc.

* Co-operatives are voluntary organizations

* Most organizations are democratic with all members having the right to vote on policy and decisions. Elected representatives are responsible to the membership

* Members mostly pay a nominal sum to become a member and receive a share in the organization. No one member is able to build up share allocations. The share capital invariably becomes the common property of all the members who have control over this capital

* In some cases, any profits (regarded as 'surpluses') are either divided equally amongst all members or are allocated to specific purposes such as re-investment into the organization or a nominated non-governmental organization (NGO) agreed by the members

* The early forms of retail co-operative distributed profits in the form of a 'dividend' which was based on the amount of purchases made by each member. At certain periods of the year, members were advised of the dividend they would receive. Each purchase recorded the share number of the member to help calculate the dividend received

* Co-operatives are independent and autonomous. Any agreement with external organizations has to be made with the agreement of the membership

* In keeping with the co-operative and self-help ideal, organizations promote the benefits of education and training as means to improve the welfare of all

* Active co-operation between co-operative movements is encouraged as a means of strengthening the organization as a whole

* Co-operatives have a concern for sustainable development of communities at a local, national and international level

* Co-operatives emphasize a concern for ethical trading and business operation.

The importance of co-operatives varies in different countries. In a number of countries around 10 per cent of the population are members of some sort of co-operative in other countries such as Germany, Argentina, Japan, Kenya, Iran, USA and Malaysia the proportion ranges from a quarter of the population to around a third. In New Zealand up to 40 per cent of the population belong to either a co-operative or a mutual society (organized very similarly to a co-operative) and in Singapore around a half of the population are involved.

The sectors of the economy represented by co-operatives are similarly varied. As well as the co-operative retail outlets the organization is involved in pharmacies, sugar, wheat, potato, coffee, dairy and meat production, forestry and fishing, schools and road building and services such as funerals, travel agents, banking and savings and credit. Millions of people around the world rely on co-operatives for their employment and their livelihoods.

Charities and Social Enterprises

Charities have existed since the middle ages. Up to the development of welfare states in most European countries in the 20th century, many charities fulfilled the function of caring for those who could not access the normal expected provision of society. Charities were often set up as a result of bequests in wills with a number of schools, hospitals and houses being set up as a result of some sort of charitable bequest. As governments absorbed the provision of the basic essentials of life into the welfare state, charities have taken on a different but related function. Many charities are now global organizations which also act as pressure groups for a particular cause such as poverty, the environment, animal welfare and disease. In addition, however, each country may have smaller charitable organizations focused on particular issues relevant to the local area.

The basis of any charitable organization is that it operates as a normal business organization but its aims are to serve the needs of the cause/charitable activity. Its income comes, primarily, from donations from the general public although there are now charities such as Oxfam and Help the Aged which run shops selling second hand and donated items. The main emphasis of the organization is on maximizing the funds they can make available to the cause they are associated with, whilst minimizing the administration costs of running the organization.

In most countries, charities are regulated to ensure that they meet appropriate standards of accounting and administration. This is designed to prevent fraud and misuse of funds. In operating like any business organization, a charity will have income (revenue) and costs. If revenue exceeds income then the charity will make a profit which is referred to as a surplus. This surplus can be used to improve the operational efficiency of the charity but is mostly used to fund the cause which the charity was set up for. In different countries the word 'charities' may not be used or familiar to the population. In India, for example, charities are more likely to be known as NGOs or non-profit organizations (NPOs).

Social Enterprises

One major development in the type of business organization in this field has been the growth of social enterprises. Social enterprises are a mix of business activity and charity. The idea of social enterprises originated in Italy in the early 1980s. The primary objective of a social enterprise is to focus on investing any surpluses (profits) into some community, social objective or business activity or issue rather than dividing the profit up between the owners of the business. As such they have been described as a 'third sector' – the private not-for-profit sector. As these enterprises have developed, there has been increasing interest from government in how social enterprises can be utilized to provide products and services that might have traditionally been seen as being within the remit of the public sector. Governments may be prepared to provide some financial support and assistance to such enterprises (for example by speeding up planning applications) as a means of providing public sector services more efficiently.

Examples of such enterprises in the UK include the provision of sports and leisure facilities in Birmingham, childcare, such as the TLC Neighbourhood Nursery in Wolverhampton in the West Midlands, People to Places, an enterprise providing accessible transport for people with disabilities and mobility problems in Berkshire, the Dead Earnest Theatre group and Fresh Pastures, a company providing milk to schools, both based in Yorkshire.

Community Interest Companies

Companies set up with the specific intention of providing community benefits in the UK are called Community Interest Companies and have the initials CIC after their names. Such organizations are set up as companies limited by share or guarantee as described above. In registering, however, the company has to provide a community interest statement which outlines the specific social purpose of the business. This is scrutinized via a community interest test and if the company passes this test then they can trade. There are a number of specific requirements of CICs. These include:

- An asset lock whereby in the event of the company folding, community assets are protected and the business cannot transfer or sell assets or profits for less than the full market value
- CICs set up as a company limited by shares have the option of setting a cap on the dividend paid to investors
- CICs must provide an annual statement of accounts and also an annual community interest company report which outlines what the company has done in relation to the community interest project it was set up to help

- Specific rules on voting rights of the chair and directors. A CIC chairperson, for example, does not have the right to a casting vote in the event of a divided vote at a board meeting.

Whilst many social enterprises have a philanthropic objective, they do operate ostensibly as any ordinary business. The main objectives of the business tend to be social and environmental and whilst they may have the objective of maximizing profit, that profit maximization goal is there to enable the organization to be able to fund or promote the cause they are working for. The cause may be helping those who are homeless, providing facilities to help local communities access water, promoting fair trade or recycling, providing affordable homes, insulation, sustainable energy projects, services for young people and so on.

Social enterprises are becoming an increasingly important sector. In the UK, it has been estimated that there are over 60 000 social enterprises with a combined turnover of £27 billion accounting for some 5 per cent of businesses with employees[2]. In other countries social enterprises have developed in different ways. The following is a short summary of social enterprise activity in other European states.

Belgium: There are only a small number of social enterprise organizations in Belgium. In 1996 the legal framework was amended to include the concept of a 'social purpose company'. The administration associated with setting up a social enterprise in Belgium is more onerous than in other countries and may explain the limited development of this form of organization.

Denmark: The concept is beginning to take hold in Denmark; there are four key areas of activity seeing a rise in social enterprise which include voluntary support groups such as self-help groups for those who have contemplated suicide, going through divorce, suffering from domestic abuse etc, co-operatives in retail, insurance and farming, education and training groups such as the 'work-integration social enterprises' (WISE) and various urban development projects.

Finland: The Finnish Act on Social Enterprises came into force in January 2004. The Act does not provide any restrictions on the use of surpluses or profits but at the same time there is little government support available for setting up enterprises. As a result there are only a handful of such enterprises at the time of writing.

France: In 2002 French law was amended to allow for the creation of a 'collective interest co-operative society' – SCIC (*société coopérative d'intérêt collectif*). This type of organization allows a wide range of stakeholders such as voluntary workers, local government and other partners to develop local projects. As in other European countries the idea of social enterprises is gathering momentum and moving on from projects designed to support greater integration of disadvantaged persons into the labour force which had been the primary focus of WISE organization in the 1990s.

Germany: Given the country's political background, the idea of a social enterprise is not seen as being distinct from the idea of a social market economy which dominates German political thinking. There are what might be recognized as social enterprises in other countries in Germany but many of these do not see themselves as being distinct in the same way that may be the case in the UK, for example. Such organizations include welfare organizations, volunteer services, co-operatives, local community and trading groups and women's movements. There are not, however, separate legal structures for these types of organizations as yet.

Italy: Italy is the home of social enterprise primarily in the form of social co-operatives. However, the concept has expanded beyond these types of organization and legislation passed in 2005 has now clarified the legal and organizational structures of social enterprises. There are a

---

[2]Source: This information was reproduced with the permission of Social Enterprise UK, the UK membership organization for social enterprises. http://www.socialenterprise.org.uk/pages/about-social-enterprise.html

number of key areas where social enterprises can develop including education and training, social tourism, culture and heritage, welfare, health and environment.

Sweden: The development of the social enterprise concept in Sweden is closely linked with the provision of public sector services which have increased in demand since the 1980s. Government has been unable to keep up with the demand and social enterprise has filled some of the gap. Child care services are a good example of this; some 10 per cent of provision is through social co-operatives.

Joint Ventures

Joint ventures refer to the formal links made between businesses to carry out some economic activity or business enterprise. The formal links may involve all parties contributing capital and subsequently agreeing to some form of sharing of cost, revenues and profits. Joint ventures can be beneficial to all parties without the formal expense of undergoing acquisition. There may be a number of reasons why businesses might want to form a joint venture. These include:

- Risk bearing economies of scale – all parties can share the risk which can be spread across a greater range of output and thus reduce unit costs
- Synergies – uniting the different strengths of each partner to create a venture in which the whole is greater than the sum of its parts
- Financial economies of scale – the joint venture may be in a stronger position to negotiate favourable rates of finance and improve their access to such sources
- Technology – all parties may be in a better position to share technology and to benefit from the economies of scale that result
- Markets – expertise and involvement in different markets can be shared leading to greater penetration of the key target market/s for all parties to the joint venture
- Parties may see the joint venture as being a way to strategically position themselves in a growing or mature market to protect or develop competitive advantage or to mount a defensive strategy against competitor threats
- Securing the supply chain – parties may join together to ensure stability of supplies for production or access to supplies which had previously not existed.

Multinational Corporations (MNCs)

MNCs represent businesses operating on a larger scale where the headquarters are in one country but where the firm has operations in a number of other countries. MNCs will typically do this to be able to access different markets (especially where the market may be restricted due to the existence of trade barriers), to better meet production needs for that local market, expand its brand, exploit the availability of resources such as labour and raw materials, benefit from tax or investment allowances and reduce transport and distribution costs.

Whilst MNCs offer extended opportunities to the countries in which they base their operations in terms of inward investment, employment and benefits to local communities, they have come in for some criticism that they seek to exploit host countries. There have been some high profile examples of firms who have appeared to have acted in a manner which has not put the interests of wider stakeholders at the heart of their operations and instead have allegedly generated negative externalities such as pollution, environmental degradation and illness. Whilst it seems clear that these sorts of issues can arise, the growing concern with reputation and realization that firms have some corporate social responsibility would indicate that the benefits that such firms provide may outweigh the costs which some impose.

BUSINESS IN ACTION

Joint Venture in Singapore

In November 2009, the Anglo-Dutch oil company, Royal Dutch Shell PLC, entered into an agreement with the state-owned Qatar Petroleum International (QPI) to create a joint venture in the petrochemical industry in Singapore. The new joint venture company is called QPI & Shell Petrochemicals (Singapore). Each company will own 50 per cent of the new entity. The agreement represents the second joint venture between the two following a deal to develop a refinery-petrochemical project with one of China's largest companies, PetroChina Company Limited. PetroChina is involved with gas and oil production and in a very short space of time has become the largest gas and oil producer in China. The company was only started in 1999 being established as a joint-stock company with limited liability by the China National Petroleum Corporation. The deal with Shell and QPI is one of the ways in which a company like PetroChina is able to expand quickly and exploit the skills, knowledge, expertise and technology of other companies in its sector.

Under the agreement, Shell will sell its interests in two existing companies to the new joint venture company. QPI & Shell Petrochemicals (Singapore) will, as a result, own 50 per cent of Petrochemical Corporation of Singapore (PCS) and around a third of The Polyolefin Company (TPC). The remaining owners of both companies are a group of Japanese companies of which Sumitomo Chemical Company is one of the leading ones.

The deal in Singapore is another example of how joint ventures can be used to focus on developing business in different areas and how such deals can be relatively complex. Qatar wants to expand its operations into the potentially lucrative Asia-Pacific market and needs the expertise Shell has in petrochemicals

to help it achieve its goal. Shell has its largest petrochemical production facility for the Asia-Pacific region in Singapore and it hopes that the joint venture will mean that Qatar will agree to supply condensate (hydrocarbon liquids that exist in gas form in natural gas (which can be separated out from the natural gas) and liquefied petroleum gas to Singapore.

The two companies involved with the joint venture include TPC which produces polypropylene, polyethylene and ethylene vinyl acetate which are used for a variety of applications including wrapping, food packaging, products such as coffee makers and bathroom equipment, thermal and insulation materials, foam and bags. Petrochemical Corporation of Singapore (PCS) produces ethylene and was itself the outcome of a joint venture between the Japan-Singapore Petrochemicals Company Limited (the consortium of Japanese companies) and Shell.

This agreement is part of an on-going partnership between Shell and Qatar to develop and expand their operations. The agreements form part of a strategic cooperation which benefits both the state of Qatar and Shell. Both have been looking at ways that they can identify projects around the world which would benefit both and give them a competitive advantage over rivals in the energy supply chain. They are, for example, building massive production facilities in Qatar itself and also in China where they plan to build a large-scale refinery and petrochemical production complex. Singapore is recognized as a major hub in the supply of petrochemicals in the region and the joint venture with Shell gives Qatar a foothold in this area. Qatar sees the Far East as its 'natural market' and a presence in Singapore allows it to monitor this market more effectively.

In establishing a joint venture, Qatar is not only able to gain access to an area where it might not have been able to easily without Shell's presence there, it also enables it to share its expertise with Shell to produce new products and secure supplies which benefit both.

THE AIMS AND OBJECTIVES OF FIRMS

The discussion about co-operatives and social enterprise organizations above helps to highlight the fact that whilst there are some similarities between different types of business organization both in the public and private sector, there are also plenty of differences. These differences are also manifested in the aims and objectives of businesses. There are a number of 'traditional' aims of businesses, typically the profit maximization assumption that underpins much of traditional economic theory of firms. However, it is now widely accepted that whilst many private sector (and increasingly public sector) organizations have to consider generating profits, the maximization of profits may not be the primary aim.

We will look at the main aims of firms in turn, dealing with objectives that have a theoretical background first.

Profit Maximization

This has been a fundamental assumption of the behaviour of firms for many years. Given that profit = total revenue – total costs, the implication is that a firm having profit maximization as an aim would be looking for ways to minimize costs but maximize revenue. In so doing there may be a variety of issues that arise which the firm would have to consider. For example, minimizing costs might involve a firm making a decision to make large numbers of its staff redundant or shifting certain aspects of its activities to low cost centres in other countries. In doing so, however, the firm has to consider trade-offs. The damage to image, motivation and reputation from such decisions can be reflected in lower sales and in the way in which other suppliers and stakeholders react to the firm. The benefits of decisions to minimize costs might be offset, therefore, by the costs to the firm in other areas of its operations. In particular, there is a growing expectation on firms to behave in an ethical manner and such decisions may be regarded as ethically suspect.

In theory, there is a level of output where the firm can achieve profit maximization. This is dealt with in more detail in Chapter 9. In summary, however, profit maximization occurs where marginal cost (MC) is equal to marginal revenue (MR). The firm will continue to expand up to this point because if it produces one additional unit of output and this additional unit adds more to revenue than to cost then it is worth producing that output as the surplus made (the difference between the two) will add to total profit. At the point where the next additional unit adds the same amount to total cost as to total revenue, there is still an incentive for the firm to produce that unit as it neither adds to total profit nor reduces it. This is the profit maximizing output. If the firm were to produce one additional unit the marginal cost of this unit would be greater than the marginal revenue and so would actually reduce total profit. It is not worth producing this additional unit, therefore. To appreciate the theory here, it is important to distinguish between marginal values and total values. Marginal values refer to the addition to total costs or revenues as a result of the production of **one extra** (or one fewer) units of production.

In reality the possibility of a business being able to recognize the precise point at which it maximizes profit is unlikely but it is certainly the case that a business might be able to recognize that it has expanded to a point where diseconomies of scale have set in and unit costs are rising. As a result divesting the business of some operations (downsizing) may be beneficial to its profits.

Maximizing Sales

An objective of maximizing sales means that the firm's attention is focused on increasing the volume of sales that it is making. This may mean that it has to identify key elements of the marketing mix and vary these in order to achieve the increase in sales. This may include aggressive pricing tactics and promotions. One of the reasons why sales maximization may be an objective is because it allows the firm the possibility of increasing market share. In adopting tactics to increase sales, the firm will incur additional costs. For example, major promotions to increase public awareness of the existence of the firm's product, will increase costs. The proviso of sales maximization, therefore, is that it must be carried out against the assumption that the firm will make at least normal profit. This is the level of profit which it must earn to keep it in a particular line of production. If the costs of increasing sales rise to a point where profits fall below this level then the firm will be forced to re-consider the strategy. In theory, therefore, the firm would seek to lower price to a point where average cost (AC) equals average revenue (AR), the point at which it will be making normal profits.

Maximizing Revenue

Revenue maximization as an objective is not the same as sales maximization. Revenue is given by price multiplied by the quantity sold (TR = P x Q). As a result a firm may have a relatively high price but sell fewer units and generate as much revenue as a firm with a lower price but greater volume. The key, therefore, is to have an understanding of the market so that the price charged maximizes sales such that revenue is maximized. The theory of price elasticity of demand is highly relevant here. The firm knows that if it reduces price the quantity demanded will increase and vice versa. The firm's revenue can rise or fall depending on the price elasticity of demand, therefore.

If a firm with a product which was relatively price inelastic were to increase its price then demand would fall but by a proportionately smaller amount, thus revenue would increase. If demand for its product was price elastic then reducing its price would result in a rise in demand that was proportionately greater than the reduction in price and again, revenue would rise. Given that the price elasticity of demand changes at every point on the demand curve the revenue maximization output would be where the price elasticity of demand was equal to 1 (unitary elasticity). At this point the marginal revenue would be zero. This is because the addition to total revenue from the sale of one extra unit would be neutral; if the price elasticity of demand was 1, then the proportionate change in demand would be the same as the proportionate change in price and so total revenue would not change, hence MR = 0.

Survival

Moving away from a theoretical background to aims, many businesses have a primary aim to survive. The success rate for new business start-ups is low both after the first year and after five years. One of the major problems facing many new businesses is successfully managing cash flow. This is one of the single most important reasons why businesses fail. It is estimated that around one in two businesses fail within the first two years and one in five fail within five years. Whether the business is making a profit or has not yet broken even, the goal of simply surviving is one that may occupy the thoughts of many businesses, especially small to medium-sized enterprises.

Profit Satisficing

It can be assumed that most private sector (and some public sector) organizations are expected to make a profit (or a surplus). What they do with that surplus is not at issue here, what is at issue is the size of the profit that a firm is prepared to accept. In the discussion about profit maximization above, we encountered the concept of normal profit. If we assume that there is a lower limit of profit that a firm must earn to stay in business (and this ignores the fact that some businesses will continue trading even though it makes a loss in the expectation that profits will return at some point in the future and it can finance those losses) then any profit earned over and above that level of normal profit is by definition abnormal profit. Profit satisficing recognizes that a firm may be satisfied with the level of profit that it is making even though there is a possibility that it could increase this profit. The firm may have other objectives that it sees as being important such as market share or social/environmental objectives that constrain profit maximization.

There may also be another reason for accepting a profit level below that of maximum profit. This is because maximizing profit might attract new entrants to the industry and provide longer-term competitive pressures or the attention of regulators. Making satisfactory profits, therefore, may not only satisfy owners/shareholders but also preserve the longer-term competitive position of the firm.

Social and Ethical Responsibility

The section above on social enterprise highlights the increasing awareness of many businesses of their social and ethical responsibilities. Most major corporations now produce environmental reports detailing the impact of the business' operations on the environment. The development of

BUSINESS IN DEBATE

Risk and Decision Making

One of the fundamental aspects of starting-up and running business is risk. Risk always has some influence in decision-making because of chance. A decision about whether to set up in business as a sole trader or a limited company is a vital one. There are obvious risks if the business fails and the owner does not have limited liability but the extent of the risk involved has to be considered. For example, if an individual decides to set up in business as a sandwich bar operating from a towed van in a lay-by, the risk to the owner of failure may be measured in small sums given the initial capital outlay to set up. For a similar individual planning on opening a new manufacturing facility the potential for financial loss is much greater even if the risk is the same (say one in five chance of surviving five years).

In the case of larger businesses, the risk may be shared amongst a larger number of owners but the challenges are no less difficult. In the aviation industry there are ongoing business battles between companies like Boeing and Airbus, national air carriers like British Airways and low cost airlines such as easyJet and Ryanair. In manufacturing, many European firms are facing challenging economic conditions in their own countries as well as fierce competition from China, India and other emerging economies. As each company makes new decisions they have to balance out the potential benefits with the risk involved. Sometimes they may get the decision-making right and sometimes not.

If risk is so important, as suggested, then it would seem to make sense that businesses and individuals are in a position to accurately consider the risk faced in making everyday decisions. If risk is not properly understood then our decision-making is affected and outcomes distorted as a result. A crucial part of decision-making, therefore, is our understanding of risk. To what extent can humans understand risk and be able to assess it accurately?

A speech in 2007 by Sir Paul Judge, Chair of the Royal Society for the encouragement of Arts, Manufactures and Commerce (RSA) Risk Commission noted some of the statistics behind everyday incidents that might concern ordinary people as they go about their daily lives:

- Chance of dying on the railways in 2003: one in ten million;
- Chance of dying while travelling by air: one in one million;
- Likelihood of a child being run over in any year: about one in 250 000;
- Chance of dying in a car: one in 40 000;
- Chance of dying on a motorcycle: one in 2500 – or 4000 times more likely than dying on a train.

The issue here is our understanding of these risks and how this affects decision-making. The risk of travelling by air is very small compared to that involved in travelling by car yet some people have a fear of flying. The fear is essentially irrational given the statistics quoted above. The RSA's analysis of the understanding of risk suggests that we are not very good judges of the risks we all face in life. The public attitude to an accident on a train, for example, that results in a loss of life seems to be out of proportion with the context of the event. If ten people die in a train accident, that is clearly a tragedy for those involved and their friends and family. The proportion of news and TV time devoted to such an incident is extensive. Similar attention is not paid to the fact that every year on UK roads over 3000 people die, that's 57.69 people every day!

What this all means is that if we do not understand and place appropriate weight on what are high risk activities then we make decisions that are not efficient. By this is meant that the relative costs and benefits are skewed. Money spent by the government on improving safety on the railways in response to the public outcry might be better spent on making the roads safer – thus saving more lives. The cost to companies like Cadbury of taking chocolate bars off the shelves because of minute traces of salmonella might be far greater than the risk involved of people eating the bars – what else could that money have been spent on not to mention the opportunity cost of the time and resources used up? Balance this against the contribution that chocolate makes to obesity and the cost of dealing with that problem.

When viewed in these contexts, our decision making might look pretty strange to a neutral observer, a Mr Spock steeped in logic and rational behaviour. Equally, the risks inherent in setting up in business are clear but the decision about what type of organization to set up as may be skewed by an inadequate understanding of risk. Further research into improving awareness of risk and its exact nature may be a valuable way of helping both individuals and businesses to make better, more efficient decisions.

Source: Adapted from http://www.bized.co.uk/cgi-bin/chron/chron.pl?id=2796

accounting procedures to fully capture the effect of and cost of business operations is a growing area. The development comes, in part, from an acceptance that firms have a responsibility to wider stakeholders than simply shareholders and that there may be sound commercial and business reasons for analyzing the costs associated with operations. Reputation, image and the opportunity to reduce costs are all possible reasons why firms may put social and ethical aims at the top of their agendas apart from any moral imperative.

SUMMARY

- Different countries have different rules and legislative frameworks for legal business structures, there are a number of similarities in the way business organizations are set up.
- Most countries will have relatively large numbers of sole traders operating in supplying local markets on a small scale. At the other end of the scale large multinational organizations are characterized by the fact that owners have the benefit of limited liability. Without such protection, the opportunities for investors contributing a joint stock of capital would be limited.
- Business organizations can be classified according to their legal structure, the sector in which they are operating and who the primary 'customer' is.
- Depending on the sector in which the business organization is operating, there will be different aims and objectives. In the private sector making profits is essential to long-term survival but this does not imply that all private sector firms aim to maximize profits.
- Many are satisfied with profit levels below the maximum possible because they have other objectives which may relate to market share, sales maximization or some social or environmental cause.
- The increased concern over the wider impact of business operations on stakeholders now means that many organizations will have some sort of social and environmental objectives and the greater awareness of the impact has led to a flourishing social enterprise sector in an increasing number of European countries which build on principles established over a hundred years ago by the founders of the co-operative movement.
- As business activity has grown and scale becomes more important, the opportunities of shared objectives can be exploited through the expansion to overseas markets where operations take place globally and away from the main headquarters as is the case with multinationals to joint ventures where individual identities can be secured but shared benefits gained.

REVISION QUESTIONS

1. Explain three advantages of a new business setting up as a sole trader.
2. What is the meaning of the term *limited liability* and why is it necessary to the establishment of large joint stock companies?
3. What is the difference between insolvency and bankruptcy in relation to different types of business organization?
4. A group of three individuals are contemplating setting up in business to produce a new invention they have developed. Outline the risks that these individuals would have to consider in relation to the type of business organization they could set up as.
5. In what way are the principles of a co-operative and a social enterprise the same?
6. Explain why an aim of profit maximization may not be advisable for a large public limited company.
7. Outline the key features of business organizations in different European countries.
8. What is the difference between a private limited company by guarantee and by shares?
9. What are the principal reasons for firms entering into joint ventures?
10. Why do firms have social and environmental objectives as well as making profit?

DISCUSSION QUESTIONS

1. Is it advisable for a business to make survival its primary, sole objective?
2. Why would any company set up as a private unlimited company?
3. Are social enterprises simply profit satisficing companies?
4. If risk is poorly understood, can any business decision be made rationally?
5. If sole traders are so risky, why do so many of them exist?

REFERENCES AND FURTHER READING

Allen, K. R. (2007) *Growing and managing a small business: an entrepreneurial perspective* (2nd ed). New York, Houghton Mifflin.

Bolton, B. and Thompson, J. (2003) *The entrepreneur in focus*. London, Thomson Learning

Gartner, W.B. and Bellamy, M.G. (2008) *Enterprise* (International edition). Mason Ohio, Cengage South Western.

GLOSSARY

Community Interest Company (CIC) A limited company set to function as a social enterprise, which adheres to strict statutory requirements for adhering to social purposes

Flotation The process of offering a company's shares for sale on the stock market for the first time

Joint Venture Cooperating firms create a legally independent firm in which they invest and from which they share any profits that are created

Limited Liability A situation where the liability (responsibility) of the owner/s of a business is limited to the amount that they have agreed to subscribe/invest

Limited Liability Partnership (LLP) A partnership in which some or all partners (depending on the jurisdiction) have limited liability

Multinational Corporations (MNC) Companies who own and control operations in more than one country

Partnership When you go into business with someone else (more commonly associated with professional services such as accountants, solicitors and doctors)

Price Elasticity of Demand The responsiveness of demand to changes in price. If demand changes by a smaller than proportion amount to the change in price it is said to be 'price inelastic' and if by more than the change in price 'price elastic'

Public Limited Company (PLC) A limited company whose shares may be purchased by the public and traded freely on the open market and whose share capital is not less than a statutory minimum (for the UK – a company registered under the Companies Act (1980) as a public company)

Social Enterprise An enterprise which lies somewhere between the for-profit and not-for-profit organization, aiming to make money, but using it mainly for social causes

Sole Trader A type of business entity which legally has no separate existence from its owner (the limitations of liability benefited from by a corporation, and limited liability partnerships, do not apply to sole traders) – the simplest form of business

Unlimited Liability A situation where the owner of a business is legally responsible for all the debts of the business

CHAPTER CASE STUDY

How a social enterprise pushed the right buttons

The latest fashion craze to hit the Bicol region (Philippines) is a set of accessories made from recycled buttons.

The fashion accessories line is sold by F.A.R.M. (short for Fabulously and Absolutely Rural-Made) based in Baao town in Camarines Sur, a province of the Philippines.

Their line includes bracelets, earrings, cocktail rings, French barrettes and layered necklaces essentially made from discarded buttons strung together with metal, leather bands or beads.

The products have been making the rounds at Bicol-based eco-fashion shows and most recently figured in the Negros Trade Fair held at SM Megamall, a large shopping mall outside the capital, Manila, in October 2009.

'So many people are curious about our product. They think it's a cute idea,' said 46-year-old F.A.R.M. owner Bernadette delos Santos. Since she founded the company in January last year, Delos Santos (a Business Management graduate from Ateneo de Manila University), described her ten months of doing business as 'phenomenal'. 'A regular businessman would not believe it. They cannot believe that I can make money from buttons. What others thought as trash, I found gold,' she said.

Without a store, the company promotes its wares on social networking site Facebook and sells its products through its blog site. The blog, launched in May this year, is a chronicle of F.A.R.M.'s activities, socio-civic programs like accessory-making workshops and the F.A.R.M. team's journey to success. The button-bracelet business, Delos Santos said, started in October last year as a sideline to her quilt and patchwork business in Baao town in Bicol. She would collect vintage buttons from fabrics she bought at 'ukay-ukay' or second-hand clothing stores and make them into bracelets as gifts for friends and family. 'The main thing here is recycling. When we hold skills workshops, I teach proper waste disposal and what they can reinvent into something useful', Delos Santos, a licensed teacher, said.

Encouraged by the response to her handmade accessories, she formally started F.A.R.M. about three months later, with a regular supplier of discarded Japanese buttons reportedly from clothing and button factories in Navotas. F.A.R.M. now sells a whole line of trinkets with colourful names like 'Zebra' for their monochromatic-themed bracelets and necklaces, 'Valeriana' for vintage dangling earrings, and 'Pinyapol' for accessories made with a mix of orange and yellow buttons.

Chunky buttons are stacked with smaller, more delicate ones, while plain buttons are paired with embellished or patterned buttons to make each accessory visually interesting. Delos Santos, a self-trained watercolour painter, designs the items herself. Bracelets are priced at P150 (€2.15), cocktail rings for P60 (80 cents) and earrings for P40 (57 cents). Delos Santos said she wants to keep prices low because many Baao residents here and abroad re-sell her products at trade fairs or in workplaces.

More than just being a 'cute idea', Delos Santos explained that her customers also appreciate the fact that a portion of sales are used to fund the college education of 'deserving students' in Camarines Sur through their 'Buttons to Hope' program. Currently, Delos Santos is putting three female students through college. Also, by training or employing housewives and a handful of farming families in upland villages of Baao, the company is able to provide income for poor families during non-harvest seasons.

Skilled workers are paid a certain amount for every accessory they make. One family is also paid to clean entire sacks of buttons and sort them by size and color. Each accessory comes with a tiny printed note detailing F.A.R.M.'s advocacies and who benefits from the company's proceeds. 'These bracelets aren't really [at the cutting edge of fashion]. But because of the cause, and the support of Baao people who are living abroad, so many people are buying. It's like there is pride when customers wear them because they know they are helping our municipality. It's very touching,' Delos Santos said.

With money from the F.A.R.M. bracelet business, the company was able to turn the entrepreneur's family organic farm, La Huerta Delos Santos in Barangay Sta. Teresita, into an eco-tourism destination called 'The Button Hole'. This serves as a venue for farming workshops by the Department of Agriculture and a hub for F.A.R.M. skills trainings.

Baao, an agricultural municipality located 455 kilometers southeast of Manila, is known in the Bicol region for producing three things: eggs, tilapia fish, as well as priests and nuns. The area is also a prime destination for agro-trade businesses like poultry and swine-raising, tilapia fingerling production, and crop-harvesting. F.A.R.M. gets most of its orders from customers abroad through the F.A.R.M. blog, which got 28 000 page visits in five months in 2009.

Regular customers – some of whom are overseas Filipino workers who grew up in Baao – come from Germany, Australia, Canada, three states in the US, United Kingdom, Sweden and Ireland. She ships them in bulk through the local post office. 'It's funny, I think the buttons have universal appeal. Because buttons are used by every race. And we found out that foreign buyers appreciate the products more because they have a social dimension. Meaning, this business is not just for me to make a profit because it helps people as well,' Delos Santos said. She said F.A.R.M. sells about 2000 bracelets at P150 each through the company's blog site every month. Sales at the Negros Trade Fair were also good, with Manila residents buying off her inventory. 'I overshot my rent of P60 000 (€858) a few days in,' Delos Santos said.

F.A.R.M. designs have been copied by other entrepreneurs in her hometown but Delos Santos said she doesn't mind. 'It's income for them. Besides, I'm confident they can't replicate the quality and uniqueness of our designs,' she said. With a relatively successful run selling button accessories and supporting the livelihood of her fellow Baao residents, Delos Santos is raring to expand her product line. She plans to establish a shirt line in Manila soon, after developing embellished shirts designed with discarded lace and linen. For now, however, Delos Santos and her team are 'quite fulfilled' with their project of making trinkets out of buttons. As F.A.R.M.-ers say, they are grateful from the 'button of their hearts'.

Source: ABS- CBN NEWS. http://www.abs-cbnnews.com/lifestyle/11/04/09/how-social-enterprise-pushed-right-buttons

Questions

- Is F.A.R.M a social enterprise? Justify your answer.
- What are the main differences between a social enterprise and any other private sector business organization?
- To what extent do you think that these differences exist in reality? Use appropriate examples to illustrate your answer.
- How does the way F.A.R.M operates highlight the way in which business responds to its environment?
- Is it ethical for a government to expect social enterprises to play an increasing role in public sector provision? Explain your answer.

9
INSIDE THE FIRM

FIGURE 9.1
Inside the firm mind map

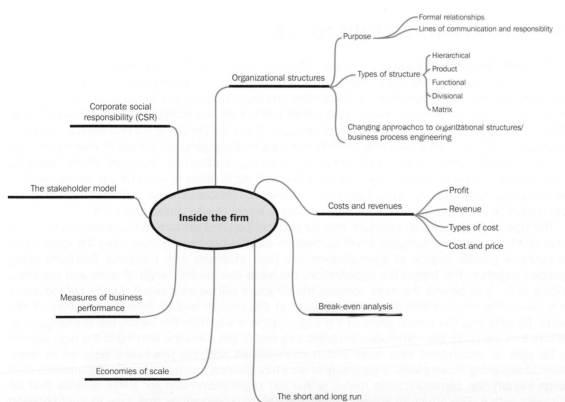

KEY CONCEPTS

Break-even | Economies of scale | Functional structure | Hierarchical structure | Line relationship | Long run | Short run | Organizational structure | Profit

INTRODUCTION

The way in which a firm operates internally can have a bearing on how it responds to changes in the external environment that it faces. This chapter looks at some of the core features of the internal operation of a business and introduces and seeks to clarify a number of important concepts. It must be borne in mind when reading through this chapter that the concepts highlighted will affect different firms in different ways; larger firms, for example, may be in a much better position to exploit the benefits of economies of scale although some benefits will be available to smaller firms.

Organizational structures tend to be classified in traditional ways – simple, functional, hierarchical, flat, divisional and so on, and this chapter will cover these main classifications. However, many larger business organizations, especially those with a global reach and multi-product output, may employ a combination of these structures. Formal structures in large corporate institutions may help to make the lines of communication and responsibility clear but such organizational structures might vary across different parts of the organization, particularly given the fact that many firms have operations in different parts of the world spanning different continents and different cultures. As a result, measures of success in one culture or part of the organization may not be the same as those in other parts. Firms, therefore, need to be aware of how their actions impact on stakeholders who may have a wide range of different views and interests in the business. The requirement for firms to take greater account of its operations on the wider stakeholder community are growing and this necessity of being aware of the importance of corporate social responsibility is changing the way that firms see themselves and their internal activities and operations.

ORGANIZATIONAL STRUCTURES

Any business beyond that of a sole trader working on his/her own will have some form of organizational structure. Organizational structure refers to the way in which an organization structures its human resources to carry out its operations and activities and the relationship of these resources with each other (for a more detailed discussion of organization structure and design see either Cole and Kelly (2011) or Kelly (2009) for an international dimension). Particular people in the firm will have different responsibilities and levels of authority and it is important for the organization to clarify what these roles and responsibilities are. The establishment of roles in an organization is an important step in helping to make sure that appropriate resources are identified and put in place to allow for the achievement of organizational aims and objectives. Clarification of roles will enable the organization to meet its goals and should be designed to make sure that everyone is aware of what those goals are.

The type of organizational structure may be partly dependent on size. Small organizations may have relatively simply structures; small to medium sized organizations may have the capacity to introduce a greater degree of specialization into their structure with particular functions being grouped together. The bigger the organization, the more diverse the range of roles and responsibilities is likely to be and the more complex the structure will be as a result. Larger organizations may have different operations in different parts of the country and in different countries of the world. Despite this the overall goals of the organization will remain the same; the challenge is to ensure that the goals are communicated effectively and to get everyone working in the organization to be able to understand their roles and responsibilities and the processes required to move towards achieving those goals. Organizational structure defines much of what the organization is. It helps identify the communication routes within the organization and for those outside that do business with it. The structure will also clarify the web of relationships that have to exist between

FIGURE 9.2

Day 1 on the new job. First task: Make coffee for the boss.

Source: Media Select International - (Patrick Currier (Patrick JPC) Reproduced with permission.

those in the organization. This may reflect the type of culture within the organization – the collection of shared attitudes, practices, values and goals in the organization. For example, an individual may have the title 'Executive Vice President' whilst another has the title 'Managing Supervisor'. The organization structure will state what relationship (if any) the one position has with the other and help to clarify what that relationship should be. Is it one of superior (higher than another in rank or authority) and subordinate? If so to what extent is the relationship hierarchical and how many rungs of the ladder exist between them? The structure will then enable those working in it to know who to go to and who they are answerable to when seeking or making decisions. The structure will also clarify the extent of formality and informality of relationships. For example, do staff who have 'superior' positions expect to be called by their first names or addressed as Ms, Mr, Mrs, etc.? To what extent do individuals in an organization have the responsibility and authority to make decisions? Who are they accountable to and for what? See Figure 9.2.

Why have a structure?

We can identify the following six major reasons:

- Organizations own and use a considerable amount of resources – land, labour and capital – and efficient use of these resources is important in controlling costs. An appropriate structure can lead to the efficient deployment and use of these resources, not least making sure that the right resources (including human) are in the right place at the right time doing what they are supposed to do for the benefit of the organization as a whole.

- Giving individuals particular roles and responsibilities helps the organization to monitor its performance as a whole in relation to the strategic aims and operational goals that have been established. Some individuals will have greater experience and knowledge of particular aspects of an organization's operation and as a result will be in a position to observe the performance of others, work with them to help them achieve their goals thus driving the organization's ambitions forward.

- All organizations have to make decisions and these decisions will always involve some element of risk. The risk might be associated with financial gain or loss but might also be related to risk to humans. For example, poor decisions related to food preparation in a restaurant could end in serious consequences to humans if not done properly whilst the consequences of developing powerful drugs to treat all manner of diseases if things go wrong, can be life threatening or create considerable suffering to victims. In 2007 a company called TeGenero tested an experimental drug, called TGN 1412 on human subjects. The drug was an anti-inflammatory drug being developed to help treat patients with diseases such as leukaemia, multiple sclerosis and rheumatoid arthritis. Six of the test subjects developed severe medical problems as a result of the drug. Facing high claims for compensation and not having extensive insurance, not to mention the damage to its reputation, TeGenero went into insolvency soon after. This incident highlights just how important organizational decision-making can be. Someone has to be held accountable for decisions and an organizational structure helps to define the different levels of responsibility and defines that accountability.

- Communication and coordination in a business is crucial to the successful execution of its operations. For communication to be a success there has to be a clear line between the sender and the receiver and a mechanism to allow feedback to be given and understood by the sender to check that the communication has been successful. The web of relationships and responsibilities makes it clear who to communicate with, when, where, how and why. Communication is the oil that lubricates the successful transmission of information throughout the organization and enables it to meet its internal and external objectives.

- The existence of some structure in an organization helps to provide specific job roles and this in turn enables a business to build-in opportunities for progression for employees. Some employees will gain an element of motivation by having the prospect of career progression and something to aspire to. For the organization it provides the opportunity to reward and also means that retaining key workers adds to the level of experience they have which helps reduce the cost of external recruitment.

- Organizational structures need to be capable of adapting to change. All businesses know that they will have to respond to and cope with change and having a structure that takes account of and facilitates such change is seen as being vital. The movement towards more flexible and less hierarchical organization structures is one reflection of the awareness of the need to respond quickly to change.

Formal relationships

Organization structures define the formal relationships between individuals and groups within a business. However, not all these relationships will be the same. Some will define the superior/subordinate relationship within an organization. Such a relationship is called a line relationship. In such a relationship authority is invested with particular individuals at different levels and tends to flow vertically throughout the organization. A sales director, for example, may be responsible for a number of sales teams in different regions. Each region might have a sales manager who reports directly to the sales director. Each sales team will have a group of sales people who report to their regional sales manager. In this example the line management structure is clear in terms of the level of authority and responsibility. Despite the lines of responsibility being clear this does not mean that the relationship between people is subservient. Many organizations recognize the importance of every individual in the pursuit of goals and this means that relationships can be relaxed and even informal. However, each person knows who they have to report to in the first instance and this makes lines of communication and the process for decision-making clear.

In some organizations, members of the senior staff may wish to appoint assistants who work closely with that person but who do not have any authority over other members of staff in the organization. Examples of these so called staff relationships include personal assistants (PAs) who have a wide range of functions and will interact with other employees but have no direct authority over them.

This idea can be extended to employing specialists who carry out a particular function but who may also not have authority over other staff. For example, many larger organizations now have dedicated IT teams that provide vital services in equipping staff with hardware and software, updating PCs, providing IT support and maintaining systems throughout an organization. The members of the IT team are unlikely to have any authority over, for example, a member of the sales or marketing team apart from implementing organization wide IT policies but the role they play in the smooth running of the organization is clear. Without the IT backup, both in the form of hardware and software, the sales team would not be as efficient. Such relationships are termed functional relationships.

In some organizations, individuals will occupy positions that cut across different departments or functions. For example, human resource departments have a particular function in their own right

BUSINESS IN ACTION

Nokia

Nokia is embarking on a sweeping overhaul of its organizational structure to try to improve the quality of its smartphones and compete more effectively with Apple.

The world's largest handset maker is splitting its mobile devices division into two units to address the challenge of combining hardware and software in smartphones.

Nokia has been criticized for failing to produce a sophisticated, user-friendly handset that can compete with Apple's iPhone.

The splitting of the mobile devices division, announced by the Finnish company in October 2009, reflects the difference between making smartphones and traditional handsets.

The first unit, called Smartphones, will be run by Jo Harlow, a Nokia veteran. She will try to raise Nokia's game in making expensive handsets that double as mini computers.

The second unit, called Mobile Phones, will be run by Rick Simonson, the company's finance director. His unit will focus on low to mid-priced handsets.

Some analysts regard Mr Simonson as a potential candidate to one day succeed Olli-Pekka Kallasvuo as Nokia's chief executive.

Giving Mr Simonson operational experience at the unit responsible for traditional handsets will be seen as an important expansion of his skill set.

The unit is extremely important to Nokia: it became the world's largest mobile phone maker by selling basic handsets in western and emerging markets.

Mr Kallasvuo said: 'After six successful years as chief financial officer, it is great to have Rick move to such an important operational role. Rick Simonson's deep knowledge of the business and its financials will be valuable for the significant part Mobile Phones plays in Nokia's business.'

Timo Ihamuotila, Nokia's global head of sales, will replace Mr Simonson as finance director.

The management rejig will build on changes to organizational structure unveiled in August.

Nokia created a Solutions unit that sought to dovetail the group's mobile phones with its portfolio of services for handsets. The unit is run by Alberto Torres, a former McKinsey consultant, and includes Nokia's mobile computer business, which is responsible for smartphones featuring a Linux-based operating system known as Maemo.

Analysts say Nokia's Symbian operating system and S60 software, used on most of its smartphones, need an overhaul. The mobile computer business will be run by John Martin, who is leaving Apple.

Source: Adapted from: www.ft.com/cms/s/0/d776564e-ba36-11de-9dd7-00144feab49a.html?catid=7#showclipthis

but they might also be expected to have an input across the organization. If a marketing department requires new staff the HR department will be responsible for working with marketing to recruit the appropriate candidate for the post/s. Other departments might identify particular training needs that are required to meet new objectives, cope with changes to production or the introduction of new technology. The HR department will be consulted in such circumstances to advise and help plan such training needs. This type of relationship is referred to as *lateral or peer relationship*. Such relationships also exist in schools and colleges where heads of department will occupy a similar position and status but have to work together on the broader organizational objectives set by the senior leadership of the institution.

Types of organizational structure

In deciding upon an organizational structure, a number of factors have to be taken into consideration. Organizational structures have people at their heart. Unlike other resources, humans respond to change and structure in different ways. The organization has to consider what human resources it possesses, how these can be organized to maximize efficiency and keep costs under control but also to increase the chances that the organizational goals of the business are achieved. Any organization may have a different structure with each having advantages and disadvantages. The outcomes of different structures may not be immediately apparent and the organization may find that its new structure does not work. It is important to remember, therefore, that structures will need to be reviewed and there may be a need for re-organization on a regular basis as the workforce changes, as markets change and as the business environment changes.

There will have to be decisions made about the basis for the structure. Will it focus on function, division, geographical region or product? Whatever structure is set up, decisions will have to be made about the roles within the structure, the relative importance of these roles within the organization, the relationships between roles and where these roles will be located. The latter point is obviously important for organizations with multi-national operations.

Having decided on the roles, decisions will then have to be taken about the extent of the authority and responsibility each is invested with and how the performance of the roles will be monitored and managed in relation to the overall goals. We must remember that the roles created have to fit in with the transformation process (see Chapter 1) and enable decisions to be made throughout the business which allow operations to be carried out efficiently. Organizations have to be aware of the potential disadvantages arising from a particular structure and, if an existing structure is being changed, how it will manage the change. An organization that has had a structure in place for many years with individuals in roles that have become highly familiar may be affected considerably by proposed change with a subsequent impact on motivation, self-esteem and productivity.

Each type of structure discussed below has its advantages and disadvantages and there is no one right approach. Each business is different, even those operating in the same industry. No two sets of employees are going to be alike and so what may work for one business may not work for another. For this reason it is not advisable for any business leader to assume that a successful structure in one business can simply be transplanted to another and work.

There are a number of organizational structures that exist and which can be represented in diagrammatic form. These diagrams highlight the main relationships between different individuals and groups within the business.

Hierarchical structure

A hierarchical structure will show the superior/subordinate relationships throughout the organization. See Figure 9.3. This is a very traditional form of organizational structure and one which increasingly is being revised in the light of the changing internal and external business environment. The lines of authority extend upwards in the organization with those at the lowest levels having less authority than those higher up. Tall hierarchical structures have many layers of responsibility throughout the business. Such structures also tend to reflect the different functions in the business – marketing, sales, administration, production and so on and the relationships between them and the staff who work in each department.

Functional structures

Functional structures may also be hierarchical but not necessarily. See Figure 9.4. Within this structure, people who do similar work (sharing a profession or specialism) are grouped together by expertise. It is a structure that focuses on the way work is done. The business structure is based around the functions that exist within it and allows individuals to exercise their particular specialism. For example, those in the marketing function may have experience and qualifications in other marketing departments whilst those in accounting and finance will have a specialism in that area. Functional structures tend to be appropriate where the business only produces a limited range of products. Where a business has a wide product portfolio especially across different markets the problems of managing the business effectively might mean that other forms of structure are more suitable. With wider product portfolios the expertise of staff in each function may be insufficient to cover the full range of products.

FIGURE 9.3

Hierarchical structure

FIGURE 9.4

Functional organization

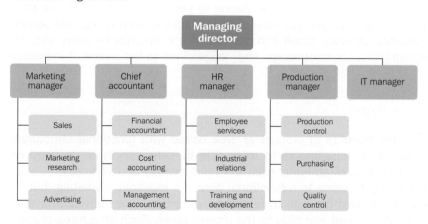

Product based structures

Here the organization is based around the range of products that the business produces. Within this structure, people are grouped according to the product(s) worked on. This structure focuses on the outputs of the transformational process, see Figure 9.5. Such an organization is suitable for a business that has a wide product portfolio or where production facilities may be based in different locations – both nationally and internationally. Each product line may in turn have its own functional departments that serve the product.

This type of structure enables a business to be able to offer a wide range of products but with the support network of functional areas. In the business above, each section of the business is able to specialize in its own area. One potential disadvantage, however, can be in making sure that each product section is coordinated with the others and that each throws its

FIGURE 9.5
Product based organizational structure

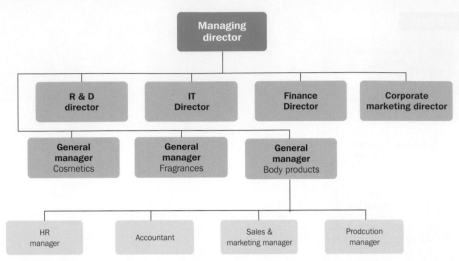

weight behind the overall corporate goals. There can develop a 'balkanization' of different products areas with each taking on its own identity and failing to integrate fully with the whole business strategy.

Area based structures

In some cases the organization may be structured according to geographical areas. Aside from area knowledge arguments the area structure may offer cost efficiencies when goods and service need to be close to the customer. Delivery, repair and maintenance costs may be lower with the area structure. The area (geographic) structure keeps knowledge close to the needs of individual countries.

Matrix structures

A matrix structure combines the benefits of product or area based with functional structures, see Figure 9.6. It allows specialist departments to exist side by side with those focused on particular products or area. The lines of authority exist both horizontally and vertically. In such a structure groups of workers might belong to a functional area, for example marketing, but its members may be assigned to different projects to lend their expertise. The individual is thus answerable both to their functional head and also to the project head. Such structures provide the element of progression for careers and flexibility for the business to utilize expertise across the organization but at the same time can create tension and confusion amongst staff who may be working for a number of different people across the business. This can create conflict between the managers of the function and the various projects as well as issues of coordination and control.

Divisional structure

There are businesses that form part of an overall business organization but which are in many respects independent. Each division of the business may have a slightly different focus but may have some common link. For example, some electronics companies have separate business areas that focus on home appliances, business systems, audio visual and so on. Each division of the business therefore is a profit centre in its own right but contributes to the overall group business

FIGURE 9.6
Matrix structure

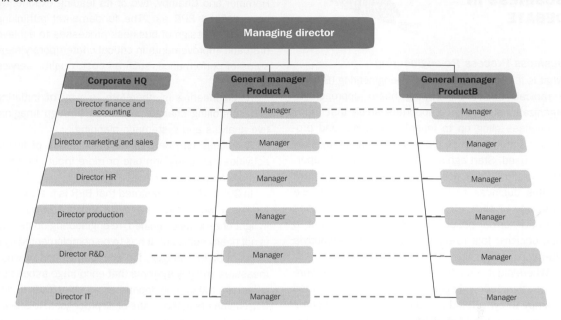

financials. Sony has divisions covering music, home entertainment, computers, optical equipment and movies. In some divisional structures, some operations will be provided centrally, for example, in some smaller organizations human resources and financial control may be overseen centrally.

Changing approaches to organizational structure

The stylized diagrammatic representations that are given above tend to oversimplify the way in which many organizations are set up. The complexity of organizations does require some element of structure but different structures may be appropriate for different parts of an organization. Many organizations now have local, regional, national and international presence. Such divisions tend to focus on North America, the emerging economies and EMEA (Europe, Middle East and Africa). The organizational structure adopted in one area is not always relevant or appropriate to another.

As a result many organizations have looked at developing more flexible structures that are designed to change with the way in which the business environment changes over time. The emphasis on hierarchy is gradually diminishing and extended layers of management seen as being too rigid and bureaucratic for a world that changes almost everyday. In addition, these hierarchical structures tend to be seen as not being conducive to innovation, a key element in maintaining and generating competitive advantage. The emphasis on organizational structure therefore tends to be more on so-called *organic structures*. These are characterized by fewer rules and regulations, more informal links between departments and functions, a greater emphasis on team work and coopera-tion and the exchange of information and ideas. The management culture in such an organization is less authoritative and places an emphasis not on difference of approach but on similarity, where good relationships are seen as being essential to generating the communication and vibrancy of new ideas and action that a business needs in order to stay competitive.

In Chapter 1 we introduced contingency theory and the idea the organization must 'fit' the challenges of the environment. We also noted that organizations may vary their structure to ensure such fit or alignment. Aside from a desire to be more creative, companies seek to compete through being responsive. This refers to the ability to make decisions quickly. Companies strive to deliver better customer service. Such goals are achieved by making the organization 'flatter' and empowering employees. Organizations are made flatter by the removal of certain ('unnecessary') management layers. Advances in ICT and business systems enable such an approach. A focus on

BUSINESS IN DEBATE

Business Process Re-engineering

What is it? Business Process Re-engineering (BPR) is a radical, back-to-the-drawing board approach to organizational change. Supporters argue that many businesses cling on to inherited systems and processes simply because those are the ones they have always used. Start again with a blank piece of paper. What would be the most sensible and effective form for this business to take? What activities can we outsource or eliminate? And what implications does this have for our headcount? Managers who want to look decisive talk re-engineering to get everybody's attention.

Where did it come from? In 1993, when belts were being tightened, Michael Hammer and James Champy threw a hand grenade into the boardrooms of the world's corporations with their book *Re-engineering the Corporation: A Manifesto for Business Revolution*. Here was the case for radical, top-down business transformation, powerfully argued: it was time to 'break the china', the authors said. Reinvent your industry and build barriers to entry by taking the tough measures others are too squeamish to pursue. For CEOs looking to justify huge 'downsizings', the book came at just the right time.

Where's it going? As a fad, re-engineering proved irresistible to a certain kind of boss. But as the recession dragged on, the wave of downsizings (later 'rightsizings') provoked outrage in the industrial world. CEOs who sacked thousands of workers and then got millions of dollars in 'compensation', were soon known as corporate killers. John Birt re-engineered the British Broadcasting Corporation (BBC) to within an inch of its life – and although the corporation may have been 'saved' for the digital age, his regime inflicted wounds from which it is still recovering. BPR may retain some of its logic today, but sensible bosses proceed with extreme caution.

Fad quotient (out of 10)

Five (and falling)

Hammer and Champy, two of its leading exponents, have defined BPR as: 'The fundamental rethinking and radical design of business processes to achieve dramatic improvements in critical contemporary measures of performance, such as cost, quality, service and speed.'

Re-engineering is, therefore, a way of initiating and controlling change processes through imaginative analysis and systematic planning.

A process can be defined as a series of linked activities that transform one or more inputs into one or more outputs.

In 2001, Hammer restated that BPR is just as valid today as it was ten years ago. He added, however, that in light of experience gained, re-engineering on its own is not nearly sufficient. It has to be complemented by a range of other changes, for example, to performance measures and pay systems that encourage a focus on corporate, rather than departmental, objectives, to putting customers at the centre of all processes, to shared responsibility and empowerment, and to moving away from confrontation towards building collaborative partnerships with suppliers and even competitors.

Managers should avoid:

- Going for BPR simply because everyone else is doing it.
- Confusing BPR with downsizing.
- Assuming you are on the right BPR track merely by introducing the latest IT.
- Focusing on individual tasks at the expense of the overall process.
- Embarking on change projects without resources and support to complete and maintain them.

Sources: Chartered Management Institute: Checklists: Operations and Quality, June 2006) and
Brainfood: Master class - Re-engineering. (Business Process Re-engineering Management Today (June 6, 2005): p.24.); and Infotrac – http://find.galegroup.com/ips/infomark.do?markListId=44802&type=markList& prodId=IPS&version=1.0&userGroupName=bized& source=gale

responsiveness is also enabled through a process orientation (horizontal) rather than a hierarchical (vertical) orientation.

One approach to organizational structure design has been that of business process re-engineering. According to this idea, businesses reflect on the fact that they are often operating in a very changed world to that in which they originated and developed. The existing structures and processes that exist might be reflective of a different era and a different organization to that which has to compete in a changed market. Re-engineering asks the basic question 'if we started again with a blank sheet of paper, how would we do things?' The answer might, of course, be 'very much the same' but it is more likely to be that things would be done very differently. The aim of re-engineering is to redesign the business structure and processes to find ways of adding value at least cost. This implies that re-engineering helps find ways of increasing efficiency and productivity and this may be partly generated through changes to the organizational structure (for further information see Hammer and Stanton (1999) or Davenport (1994)).

For almost a century scholars have been writing about the environment and its impact upon business; environmental determinism theory states that: 'internal organizational responses are wholly or mainly shaped, influenced or determined by external environmental factors'. Back in the 1960s Chandler famously argued that 'structure-follows-strategy' (and strategy must fit the external environment). The work of Pugh and others was instrumental in shaping theories about internal context (internal environment) and organizational form. Externally, the contemporary turbulent environment calls for flexible, adaptable and responsive structures; historically, a more predictable environment favoured the bureaucratic/hierarchical approach.

COSTS AND REVENUES

If you are relatively new to a business course you can be forgiven for being slightly confused at the terminology that is required throughout your course. One of the problems facing students on business related courses is that some of the terms and concepts use are also used in everyday language. The way these terms and concepts are used in everyday language is not the same as the more precise use in business. One such example is the term 'cost'. In business, cost has a very precise meaning but in everyday language we use it in a variety of ways and this is where confusion can arise. For example, we often say 'I bought a top up for a new mobile phone which cost me €25' or news headlines will say 'the cost of electricity is set to rise'. In these two cases the term 'cost' is being used when 'price' would be more accurate. Cost in business relates to production whereas price is related to sales and revenue.

There are many costs associated with managing the firm and the costs are influenced by environmental variables discussed in Part Two this book. In the next section of Chapter 9 we explore costs in more detail. Whilst reading about costs you should consider how they may be affected by the factors in the external environment and draw on the knowledge you gained from reading Part Two.

Cost

To produce anything – whether it is a product or a service, a business has to use a variety of resources usually classified under the general headings of *land, labour and capital.* Land is any of the natural resources of the earth; labour is all the human effort, mental and physical that goes into production and capital is the equipment and plant used not for its own sake but for the contribution it makes to production. In acquiring these resources a business will incur cost. It is usual to classify these costs in relation to the factor inputs outlined above. The cost of land is termed 'rent' (note this, again, is different to the everyday use of this term); the cost of acquiring labour is wages (this term also includes salaries) and the cost of acquiring capital is interest.

Any business will incur these costs in setting up and operating their business. For very large businesses the only real difference is the number of noughts on the accounts! However, there will be different types of cost that a business will incur in relation to the amount it produces and these are classified as follows:

Set up costs

All firms will have to incur some costs before the business ever sells anything and receives any income from those sales. These set up costs may include the purchase of raw materials, stock, component parts, plant and equipment, premises and so on.

Sunk costs

Making any decision in business usually involves some consideration of the cost involved. However, in some cases, costs that have been incurred have to be ignored as they are not relevant to the decision. These costs are referred to as sunk costs. Sunk costs cannot be recovered which is the reason why they are not relevant to decision making. For example, a business buys a piece of software for part of their IT system at a price of €5000. Within two months a new system becomes available which renders the software redundant. It is highly unlikely that the business will be able to recover the money it paid out for the software and will have to write off the sum as a result. It should not influence its decision-making in terms of adopting the new system because it has no bearing on the merits of the new system. This has to be considered on its own merits. It would not be seen as being rational for a business to make a decision on the new system on the basis of 'losing' €5000 spent on the software.

Fixed costs

Fixed costs are those that are not dependent on the amount being produced. They are incurred regardless of whether any output is produced. For example, businesses will have to pay for insurance such as public liability and employers' liability, they will have to pay for marketing services such as market research, have to take into account salaries of staff and will incur numerous administration costs. None of these costs are dependent on the amount of goods produced. However, they can, of course, change; insurance and rent may be subject to an annual review as might staff salaries for example. The term 'fixed' therefore, is in relation to the level of production. The definition of fixed costs, however, usually assumes that they are fixed within a relevant period of time or scale of production. See Figure 9.7.

Fixed costs will need to be considered in relation to the amount of output a firm produces. Here we need to distinguish between total fixed costs (TFC) and unit or average fixed costs (AFC):

$$AFC = \frac{\text{Total fixed costs}}{\text{Output}}$$

Total fixed costs stay constant over a given period of time or scale of production but average fixed costs will fall over a range of output. This is because the total fixed costs will be spread over that range of output. For example, assume a business incurs fixed costs of €20 000 per month. If the total output run during that month is 20 000 units then the AFC = 20 000/20 000 = €1 per unit. If, however, the firm only produces 2000 units per month then the AFC becomes 20 000/2000 = €10 per unit.

Variable costs

Variable costs are distinguished from fixed costs in that they vary in direct proportion with production levels, see Figure 9.8. If a furniture manufacturer, for example, sees a large rise in demand for its product it will require more raw materials such as timber to meet the demand. The raw material costs would be classed as variable costs. Other costs that would rise in proportion with output would be labour costs *associated directly* with production and the cost of power and fuel. It is normally assumed that variable costs rise in a linear fashion in direct proportion to output. This means that doubling the level of output would lead to a doubling of variable costs. In reality variable costs may not behave in an exactly linear fashion but the general principle still applies. What this implies is that the average variable cost or unit cost is constant over that output level. Average variable costs (AVC) are found by using the following formula:

$$AVC = \frac{\text{Total Variable Costs}}{\text{Output}}$$

If the furniture manufacturer we referred to above makes 500 coffee tables in one month and the variable costs are €37 500, the average variable cost per table would be 37 500/500 = €75. If in the next month output rises to 1000 then the variable cost would double (assuming raw material prices remained constant) to €75 000. The AVC will still, however, be 75 000/1000 = €75.

Marginal costs

Many business decisions are made on the basis of cost but one important cost element that must be considered is marginal cost, see Figure 9.10. Marginal cost (MC) is the cost of the next additional unit produced. It can be expressed in the formula:

$$MC = TC_n - TC_{n-1}$$

where TC_n is the total cost of producing n number of units and TC_{n-1} the total cost of producing one fewer units.

MC has an important role in pricing. For example, take the case of an airline operating a route between London and New York. The total cost of the flight will include the cost of the aircraft in the first place, the staff costs of the pilots and cabin crew, fuel, food and entertainment and airport charges. The number of passengers on board is the 'output' but the additional cost of seating one extra passenger is minimal. There will be the cost of an extra meal, there will be some effect on the weight of the aircraft which affects fuel load and so on. However, for one extra passenger this sum is likely to be dwarfed by the fixed costs of flying the route.

Assume that the total cost of the flight is €150 000 of which the fixed costs are €125 000. The flight will operate whether there is one passenger or a full quota of 400. The firm is able to operate a pricing structure that enables it to exploit its knowledge of marginal cost to maximize the revenue for the flight. There will be some passengers who book in advance at, say, a price of €550 per seat. If the flight manages to pre-book 150 passengers this way the revenue from these passengers will be €82 500. The firm still has a margin of €67 500 to generate to break-even on the flight. Basic demand theory tells us that if prices are lowered it will lead to an increase in the quantity demanded. The airline may offer discount prices up to and including the day of the flight to try and ensure that the plane is as full as possible.

It might offer a range of seats at a discount price of €400 which encourage an extra 100 passengers bringing the total revenue generated to €122 500. The airline knows that it still needs to generate more revenue and so continues to discount prices to encourage more sales. From the information above we know that the variable costs of the flight are €25 000 and with a maximum quota of 400 seats, the variable cost per passenger is €62.50. This is the marginal cost per passenger; the cost of seating one extra passenger on the plane. In theory, therefore, the firm could offer seats at a price of €62.50 to ensure the capacity is fully utilized. The firm may continue to discount prices down to this price to fill the plane. Any price above €62.50 not only covers the marginal cost but also makes a *contribution* to the fixed costs which give the firm considerable flexibility in its pricing options. For passengers, therefore, the fares they pay might be very different for exactly the same flight depending on when they booked, what deals they were able to get and so on.

FIGURE 9.10

Marginal costs

The marginal cost curve shows additional units can be produced at lower cost initially but then begin to rise as additional units are produced.

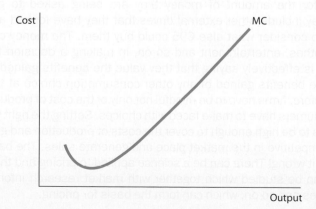

BUSINESS IN ACTION

Train ticket pricing

Train operator South West Trains, which operates services from London Waterloo to the south coast and the south west of England, often sell single tickets for rail journeys for just £1.

Not every ticket is priced at this level and there are restrictions that apply. In one case, 3000 single tickets were made available between London, Portsmouth and Southampton. Passengers had to book in advance by phone or use a special website – megatrain.com – to access the tickets.

These are tickets that could be used on off-peak services and were also not valid for use on Sundays. The tickets were offered at substantially lower prices than normal with many priced at less than £10. This is in comparison to a standard day single which is priced at around £25 between London and Southampton for example.

In reality many airlines offer cheaper seats on schedule flights several months in advance and the closer the flight gets to departure the prices actually rise reflecting the relative demand and supply of seats. However, the principle of marginal cost pricing outlined above can be relevant to airlines.

Marginal cost is important in any firm where the vast majority of the costs incurred in production tend to be fixed costs. In the case of vehicle rental, for example, the cost of hiring out a vehicle to a customer is mostly fixed – whether the customer has it for one day or for a week makes little difference to the overall cost to the hire firm. As a result, even if a customer only wanted the car for a half day, the firm would have to charge a full rate to cover the total costs of hiring the vehicle out. However, they do have some flexibility in the pricing that they can offer over a longer period of time because the marginal cost is relatively small.

Revenues

The revenue a firm receives is the money that it generates from selling its products or services. It is calculated by multiplying the price charged (P) by the quantity sold (Q) – both of which are influenced by the external environment:

$$TR = P \times Q$$

The price is the amount of money that the customer is asked to give up to acquire the good or service. In making a consumption decision, the customer is being asked to make a sacrifice. If, for example, an external disc drive for a PC is priced at €95 the consumer is faced with a number of issues. They will have to consider whether the price represents value for money and to do this they will have to consider whether the product will fulfil the function that they require it for and whether it seems to be a quality product, but they will also have to consider what other consumption options are available to them for the amount of money they are being asked to give up. The other consumption options may include other external drives that they have looked at from competitors but they will also have to consider what else €95 could buy them. The money could also be spent on weekly shopping, clothes, entertainment and so on. In making a decision to buy the external hard drive the customer is effectively saying that they value the benefits gained from consumption of this product above the benefits gained of any other consumption choice at that time.

In setting prices, therefore, firms have to be mindful not only of the cost of production but also of the value decisions that consumers have to make faced with choices. Setting the right price is therefore an important decision. It has to be high enough to cover the costs of production and generate some profit but low enough to be competitive in the market place and generate sales. The balance is not always easy and many firms get it wrong! There can be a science applied to pricing and there are a number of *pricing strategies* that can be studied which together with market research information, data about estimated price elasticities and so on, which can form the basis for pricing.

FIGURE 9.11

Total revenue

Panel (a) shows a linear total revenue curve rising as sales rise. This assumes that the firms sell each extra unit at the same price. In Panel (b) total revenue is depicted in curvilinear fashion. This assumes that at some point firms will have to adjust price in order to sell additional quantities; as sales increase successive units may only be sold if price is lowered hence the TR curve eventually slows and then falls as sales increase.

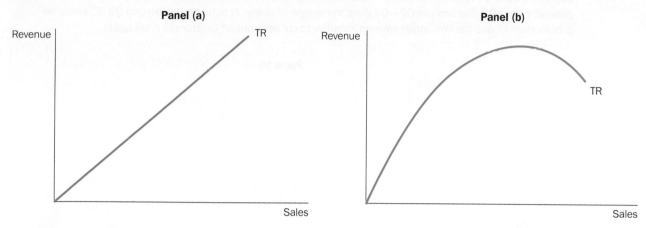

Ultimately there are a very large number of other factors including competition, packaging, placement, the product itself, the economic climate, and the people associated with the selling amongst many others that will determine whether the price set is appropriate for the product and will generate sufficient sales to enable the firm to make profit. Further analysis of the role of price in markets will be covered in Chapter 11.

As with our study of costs, there are a number of basic concepts associated with revenue that we must consider. *Total revenue* rises in a linear fashion in relation to the volume of sales, see Figure 9.11. Assuming that price is constant, as sales volumes rise the total revenue will also rise. However, the rate at which total revenue rises will be unlikely to stay constant over large sales volumes. It is normally assumed that to sell increasing amounts of a product a firm will have to lower price and so the actual total revenue curve will be more likely to be curvilinear.

As with costs, we can identify average revenue by taking the total revenue and dividing it by the number of sales (Q):

$$AR = TR / Q$$

Marginal revenue is the addition to total revenue from the sale of one extra unit of output:

$$MR = TR_n - TR_{n-1}$$

where TR_n is the total revenue received from selling n units of output and TR_{n-1} the total revenue received from selling one fewer units of output.

Profit

Putting total revenue and total cost together gives us a calculation of profit, see Figure 9.12. Profit is the difference between total revenue and total costs given by the formula:

$$Profit = TR - TC.$$

If TR is greater than TC then the firm will be making profit and if TR is less than TC then the firm will be making a loss.

However, we have to be careful when looking at this simple interpretation because the actual calculations of profit or loss will be dependent on a large range of factors including the time period being considered, how to account for stock levels, when to recognize revenues (the revenue does not always arrive at the time that a product is sold because of trade terms, delayed payment and so

FIGURE 9.12

Profit

Panel (a) shows a linear cost curve suggesting costs rising in direct proportion to output, Panel (b) and the curvilinear total revenue curve from Panel (b) in Figure 9.11. Panel (c) puts these two curves together. At output levels below Q1, the firm makes a loss. At Q1 it breaks-even where total costs = total revenue. At output levels between Q1 and Q3 the firm makes profit because TR is greater than TC with the point where profits are highest given at output Q2. The amount Q2 – Q1 gives the margin of safety. At output levels beyond Q3, TC would be greater than TR and the firm would have an incentive to cut back output to return to profit again.

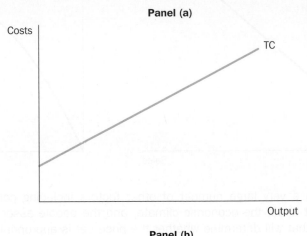

Panel (a)

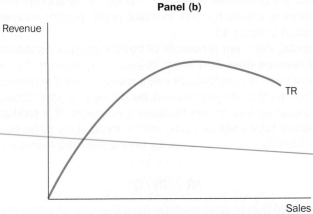

Panel (b)

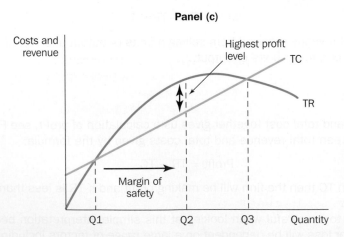

Panel (c)

on), apportioning different types of costs, the effect of changes to exchange rates and so on. This complicates the picture in many businesses and is governed by accounting rules.

For this analysis, however, we will assume a more simplistic approach to calculating profit as given by the formula above. The level of profit that a firm generates is an important consideration. In many economics textbooks there is an assumption that the main objective of a firm is to maximize profits. This implies that the difference between total cost and total revenue (as discussed in the previous chapter) must be at a maximum. In practice the objectives of a firm are more complex than simply profit maximization although there is no denying the fact that a firm must make some profit over a period of time to survive.

In many cases, firms may not realize profits for some considerable time. The set up costs of a new venture have to be incurred before any product is sold and generates revenue and it will take some time before the revenue generated is sufficient to cover the cost of production and the firm moves into profit. What will be important to the firm is to make sure that the price charged is at least sufficient to cover the variable costs of operation but in most cases will be above the variable costs. The difference between the selling price and the variable cost is called the contribution. If the selling price is €10.50 and the variable costs of production are €4.00 then the contribution will be €6.50. This will represent the contribution to the fixed costs. This concept will become clearer when we look at break-even analysis later in this chapter.

Most firms will have some idea of a level of profit that represents an appropriate level of return for the risk involved in a project. The return is invariably expressed as a percentage relating the cost of the project and the revenue generated. The simplicity of this ratio does hide the fact that in practice the picture will be complicated by the flows of revenue over a period of time as stated above. The concept of *profit margin* is appropriate for us to consider the main features of profit in this context. The profit margin is simply the difference between the selling price and the cost of production. It is mostly expressed as a percentage. If the selling price of a PC is €500 and the cost of production, calculated on a per unit basis, is estimated at €400 then the profit margin on each unit is €100 or 20 per cent. Some products sell large volumes and the profit margin on each might be very small. The total profit, however, can still be large when considering the volumes sold. Other products may sell very small volumes but have relatively high profit margins. These types of products are likely to be products that are perceived by consumers as having very high value added and/or are highly specialized items.

In assessing the level of profit and deciding whether it is appropriate a firm will consider a variety of other factors including interest rates, the time value of money (calculated through the use of present value) inflation and the return from alternative investment opportunities. The lowest level of profit that is required to keep a business in a particular line of production is referred to as normal profit. Exactly what normal profit might be is not possible to quantify as it will vary in different situations. For the sake of illustration, however, consider a computer expert who goes into business on his/her own repairing and maintaining PCs. They might consider the level of normal profit to be equivalent to the amount they could earn by working for someone else. If this salary level was €35 000 a year then that is the minimum that the individual would want to earn as profit from their business venture. In this case, this would be the level of normal profit.

If the level of profit generated was actually €50 000 a year then this would be regarded as being abnormal profit. Abnormal profit is any amount over and above the level of normal profit. In theory abnormal profit could all be taxed away without affecting the existence of the business. In our example above, if €15 000 of the €50 000 was taxed then the individual would stay in his/her line of business because they would still be earning normal profit. In reality, the higher the level of abnormal profit the greater the incentive to continue producing and whilst tax on company profits does take a proportion, many firms can and do make considerable profits. Some of this abnormal profit will be used to invest back into the business to improve its competitiveness and the quality of its products and service to its customers.

Profits generated below the level of normal profit are called *sub-normal profit*. In the short term, businesses might stay in a particular line of production but in the longer term the return is not sufficient to encourage them to stay and they may choose to leave the industry. In our example, if the individual earns less than €35 000 a year then it would be worth their while closing the business and getting employment with a firm paying a salary of €35 000.

Profit Maximization – The Theory

The output level where a firm would be making maximum profit would be the point where the difference between the total cost and total revenue curves was at its greatest. Exactly what this output level would be is more difficult to define in practice but if a firm had information about its marginal costs and marginal revenues it could make decisions about whether any increase or decrease output would add to profit or reduce total profit. The point of profit maximization would occur where MC = MR. It is worth a firm continuing to expand output up to a point where the marginal cost is equal to the marginal revenue, that is where the addition to total cost is the same as the addition to total revenue as a result of producing and selling one extra unit.

The logic of this is relatively straightforward providing you remember that marginal cost and marginal revenue is referring to ONE extra unit of output/sales and is the ADDITION to total cost/revenue from the production/sale of that additional unit. If we refer back to our example of the airline above, we identified that the MC of one extra passenger was €62.50. If the airline is trying to calculate whether taking an extra passenger on board was worth it, it could look at the MC and MR associated with that extra passenger. We assumed that the capacity of the aircraft was 400. At present there are 395 seats sold and the firm is contemplating reducing price to fill the last few seats. It offers seat prices at €90 and one person buys a seat at this price. Is it worth selling that seat? The MC is €62.50 but the MR of selling the seat at that price is €90 so the **addition** to the profit generated for the airline is €27.50. Put yourself in the position of the airline – would you rather receive €27.50 or nothing which is what you would get if you did not sell the seat?

The airline then drops the price to €75 and another person buys a ticket at that price. The MC is still €62.50 but the MR is now €75. Is it worth selling the seat? The addition to profit would now be €12.50. Again, this is the **addition** to profit and as such there is no reason why the firm would not sell the seat. If the firm can find that the only way they can sell the 398th seat is by reducing the price to €60 then the issue becomes different. The MC of taking the passenger is €62.50 but the MR is €60. This means that profit would fall by €2.50. Logically the firm would not sell this ticket preferring to keep the seat vacant rather than selling it at this price and reducing profit.

BREAK-EVEN ANALYSIS

For small firms just setting up, to large firms planning new projects, break-even is an important concept, see Figure 9.13. It is a simple idea with powerful implications. A firm will break-even when the total costs of operating are just covered by the revenues that it is generating. In other words:

Break-even is the point where TC = TR.

An example is perhaps the easiest way to explain this concept.

Assume that a chemical plant in Germany, OrgChem AG, is approached by a company in Egypt, El Hadj, that require the development of a chemical compound which will be used in the production of a new anti-depressant drug. El Hadj have carried out initial small scale tests but now require larger quantities of this particular chemical to be made as it continues the testing regime and need the expertise of OrgChem to produce larger quantities.

OrgChem will need to consider the costs of engineering the chemical, setting up its plant to produce it and the costs of distribution and so on. In other words, it has to consider the fixed costs and the variable costs associated with the production of the product. At the same time it also has to consider the revenues that it will generate from the Egyptian company in selling the compound to it. We know that the fixed costs are constant regardless of output in the short run. The variable costs will rise the more of the compound they produce. Together the total costs will rise with the level of output. This output can be sold – but for what price? OrgChem will need to think about the price per unit of the compound (per kilo let's say) that they will charge. If they decide on a low price then they will need to sell a large amount of the compound to cover the costs of development and production. If they charged a higher price then they would not need to sell so many in order to cover the costs. Which price do they settle on?

FIGURE 9.13

Break-even analysis

The diagram represents the position for OrgChem with fixed costs at €50 000 and variable costs rising at €50 per unit. If the firm set price at €75 it would only need to sell 2000 kilos to break even. At a price of €60 it needs to sell 5000 kilos to break even. If it sells 10 000 kilos per month it has a margin of safety of 5000 kilos. At any output/sales level above 5000 kilos per month the total revenue is greater than the total costs and so the firm makes a profit. At a price of €60 at any output/sales level below 5000 kilos the total costs are greater than the total revenue and OrgChem makes a loss.

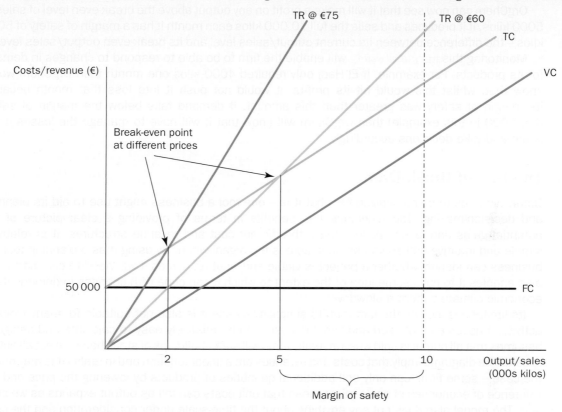

Break-even analysis allows OrgChem to plug these different scenarios into its model to form the basis of discussion about its strategy and what price it charges.

Let us assume that the fixed costs are estimated at €50 000 per month and the variable costs per kilo at €50. How many units does the firm need to sell each month to cover its costs? This will, of course, depend on the price per kilo it charges. We can use the break-even formula to calculate the number of units it needs to sell to cover these costs. The formula is:

$$\text{Break even} = \frac{\text{Fixed costs per period of time}}{\text{Contribution}}$$

The contribution is the selling price minus the variable costs per unit.

If it chose to fix price at €60 per kilo it would need to sell:

$$\frac{50\,000}{60-50} = 5000 \text{ kilos per month to break-even}$$

If the firm chose to fix price at €75 per kilo then it would need to sell:

$$\frac{50\,000}{75-50} = 2000 \text{ kilos per month.}$$

The price OrgChem decides to charge El Hadj is important, therefore. If it settles on a higher price it does not need to produce as much before it breaks-even. However, at a higher price it needs to consider whether El Hadj would be willing to pay that amount for the product. Let us assume that El Hadj is only willing to pay €60 per kilo. This would mean that OrgChem now needs to plan production levels to produce at least 5000 units per month. The contract with El Hadj may be for a fixed amount of the chemical compound over a period of time. Assume that the Egyptian company has agreed to purchase 10 000 kilos per month over a contract period of a year.

OrgChem can now see that it will make a profit on any output above the break-even level of sales of 5000 kilos. If it produces and sells the full 10 000 kilos each month it has a margin of safety of 5000 kilos – the difference between its current output/sales level and its break-even output/sales level.

Monitoring this margin of safety will enable the firm to be able to respond to changes in demand for its products. For example, if El Hadj only required 4000 kilos one month then OrgChem would know that, whilst this would hit its profits, it would not push it into loss that month because its margin of safety was greater than this amount. If demand falls below the margin of safety (i.e. 5000 in this example) then OrgChem will know that it will have to manage the losses it will make and take decisions accordingly.

The Use of Break-Even

Break-even has to be recognized for what it is – **one** tool a business might use to aid its planning and decision-making. The technique has benefits in terms of providing a clear picture of the potential gains and losses associated with different cost and revenue structures. It is relatively simple and intuitive and so can be used across the organization. By using it as a planning tool the business can identify whether a project is viable and what resources it will need to commit to it. It also enables it to have some idea of the extent to which it can cope with changes in demand if the economic climate suffers a slowdown.

Its limitations include the fact that its simplicity means it is also not suitable for many types of activity. It assumes that fixed and variable costs can be relatively easy to calculate and assign; it assumes that all output is sold when in reality firms will suffer build-ups of stock because not all output is sold. The diagrams imply that costs and revenues are a linear function and in reality this may not be the case – some firms can only sell additional quantities of products by lowering the price and the existence of economies of scale might mean that unit costs can fall as output expands as we shall see. The model also does not say anything about the time-scale under consideration and the price elasticity of demand. We assumed above that OrgChem can decide on a price but in reality a firm would have to take into account the market it was operating in and how buyers would respond to different prices and how competitors would respond to any changes in price the firm decides to make. The dynamic nature of the business world means that nothing stays very stable for very long and so a break-even analysis may have a limited life-span and thus validity.

THE SHORT AND LONG RUN

So far we have looked at costs without giving consideration to the time period under analysis. We have said that fixed costs are not dependent on the amount produced but this does not mean that they never change. Firms are able to look at costs in the short run and in the long run. The short run is the period of time within which some factors of production cannot be altered. In the long run, all factors of production can be altered. This implies that the firm will face different cost structures in the short run compared to the long run. For example, if a firm is operating at or near to full capacity but is facing an increasing demand for its product it may consider expanding. This may involve expanding existing premises, or building new plant. The time period before this new capacity comes on stream might be five years. In this case the short run is five years and the long run any period over five years. In the short run, therefore, some of its factors of production (its existing plant) will be fixed and cannot be increased quickly. The firm will have to manage its operations to cope with the increasing demand. This may involve changing factors of production that are adjustable in the short run such as re-organizing production, expanding its workforce and investing in new machinery and equipment but ultimately it can only solve the capacity problems by expanding its operations by changing all the factors of production and building a new production facility.

The total cost curve associated with its operations in the short run will be different to that in the long run. In the long run it will be operating at a different scale of production. Let us assume that a firm's current capacity is 1 million units per year. It can make some changes to its operations in the short run and so increase this to 1 100 000 but if demand is rising faster than this then it needs to be able to increase total capacity. Once its new plant is constructed and operational the firm can now produce a total of two million units per year – it has doubled its capacity; it is now operating at a different scale. The total costs of operating a business with a capacity of two million units a year will obviously be larger but the average or unit costs could actually fall. To see why we need to introduce the concept of economies of scale.

ECONOMIES OF SCALE

Economies of scale are the advantages (refer back to Chapter 6 and the pursuit of cost advantage) of large scale production that result in lower costs per unit produced. In our example, assume that the total cost of operating the plant when capacity was one million units was €30 million per year. If the firm operated at full capacity this would mean that the average or unit costs would be €30. After the new plant becomes operational the scale of production has now changed and the capacity of the firm is two million units per year. What happens to the total costs after this increase in scale? It is almost certain that they will rise – after all the firm will have had to finance the building of the new plant but the crucial point will be the proportionate increase in cost in relation to the increase in output.

If the total costs increased in direct proportion (i.e. were now €60 million) the unit costs would remain at €30. However, it is likely that the total costs would increase by a smaller proportion than the increase in output in which case unit costs would fall. If the total cost of operating the new capacity increased to €50 million then the unit costs would now fall to €25 (€50 million / 2 million).

Economies of scale are an important reason why many firms look to expand the size of their operations. Lower unit costs can mean that the firm can be more competitive against its rivals and have more options to manipulate its competitive position. It could, for example, use the reduction in unit costs to reduce its selling price and be more competitive in the market place. It could maintain its selling price (and if it was facing strong demand then there might be every reason to do so) and as a result increase the size of its profit margin. This might be something that its shareholders would welcome and also benefit its stock price as a result.

The sources of economies of scale come from a range of the businesses' operations. There are *technical economies of scale* associated with operating on a large scale. In industries such as oil, chemicals, energy supply, telephony and communications, the efficiency of the business is largely dependent on being able to operate on a large scale. Fixed costs can be spread out across a larger range of output and so reduce the average cost. These firms can purchase and utilize very large and efficient pieces of equipment which smaller firms cannot afford. Such equipment often helps to increase productivity considerably and so help reduce unit costs.

Large firms are also able to negotiate advantageous prices and sources of funding compared to smaller firms. *Commercial economies of scale* refer to the benefits large firms can gain by buying large quantities of goods from suppliers. If a small firm goes to a supplier of tomatoes in Italy and wishes to purchase five tonnes of tomatoes a month the price they are quoted is likely to be higher than that quoted to a large company buying 500 tonnes a month. The supplier would be willing to negotiate lower prices because they can be assured of selling their output. If the farm's total output of tomatoes was 600 tonnes a month then dealing with a large number of buyers each wanting small amounts is more expensive than dealing with one major buyer willing to take most of the output off the hands of the farmer. For the buyer it means that a negotiated lower price reduces the unit cost per tomato bought.

Equally, larger firms looking to raise funds to cover an overdraft or for expansion can not only afford to employ specialists in the capital market to manage the process for them but because they may be deemed as being less risky can acquire additional capital at lower rates of interest. These are referred to as *financial economies of scale*. This again, gives them an advantage over their smaller rivals.

Managerial economies of scale refer to the benefits that firms can gain by employing specialists in the different functional areas. Having a specialist human resources (HR) department may involve additional cost but if the benefits in terms of additional revenue and efficiency that arise from having this department are greater than the costs the unit costs will fall. The HR function may be able to ensure staff are productive, that recruitment is efficient and effective and that motivation is a focus for the business. Smaller firms trying to handle all these aspects of human resource management may be able to do the job but they will have to juggle this along with all the other things they have to manage and so are unlikely to be as productive and efficient.

Larger firms are also in a position where they are able to diversify their activities – not put all their eggs in one basket. This enables them to benefit from *risk-bearing economies of scale*. If one part of the business suffers a downturn in demand, for example, the larger firm is able to cope with this by perhaps relying on other aspects of the business to be performing better whereas a small firm which just specializes in one area can be badly hit if that area suffers a fall in demand.

The economies of scale described above are classed as internal economies of scale. These are the benefits that arise as a result of the growth of the firm itself. However, there are also benefits that a firm can derive as a result of the growth of an industry in a particular location. These are called external economies of scale. For example, wine growers in France may be able to benefit from the supply of skilled labour that exists in the area or from research and development carried out by educational institutions and other organizations. Some industries benefit from specialist services, advice and ancillary operations located in and around the area where the industry is concentrated. For example, the concentration of chemical plants in the North East of England on Teesside has led to specialist fire, emergency and waste disposal services being located in the region. Chemical firms located here can take advantage of these specialist services and this helps to reduce unit costs. In the City of London and in Frankfurt, the concentration of the financial services industry means that there are benefits that arise to firms in that industry locating there including important communication networks, specialist financial businesses and so on.

Whilst economies of scale are associated with large firms, smaller firms may also find ways of benefiting from economies of scale by joining together in associations to try and take advantage of commercial economies of scale or share resources and technologies. Joint ventures and coopera-tive movements are good examples of where this happens.

Economies of scale are not always appropriate for all businesses. Many small firms survive in competitive markets because they provide specialist services or unique bespoke products that do not lend themselves to the sort of mass-market output associated with large scale production. For example, there are firms that produce kitchens and mass produce identical units which can be fitted into homes. The cost per unit of such products is much lower than that of a firm providing an individually designed bespoke fitted kitchen. Buyers of the latter can justifiably claim that what they have is unique and may be prepared to pay higher prices for such individuality.

MEASURES OF PERFORMANCE

Most business organizations will have to have some sort of measure of performance against which to judge themselves in relation to their own aims and objectives and against that of their rivals. We saw in Chapter 8 the growing role of social enterprises in the European economy and operating with the aim of achieving some sort of social objective is one way of measuring performance. However, we will look at three more traditional ways to measure performance – profit, sales growth and return on capital employed (ROCE).

Profits

Generating profit is one of the most obvious ways in which a business might measure success; the more profit it makes the more successful is its performance. We have established the difference between *normal* and *abnormal profit*; this immediately helps to provide some benchmark about performance; if any performance benchmark is beaten the firm can be said to be performing well.

Typically firms will make further distinctions on profit. This allows the firm and other interested stakeholders to be able to see how it is performing in different ways. *Gross profit* is the difference between the total revenue and the cost of sales – the amount it costs the business to produce what it sells. This does not take into consideration the overheads – the fixed costs of production. Gross profit allows the firm to see how it is performing in relation to sales revenue and its variable costs; sales revenue might have increased, for example, but if the cost of sales has increased by a greater proportion then its gross profit may fall. Budgetary processes will invariably be able to identify the reasons for increasing cost of sales, due to higher import costs as a result of a devaluation of the currency, for example, but for external stakeholders, such information will be useful as a contribution to the information they consider when making investment decisions.

Net profit takes into account not only the cost of sales but also the overheads involved in production. This is usually presented as *profit before tax*. Different businesses present profit data in different ways depending on the country they are operating in, the accounting rules and conventions being adhered to and the type of audience the information is aimed at. Formal end of year accounts published in the annual report to shareholders may be more detailed than those released to the press. Interim statements showing performance over a period within a year, such as a quarter or half-year results, may be simpler to interpret. Figure 9.14 is an interim statement from the shipping and distribution firm A.P. Moller – Maersk. The company has its headquarters in Denmark and so has given its results in both Danish Krona and US dollars.

The results show that its sales revenue rose from almost DKK63 billion in the first quarter of 2009 to just over DKK71 billion in the same period of 2010. Its gross profit for the first quarter of 2010 came in at nearly DKK18 billion which implies that its cost of sales was around DKK53 billion. From this figure it subtracted various costs such as depreciation and amortization and gains from the sale of assets. It also subtracts something called 'financial items' to show a net profit of DKK9.678 billion. *Depreciation* is the write-down that firms make to its assets as they suffer from wear and tear and thus lose their value over time. *Amortization* is a similar term but is often used to take account of the reduction in value of intangible assets such as brand recognition, intellectual property such as patents or trademarks – assets that are not physical in nature but have some value to the firm.

Profit margin relates profit to turnover (sales revenue). In general the higher the profit margin the better. A profit margin of 10 per cent means that the firm makes 10 cents profit for every €1 of goods sold. Narrow margins tend to be associated with products which are high volume, mass market products and are sold in highly competitive markets. Wide margins are associated with products that are low volume, high value with a relatively high degree of monopoly power in their market. There are two ratios that firms use to measure profit margin:

FIGURE 9.14

Key figures for the period 1 January – 31 March	DKK million			USD million		
(Unaudited)	2010	2009	Change	2010	2009	Change
Revenue	71,019	62,970	13%	13,200	11,024	20%
Profit before depreciation, amortisation and impairment losses, etc.	17,828	11,406	56%	3,314	1,997	66%
Depreciation, amortisation and impairment losses	7,245	7,323	-1%	1,346	1,283	5%
Gain on sale of ships, rigs, etc.	513	142	261%	95	25	280%
Profit before financial items	11,200	4,433	153%	2,082	776	168%
Profit before tax	9,678	1,741	456%	1,799	305	490%
Profit/loss for the period	3,440	-2,132	n/a	639	-373	n/a
Cash flow from operating activities	11,066	10,685	4%	2,072	1,876	10%
Cash flow used for capital expenditure	-6,223	-13,550	-54%	-1,157	-2,372	-51%

Source: The A.P. Moller – Maersk Group: Interim Management Statement. Available at: http://files.shareholder.com/downloads/ABEA-3GG91Y/919893242x0x373579/79dcf7b1-1d3e-40df-a28f-185312b38e34/apmm_interim%20management%20statement_12%20may%202010.pdf

Gross profit margin relates gross profit to sales as a percentage:

$$\text{Gross Profit Margin} = \frac{\text{Gross Profit}}{\text{Turnover}} \times 100$$

Net profit margin relates net profit to sales as a percentage:

$$\text{Net Profit Margin} = \frac{\text{Net Profit}}{\text{Turnover}} \times 100$$

Comparisons of profits over a period of time give external stakeholders some guide as to how a business is performing. Profit is a financial measure but many firms may also have other non-financial objectives against which they may measure themselves. These might include environmental and social objectives covered elsewhere in this book.

Sales Growth

Growing sales shows that a business is attracting more custom over a period of time. Given that businesses exist to satisfy customers, whether this be in the B2B or B2C realm, so increasing sales is one measure of performance. Sales can be measured in physical units or as the value of sales – the number of units multiplied by the price they were sold at. It is important to distinguish between a rise in the level of sales and a rise in the rate of growth of sales – both may be monitored.

Schwan-STABILO is a German manufacturer of stationery items. It manufactures the STABILO-BOSS highlighter pen. In the first quarter of the year it might sell 50 million of these pens worldwide and in the second, 54 million. The level of sales has increased by four million. In the third quarter it might sell 53 million and in the fourth, 45 million. As the year has progressed its level of sales has increased – the total sales are 202 million.

It can compare this to the sales in the previous year (let's assume they were 198 million) and conclude that its performance is improving because the level of sales has risen.

However, when we look at what has happened in the second year a different picture may emerge. Sales grew by 8 per cent in the second quarter of the year but whilst the level of sales was 53 million in the third quarter, the growth in sales was negative at −3.7 per cent compared to quarter two. In quarter four sales were again down on the previous quarter at 45 million, a fall of 15.09 per cent on the previous quarter. The firm might want to investigate the reasons for the fall in the growth of sales and whilst it might be pleased that overall sales had risen it may want to get some answers about the changing growth in sales. Is the fall in growth due to some seasonal factor, is it a one-off event as a result of some external factor such as a slowdown in growth or is it the start of a more serious trend as a result of a change in demand or the effect of competition?

Many firms will keep a careful track of its sales on a regular basis – in some cases this might be daily, weekly and monthly not only because it is an indicator of performance but also because changing sales patterns can have an effect on cash flow.

ROCE

Return on capital employed is a measure of the efficiency with which a business uses its assets to generate profit. Take two Polish coal mines belonging to different firms, both are exactly the same size and employ the same number of workers and assets valued at €1 million. Firm (a) generate profits of €250 000 while Firm (b) generates profits of €100 000. It is easy to see in this example that Firm (a) is performing the better of the two as it uses its assets more effectively than Firm (b). For every €1 of capital it owns it generates profits of €0.25 whereas Firm (b) uses those same assets and only generates €0.10 in profit.

In reality, of course, few firms are identical even if they do operate in the same industry. ROCE is a ratio which will tell us the relative efficiency of firms in the way they utilise their assets to generate profits. It is given by the formula:

$$ROCE = \frac{\text{Profit for the Year}}{\text{Equity Shareholders' Funds}} \times 100$$

Generally – the higher the ratio, the more effective the firm is in using its capital assets. If Firm (a) in our example had €10 million in capital assets and generated profits of €1.5 million whereas Firm (b) had €30 million in assets and generated €5 million, ROCE can offer us some comparison of performance. Firm (a) has a ROCE of 15 per cent and Firm (b) has a ROCE of 16.6 per cent. This suggests that Firm (b) is performing better than Firm (a). This may be due to its size (it may be benefitting from economies of scale) or many other reasons such as how it organizes its plant and equipment, how it utilizes its labour force, their levels of motivation, the quality of its management processes and so on.

THE STAKEHOLDER MODEL

Stakeholder responsibilities were introduced in Chapter 7. The stakeholder model is a way of looking at the interaction between a firm or other organization and those individuals and groups who have some interest in the business. The model generally classes stakeholders into two categories, internal and external. *Internal stakeholders* are directly associated with the organization such as employees, management and owners/shareholders. *External stakeholders* are not directly involved in the organization but are affected by it such as consumers, suppliers, local and national government, the local community and the environment.

It is now widely accepted by many businesses that they have wider responsibilities than simply generating profits for owners. They recognize that some balance has to be struck between the operation of the business in relation to its aims and objectives and the wider interests of its other stakeholders. These responsibilities were outlined in Chapter 7.

The acknowledgement that an organization's operations have a wide impact is part of the drive to develop a greater degree of corporate social responsibility (CSR).

CSR – AN INTRODUCTION

A detailed look at CSR is beyond the scope of this book but this will serve as an introduction to some of the main issues that are raised by this idea. CSR is a measure of the impact that a business has on society and the environment as a result of its business actions, and the extent to which a business recognizes and acts on the responsibilities it has in relation to this impact.

Chapters 2–7 covered a range of the external environments that businesses interact with and have an impact on in some way or another. It is sometimes tempting to think only of the negative impact that organizations have and these are certainly important. However, organizations, both business and other organizations, can generate many positive effects on a wide range of stakeholders. Many organizations are aware of the fact they their actions are scrutinized in ever more detailed ways as the Internet, legislation such as freedom of information laws, social networking sites such as Facebook and Twitter, viral marketing techniques and the so-called 'blogosphere' mean that information can be circulated very quickly to millions of people. Whilst many organizations are able to retain some element of privacy and secrecy about what they do it is becoming increasingly difficult to sustain. Negative information can be very damaging to a business and destroy many years of hard work not to mention rendering worthless millions of pounds of investment in building brands and reputation. The main problems facing most organizations is in finding the appropriate balance to meet its wider social responsibilities but also work towards achieving its aims and objectives. Table 9.1 highlights some of the positive and negative effects of the operations of organizations.

The table highlights the fact that whatever organizations do they run the risk of facing some criticism. It is unlikely that any organization will fulfil the needs and wishes of all its stakeholders at once but there is no doubting that more and more businesses recognize that they have to find ways of balancing their aims and objectives with the wider needs of all the organizations' stakeholders.

TABLE 9.1 Factors influencing corporate social responsibility

Action	Positive effect	Negative effect
Closure of a part of the business	Enables the firm to control its costs and boost profitability.	Creates job losses, impacts on local businesses and communities, affects suppliers and other related businesses.
Building market power	Improves security for employees and helps improve profits.	May lead to consumers facing higher prices and reduced choice. Rivals are prevented from competing effectively.
Use of energy and resources	Generally means the business is producing goods and services and this can lead to an improvement in the standard of living.	Production uses up non-renewable resources, can drive up prices (e.g. oil) and creates waste which needs to be dealt with.
Outsourcing	Can improve efficiency, lead to lower costs and thus boost the profitability of the business. Boosts local economy of region where outsourcing is allocated.	May mean domestic workers are made redundant. Customers may not feel they are getting the best service.
General operations	Create jobs and wealth not only in domestic countries but in other countries where organizations locate and operate. Successful organizations help improve the standard of living giving people a wider choice and better quality often at cheaper prices.	Contributes to pollution and the potential damage to the environment. Pollution manifests itself in the form of noise, odour and air pollution. They are often external costs and so the burden of dealing with them falls to a third party. Increased distribution by air, rail, sea and road leads to increased pollution and congestion. Are the benefits of being able to eat strawberries all year round, for example, worth the costs involved?
Business growth	As organizations grow they tend to employ a more diverse range of people (ethnic minorities, disabled people, those with different lifestyles and so on) and this helps social integration and cohesion. Growth also improves employment opportunities.	Businesses become too powerful and can use market power to drive down prices and extract unreasonable concessions from suppliers and other groups they deal with. Can exploit their power to ride roughshod over the law and in some cases may abuse the law (especially in cases where national governance is weak or corrupt).
Local community projects/ charitable acts	May organizations are involved in acts of charity and involvement with local communities which benefit disadvantaged groups. Sponsorship provides a source of funding for activities which otherwise might not take place.	May be used in a cynical way to boost reputation and/or market power.

SUMMARY

- An organizational structure helps to define the types of relationships, lines of communication and roles and responsibilities in a business. The right organizational structure can help to promote and achieve the strategic goals of a business. There are a number of models which stylize organizational structures which include hierarchical, functional, product or area based, divisional and matrix. Each has different advantages and disadvantages.
- Modern business organizations are highly complex and many will make use of different structures at different times and in different situations. One of the key moves in organizational structures in recent years has been the move to more organic flexible structures that are able to adapt to and cope with change rather than mechanistic highly hierarchical structures that are too rigid and stifle innovation and creativity.
- Business process re-engineering is a method that has been promoted as being a way in which a business can re-organize itself based on adding maximum value at least cost.
- There is often confusion between the terms 'price' and 'cost'. Price refers to the amount an individual has to give up to acquire a good or service. Cost refers to the money spent by organizations on factor inputs used in production. Businesses costs are classified according to their relationship with production.
- Profit is the difference between the firm's revenue and its cost of production.
- Break-even analysis is one tool a business can use to help plan.
- Cost structures are different in the short run and long run.
- Larger firms can benefit from economies of scale which reduce unit costs.
- Firms have different measures of performance, three of which include measures of profitability, sales growth and the return on capital employed.
- The stakeholder model helps to identify those with an interest in an organization's operations.
- Many organizations now take corporate social responsibility seriously and try to find a balance to meeting different stakeholder needs.

REVISION QUESTIONS

1. Outline **three** reasons why an organization needs a structure.
2. Describe the main features of a hierarchical, matrix and flat organization structure. State two advantages and two disadvantages of each.
3. Explain the difference between cost, price and revenue.
4. Using an example in each case, distinguish between total, average and marginal costs.
5. Explain the value of break-even analysis to a business and outline its limitations.
6. Why is it important for a business to distinguish between the short run and the long run in making decisions?
7. Discuss the benefits and limitations of economies of scale.
8. Discuss the value of profitability ratios, ROCE and sales revenue as measures of business performance.
9. Why are organizations becoming increasingly aware of the need to address a range of stakeholder needs?
10. Explain the importance of corporate social responsibility to business organizations.

DISCUSSION QUESTIONS

1. Do organization structures necessarily limit an organization's flexibility in the modern world?
2. How relevant are marginal costs to business decision-making?

3. To what extent is break-even analysis of value to a business organization?
4. 'Economies of scale are only relevant to very large organizations'. Discuss.
5. Corporate social responsibility is merely a marketing tool for organizations to gain some competitive advantage over rivals. Do you agree with this statement?

REFERENCES AND FURTHER READING

Cole, G. A. and Kelly, P. P. (2011) *Management: Theory and Practice*, Ed. 7. Cengage Learning EMEA

Davenport, T. (1994) 'Managing in the New World of Process', *Public Productivity & Management Review*, Vol. 18 no 2, Winter 1994, 133–147

Hammer, M. and Stanton, S. (1999) 'How Process Enterprises Really Work', *Harvard Business Review*, Nov/Dec99, Vol. 77 Issue 6, 108–118

Kelly, P. P. (2009) *International Business and Management*, Cengage Learning EMEA

GLOSSARY

Abnormal Profit The amount over and above normal profit

Authority The right to make particular decisions and to exercise control over resources

Average Revenue The average amount received by a firm from sales found by dividing the total revenue by the level of sales

Break-even The level of output and sales where sales revenue is just sufficient to cover the costs of production

Business Process Re-engineering The analysis and design of workflows, structures and processes in an organization with the aim of re-thinking the way an organization operates and to improve its operation and efficiency

Contribution The difference between the selling price and the variable cost of production

Corporate Social Responsibility A measure of the impact that an organization has on society and the environment as a result of its actions, and the extent to which the organization recognises and acts on the responsibilities it has in relation to this impact

Culture The collection of shared attitudes, practices, values and goals in an organization

Economies of Scale The advantages of large scale production that result in lower costs per unit produced (average costs)

External Economies of Scale The benefits of large scale production that arise from the growth of the industry particularly if that industry is concentrated in a particular area

Functional Relationship The formal relationships within an organization between people in a specialist or advisory position, and line managers and their subordinates. This occurs when a person offers a common service throughout all departments of the organization

Functional Structure The organization is structured according to functional areas such as finance, marketing and HR

Hierarchical Structure A type of organization structure based on layers of authority with power concentrated at the top

Internal Economies of Scale The benefits of large scale production that arise from the growth of the firm

Line Relationship The links, as shown on an organizational chart, that exist between managers and staff whom they oversee directly

Long Run The period of time when all factors of production can be altered

Marginal Cost The cost incurred in producing one more unit of production

Margin of Safety The difference between the current output and the break-even output

Marginal Revenue The addition to total revenue from the sale of one extra unit

Matrix Structure A matrix structure is a combination of structures which could take the form of product and geographical divisions or functional and divisional structures operating in tandem

Normal Profit The minimum amount of profit required by a firm to keep it in its present line of production

Organizational Structure The way in which the interrelated groups of an organization are constructed

Price The amount of money consumers give up to acquire a good or service

Product Structure The organization is structured according to related products or services

Profit The difference between total revenue and total costs where total revenue is higher than total costs

Profit Centre A part of an organization that directly adds to its profit, run as a business with profit objectives; it is a subset of the business for which senior managers want to track income and expenses

Short Run The period of time in which some factors of production cannot be altered

Staff Relationship A link between workers in advisory positions and line employees – Staff employees use their specialized expertise to support the efforts of line employees who may choose to act on the advice given

CHAPTER CASE STUDY

Vodafone

In April 2006 Vodafone announced changes to its organizational structure to better focus the business according to the different market and customer requirements.

In May 2006 Vodafone announced losses of €15 billion: that's €15 000 000 000! Just try and think of this sum – fifteen thousand million. It is difficult enough trying to think of what fifteen thousand pounds looks like, never mind fifteen thousand million! The problem was quite simple – their revenue was not as high as their costs. The operating profit was healthy at €8.8 billion but the firm had spent out a lot of money on acquisitions and the licences for 3G technology. The revenue growth it was hoping for from this had not materialized despite recruiting an additional 21 million customers. It also announced that it expected sales growth to fall in 2007. The costs, and the cause of this particular loss, came, essentially, because the firm had to write off the overvalued German business, Mannesman, which it bought in 2000.

Vodafone still exists despite the massive losses, and it is unlikely that the firm is going to 'go bust' in the near future. Instead, it is looking ahead to doing something about the cause of the losses that it is facing. This means trying to find ways to boost its revenue and also looking at its cost base and doing something about cutting those. To raise revenue is a more challenging task than cutting costs in many ways. Cutting costs is within the firm's control to a large extent but persuading customers to buy your services as opposed to those of a rival is something that is not within the direct control of the firm. Vodafone is trying to boost its revenue by persuading customers with landlines to switch to using mobiles and offering customers a high speed internet service through existing landlines. Both of these strategies might work, but there again, they might not.

The success of the strategy will depend on the extent to which it can boost its revenue and the cost involved – not only financial but in terms of the loss in skills and the impact on productivity through falling morale – of its cost cutting programme. That it is making a loss – a huge loss – does not mean that the firm will automatically 'go bust'. It does mean it must do something about rectifying the problem; the remedy, therefore, is equally simple – cut costs and boost revenue

Source: Adapted from Biz/ed 'In the News' http://www.bized.co.uk/cgi-bin/chron/chron.pl?id=2611

Questions

- Why might Vodafone have decided to change its organizational structure?
- Examine the extent to which a new structure is likely to meet its goals as stated in the first lines of the case study.
- What was the main reason for the losses announced in 2006? What sort of cost would this be classified as? Justify your reason.
- How can Vodafone make such a loss yet continue in business?
- Assess TWO possible strategies that Vodafone might use to reverse the losses it has announced in the future.
- Research Vodafone's performance since 2006. In the light of Vodafone's results since 2006, comment on its performance in the light of its restructuring.

10
THE BEHAVIOUR
OF FIRMS

LEARNING OBJECTIVES:

1 Explain the key principles and sources of competitive advantage

2 Identify the importance of core competencies and core markets

3 Explain the meaning and significance of strategy to business decision-making

4 Outline the major forecasting techniques used by business

5 Evaluate outsourcing as a business option

6 Evaluate the key sources of business finance

7 Review the costs and benefits of research and development (R&D)

FIGURE 10.1

The behaviour of firms mind map

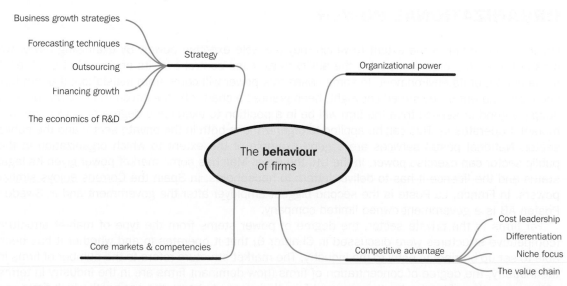

KEY CONCEPTS

Competitive advantage | Strategy | Forecasting | Strategic planning

INTRODUCTION

Imagine a situation where you were the only firm producing a vital good that everyone on the planet needed to buy on a regular basis in order to survive. How would you behave? What price would you charge? Would you seek to maximize profit? Would you act in a socially responsible manner given your awareness of the importance of the good you produce and your situation as the only producer? How would you treat your workers? How would you interact with your suppliers and customers? Now imagine the same good – still vital – but your firm being just one of thousands across the world that produce the good. Now how would you behave?

It is likely that your behaviour would be different in each of these two situations. This chapter will look at how firms behave in different market situations and under different internal circumstances, see Figure 10.1. When we refer to firms' behaviour we are looking at the prices they charge customers, what level of profits they make, what sort of investment decisions they make and why, how they look to gain advantages over their rivals (if they have any), the decisions made on the level of output, how they deal with their stakeholders and what strategies they adopt for the future.

The answer to many of these questions will be dependent on the type of market structure they operate in (refer back to Chapter 6). By market structure we mean the number of competitors a business faces in trying to sell its products in the market in which it operates. Some markets have a large number of sellers; others face buyers who have differing degrees of market power. The type of market structure will have an effect on the freedom the business has to make decisions to boost its own position.

This chapter builds upon Chapter 6 (the competitive environment) and will also look at some of these internal decisions and how they might be affected by the type of market structure. This will include decisions the business might make on where it locates certain of its operations, how it is able to raise finance, what its decisions are with regard to investing in research and development and new technology, the impact on efficiency and how it may attempt to build advantages over its rivals that allow it to pursue its strategic aims.

ORGANIZATIONAL POWER

Organizations differ in the extent to which they are able exercise power. By exercising power we mean whether the organization has the ability to exercise control over its environment or at least some aspect of its environment. In some cases this power will come from legislation; if a firm has acquired a patent or registered copyright, been granted a charter by the government or a licence to supply a good or service then the firm will be in a position to exercise a degree of power over the market it operates in. This can be applied to organizations both in the private sector and the public sector. National postal services are a good example of the extent to which organization in the public sector can exercise power. In the UK, the Royal Mail has some market power given its legal status and the licence it has to deliver letters to households, in Spain the Correos enjoys similar powers, In France, La Poste is the second biggest employer after the government and in Sweden Posten AB is a government owned limited company.

For firms in the private sector, the degree of power stems from the type of market structure (competitive structures were discussed in Chapter 6) that it operates in and whether it has been able to set up barriers to entry to the industry. The market structure refers to the number of firms in the industry, the degree of concentration of firms (how dominant firms are in the industry in terms of the proportion of total sales they account for – their market share), the ease with which firms can enter and exit the industry and factors such as the degree of diversification of firms in the industry and the extent to which firms have amalgamated. In some respects the power of a firm is influenced by the market it operates in; such power may be restricted by external factors over which it has little control but firms are also trying to find ways in which they can increase the market power they have. In so doing they increase their own control over affairs and thus are better able to direct things according to their aims and objectives. Aspects of power are related to competitive advantage, a matter we focus on next.

COMPETITIVE ADVANTAGE

It is tempting to think that any advantage one firm can gain over another represents some form of competitive advantage – and to an extent this might be true. However, technically, competitive advantage occurs when the edge the firm has over its rivals fulfils two criteria:

1 The advantage has to be defensible (i.e. it is not easy for rivals to simply copy the advantage)
2 The advantage has to be distinctive (i.e. it has to be something that clearly sets it apart from the competition in the market).

As was noted in Chapter 6, some writers distinguish between competitive advantage and sustainable competitive advantage. Defensible advantages are sustainable.

When customers (stakeholders in the external environment) have a choice, organizations must compete for their business. With this in mind we might ask how companies compete. A firm can develop cost leadership, product differentiation, and business innovation strategies to confront its competitive forces. Companies may also compete by being more responsive than rivals. An organization may compete by offering customers what they want at the lowest price/cost and/or may differentiate their products and services in such a way that the customer is prepared to pay a premium price for them. Cost leadership requires the organization to find and exploit sources of cost advantage (efficiency gains), typically selling a standard, no-frills product or service whilst differentiation necessitates the organization providing something unique and valuable to buyers (effectiveness). They represent two fundamentally different approaches to business strategy and two of the three generic strategies referred to by Porter (1996). A third source of competitive advantage is based on focus. Cost leadership and differentiation are industry-wide sources of competitive advantage whilst focus strategies seek out competitive advantages for particular market segments. Differentiation is important to competition. If rivals are selling the same (homogenous) product then it becomes difficult for the producer to set the price. Consequently, competitive behaviour is limited and individual organizations have little market power. Products may be differentiated through features, value added and through marketing. Creating real or perceived differences in the product empowers the organization, enabling a range of pricing strategies. Companies that are more responsive may also have an advantage over their sluggish rivals. Responsiveness is enabled through resources (information) and capabilities (flexibility). Speed of response as a source of competitive advantage is termed time-based competition. Organizations identify sources of competitive advantage through the use of frameworks such as the value chain, discussed later. Focusing on the way the organization may use its resources may allow the organization to identify how it can be different and unique or where it can be more efficient.

In Chapter 6 (country competitiveness section) we discussed factors of production, the key factors (resources) which contribute towards making goods and delivering services – the input and transformational resources organizations use to create what customers want. For a manufacturing company, typical factors engaged will be: management and employees, raw materials, plant and equipment. Wernerfelt (1984) explored the usefulness of analyzing organizations from the resource (input and transformational process) side rather than from the product (output) side. Looking at organizations in terms of their resources has a long tradition in economics; however, analysis is confined to categories such as labour, capital, and land. Wernerfelt argued that we can identify types of resources which can lead to high profits. He discussed resources and profitability; by a resource he meant anything which could be thought of as a strength or weakness of a given organization. More formally, an organization's resources at a given time could be defined as those (tangible and intangible) assets which are tied semi permanently to the organization. Examples of resources are: brand names, in-house knowledge of technology, employment of skilled personnel, trade contacts, machinery, efficient procedures, capital, etc. Wernerfelt posed the question: 'Under what circumstances will a resource lead to high returns over longer periods of time?'

The resource-based view (RBV) theory is the perspective on strategy stressing the importance of capabilities (sometimes known as competencies) in determining competitive advantage. The fundamental principle of the RBV is that the basis for competitive advantage of an organization lies primarily in the application of the bundle of valuable resources at its disposal. The bundle of resources, under certain conditions, can assist the organization, sustaining above average returns. Such resources must be valuable and must enable the achievement of goals. Which resources matter? There are two fundamental resource categories within the RBV model: tangible and intangible resources. Tangible resources include factors with an accounting value, as recorded in the organizational balance sheet. Intangible resources, on the other hand, include factors that are non-physical (or non-financial) in nature and are rarely, if at all, included in the organizational balance sheet. Intangible resources can be defined as either assets or capabilities. If the intangible resource is something that the organization 'has', it is an asset. If the intangible resource is something the organization 'does', it is a capability. Thus, resource constructs may be conceptualized as: tangible resources which include financial and physical assets; and intangible resources which include intellectual property, organizational assets and reputational assets; and intangible resources that are capabilities.

Thus far we have discussed competitive advantage in terms of factors enabling an organization to earn a higher rate of profit. However, in the face of rivalry, competitors are likely to try and imitate and copy the advantages of others so they are not disadvantaged in any way. For example, a new piece of technology, procured off-the-shelf, which reduces costs or differentiates the product offering can also be purchased and used by a competitor (imitation). With this in mind, companies seek out sources of sustainable competitive advantage. This is the prolonged benefit a firm achieves by creating a product or service that is valued by its target market and cannot be readily duplicated or replaced by the competition. The central proposition of the RBV is that not all resources are of equal importance in contributing to organizational performance. The resource-based literature describes resources in terms of their value, rareness, inimitability and non-substitutability (VRIN).

Organizational assets may be [intangible] assets that can resist the imitation efforts of competitors, i.e. some organizational assets may be difficult to duplicate and may therefore be strategically more important. For example, reputation is argued to be an important and sophisticated asset; reputation is built, not bought, suggesting it is a non-tradable asset that may be much more difficult to duplicate than tangible assets. Capabilities, as ultimately reflected by organizational know-how, are argued to be the principal source of organizational performance; the productivity and performance of any organization is solely dependent upon the know-how of its employees. Lastly, the ability to build and maintain relationships external to the organization is not only essential for competitive success; it is largely reflective of the knowledge-generating, knowledge-sharing and learning ability of the organization. In other words, building and maintaining external relationships is critical for the organization and largely consists of a 'collective', organization-wide effort of the know-how of a variety of employees and managers. Although intangible assets may be resistant to competitor duplication, capabilities are viewed as a 'superior' intangible resource. Furthermore, intangible assets have been described as resources that are created as a result or outcome of capabilities. Thus, capabilities can be considered a higher-order and more important resource. Consequently, the RBV literature largely favours capabilities as the most important determinant of organizational performance. Furthermore it has been argued that the strength of some resources is dependent upon interactions or combinations with other resources and therefore no single resource – intangible or otherwise – becomes the most important for organizational performance.

As noted earlier, dominant theories about the sources of competitive advantage cluster around the internal or external environment. The dominant paradigm in the 1980s was the competitive forces approach developed by Porter (1979) which focused on the external environment. The key aspect of the firm's environment is the industry or industries within which it competes. Industry structure strongly influences the competitive rules of the game as well as the strategies available to firms. In the competitive forces model, five industry-level forces determine the inherent profit potential of an industry. The approach can be used to help the firm find a position in an industry from which it can best defend itself against competitive forces or influence them in its favour. Such an approach emphasizes the exploitation of market power. Later, the 'resource-based perspective,' was proposed, with an internal focus, emphasizing firm specific-capabilities as the fundamental determinants of organizational performance. This perspective represents a strategy model emphasizing efficiency. The RBV approach sees organizations with superior systems and structures being profitable not because they engage in strategic investments that may deter entry and raise prices above long- run costs, but because they have markedly lower costs, or offer markedly higher quality or product performance. Organizations which are able to accumulate resources and capabilities that are rare, valuable, nonsubstitutable and difficult to imitate will achieve a competitive advantage.

Later work saw the introduction of the concept of 'dynamic capabilities' to address changing environments. This approach emphasizes the development of management capabilities, and difficult-to-imitate combinations of organizational, functional and technological skills. The term 'dynamic' refers to the capacity to renew competencies so as to achieve congruence with the changing business environment. Certain innovative responses are required when time-to-market and timing are critical, the rate of technological change is rapid, and the nature of future competition and markets difficult to determine. The term 'capabilities' emphasizes the key role of strategic management in adapting, integrating and reconfiguring internal and external organizational skills appropriately, as well as resources, and functional competencies to match the requirements of a changing environment. Organizations rely increasingly on information technologies, including process, knowledge, and communication technologies, to enhance their agility. Agility is the ability to detect and seize opportunities for innovation by assembling necessary assets, knowledge and relationships with speed and surprise. As contemporary organizations face intense rivalry, globalization and time-to-market pressures, agility is considered to be an imperative for business success. Agile organizations sense opportunities for competitive action continually in their product-market spaces and gather together the necessary knowledge and assets for seizing those opportunities. Agility underlies organizational success in continuous enhancement and redefinition of value creation, capture and competitive performance through innovations in products, services, channels, and market segmentation. The convergence of computing, communications, and content technologies offers organizations significant opportunities for enhancing agility. Contemporary organizations make significant investments in information technologies (such as Web services, data warehousing, customer relationship management, or supply chain management technologies) to leverage the functionalities of these technologies in shaping their business strategies, customer relationships, and extended enterprise networks. In particular, the disruptive forces of digitization, unbundling of information and physical value chains, and disaggregation of organizational infrastructures for customer relationship, manufacturing, procurement and supply chain fulfilment have heightened the significance of IT in enabling agile competitive moves. Dynamic capabilities permit organizations to combine flexibly different IT and business resources and stimulate competitive actions through innovations in products, services, and channels.

Porter (1996) suggests that attempts to achieve both cost leadership and differentiation may be incompatible with each other simply because the pursuit of differentiation is often associated with higher costs; cost leaders tend to sell more standardized products. Whatever the strategy adopted, a focus allows the firm to continue to find new ways to cut costs or to achieve differentiation. Porter places great emphasis on what he refers to as the value chain. A firm is made up of many activities which are all individual or discrete but related. For example, firms have human resources departments, procurement, finance and accounts sections, design functions, logistics, marketing and sales, customer service, operations which includes the transformation process, assembly, packaging, maintenance and so on.

The importance of these discrete functions will be dependent on the type of business, for example, a firm operating in the service industry may place more emphasis on marketing and sales than a firm in manufacturing where assembly, testing, machine maintenance and packaging may be more important.

BUSINESS IN DEBATE

IBM

The European Commission (EC) has decided to initiate formal antitrust investigations against IBM Corporation in two separate cases of alleged infringements of EU antitrust rules related to the abuse of a dominant market position. Both cases are related to IBM's conduct on the market for mainframe computers (machines that handle high-volume processing). The first case follows complaints by software producers T3 and Turbo Hercules, and focuses on IBM's alleged tying of mainframe hardware to its mainframe operating system. The second is an investigation begun on the Commission's own initiative of IBM's alleged discriminatory behaviour towards competing suppliers of mainframe maintenance services. Mainframes are powerful computers which are used by many large companies and government institutions worldwide to store and process critical business information. It is estimated that the vast majority of corporate data worldwide resides on mainframes. In 2009 approximately €8.5 billion worldwide and €3 billion in the European Economic Area were spent on new mainframe hardware and operating systems.

IBM is alleged to have engaged in illegal tying of its mainframe hardware products to its dominant mainframe operating system. The complaints contend that the tying shuts out providers of technology which could enable the users to run critical applications on non-IBM hardware.

In addition, the Commission has concerns that IBM may have engaged in anti-competitive practices with a view to foreclosing the market for maintenance services (i.e. keeping potential competitors out of the market by delaying access to spare parts), in particular by restricting or delaying access to spare parts for which IBM is the only source.

The initiation of proceedings signifies that the Commission will further investigate the cases as a matter of priority.

Source: adapted from: http://europa.eu/rapid/pressReleases Action.do?reference=IP/10/1006&format=HTML&aged=0& language=EN&guiLanguage=en © European Union, 1995–2012. Reproduced with permission.

Additional information:

The production of mainframe computers is part of the core business of IBM. Analysts estimate that around 20 per cent of its revenues are attributable to the sale of mainframes and that these sales, along with software and services associated with mainframes, contribute to around 40 per cent of its profits. The company said that it would fully cooperate with the investigation but rejected any suggestion that it was behaving in an anti-competitive manner saying: 'IBM is fully entitled to enforce its intellectual property rights and protect the investments we have made in our technologies'.

'Tying' refers to the act by a business of offering two separate but related products as part of a sale. The tied product is made available on condition that the other product is purchased. (In the case of Microsoft, the EU alleged that availability of its Internet Explorer browser and Windows Media Player software came bundled with its Windows operating system – these were the 'tied' products.) In such a case there is less of an incentive for the purchaser to look for or purchase the tied product. One concern with tying is that a firm like IBM might use its monopoly power in one market as a means of limiting competition in another market.

IBM pointed out that 'The mainframe server is a small niche in the overall, highly competitive server landscape'. IBM also suggested that T3 was a company which was partly owned by Microsoft and that this was the reason why the allegations had been brought against it: 'There is no merit to the claims being made by Microsoft and its satellite proxies', it said. T3 and Turbo Hercules produce what are called 'emulator technologies'. This is technology that makes software think that it is running on an IBM mainframe when it is not which then allows users to buy cheaper servers rather than the more expensive IBM equipment. IBM's argument is that 'by attempting to mimic aspects of IBM mainframes without making the substantial investments IBM has made and continues to make... they are violating IBM's intellectual property rights'.

Analysts have also pointed out that existing customers of IBM may have been with the business for some time and have come to rely on IBM for their systems; the costs to these companies of looking to switch from IBM would be high.

Either way, it is important for the firm to focus on ways in which it can either gain cost leadership or differentiation in each of these discrete functions if it wants to gain competitive advantage. The development of just-in-time stock control systems and *Kanban* are examples of where firms may be able to gain significant advantages over their rivals which in turn allow them to be able to be more competitive on price or to justify premium pricing. Gaining a significant cost advantage through the development of a more efficient and productive packaging system, for example, may not be something that sets the pulse racing but could be a crucial factor in giving a firm cost advantage or differentiation.

CORE MARKETS AND COMPETENCIES

Closely linked to competitive advantage are the ideas of core markets and core competencies. Core competencies are the things that a firm is especially good at and which it can do better than its rivals. In many cases, these core competencies are focused on a particular aspect of the market – a firm's core market. The core market may be related to the product that the firm became known for and which provides it with its main sales. Over a period of time, firms do diversify into other markets or develop new variants of its original product to satisfy different markets. Canon, for example, has a particular expertise in optical technology. It is mostly associated with cameras but has branched out into different markets such as photocopiers, printers, scanners, medical equipment and video and film recording technology. These are quite diverse markets but at the heart is Canon's core competence – its experience in developing and utilizing technology to capture images. Whilst Canon could further diversify into other technology markets (developing hand held devices, mobile phones, etc.) these are not its core markets. Breaking into the mobile phone market, for example, may be possible for Canon and it could trade on its reputation and the quality of its brand. However, it would be moving away from its core competence and it may be that it finds it more difficult to compete in a relatively unknown market (for Canon).

The idea of core competencies was developed by Gary Hamel and C.K. Prahalad. Where it differs from Porter's Five Forces model is that it bases strategy on a so-called inside-out approach; rather than basing strategy on the market, competition and the customer – external factors – the core competencies model bases strategy on the ability of the firm to use its expertise to develop new products at lower cost and quicker than rivals. Such competencies allow a business to be able to develop 'unanticipated' products using the combined expertise, skills and technologies that allow the business to not only do things better than their rivals but also to be more flexible and adapt to changing market conditions.

These core competencies are developed through sharing, learning, developing the right culture and being able to weld together the technologies within the firm to allow the business to access a wider variety of markets, improve customer perceptions of value added and to make it much harder for competitors to imitate the business model or its products. Care needs to be taken that core competencies do not become straightjackets which prevent the firm from continuing to learn and adapt. For example, if Canon had not adapted to the developments in digital imaging it may not have been able to compete effectively with its rivals and find new markets such as those in healthcare. Examples of the types of generic core competencies that might exist in firms include:

- Communication
- Teamwork
- Problem solving
- Personal spirit
- Innovation
- Design
- Customer acquisition
- Customer service
- New product development

- Project management
- Adaptability
- The ability to learn and, crucially to 'unlearn' (to shake off the shackles of tradition, routine and entrenched views, opinions or perspectives)
- Empowerment of employees
- Leadership throughout the business

BUSINESS IN ACTION

Core Competencies: Eight Ways to Develop Your Worker's Core Competencies

By James Adams

As a manager, you face plenty of challenges. You get pressure from your management and employees. You get pressure from the customers that are served. You want your employees to be faster, stronger and more committed to the job. Here are some ways to get the best out of your employees.

1 Research all the time: Information for self improvement is found everywhere, from the latest magazines to trade journals. Read everything, because you never know where or when you will receive insight on something important within your field. Be on the lookout for more efficient ways to do your job.

2 Listen to your employees: You trust your employees to offer their best suggestions and ideas. Listen to what they say, because they are working directly with the customers and equipment. If your employees come up with some great solutions, implement them and give credit where it is due. If the solution does not work, take the blame and responsibility for the setback.

3 Be enthusiastic: Be enthusiastic about the tasks that you perform. Your employees will see that and, if they trust you, try to emulate your behaviour. Focus on the tasks you enjoy within your job. If you find yourself flagging, remember that there is some truth to the statement 'fake it till you make it'.

4 Be encouraging to others: Enthusiasm and encouragement is contagious. Create an environment that your employees feel comfortable with you and want to earn your respect. People will work very hard for a pat on the head. There are many cases where an employee will work harder for recognition than money. When you provide a foundation of trust and respect for your employees, you empower them with the tools they need to succeed.

5 Provide realistic, clearly defined goals: Have you ever had a manager who could not tell you what your division's overall goals were? Shy away from ambiguity about the company's goals. Tell your employees for what they are aiming and give them tactics to complete the goal. There should be a reward tied to achievement of the goal. This reward does not have to be money, it could be a small trophy or a great parking space.

6 Cross Training: As a manager, you are in charge of a small team. Cross train your employees so they can get the full extent and breadth of the duties of their teammates. This advances the team as a whole, preparing you for the absence of employees. Cross trained employees respect their teammates and will generally push themselves to learn more. There are some employees who learn better by teaching their co-workers.

7 Internal knowledge sharing: Share your knowledge with your employees and encourage other divisions to share their ideas. This provides your employees with a bigger picture view of the company and teaches them new job skills and responsibilities. Make a calendar and schedule classes or meetings which everyone can attend.

8 External Trainer: Try bringing someone in from the outside. This is the most expensive way to train and develop core competencies, but it offers advantages over in house training. Training enhances the skills of everyone within the division and raises the bar for excellence.

There might be areas that everyone is weak in. Bringing an external trainer to your company for a day or two will get everyone up to speed.

Find out more about your employees' motivations and passions. Play into personal enthusiasm and show that you care about them. Lay the foundation for your own employees to push and motivate themselves, and both you and your team will go far.

Source: www.noobpreneur.com/2010/08/11/8-ways-to-develop-your-workers-core-competencies/

STRATEGY

Strategy refers to the way a business looks into the future and determines ways in which it can turn goals into reality. Strategy requires that the business considers three main questions:

1 Where do we want to be at X point in the future? This represents the long-term aim of the business.

2 Where are we now? Strategy requires that some analysis is made of the current position of the business so that it can identify its strengths, weaknesses, opportunities and threats and how far away it is from its long-term aim/s.

3 How are we going to achieve our aims? The business may well formulate a plan or set of broad objectives that will help it to be able to pursue its aims and to monitor and evaluate progress.

Traditionally, the first stage of strategic planning may involve thinking about what the business might need to do 10–20 years ahead – this is referred to as *futures thinking* (see futurist). The business might then think through a series of key strategic themes which will help it inform decision-making. These help the business respond to changed circumstances but at the same time provide a framework or the scaffolding for making decisions and maintaining its strategic direction. These are called *strategic intents*. The firm may then develop a vision encompassing and defining the strategy which it will communicate to its internal stakeholders which allows the firm to be able to share the goals and ambitions of the business.

Once the strategy is underway systems will have to be in place to enable the firm to analyze its position and receive feedback in relation to its aims and objectives and provide the opportunity of responding to changes, adapting the objectives and feeding this back into the business planning process. Such feedback may include data from sales, profit, teams in the field, etc. used to evaluate the progress and success of the strategy and to inform of changes to the strategy in the light of that data.

More recently the planned approach to strategy formulation has been criticized. Over the past century scholars and practitioners have labelled many types of strategy and discussed alternative processes of strategy formation (see Cole and Kelly 2011). It is common for scholars to distinguish between planned (intended) versus emergent strategies. The planning mode depicts the process as a highly ordered, neatly integrated one, with strategies spelled out on schedule by a purposeful organization; planning theory postulates that the strategy-maker 'formulates' from on high whilst the subordinates 'implement' lower down. Conversely, strategy may also be described as 'a pattern in a stream of decisions' (realized strategy). Emergent strategies are realized strategies that were never intended. In other words, the strategy-maker may formulate a strategy through a conscious process before he/she makes specific decisions (formulation), or a strategy may form gradually, perhaps unintentionally, as he/she makes decisions one by one (strategy formation). Strategy making under the planning view, typically includes:

1 Environmental analysis;

2 Objective setting;

3 Distinctive competence selection or the choice of tools and competitive weapons with which to negotiate with the environment;

4 Power distribution, or the determination of authority and influence relationships amongst organizational subunits;

5 Resource allocation or the deployment of financial and physical resources to carry out a strategy; and

6 Monitoring and control of outcomes, or the comparison of intended and manifested strategy contents.

Strategic choices are concerned with decisions about the organization's future. In the following sections we consider forecasting techniques and choices about growth and how to finance it, outsourcing and investment in R&D.

Business growth strategies

One of the strategic aims of the firm may well be to grow. There are a number of main strategies that a business can pursue in this respect. They include:

- Diversification – finding new products and markets not necessarily related to its core markets which it can exploit.

- Joint ventures – this involves setting up a partnership with another firm who may have different opportunities, markets or skills, and which allow the business to develop new products or exploit new markets. The joint-venture allows a business to be able to exploit synergies and scale advantages thus reducing unit costs and also avoiding some of the need to spend large sums on research and development.

- Franchising – an increasing number of firms find that a relatively cost-effective way of growth is to issue franchise licences. These allow entrepreneurs to set up in business independently but with the right to use the franchiser's brand and support.

- Exporting – breaking into new markets may also mean exporting products abroad. This is not a challenge to be undertaken lightly but for many businesses is an essential part of business growth.

- Mergers and acquisitions – these are external methods of growth and involve joining together with another firm on an agreed voluntary basis (merger) or acquiring another firm by taking it over. In many cases a merger means that some element of each firm's identity is retained in the new entity. This requires that the business acquires control over the business and its assets and is likely to mean that the acquired business loses its identity.

- Alternative investment market (AIM) – this is a way in which smaller companies can float on the stock exchange and gain exposure to the wider business world and raise capital. AIM has been specifically set up for this purpose and has provided a large number of small firms the opportunity of being able to grow which may not have existed prior to AIM. Firms who float on AIM are sometimes referred to as 'fledgling public limited companies'.

There are also a number of other methods by which a business will seek to grow.

Market dominance

This refers to attempts by a business to gain additional market share or find a way in which it can secure some control over the market either through being able to influence price or exercise control over supply. Market dominance can be achieved internally through re-investing in the business and building up capability and expertise. To do this businesses may use profits to plough back into the business for research and development, investment in new plant and equipment and expansion into new markets. The trade-off is the lack of dividends available to shareholders. The prospectus of the business may have made it very clear that one of its aims was growth and market dominance and to do this in the early years of the business' development would mean no dividends being paid.

For many businesses it will be important to identify its core competencies and to focus on these as a means of generating internal growth. If the business can do this then it may be in a position to be able to concentrate on new product development and so keep ahead of its rivals and establish some element of market leadership. The other way of growing, often a much quicker way, is to engage in merger and acquisition, build the business and gain market dominance as a result. Such methods not only lead to greater dominance within the country that the business initially operates in but also globally.

Businesses may also employ other strategies to change the way they operate, target particular aims or attempt to gain greater market dominance. These include re-engineering, delayering (flattening the management structure, removing bureaucracy, speeding up decision making and downsizing – selling off unwanted parts of the business – similar to contraction. The purpose of these strategies is to improve productivity and efficiency and to gain some cost advantage as a result which may in turn lead to some competitive advantage.

Forecasting techniques

In order for a business to be able to establish any sort of strategic plan, some degree of forecasting will be necessary, both of sales and costs. This is not easy and is fraught with potential difficulties simply because a business cannot see into the future. It can employ statistical techniques to try and estimate future sales and costs but these will invariably be associated with various degrees of risk and error. All stakeholders will need to be aware of the probabilities that the business' forecasts are likely to be wrong!

The main techniques used to forecast includes extrapolation, the use of moving averages and test markets. Extrapolation bases forecasts of the future on the basis of historical patterns. Relevant data is collected over a number of years and analyzed in various ways to allow a projection to be made for the future based on this analysis. There are a number of statistical techniques that can be used to improve the accuracy of the analysis and extrapolation and to a large extent the quality of the forecast will be dependent on the accuracy of this analysis and the data used in compiling historical trends. In addition, the more volatile the markets that firms operate in the more difficult it is to use extrapolation because the reliability of past data is even more unpredictable.

The weaknesses of this method (and indeed other techniques of forecasting) is that few people are capable, regardless of the degree of sophistication of the statistical devices employed, of predicting so-called 'Black Swans', events that can cause considerable impacts on businesses but which simply could not be foreseen. In recent year's natural disasters, economic events, terrorist attacks have all led to global changes but few people were in a position to be able to forecast them and build them into statistical models.

Moving averages allows analysts the opportunity of being able to smooth out the fluctuations in data which can occur over short periods of time in time-series data. The sort of data that can lead to short-term volatility includes seasonality and economic cycles. In so doing the analyst can identify more long-term trends which can then be used to help in forecasting.

Test markets provide businesses with a way of reducing the risk involved in launching new products. It works by the business selecting a small but representative area in which to launch the product for a limited period of time. The results of the test can then be analyzed and used to help the business plan and forecast sales nationally or, indeed, globally. It might be that the results of the test market are disappointing and the product does not perform as well as expected. As a result the business may decide that it is not worth its while launching nationally and cancel the project. Either way the information enables the business to be able to have information on which it can forecast future sales and costs and as a result make decisions. If the test market is very successful then it may be that it can analyze the results and use these to forecast national sales or plan to allow it to put in place sufficient capacity to meet expected demand. If this is necessary then it can have a clearer picture of the costs it may have to face in continuing to support the product in the future.

FIGURE 10.2

EMMA BEGAN TO SERIOUSLY THINK ABOUT OUTSOURCING HER MATHS HOMEWORK TO INDIA.

Source: Media Select International – (Patrick Currier (Patrick JPC) Reproduced with permission.

Outsourcing

The rise of globalization has led an increasing number of firms to look at ways in which they can seek to gain some competitive advantage through reducing costs or improving efficiency by contracting out some of their operations (see outsourcing and Figure 10.2). This may be abroad but does not necessarily have to be. The organization who is contracted to carry out the operation takes on the responsibility of carrying out the operation to specified and agreed standards often based on a pre–determined service level agreement. Examples of the types of operations which can be outsourced include customer service functions, market research, information technology, accounting and other financial operations such as payroll and marketing functions such as product design and advertising.

Outsourcing can help reduce unit costs and allow firms to gain some benefits which may give them a competitive advantage. Carrying out the process is not cheap, however, and does bring with it some degree of risk. These include a loss of control, possible problems over product or service quality and damage to reputation if ethical procedures are compromised.

Financing growth

In order to grow, firms need finance. We have already seen how some firms will use profits to be able to re-invest in the business and grow. If internal sources of finance are not available or if the firm does not want to use this source of finance then it has a number of options available:

Bonds – bonds act as an IOU enabling firms to borrow money, often over long periods of time at fixed interest rates. The initial sum is called the *principal* and the interest rate associated with the bond called the *coupon*. The bond holder has primacy of claims to payment in the event of the business failing. Larger firms make significant use of bonds as a means of raising capital. Bond holders do not have to hold onto the bonds for the whole period until maturity and can sell them on the bond market.

Bank loans – bank loans are often used by small to medium sized companies and provide an important source of credit line for such businesses. Loans can be negotiated for a fixed period at either fixed or variable interest rates. Bank loans can be a useful source of finance in both the short and long-term but the risks associated are relatively high – some banks can demand repayment of the loans and place the business in a financially challenging position. Interest payments can also be high, especially if the bank deems the borrower to be of high risk.

Share capital – listed companies will often raise additional funds for expansion through additional share (equity) offerings. These offerings can include new shares being issued through an initial public offering (IPO) either through the stock market or the alternative investment market (AIM), additional shares being made available in the business and rights issues, which give existing shareholders the right to purchase more shares at discounted prices.

Debentures – debentures are loans that are usually secured and are said to have either fixed or floating charges with them. A secured debenture is one that is specifically tied to the financing of a particular asset such as a building or a machine. Then, just like a mortgage for a private house, the debenture holder has a legal interest in that asset and the company cannot dispose of it unless the debenture holder agrees. If the debenture is for land and/or buildings it can be called a mortgage debenture.

Debenture holders have the right to receive their interest payments before any dividend is payable to shareholders and, most importantly, even if a company makes a loss, it still has to pay its interest charges. If the business fails, the debenture holders will be preferential creditors and will be entitled to the repayment of some or all of their money before the shareholders receive anything.

A debenture issued with a floating charge means that the interest rate is not fixed and such debentures are usually not tied to any specific asset such as land or buildings. Debentures have been used in recent years in relation to the financing of sports stadia. Part of the funds raised for stadium developments like those at Wembley, Arsenal, the rugby stadium at Twickenham and the cricket stadium at Trent Bridge in Nottingham are financed by debentures. The debenture holders usually also receive access to boxes at the stadium for their use throughout the period of the 'loan'.

Venture capital – venture capital is invariably used by firms in the early stages of development or growth where there is a high potential for the business to be successful. Venture capitalists tend to be groups of institutional investors or companies set up with the expressed intent of searching out investment opportunities (private equity companies). These groups or companies will agree to invest into a business and take on some role within the business either on the management side or offering advice on technical or managerial issues. The aim of the venture capitalist is to realize relatively swift returns on their investment sometimes through taking a relatively small but potentially successful company, growing it quickly and then floating the business on the stock exchange.

The economics of R&D and technological innovation

Fundamental to the growth potential for many businesses is investment in research and development (R&D) and technological innovation. R&D is important because it provides opportunities for businesses to not only develop new products for new markets but also to develop new technologies that can help them cut costs and as a result put them in a better position to be able to generate and exploit competitive advantage. The economics of R&D is essentially simple – the cost of investing in R&D has to be outweighed by the benefits. Such costs and benefits will be taken into consideration in the context of present values given that the stream of benefits are likely to be spread over a number of years in the future. Firms will also consider the relative risks associated with investment in R&D; in some cases the risks of new developments failing are relatively large and this has to be factored into decisions about starting, continuing and finalizing R&D projects.

One problem facing firms in developing projects is the asymmetry of information between those involved in R&D and those who finance such projects or have to find commercial uses for new developments. These are not always the same people, especially if the firm is a large global operator. There may be an incentive, therefore, for those involved in R&D to keep some information secret including the full consequences of the research and new products and processes which might result. Without this information those responsible for financing continuation of the R&D may not be willing to invest more funds in the project if they do not know the full extent of the possible commercial viability of the projects. Such asymmetric information may also mean that the firm is not able to profit as much as it could do from R&D.

In addition, it has to be recognized that R&D (expertise and outcomes) take time to accumulate and in so doing will require resourcing. Firms have to appreciate that the use of these scarce resources has an opportunity cost which it is prepared to accept. In some cases, R&D is carried out in the context of commercial operations where the key consideration will be the private cost and benefit, when in reality the development might yield significant social benefits (and possibly costs). These, typically, are not taken into consideration by the firm and as a result it may be that R&D and its benefits are underprovided. If this is the case there is an argument for governments stepping in to subsidize such activity so that the social benefits can be internalized. Specific legal protections may need to be in place to encourage firms to engage in R&D because if they cannot gain the benefits of many years of research (and many millions of euro) then there is no incentive for them to carry out such activity. Firms will consider the length of time that their developments will be protected during which time they can generate abnormal profits before rivals copy ideas and products and the market price falls, reducing margins and profits. This is despite the fact that the spillover effects of a wider availability of the product will not only reduce industry costs but increase the social marginal benefit.

Investing in research and development can be likened to investment in physical capital in that it can help the business improve its productivity and/or its sales potential at some point in the future. However, it may be that the outcome of R&D leads to the firm being able to substitute labour in the longer-term as part of the process of improving productivity.

If R&D is successful it can lead to competitive advantage for the business but in so doing has other benefits which are not as obvious. Successful R&D tends to persuade firms to continue to invest in such activity which often means that they are more likely to continue to invest, which in turn means more success and the gap between them and rivals widening even further. This can certainly mean that firms with successful R&D can gain some element of market domination and also gain benefits of economies of scale which reduce the unit costs of R&D.

SUMMARY

- This chapter has introduced further detail about the firm and its internal environment. It has looked at the meaning of organizational power in the context of the extent to which the firm is able to exercise control over some element of its environment, in particular the price it charges for its product or the amount it supplies to the market.
- The degree of organizational power depends to a large extent on the market structure that the firm operates in. If a firm operates in a highly competitive market it may have limited ability to influence the market; if it is able to differentiate its product in some way it may be able to have some influence.
- Firms operating in imperfectly competitive market structures may be able to exercise greater degrees of market power; in general the fewer firms there are in the industry the more market power the firm has.
- Typical of many industries is the oligopolistic market structure where the industry is dominated by a relatively small number of large firms. In this sort of structure, firms may be able to differentiate their product significantly or have to rely on some form of non-price competition. In such industries, the incentive to engage in some form of collusive behaviour exists.
- Firms in some industries may exert monopoly power where they are able to control either price or supply and can do so because they are the only or dominant firm in the industry. Because of the potential for consumers to be exploited, firms with monopoly power may be subject to regulation.
- One key driver for any firm is to gain some element of competitive advantage over its rivals. This is not simply any advantage but one which is both distinctive and defensible. Competitive advantage can arise through some sort of new product development which is different to that which is on the market at present (and which consumers value) or through finding a way to gain a cost advantage. This might be done through various strategies designed to help the firm grow or gain competitive advantage and thus gain market dominance.
- Growth can take place either internally or externally with the latter often involving some form of acquisition through merger or takeover.
- Internal growth may rely on the firm being able to identify and exploit its core competencies – the things it does better than its rivals.
- Firms will also look at other ways of building competitive advantage through outsourcing, for example or through investing in research and development. To grow, firms invariably need to raise finance, unless they generate sufficient profits to be able to re-invest in the business.
- The main sources of finance include issuing shares to build equity capital or revert to loan capital principally through bank loans, debentures or bond issues, the latter being primarily appropriate for larger firms. For firms in the process of growing but with the potential for success, venture capital may be an appropriate method of securing capital although it does mean that the business has to surrender some control to the venture capitalists who agree to invest in the business.

REVISION QUESTIONS

1. Explain **two** sources of organizational power.
2. Why is it necessary for a competitive advantage to be both distinctive and defensible?
3. Can a firm both differentiate and cut costs to gain competitive advantage? Explain.
4. What problems might arise if a firm expands outside its core markets?
5. Alitalia, an Italian airline, decides to reduce the price of all seats on its flights by 20 per cent. Would this give it competitive advantage? Explain.
6. What are core competencies?
7. Outline **five** different business growth strategies.
8. Outline **two** techniques a business might use to forecast future sales and identify **one** potential problem associated with this technique.
9. What is outsourcing? Give **one** advantage and **one** disadvantage of outsourcing to a business.
10. Under what conditions would a business consider that a research and development project is worth pursuing?

DISCUSSION QUESTIONS

1. Can any advantage a business develops over its rival really be 'distinctive and defensible'?
2. Discuss the circumstances under which a firm outsourcing its call centre operations abroad might regret the decision.
3. If forecasting techniques are so inaccurate then what is the point of any firm using them?
4. To what extent would you agree that it is essential to confer monopoly power on the outcomes of firms who carry out research and development in order to encourage such investment?
5. Does collusion between firms always lead to socially undesirable outcomes?

REFERENCES AND FURTHER READING

Cole, G. A. & Kelly, P. (2011) *Management: Theory and Practice 7e*. Cengage Learning.

Porter, M. E. (1979) How competitive forces shape strategy, *Harvard Business Review,* Mar/Apr, Vol. 57 Issue 2, 137–145

Porter, M. E. (1996) What Is Strategy?, *Harvard Business Review,* Vol. 74 Issue 6, 61–78

Wernerfelt, B. (1984) 'A Resource-based View of the Firm', *Strategic Management Journal* 5, no. 2, April–June.

GLOSSARY

Bond Long term debt instrument issued by companies to raise funds

Core Competencies The things that a firm is especially good at and which it can do better than its rivals

Debenture An unsecured loan certificate issued by a company, backed by general credit rather than by specified assets

Forecasting Means predicting the future. It is the process of estimation in unknown situations by use of qualitative (such as scenario-based) data, or quantitative (such as time series, cross-sectional and longitudinal) data

Franchising A form of licensing granting the right to use certain intellectual property rights, such as trade names, brand names, designs, patents and copyrights

Futurist A person who studies the future and makes predictions about it based on current trends

Outsourcing The practice of having goods or services provided by an outside organization

Strategic Planning The process of deciding on the long term objectives and policies of an enterprise

Strategy Strategy is the direction and scope of an organization over the long term, which achieves advantage in a changing environment through its configuration of resources and competencies with the aim of fulfilling stakeholder expectations

Value Chain A collection of discrete but related production functions in a business that enable it to design, produce, market, deliver and support its product

Venture Capital Capital invested in a project in which there is a substantial element of risk, typically a new or expanding business

CHAPTER CASE STUDY

Competitive Advantage and the Jewellery Industry
Jewellery Services are Key to Competitive Advantage

By Tim Malone

Having the right staff on hand to deliver the right types and quality of services for today's convenience oriented customers is very important. There are four unique characteristics of jewellery services that managers should be focused on in order to consistently provide and incrementally improve services. Services differ from the physical inventory in that they have the following characteristics: intangibility, inseparability, variability and perishability. No jewellery service can be physically held or touched prior to acquisition as compared to the inventory which can be examined by shoppers. Prospective customers must evaluate jewellery service quality and quantity often before committing to a transaction exchange. How do you signal your prospective customers regarding the services they should expect to receive?

A service is generally produced and consumed at the same time so production and consumption are inseparable. Jewellery products go through quality evaluations during production and certainly before consumers are exposed to products. Services are extremely variable because they are offered by every jewellery store, but the quality and quantity of services vary widely. Therefore, jewellery customers are exposed to multiple levels of services through their multiple shopping experiences. A branded product will have the same product qualities regardless what store a customer purchases it from. However, the services provided by each retailer will be different. Competitive advantage can be gained through offering the right added value services.

Due to the unsteady demand for services it can be very difficult to always have the staff necessary to meet all customer expectations for service. Peak demand in the jewellery industry is usually associated with holiday occasions. However, many stores track store traffic trends to plan staffing to meet peak shopping hours during each week. Over staffing can be more expensive than over stocked inventory. Jewellery services are very important as they make up part of the total shopping experience. Today, convenience is very important and having the right services to provide with the right staff trained for the right customers is key to creating competitive advantage in the jewellery industry.

Take another look at each service offered by the company. Too often stores continue to offer more and more services without trying to purge those services that don't generate the level of customer loyalty desired. Every service costs money to provide. Therefore, all services must be managed and evaluated to be sure that each service provides the desired return on investment. When was the last time you evaluated each service offered by the company to insure each one is effectively creating competitive advantage for the company?

Source: http://www.jckonline.com/blogs/memo-to-merchandisers/2010/08/10/jewellery-services-are-key-to-competitive-advantage.

About PANDORA

PANDORA designs, manufactures and markets hand-finished and modern jewellery made from genuine materials at affordable prices. PANDORA jewellery is sold in more than 65 countries on six continents through over 10 000 points of sale, including around 700 concept stores.

Founded in 1982 and headquartered in Copenhagen, Denmark, PANDORA employs over 5300 people worldwide of whom 3600 are located in Gemopolis, Thailand, where the company manufactures its jewellery. PANDORA is publicly listed on the NASDAQ OMX

Copenhagen stock exchange in Denmark. In 2011, PANDORA's total revenue was DKK 6.7 billion (approximately EUR 893 million).

For more information, please visit www.pandora.net

Source: http://www.pandora.net/en-GB/pandora-company/about-pandora. Reproduced with permission.

Questions

- Is there a difference between the sources of competitive advantage for a product compared to a service?
- What sort of market structure is the jewellery industry? Explain your reasoning.
- 'A branded product will have the same product qualities regardless what store a customer purchases it from.' What do you think is meant by this statement?
- Given the 'unsteady demand for services' in the jewellery industry, what core competencies might retailers focus on in order to improve customer satisfaction?
- Describe the different markets that firms selling jewellery might be targeting.
- What do you think is PANDORA'S core market?
- If PANDORA wished to expand its business, what would be the most appropriate source of finance? Explain.

PART FOUR
MARKETS

Having investigated the factors and analytical tools used in the study of the external and the internal environment of the organization, Part four focusses on *markets*. There are three chapters in this part of the book:

Chapter 11: Markets

Chapter 12: The Role of Government

Chapter 13: International Markets and Globalization

The firms, discussed in Part 3, are the sellers who aim to meet customer demands. In Chapter 11 we consider how buyers and sellers interact with each other. Sellers are in business to make a profit and, as such, are concerned with ways of increasing revenue and keeping costs to a minimum. Buyers, on the other hand, seek to gain value from their spending and are thus concerned with obtaining value for money. Buyers represent demand in the market. Yet their spending power and needs (and therefore demand) are dependent upon many of the factors discussed in Part 2 of the book. Consequently, in this chapter we explore, in more detail, the factors affecting supply and demand – the way markets work. There are a number of reasons why markets cannot be left fully to their own devices and so in Chapter 12 we explore the role of Governments.

Finally, in Chapter 13 we explore International Markets and Globalization. Globalization has featured in many chapters of this book. However, this chapter is dedicated to the topic and we start by explaining what is meant by Globalization, discussing the globalization process, drivers and trends. We then link the concept with Part 2 of the book, evaluating how global forces shape the national (PESTLE) environment. Next we examine how organizations may respond (strategically) to the challenges and opportunities presented through globalization. We finish with an evaluation of globalization from a multiple stakeholder perspective, identifying the 'winners' and 'losers'.

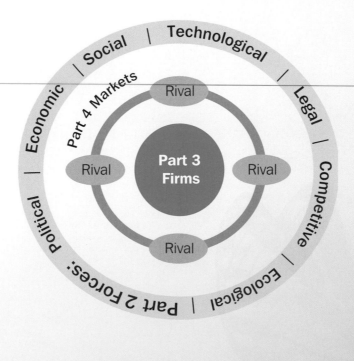

11
MARKETS

FIGURE 11.1

Markets mind map

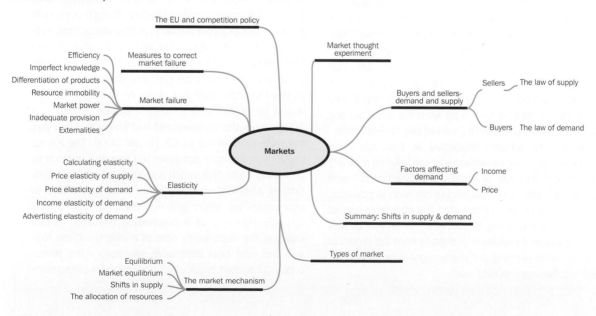

KEY CONCEPTS

Demand | Law of demand | Supply | Law of supply | Market failure

INTRODUCTION

Perhaps few of the subject areas you will study will be as familiar as this one but in many respects few people stop to think about the mechanics of markets and much is simply taken for granted – until things go wrong. This chapter, which builds upon Chapters 3 and 6 in particular, will help you to think about your everyday interaction in a new light and improve the way in which you are able to analyze a wide range of topical issues that arise every day. The familiarity with markets comes from the fact that virtually every human being is a consumer on the one hand and many are also involved in production on the other whether as an employee or as an employer. Often we do not make connections between the two. We might be working for a firm which is attempting to squeeze profits from its operations which as employers or employees we may think is a good thing only to later complain when the price of our favourite drink has gone up – again! See Figure 11.1.

We will refer to buyers/consumers in relation to the demand for goods and services in a market and to sellers/producers in relation to supply. These are the two crucial elements that make up any market. When these two elements are put together, the common factor linking the two is price. The behaviour of both consumers and producers (acting independently for most of the time) helps to determine price. Prices in turn are the signal through which scarce resources are allocated to different uses in many economies throughout the world. Changes in prices act as the signal for resources to move to different uses. In analyzing resource allocation we may be concerned with two aspects – efficiency and equity.

A Market Thought Experiment

You walk into a supermarket with the intention of buying various goods including a jar of coffee. In the relevant aisle you are faced with a number of different jars of coffee all different sizes, different strengths and blends, different qualities, different brands and, of course, different prices. Which do you choose? You may decide to go for the jar that you always buy – the remnant of a key decision made some time ago. You may not be totally wedded to that particular brand but willing to look around at what takes your fancy. It may not take you long to take a jar from the shelf but the mental thought processes involved are considerable.

What has actually happened is that you have assessed the choices available to you, filtered a variety of different features of each as outlined above and arrived at a decision. That simple decision is powerful. It is powerful because every time you make this type of decision you are acting as part of a market and as well as processing a multitude of signals from the producer you are also sending out many signals to producers. Such is the way markets work.

Let us assume that you have decided to purchase a 100g jar of Carte Noire instant coffee. In deciding to purchase this particular coffee you have made a decision that the money that you have to give up to acquire it (assume it is €3.20) is worth it in terms of the satisfaction (sometimes called utility) that you will get for it. Equally your decision is also associated with the idea that you value this particular coffee at this time more than any of the other coffees available which you could have bought. You may have decided to buy the Carte Noir but close on the value stakes was a jar of Kenco Rich instant Coffee. It was in a 200g jar but the supermarket had kindly told you that the price worked out at €3.10 per 100g. The Kenco coffee was cheaper per gram but you still decided to go for the Carte Noir which suggests there were other factors affecting your decision than just price. In economics we often ignore price and look at the opportunity cost of a purchasing decision. In this example the opportunity cost of buying the Carte Noir was the next best alternative sacrificed – the Kenco coffee. This often helps us to understand a consumer's interpretation of value; in this case you, the consumer, are saying that you place a higher value at the time you decided to choose this coffee on one product than another. This information is of value to a producer. For the manufacturers of Carte Noir your decision is some confirmation of the care they have taken to produce the product, the quality, the way they advertise and promote it and the price they have put on the product. For the manufacturers of Kenco, your decision is a slap in the face – it is telling them that you do not think that they are offering you what you want and so you have decided their product does not give you the value you are looking for. It might be the price is wrong; it could be the packaging, where it appears on the shelf, the fact that you have never tried it and so do not have confidence that it is any better than what you normally buy or a host of other reasons. So, despite the best efforts of Kenco having that jar in the supermarket shouting 'buy me' you did not take them up on the offer.

This story has so far been based on the individual decision of one person in relation to one product – a jar of coffee. Now scale the story up to include every person in the region you live and then every person in the country you live in and then, every person in the whole world. When you jump from an individual decision to a global one the picture becomes incredibly complex. This global scale, however, is at the heart of the so-called invisible hand of the market outlined by Adam Smith, the Eighteenth Century economist who attempted to formalize the study of economics and the working of markets in his 1776 book, *An Inquiry into the Nature and Causes of the Wealth of Nations*. The debate about the extent to which free markets should be the dominant philosophy of policy makers is beyond the scope of this book. We will assume, however, that the private decisions of millions of people are dominant in the economy.

The seemingly insignificant importance of your individual decision about which coffee (and every other product) you buy is put into some context when viewed as being one in many similar such decisions being carried out across the world. In some cases the decisions will be more local such as whether to employ electrician X rather than Y to rewire a house and in others the market will be truly global with decisions made by individuals in New Zealand playing as much a part of the market as those made in Angola or Sweden. And, of course it is not only individuals who are making these decisions, it is companies, organizations and governments. Companies and organizations buy raw materials, equipment, machinery, buildings, land and labour; governments will buy hospital and road services, military equipment, snow ploughs, education services, justice and law and order and so on.

The common factors in this story are that there are buyers and sellers, who represent the demand and supply of products, and who interact in markets which bring buyers and sellers together. Price is the signal which tells consumers whether something is worth buying and also tells producers whether a product is worth producing or not. As these forces play out in markets, resources are allocated to different uses. Let us extend the story for a moment to see how this might happen.

Assume that a large number of people shopping for coffee make the same decisions as you did and buy Carte Noir. For the manufacturers of this product high sales are a signal that it is worth continuing to produce and indeed to increase production. As the firm organizes itself to increase production, more resources are pulled in; more coffee beans are bought from farmers, new equipment may be purchased to help process the coffee beans, new orders are received by distribution firms, more people are hired to help manage the expansion in production and so on.

For Kenco the situation is quite different. They are seeing stocks of their coffee build up as sales slow down. They tell coffee growers that they will be cutting back purchases of coffee beans, workers at processing plants may be given redundancy and indeed whole plants may have to shut down. The workers who have been made redundant will have to find new jobs (maybe with Carte Noir?) and some will move into completely different types of work. Kenco may decide to focus on developing a new product which it may feel is going to be able to compete in the market and given the external pressures on such firms to treat workers in the supply chain fairly they may decide to link up with an organization which promotes ethical production of coffee. Kenco diverts resources into the production of this new product and employs people to develop the marketing campaign which will improve its chances of success.

All these changes have occurred because you decided to buy one brand of coffee over another! If you are feeling slightly guilty – don't. This is how markets work; they are dynamic, evolving and because of this, fascinating. The problem is that analyzing markets, because of their complexity, can be almost impossible unless we have a framework to help us understand the main processes involved. That is why we use a model of the market mechanism to help. We will develop this model as the chapter proceeds. Just remember that a model is designed to present a simplified view of reality to aid analysis and is not meant to be reality. We can look at how a model works as a stylized representation of reality to help understand events and make predictions and then when reality catches up we can use the model to explain why things may have happened differently to that which the model initially suggested.

As we begin our journey into markets keep in mind the story we have presented here and try to think about it when you make your purchasing decisions. It can help to develop thinking and understanding when you do such things because in so doing you will notice things that you may have ignored or taken for granted in the past.

BUYERS AND SELLERS – DEMAND AND SUPPLY

In developing the model of how markets work we need to understand the basic elements of the market. Markets consist of two players – buyers and sellers. Buyers represent the demand for products and sellers represent the supply of products on the market. These two elements are completely independent but interact with each other in different ways. We are going to look at sellers first.

Sellers

We are going to assume that sellers are in business to make a profit and as such are concerned to find ways of increasing revenue and keeping costs to a minimum. They are interested in selling more rather than less but if they increase production then their costs will also rise and so offering more for sale means that they will be looking for higher prices to partly offset those rising costs. There is nothing technical or complex about these basic assumptions. They are in many respects common sense – put yourself in a producer's position, would you rather sell five million units at €1 each or at €10 each? Selling at €10 each is **more likely** (although not guaranteed) to give you a bigger profit than if you sold your five million units at €1 each. How much profit you make depends on your costs of production in relation to the price that you are able to get from selling your products.

Assume we conduct a survey of different producers in the market for electric hair straighteners in order to produce a schedule for supply. If we asked them the question of how many pairs of straighteners they would be **willing and able** to supply to the market at different prices (note the emphasis on willing and able) it is likely that we would get back data which confirms the law of supply. This law states that suppliers will offer more for sale to the market at higher prices.

If we took all the individual supply schedules from each firm in the survey and added them together at the different prices in this market we would get the market supply curve as shown in Figure 11.2. (The term 'curve' is used but we present the relationship here as a linear curve.) As we develop our model we will use both supply and demand curves. It is essential that you remember that these curves, individually, do not tell us **what** will be bought or sold, only the amount sellers and buyers **would like** to sell or buy at different prices.

The supply curve shows the law of supply and demonstrates a positive relationship between price and quantity supplied.

Figure 11.2 shows a supply curve (for hair straighteners) which slopes upwards from left to right. Reading this particular graph tells us that at a price of €10 suppliers are willing and able to offer 5000 straighteners onto the market. If the price were at €35 then suppliers would be willing and able to offer 20 000 for sale in the market. We have emphasized the idea of being *willing and able* to offer products for sale; producers must not only want to offer products for sale in the market they must be in a position to be able to do so – they must have the capacity to supply the products in the market.

FIGURE 11.2

The market supply curve

Figure 11.2 shows the relationship between price and quantity supplied. At higher prices, firms are willing to offer more products for sale than at lower prices. There is a positive relationship between price and quantity supplied.

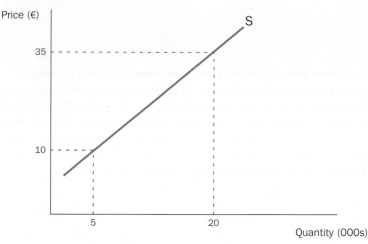

The supply curve also shows all other points linking price and the quantity supplied by producers in this market. The market supply curve reflects the fact that there will be lots of different types of firms in the market – some big and some small – with each having different capacities and factors affecting what they are able to supply. These factors determine where the supply curve actually lies on the graph. If, for example, the cost of producing hair straighteners was very high or the raw materials very expensive to access then the supply curve may be further to the left of the curve in Figure 11.2, whereas if the cost of producing straighteners was low and there were levels of technology which were high and freely available then it may be the supply curve would lie further to the right of that in Figure 11.2.

It is important to remember, therefore, that the supply of products in a market is not fixed and various factors could cause it to move around. These factors are those that affect the ability of sellers to produce products. For farmers the weather during the growing season is a key factor affecting the size and quality of the harvest, for the banking sector the availability of highly skilled individuals will affect the cost of carrying out their activities; the more highly skilled the individuals the higher the salaries that have to be paid to persuade them to work for the institution. Over the last few years changes in technology have lowered the costs of production of mobile and smartphones which has enabled firms to supply more to the market because technology has increased productivity so much.

In order to facilitate analysis we classify the factors affecting supply as summarized in the formula below which says supply (S) is a function of (is dependent upon – =f) all the factors within the brackets.

$$S = f (P_n, P_n..P_{n-1}, H, N, F_1..F_m, E, S_f)$$

Where:

- P_n = Price
- $P_n..P_{n-1}$ = Profitability of other goods in production and prices of goods in joint supply
- H = Technology
- N = Natural shocks
- $F_1 ... F_m$ = Costs of production
- E = Expectations of producers
- S_f = Social factors

Refer back to Chapter 3 for discussion about factors influencing production costs; Chapter 4 on social factors, Chapter 5 on technology and Chapter 6 on price.

FIGURE 11.3

Shifts in the market supply curve

*Figure 11.3 shows changes in any of the factors affecting supply **other than price** can cause a change in supply. Factors negatively affecting producers such as a rise in the costs of production cause the supply curve to shift to the left. At every price suppliers will now be willing and able to offer less to the market than before. If factors change which affect producers in a positive way then the supply curve shifts to the right. At every price suppliers are now willing and able to offer more for sale. In the figure an initial supply curve S is shown along with a price of €20. A shift of the supply curve to the left causes a fall in supply at €20 of 7000 to 5000 whereas a rise in supply at a price of €20 causes an increase in supply to 20 000, a rise of 8000.*

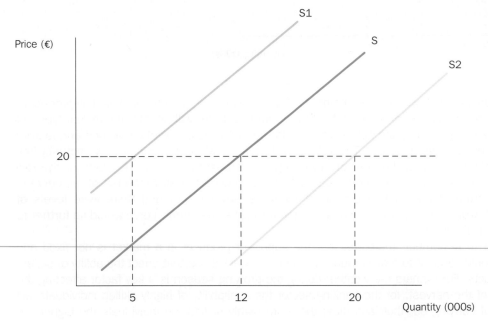

A change in any of the factors above **other than price** will cause the supply curve to shift either to the left where less will be supplied at every price or the right where more will be supplied at every price. This is shown in Figure 11.3 and is best illustrated using an example.

Manufacturers of hair straighteners will use various resources in the production of the product, Anything which affects the cost of production will affect the amount firms are able to supply. If there is an increase in the cost of buying in ceramic plates for the straighteners then it will now cost the firm more to produce the same amount than before. This is shown as a shift in the supply curve to the left. If costs fall for some reason then the supply curve would shift to the right because more can now be produced at the same price as previously.

The manufacture of hair straighteners involves technology both in the design and the production process. Improvements in technology can lead to improvements in productivity which mean that more can be produced in the same time period lowering unit costs. As a result the supply curve shifts to the right. Equally, if some new technology became available such as a water based shampoo which leaves hair dead straight after washing then manufacturers of hair straighteners could find themselves at a competitive disadvantage and some firms may leave the industry.

This means the supply curve for straighteners shifts to the left. This would also happen if manufacturers had expectations about the market which cause them to adjust supply. It could be that a severe economic downturn would lead manufacturers to expect sales to fall dramatically and so they decide to cut back production in anticipation. The reverse could also occur, of course.

Other factors that could cause the supply curve to shift are natural shocks and social factors. If, for example, an earthquake in a major copper producing region of the world was to cut supplies of copper dramatically then firms using copper in production may find supplies hard to acquire and if they can acquire them, they only do so at a very high price. As a result supplies of straighteners may fall and the supply curve shifts to the left. If a major discovery of new supplies of copper occurred then prices might fall and copper becomes easy to access. The supply of hair straighteners as a result could increase, shifting the supply curve to the right.

Social factors are an important factor affecting supply. Concerns over the environment (Chapter 7), over the use of energy, health issues and so on can all affect supply. At the time of writing straight hair is fashionable. If for some reason fashions changed and the social norm moved to having curly hair then hair straighteners might become largely redundant and firm might look to move into another line of production, for example the production of curling tongs. Manufacturers of straighteners might feel that it would be relatively easy given their technology and expertise to be able to switch production to the manufacture of curling tongs which would shift the supply of straighteners to the left (but the supply curve of curling tongs to the right). Producers often look at the relative profitability of products which are substitutes in production (such as curling tongs and straighteners) in making decision whether to supply the market. Some goods are in joint supply – an increase or decrease in one good automatically affects the supply of another; wool and lamb being an often used example.

Summary

The law of supply states that the amount sellers are willing and able to offer for sale in a market rises when prices are higher and falls when prices are lower. The change in supply which occurs when price changes is referred to as a *change in quantity supplied*. Other factors affecting supply can also change and when they do they cause a *change in supply*. A change in supply will be the result of a shift in the supply curve either to the left when supply is reduced or to the right if supply rises.

Buyers

From the buyers' side we are going to assume that they prefer more to less, that buyers are seeking to get value from their spending and are thus concerned with getting value for money. Buyers represent demand in the market. Every individual has their own schedule of demand which is determined by a wide range of factors including income (Chapters 3 and 4) and tastes. One person may be prepared to pay a relatively large sum of money for a product that someone else would not buy at any price! Some people are in the fortunate position of having very high salaries whereas others barely have enough to live on; buyers' behaviour will change when the prices of other goods change, and the size and structure of the population (Chapter 4) can also have a powerful effect on demand.

Whatever the personal situation of buyers they have one thing in common; virtually everyone would rather buy more goods at lower prices than they would at higher prices. If we continue with the example of hair straighteners, for any quality pair of straighteners on the market, if a survey was conducted asking people what they would be **willing and able** (again, this is important) to purchase at different prices, the chances are that there would be more people willing and able to buy straighteners at lower prices than at higher prices. This is called the law of demand.

As with supply we can model this law using a very similar diagram. This time, however, the relationship between price and quantity demanded is negative; there is an inverse relationship between quantity demanded and price as shown in Figure 11.4.

FIGURE 11.4

The market demand curve

Figure 11.4 shows the relationship between price and quantity demanded. At higher prices there are a relatively small number of buyers willing and able to buy products whereas at lower prices far more people are willing and able to purchase the good.

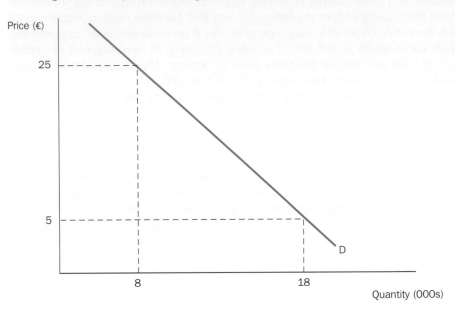

In Figure 11.4, the demand curve is shown as a downward sloping curve from left to right. At a price of €25 there are 8000 people willing and able to buy straighteners in this market but if the price were €5 there would be 18000 people willing and able to purchase straighteners. As with supply we place the emphasis on *willing and able* because it is not sufficient to want to buy something, the buyer must have the means to be able to buy it. This is called effective demand.

FACTORS AFFECTING DEMAND

Factors affecting demand were first highlighted in Chapter 3 (refer back to Figures 3.3–3.6). As with supply, the demand curve in a market is not fixed and will shift to the left meaning less is demanded at every price, or to the right meaning more is demanded at every price. There are a variety of factors, apart from price, that cause a shift in the demand curve. These are summarized in the formula below which says demand (D) is a function of (is dependent upon – =f) all the factors within the brackets.

$D = f(P_n, P_n...P_{n-1}, Y, T, P, A, E)$

Where:

- P_n = Price
- $P_n...P_{n-1}$ = Prices of other goods – substitutes and complements
- Y = Incomes – the level and distribution of income
- T = Tastes and fashions
- P = The level and structure of the population

FIGURE 11.5

Shifts in the market demand curve

Figure 11.5 shows how shifts in the demand curve affect demand. A rise in demand will occur if the demand curve shifts to the right (from D to D1) At a price of €15, demand would rise from 18 000 to 27 000.

If a change in a factor caused demand to shift from D to D2 then the demand would fall. At a price of €15 demand would now be 7000 compared to the 18 000 prior to the shift in demand.

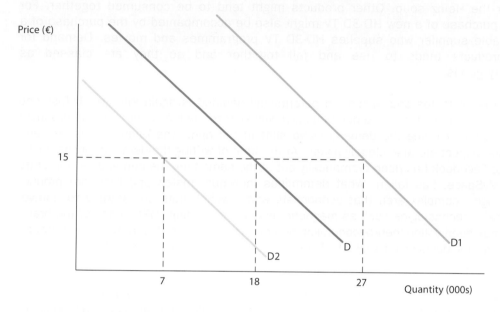

- *A* = Advertising
- *E* = Expectations of consumers

Changes in these factors will cause the demand curve to shift either to the right or to the left as shown in Figure 11.5.

The initial demand curve is given as D. At a price of €15 demand is 18 000. A shift of the demand curve to the left or right will mean that at all prices buyers are willing to buy less or more than previously. A shift in the demand curve to the right to D1, leads to demand rising to 27 000 at a price of €15. If the demand curve shifted to the left to D2 rather than D then demand would fall from 18 000 to 7000.

Again, there is nothing too complex about these factors, they are mostly common sense.

Income – If, for example, your income increases then it means you are in a position of being able to buy more of everything. If you receive a salary increase of 5 per cent you may feel that the high quality straighteners you had your eye on for some time is now something you can afford. Equally, when people lose their job their incomes tend to fall and buying behaviour has to change as a result. It can mean that you buy less food in your weekly shop or buy cheaper products such as supermarket own brand which you would not normally purchase. A fall in income will shift the demand curve for most goods to the left whilst a rise will shift demand to the right. This is not, however, the case for every good. If an unemployed person does decide to switch from buying tins of Heinz soup to buying a supermarket own brand then demand for this product has risen when income has fallen. This type of product is called an inferior good. Notice that the demand for the Heinz soup has fallen as income has fallen. This product would be classed as a normal good.

Changes in the prices of other goods – The demand curve might also shift in response to changes in the prices of other goods. These other goods can be classed as substitutes and complements. If the price of Heinz soup rises then some buyers will think twice about whether the higher price really represents the same value for money as it used to. It might just tip the decision making in favour of purchasing a cheaper brand. This cheaper brand may be almost as good quality in the eyes of the buyer. The cheaper brand is a substitute for the Heinz soup. Other products might tend to be consumed together. For example, the purchase of a new HD-3D TV might also be accompanied by the purchase of a satellite or cable supplier who supplies HD-3D TV programmes and movies. Demand for these two products tends to rise and fall together and so they are classed as complementary goods.

Tastes – The role of tastes and fashion in determining demand is again intuitive. If fashions change away from a product then the demand curve will shift to the left whereas those products which are in fashion will see the demand curve shift to the right. The relationships between products in this respect are also closely linked. At the time of writing the demand for the social networking site Facebook has risen dramatically but at the same time the demand for one of its competitors, MySpace, has fallen. What determines individual tastes and therefore product choices is a highly complex area that economists and psychologists are starting to unravel through the use of technologies such as magnetic resonance imaging (MRI) scans of the brain. This research has been called 'neuroeconomics' or 'neuromarketing' and is throwing new light on possible reasons for decision-making which we have not understood prior to the use of this technology.

Population – It is also fairly obvious that the more people there are the more demand there will be for a product. It is not only the size of the population which has an effect on demand, however. The structure of the population – how it is made up (see Chapter 4 Figure 4.2) – is also of considerable importance. In Iran, for example, there is a much higher proportion of young people in the population and only 5.4 per cent of its population are over 65. In Finland 16.8 per cent of the population are over 65, in Armenia it is 10.6 per cent, 16.2 per cent in the UK and 20.3 per cent in Germany. Younger people tend to have different wants and needs than older people and so the demand for products in a country like Germany is going to be different to that in Iran.

Advertising – Advertising plays a role in influencing demand. It used to be thought that adverts were simply designed to try and increase sales but this simple view has now been supplanted by a far more sophisticated set of explanations. Researchers have found that humans react to advertising in many different ways dependent on a whole host of factors. The use of MRI scanning, as outlined above, has helped to shed some new light onto the process involved. However, we can generally surmise that increased levels of advertising of a product will generally help to increase demand whereas if a firm stops advertising or a rival firm increases its advertising, demand for the product will fall.

Expectations – Finally, we can look at the expectations of buyers as having an effect on demand. If buyers expect prices to rise for example, because of an increase in taxes or duties, then demand tends to rise in the short-term. If buyers are pessimistic about the economy they may tend to 'tighten their belts' and reduce spending on some types of products and this can affect demand considerably. The recession in the latter part of the first decade of the twenty first century in Europe and across the world led to considerable changes in patterns of expenditure as buyers adjusted to new situations and their expectations of future events. Many people in Spain, Portugal, Greece and Ireland lost their jobs as a result of government spending cuts but in the months prior to the cuts being announced public sector workers cut back spending in anticipation of the possible threat of losing their jobs.

TABLE 11.1   Summary of the causes of shifts in supply curves.

Factor	Shift in Supply	Effect on Supply
Increase in profitability of substitute product	Left	Fall in Supply
Decrease in profitability of substitute product	Right	Increase in Supply
Increase in profitability of product in joint supply	Right	Increase in Supply
Fall in profitability of product in joint supply	Left	Fall in Supply
Improvement in technology	Right	Increase in Supply
Decrease in technology	Left	Fall in Supply
Negative natural factor affecting supply	Left	Fall in Supply
Positive natural factor affecting supply	Right	Increase in Supply
Increase in costs of production	Left	Fall in Supply
Fall in costs of production	Right	Increase in Supply
Pessimistic expectations of producers	Left	Fall in Supply
Optimistic expectations of producers	Right	Increase in Supply
Positive social factors	Right	Increase in Supply
Negative social factors	Left	Fall in Supply

SHIFTS IN SUPPLY AND DEMAND – A SUMMARY

TYPES OF MARKET

We are now in a position to be able to put the two elements of markets together to see how they interact and how prices are determined. Before we do it is worth noting that the model developed here applies to lots of different types of markets. Every day across the world, millions of different currencies are exchanged on highly organized markets dealing in foreign currency, shares, bonds, derivatives, commodities such as gold, platinum, tin, copper, sugar, cotton and cocoa amongst others. These markets are international and bring together buyers of these products into contact with sellers. Many people will be familiar with street markets and farmers markets. In this case traders will bring their wares to the market and buyers visit if they are looking to buy a particular product. Then there are online markets where buyers and sellers never actually meet but are brought together by technology. Businesses will buy and sell products to each other in B2B

TABLE 11.2   Summary of causes of shifts in demand curves.

Factor	Shift in Demand	Effect on Demand
Increase in the price of a substitute	Right	Increase in Demand
Fall in the price of a substitute	Left	Fall in Demand
Increase in the price of a complement	Left	Fall in Demand
Fall in the price of a complement	Right	Increase in Demand
Rise in incomes – normal good	Right	Increase in Demand
Fall in incomes – normal good	Left	Fall in Demand
Rise in incomes – inferior good	Left	Fall in Demand
Fall in incomes – inferior good	Right	Increase in Demand
Change in tastes/fashion to the product	Right	Increase in Demand
Change in tastes/fashion away from the product	Left	Fall in Demand
Increase in population	Right	Increase in Demand
Decrease in population	Left	Fall in Demand
Change in Structure of the population	Left or Right – dependent on the nature of the change in structure	Increase or Fall in Demand Depending on Shift in Demand
Increase in advertising	Right	Increase in Demand
Decrease in advertising – or campaign by rival product	Left	Fall in Demand
Negative expectations of buyers	Left	Fall in Demand
Positive expectations of buyers	Right	Increase in Demand

markets and everyday millions of people around the world will go to shops, restaurants, leisure facilities and so on and in so doing are taking part in markets.

We talk, therefore, of a market for groceries, a market for reinforcing steels, a market for cement, a market for insurance services and so on. Even within these markets there may be further granulation – the market for insurance services can be divided into highly sophisticated marine insurance involving risks in international shipping, to life assurance and the insurance of property and personal belongings from fire, theft and damage. It is precisely because there are so many markets that a general model is used to help understand what happens when things change.

THE MARKET MECHANISM

Before we get into the detail of how the market mechanism determines prices and allocates scarce resources it is useful to establish the process by which this analysis is carried out. We will make use of what is called *comparative static analysis*. This means we compare one situation with a different one and then look at the changes which have occurred as a result. Some textbooks give the impression that changes are almost instantaneous and this can sometimes lead to misunderstanding and confusion. It must be stressed that there is a time period involved between changes in markets – sometimes the changes can lead to new market situations very quickly which is often the case with highly organized financial markets where information exchange is rapid; in other cases the changes may be very slow to have an effect; changing fashions can take time to feed through to buyers and so markets may take many months to adjust. It is worth bearing these practical issues in mind as we proceed through the analysis.

There are several stages to the analysis:

1 We begin the process by assuming that the market is in equilibrium, Equilibrium is defined as being a state of rest. In equilibrium there is no incentive for either buyers or sellers to change their behaviour.

2 We then introduce some change – this will be one of the factors affecting supply or demand. In introducing the change we assume all other factors are held constant. Economists often use the term *ceteris paribus* which translates to 'other things being equal'. We then decide whether the change is going to affect supply or demand.

3 Having identified whether supply or demand is affected first we decide on the direction of the shift in the curve.

4 A shift in either the supply or demand curve (or both) will put the market into disequilibrium and create either a shortage or surplus in the market.

5 We finally look at the way in which the shortage or surplus affects buyer and seller behaviour and as a result what happens to price as the market re-establishes equilibrium.

Market equilibrium

The market is said to be in equilibrium when the supply of a product at a particular price is the same as the demand for the product at that price. At this price the market is said to have cleared (the market clearing price), that is, there is no shortage or surplus in the market and as such no incentive for either buyers or sellers to change their behaviour.

Shortage – If a shortage existed in the market (demand being greater than supply at a particular price) there would be more buyers looking to purchase goods at that price than sellers willing to offer the product for sale. In their desire to acquire the product buyers would be prepared to pay higher prices but as price gradually rises some buyers decide that the price has gone beyond what they believe gives value for money and so drop out of the market. At the same time, sellers are faced with a demand for their product which they cannot, at that moment in time, satisfy. As prices are bid up, it provides an incentive for producers to seek out new resources to expand production in the knowledge that they are likely to be able to sell the additional supply. These new resources do increase costs and so producers will be expecting higher prices to cover these additional costs.

These different forces continue to act on the market until the price has risen to a point where the supply of the product once again is the same as the demand at the new price and a new equilibrium position has been established.

TABLE 11.3

Market Situation	Supply and Demand	Direction of Price
Equilibrium	S = D	No pressure on price to change
Shortage	S < D	Pressure on price to rise
Surplus	S > D	Pressure on price to fall

Surplus – Where a surplus exists in a market at a particular price, the amount buyers wish to purchase is less than the amount suppliers would like to offer for sale at that price; sellers are left with unsold stocks. There is an incentive for them to try to offload these unsold products by lowering the price and in so doing encourage buyers to enter the market when the higher price did not reflect value for money for some buyers. As the price falls, however, some sellers feel that they are unable to offer products for sale because it is simply not worth their while to do so; for some sellers the cost of production would be higher than the new lower prices which are reigning in the market. As a result some sellers will leave the market. Again, these opposing forces will continue to work their way through the market until a new lower price brings about a new equilibrium where the amount sellers are willing to offer at a particular price is the same as the amount buyers wish to purchase at that price.

Summary

We will now look at this using our diagrammatic model of supply and demand. We will use the market for a particular brand of hair straighteners (we will call this *Str8*) as the context to explain how the market mechanism works.

Shifts in Demand

Panel a) of Figure 11.6 shows the market for *Str8* straighteners in equilibrium; the price of straighteners is €75 and the amount bought and sold at this price is 50 000 every time period. Imagine that a report in a tabloid daily newspaper highlights a case of a pair of *Str8* straighteners catching fire and burning down a house injuring three people. The social networking and viral media seizes on this story and it soon becomes clear that this is not the first time this has happened with a pair of these straighteners.

BUSINESS IN DEBATE

Cocoa

In the latter half of 2010 controversy arose on the commodity markets over the actions of a hedge fund manager who acquired a large amount of cocoa which could, according to some reports, lead to a rise in the price of chocolate. Anthony Ward runs the Armarjo fund. Mr Ward bet on the price of cocoa rising and bought futures contracts to buy cocoa beans on the London International Financial Futures and Options Exchange (LIFFE). The contracts gave Mr Ward the right to take delivery of the cocoa and in

July he did just that. Mr Ward took delivery of the cocoa beans after exercising this right on 24 100 contracts. What this meant was that he took delivery of around 7 per cent of the world's yearly output of cocoa valued at €750 million which, it was reported, would be stored in LIFFE's warehouses in the Low Countries. It was reported that Mr Ward planned to sell the cocoa on.

It was argued that Mr Ward's actions allowed him to 'corner the market', gain control of supply and thus be in a position to exploit the resulting rise in prices. This so called 'market squeeze' angered those who were on the other side of the contracts, i.e. the ones who had to ensure that they acquired enough cocoa beans, at whatever price to fulfil the contracts.

Others pointed out that Mr Ward had not done anything illegal or against market rules – he simply bet that the price of cocoa was going to rise.

The cocoa harvest in Africa was due around September and October 2010 and if it was poorer than expected then Mr Ward could stand to benefit from rising prices. Critics argued that by acquiring such a significant proportion of the world cocoa output, Mr Ward could himself contribute to any shortage in supply and thus drive up prices further meaning he would be able to make even more profit.

Mr Ward is reported to have started buying contracts at around £2481 per tonne and at the time the contracts were due for completion, the price had risen to £3152. Mr Ward could have taken the profit there and then but the fact that he exercised the contracts and took physical delivery implies he believed the price would continue to rise. This prompted cocoa buyers to complain to LIFFE that speculators will force the price of cocoa up and has fuelled rumours that prices of chocolate products would rise for Christmas 2010.

However, after July prices began to fall. In October, trading in cocoa in London was at around €2192 per tonne which meant that cocoa was trading at 30 per cent below its July high. The reason for the easing of prices is that improved weather conditions meant a bigger crop than forecast and traders also believe that the 2010–11 harvest was also going to be much better than had been the case over the last four years where shortages have been characteristic of the market. Forecasts were being made of a 15 per cent increase in output from the Ivory Coast which accounts for two fifths of global supply and also a rise in output in other cocoa producing countries such as Ghana.

The high prices also contributed to the expected increase in supply. As theory suggests, high prices will encourage producers to seek to expand supply but in doing so they incur additional costs. Cocoa farmers have been reported to be buying more fertilizers and pesticides in an attempt to help increase yields. In addition some farmers planted new trees, some of which are needed to replace older trees which were less productive. In the longer term this will increase output (other things being equal.)

However, despite the optimism being expressed about the crop for 2011, traders were warning of caution; a great deal can happen in a short time, in particular the size of the crop is very much dependent on weather conditions and this is not something that is easily forecast. What of Mr Ward? It seems he might not have made a billion but he had, reportedly, managed to cushion some of the fall in prices by appropriate hedging strategies on short positions (trades made in the expectation that prices will fall).

The whole saga sounds quite glamorous and some news reports portrayed Mr Ward as some sort of Bondesque villain. The reality may be less exciting – even if Mr Ward did succeed in generating $1 billion from the trades he made. Anthony Ward has spent over 30 years in the business and colleagues describe him as being as near to an expert in matters cocoa as it is possible to be. His attention to detail means that he has even set up weather stations in cocoa producing countries to monitor the weather and help give better information about the possible size of cocoa harvests. The fragility of such knowledge needs to be put into perspective; in 1996, Mr Ward took a similarly large position on the cocoa harvest and his bet backfired when the harvest was plentiful; he made substantial losses.

Source: adapted from Biz/ed In the News www.bized.co.uk/cgi-bin/chron/chron.pl?id=3696 and www.bized.co.uk/cgibin/chron/chron.pl?id=3654

Is supply or demand likely to be affected first here? It will be likely that demand is the first thing to be hit (although it could be argued that *Str8* might take the product off the market if they are dangerous; however, we will assume that *Str8* insists that there is nothing wrong with the product and that these incidents are very unusual).

Assuming the news becomes widespread the demand for *Str8* straighteners would fall; whatever the price fewer people are now willing to buy this product. Note, not everyone will cease buying the product, some people will still be prepared to buy *Str8* straighteners because they have not had any problems with the product before and do not believe all the hype.

The fall in demand is shown in Panel b) of Figure 11.6 as a shift of the demand curve to the left from D1 to D2. At a price of €75 the manufacturers of *Str8* straighteners find themselves with lots of unsold goods – they could not see this change coming and have not had time to adjust production to take account of the news and the sudden fall in demand. There is now a surplus in the market, therefore, of 30 000 as highlighted in Panel b). At €75 only 20 000 people are now

FIGURE 11.6

The market mechanism

Panel a) in Figure 11.6 shows the initial equilibrium in the market for Str8 straighteners with price at €75 and the amount bought and sold at 50 000. Panel b) shows how, following the adverse publicity, the demand curve shifts to the left to D2. At a price of €75 demand is now just 20 000 but Str8 are still offering 50 000 for sale in the market. The surplus in the market is 30 000 units. The surplus put pressure on price to fall; at a price of €65, buyers are willing to purchase 25 000 and Str8 is willing to offer 45 000 for sale – the size of the surplus has shrunk but a surplus still exists.

Price will continue to fall until a new equilibrium is reached at a price of €45 when 35 000 units are demanded and Str8 is willing to offer 35 000 for sale. The market has now cleared.

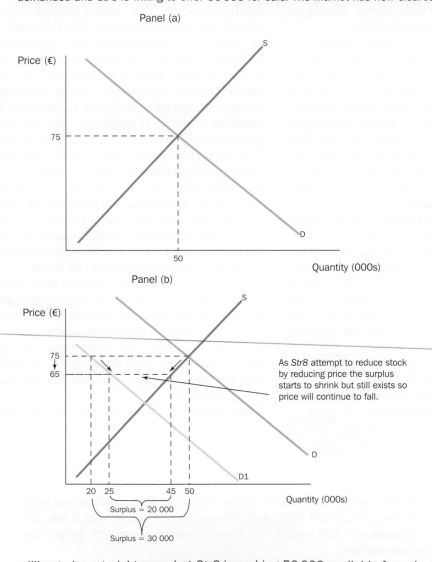

willing to buy straighteners but *Str8* is making 50 000 available for sale. With this excess supply in the market *Str8* cuts prices to try and encourage sales. As the price falls to €65 (for example) the demand is now 25 000 – some people are now prepared to pay for the straighteners at the lower price when before they were not. The lower price, however, means that *Str8* is willing to offer less to the market. The pressure on price to fall will continue until equilibrium is restored. This may take some time, possibly several weeks or months in this example. The new equilibrium price will be €45 and 35 000 will be bought and sold as shown in Panel c). The result of the change in demand has been to bring about a new lower price in this particular market with a lower number of straighteners bought and sold.

FIGURE 11.6

The market mechanism *(Continued)*

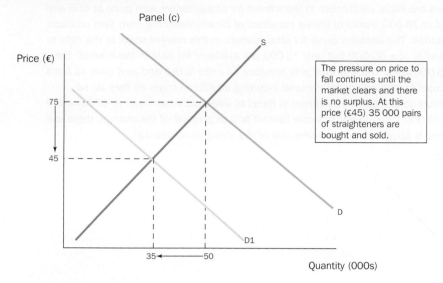

Panel (c)

The pressure on price to fall continues until the market clears and there is no surplus. At this price (€45) 35 000 pairs of straighteners are bought and sold.

We can extend our analysis by looking at what might happen in the rest of the market for straighteners. Other manufacturers might see the demand for their straighteners rise as a result of the problems faced by *Str8*. Assume that the price of straighteners in the rest of the market was €65 and the amount bought and sold 75 000. As a result of the problems faced by *Str8* buyers look to switch to other manufacturers and so demand in this market would rise as shown by a shift in the demand curve to the right from D to D1 in Figure 11.7. In this market there would now be a shortage of straighteners as manufacturers are faced with a rise in demand which they did not anticipate. The shortage will cause price to rise (for the reasons outlined above) and eventually a new equilibrium will occur when price is €72 and the amount bought and sold in the market will be 83 000.

Shifts in Supply

In the previous example we looked at what can happen to markets when demand shifts. Equilibrium in markets can also be disturbed by factors affecting supply. Assume that the price of copper on international commodity markets rises sharply. Copper is a metal used in electrical cables used on products like straighteners.

Assume that the market for straighteners is at the level outlined in Panel a) of Figure 11.8. The price of a pair of straighteners is €75 and the amount bought and sold in the market is 50 000. As a result of the higher price of copper, the cost of production of straighteners is now higher. Manufacturers will now face a higher cost of production for producing any amount of their product. At a price of €75, therefore, manufacturers are willing to supply fewer straighteners to the market because it now costs more to make each pair. The supply curve for straighteners will shift to the left so that at any price there are now fewer straighteners being made available on the market. This shift to the left is shown in Panel b). The effect on the market is that at the existing market price of €75 there are now fewer straighteners available for sale – supply has dropped to 40 000 units – while demand is still at 50 000 units. As a result the market is facing a shortage with demand for straighteners higher than available supply. Market forces now kick in and price starts to rise as buyers are prepared to pay more to get their hands on straighteners. As the price gradually rises some buyers start to think that the price they are being asked is not worth it and so they drop out of the market whereas suppliers, seeing prices rise, are encouraged to offer more for sale. Once again the process continues until a new equilibrium is reached. In this example (as shown by Panel c)) the new market price for straighteners will be €78 and the number of straighteners bought and sold in the market now 46 000.

The Allocation of Resources What we can see from this simple example is a snapshot of the dynamics of markets which takes place in every market all around the world every day. In our first

FIGURE 11.7

The market for straighteners

Panel a) in Figure 11.7 shows the initial equilibrium in the market for straighteners with price at €65 and the amount bought and sold at 75 000. Panel b) shows the effect of buyers switching from Str8 products to those in the rest of the market. The demand curve for straighteners in this market shifts to the right to D1. At a price of €65 demand is now 90 000 but only 75 000 are available for sale in the market. The shortage in the market is 15 000 units. The shortage puts pressure on price to rise and as it does so firms look to increase output to cater for the additional demand incurring additional costs as they do so. Eventually the market will return to equilibrium as shown in Panel b) when price has risen to €72 and the amount bought and sold is 83 000. The market has now cleared and as a result of the change, there is a higher market price and more is bought and sold in the rest of the straightener market.

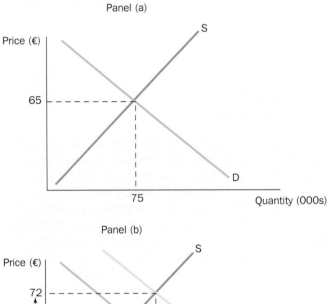

Panel (a)

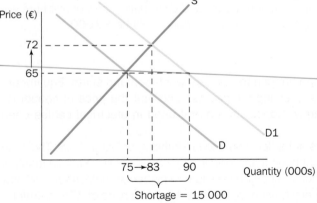

Panel (b)

example of *Str8,* the damage of the bad publicity has affected its market in a negative way as far as it is concerned. It now sells fewer items and may even have to take decisions to close plant and lay off workers as a result. For those buyers still willing to pay for products from *Str8* the situation is positive in that they now face lower prices for the product. For other manufacturers elsewhere in the market as a whole the news is positive if they receive customers who have switched from *Str8.*

In our second example where supply of straighteners was affected by a rise in the costs of copper, supply fell. This might have been caused in part by some manufacturers leaving the industry; it may have been that some were only just making enough to survive anyway and this rise in costs just tipped them over the edge causing them to take the decision to close or shift production to other more profitable items.

What we do need to recognize in this process is what is happening to resource allocation. Remember that one of the benefits of markets is that they allocate scarce resources to competing uses. Societies have found various ways of trying to allocate scarce resources and markets are one

FIGURE 11.8

A shift in supply

Panel a) in Figure 11.8 shows the initial equilibrium in the market for straighteners with price at €75 and the amount bought and sold at 50 000. Panel b) shows how, following the rise in raw material costs the supply curve shifts to the left to S2. At a price of €75 supply is now just 40 000 but buyers are willing to purchase 50 000 in the market. The shortage in the market is 10 000 units. The shortage puts pressure on price to rise; at a price of €76, buyers are willing to purchase 48 000 and sellers are willing to offer 42 000 for sale – the size of the shortage has shrunk but a shortage still exists. Price will continue to rise until a new equilibrium is reached at a price of €78 when 46 000 units are demanded and producers are willing to offer 46 000 for sale. The market has now cleared.

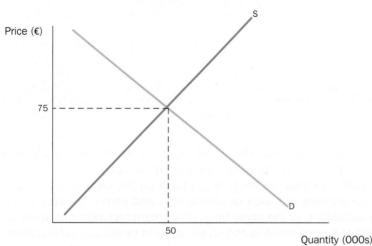

Panel (a)

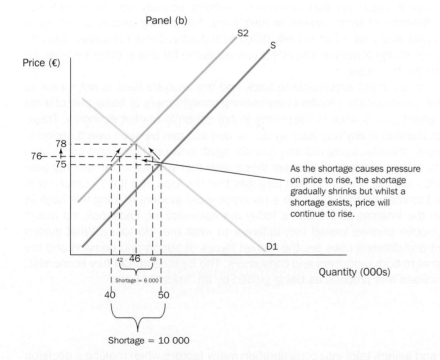

Panel (b)

As the shortage causes pressure on price to rise, the shortage gradually shrinks but whilst a shortage exists, price will continue to rise.

FIGURE 11.8

A shift in supply *(Continued)*

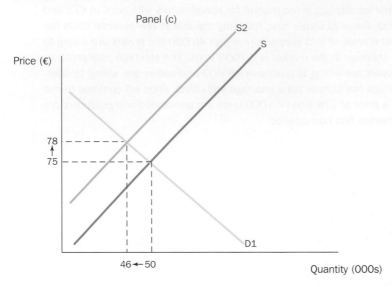

of the systems that is most widely used throughout the world. In the example we have given resources are shifting between different uses – you have to view the big picture here!

For *Str8* the bad publicity has meant that they are likely to cut back on the order of some raw materials, maybe close plants, lay-off workers, cut back on distribution and so on. The resources used in these activities will now be redundant. At the same time, other manufacturers may have to scale up their operations to cope with the extra demand and so will draw in resources to help them do that. It may even be that some workers who used to work for *Str8* secure a job at a rival manufacturer! In other cases it could be that redundant workers actually decide to use the experience to change the direction of their careers or their lives. Some may decide to set up in their own business, others may find work in an entirely different industry. Other resources such as the steel used in production of straighteners is now effectively available for use in other firms which may offer greater returns to the business.

All this resource movement is almost impossible to track and the analysis here is not meant to suggest that a lump of metal automatically transfers from making straighteners to being part of a rail for a tram system. But, in effect that is what is happening in any dynamic market economy. These resource allocations are not planned in any way but they do happen and can be seen over a period of time. In Germany, for example, manufacturing industry has changed; new products have come onto the market and old products have disappeared. It is rare these days that you see a cathode ray tube TV and most monitors for PCs are flat; it was not that long ago that the idea of a flat TV screen was science fiction and it is hard to imagine that if you are a twenty-year-old student reading this book in 2012, when you were born the Internet as we use it today did not exist; no Facebook, no music downloads, no DVDs and mobile phones looked very different to what they do today. What guides resources to these different and differing uses are the market forces of supply and demand and the fact that price acts as a signal to both producers and consumers. The Eighteenth Century economist, Adam Smith, famously described this process as being guided by an 'invisible hand'.

ELASTICITY

We have seen how buyers and sellers take into consideration many factors when making a decision to buy or sell. We have also seen how the law of demand and supply relate the amount buyers and sellers wish to buy to price. There is a positive relationship between price and the quantity supplied and an inverse relationship between price and quantity demanded.

BUSINESS IN ACTION

Commodity Markets

On September 21st 2010 the price of cotton on world markets hit $101.50, a rise of 2.14 per cent on the day. This piece of news may not seem that remarkable but this is the highest price cotton had been since 1995 and before that you had to go back to the American Civil War in the latter part of the 19th century to find cotton prices above $1 per pound. Prices have risen sharply since the beginning of the year rising by a third with most of the increase occurring after August when prices rose by 30 per cent.

The reason for this is good old-fashioned supply and demand. On the supply side floods in Pakistan in the summer of 2010 decimated cotton growing areas and bad weather also affected crops in China which is not only one of the largest growers of cotton but also one of the biggest users. It was estimated that supply would drop by over 20 per cent compared to 2009. India is the second largest supplier of cotton and it was considering an export ban which would have added to the supply side pressures.

The reports of a drop in supply caused a scramble to buy cotton. China itself had to import over 50 per cent more in 2010 to offset the fall in its cotton harvest and clothing manufacturers around the world were looking to buy on the futures market. This has led to a shift in the demand curve for cotton to the right and when demand rises and supply falls the effect is a rise in price. (The effect on quantity bought and sold will depend on the relative strength of the movement of both supply and demand.) As prices rose another demand side effect could be identified – speculators. If there is the prospect of price rising in a commodity market it is not long before hedge funds and other speculative investors sit up and take notice and spot the opportunity for making money. Speculators increase the demand for the commodity and help push prices even higher.

In the United States, one of the world's largest cotton exporters, harvesting was in full swing in order to try and meet the demand from key milling centres in places like Colombia and Mexico as well as China. For cotton producers that do have supplies to send to market the high price was a boost to their revenue. For cotton users the news is not so good; they faced higher input costs and so the prices of clothing were likely to rise. Some analysts suggested that the era of cheap clothing was coming to an end.

By late October 2010 cotton prices had continued to rise with a pound of cotton fetching $1.25 on US futures exchanges. A futures market provides traders with some protection against rising prices.

Usual market analysis tells us that as prices rise, suppliers are willing to offer more for sale on a market. Cotton merchants are no different; they would rather offer cotton for sale at higher prices than lower ones so the futures market can be a way of locking in high prices for the commodity for delivery at a point in the future. An example may serve to highlight the situation that can arise for cotton traders (and those involved in other types of futures contract) when high prices can actually be bad news for them.

Imagine a cotton grower who is attempting to market her crop; whilst the harvest will usually occur once a year, she wants to get buyers for her crop throughout the growing period, not simply wait until the crop has been harvested and then try to sell it. They do this by using the futures market. Contracts are agreed for delivery of a specified sum of cotton at some point in the future at a price fixed at the time the contract is taken out. Such contracts serve to give both buyers and sellers some degree of certainty and aid planning. The buyer of the cotton may be a final user but may also be an intermediary between the grower and the final user. In making the contract the buyer has agreed a price but runs the risk that if prices fall as the contracts come to be honoured they could be out of pocket - they could have bought the cotton they need at a cheaper price. To offset this risk, buyers may hedge their purchase of the contracts by selling a futures contract for the same amount of cotton.

It must be remembered that a futures contract is a legally binding agreement – the buyer must deliver the contract. Trade rules dictate that the seller of the futures contract must put up some collateral called a 'margin' as a sign that they will honour the contract. If cotton prices continue to rise then the risk the buyer has in the forward contract he sold increases – there is more of a risk that he will not be able to honour that contract because it is costing him far more than he thought. When this happens a so-called 'margin call' is triggered and the buyer now has to put up more collateral. This obviously affects cash flow and in some cases can seriously impact on liquidity in the market (defined here as the ability of traders to make deals). When prices of cotton were rising in September 2010 some growers reported that they could not sell any cotton because margin calls had led to the market freezing up temporarily as positions were amended and unwound.

One US cotton company has said that the 7.8 per cent price increase which occurred up to around September increased the margin call requirement by $1 billion and since prices began rising, some $5 billion had been required. This put a huge strain on intermediaries and causes potential problems not only to them but also to growers who may find greater problems accessing the cash for their crops. High prices can, therefore, be a blessing to some suppliers – but not to everybody; a useful point to remember when conducting any analysis.

Source: Adapted from Biz/ed 'In the News' www.bized.co.uk/cgi-bin/chron/chron.pl?id=3688 And www.bized.co.uk/cgi-bin/chron/chron.pl?id=3712

In the introduction to this chapter we walked you through a thought experiment – let's return to that experiment. Whenever you go shopping you have to make many decisions between lots of competing products (usually). In the course of a shopping trip we make innumerable mental calculations which we are really not aware of but which do happen. Let us assume that we are used to paying €4.50 for our usual jar of Carte Noir coffee but as we go to grab the jar this time we see that the price has increased to €5.20. The reason for the increase in price is not really our principle concern (it may be due to a rise in the world price of coffee beans, increased processing or distribution costs, increases in the cost of packaging or many other supply side reasons), what we are concerned with is whether this new price represents value for money compared to what we have been used to paying.

Different customers will react in different ways; some will immediately leave the jar alone and look for a cheaper alternative. Others will look more closely at prices of other products, weigh up what they know about Carte Noir against other brands, maybe consider ethical issues associated with different brands or even recall marketing messages such as advertising campaigns or news items about coffee production and then make a decision. Some buyers will continue to stay loyal to Carte Noir and others will switch to another brand or even to another product altogether – tea, for example.

In this example the price of Carte Noir has increased from €4.50 to €5.20. It is useful to represent this price change as a percentage. To do this we take the difference in the prices (€0.70) and divide it by the initial price (€4.50) and multiply the result by 100. The percentage increase in Carte Noir is, thus (0.70/4.50) x 100 = 15.5 per cent. We know from the law of demand that when price rises the quantity demanded will fall, however, what we have not looked at so far is *how far* demand would fall. Would demand fall by more or less in percentage terms, compared to the percentage change in price?

This is very important. For sellers, price changes are a feature of business and they know that when price changes demand will also change. A firm's total revenue is determined by the price it charges and the amount of products it sells. If Carte Noir sells four million jars of coffee every month at an average price of €4.50 then its monthly revenue is €18 million. If Carte Noir has to increase price to €5.20 the reaction of consumers to this 15.5 per cent price increase is important to its revenue.

If, for example, many buyers now felt that the price rise represented poor value for money and they switched to other products the effect on demand might be significant. Assume that as a result of the price rise Carte Noir saw sales fall to 3.2 million, then its revenue would now be 3 200 000 × €5.20 = €16 640 000 per month, a fall in revenue of €1.36 million a month. This is clearly a serious situation for Carte Noir.

Compare this situation, however, with a different scenario. Assume that as a result of the rise in price customers stay loyal to Carte Noir for whatever reason and so the effect on sales is only minimal. If sales fall to 3 720 000 then Carte Noir's revenue will be €19 344 000 so the rise in price has actually increased its revenue. This is clearly a better situation for Carte Noir than the previous situation.

What is the reason for the difference between these two scenarios? It is simply the amount by which demand has changed in response to the rise in price that is the explanation. We have already worked out that the rise in price was 15.5 per cent. If sales dropped by 800 000 this represents a percentage change in demand as a result of the rise in price of minus 20 per cent. Because the percentage change in quantity demanded is greater than the percentage change in price the effect on Carte Noir's total revenue has been to reduce it. In the second scenario the percentage change in quantity demanded was minus 7 per cent, which is less than in proportion to the rise in price. In this case the fall in demand is relatively small in comparison to the change in price and so the effect on revenue has been to actually increase it.

If we look at the concept from the supply side of the market, similar principles apply. Carte Noir will respond to changes in price in the market caused by changes in demand but the extent to which supply changes in response to a change in price will vary depending on the circumstances. If, for some reason, a large shift in demand caused price to rise for Carte Noir's products they would wish to expand output to meet the demand. However, the extent to which they can do this is determined by the availability of the right quality beans, the harvest, weather conditions, capacity, whether they have the right labour in the right place, whether managers expect this to be a permanent increase in demand or simply transitory and so on.

In response to a 10 per cent increase in price, for example, Carte Noir might like to increase supply but conditions make it very difficult to enable it to expand output by very much at all. If output could increase by something less than the percentage increase in price then we would say that supply was not very responsive to the change in price. If Carte Noir was able to expand output quickly by more than the 10 per cent increase in price then we would say that supply was more responsive to changes in price. Again, the extent to which suppliers can respond to changes in price will have an effect on their total revenue as they try to meet changed market conditions.

In some cases it is simply not possible at all to respond to a change in demand regardless of how much a firm might want to. For example, If Barcelona were to qualify to play AC Milan in the final of the Champions League and the final was scheduled to be played at the Stade de France in Paris, the demand for tickets to see this match might be far greater than the available supply of tickets. At the time of writing the capacity of the Stade de France is 80000; if demand for tickets were 150000 we would expect the price of tickets to rise but no matter how far price rose it would be extremely difficult if not impossible for the authorities to meet the shortage with extra seats. In this example the supply is totally unresponsive to changes in price.

A More Formal Analysis

We can formalize our discussion of how far supply and demand change in response to price by introducing a little terminology and some simple maths:

- The responsiveness of quantity demanded to a change in price is called price elasticity of demand (*ped*).

- The responsiveness of quantity supplied to a change in price is called price elasticity of supply (*pes*).

- The more responsive quantity demanded and supplied are to changes in price the more *elastic* the relationship is said to be.

- Where quantity demanded and supplied is not very responsive to changes in price, the relationship is described as being *inelastic*.

- There are differing degrees of elasticity, therefore, across a scale. The more responsive quantity supplied and demanded are to changes in price the more elastic is the relationship and the more unresponsive quantity demanded and supplied are to changes in price the more inelastic is the relationship.

- In order to quantify the relationship we use a simple formula which is:

$$Ped = \frac{\text{Percentage Change in Quantity Demanded/Supplied } (\% \ \Delta Qd/s)}{\text{Percentage Change in Price } (\% \ \Delta P)}$$

If the percentage change in quantity (the numerator) is greater than the percentage change in the price (the denominator) the relationship is said to be elastic. The numerical value from this calculation will be a number greater than one.

* If the percentage change in quantity (the numerator) is less than the percentage change in the price (the denominator) the relationship is said to be inelastic. The numerical value from this calculation will be a number less than one.

Calculating Elasticity

We can now move to showing how elasticity can be calculated using the example of Carte Noir we have outlined above. Note that this analysis is using the simplest method of calculating elasticity. There are a number of different and more complex ways of doing the math but these are beyond the scope of this book. If you are interested in looking at different ways to calculate elasticity using more accurate mathematical tools then look at McGuigan, Moyer and Harris, (2008) *Economics for Managers (12th Ed)*, Cengage Learning International Edition, Chapter 3.

Price Elasticity of Demand

Remember that a jar of Carte Noir was €4.50 and that price rose to €5.20 – a percentage increase of 15.5 per cent.

Scenario 1

Quantity demanded falls by 800 000 from 4 million to 3.2 million. The percentage change in demand is thus the change in demand divided by the original demand multiplied by 100 (800 000/4 000 000) x 100. The percentage change in demand is thus 20 per cent. Substituting both percentage changes into our formula gives us:

$$Ped = \frac{\% \, \Delta Qd}{\% \, \Delta P}$$

$$Ped = \frac{20}{15.5}$$

$$Ped = 1.29$$

The fact that the number for *ped* is above 1 tells us that the relationship in this scenario between price and quantity demanded is elastic. If the change in quantity demanded had been even more marked, 30 per cent for example, then *ped* would have been 1.93 – even more responsive to the change in price.

If this was the case facing Carte Noir the figure of 1.29 would tell them that for every 1 per cent change in price the quantity demanded would change by 1.29 times. If price rose by 5 per cent then demand would fall by 1.29 x 5 per cent = 6.45 per cent. If they reduced price by 7 per cent then demand would increase by 7 x 1.29 = 9.03 per cent.

Scenario 2

Quantity demanded falls by 280 000 from 4 million to 3.72 million. The percentage change in demand is thus the change in demand divided by the original demand multiplied by 100 (280 000/4 000 000) x 100. The percentage change in demand is thus 7 per cent. Substituting both percentage changes into our formula gives us:

$$Ped = \frac{\% \ \Delta Qd}{\% \ \Delta P}$$

$$Ped = \frac{7}{15.5}$$

$$Ped = 0.45$$

The fact that the number for *ped* is less than one tells us that the relationship in this scenario between price and quantity demanded is inelastic. If the change in quantity demanded had been even lower, 3 per cent for example, then *ped* would have been 0.19 – even less responsive to the change in price.

If this was the case facing Carte Noir the figure of 0.45 would tell them that for every 1 per cent change in price the quantity demanded would change by 0.45 times. If price rose by 6 per cent then demand would fall by 0.45 x 6 per cent = 2.7 per cent. If they reduced price by 9 per cent then demand would increase by 9 x 0.45 = 4.05 per cent.

Price Elasticity of Supply

Let us now apply a similar analysis to supply. If, as a result of a rise in price of 5 per cent, Carte Noir is only able to increase quantity supplied by 3 per cent then our formula will give us:

$$Pes = \frac{\% \ \Delta Qs}{\% \ \Delta P}$$

$$Pes = \frac{3}{5}$$

$$Pes = 0.6$$

In this case quantity supplied is not very responsive to the change in price and *pes* is inelastic. If Carte Noir was only able to increase quantity supplied by 1.5 per cent in response to the 5 per cent price increase then *pes* would have been 0.3, even more inelastic or unresponsive. A *pes* of 0.6 would mean that for every 1 per cent change in price the quantity supplied would change by 0.6 times. A fall in price by 13 per cent would lead to supply also falling but by 7.8 per cent.

If, on the other hand, Carte Noir was able to increase quantity supplied by 12 per cent in response to the increase in price of 5 per cent then the *pes* would be:

$$Pes = \frac{\% \ \Delta Qs}{\% \ \Delta P}$$

$$Pes = \frac{12}{5}$$

$$Pes = 2.4$$

In this scenario quantity supplied is quite responsive to the change in price and *pes* is elastic. For every 1 per cent change in price, quantity supplied would change by 2.4 times. A fall in price of 6 per cent, for example, would lead to a fall in quantity supplied of 2.4 x 6 = 14.4 per cent.

Representing Elasticity Diagrammatically

We can show the effects of different elasticities using our market model. When we take into account elasticity the slope of the supply and demand curve will be different for different products. If we assume that we are using the same scale on different diagrams then both supply and demand curves can be shown with different elasticities. The more steep the slope of the supply and demand curve respectively the more inelastic they are and so the less responsive they are to a change in price. The shallower the slope of the supply and demand curve the more elastic they are, in other words they are more responsive to changes in price.

We can now represent markets not only in relation to the level of demand and supply at any particular time, i.e. where on the diagram the curves are drawn, but also the degree of response they have to changes in price. Figure 11.9 illustrates how the effect of a change in demand can have different effects on the market depending on the degree of elasticity of the supply curve.

FIGURE 11.9

Price elasticity of supply

Panel a) in Figure 11.9 shows the market for coffee beans, a commodity traded on international markets. Panel a) shows two supply curves, Si and Se. Si is relatively steep and would be associated with a relatively inelastic supply – the ability of farmers to increase supply of coffee beans in response to a rise in price would be limited. Se on the other hand shows a supply curve that is relatively elastic. If this were the case farmers would be able to respond more easily to changes in price and increase the supply of beans.

Panel b) shows the effect of an increase in demand on the market for coffee beans if supply was relatively inelastic. The percentage increase in price is greater than the percentage increase in the amount bought and sold and total revenue rises.

Panel c) shows the market changes if the supply curve was relatively elastic as shown by supply curve Se. In this case the increase in demand would lead to only a small rise in price but a relatively large increase in the amount bought and sold.

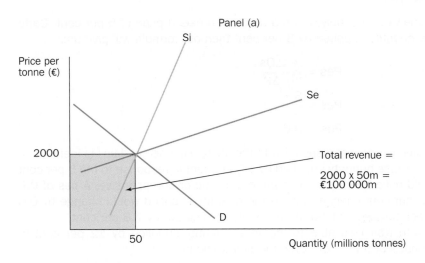

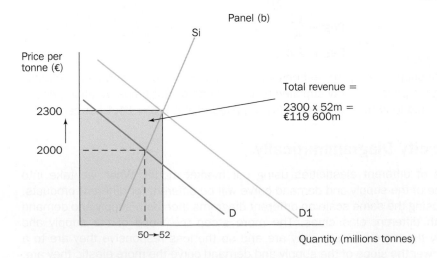

Figure 11.9 represents the market for coffee beans. Growers of coffee beans represent the supply of coffee beans in the market and coffee retailers and processors represent the demand for coffee beans. Commodities like coffee are traded on international markets. In Panel a) the initial market equilibrium is given as a price of €2000 per tonne and a quantity bought and sold of

FIGURE 11.9

Price elasticity of supply *(Continued)*

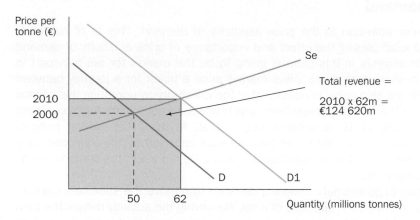

Panel (c)

50 million tonnes a year. Panel a) also shows two different supply curves, Si and Se. Si is relatively steep and would represent a supply curve which is relatively inelastic, i.e. not very responsive to changes in price (we assume that the scale on the axes are common and therefore the slope of the curve can be taken as an indicator of the relative average elasticity of the curve). If this were the case then it would not be easy for coffee growers to respond to a change in price by increasing the supply available on the market. Supply curve Se shows a more elastic supply. The curve is shallow and implies that growers can respond to changes in price by increasing supply relatively easily. The shaded area highlights the total revenue received from the sale of coffee beans in the market. At the price of €2000 per tonne and 50 million tonnes purchased, total revenue for growers is €100 000 million.

Panel b) highlights what happens in the market if demand for coffee beans rose as shown by a shift in the demand curve to the right from D to D1 and where the supply curve was inelastic. The shift in demand means that at the initial equilibrium price buyers now wish to purchase more than the available supply and so there is a shortage in the market. The shortage triggers the usual process we have already described and there is pressure on price to rise. As price rises suppliers would like to offer more for sale but given the relatively inelastic supply curve it is hard for producers to suddenly respond to the price rises by increasing the amount of beans for sale on the market. This could be due to the fact that there is a limited number of plants, the harvest is still several months away and stocks of beans are limited. With a crop like coffee beans, increasing supply quickly can be difficult. The result is that when the market reaches the new equilibrium we can see that the price has risen to €2300 per tonne, a rise of 15 per cent but because the farmers have difficulty increasing supplies, the amount bought and sold has only increased by a relatively small amount – by 2 million tonnes a year. The effect on farmers is that their total revenue will increase to €119 600 from €100 000 prior to the change in demand.

Panel c) shows what would happen if the supply curve was much shallower and therefore more elastic. An identical increase in demand would now mean that the shortage would be much greater but because supply is elastic it is much easier for farmers to increase supply. This might be because they have large stocks in reserve which can be put on the market now that price is rising. However, the fact that the supply curve is elastic means that the new equilibrium price is only just higher than the initial one at €2010 per tonne, a rise of just half a per cent whereas the increase in the amount bought and sold has risen considerably to 62 million tonnes per year, a rise of 24 per cent. In this case total revenue for growers has risen to €124 600 from the initial €100 000.

This shows that the degree of elasticity of supply in a market can lead to different outcomes for both the market as a whole and for suppliers. If supply was relatively elastic, coffee drinkers might find that the effect on the price of a cup of coffee in a coffee shop was negligible but in the initial case when supply was inelastic, the steep rise in the price of coffee beans might well be translated along the supply chain to consumers who may see the price of a cup of coffee rising quite sharply.

Price Elasticity of Demand

We are now going to turn our attention to the price elasticity of demand. This is of particular importance because we see examples of the effect and importance of price elasticity of demand every day. The basis for our analysis in this case is going to be the market for rail transport in Germany. We are going to assume that at the initial market price a ticket for a journey between Munich and Berlin is €90. We are also going to assume that the rail company operating this service is in receipt of a subsidy from the German government which helps it keep prices for passengers relatively low. Panel a) of Figure 11.10 represents this market. At the initial market price of €90, 500 000 journeys are made each month. The total revenue received by the train operating company is €45 million per month. The two demand curves Di and De represent the demand for rail travel with different price elasticities.

Now assume that the German government makes a decision to remove the subsidies given to train operators. A subsidy is, in effect, the opposite of a tax. Removing the subsidy means the train operator now has to find more of its own funds to finance its operations; the effect is the same as an

FIGURE 11.10

Price elasticity of demand

Panel a) in Figure 11.10 shows the market for rail transport in Germany. In this market a train ticket between Munich and Berlin is €90 and there are 500 000 journeys made each month. The demand curve is depicted as being relatively inelastic suggesting that demand is not very responsive to changes in price.

In Panel b) the supply curve shifts to the left when the government removes the subsidy to the train operating company. The effect is to increase the equilibrium price for a ticket from €90 to €130, a rise of 44.4 per cent. However, despite this sharp increase in price the amount of journeys taken falls by only 15 000 to 485 000, a percentage decrease of only 3 per cent. Panel c) contrasts this with a situation where the demand curve for train journeys between Munich and Berlin is price elastic. The demand curve De is now much flatter. The removal of the subsidy now leads to a much smaller rise in price from €90 to €95 – a percentage change of 5.5 per cent – but the number of journeys taken decreases considerably from 500 000 to 240 000, a fall of 52 per cent.

In Panel b) the total revenue of the train companies increases from €45 million to €63.05 million whereas in Panel c) the train operator faces a fall in revenue from €45 million to €22.8 million per month.

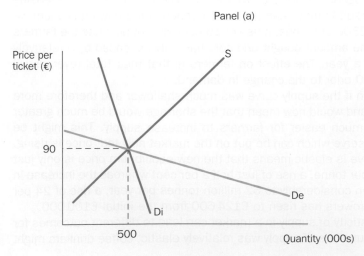

Panel (a)

FIGURE 11.10

Price elasticity of demand *(Continued)*

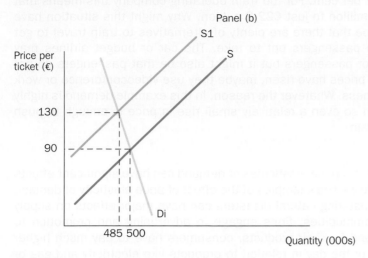

Panel (b)

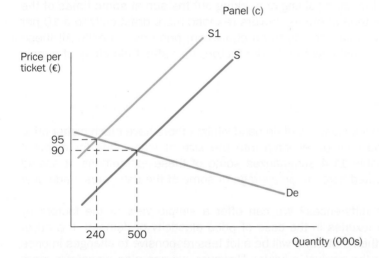

Panel (c)

increase in the cost of production and so shifts the supply curve to the left from S to S1 meaning fewer journeys are offered for sale at each price.

In Panel b) we observe what happens to the market if the demand curve was relatively inelastic as shown by the steep curve Di (again, we are assuming the scale on each axis here is the same). The shift in supply means that at a price of €90 there is now a shortage, more passengers looking for tickets than currently available. The fact that the demand curve is relatively inelastic, however, means that prices are forced up quite considerably. The market ends up in equilibrium with a new price of €130 per ticket, a rise of 44.4 per cent but only a relatively small drop off in the number of journeys made of 15 000 – 3 per cent. The total revenue for the train operating company rises from €45 million to €63.05 million.

There might be a number of reasons for this outcome. Passengers may rely upon the train for their journeys and there might not be many suitable or convenient options open to them, as a result the use of the train for their journey is almost a necessity. Whilst passengers may complain about the rise in the price of a ticket a large proportion are still willing to pay the higher price to make their journey. Demand, in this example is highly unresponsive to changes in price.

If we compare this outcome with that in Panel c) we see quite a different situation. In Panel c) the demand curve is shallow implying that it is relatively elastic and responsive to price changes. The same removal of the subsidy shifts the supply curve as in Panel b) and the shortage forces price upwards but this time the new equilibrium price has only risen by 5.5 per cent to €95 and the number of journeys taken has dropped dramatically from 500 000 per month to just 240 000, a fall of 52 per cent. For the train operating company this means that total revenue has fallen from €45 million to just €22.8 million. Why might this situation have arisen? One of the reasons could be that there are plenty of alternatives to train travel to get between Munich and Berlin which passengers opt to take. The car or budget airlines may provide more compelling options for passengers but it might also be that passengers do not have to make the journey now that prices have risen, maybe they use videoconference or work from home if they travelled for business. Whatever the reason, in this example demand is highly responsive to changes in price and so even a relatively small rise in price is enough to push passengers away from using the train.

Summary

These two scenarios show how different price elasticities of demand can have significant effects on market outcomes. In everyday life we see examples of the effect of price elasticity of demand and supply on a regular basis. Devastating natural disasters can have major effects on supply and the elasticity of supply for commodities, firms engage in advertising and promotion to reduce the price elasticity of demand for their products, consumers have to pay much higher prices for goods at different times of the day in relation to products like electricity and gas or train journeys, holiday makers find that going skiing or seeking out the sun at some times of the year is significantly more expensive than at others, buyers respond more drastically to a 10 per cent increase in the price of 3D TVs than they do to an equivalent price rise in milk. All these changes are to do with elasticity. We will now turn to the factors that affect elasticity of supply and demand.

Determinants of Elasticity

Some products will have a very low price elasticity of demand whilst others have much higher price elasticities. There has been a good deal of research into the size of elasticities for different products with regard to demand. Table 11.4 summarizes some of these estimations. It should be noted that the estimations presented here are an average of some of the estimates made over a number of years.

What are the reasons for these differences? We can offer a simple view of the factors by classifying goods as necessities or luxuries in the case of price elasticity of demand. If a buyer believes a product is an 'essential' then that buyer will be a lot less responsive to changes in price of the product than if they consider the product a luxury. However, we can also pinpoint a more specific number of factors which determine elasticities. These include:

1 **The time period under consideration**

   For both the price elasticity of supply and demand, time is an important factor. The longer the time period under consideration the more elastic the demand and supply a product tends to be with respect to price. This is because over time consumers and producers can change their behaviour and adjust to price changes more effectively. For example, if the price of feedstuffs rises significantly, many cattle farmers find it difficult to adjust herds quickly and so have to keep buying the feedstuff. However, over a period of years they may decide to reduce their herd, change feeding practices, look for alternative cheaper feedstuffs or even change the type of farming they carry out. In the very short run the *ped* for feedstuffs is almost completely inelastic whereas over a 2–3 year time period the demand is likely to be more elastic.

2 **The availability of resources and factors of production**

   For suppliers, the ease with which they can adjust supply may depend on how easily they can access resources to be able to expand production. Some industries have long lead times in production especially where high levels of technology are involved whereas others might need specialist labour in order to expand and it may take time to access such labour.

TABLE 11.4 Estimations of the price elasticity of demand for a selection of products.

Product	Ped
Tobacco	0.4
Milk	0.3
Wine	0.6
Shoes	0.7
Cars	1.9
Particular brand of car	4.0
Movies	0.9
Entertainment	1.4
Furniture	3.04
Fuel	0.4
Bread	0.25

In general, therefore, the easier it is for a firm to access resources needed for production the more elastic will be supply with respect to price; if accessing resources is difficult and time consuming then the *pes* will be highly inelastic.

3 Plant limitations

Some suppliers have spare capacity which allows them to respond to changing market conditions quickly whilst others may have to build new plant in order to release capacity. In the former case, the *pes* will be more elastic than in the latter situation. The *pes* of electricity supply, for example, is highly inelastic in the short run once capacity has been used up because it can take many years to build the generating plant and distribution infrastructure to bring new capacity online.

4 The proportion of income taken up by the product

Some goods represent a very small proportion of total income; if the price of a €2 ball point pen rises by 15 per cent it is unlikely that large numbers of buyers will be put off purchasing a pen but if the price of a €1000 three-piece suite rose by 15 per cent the situation might be quite different. A larger proportion of consumers might feel that the higher price now made the item too expensive and so put them off buying. In Table 11.4, the estimation of the *ped* for furniture is quite high at 3.04 which supports this explanation.

5 The availability and closeness of substitutes

The price elasticity of demand and supply is affected by the availability and closeness of substitutes in consumption and production. If the price of taxi fares rises then consumers in urban communities might substitute using a taxi for public transport and so the *ped* of taxi journeys might be relatively elastic. In remote rural areas where there is very little public transport, taxi journeys may have a far lower *ped* reflecting the fact that consumers have little choice.

In production, if a supplier can easily substitute one raw material or component part for another then the *pes* is likely to be relatively elastic if price rises because they can use the substitutes to help expand production. If it is not possible to substitute other components or raw materials then it may be much harder for the producer to be able to expand production quickly and easily in response to a price change.

6 **The breadth of the definition of the product**

The degree of the *ped* can change according to how we define the product. In Table 11.4, cars in general have a relatively high *ped* of 1.9, elastic but not as elastic as that of a particular brand of car which is given as 4.0. We would expect the *ped* for foodstuffs in general to be more inelastic than that of a particular foodstuff such as tinned rice pudding. This is because the more broadly the product is defined the fewer substitutes it is likely to have. Take the case of central heating systems. Central heating as a whole may have a *ped* of (say) 1.2 but for a particular type of central heating system the elasticity may be higher. Gas central heating, oil fired central heating, Calor gas heating systems and electric central heating may all have a similar *ped* (say 1.9) but focusing on a particular company selling a gas central heating system, the *ped* is likely to be even higher at 2.5. This reflects the fact that if a buyer is thinking of installing a central heating system there are a relatively small number of choices available but if choosing a gas central heating system, for example, there might be a large number of firms for the buyer to choose from so there are more substitutes and the *ped* will be higher as a result.

Other types of elasticity

The basic concept of elasticity relates the proportionality of changes in one factor to changes in another. We can use this concept, therefore, to look at how demand changes with respect to other factors that influence it. The main ones are highlighted below.

Income elasticity of demand

Income elasticity of demand relates changes in demand to changes in income. We can identify two basic types of goods in this relationship, normal goods and inferior goods.

A normal good is one where demand rises in response to a rise in income and falls in relation to a drop in incomes

An inferior good is one where demand falls when income rises and rises when income falls. The reason for this is that if incomes rise, consumers will look to substitute other goods which they would rather buy but previously may not have been able to afford. Equally, if incomes fall, maybe due to the loss of employment, then some consumers will look to buy goods that they believe represent better value for money, buying own brand items in supermarkets rather than more expensive branded goods, for example. The more sensitive a good is to changes in income the more elastic and vice versa.

The formula for income elasticity of demand (Yed) is:

$$\text{Yed} = \frac{\text{Percentage Change in Quantity Demanded}\ (\%\ \Delta \text{Qd})}{\text{Percentage Change in Income}\ (\%\ \Delta \text{Y})}$$

If incomes rise/fall by 5 per cent but the demand for the latest 3D televisions rises/falls by more than 5 per cent then demand is income elastic. If incomes rise/fall by 2.4 per cent but the demand for broccoli rises/falls by less than 2.4 per cent then demand is income inelastic.

Cross Price Elasticity of Demand (Xed)

Cross price elasticity of demand relates changes in the prices of substitutes and complements to the demand for other goods. For example, if the price of a ticket to the cinema rose by 10 per cent we might expect cinema goers to substitute a trip to the cinema with the purchase of a movie DVD. Cross price elasticity measures the extent to which these two goods are related. If as a result of

BUSINESS IN ACTION

Income Elasticity of Demand

In times of economic slowdown some businesses are affected more than others. The extent of the effects will depend on the type of business, the market it operates in and the nature of the product sold. Food retailers, for example, might see changes to the type of products being bought by consumers but the overall level of sales tends to stay fairly stable. Consumers might decide to buy value products in stores rather than products that might be better quality but they still have to eat. Supermarkets like Sainsbury's, Auchan and Carrefour are big enough to be able to adapt to changing demand with limited impact on their overall sales.

Other businesses tend to be affected more significantly. Marks & Spencer (M&S) in the UK and Praktiker, a DIY chain covering much of southern Europe are typical of the sort of business that we might expect to see affected by economic slowdown. A major part of the market for these types of businesses are people in middle income brackets, the products they sell have plenty of substitutes and are not classed as 'necessities'. This means that consumers are able to defer spending of their discretionary income and firms like M&S and Praktiker tend to suffer as a result.

Not all firms who sell 'luxuries', however are affected by slowdown in the same way. Luxuries tend to have the characteristics of being subject to choice – consumers might like to buy them but they are not considered essential and so they tend to be foregone (albeit temporarily perhaps) when finances are tight. As a result the income elasticity of demand for these products tends to be positive and also relatively high. This means that they are sensitive to changes in incomes, if incomes fall then we would expect the demand for these products to also fall but by a larger proportion than the fall in incomes.

Some products classed as luxuries might not behave in this way. Some businesses that target their products at the very top of the market might also hope to be more immune from changes in economic activity. Take the Danish luxury electronics manufacturer Bang and Olufsen (B&O). The company targets its products at the high end of the market; the products it sells such as TVs, home entertainment systems and hi-fis are high quality and tend to be priced accordingly. The sort of market they are aiming at could be thought of as being one where the income elasticity of demand is relatively low – if you can afford to pay for a B&O system then price is not really the issue as your income is high enough for price to not be a major concern!

However, during the global recession of 2008–2009 the company issued a number of warnings with regard to its profits. The company suffered a sharp fall in profits in 2007 and sacked its boss, Torben Sorenson, in January 2008. It then issued another profits warning in March of that year and in July made another announcement saying that it expected profits to be down around 30 per cent on its previous estimates for the year to May 2008. It also warned that its full year sales figures would be down by over 5.5 per cent. The main markets for B&O are in Germany, Denmark, the UK and the US.

It seems that the slowdown in its main markets affected the business despite the fact that it might normally hope that the high quality, high end products it sells would be protected to an extent from such a slowdown. There could, of course, be other reasons for the downturn in its prospects. The marketing mix in some way might need adjusting and it might not be meeting customer needs. The analysis of the state of the business and the strategies to help it overcome the problems it is experiencing was to be the job of Kalle Hvidt Nielsen who became the head of the business on August 1st 2008.

Source: adapted from Biz/ed In the News: www.bized.co.uk/cgi-bin/chron/chron.pl?id=3128

the rise in price of cinema tickets demand for movie DVDs rises by more than 10 per cent then the Xed would be elastic. If demand for movie DVDs rose by less than 10 per cent then the Xed would be inelastic.

If the price of bus fares fell by 5 per cent and the demand for taxis fell by more than 5 per cent then the Xed would be elastic and vice versa.

The *Xed* for goods which are substitutes will exhibit a positive relationship as in the example of bus fares and taxis above, whereas the relationship between goods which are complements would be negative. If the price of TVs rose then we might expect the demand for satellite or cable services to fall and vice versa. The formula for Xed is:

$$Xed = \frac{\text{Percentage Change in Quantity Demanded of Good X} \, (\% \, \Delta Qdx)}{\text{Percentage Change in Price of Good Y} \, (\% \, \Delta Py)}$$

Advertising Elasticity of Demand

The advertising elasticity of demand *(aed)* relates the proportionate change in demand of a product to a change in advertising expenditure. If BMW increased spending on advertising a particular model by 10 per cent and demand rose by 15 per cent then the *aed* would be elastic. If demand rose by a smaller proportion than the change in advertising expenditure then the *aed* would be inelastic. The formula for *aed* is:

$$aed = \frac{\text{Percentage Change in Quantity Demanded} \, (\% \, \Delta Qd)}{\text{Percentage Change in Advertising Expenditure} \, (\% \, \Delta Ae)}$$

One of the problems with estimating the *aed* is the extent to which the firm can make a direct link between changes in advertising expenditure and changes to sales.

Changing Consumer Trends

Consumer trends are forever changing; for any business, whether they be B2C or B2B, the needs of consumers are of vital importance so keeping up with changing trends is important. National governments do collect data on consumer trends and specialist market research companies such as Mintel also publish detailed reports on trends. What follows is a short summary of some of these trends.

Ageing populations: A number of EU countries have an increasing proportion of the population in the 65 and over age range (refer back to Chapter 4, Figure 4.8). In addition, improvements in health care and lifestyle mean that people are living longer. The needs of the retired classes will become increasingly important in the next 50 years. This affects a wide range of goods and industries, for example, cars may have to be designed to better suit the limitations that elderly people invariably suffer, housing needs are likely to change with the demand for smaller housing likely to rise, insurance and health care needs will vary as will the demand for certain types of social services not to mention the pension requirements of those who have retired.

Online retail sales: The development of the Internet and the greater access to fast connection and download speeds means that more and more people are using the Internet to buy goods and services and this is likely to be a continuing trend in the coming years (refer back to Chapter 5, Figure 5.5 for example). In November 2010 Christmas sales (defined as a six week period from mid-November to the end of the year) for that year in Europe were forecast at being €32 billion, a rise of over 51 per cent compared to 2008 and represents 10.3 per cent of total retail spending.[1] In July 2012, online and catalogue only retailers saw sales rise by 19.5 per cent over the previous year. Businesses across all sectors are now looking at ways to exploit this growth and traditional retailers are also having to change the way they operate to come to terms with the rise in online sales.

Free-from and niche market foods: As the boundary of medical science advances, the number of people who discover they have allergies or intolerances to certain foods increases, and as a result food producers have opportunities for filling those market needs. As a result the market for these types of products is expanding; gluten free products for celiacs (people who have intolerance to wheat based products which contain gluten) has increased by 100 per cent since 2007 and the market has expanded by over 20 per cent. Products which help digestion such as those with pre

[1]Source: 'Christmas 2010: European Assessment' commissioned by Kelkoo and conducted by the Centre for Retail Research, Nottingham in September 2010. Reproduced with permission with thanks to the Centre for Retail Research

and pro-biotic ingredients (ingredients that help the development of beneficial bacteria in the body and microorganisms that provide some benefit to humans) are seeing double-digit growth in Europe, led by manufacturers such as Danone. Food manufacturers are increasingly looking at ways in which the growing number of people with some sort of food intolerance or a requirement to improve their digestion, for example, can be catered for and this type of niche market is likely to grow as awareness and medical diagnosis increases.

Green and Ethical Consumerism: The debate over climate change has led to a burgeoning new industry in green and ethical consumerism (refer back to Chapter 7). This covers a wide range of industries from energy production and the manufacture of more efficient products through to the growth in recycling, the reduction in packaging and the whole concept of a product life cycle and its impact on the environment. Closely linked to this is the notion of ethical consumerism. Firms in all sectors are having to take increasing account of the effect of their operations on the environment and the extent to which they balance the needs of different stakeholders. For example, the spotlight on the use of cheap labour is much brighter than ever before given the speed with which 'bad news' can spread via the web and social network sites. Businesses are keen to demonstrate that they do adhere to some basic standards in making products available to consumers and indeed many may see a green and ethical approach as a useful marketing tool in capturing market share. The danger is that consumers perceive such an approach as being cynical and don't believe the claims that firms make. Indeed, there are many people who would suggest that the whole notion of green consumerism is an oxymoron – any purchase of a product involves the use of resources and the production of waste.

A number of EU governments have pledged investment into green/clean technologies and this is likely to be a future growth area. Such technologies include wind power, energy conservation, improving the efficiency of new buildings, heat exchange technologies, CO_2 capture and storage, the removal of pollutants from the environment (termed environmental remediation), biofiltration, new types of fuels such as hydrogen cells, thermal depolymerization which aims to convert some types of waste products such as plastics and biomass into light crude oil and the use of nanotechnology.

Ultimately the success of these technologies will be dependent not only on government regulation and laws but also how commercially viable they can become. A number of vehicle manufacturers, for example, have invested in hydrogen cell technology but at the time of writing the cost of manufacturing vehicles using this technology would make the purchase price prohibitive.

MARKET FAILURE

When particular assumptions are made about markets, they can be an excellent means of allocating resources efficiently. There are few countries in the world that do not use markets as the main way in which resources are allocated. If we assume high levels of knowledge on the part of both buyers and sellers, ease of movement of resources from one use to another, a large number of firms who are not in a position to dominate or control the market and an assumption that price does act as an appropriate signal to both buyers and sellers, then markets can and do work.

However, to expect these assumptions to always hold true is unrealistic and when some or all of these assumptions break down the market may not allocate resources efficiently. When this happens the market is said to fail (an idea first discussed in Chapter 2). Market failure can manifest itself in a number of ways. However, before we look at ways in which markets can fail it is useful to have some definition of efficiency as a benchmark for judging the efficiency of markets.

We can identify four key definitions:

- **Social Efficiency** occurs where the external costs and benefits are accounted for in decision making. External costs and benefits arise when someone other than the decision maker is affected by the decision. For example, in October 2010, an aluminium plant in Hungary was identified as the source of a leak of a highly toxic sludge which not only killed nine people and injured many more but threatened to leave behind a pollution problem that would persist for many years and also threatened the River Danube. The cost of cleaning up the pollution and the effects it had on residents living near the spill were not costs borne by the plant itself.

- **Allocative Efficiency** occurs when society produces goods and services at minimum cost that are wanted by consumers. This may seem fairly common sense but there are plenty of examples of goods which go to waste – millions of tonnes of food, for example, are thrown away by EU households every year.
- **Technical Efficiency** occurs where the production of goods and services takes place using the minimum amount of resources necessary.
- **Productive Efficiency** refers to the production of goods and services at lowest factor cost.

Given our benchmarks and the summary of assumptions about the operation of markets above, we can now identify the main sources of market failure.

Imperfect Knowledge

In many markets buyers and sellers do not have perfect knowledge of the products they are buying and selling and in many cases adequate technical knowledge of products is lacking. Smart phones are a good example of such a lack of knowledge. In making decisions to purchase a smart phone few buyers have a complete understanding of the technology they are investing in and few will utilize all the functions of the phone. This may mean that our purchasing decisions are not as efficient as they could be.

In addition firms use various means to influence our purchasing decisions – advertising, for example, can mislead or mis-inform buyers. Producers are invariably unaware of all the selling opportunities that exist and the expansion of the global economic environment is making it even harder for firms to have a complete understanding of all the markets they operate in or could potentially exploit. In terms of production, we make assumptions that producers are able to accurately measure productivity and shift resources around in order to maximize technical and productive efficiency. In many cases it is very difficult for firms to accurately measure productivity and as a result inefficiencies can arise which go unchecked.

We are also becoming far more aware of the importance of cognitive processes in buying behaviour. Developments in behavioural economics have highlighted the fact that people do not always make decisions based on a rational assessment of the costs and benefits but on such things as past experience, reference points, what friends and relatives may have bought or talked about, what we are familiar with and so on.

As a result of imperfect knowledge buyers and sellers will make decisions which can lead to an inefficient allocation of resources.

Differentiation of Products

We have seen how different market structures (Chapter 6) attempt to manipulate the market to their own advantage. One of the key ways many firms try to do this is by attempting to differentiate their product from that of their rivals. One way of doing this is branding, Branding is an attempt to get the consumer to make an association with a product which will mean that they are more likely to choose it above another similar product. Branding is not simply associated with expensive products but with an attempt to create some sort of identity which consumers will recognize and act upon. However, if we look at expensive brands such as designer labels we have to ask whether the fact that an item of clothing or jewellery, for example, might be priced three times as much as another non-branded item are they three times the quality? They may indeed be better quality but does the price premium consumers are paying give them an appropriate signal as to the true value for money?

Other forms of differentiation include technology and labelling and product information. Do buyers fully understand what they are buying and what the consequences of that purchase may be? For example, a business might have high ethical and green aspirations in its procurement activities but does it fully understand the environmental and green claims made by a supplier of a piece of equipment? If it does not then the damage to the environment in the longer term may be much higher than the buyer can anticipate or know at the time of purchase.

Resource Immobility

The assumption that resources are mobile and can move from one use to another holds up to an extent but it is clear that some factors of production are not perfect substitutes for another and also that factors are not fully mobile. For example, labour is both geographically and occupationally immobile in some cases. Someone with skills in tool making made redundant in northern Germany may not be in a position to take a job available in a human resources department of a corporation based in Belgium. Capital can also be immobile, plant designed for a specific task or process cannot suddenly be utilized in another role although many manufacturing firms are increasingly looking at ways to improve the interchangability of component parts and products to improve this aspect of production. In some cases however, it is almost impossible to imagine an alternative use for some products; what other purpose could the channel tunnel serve other than being a vehicle and rail tunnel? Equally whilst some land can be utilized for many different purposes there are restrictions. The obvious ones are physical; if there is a shortage of land for building in southern Spain it is simply not possible to move land from northern Spain where there may be a surplus! In other less obvious cases, regulation and legal issues may prevent land reverting to alternative uses. Planning regulations, environmental protection legislation and so on can all severely restrict the way in which land can be utilized meaning that inefficiencies may arise and continue to exist in terms of resource allocation not only from land use but in relation to other aspects of the economy such as shortages of certain types of labour or office space, for example.

Market Power

We saw in Chapter 10 how firms who are able to exercise some degree of market power can influence price and or output. If a firm can influence price and/or output then by definition market signals will be interrupted. Key ways in which market power can be manifested is in the existence of collusion, price fixing agreements, the existence of abnormal profits in the long-run, the rigging of markets and the erection of barriers to entry.

Inadequate Provision

We have covered merit goods and public goods in both Chapter 1 and Chapter 8. To briefly recap, merit goods can be provided by the market but consumers may not be able to afford or feel the need to purchase them – the market would not provide them in the quantities society needs. For example, would sports facilities, nurseries, schools, colleges, universities – which could all be provided by the market – be provided in sufficient quantities to satisfy society and allow everyone who wants to use them to be able to afford to do so? The answer is probably 'no' so governments step in to provide for these needs, in other words to fill the gap left by the market.

Public goods have the characteristics of non-excludability and non-rivalry, an individual paying for these products could not prevent anyone else from also benefitting from the product and cannot exclude those benefits from them. They also have the characteristic that there are large external benefits relative to cost. For example, the provision of defence, street lighting and justice are all socially desirable but would not be profitable for private firms to produce because of the characteristics outlined. It is likely therefore that under a pure market system such products would not be provided at all.

De-Merit Goods

These are products which are the opposite to merit goods – they are products which society over-produces and which generate greater social costs than benefits. Tobacco and alcohol, recreational drugs and gambling might be examples of these types of products.

External Costs and Benefits

External or social costs are the cost of an economic decision to a third party while external benefits refer to the benefits to a third party as a result of a decision by another party and are collectively referred to as externalities. With external costs, decision makers do not take into account the cost imposed on society and others as a result of their decision, for example pollution, traffic congestion, environmental degradation, depletion of the ozone layer, misuse of alcohol, tobacco, anti-social behaviour, drug abuse and poor housing. External benefits are the by-products of production and decision making that raise the welfare of a third party, for example education and training, public transport, health education and preventative medicine, refuse collection, investment in housing maintenance and law and order.

External costs and benefits arise because the decision-maker does not have to take them into account, possibly because they are unaware of the extent of the cost or benefit they are imposing or possibly because they do not care that someone else has to pay or would benefit. In the case of both external costs and benefits, price does not reflect the true costs and benefits of production or consumption and so either too much is produced (in the case of external costs) or too few are produced (in the case of social benefits). It follows that in markets where social costs are imposed on society the price is lower than would be the case at a socially efficient output; where social benefits are bestowed, the price is higher than the socially efficient outcome. An example of each may serve to highlight this.

Whenever an individual climbs into a car to make a journey they incur a number of private costs: the wear and tear on the vehicle, a proportion of the insurance costs that have to be paid on the vehicle, the cost of fuel and so on. However, there are also a number of external costs that the driver does not take into account which include the risk that they could be involved in an accident which kills or injures another person, the possible health costs of treating those injured in an accident, the costs of police time attending the scene, not to mention the pollution from the vehicle, adding to congestion and the wear and tear on the road network.

The true cost of a road journey is therefore much higher than the one paid by the driver. The result is that more journeys are made than would be the case if the true price of a road journey was reflected in that paid by the driver. Price does not act as an appropriate signal to drivers of the costs involved and so the market fails to allocate the socially efficient number of journeys.

Many European countries provide financial assistance to their citizens to help pay for education. Education not only provides benefits to the individual but to the wider economy and society as well. A better educated workforce is likely to be more creative, more productive, live a healthier lifestyle and help to create wealth and generate more tax revenues whilst relying less on state benefits. Society as a whole benefits from these things which, if left to the market may not be available simply because not everyone would be able to afford to access the education they need. If education was purely provided by the market the result would be that the price would be too high and so an insufficient amount of education would be provided. In this case the price does not act as a signal to reflect the true benefits of education and so is under-provided compared to the socially efficient market outcome.

Inequality

Inequality can be a manifestation of market failure. This is partly to do with the distribution of factor ownership which may not necessarily link to a measure of how productive factors of production are but could be due to inheritance, for example. Income is also not distributed equally within an economy and this can also be due to barriers to entry into certain types of employment, discrimination, lack of knowledge about the availability of jobs, social disadvantages and so on. The result is that some people and some groups of people have significantly higher incomes than others. We can see examples of considerable differences in income and wealth distribution across Europe, some of which may be due to market failures.

MEASURES TO CORRECT MARKET FAILURE

There are a number of measures that governments take to correct market failure. Some are designed to make price signals more effective and others are deliberate attempts to influence price signals to achieve desired objectives.

- **State provision –** when the market fails to provide products that people need then the state invariably steps in. Most European states provide public goods such as defence and justice and invariably offer state funded health and education systems through the tax system. Welfare systems provide citizens with the basic means of survival to reduce the incidence of poverty.

- **Extension of property rights** – property rights are the conferring of the rights of ownership. If I am the legal owner of my house and you decide to throw a brick through the window I have a legal redress against you for damages to my property. The threat of this legal redress is sufficient for you to think twice about the consequences of throwing the brick through my window!

  Negative externalities such as pollution and the over exploitation of natural resources may occur because of inadequate property rights. If rights of ownership of land, the sea, sky, etc. were extended then behaviour can be moderated. For example, if agreement can be reached on who owns the seas in which over-fishing is currently taking place then it can be possible to prevent those who do not have the rights to fish from exploiting the area. In addition, those who have ownership over the area have an incentive to fish it responsibly because to abuse it would be detrimental to their own livelihoods.

  Equally, if property rights can be established for rivers and waterways then those who pollute them can also be prosecuted. The difficulty comes in establishing who should have the rights and how far such rights extend. Is it possible, for example, to establish property rights for the air that surrounds us?

- **Taxation and Subsidies** – taxes and subsidies are a common method adopted by governments (Chapter 3) to correct market failure. Taxes can be imposed on goods which are subject to over-production and which confer negative externalities on society whilst subsidies can be levied on products deemed beneficial to society but which are currently under-produced. Both taxes and subsidies lead to changes in buyer and seller behaviour; sometimes the tax or subsidy has a distorting effect on behaviour which was not intended and which may even lead to a more inefficient outcome or at least an inefficient outcome in a different market.

- **Regulation** – where perceived market failures arise governments may decide to intervene by regulating to try and correct the market failure (Chapters 2, 3 and 12). The financial crisis of 2007–2009, for example, raised a number of issues about the behaviour of banks and other financial institutions. One of the market failures identified in this instance is referred to as moral hazard – the tendency of individuals to behave inappropriately when they are not subject to facing the consequences of their actions. Concerted international action has and is being taken to try and introduce new regulations that help to reduce moral hazard and to improve decision-making in the financial services industry. In other areas of industry there are numerous regulations which aim to improve decision-making and behaviour to the benefit of stakeholders. Health and safety, food preparation and manufacture, record keeping in farming, the monitoring of privatized monopolies, safeguarding standards in education are just some of the areas where regulation is in place.

  As with any interference in the market, there is the possibility that whilst regulation is intended to be well meaning and bring benefits to wider stakeholder groups, there is always the possibility of over regulation, excessive 'red tape' and bureaucracy simply increases the costs of a business and some would argue outweigh the wider benefits.

- **Prohibition** – in some cases, market failure can be combated through legislation. This might take the form of laws banning certain activities that are deemed to generate excessive private and social costs. Laws banning the abuse of non-medicinal drugs, some types of pornography, prostitution, guns, knives and in many European states smoking in public places are all designed to try and improve overall welfare. In some cases it is argued that prohibition merely drives the problem underground with the result that those affected are at greater risk than if the market were legal but regulated.

- **Positive discrimination** – In order to reverse the effects of discrimination a policy of positive discrimination has been used in a number of countries. The aim is to give those who may have been discriminated against a chance to gain a more proportionate representation in employment and positions of authority than might be the case if left to the market. Such policies have been actively pursued by Denmark and Sweden, for example, in order to improve the representation of women in government and employment. In Sweden the policy is called *positiv särbehandling*. The terms of the 1991 Equal Opportunities Act provides for:

  …positive action, *i.e.* giving a less qualified person of one gender preference over a better qualified person of the opposite gender, subject to the condition (in line with the Instrument of Government) that it forms part of efforts to promote equality of opportunity and therefore represents a systematic policy; this means, typically, the express backing of an equal opportunities agreement or equality plan. Since such reverse discrimination is permitted in order to promote the overriding interest of equality of opportunity, it is deemed not to constitute unfair treatment within the meaning of the Act. Positive action is restricted to hiring, promotion and training for promotion and is not permitted in matters relating to terms and conditions of employment.[2]

  There are critics who argue that positive discrimination is merely another form of discrimination and that such measures should not override fairness in treating people on an equal basis. However, proponents claim that discrimination can be so deep rooted that such measures are an essential step to redressing the balance and that the benefits outweigh the costs.

- **Redistribution of income** – Steps to redistribute income are implemented primarily through national tax and benefits systems. Basically, those who are better off in society pay a greater proportion of income in taxes which is then given to those who are the poorest through the welfare state. Most EU countries have a progressive tax system for income tax where the wealthy are taxed at a higher rate than those who are poorer. If the poor are given a helping hand in this way then they will be in a better position to be able to make a contribution to society and to take a more active and full part in employment. Ultimately everyone gains.

  This simple justification, however, hides a myriad of complex issues which many EU states struggle to come to terms with. The theory in relation to equity and efficiency in the tax and benefits system is easy to define; in practice the edges are far more blurred and complex to implement as has been witnessed in many EU countries that have been trying to reform the tax and benefits system to bring public spending under control. As already noted, any tax system will lead to a distortion of market signals with possible outcomes that might be worse than the problems that were originally the target of the action.

[2]Source: http://www.eurofound.europa.eu/emire/SWEDEN/ANCHOR-POSITIVS-AumI-RBEHANDLING-SE.htm © European Union, 1995-2012. Reproduced with permission.

SUMMARY

- In this chapter we have looked at markets and how models are developed to help us understand how markets work. We have seen that markets consist of sellers and buyers who represent supply and demand.
- There are many different types of markets ranging from highly organized commodity and stock markets through to street markets which many people are familiar with and use regularly. Markets bring together buyers and sellers to agree a price. Price acts as a signal to both sellers and buyers to give them some idea of value for money and whether a product is worth producing or not.
- Price is determined where supply is equal to demand at which point the market is in equilibrium. Changes to either supply or demand, or both, cause shortages and surpluses to occur which in turn create pressure on price to either rise, in the case of a shortage, or fall when a surplus. This process will continue (and can take some time) until equilibrium is restored.
- The concept of elasticity was introduced which relates the proportionate change in one variable to changes in another. This allows us to be able to look at the sensitivity of supply and demand to changes in price and in the case of demand, other factors such as income and the changes in the price of other goods. There are a number of factors which influence elasticity including the time period under consideration, the proportion of income devoted to the product, the ease with which producers can access raw materials and component parts, the extent to which the product is defined and the availability and closeness of substitutes and complements.
- Having an understanding of the market is an important element of any business planning. One aspect of this is having some understanding of broad trends in consumer spending. The changing structure of the population with a trend towards an ageing population, an increasing interest in green and ethical issues, the development of niche foods and online retailing are some of the important trends occurring across Europe.
- Dynamic and forever changing markets mean that resources are constantly moving from one use to another. One of the benefits of markets is that they allocate scarce resources to different uses. However, we also saw that imperfections in the market can lead to market failure. In such circumstances the market fails to allocate resources efficiently and the state may step in using a variety of methods including taxes and subsidies to ensure that market failures are corrected.
- In order to limit the effects of excessive market power, governments and the EU authorities monitor competition and take action to deal with cases where anti-competitive behaviour which breaches regulations or legislation has taken place.

REVIEW QUESTIONS

1. Give a definition of a 'market'. Give five different types of market and briefly outline their main characteristics.
2. What does:
   a. The law of supply and
   b. The law of demand
      state?
3. Briefly outline three factors which could cause the supply of computer printers to:
   a. Rise and
   b. Fall
4. Briefly outline three factors which could cause the demand for tractors to:
   a. Rise and
   b. Fall

5. Use a supply and demand diagram to show what would happen in the market for wheat if a drought reduced the harvest by a significant amount. Provide an explanation of the process by which the market would change and state clearly what you would expect to happen to both price and the amount of wheat bought and sold. Refer to the diagram in your answer to help illustrate the points you are making.

6. Explain the concept of price elasticity of supply and demand.

7. Provide an estimation of the price elasticity of demand and supply for the following five products and justify your estimation:
   a. Butter
   b. Lurpak Butter
   c. A top of the range espresso coffee making machine
   d. Oil
   e. Flights between Frankfurt and New York

8. The government imposes a €5.00 tax on a packet of 20 cigarettes which has to be paid by the tobacco producer. Use a supply and demand diagram to show what is likely to happen to the price and amount bought and sold of cigarettes. Using your diagram explain what happens to the total revenue of tobacco firms as a result of the tax.

9. Explain the concept of market failure and outline two ways in which such failure can be corrected. You should use a specific example to help illustrate your answer.

10. Why does excessive market power lead to a misallocation of resources?

DISCUSSION QUESTIONS

1. Should the provision of all products be left to the market? Explain your reasoning.
2. 'Taxes and subsidies merely distort market forces and lead to a worse allocation of resources.' Do you agree with this statement? Explain your answer.
3. If governments want to raise large sums in tax revenue they should always look to tax products with a highly elastic demand. Is this true? Explain.
4. 'Pirated movies and music is the direct result of market failure. Extending property rights is the only way to solve the problem.' Do you agree with this statement? Explain your answer.
5. 'The more effective price acts as a signal to producers and consumers the more efficient resource allocation will be.' Explain this statement.

REFERENCES AND FURTHER READING

Smith, A. and Butler-Bowdon, T. (2010) *The Wealth of Nations: The Economics Classic. A Selected edition for the contemporary reader*. Capstone

McGuigan, Moyer and Harris (2008) *Economics for Managers* (12th Ed), Cengage Learning International Edition, Chapter 3.

Mankiw and Taylor (2011) *Economics* (2e). Cengage Learning, Chapters 4 and 5

Mankiw, Taylor and Ashwin (2013) *Business Economics*. Cengage Learning

Cassidy, J. (2010) *How Markets Fail: The Logic of Economic Calamities*. Penguin

Prasch, R. E. (2008). *How Markets Work: Supply, Demand and the 'Real World'*. Edward Elgar

GLOSSARY

Advertising Elasticity of Demand The responsiveness of quantity demanded to a change in advertising expenditure

Complement A good which tends to be purchased along with another good

Cross Price Elasticity of Demand The responsiveness of quantity demanded of one good to a change in the price of another good

Demand The number of buyers willing and able to purchase a product at different prices

Effective Demand The amount an individual is willing and able to purchase at different prices – not simply what they would like to buy

Equilibrium A situation in a market where supply and demand are equal; the market is in a stable position with no incentive on the part of either buyers or sellers to change their behaviour

Income Elasticity of Demand The responsiveness of quantity demanded to changes in income

Inferior Good A good where demand falls as a result of a rise in income or rises as a result of a fall in income

Market Clearing Price The price in a market at which demand equals supply and there are no shortages or surpluses

Market Failure A situation which arises in a market when the allocation of resources is not efficient

Market Mechanism The process by which supply and demand interact with each other to allocate resources in a market

Moral Hazard A situation which arises when economic actors make decisions which may be inappropriate and are protected from the consequences of those decisions usually due to some form of asymmetric information

Normal Good A good where demand rises when incomes rise and falls when incomes fall

Opportunity Cost The cost expressed in terms of the value of the next best alternative foregone (sacrificed)

Price The amount of money an individual agrees to give up in order to acquire a product

Price Elasticity of Demand The responsiveness of quantity demanded to a change in price

Price Elasticity of Supply The responsiveness of quantity supplied to a change in price

Substitute A good which can be used instead of another

Supply The number of sellers willing and able to offer products for sale at different prices

The Law of Demand The idea that assuming other factors are held constant, the quantity demanded of a product will fall when the price of the product rises

The Law of Supply The idea that assuming other factors are held constant, the quantity supplied of a product will rise when the price of the product rises

CHAPTER CASE STUDY

'Institutional prejudice' restricting audit market

If you are a business looking to secure the services of a firm to audit your accounts or to get financial advice, then you will need to approach a firm of accountants. The question is, who do you choose? Large firms may well end up using one of the four dominant players in the market. The so called 'Big Four' are Ernst & Young, KPMG, Price Waterhouse Coopers (PWC) and Deloitte. These firms have grown to be dominant because they have economies of scale, can employ the brightest and best talent, have a reputation for quality and high standards, are able to market themselves and their services effectively and have networks and contacts that reach into every corner of the financial services industry.

Of course, these are not the only firms that offer financial services and can carry out company audits. There are many thousands of audit firms across Europe – a glance at the Yellow Pages or an online search in the region you are studying will reveal plenty of firms. Fact remains, however, that if you are a large firm such as a blue chip FTSE 100 company or similar in other European markets, you are more likely to have employed the services of one of the Big Four. Second question to ask is 'Why?'.

Small and medium sized accounting firms may well serve relatively local markets and given that most large firms are national or international in scope, the services offered by the Big Four tend to be seen as being more relevant. With offices around the world, the likes of Ernst & Young can provide lots of local expertise and convenience as well as advice to large corporations who are operating globally. The reputation of the Big Four goes before them; for blue chip companies, securing the services of such a reputable firm is a low risk option whereas going for a small or medium sized firm may mean that there is a much greater perceived risk. What if the small firm does not have the experience or expertise to deal with the complex financial structures and transactions that characterize large corporations?

Reputations, however, do not come cheap. The Big Four are able to exploit their reputations by charging premium prices for the privilege of accessing all that expertise and global spread. For the smaller audit firms it seems the dominance of these giants in the industry is placing them at a distinct disadvantage. Some argue that the lack of real competition they face means they are more likely to not provide the very best service whereas smaller firms have to constantly prove they are worthy of being hired and retained. Why would large firms take the risk of employing them, even if they were cheaper?

Some of these smaller firms have raised concerns about what they see as being excluded from the market especially in being hired by the larger corporations. They have argued that there is almost a bias against them by larger companies when choosing who to hire (or re-hire) to audit their books that is not justified by the quality of the service and the expertise they offer. Being smaller does not mean they are not capable of providing a first class service to larger businesses.

So what can they do to combat this perceived bias? One way would be to try and grow in order to rival the Big Four but many see the investment necessary as being too large to be able to overcome this perception – only when reaching a critical size would they be deemed big enough to be an 'equal' of the Big Four. So if the market is uncompetitive then should there be greater regulation? Should governments or the EU intervene to ensure that smaller firms are able to put in tenders for auditing work on a more equal footing than the Big Four in some way? Research suggests that intervention which forced some of the medium to large firms in the wider stock market indexes such as the FTSE 250 or the FTSE 500 to use smaller or medium sized firms would mean a considerable change in the size of the market open to them worth millions of euro a year. Government could lead the way in this respect by using some of the smaller and medium sized firms rather than the Big Four.

One other option that has been suggested is to adopt something which is a legal requirement in France and that is to have more than one firm auditing the books of a business with the aim of providing a more effective service to the firms being audited. This is not a case of one firm checking another but a requirement for two (it could be more) firms to work together on bringing a combined expertise to viewing the finances of a firm and providing the certainty that their books are not only accurate and free from fraud or 'dodgy dealing' which might be detrimental to shareholders and other stakeholders, but also that any advice provided is seen as being more objective. Opening up the market to joint audits means that there is more likely to be increased opportunities for small and medium sized firms to be engaged.

As with any proposal, there are those that do not see joint audits as a solution. For the hiring company the potential for a joint audit to cost more both in terms of money and time not to mention the potential for discord between the auditors and lack of clarity over the division of responsibilities. What happens if one of the firms employed is not as efficient or effective as the other – would this mean that firms being audited get a less than efficient and accurate service?

Questions

- Outline the two 'players' in the market for audit services. In this instance what is the price that operates in the market?
- What type of market structure do you think the audit industry is? Justify your answer.
- Is the fact that FTSE 100 companies tend to use one of the 'Big Four' an indication of market failure? Explain your answer.
- What factors do you think would determine the price elasticity of demand for audit services? Explain your reasoning.
- Some of the larger accounting firms may be able to charge a premium price for services to their biggest clients. Does this mean price is not fulfilling its role as a signal to buyers and sellers?
- Consider some of the advantages and disadvantages of joint audits such as those operating in France.
- To what extent do you think regulation would help to address the concerns of small to medium accounting firms?

12

THE ROLE OF
GOVERNMENT

FIGURE 12.1
The role of government mind map

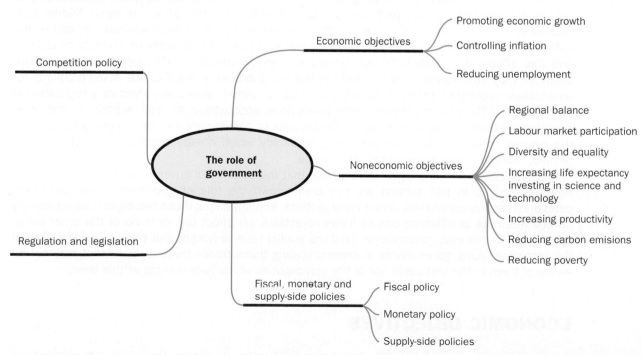

KEY CONCEPTS

Fiscal policy | Monetary policy | Productivity | Public goods

INTRODUCTION

In Chapter 2, we outlined role of government as part of the political and economic environment. Let us remind ourselves of the main role of governments in most societies, see Figure 12.1.

* managing the economy
* protecting the vulnerable
* protecting the environment
* providing public services (e.g. health) and infrastructure (e.g. transportation)
* defence and national security
* education
* foreign policy
* ensuring employment and the distribution of income

Notice that we have used the phrase 'most societies' above. This is because many governments across the globe operate within a democratic system and are deemed to be accountable for their actions and decisions. If the decisions they make are not seen as being appropriate for the 'good of society' then voters are at liberty to make their views known at the next elections and the government can change as a result. This acts as an influence on government decision making but may also mean that difficult, necessary but unpopular decisions may not be made and as a result efficiency can be compromised both at the level of the economy as a whole and to individual businesses.

There are, however, some countries where the democratic process is weak or even non-existent and in these cases the influence on government decision making may be much less powerful or subject to influence by one particular group of people or organization. In some Middle East countries, tribal or family influence on decision-making is very strong whereas in others the influence of the military may be significant. In some countries the process of governance is weak and this affects the capacity of businesses to operate effectively. Corruption and bribery, for example, may be endemic in some parts of the world and as a result cause many problems for businesses seeking to carry out activities in these countries, especially given new legislation in some parts of the west on bribery which holds firms accountable for their actions. In still other countries (Somalia being one example), the process of government may be almost paralyzed and the country is subject to lawlessness and instability which means conducting, what might be termed, 'normal' business is almost impossible.

Our discussion in this chapter will assume that the process of government and governance is relatively strong. In this context we can break down the role of government into two broad categories, economic and non-economic objectives. In many cases these two objectives are closely related attempts to influence one of these objectives will affect one or more of the other set of objectives. To this end, governments (and the public) have to accept that trade-offs occur. One of the problems facing governments is communicating these trade-offs to a public that may not be aware of them in the first place nor of the complexities of decision-making at this level.

ECONOMIC OBJECTIVES

Economic objectives can be seen as being essentially macro in nature. They refer to the key macro-economic indicators of a country's 'health' and well-being. The main objectives are generally:

- Promoting Economic Growth
- Controlling Inflation
- Reducing Unemployment and Maintaining Full Employment

Each is discussed in more detail next.

Promoting Economic Growth

Economic growth is important because it acts as a driver to other issues governments will be interested in monitoring and promoting. In many developed economies the level of economic growth is likely to be modest with growth rates of between 1 and 3 per cent being typical. In developing countries, growth rates into double digits is equally typical but this tends to be a combination of rapid growth and the fact that some of these economies are starting from a very low base.

In many European economies, a growth rate of around 2 per cent is seen as being the minimum required to help generate improvements in the well-being of the country. At 2 per cent growth, it is likely that jobs are being created at a faster rate than those being lost. Businesses will be expanding in some sectors of the economy in the face of increasing aggregate demand and employers will be taking on new workers. Of course, there will be some businesses that will be facing falling demand possibly because the product or service they are offering has reached the decline stage of its life cycle or because of changes in tastes, technology, etc. In these cases firms may be closing or contracting and jobs are being lost. There are two important elements in this process. First, is the rate at which jobs are lost lower than the rate at which new jobs are created and secondly, the ease with which those who lose their jobs can move into new employment. The government has a role to play in this respect.

Growth rates of around 2 per cent are also seen as being sustainable in terms of avoiding pressure on prices. If aggregate demand in an economy grows at a faster rate than the capacity of the economy to grow (i.e. aggregate supply) then there will be a build up of inflationary pressure which can be damaging. Governments have a role to play here as well.

Controlling Inflation

Inflation is a general rise in the price level. In simple terms, government statistical services identify a range of products which are used by the public every day and monitor the prices of these products. A system is also devised to attach weights to these products to take into account their relative importance in the spending of households. For example, a rise in the price of a product which accounts for a large proportion of consumer spending (petrol, for example) might have a more significant effect on households than a similar rise in the price of a product which accounts for only a small proportion of spending (on a ball point pen, for example).

Over a period of time the prices of some of these products will rise and others will fall. Some will rise by a relatively large amount and others by a much smaller amount and equally some products will see prices fall by a considerable amount whilst others may hardly fall at all. The price of some goods will not change at all over the period. All these price changes are expressed as an average by the statistical service and published each month. The majority of European countries publish the consumer prices index (CPI) as their preferred measure of inflation.

Inflation is not necessarily a 'bad' thing – it depends on how fast prices are rising. If the CPI is reported as 4.5 per cent over a period of a year this might be seen as being too fast a rise whereas most governments either have official or implied targets for inflation of around 2 per cent. Some inflation can be regarded as 'good' because it suggests that the economy is expanding and there is an incentive for businesses to increase output, invest and grow as a result. However, if prices rise too quickly then it may be that businesses will face uncertainty on future prices for inputs, on what prices to charge customers, on planning and deciding on investment strategies.

As a result governments adopt policies (or give other institutions or bodies the responsibility) to try and keep inflation under a degree of control. Past experience suggests this is not easy to do. Inflation is affected by a number of different trends and pressures, some of which can be controlled to an extent and others which are much harder to control. For example, a rise in the global price of oil will put pressure on the price of lots of other products which rely on fuel to rise as well. A government has little control over such price rises. If it decides to increase an indirect tax which in turn pushes up prices to consumers (as happened in the UK where the government wanted to raise tax revenue to help cut budget deficits) this might see inflation rise faster in the short term but the effect will be temporary as the tax rise will eventually drop out of the statistical calculations.

Many businesses, therefore, will be interested in inflation statistics as a means of gauging how the economy is performing in general but will also want to be mindful of the underlying trends in inflation and possibly looking at particular trends in prices which affect them more directly. A company involved in logistics, for example, will be likely to be affected far more by a significant rise in the oil price than will a business who provide web services.

Governments may want to set a target for inflation but it is important to remember that individual businesses will be affected in different ways depending on what is happening to particular prices which they have to pay to suppliers or which they have to charge consumers.

Governments will seek to control inflation either through monetary policy, fiscal policy or supply side policies which were introduced in Chapter 3 but will be further developed here. The principles of each of these reflects a degree of common sense but the complexities of achieving such targets in reality is much more challenging.

Reducing Unemployment and Maintaining Full Employment

Unemployment can be looked on in one respect as those who are without a job but the definition of unemployment is more specific to take into account subtleties in the circumstances of individuals. Some people, for example, women or men who choose to stay at home and look after young children, do not have a 'job' in that they are not employed. These people are not classed as unemployed, however. The definition of unemployment is those people who are out of work and actively seeking employment.

It is not simply a case of reducing unemployment which may be a target of policy. Governments will also seek to try and maintain full employment defined as a situation where economic output is at a level which enables everyone who wants work to find a job.

Most governments have support mechanisms in place in the form of welfare benefits to help support those who do not have a job but are seeking work. If unemployment rises, the burden on government finances increases because governments will have to spend more on this support. In addition, if people are out of work they tend to spend less because their incomes are lower and this can have a knock-on effect to other businesses. Restaurants, cinemas, furniture stores, and other forms of leisure and entertainment businesses may see sales of their products decline as a result of higher unemployment and they may be forced to reduce the size of their workforces in turn adding to the unemployment problem. If people cut spending because they are unemployed then government revenue in the form of indirect taxes may fall and revenue from direct taxes such as income tax and national insurance will also decline. The net effect is to increase government spending but cut revenue and may force the government into having to increase borrowing.

The effects of rising unemployment can also affect government and society in wider ways. There are well documented social effects on those who are unemployed, especially if they remain unemployed for long periods of time. These can include depression and anxiety, problems with drug and alcohol abuse, links to crime and family breakdowns. If these effects take place then it is often public sector services such as the emergency services, health services, social workers and so on, which have to deal with the effects. These are often supported by government funds and as a result puts a further strain on government finances.

There are also economic effects of unemployment. For one, there is an opportunity cost of unemployment in the form of the output which those who are unemployed could have generated. Workers who are without jobs but want one may find their skills start to become outdated, especially if they are out of work for some time. The cost of retraining and support systems for these people then increases. For all these reasons governments would like to preside over falling and low unemployment rates. Again, governments might seek to influence both employment and unemployment by utilizing the three policies mentioned above – more later in the chapter.

NON-ECONOMIC OBJECTIVES

These can be considered as being primarily micro in nature. The term 'non-economic' is a little misleading because they could easily be seen as being closely linked to 'economics' and indeed they are. However, whilst most governments will be interested in targeting appropriate macro targets such as growth, inflation and unemployment, the non-economic targets might differ. The following provides a brief overview of the sort of objectives governments might have in relation to this area.

Reducing poverty

Regardless of the size of the country and its apparent wealth there will be some poverty which exists. Poverty is a relative concept – in other words it depends how you look at it. To a billionaire, someone earning €70 000 a year may seem 'poor' but to another person who only earns €200 a year, that €70 000 may seem like a fortune. For this reason there is a definition of the poverty line which is widely accepted. Families will be below the poverty line if earnings are less than 60 per cent of median income.

The median income is that which divides the income earning distribution in half so that 50 per cent of individuals across the income range have incomes at or below the median and 50 per cent have incomes at or above the median. If the median income is €22 000 then the poverty line would be at €13 200.

At and below this level of income, families may face a number of problems. Apart from not having as much access to things that many other people would consider 'normal' such as food, clothing, entertainment and leisure, there are likely to be an increased risk of health and social problems. Incidences of family breakdown, for example can be higher amongst families in poverty and there may also be an increased likelihood of involvement with crime in some way.

For these reasons, as well as the moral obligation that exists for many governments, there is an imperative to adopt policies that seek to reduce poverty levels. This could be targeted even more specifically at particular groups in society such as child poverty. Fiscal policy may be a key way in which governments can influence poverty levels through the manipulation of the tax and benefit system to improve incentives and also to help support the most vulnerable in society.

In doing this, governments invariably face a trade-off. Provide too adequate a support mechanism and have the wrong incentives and the number of people remaining in poverty might even increase, especially if the difference between being in work and earning and receiving welfare benefits is skewed towards being better off out of work than in. There will always be some in society who attempt to abuse the welfare and benefits system and these people often get portrayed as the norm. As a result, the public at large may get a skewed impression of those people who are living in poverty which may not accurately reflect the difficult circumstances many have to live in.

Reducing carbon emissions

In Chapter 7 we discussed concerns over the amount of carbon emissions which have been the result of human activity, in particular with regard to business activity. There are a number of government policies designed to promote the reduction in carbon emissions and these can affect businesses in different ways. In some cases it may be an adjustment of the tax system to provide incentives to reduce undesirable behaviour and promote 'good' behaviour (i.e. operations that reduce carbon emissions). In others it may be changes to legislation to force businesses to adjust and still others the provision of grants or investment in more environmentally friendly business operations. Whatever the policy, there will be businesses who will be affected both positively and

BUSINESS IN ACTION

Middlescence

Many people reading this article will have some understanding of the term adolescence – you might actually have been going through it recently or you might be on the receiving end of it as a relative of teenagers. Adolescence has been characterized as a time of frustration, pent-up anger, confusion and alienation. Don't worry, however, if you are feeling those sensations, they will go away – but perhaps only for a time.

A Harvard Business Review article in 2006 has identified similar feelings in a completely different group of people. The feelings are those felt by people in the 35–55 age range, normally solid members of the public, hardworking, reliable and dependable – in fact, the very backbone of many businesses throughout the world. The problem is they are facing what the authors, Robert Morison, Tamara Erickson and Ken Dychtwald call 'Middlescence'. It is a feature of so many businesses that managing this is seen as being a vital aspect to improving productivity in the workforce and maintaining motivation.

Morison *et al.* identified a core of workers who have reached a stage in their career where the excitement of the possibilities of promotion have largely evaporated; they have reached senior management positions, are loyal, committed, often work long hours but are, according to Morison *et al.* 'bored, burned out and bottlenecked'. Because these workers are so solid and reliable, they tend to be forgotten whilst the focus goes on the energetic, enthusiastic and dynamic but possibly less productive and reliable younger employees.

The neglect of this group of workers can cause many problems. Morison *et al.*'s research suggests that around a third of workers in this group can feel disaffected, are not energized by their work and feel they are in dead-end jobs. They face real challenges in balancing their work, family and life demands. The consequences for a firm are that these workers might leave, which constitutes a waste of talent. Around a fifth say they would like to have another job. It may be that they stay where they are, but then the firm has a rump of unhappy people, often in key posts, which is not good for business.

Morison *et al.* suggest that the desire has not left these people but that a firm would be advised to find ways of tapping into this drive to help maintain a healthy atmosphere in the workplace. Morison *et al.* make it clear that offering promotions is not a practical way of doing this but suggest that there are other tactics that can be used. These include offering sabbaticals to workers to provide them with opportunities for further education or social enterprise work; new training can be given to refresh skills and provide new challenges; also, they can be encouraged to use their skills and expertise to provide mentoring for other workers.

Such tactics may help to provide additional needs that such a group of workers might require. We can link this back to the high-profile motivation thinkers such as Maslow and Herzberg, who suggested that things like recognition, belonging and cognitive and aesthetic needs were important aspects of motivational strategies in the work place.

Morison *et al.*'s study suggests that there is massive unlocked potential sitting in many businesses that could be unleashed and which could offer significant benefits to a business. Ignoring the needs of the middlescents could lead to stagnation and inertia that is not conducive to a dynamic and forward-looking business which prizes productivity.

Source: www.bized.co.uk/dataserv/chron/news/2602.htm

negatively. Some businesses with out-dated machinery and equipment, for example, may find that they will have to invest significant sums to meet new regulations, requirements or laws and they simply cannot afford to do so and so become insolvent. Others will see opportunities to seek out new markets and present themselves in a new light which can give a significant marketing boost. There will be opportunities for new businesses to be established at the cutting edge of new technologies designed to help reduce carbon emissions.

Increasing productivity

One of the keys to improving economic growth is to increase productivity not only of labour but also of land and capital. Productivity is measured as the output per factor of production per period of time. Let us use the example of two businesses each producing smart phones. If productivity per worker at Firm A is 50 units per hour whilst at Firm B the productivity is 30 units per hour, then Firm A, other things being equal, can have some significant advantages. Cost per unit can be lower in firms where productivity is high and in effect the firm is getting more output out of using a smaller amount of resources (the definition of efficiency).

One of the key ways to promote economic growth is to encourage greater productivity. Countries where productivity is relatively high tend to have stronger growth rates and so governments are keen to promote ways in which businesses can increase productivity.

These ways can be diverse but include such things as improving the education and training system in the country, investing in science and technology and providing tax and grant incentives to firms which invest in research and development. Governments might also look at the tax system and at the extent to which bureaucracy or 'red tape' can be cut to help businesses improve their efficiency. One interesting statistic that gives an indication of this sort of issue is the speed at which it takes a business to set up in different countries. See Table 12.1.

For example, the World Bank Doing Business Report suggests that the legal and formal channels required to start-up a business in Zimbabwe was on average 90 days. The Southern Africa Development Community (SADC) average was 42.5 days. In the Kyrgyz Republic the number of procedures required to set up a business is two, in Greece it is 15. In Macedonia FYR it takes an average of three days to start a business, in Suriname it is 694 days.

What this data shows is that support for entrepreneurs and businesses and by implication, productivity, can be significantly affected by the amount of bureaucracy and red tape that exists within government. Some governments, therefore, will actively seek to find ways of cutting the barriers that businesses face in setting up, expanding and being able to improve efficiency.

TABLE 12.1   Where is starting a business easy—and where not?

Easiest	RANK	Most difficult	RANK
New Zealand	1	Iraq	174
Australia	2	Djibouti	175
Canada	3	Congo, Rep.	176
Singapore	4	São Tomé and Principe	177
Macedonia, FYR	5	Haiti	178
Hong Kong SAR, China	6	Equatorial Guinea	179
Belarus	7	Eritrea	180
Georgia	8	Guinea	181
United States	9	Chad	182
Rwanda	10	Guinea-Bissau	183

From www.doingbusiness.org/reports/global-reports/doing-business-2011/~/media/FPDKM/Doing%20Business/
Documents/Annual-Reports/English/DB11-Chapters/DB11-SB.pdf – see page 1 Table 3.1

Investing in science and technology

Closely linked to productivity is a desire to invest in science and technology. Advancements in science and technology are associated with increases in productivity and economic growth. If a country has skills in these areas then it helps to increase global competitiveness and as a result enables producers to win more export orders. Increasing exports is a factor in economic growth and so governments are keen to divert resources to these growth generating areas. For businesses, both existing and those yet to be created, the benefits of government investing in science and technology are that they may receive help to invest themselves, to acquire skilled workers, access facilities, improved infrastructure and be able to grow or start-up.

Increase life expectancy, health and welfare

Improved health facilities are a key factor in helping to raise average life expectancy. Having better equipped hospitals, highly qualified doctors and nurses and access to medicines and the latest technology is only one part of the story, however. Complementing these is the necessity of education programmes to help the population understand how to help themselves. In the developed world, obesity, heart disease and diabetes are three major challenges facing governments and health authorities. In the less developed world, AIDS, malaria and tuberculosis are significant problems. In both situations there is an important role for government to play in improving education and awareness of these problems.

Encouraging people to take more exercise, eat a balanced diet and reducing consumption of alcohol and tobacco are all ways which can help to improve overall health and increase life expectancy. In the less developed world, education on safe sex, the use of condoms and the dangers of AIDS as well as providing help with simple preventative measures to reduce instances of malaria, such as mosquito nets as well as making medication available, are ways which can help reduce the instances of major killers in these countries.

There are problems which can arise as a result of improving life expectancy not least from the adjustments that need to be made due to an ageing population, which many countries are facing. With an increasing proportion of the population over the age of 65 in many countries, governments have to adjust to the tax and benefit implications and in addition there are opportunities for businesses to target this market segment more specifically. The construction industry may see a change in the demand for the type of housing required by people, car manufacturers may see opportunities for developing vehicles that help those with the infirmities of old age, the leisure and entertainment industry may also see changing patterns of demand and businesses may have to adjust to changing employment demographics as they may see an increase in the proportion of their workforce who are middle aged and above along with the problems that this could create – see the Business in Action article later in this chapter.

Overall, therefore, a healthy population is more able to work, more productive, takes less time off, is more able to access the labour market, contributes more to the economy in terms of paying taxes and takes less from the economy from accessing welfare benefits and health services. It is for these reasons that governments invest in improving measures to extend life expectancy.

Diversity and equality

The trend to increasing diversity within countries and the workplace was discussed in Chapter 4. In addition to the many different nationalities that many countries now see, there is an increased awareness and understanding of the needs and frustrations of those who are classed as disabled or those who choose to follow a different lifestyle. Legislation has been passed across Europe to help combat discrimination in the workplace against race, religion, colour, ethnic origin, gender and sexuality. Proponents of such laws and regulation argue that society is all the richer for this diversity and recognition of diversity and equality in the workplace is an essential element of 'modern business'. Critics argue that there are clearly some areas where equality and diversity should be embraced but suggest that there are boundaries which need to be in place to preserve fundamental morals. There are, for example, moves by the UK government to legalize marriage between same sex couples. At the time of writing, same sex couples can access various legal rights which married couples can gain through civil ceremonies. Pressure groups have been arguing that the full rights that come with formal marriage should also be available to same sex couples and the Coalition Government signalled its intention to move on this at the Conservative Party conference in Autumn 2011.

Different countries will have very different views on such developments depending on their cultural and religious background. Not all governments, therefore, will actively promote some of the changes outlined above – indeed, there may be some societies where issues such as same sex relationships is strictly taboo. Being sensitive to these different cultural, religious and societal norms is an important focus for companies who are conducting business in different regional markets. Views on diversity and equality are going to be very different in countries like Saudi Arabia and Iran to Belgium and the Netherlands and so awareness of what societal norms are is an important part of business.

Labour market participation

Labour market participation refers to the proportion of the population of working age who are either in work or actively seeking employment. Governments may be interested in increasing the labour market participation rate because the more people who are in work or seeking work the higher the revenues from income related tax, the more likely those people are to spend and thus increase indirect tax revenues and lower the spending by governments on benefits. As a result, government income is higher and expenditure lower thus reducing the need to borrow and freeing up funds to invest in long term supply-side improvements to the economy.

In addition, the economic objective of reducing unemployment, brings social benefits which arise when people are in work. Part of the drive to increase the labour market participation rate is the desire to increase the proportion of women in the labour market in many countries. This may also be linked to policies to improve equality and diversity and to better reflect the gender balance in society.

Regional balance

Most countries have regions which are economically more prosperous than others. In the UK, parts of the south west, north east and north west are relatively poorer than parts of the south east, for example. In Germany, the unification of East and West Germany brought its own economic problems given the economic state of the East in comparison to the West. The German government introduced a 5.5 per cent Solidarity Tax following unification to help raise funds to invest in the East, a tax which was not universally popular amongst Germans. In Italy the per capita income of those living in the north of the country is almost twice as high as those living in the south, see Figure 12.2.

In other parts of EMEA there are similar disparities. These may manifest themselves in differences between prosperity levels between urban and rural areas but even within particular urban or rural areas there can be significant differences in prosperity.

Governments can do a great deal to help alleviate some of these regional disparities although the evidence suggests that regional policies have not always been as cost effective as they might seem in theory. It is not simply a case of providing incentives, tax breaks, employment subsidies, grants, investment incentives, taking direct action (such as moving key government functions to 'poorer' regions) and using regulation or legislation to force or promote economic development in targeted areas (such as easing or enforcing planning laws, making available brownfield sites for development and so on). It is also a case of trying to influence deep (often historical) and cultural structural rigidities and prejudices. These can be more difficult to change quickly. For example, in the UK, the BBC has taken a decision to move some of its broadcasting to a new development at Salford Quays near Manchester from its traditional main broadcasting base in London. The Corporation claim there are economic and social reasons for re-locating to the north west of England but a number of presenters and other staff expressed concern about the move. Some,

FIGURE 12.2

Regional disparities in Italy

Figure 12.2 shows two sets of statistics highlighting the extent of regional disparity in Italy. Panel 1 shows the differences in GDP per capita across the country with a clear north-south divide and Panel 2 shows similar disparities in relation to unemployment rates within the country.

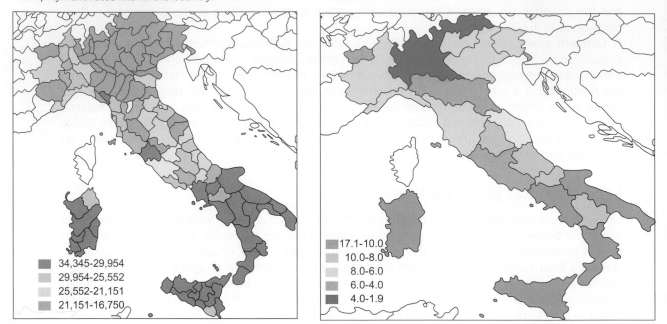

34,345-29,954
29,954-25,552
25,552-21,151
21,151-16,750

17.1-10.0
10.0-8.0
8.0-6.0
6.0-4.0
4.0-1.9

Source: Lusinyan, Lusine; Morsy, Hanan; Zoli, Edda (EUR); and Eyraud, Luc (FAD) (2011) *Italy: Selected Issues* (page 5) Available at:http://www.imf.org/external/pubs/ft/scr/2011/cr11176.pdf

for example, have said that it would be harder to get key political figures on news shows because government is based in London and so it would not be feasible for top politicians to simply fit in a visit to the Manchester studio in the same way as they were able to do when the studios were based in London. Others have simply said they do not want to relocate their families to the north west and claimed that the move is political rather than economic.

FISCAL, MONETARY AND SUPPLY-SIDE POLICIES

In order to achieve the various economic and non-economic objectives outlined above, three key policies are used which were outlined in Chapter 3.

Fiscal policy refers to the manipulation of government income and expenditure to achieve particular objectives. Government income is generated through taxation. Governments spend this income on a wide variety of goods and services which are classed as public and merit goods. **Public goods** have the characteristic that when supplied one individual's use of the good does not prevent anyone else from also using and gaining the benefits of that good. A classic example is street lighting. Street lighting is a service – if one person benefits from being able to see where they are going then no other individual can also be prevented from benefiting from the lighting. In this case the good is said to have the characteristic of being excludable – no one else can be prevented from benefiting from the street lighting once it is provided.

At the same time if one individual gains the benefit of the provision of street lighting it does not reduce the benefit that any other individual can gain from that provision. In this case the provision of street lighting is said to be non-rival. Because of these two characteristics it is not possible to provide services such as street lighting, defence, justice and knowledge creation through normal market processes where a price is charged so governments tend to take on the responsibility of providing these services to the benefit of all, funded through general taxation.

BUSINESS IN ACTION

Taxation

London risks losing the showcase end-of-season ATP World Tour Finals because of the high rate of tax, world number one Rafael Nadal said at the Shanghai Masters on Thursday.

The Spaniard believes the 50 per cent tax on players' appearance fees, winnings and a proportion of their worldwide endorsement earnings could see the glamour event featuring the top eight men being staged elsewhere unless the law is changed.

'It is really tough what is happening today in the UK with the tax. There are a lot of things that are really positive. This (tax) thing is probably really negative,' he said after losing in the third round to German Florian Mayer.

'What I believe in my heart, is that London is a fantastic event. There's a full crowd at every match, a fantastic stadium. But London is not the only city in the world,' he said.

The five-year contract for the ATP World Tour Finals, staged at the 02 Arena, comes up for renewal in 2013 but Nadal indicated that growing discontent could see players pushing for the event to be moved to a more favourable tax environment.

'The tax regime from UK is complicating a lot of things because to go and play at Queen's, the problem is not to win. The problem is I can lose money because I go there.'

'I play for one week, and they take out money from my sponsors. That's a lot,' he said of the Wimbledon warm-up event he has decided to skip next year in favour of playing at Halle.

'I'm going play at Wimbledon. I'm going to play in the World Tour Finals. So that is a lot of weeks, a lot of tax. It is becoming more and more complicated to play in the UK at the moment,' he said.

However, a change to the tax regime could help London renew its contract for the ATP finals, added the Spaniard.

'So (if there is a tax) change, the chances of keeping the World Tour Finals in London are going to be very, very high,' he said.

Nadal dismissed suggestions in the British media that he had decided to play the Halle event in Germany instead of Queen's because he had been offered a higher appearance fee.

'For the last four years, I have played at Queen's. So we thought it is the right moment to change. I am not changing because Halle is paying me more money than Queen's. That's not the reason,' he said.

Wimbledon chief executive Ian Ritchie called on the government earlier this year to change the tax laws or risk Britain losing some of tennis's marquee events.

Government rules state that sportsmen and women competing or even just practising in the UK are taxed a proportion of their income from endorsements and sponsorships even if those deals have nothing to do with Britain.

The rules are the reason triple Olympic champion sprinter Usain Bolt has stayed away from the London Diamond League meetings and there are also fears they could affect some of the country's smaller golf tournaments.

The same argument does not apply to merit goods. Merit goods have the characteristic of being able to be provided by the market system but if provision was exclusively through this system there would be under consumption by the population as a whole which is deemed to be disadvantageous to society. Examples of merit goods include public health provision and education – in its widest sense. Some economies have health systems which rely more heavily on an individual taking out insurance to cover their health needs. However, not everyone will be able to afford such insurance or take the risk that they might be able to get away with avoiding the cost of doing so. If this happens and the individual falls ill or is involved in an accident and does not have insurance cover they are liable for the costs of their health treatment and this could result in serious financial problems for the individual and their family.

These governments would provide a safety net for those who are unable to provide for themselves. In other cases, the state takes on a greater role in health care provision and provides such series free of charge at the point of use to everyone in society. This service is funded out of general taxation.

Spending by governments on health, education, social welfare, justice, the environment, defence, prisons, the emergency services and transport amongst other things, is significant in most countries. This spending is partly funded by the tax receipts from direct and indirect taxes such as taxes on incomes and taxes on spending. The difference between what a government receives in tax revenue and what it needs to spend on services is either funded by borrowing (in which case the government is running a budget deficit) or if tax receipts are greater than spending by either paying off debt or building up a budget surplus.

The decisions by government on what it will focus its spending on and how it raises the funds to do so have important and widespread implications. Taxes not only raise revenue but have important effects on incentives. Increase income taxes and some people will question whether the effort of being enterprising or working harder is now worth the effort. As a result economic growth could be affected.

Taxes can also be used to provide incentives to make people behave in what are deemed to be desirable ways. For example, taxing pollution may force businesses to think of ways to reduce pollution or invest in new technologies, taxing goods which are considered dangerous or a threat to health such as tobacco can help to reduce consumption.

On the spending side, governments can choose to spend money on services which help to meet their various objectives. For example, if an objective is to reduce child poverty, decisions may be made to subsidize child care services so that families can afford to go out to work or invest in improving housing and educational support at an early age. In times of economic slowdown, government may manipulate its tax and spending to provide a stimulus to the economy in the hope of supporting a recovery.

Given that government activity accounts for a significant proportion of total GDP in many countries, fiscal policy can prove to be a powerful tool in helping governments meet their various objectives. In theory, the transmission mechanisms are simple but in practice the links between fiscal policy and achieving desired objectives is much more complex and subject to intense debate. The principle, however, is clear.

Given that monetary policies were discussed in detail within Chapter 3 we focus on supply side policies here.

Supply-Side Policies

In this section we are going to look at supply-side policy. The aim of this policy is to shift the aggregate supply curve to the right, increasing the long term productive capacity of the economy. By their very nature they tend to be long-term policies. It is also sometimes difficult to tease out such policy from fiscal and monetary policy since they are to some extent closely linked. For example, a decision to change tax allowances on direct taxes so that individuals can take home pay might sound like fiscal policy but the effects might find their way through to incentives which help boost the supply side.

There are many arguments about how effective they are, for example, to what extent does lowering taxes increase incentives, reduce welfare dependency and increase the urge to find work. Supply side policies are specifically designed to influence the productivity and efficiency of the economy. A key feature of policy is the aim to open up markets and de-regulate to improve efficiency in the working of markets and the allocation of resources. The main areas of policy can be summarized as follows:

- **The Labour Market**

The intention of policy is to reduce impediments to free markets, reduce bureaucracy and 'red tape' which lead to inflexible labour markets. Part of this process might be legislation or regulation designed to reduce the power of trade unions, establish wider use of short term contracts, bring in more flexible working arrangements, make so called hiring and firing easier, improving the flexibility of contracts, terms and conditions and pay.

Clearly these are very sensitive areas and there is criticism that such policies put the needs of employers above those of workers which can lead to exploitation.

Tax and Welfare Reform

In many countries the tax and welfare benefit system is extremely complex. Critics argue that support networks through the welfare system have become so comprehensive that they are subject to widespread abuse and act as a major disincentive to find work and exit the state benefit support system. Bringing in reform of the system and a stricter benefit regime along with tax reform would help to encourage people to find work.

Education and Training

This could be supported by improving access to training and education and making it easier for people to overcome both geographical and occupational mobility of labour. This might include measures to help provide support for accessing housing and information centres to help match those people looking for jobs with those who have vacancies.

Indeed, this area is considered of increasing importance so much so that in 2010, the Nobel Prize Committee awarded the 2010 Economics Prize to three economists, Peter Diamond and Dale Mortenson from the United States and Christopher Pissarides, a British-Cypriot based at the London School of Economics. The three were given the award for their work on labour markets and how they differ from normal markets.

Their work has covered what is known as 'search and matching theories'. Under normal circumstances, markets are assumed to be in equilibrium when supply equals demand. When something happens to disturb that equilibrium, market forces work to restore equilibrium. The work of these three economists has shown how labour markets can operate differently and that unemployment can remain at high levels even though there are plenty of vacancies. Government policy and labour market regulation may have important consequences for labour markets and can contribute to the disequilibrium rather than helping to clear the market.

Some of the reasons include the time it takes for those who are unemployed to find work – there are search costs involved. For employers there are transaction costs to hiring labour and whilst there may be employers looking for labour and labour looking for work both parties need to be put in touch with each other and agree to a transaction. Even if the two parties do come together a transaction may not be guaranteed (i.e. the supplier of labour gets a job) because there may be incentives for both sides to see if they can get a better outcome for themselves. In addition, policies regulating the ease with which employers can hire or fire workers and the benefits or unemployment insurance that exists in a country can also influence when labour becomes unemployed and how long they stay unemployed. If for example, unemployment benefit is relatively generous then it may be that workers take more time to find work because they have some degree of support to live on whilst they find 'the right job'. It is entirely possible, therefore, that vacancies can remain unfilled even when there are high levels of unemployment.

The research carried out by the laureates is helping economists and policy makers gain a better understanding of policies to use to help reduce high levels of unemployment. They have brought a different perspective to the debate on how best to deal with the frictional aspects of structural unemployment, which seems to be a problem for a number of countries following the financial crisis where jobs have been lost in one sector but workers have found difficulty moving to other sectors of the economy where vacancies exist.

A number of governments across the EMEA region have set targets to increase the number of people entering higher education and also improving vocational education to help improve the sort of skills that many businesses suggest are not always evident from mainstream schooling. One of the problems with such policies, however, is that vocational skills are not always seen as being as 'valuable' as academic ones mainly due to a prejudice about what 'education' really means. Policies designed to increase participation rates at university can be seen as being popular, however, it is also important that governments are aware that increasing rates needs to be matched by the opportunities that exist after university. An increasing number of graduates flooding the labour market with a limited number of vacancies available can lead to frustration and disenchantment in young people. Indeed, the political changes that took place in Egypt in the early part of 2011 can be attributed in part to the increasing number of young people in that country leaving university with no prospects for jobs. The Egyptian government invested heavily in encouraging university entrance but for many the prospects of jobs at the end of the process were very limited.

Incentives and technology

A key part of supply side policies is to change thinking/expectations, create incentives and foster an entrepreneurial spirit and to embrace the 'knowledge driven economy' amongst the population. This is done partly through reform of the tax system to create those incentives and give people a reason for wanting to start up new businesses. Other incentives may also be given through grants to help start up or develop businesses, low rent business premises, the chance to use cheap office space to work in during the early phases of a new business – so called 'business incubators' – subsidies to help employ new workers and as mentioned above, regional policies to encourage enterprise, expansion investment and location.

Put together these policies will, it is hoped, create an economic climate such that enterprise can flourish and there are sufficient incentives to persuade people to be creative, start new businesses and develop existing ones. If they work then they can generate more of a focus on business and productivity and a removal of the causes of market failure which leads to inefficiency. Assuming they are successful such policies can lead to a long term shift of the aggregate supply curve to the right but at the same time critics argue that too much of a focus on enterprise can lead to the opportunity for those most vulnerable in society to be exploited and left behind.

REGULATION AND LEGISLATION

The case for regulation and some of the key regulations in operation across the EU has been covered in Chapter 2. In this chapter we are going to present a brief analysis of the costs and benefits of regulation.

It is important to remember that effectively regulation is deemed necessary because businesses cannot be trusted to carry out operations themselves to standards where, in the eyes of society, stakeholders are protected sufficiently. Because of this view, the state steps in to protect stakeholders. In some cases, industries are subject to self-regulation. In this situation, an agreed code of practice governing behaviour may be established and businesses in the industry volunteer to abide by the code. Whilst the code is often not legally binding, there is the prospect that if businesses do not conform then the government could step in and legislate so this acts as a suitable incentive for appropriate self-regulation.

Some industries such as the utilities (gas, electricity and water) are heavily regulated because they are deemed to be natural monopolies and whilst attempts have been made to inject competition into these industries in many countries, there are still perceived problems of lack of choice and accusations over unfair pricing by firms in the industry. The food industry is also heavily regulated, perhaps for obvious reasons – to help protect consumers but also to educate consumers so that they can make more informed decisions about what they buy and eat.

It should be immediately obvious that there is a tension between increasing regulation and the points raised in the section about supply-side policy above. The more regulation businesses face the more controls they have over what they can and cannot do and as a result the more likely it is that incentives will diminish. Many businesses complain that they have to abide by so many regulations relating to health and safety that it becomes almost impossible to carry out work efficiently. When meeting regulations, businesses incur additional costs which are either passed onto the consumer in the form of higher prices or which have to be absorbed by the business in some way thus reducing profit margins and in some cases making it financially unviable to carry out work.

Supporters of regulation argue that without it there is always a powerful incentive for businesses to cut corners and this results in negative effects on stakeholders. The financial crisis of 2007–2009 has led to a great deal of soul searching about the extent to which the financial and banking system took advantage of the relatively light regulation which existed and which many leading finance ministers across Europe and the US subscribed to. The result was, so goes the argument, that excessive risks were taken because the right regulatory framework was not in place and the result was the near collapse of the banking and financial system.

The advertising, tobacco and alcohol industries are other examples where consistent accusations are levelled against firms that they behave inappropriately. In the case of advertising and alcohol there are self-regulatory frameworks in place but the incidents of complaints about behaviour are numerous and regular. Critics of self-regulation cite these complaints as evidence that stricter regulation is needed possibly through legislation.

The picture in parts of Europe and the UK is one of accusations of too lax a regulatory structure across many industries and too harsh a one on the other hand. This highlights the difficult balance that governments face over the issue. In other parts of the EMEA region, there may be accusations that regulation is almost non-existent and as a result there are suggestions that global businesses can exploit the lack of regulation by setting up operations in those regions and produce at lower cost. Many businesses are very aware of the extent to which such accusations could damage their reputation and so go to great lengths to show how they monitor operations in these regions to ensure that exploitation is avoided and high standards are maintained. One of the main reasons for the efforts which such businesses go to is the fact that the viral networks afforded by the Internet mean that it is very difficult for information to be contained and so it is almost imperative that these businesses do what they say they do. If they do not then information publicizing the negative side of their operations leaks out very quickly and can damage reputations.

In parts of the Middle East the degree of regulation varies considerably. A number of countries have been accused of having weak regulatory structures which can make it more difficult for businesses to operate. This is because the levels of corporate governance which many businesses will aspire to are different in other countries. Again, businesses could find that they are accused of exploiting weak regulatory regimes to cut costs. The problems, however, might outweigh the benefits. Issues related to corruption, bribery, fraud and lack of health and safety can damage reputations as outlined above.

However, it is also the case that many countries in the Middle East region recognize that in order to be able to take part in wider global business development, having the right regulatory structures in place is an important part of their individual development and integration into the world economy.

Financial regulation is one such example where this is taking place. The formation of the Gulf Cooperation Council (GCC), consisting of Bahrain, Kuwait, Oman, Qatar, Saudi Arabia and the United Arab Emirates (UAE) in 1981 aimed to promote the interests of members and improve coordination and integration between them and has led to a number of initiatives to align financial regulation with those of the rest of the world.

In recent years the growth of the financial sector in GCC countries has led to an acceleration of improvements in regulatory structures. In 2003, for example, Saudi Arabia set up the Capital Market Authority to regulate capital markets, four years later a code of practice for hedge funds was issued by the Dubai Financial Services Authority, the Qatar Financial Centre Regulatory Authority was established in 2005 and in Bahrain, the central bank issued a rule book in 2004 covering regulatory issues which is regularly updated and there are strict rules governing the amount of paid-up capital and reserves held in the banking sector in the UAE.

The result of these and other reforms has meant that there is a considerable degree of compliance with global banking and financial regulation which have been part of the Basel agreements. A key driver for these changes has been the desire to become more closely integrated with the global financial system and it is recognized that if inward investment as well as internal financial expansion is to be generated, having standards which are recognized by the majority of the rest of the financial world is essential. For countries like Saudi Arabia, it is also important that it diversifies its economy away from an over reliance on oil given that reserves will run out at some point and that the world will seek alternative sources of energy in the face of the concerns over climate change and finding alternative sources of energy.

COMPETITION POLICY

We have seen in Chapters 6, 10 and 11 how firms with market power can affect market outcomes so that prices can be higher than in competitive conditions or supply will be restricted. Many national governments have a body charged with overseeing and monitoring competition. There are now over one hundred different legislative entities (jurisdictions) around the world. Part of the reason for the increase in the establishment of competition laws and jurisdictions is the fact that many more countries are embracing market principles and with market principles comes the potential for market failure of which abuse of market power is one.

This expansion is uneven, however. In the Middle East only around half of the countries which could be said to comprise this 'region' (Algeria, Bahrain, Egypt, Iran, Iraq, Israel, Jordan, Kuwait, Lebanon, Libya, Morocco, Oman, Palestine, Qatar, Saudi Arabia, Sudan, Syria, Tunisia, Turkey, the United Arab Emirates and Yemen) have what could be described as 'developed' competition law and policy. We might not be particularly surprised at this given the very diverse nature of the 'region'. The origin and development of competition law and policies that do exist are closely intertwined with the cultural, historical and religious identity of the country concerned.

For example, in Israel the competition laws reflect that country's ties with the UK and the original competition law laid down in the 1959 Restrictive Business Practices Law was very similar to UK competition law at that time. In Turkey competition law has evolved as the country has moved closer to being tied with the European Union – something that a number of other countries have also begun to do even if they have no intention of ever joining the EU. In other cases, the development of competition law has been closely aligned with Islamic teaching and principles which go back many centuries. It is perhaps safe to say that the more liberalized economies in the Middle East become, the more likely competition jurisdictions will become an imperative. This is especially the case as countries seek closer ties to other nations across the globe as a means of attracting inward investment and helping promote growth. This, in turn, is a means of helping people to escape from the poverty that blights some regions in countries in the Middle.

In Europe, each country has a competition authority. The UK has the Competition Commission, in Germany the competition authority is the Federal Cartel Office (Bundeskartellamt), in France the French Competition Authority began discharging its regulatory powers following reform of competition regulation in 2009 and in Italy the Antitrust Authority (Autorità garante della concorrenza e del mercato) monitors competition legislation. Each national competition authority will share information and cooperate both with each other and with the EU Competition Commission through the European Competition Network (ECN). The aim of the ECN is to coordinate activities so that EU competition law is enforced in member states. Different countries will have national competition legislation but any such laws have to dovetail with EU competition legislation. In the UK, the Competition Act 1998 and the Enterprise Act 2002 cover breaches of competition within the UK but when such breaches involve cross-border activity, EU competition law takes precedence.

In South Africa The Competition Tribunal is the body charged with adjudicating over competition issues. The Competition Commission carries out the investigations into alleged abuse of market power and restrictive practices. It then refers its findings to the Tribunal which makes a judgement on the issue.

Competition law covers three main areas:

* Dealing with cartels and restrictive business practices such as market rigging.
* Acting against illegal pricing practices such as price fixing, price gouging (deliberately raising price to exploit periods of market shortage, a practice which is often reported during the Muslim Holy month of Ramadan, for example) and predatory pricing where prices are set below cost with the intention of squeezing out competition.
* Overseeing merger and acquisition activity including the operation of joint ventures.

These areas are going to be ones which apply across competition authorities worldwide. Indeed, in 2001, a network was established to help provide national competition agencies with a forum to discuss and improve competition laws. The International Competition Network (ICN) now has over 100 competition agencies as members covering over 90 different jurisdictions. Membership is entirely voluntary and helps to improve the convergence of competition law and regulation and helps countries which are establishing competition laws to be able to do so more effectively and efficiently.

As a virtual organization, members can share ideas and information and recommendations can then be made to national competition authorities. Whether these recommendations are then taken up is dependent on the individual competition authorities; any of the work carried out by the ICN and its recommendations have no legal status.

BUSINESS IN DEBATE

Advertising and Business Ethics

Business ethics is a tricky subject. The following case highlights the dilemmas facing regulatory authorities and businesses with regard to the way in which advertising is carried out. The Advertising Standards Authority (ASA) is an independent body in the UK set up by the advertising industry to adjudicate rules on advertising. The ASA will deal with a variety of different types of advertising and through different media but in essence the principles they work to is that advertising should not mislead, cause harm, or cause offence. Complaints by members of the public are investigated by the ASA and the body makes a ruling which can include banning the advert.

Ultimately, the ASA cannot force a business to withdraw advertising – most do if an adjudication goes against them. However, if the business does not respond to the decision made by the ASA, the body does have the right to refer the offending business to the Office of Fair Trading (OFT) and Ofcom, the industry regulator in the UK. These both have greater powers to act.

Ryanair is no stranger to clashes with the ASA over its various promotions but on this occasion the budget airline refused to accept the ASA ruling. The advert in question was designed to promote its latest fare deals. The advert was titled 'Hottest Back to School Fares' and featured a female model dressed in what was interpreted as school uniform. The model had a bare midriff, short skirt with the top slightly open, a shirt and tie and knee-length socks

and she was stood amidst a classroom full of desks.

The advert was featured in three daily UK newspapers; the *Daily Mail*, the *Scottish Daily Mail* and *The Herald*. The total readership of the three newspapers is around 3.5 million. The advert initially generated 13 complaints from the public. The substance of the complaints was that the advert was offensive and that it promoted a male dominated sexual fantasy that used school girls and was inappropriate.

Ryanair received a substantial amount of publicity over the advert as a result of the ASA ruling prompted by the response it gave to that ruling. It criticized the ASA for being unelected and referred to its members as 'dimwits'. Ryanair refused to pull the advert although the newspapers who ran it said they would not publish it again. Ryanair pointed out that the number of people complaining was tiny in comparison to the number of people who are likely to have seen the advert and suggested the ASA were not capable of ruling on a fair and impartial basis.

This was not the first time that Ryanair has taken issue with the ASA. Previous adverts have been subject to adjudication by the regulator. These included an advert by Ryanair offering two million tickets for £10. Complaints were received that such tickets were not available on Fridays or Sundays and that the adverts were therefore misleading. Other cases included claims by Ryanair that its flights from London to Brussels were both faster and cheaper than the trip by Eurostar, claims over the environmental friendliness of its operations and adverts warning customers that 100 per cent mark-ups on its prices by ticketing agents amounted to customers being ripped off.

The ASA, it seems, finally lost patience with Ryanair. It claims that Ryanair is consistently flouting the rules that all players, in what is a highly competitive market, have to abide by. When the ASA makes a ruling in response to complaints Ryanair simply 'throws its toys out of the pram' they say. Ryanair, however, has a different view.

Ryanair says that it has answered some of the accusations against it and that it is persistently targeted by the regulator. The company claims that the ASA's rulings are 'unfair, biased and untrue' and that the regulator 'demonstrated a repeated lack of independence, impartiality and fairness'. Ryanair gives examples where it has received adverse judgements whilst others in the industry have not, for example, Ryanair was asked to put 'from £10' on some of its adverts to show that prices might be more than this amount but easyJet were not made to do the same.

The ASA has no power to enforce its rulings but it can refer companies to the Office of Fair Trading (OFT). It rarely does this – the last case was in 2005 – but it has decided that it now has no option but to refer Ryanair to the OFT for further investigation. Ryanair has welcomed this referral and argues that an impartial third-party investigation will give it the chance to have its claims that it is being treated unfairly heard and that its advertising policies will be vindicated. The ASA hope that it will be able to show that Ryanair are not complying with the rules of self-regulation that all in the industry have to abide by and that they will be forced to abide by the code of conduct for advertising in the future.

The whole issue raises important ethical questions for discussion.

Ryanair do push the boundaries in their advertising but is that necessarily a bad thing? When does an advert become inappropriate and offensive? How fair and impartial can a regulator be, especially when it begins to use language like 'throwing its toys out of the pram'?' Should businesses use women in 'provocative' poses for advertising? Is the use of male dominated fantasies to advertising acceptable? Should children (even if the model was not a child) be depicted in adverts in such a way? Was the advert sexually provocative? Should the decision by 13 people to complain be the basis for making such a ruling? Should the ASA seek the views of those who might not be offended by such an advert? Was Ryanair right to reject the ASA's ruling and did the furore over their rejection merely serve to bring the advert to a much wider audience than might have been the case otherwise?

Source: adapted from www.bized.co.uk/dataserv/chron/news/3019.htm and www.bized.co.uk/dataserv/chron/news/3066.htm

BUSINESS IN DEBATE

Europe's Demographic Future

Where do we find the most pronounced effects of demographic change? Why is it that youth unemployment is especially high in certain regions? In what countries or regions is the job situation so poor as to induce people to emigrate? Based on a total of 24 indicators, the Berlin Institute has analyzed and assessed the sustainability of 285 European regions. Green means good prospects, while the red indicates problems for the regions in question, and the deeper the red, the more problematic the situation is. Even a first, cursory glance at the map reveals a marked east–west disparity.

The present study assesses the sustainability of 285 European regions on the basis of 24 demographic, economic, social and environmental indicators. All EU countries as well as Iceland, Norway and Switzerland, all three of them non-member states, have been included in the study. The diversity of the data that went into the making of the present assessment ensures that we have come up with a differentiated picture: In addition to economic performance, the factors that count here include e.g. population, age composition, employment levels for young people, women and older persons, investment in research and development, but also pollution of the atmosphere with carbon dioxide, a climate gas. The sustainability of Europe's regions depends in important ways on all of these factors.

The study spells out the implications of demographic change, showing that individual countries are not only affected in very different ways by it but that these countries also deal quite differently with the challenges it poses. All countries are faced with problems that they need to solve. Many have good ideas. But none is in possession of a magic formula. It is that that makes Europe, with its diversity of cultures and sensibilities, a marketplace of ideas, of successes and failures, that everyone would do well to have a good look at.

The best scores were given to regions in northern Europe, which also have high fertility rates, and the field is led by Iceland, a small, exceptionally prosperous, and highly developed nation. The capital cities of Stockholm and Oslo did particularly well in this connection. Six of Switzerland's seven regions are ranked among Europe's ten best. All these regions are typified by relatively stable demographic structures as well as by high aggregate value added, good education levels, and impressive employment levels — also for older persons. Ireland and the UK also rank high, as do the Benelux countries, France, Germany's southern regions, Austria, and some regions in northern Italy and northeastern Spain.

Just about all of the regions that scored on the lower end of the scale are remote rural regions, e.g. in southern Italy or Greece, and regions in Bulgaria, Romania, and Poland that have been hard hit by radical structural change. These regions are affected by an array of negative demographic phenomena: very low fertility rates, massive outward migration of young people, and the marked aging of the remaining population that this entails — and to make things worse, the latter is as a rule not particularly well off in social terms.

If we look at the map presenting the overall ranking, we cannot fail to notice a clear-cut east–west divide. What this shows is that in eastern European countries the transition from a planned to a market economy is far from complete. But it also shows how important its is to get started with reforms as early as possible. To cite an example, the Baltic nations, the first countries of the Soviet Union to declare their independence and seek orientation in western Europe, have already caught up with the weaker regions there. The same goes for the Czech Republic and Slovenia, which, even in the context of the East Bloc, were relatively highly developed and wasted little time in getting to work on reforms when the opportunity came. Other countries, like Bulgaria and Romania, both new EU member states that were plunged into a decade of political and economic crisis when the Iron Curtain was lifted, necessarily lag behind on reforms.

In addition, many countries themselves have a marked north–south divide: In the north (Sweden, Finland, the UK) and in Germany the southern regions tend to be better off in relation to the other regions in their countries.

Very generally speaking, Europe's successful regions are located in an oval area extending from Stockholm and Oslo though London, Paris, and the Alemannic region, including Switzerland and southern Germany, to western Austria. Germany continues to bear the marks of the old border demarcating the east–west political systems. The boundary separates Germany's needy east from its more prosperous west, and here in turn the south ranks appreciably higher than the north. Despite the massive subsidies that have been pumped into Germany's new eastern states, the latter have not yet been able to close the gap on the west. While the capital regions of most countries — the headquarters of major corporations that attract young and qualified persons — tend as a rule to be among these countries' most dynamic and youngest regions, Rome and Berlin in particular have at best an average ranking. The Czech Republic and Slovenia, indeed even the capital regions of Hungary and Slovakia, have better prospects for the future than eastern Germany.

Source: The Berlin Institute – www.berlin-institut.org/selected-studies/europes-demographicfuture.html

SUMMARY

- This chapter is designed to support some of the earlier chapters in the book which provided an outline of the political and economic environment in which governments operate.
- Governments do differ across the world with some operating in systems which hold individuals accountable for their actions and others where the ruling elite have a significant amount of power and protection from criticism and questioning about their policies and actions.

- However, we can generalize to an extent and look at some basic economic and non-economic objectives that most governments will have. These two sets of objectives are closely interlinked. If policies can be adopted which improve incentives through the reform of tax systems then economic growth might increase which helps to boost employment and reduce unemployment.
- Readers should note, therefore, that whilst the book presents these objectives discretely, in reality they are all highly connected.
- In addition, stating an objective is one thing, achieving them without causing problems or affecting other objectives is extremely difficult. Faster economic growth might help reduce unemployment but it might also lead to inflationary pressures building up.
- To achieve these objectives, governments (or their nominated agents such as central banks) adopt three main types of economic policy: fiscal, monetary and supply-side.
- In most cases these policies will not be used in isolation but together in an attempt to achieve objectives.
- Some governments place more of a reliance on one policy than another invariably determined by their political and economic affiliations but we can generalize to say that after the financial crisis all three policies need to be utilized in a coordinated manner to help steer the economy through difficult periods and achieve objectives.
- Finally we took a brief overview of some of the issues facing governments in deciding appropriate regulatory frameworks to help protect stakeholders from potential market failure and also how competition laws and policy targets key areas of abuse of market power.

REVISION QUESTIONS

1. State six key roles of government in the political and economic environment – three from the political and three from the economic.
2. Explain why:
   a. Economic growth
   b. Control of inflation and
   c. Reducing unemployment are key economic objectives of government.
3. Identify and briefly outline four non-economic objectives of government.
4. Using the four non-economic objectives you have outlined above, explain how the three main economic objectives of government can directly and indirectly influence these four non-economic objectives.
5. Analyze how a cut in taxation and interest rates could lead to an expansion of economic growth.
6. Explain how cuts in taxation might lead to an increase in productivity and in the rate of business start-ups (hint, you might need to think about what sort of taxation is being cut).
7. Explain the difference between regulation and self-regulation.
8. Evaluate the merits of regulation as it applies to an industry of your choice.
9. Describe the key objectives of competition policy and laws.
10. To what extent are globalization and liberalization important in the development of more consistent competition policy and laws across the world?

DISCUSSION QUESTIONS

1. Achieving all a government's economic goals at any one time is impossible. Do you agree with this statement? Explain your reasoning.
2. Distinctions between economic and non-economic objectives are irrelevant – they are all economic. Explain.

3. A target of boosting economic growth is at odds with a desire to cut carbon emissions. Explain why this statement may be a) true and b) false.

4. Self-regulation will never be an effective means of regulating any industry. To what extent do you agree with this statement?

5. The fact that there has to be competition laws shows that market failure is pervasive and implies a greater role for government. Do you agree?

REFERENCES AND FURTHER READING

Tullock, G., Seddon, A., Brady, G.L. and Seldon, A. (2002) *Government Failure: A Primer in Public Choice.* Cato Institute

Kingston, S. (2011) *Greening EU Competition Law and Policy.* Cambridge University Press

Lyons, B. (Ed). (2009) *Cases in European Competition Policy.* Cambridge University Press

Mankiw and Taylor (2011) *Economics* (2e). Cengage Learning, Chapters 33, 34 and 35

Chamberlin, G. and Yueh, L. (2006) *Macroeconomics.* Cengage Learning

GLOSSARY

Efficiency Where maximum output is obtained through using minimum resources in production

Fiscal Policy The manipulation of government income and expenditure to influence economic activity and achieve various desired economic and non-economic objectives

Full Employment A level of output (national income) at which everyone who wants to work is able to find a job

Merit Goods Goods that are deemed beneficial to society as a whole which could be provided by a market system but which would be under-consumed by the public at large as a result

Monetary Policy The process of influencing the price of and supply of money in circulation to influence economic activity and bring about desired objectives

Poverty Line A level of income below which a family is considered to be in poverty measured by earnings less than 60 per cent of median income

Productivity The output per period of time of a factor of production

Public Goods Goods that are neither excludable nor rival

Unemployment Those people of working age who are out of work and actively seeking employment

CHAPTER CASE STUDY

Too many cooks

By Emma Cosgrove

October 2011

Who's carrying the can over Lebanon's food policy?

Stated with as much trepidation as is needed vis-à-vis any remark regarding an undertaking dependent on the Lebanese government, it is reasonable to assume that there will be a food safety law on the books shortly. And where food safety is concerned, Lebanon has nowhere to go but up.

Currently, the duties performed in other countries by a central body, such as the United States Food and Drug Administration, are being done by a plethora of different ministries with several layers of authority that overlap and collide in a manner that perhaps only Lebanese legislation could have conjured up.

Even industry players and government employees will say that the duties of ensuring food safety are so sporadically spread throughout the ministries of health, agriculture, interior, industry and economy and trade that coordination is next to impossible. Furthermore, the funds and skilled manpower needed to support activities such as testing products for labeling accuracy are next to nil. The food safety law, which is currently undergoing a revision by several ministers – who have already had at least one extraordinary cross-ministerial meeting as Executive goes to print – creates just such an authority.

'In Lebanon in particular [an independent authority] is really important because, the way that it is now, the responsibilities are fragmented among all of the ministers,' said Zeina Kassaify, professor of nutrition and food sciences at the American University of Beirut and president of the Lebanese Association for Food Safety.

The Lebanese Food Safety Authority will theoretically be able to function unhindered by the territorial posturing of the ministries and the glacial pace of cabinet decisions.

Unified authority

The authority will have jurisdiction over the farming, production, makeup, packaging and storage of all food items produced or distributed in Lebanon where and whenever their safety is of concern. The authority will also have control over labeling requirements and investigations into the accuracy of labelling, and will also be in charge of inspecting the supply chains of operators and ensuring that proper records are kept.

The food safety authority will also have the opportunity to make regulations regarding genetically modified food – a controversial issue in Europe and the United States and a legislatively nebulous one in Lebanon.

Advising the authority will be a council of experts from public and private sector organizations such as the Lebanese Standards Institution, the Federation of Lebanese Chambers of Commerce and the Consumer Protection Association.

The authority will be governed by a managing board made up of experts from a variety of existing government offices, which points to perhaps the most radical and the most important structural element of the food safety authority: it belongs to no ministry. The authority falls under the tutelage of the Council of Ministers and receives an allocation in the government's budget just like any ministry, although it is not subject to oversight by the Civil Service Board or the Central Inspection Board as per the initial draft law.

Though this arrangement may be a good thing where autonomy is concerned, the authority is also at the mercy of the Council of Ministers' leisurely decision-making schedule, as any measure must be ratified by decree from the Council of Ministers.

The designers of this law have, however, kept emergencies in mind and given the authority the power to take immediate decisions regarding item recalls and import restrictions during times of crisis. These decisions need only be alerted to the Council of Ministers.

Kassaify describes the authority in these cases as a facilitator, linking the ministries under one authority, assigning response work and coordinating information from each ministry.

'An outbreak is not just people getting sick. You have to go follow the source, you have to see who is responsible, you have to go and close down places, you have to follow it in the courts and you have to prevent things from happening again,' she said.

An unknown quantity

If the scheme sounds like it will shake things up within some ministries, it will. And there has been a marked amount of pushback from related ministers who believe that they are losing power and influence by forfeiting some of their responsibilities. As Executive went to print, these very ministers were making changes, and only when the law is resubmitted to the Council of Ministers and then moves on to Parliament will we know if its spirit has remained intact.

Kassaify, who was not consulted in the drafting of the law, was a supporter of the original scheme, but is wary about the most recent round of changes and said she could not throw her support behind the new version until she has seen it.

Guidelines and regulations for individual sectors and distribution points will be decided by the authority's many departments if the original scheme survives, and though the formation of the authority will be a good sign, these will show how serious the government is about making Lebanon a safer place to eat.

Source: www.zawya.com/story.cfm/sidZAWYA20111018083633/Too_many_cooks © Executive 2011 Contribute to Zawya Select

Questions

- Why do governments set up and administer food safety laws and regulation?
- The case study suggests that different parts of government in Lebanon have differing degrees of responsibility for food safety. What problems might this present and how would you advise the Lebanese government solve these problems?
- 'The Lebanese Food Safety Authority will theoretically be able to function unhindered by the territorial posturing of the ministries and the glacial pace of cabinet decisions'. What do you think Zeina Kassaify means by this comment?
- Why are 'proper records' across the supply chain for food an important aspect of regulation?
- Does the situation in Lebanon prior to the planned unification in the law highlight the fact that the market mechanism is more likely to fail than to be an efficient allocator of resources?
- Are laws or regulation the most effective way of protecting public health and advancing food safety standards in a country like Lebanon?

13
INTERNATIONAL
MARKETS & GLOBALIZATION

LEARNING OBJECTIVES:

1   Explain what is meant by globalization, discussing the globalization process, drivers and trends

2   Evaluate how global forces shape the national (PESTLE) environment

3   Examine how organizations may respond (strategically) to the challenges and opportunities presented through globalization

4   Evaluate globalization from a multiple stakeholder perspective, identifying the 'winners' and 'losers'

5   Explain what is meant by internationalization, commenting on alternative market entry methods

6   Discuss the classification of multinationals, describing the multidomestic organization, global company and transnational enterprise (TNE)

FIGURE 13.1

International markets & globalization mind map

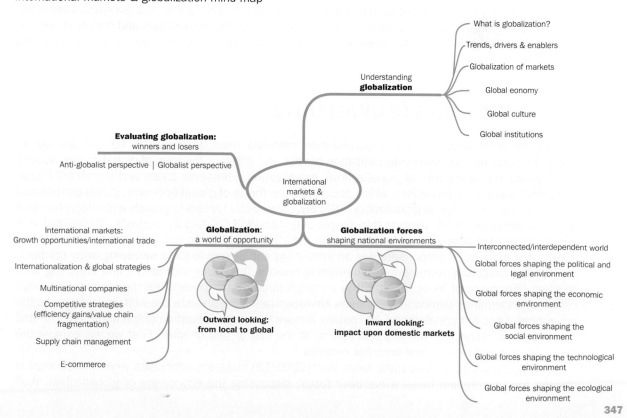

347

KEY CONCEPTS

Geographic scope | Global culture | Globalization | Interconnectedness | Interdependence | Multidomestic organization

INTRODUCTION

Globalization, a process that gained momentum throughout the latter part of the 20th century now seems to touch and impact upon every person worldwide and every type of business activity in all sizes of organization. More importantly, in the context of this textbook, its forces play an increasingly significant role in shaping national business environments. Furthermore, such forces may manifest as threats and opportunities. Threats in terms of increased competition, challenges in terms of constraints posed through legislation, codes and standards and opportunities for growth and efficiency gains. Undoubtedly there are winners and losers, advantages and disadvantages, supporters and critics. Globalization is about the interconnectedness and interdependence between people, organizations and governments. It has been facilitated by technology, political and economic integration, international trade and the motivation of consumers, investors, politicians, workers, tourists and a range of people throughout the world. See Figure 13.1.

Globalization is a complex concept which we seek to explain in the first section of this chapter. Having explored the concept from a number of perspectives we then evaluate how it is shaping the national environment where businesses may operate. The forces behind globalization are many and varied; globalization is a supranational concept whose forces influence the political, economic, social, technical, legal and ecological and environmental factors discussed during this book. Throughout the chapter we will evaluate whether globalization is associated with the homogenization of markets and cultures and the harmonization of political and economic systems. We will also consider the implications for business in terms of standardization and differentiation. Having considered the impact upon an organization's domestic (national) environment, particularly in terms of threats and new challenges, in the third section of this chapter we evaluate globalization as an opportunity for organizations to expand and achieve efficiency gains. Not everyone shares the same view of globalization so in the final section we evaluate the advantages and disadvantages of globalization. Taking a multiple stakeholder perspective we review the opinions of critics and supporters alike.

UNDERSTANDING GLOBALIZATION

One of the main questions most globalization theorists have dealt with is how to provide an adequate classification and systematization of vast and different theories of globalization. According to globalists (advocates of globalization), globalization represents a real and significant historical process without a precedent, which generates new forms of global economy, global politics and global culture. What then is globalization? Simply, globalization refers to growth and integration to a global or worldwide scale. Despite this simple definition Wolf (2005:13) suggests, 'Globalization is a hideous word of obscure meaning, coined in the 1960s, and came into ever greater vogue in the 1990s. For many of its proponents it is an irresistible and desirable force sweeping away frontiers, overturning despotic governments, undermining taxation, liberating individuals and enriching all it touches.' For many of its opponents it is a malign force that impoverishes the masses, destroys cultures, undermines democracy, imposes Americanization, lays waste the welfare state, ruins the environment and enthrones greed. We outline a more thorough evaluation of the arguments for and against globalization, the winners and losers, at the end of this chapter. First we will explore the meaning of this 'hideous' and complex concept.

Defining globalization is no trivial task. Wolf (2005:13) suggests difficulties when the concept is defined too broadly and takes a narrower focus, discussing the economics of globalization. Wolf believes the simplest of all definitions comes from Anne Krueger (the first deputy Managing Director of the IMF) who, in 2000, defined globalization as: 'a phenomena by which economic agents in any given part of the world are much more affected by events elsewhere in the world' than before. Wolf offers a more 'technically precise version of this process: the integration of economic activities, across borders, through markets'. Others have defined globalization as the free movement of goods, services, labour and capital thereby creating a single market in inputs and outputs; and full national treatment of foreign investors so that economically speaking there are no foreigners. Brink Lindsey defined (Liberal) globalization in relation to increasing integration of markets across political boundaries, falling government-imposed barriers to international goods, services and capital and the global spread of market-oriented policies. This definition emphasizes what we are talking about is movement in the direction of greater integration (a process), as both natural and man-made barriers to international economic exchange continue to fall. Wolf argues a necessary consequence of such a process of integration is the increased impact of economic changes in one part of the world on what happens in the others. A possible endpoint for such a process might be a world with no policy barriers to the movement of goods, services, information, capital or people.

As was mentioned above, many describe globalization as a process. Goldin and Reinert (2012:5) present an historical overview of globalization (summarized by ourselves in Figure 13.2 the process of globalization). They describe three main stages commencing in 1870. The first stage (the birth of the modern world economy) continued until 1914 and was characterized by the global integration of capital markets. Punctuated by two world wars and the Great Depression, the second stage followed in the late 1940s. The period between stages one and two witnessed a reversal of many aspects of globalization, with increased nationalism and conflict. The second stage began with the establishment of the IMF, what was to become the World Bank, and the General Agreement on Tariffs and Trade (GATT). During this stage, capital flowed from the United States as did various management theories and practices which relied upon economies of scale in

FIGURE 13.2

The process of globalization

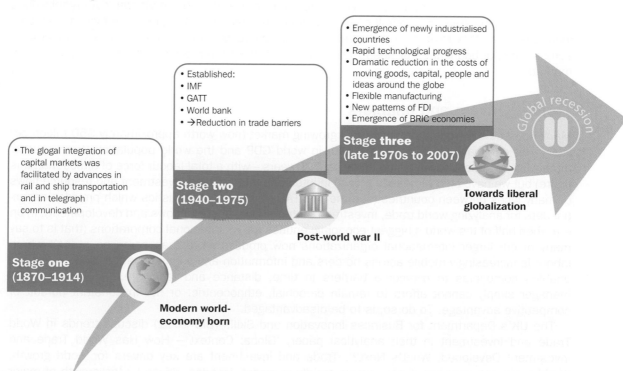

manufacturing. There were reductions in trade barriers and resultant increases in exports and imports as a result of liberalization. The third 'modern stage globalization' began in the late 1970s. The newly industrialized countries of East Asia emerged and rapid technological progress was witnessed. This led to a dramatic lowering of the costs of moving goods, capital, people and ideas across the globe. New flexible manufacturing technologies meant that firms relied less on economies of scale. In this stage, Japan emerged as an important, new source of foreign direct investment (FDI) and a new set of developing economies emerged (see for example Brazil, Russia, India and China). This third stage came to an end with crisis in the form of the global recession in 2008.

Thus, globalization – the opposite of protectionism (policies reflecting the belief that domestic manufacturers and workers need to be safeguarded from foreign competition) – refers to the growing interdependency between nations and organizations through international trade and factor mobility (integration). As can be seen from previous paragraphs, a variety of meanings have been attached to the concept. For some it is the extension of operational supply chains to cover the whole world; a trend away from distinct national economic units and towards one huge global market; the increase of international trading and shared social and cultural values, and the intensification of worldwide social and business relationships which link distant localities in such a way that local happenings are shaped by distant events, and vice versa. Globalization and the globalization process mean different things to different people. Many have discussed the concept of cultural globalization, i.e. whether there is a global culture or set of universal cultural variables; economic globalization considers the increased interdependence of national economies and the trend towards greater integration of goods, labour and capital markets; geographical globalization refers to the idea of compressed time and space as a result of reduced travel times between locations and the rapid (electronic) exchange of information. Knowledge and production previously confined to certain geographical areas may now cross borders and be made available because of the rapid transfer of information and transport innovations. Consequently some argue that location no longer matters. Despite this, others argue that geography is becoming more, not less, important. Institutional globalization is typified through organizations such as the international Monetary Fund (IMF), World Bank and World Trade Organization (WTO) which seek to make markets more flexible and demolish international barriers to trade. Scholars also discuss the concept of political globalization and the relationship between the power of markets and multinational organizations versus the nation state. As a result of globalization, the international organization faces the global–local dilemma. This relates to the extent to which products and services may be standardized across national boundaries or need to be adapted to meet the requirements of specific national markets.

Trends, drivers and enablers

Many now see the world as a single and growing market (now worth approximately $50 trillion per year). Not only have we witnessed growth in world GDP and the world population (from approximately five to almost seven billion in the past 20 years – with a total labour force of almost half this figure) but we have also witnessed growth in international trade and investment and resource flows of many types between countries (see the UNCTAD Handbook of Statistics which provides essential data for analyzing world trade, investment, international financial flows and development). In an era when half of the world's biggest economic entities are multinational corporations (that is to say many of our larger international organizations now produce more than some countries); where labour is increasingly mobile across borders and information and communication technology (ICT) enables companies to overcome barriers in time, distance and language, the contemporary manager simply cannot afford to remain parochial, ethnocentric, or not in constant pursuit of competitive advantage. To do so, is to be disadvantaged.

The UK's Department for Business Innovation and Skills (BIS 2011) discuss trends in World Trade and Investment in their analytical paper, 'Global Context – How Has World Trade and Investment Developed, What's Next?'. Trade and investment are key drivers for world growth. World trade and investment have grown rapidly in recent decades, driven by the growth of major emerging markets, rising incomes, greater taste for variety, enhanced integration of the world economy, especially the growth in global supply chains, continuing trade liberalization and reductions in communication and transportation costs. Whilst there has been a rapid expansion in trade and investment, growth has not been uniform. Developed countries still account for the majority share of trade and investment, but the most rapidly growing suppliers of exports have been emerging markets including much of Asia, but also less widely recognized successes in Africa, South America and Central and Eastern Europe. The crisis to the global economy caused a sharp fall in world trade, the worst fall since the Great Depression. At the worst point, in early 2009, exports of goods by the leading economies had fallen by a third compared with a year earlier. Even after a recovery started later in 2009, the value of exports still ended 23 per cent lower in 2009 compared with 2008 (see Figure 13.3). Over time there are likely to be significant changes to the distribution of global wealth, growth and trade. Emerging markets, especially China and India, but also many other emerging and developing countries will contribute a far greater share of global trade and wealth. Firms will need to adjust to these shifts.

Although exports by developed countries have been increasing, their share of world exports of goods has been falling. All members of the OECD, except Turkey, have seen their share of world exports decline. This reflects the rapid export growth of major emerging markets, such as China, but also the significant growth in many other emerging and developing countries, in Africa, Latin America and Central and Eastern Europe as well as in Asia. One of the outcomes of international investment is that much trade is now carried out within multinational firms, (BIS 2011). The majority of employment of foreign affiliates is now located in emerging or developing economies and China now hosts the largest number of employees. There has been an increase in the proportion of multinationals based in emerging markets. In 2008 more than a quarter of the 82 000 multinationals counted by UNCTAD came from non-developed countries. They account for nearly one tenth of the foreign sales and foreign assets of the top 5000 multinationals in the world, compared with only 1–2 per cent in 1995.

FIGURE 13.3

Growth of export trade: values and shares of merchandise exports and imports, shows the value of total merchandise exports by geographical region, economic grouping

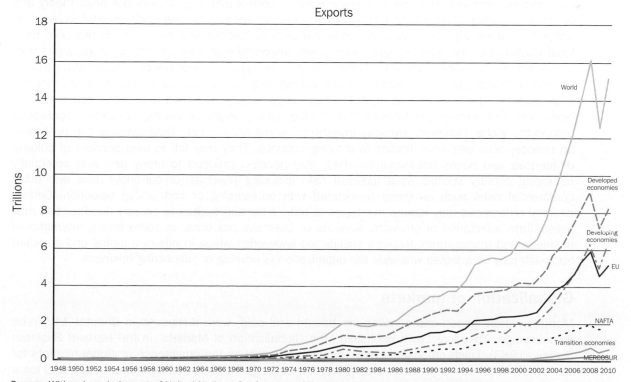

Source: With acknowledgment of United Nations Conference of Trade and Development (UNCTAD 2012)

As can be seen from Figure 13.3, there has been significant growth in international trade over the past three decades. Cross border trade now amounts to over $15 Trillion. However, it is not just goods and services that flow between countries, so too do finances, people, technology, knowledge and other resources. Consumers and investors not only buy and sell across country boundaries but also invest in other countries, see foreign direct investment (FDI). Organizations undertake FDI for a variety of reasons such as setting up offices, manufacturing, operations and distribution facilities. Additionally, in some cases, trade takes place using electronic channels (see e-business/commerce). Online shopping is now valued in the $ trillions; not surprising when we consider there to be over two billion Internet users worldwide (www.internetworldstats.com/stats.htm). At this point, we might ask why international business has grown so much over the past 30 years. There are many explanations for the growth of international business. The (social, political and economic) pursuit of 'free trade' has also eroded barriers and borders. This has been further enabled through the wide scale adoption of ('open') Information and communication technologies which enable trade, communication and collaboration – eroding barriers in time, space and language and integrating financial, political and legal systems. Liberalization has not only resulted in increased mobility of people as workers and migrants but also in the movement of capital, goods and services. Consumers want choice, quality and low-cost products sourced from around the world. E-commerce and the MNC now bring the world to the doorsteps of businesses and consumers everywhere. With the phenomenal growth of E-Commerce, anyone can be open for business on an international level 24 hours a day, no matter where the business is physically located. In other words, one location can serve the business needs over the entire globe.

Companies may now not only import and export more easily but can also establish their operations overseas. There has been a rapid growth by Transnational Corporations (TNCs) in the production of goods and services outside their home countries. The majority of the 'top' 500 global companies are headquartered in America, Europe and Japan (the Triad). However, the whole shape of international business is evolving. For example, developing economies now produce almost half of the world's outputs. Organizations now source, manufacture, market and conduct value adding activities on an international scale. This poses new management challenges and necessitates the rise of the international manager or manager within an international organization who can acquire the requisite business knowledge and skills to enable the organization to perform in our ever-increasing globalized business environment. Not only is there a need to understand international business theory and practice, because international business activities are increasing, but there is also a need to understand domestic business since international organizations and their subsidiaries also have local challenges. The number, size, activity and importance of international organizations are of significant and growing importance. However, it is not just the multinational corporation that is embracing global opportunity; international business may now be conducted by small and medium enterprises. In some cases organizations may simply engage in import and export activities from home, enabled through the Internet and in other cases organizations may establish operations around the globe. However, overseas investment is not without risk. Organizations can behave in an unacceptable way when trading in a foreign country. They may fail to take account of cultural differences and needs (cross-cultural risk), may become exposed to many new and potentially damaging country specific risks (political risk) including financial (or currency) risks and other commercial risks such as those associated with outsourcing or partnership selection. Certain national differences may require managers to tailor their approaches to country needs – this may necessitate adaptation of products, services or business practices. In some areas, international business and management requires specialized knowledge whilst in others a global and standard approach may be adopted wherever the organization is working or conducting business.

Globalization of markets

Markets, where goods and services are bought and sold, were discussed in Chapter 11. Three decades ago, Theodore Levitt published 'The Globalization of Markets' in the *Harvard Business Review* (1983). Levitt proposed a new commercial reality as the emergence of global markets for standardized consumer products on a previously unimagined scale of magnitude. 'A powerful force drives the world toward a converging commonality, and that force is technology,' Levitt (1983).

Technology, by proletarianizing communication, transport, and travel, drives the world toward a converging commonality. Well-managed companies have moved from emphasis on customizing items to offering globally standardized products that are advanced, functional, reliable and low priced. They benefit from enormous economies of scale in production, distribution, marketing and management. He argued companies must learn to operate as if the world were one large market – ignoring superficial regional and national differences. According to Levitt, back in 1983, the globalization of markets was at hand. With that, he predicted, the multinational commercial world nears its end; and so does the multinational corporation. The multinational and the global corporation are not the same thing. The multinational corporation operates in a number of countries, and adjusts its products and practices in each – at high relative costs. The global corporation operates with resolute constancy – at low relative cost – as if the entire world (or major regions of it) were a single entity; it sells the same things in the same way everywhere. Levitt was discussing two different strategies, a matter we explore later in this chapter. More recently Abdelal and Tedlow (2003) acknowledged Theodore Levitt was one of the first scholars to write a high-impact article on globalization aimed at business managers. Decades later, 'The Globalization of Markets' is still widely read, they wrote. Rather than agreeing with Levitt, however, most observers believe that his arguments are flawed and many of his predictions have not been borne out. The era of the 'multinational corporation' was drawing to a close, Levitt asserted. However, this has not proven to be true. Despite this, there are many global companies, in support of some of Levitt's predictions. The future belonged to the 'global corporation'. The global corporation did not cater for local differences in taste. The global corporation was being called forth by a new era of 'homogenized demand'. Abdelal and Tedlow (2003) discuss ways to think about globalization. They suggest that we can think about globalization as an actual process of economic integration – the acceleration of flows of goods and capital, and perhaps many other things as well. In this sense, there may exist not a single globalization process, but many linked processes of globalization, each of which demands an answer to the question: 'The globalization of what?' Thus, we hear and read about the globalization of finance, of trade, of policy ideas, of culture, of almost anything. This is perhaps the most common way people think and talk about globalization, and it is useful.

So what is meant by the term the 'globalization of markets'? For many the globalization of markets means the expansion and access of businesses to reach the needs of customers worldwide. It may be described as the moving away from an economic system in which national markets are distinct entities, isolated by trade barriers and barriers of distance, time, and culture, and towards a system in which national markets are merging into one global market. In the next two sections we explore further the aspects of economic and cultural integration.

Global economy

When the term *economy* is discussed it refers to the wealth and resources of a country or region, generally in terms of the production and consumption of goods and services (see Chapter 3). An economy consists of the economic system of a country or other area (the structure a nation or society uses to meet the problem of scarcity e.g. Market Economy – based on private ownership of property with little inference from government regulation, or Command Economy – the state directs the economy); the labour, capital and land resources; and the manufacturing, trade, distribution, and consumption of goods and services of that area. Economic activity refers to actions that involve the production, distribution and consumption of goods and services at all levels within a society. The term Global economy is used to describe an integrated world economy with unrestricted and free movement of goods, services and labour transnationally. The economies of most of the world's nations have become increasingly interconnected. International economic activity includes the world-wide integration of markets for goods, services, labour and capital. Thus the global economy can be considered as economic activity spanning many nations of the world, with little regard for national borders. Some consider the development of an increasingly integrated global economy, marked especially by free trade, free flow of capital, and the utilization of cheaper foreign labour markets as the definition of globalization, see for example the Merriam-Webster Dictionary.

'Sweeping changes are afoot in the global economy. As the second decade of the 21st century unfolds and the world exits from the 2008–09 financial crisis, the growing clout of emerging markets is paving the way for a world economy with an increasingly multipolar character. The distribution of global growth will become more diffuse, with no single country dominating the global economic scene.' Authors of the publication 'Global Development Horizons 2011' (World Bank, 2011) project that today's emerging economies will grow, on average, by 4.7 per cent a year between 2011 and 2025 and their share of global GDP will expand from 36 per cent to 45 per cent. Advanced economies, meanwhile, are forecast to grow by 2.3 per cent over the same period, yet will remain prominent in the global economy, with the euro area, Japan, the United Kingdom, and the United States all playing a core role in supporting the global economic engine. By 2025, six major emerging economies – Brazil, China, India, Indonesia, South Korea, and Russia – will account for more than half of all global growth and the international monetary system will no longer be dominated by a single currency. As economic power shifts, these successful economies will help drive growth in lower income countries through cross-border commercial and financial transactions. Over the past two decades, the world has witnessed emerging economies rise to become a powerful force in international production, trade and finance. There has been a steady rise in the share of international trade flows by developing countries, from 30 per cent in 1995 to an estimated 45 per cent in 2010. Much of this rise has been due to an expansion of trade not between developed countries and developing countries, but amongst developing countries. Similarly, more than one-third of foreign direct investment in developing countries currently originates in other developing countries. The Industrial Revolution brought Western European economies to the forefront. In the post-World War II era, the United States was the predominant force in the global economy, with Germany and Japan also playing leading roles. In more recent years, the global economy has begun yet another major transition, one in which economic influence has clearly become more dispersed than at any time since the late 1960s.

Globalization and culture

Whilst Levitt implied the emergence of a global culture, Hofstede (1984), writing at the same time dismissed the idea. Hofstede widely regarded as a pioneer of (national) cultural studies, commented on worldwide trends. He acknowledged that technology plays an important role as a force towards change (Hofstede 1984:233). 'As all countries are gradually exposed to the products of the same scientific discoveries in the form of modern technology, and as these play an important role in culture change, some authors have concluded that all societies will become more and more similar. In the "comparative management" literature of the 1960s we find the "convergency theory" which implies that management philosophy and practice around the world will become more and more alike. However, whilst technological modernization leads to partly similar developments in different societies, "it does not wipe out differences among societies and may even enlarge them".' (Hofstede 1984:234).

BUSINESS IN ACTION

Forbidden City: Starbucks 'tramples over Chinese culture'

Beijing's Forbidden City palace considered closing a Starbucks on its grounds after protests led by a state TV personality who said the presence of the American coffeehouse was eroding Chinese culture...

In January 2007 an online campaign against Starbucks was started by blogger Rui Chenggang who said, 'The Forbidden City is a symbol of China's cultural heritage. Starbucks is a symbol of lower middle class culture in the West. We need to embrace the world, but we also need to preserve our cultural identity. There is a fine line between globalization and contamination.'

Chiu *et al.* (2011) investigate the social and cultural implications of globalization – how people make sense of and respond to globalization and its sociocultural ramifications; and how people defend the integrity of their heritage cultural identities against the 'culturally erosive' effects of globalization. They commence their article by defining globalization broadly as a process of *interaction* and *integration* amongst the peoples, companies, and governments of different nations. This process is driven by international trade and investment and aided by information technology. Globalization has led to rapid diffusion of economic, political and cultural practices across national borders, creating optimism in global acceptance of the finest universal values of humanity as well as fear of erosion of local cultural traditions. Globalization has fuelled economic developments in both developed and developing countries, but has also intensified both positive and negative interdependence amongst national and religious cultures. 'Globalization has transformed the cultures and life practices in all countries', they argue. Chiu *et al.* (2011) then discuss the Cultural and Intercultural Implications of globalization. With the advancement of globalization, many people have experienced an increase in the frequency and intensity of exposure to other cultures. Globalization has resulted in experiential compression of time and space; people in global cities frequently experience traditional and modern cultures (and their symbols) at the same time and cultures (and their symbols) from different geographical regions in the same space. Social scientists have different views on the possible cultural impacts of globalization. Some writers believe that exposure to foreign cultures is a profoundly enriching process that opens minds to new experiences, removes cultural barriers, strengthens the cultural diffusion of human rights and democracy, and accelerates cultural change. These writers envision the emergence of a multicultural global village, where people from different nation-states and cultural backgrounds can exchange their ideas and practices freely and appreciate those of others. In contrast, some scholars believe that increased cultural exposure may incite parochial and exclusionary resistance against foreign cultures, as well as collective movements that aim at reaffirming local cultures. These reactions, according to some, could lead to conflict. For example, there are concerns in France that American restaurant chains may crowd out French cuisines with fast food. There are also concerns over the massive emigration of US-dominated popular culture (e.g., Hollywood movies) to the world. In some countries, the spread of US popular culture and its attendant American values and beliefs has evoked xenophobic anxieties over and incited nationalistic reactions toward the Americanization of world cultures.

People on the receiving end are often concerned that globalization will ultimately lead to homogenization of cultures. Indeed some writers refer to the 'Global Citizen' (think of themselves as a citizen of the world and not a particular country); yet others discuss global culture – a shared way of thinking throughout the world (people from around the world being more alike than different). Developing countries aspiring to become industrialized nations may treat Western economic powers as reference nations not only in the domain of economic development, but also in the realm of cultural restructuring, argue Chiu *et al.* (2011). Global culture has been characterized as new, modern, scientific and results-oriented. It privileges consumerism, individualism, competition and efficiency. These values may be identified or considered as the values separating advanced societies from economically backward traditional economies. Thus, global culture may become the reference culture for some developing countries that seek to emulate Western economic powers by embracing global values. Consequently, global culture exerts its hegemonic influence on some local cultures via voluntary submission to global culture (van Strien, 1997 cited in Chiu *et al.* (2011)). Furthermore, globalization has brought rapid changes in consumption patterns and the spread of global 'brand-name' goods. An expanding consumerist culture with its attendant global marketing strategies such as global advertising tends to exploit similar basic material desires and create similar lifestyles.

Living in a culturally mixed environment can engender anxiety and discomfort. Fear of global culture's hegemonic influence on the local culture often takes the form of contamination anxiety – the worry that the global culture will contaminate the local culture. Such contamination fear was responsible for the closedown of the Starbucks coffee shop in the Imperial Palace Museum in Beijing in 2007. On the other hand, people are also often willing to appropriate ideas from foreign cultures. Cultural mixing in a global society confers intercultural learning opportunities that invite integrative response, whilst, at the same time, presenting potential identity threats that evoke exclusionary reactions. Some writers have focused on the benefits of globalization, discussing how globalization can enhance creativity and promote a global mind-set or new ethics (e.g., cosmopolitanism). Meanwhile, others have written about the drawbacks of globalization, focusing on negative reactions ranging from fear of cultural erosion to culturocentric xenophobia. As globalization proceeds, individuals are exposed to many novel ideas from other cultures. Thus, globalization can be a profoundly enriching process if people are open to new experiences and willing to learn from other cultures. On the other hand, increased cultural contacts can evoke fear of cultural contamination and erosion.

Writers on globalization and culture identify several possibilities: (1) the preservation of national cultures and difference between nations; (2) the enrichment of national culture but difference between nations continues and (3) the homogenization of national cultures and development of a global culture; essentially one world culture, i.e. the loss of national cultural diversity and the development of one culture to be experienced by all people. From a marketing perspective, this would essentially enable a company to standardize its products and business practices; removing a need to differentiate and be 'local'. It would seem that there can be evidence of each perspective and that, as the process of globalization may not yet have reached its end point, the impact of globalization on national cultures remains in a state of change.

Global institutions

Earlier, see Figure 13.2, we suggested that globalization was an on-going process that could be decomposed into stages over time. In the model presented, stage two was characterized by the creation of several key global institutions; these are organizations with an international membership, scope, or presence. We have seen an emergence of institutions needed to help manage, regulate and police the global marketplace. The institutions have been described in previous chapters of this book and a brief summary is presented here.

- The United Nations (UN), founded in 1945, is committed to maintaining international peace and security, developing friendly relations amongst nations and promoting social progress, better living standards and human rights. Although best known for peacekeeping, peace building, conflict prevention and humanitarian assistance, there are many other ways the UN affects our lives. The organization works on a broad range of fundamental issues, from sustainable development, environment and refugee protection, disaster relief, counter terrorism, disarmament and non-proliferation, to promoting democracy, human rights, gender equality and the advancement of women, governance, economic and social development and international health, expanding food production, and more, in order to achieve its goals and coordinate efforts for a safer world for this and future generations.

- The World Trade Organization (WTO) deals with the global rules of trade between nations. Its main function is to ensure that trade flows as smoothly, predictably and freely as possible (liberalizing trade). The WTO is run by its member governments.

- The International Monetary Fund (IMF) is an organization of 187 countries, working to foster global monetary cooperation, secure financial stability, facilitate international trade, promote high employment and sustainable economic growth, and reduce poverty around the world. The IMF has played a part in shaping the global economy since the end of World War II. The IMF's fundamental mission is to ensure stability in the international economic system.

- The World Bank is a vital source of financial and technical assistance to developing countries around the world.

Throughout this section we have explored several explanations of what is meant by the term globalization. Interestingly, Abdelal and Tedlow (2003) suggest the best tool for managers to understand their markets may be neither globalization nor internationalization. There are other ideas about how best to describe the world economy and the markets that compose it. 'Regionalization', for example, is another lens through which to view markets. Throughout this book we have commented on this concept, with particular attention to the EU. Throughout the remainder of this chapter we continue to explore the concept of globalization. In the next two sections we consider two viewpoints in particular. Firstly we consider the inward looking, domestic perspective and consider how global forces are shaping national environments. Following this we take an outward looking perspective and consider the world of opportunity – how global forces expand an organization's markets.

GLOBALIZATION FORCES: SHAPING NATIONAL ENVIRONMENTS

Goldin and Reinert (2012) define globalization as an increase in the impact of forces, which span national boundaries, on human activities (economic, social, cultural, political, technological or even biological – all of which can interact). We have summarized the relationship between global forces and the national environment in Figure 13.4 Globalization and the national (PESTLE) environment. Indeed, throughout Chapters 2 to 7 of this book we have commented upon how global and regional forces have impacted upon national environments and will highlight key examples in this section. Managers of domestic firms must understand how their local environment is changing as a result of such forces. Whilst, in some cases, such changes may be viewed as challenges or even threats, In the next section we explore the opportunities and benefits globalization may bring to those firms seeking growth through overseas sales or efficiency gains through value chain fragmentation or gains through other aspects of the way they manage their supply chains.

FIGURE 13.4
Globalization and the national (PESTLE) environment

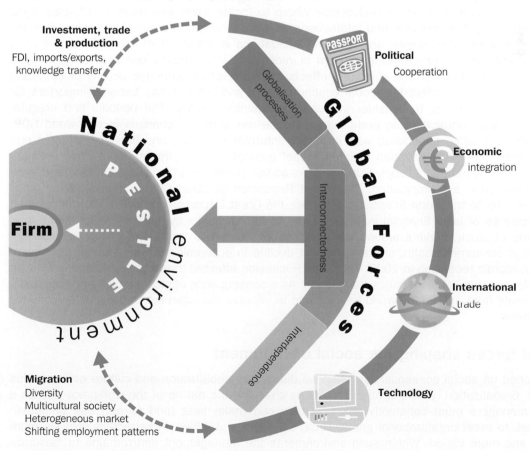

Within Figure 13.4 we emphasize an interconnected /interdependent world. The extent to which the behaviour of one country depends upon others is a matter of Interdependence and the state of being interconnected – connected reciprocally is a worldview which sees a oneness in all things.

Global forces shaping the political and legal environment

In Chapter 2 we noted that whilst it remains important to consider specific governments within particular countries, current political trends seem, especially in Europe, to be moving away from exclusive state and sovereign control to a model of multilevel governance. Under such a model, governance takes place on a number of spatial scales – national, subnational and supranational. In the case of the latter, there is a level of political authority above the nation-state e.g. the European Union (EU). Ever since the Second World War, the European integration *process* has always hesitated between two opinions or two approaches: certain states favour federalism (e.g. Germany) whilst others favour intergovernmentalism (e.g. the UK). The federalists support greater political integration whilst the intergovernmentalists promote economic without political integration. The central component in European integration from a business point of view is the single market, with its 'four freedoms': the free movement of goods, services, capital and people. The EU is not the only supranational organization of which European companies must be aware. The need to be aware of world politics is emphasized by Haynes *et al.* (2010:698) who argue, 'there seems little doubt that governments have become less and less able fully to control events in their states in the face of globalization'.

Global forces shaping the economic environment

Globalization encourages internationalization and the fragmentation of value chains. Firms must examine their primary activities and decide where to locate them worldwide. In Chapter 3 we discussed the global economy and international business cycles. The global economy, like any economy, is affected by regular and recurring fluctuations in the levels of economic activity. If a country's economy is experiencing a boom or recession, its domestic demand for goods and services can be affected. The combined effects on the level of economic activity of individual countries will in turn affect the global economy. More and more it has become important for government economists to consider International business cycles. The periodic and irregular expansions and contractions in world output can be measured by changes in real world GDP. Globalization is often associated with increased international trade and financial linkages and consequently the synchronization of international business cycles. International trade linkages generate both demand and supply-side overflows across countries, which can increase the degree of business cycle synchronisation. The 'Great Recession of 2008–09' is considered by many economists to be the worst financial crisis since the Great Depression of the 1930s. It resulted in the collapse of large financial institutions, the bailout of banks by national governments, and downturns in stock markets around the world. It contributed to the failure of key businesses, declines in consumer wealth, and a significant decline in economic activity, leading to a severe global economic recession in 2008. The Great Recession affected the entire world economy, with higher detriment in some countries than others. As a consequence of global cycles and recession, governments from around the world have sought to improve management of the global economic environment.

Global forces shaping the social environment

We touched on social consequences when we discussed globalization and culture earlier in this chapter. Globalization, amongst other factors, is changing the nature of the workplace and as a result, managers must constantly ask how they can make best (and fairest) use of human resources to meet organizational goals. Today's workforce is older, more racially diverse, more female and more varied. Within such environments the management aim remains to maximize benefits and minimize costs and to enable all workers to achieve their full potential. In Chapter 4, see Figure 4.2, we illustrated the relationship between globalization and the PESTLE factors. Liberalization leads to increased migration and this can lead to changes in the social environment, impacting upon national culture, increasing diversity and introducing the concept of multiculturalism. For example, migration is dependent upon the government's immigration policy – itself swayed by the actions of other governments and in the case of European countries by EC policy. The implications of migration policy for business are then influenced by legal forces in terms of the law. Various equality laws seek to outlaw discriminatory practices. Immigration impacts upon culture, making the society more heterogeneous and multicultural; immigrants bring their values, traditions and cultural practices which may then alter the cultural characteristics of the host country. Migration is the main driver of population growth in most of the EU-27 Member States and plays a significant role in the population dynamics of European societies; in recent years, the increase in the population of the EU-27 Member States has mainly been due to high net migration rates.

Global forces shaping the technological environment

Ultimately, much of research, science and technology manifests as goods, supplied through business to solve everyday living problems, and provide entertainment. Technological diffusion refers to the spreading of new technologies within and between economies. Communication technologies and behaviours impact upon diffusion. For example, the UNESCO Science Report (2010) comments upon the number of Internet users – a variable used to gauge whether easier access to information and knowledge has provided opportunities for a more rapid diffusion of science and technology. The proliferation of digital information and communication technologies is increasingly modifying the global picture. By making codified information accessible worldwide, it is having a dramatic effect on the creation, accumulation and dissemination of knowledge, whilst at the same time providing specialized platforms for networking by scientific communities operating at a global level. A similar concept to diffusion is technology transfer – a process of acquiring technology from another country, especially in manufacturing; whereby skilled workers in the host country are able to learn from the technology of the foreign investor. Globalization has had a significant impact upon technology transfer.

Technological determinism is the view that there is an inevitable direction in which events move. For technological determinists, the cause is technology. According to technological determinists, certain key technologies are the primary movers in developments in organization, the economy or even society itself. Technology (symbolized by the mobile phone and the Internet) has increased our capacity to communicate and access information. This leads to a better informed population. It also has made globalization more difficult to prevent (Wolf 2005:17). However, whilst technology may dictate some aspects of liberalization, Wolf indicates that governments can continue to control the movement of physical things; they can regulate the movement of people and impose barriers upon the movement of capital. Furthermore, transportation costs remain an obstacle to mobility. Wolf suggests that changes in technology and the economy also have complex cultural, social and political effects. Changes in how people are able to earn their living, in what they can buy, in how readily they can move from place to place, in how easily they can transport things, in how they can disseminate and access information and ideas, transform human societies and the individuals who live within them.

Global forces shaping the ecological environment

We examined the sustainable and ecological environment in Chapter 7. Sources of environmental impact, such as globalization, are shown in Figure 7.2. Warming of the climate system is indisputable, as is now evident from observations of increases in global average air and ocean temperatures, widespread melting of snow and ice and rising global average sea level. Climate change is caused by many and impacts upon all countries. The United Nations Framework Convention on Climate Change (UNFCCC) and other global institutions, through agreements, create forces which impact upon regional and national environmental policy. Europeans are feeling the effects of global warming: droughts, floods, heatwaves and forest fires are all becoming more frequent. Such changes are largely the result of billions of tonnes of carbon dioxide (CO_2) released daily into the atmosphere from burning coal, oil and natural gas. These fossil fuels provide us with the energy needed to run cars, heat homes and light offices. However, as a consequence of excessive use of fossil fuels, our environment is, and will continue to suffer, as will our economy and society. The growing evidence of the cost of climate change points to one simple conclusion: 'we cannot afford to do nothing' (European Commission 2009: p7). Earlier in this book we noted that combating climate change is a key priority for the EU. Europe is working hard to cut its greenhouse gas emissions substantially whilst encouraging other nations and regions to do likewise. At the same time, the EU is developing a strategy for adapting to the impacts of climate change which can no longer be prevented. As is the case for all the countries of the EU, the UK has been influenced by global bodies and remains tied to EU policy. Environmental policy is one of the most important and far-reaching areas of EU legislation. The EU is the leading authority in this area, with up to 80 per cent of UK legislation on environmental affairs estimated to derive from the EU. Changes to the Treaty of Rome, agreed in the Treaty of Amsterdam, gave sustainable development a much greater prominence in Europe, by making it a requirement for environmental protection concerns to be integrated with EU policies. In 1999, the UK government outlined how it proposed to deliver sustainable development in 'A Better Quality of Life'. This strategy set out the framework for action to deliver SD in the UK; a vision of simultaneously delivering economic, social and environmental outcomes.

GLOBALIZATION: A WORLD OF OPPORTUNITY

In the previous section we commented on how the domestic environments of business (the PESTLE factors) were being shaped by global forces. In many ways, such changes may be perceived as threatening. Globalization can bring increased competition and costly constraints through legislation, codes or standards. In this section we take an outward perspective and discuss how firms can benefit by penetrating the global marketplace to grow sales and reduce costs. A more complete discussion on the benefits of globalization will be presented at the end of this chapter. Business benefits are clustered around production and the supply chain, investment, sales growth and the pursuit of advantage. Globalization of production refers to the sourcing of goods and services from locations around the globe to take advantage of national differences in the cost and quality of factors of production like land, labour, and capital. Globalization through increased competition forces companies to locate particular operations (activities and resources) in those places where they can be performed most efficiently. Organizations do this by relocating production facilities to other countries or by outsourcing certain activities to companies in other countries. However, globalization and the Internet do not merely benefit the larger organization, they have created unprecedented opportunities for small and medium-sized businesses. Throughout this section we consider the way a firm's strategy may be influenced by globalization.

Internationalization and global strategies

Whereas globalization is a process impacting upon the firm, Internationalization refers to the firm's process of entering foreign markets and exploiting the benefits liberalization brings. Geographical scope describes the multinationality of the organization. Global strategies change the locations from where organizations may purchase inputs, sell outputs to, locate activities performed in the value chain and find intellectual capital. Internationalization is a significant force shaping the competitive environment of business. Internationalization occurs through trade and direct investment and has implications for strategy formulation or formation either in terms of opportunity to expand markets or through the threats posed by overseas competitors. International strategy is concerned with choices about where the organization offers its products and services and where it locates value adding activities. Organizations pursue international strategies for a number of reasons: homogenization of customer demand (globalization) leading to economies of scale, access to different markets for economies of scope and growth and to serve the needs of global customers. By internationalizing, the organization is able to broaden the size of its market. International strategy considers not only where to locate facilities and activities but also how to enter different markets, i.e. the appropriate entry mode (to be discussed later). There are a number of benefits associated with such strategies. Such a strategy should enable efficiency advantages. Firstly there is opportunity to produce more, which may enable economies of scale through both experience and the ability to spread fixed costs over a greater number of units. Secondly there will be scale benefits in the ability to replicate knowledge and technology within the organization. Once created, knowledge can be reused at close to zero cost if it can be transferred. As has already been mentioned, efficiencies may also be gained from locating different activities in different places. Furthermore, organizations may make use of positive cash flows in one region to cross subsidize and invest in another region. However, organizations have fundamentally different views of world markets and these are reflected in strategy. Two broad generic international strategies can be distinguished: (1) the global strategy – assumes a single market and offers a standard product(s) to meet customer needs wherever customers are located. This is essentially a cost leadership strategy, exploiting economies of scale and other cost efficiencies; (2) the multidomestic strategy – assumes variance in customer needs according to their location and therefore issues a differentiation strategy, adapting products and services to meet unique local requirements. The extent to which services may be standardized across national boundaries or need to be adapted to meet specific local requirements is often referred to as the global–local dilemma. In practice, organizations rarely pursue a pure and a single generic strategy and seek out a position between the two. Most large multinational organizations face the need to tailor their product or service to some extent. Whilst there are many benefits to an international strategy such as economies of scale and scope, access to new markets for growth and the exploitation of location advantages, the organization becomes much more complex, requiring more money and time to be spent on coordination, collaboration, communication, formalization and control. Consequently not all organizations benefit from internationalization in the same way and some may not benefit at all.

As was noted, a global strategy is one that views the world as a single market. This means that customers are assumed to be similar across country boundaries and that there is therefore little or no need for differentiation at the country level; consequently, more decisions are likely to be made at the headquarters. However, laws and government regulations, variance in disposable income, national culture and country infrastructure may impact upon products and services and the means by which they are delivered to customers. Global strategies are very much about integration whilst other international business strategies may focus on differentiation. In the case of some products and services there are national differences in customer preferences and as a consequence the organization must consider customer needs in different locations. Products and services must then be designed or adapted to meet those needs. However, in some cases common basic designs and common components can reduce the cost of national differentiation. Flexible manufacturing systems, computer-aided design and manufacture with lean production processes help create customized products at a lower cost. Reconciling conflicting forces for global efficiency and national differentiation represents one of the greatest strategic challenges facing the international or multinational corporation. Many organizations opt for a hybrid approach – one of global localization, i.e. 'glocal' (transnational). In such cases the organization will seek to standardize aspects of the product or service and primary activities where scale economies are substantial and will differentiate where national preferences are strongest. Whether or not the international organization pursues a global or a local strategy will impact upon the organizational structure and management systems (the internal environment of the firm). Business units such as IT, research and development and procurement can be more centralized or at least organized at a global level since it is likely that scale economies can be attained through sharing such resources across the whole organization. The downstream and primary activities of marketing and customer service and the secondary activities associated with human resource management are more likely to reflect local differences. Whilst manufacturing lies somewhere in between, it has strong globalization potential, being located near raw materials, low-cost or highly skilled labour. Whether pursuing a global, multidomestic or glocal strategy, the international organization will establish operations, sales and other facilities in other countries therefore we next consider market entry strategies.

Market-Entry Strategy

As has already been noted in this chapter, globalization is associated with the erosion of country boundaries and this makes the establishment of overseas operations, through FDI, an easier task to accomplish. Having decided which markets to enter, for the majority of organizations, the most significant decision they are likely to make next is how they should enter new markets. In this section we examine the different market entry options open to organizations to enable them to select the most appropriate method for their given situation. There are advantages and disadvantages with each market entry method and critical in the decision-making process is the organizational assessment of the costs and risk associated with each method. There is no ideal market entry strategy and different market entry methods might be adopted by different organizations entering the same market. There are a variety of ways in which organizations can enter foreign markets (for further discussion, see Kelly 2009). The main ways are direct or indirect, marketing only or production in a foreign country. Alternative market entry methods include:

* products are supplied from the organization's domestic operations
* indirect exporting (the simplest and lowest cost method of market entry-products are sold overseas by other organizations)
* direct exporting (the organization becomes directly involved in the presence of exporting)
* products are supplied from the organization's overseas operations
* foreign manufacturing strategies without direct investments (contract manufacturer, franchising and licensing)
* cooperative strategies (joint ventures and strategic alliances)
* foreign manufacturing strategies with direct investment (wholly-owned subsidiary, company acquisitions and mergers)

There are many alternative ways (modes) to enter a new market:

Stage 1: No regular export activities

Stage 2: Export via independent representatives (agents)

Stage 3: Establishment of an overseas sales subsidiary

Stage 4: Overseas production/manufacturing units

Many factors determine the market entry mode such as availability of resources, attitudes to risk, attributes of the served market, product considerations and environmental factors. Market-entry modes can be classified according to whether they require indirect or direct organizational involvement and whether they involve both marketing and production or solely marketing. As the organization becomes more involved in marketing and production, the risk and control of the organization increases. The mode of entry or extent of internationalization is a reflection of the value chain activities, i.e. which are insourced or outsourced, undertaken at the home or served country. With regard to marketing and sales, organizations may simply export from the home country or may establish a foreign sales office. With regard to production they can licence, franchise or contract out production or invest in their own production facility in the target country market (direct foreign investment). There are many choices. Each market entry method reflects a different level of organizational involvement in international operations. The level of involvement has significant implications in terms of levels of risk and control. When deciding on market entry strategy, the organization should ask questions such as:

* what level of control over international business is required?
* what level of risk are we willing to take?
* what cost can we afford?

The market entry strategy should recognize time as a determining factor. The building of marketing information systems, operations, distribution channels and creation of brand awareness through promotion take time, effort and money. Brand names do not appear overnight and large investments in promotion campaigns are needed. In the context of this chapter, the internationalization process not only benefits the firm but also consumers, workers and stakeholders in the value system.

Multinational companies

Approximately half of the world's top 100 economic entities are now companies. So far we have discussed the idea of internationalisation, noting that not all organizations become multinational. However, we should not treat 'multinational' as a simple term. Multinationals are not always the same. The most popular classification of multinationals in the international business literature is probably Bartlett and Ghoshal's (1987) technology of strategic postures: global, multi-domestic and transnational. Multinationals may be:

- **Global companies** which promote a convergence of consumer's preferences and strive to maximize standardization of production, which makes centralization and integration profitable. They benefit from home country specific advantages and export these abroad by creating replicas of the parent company. Strategic decisions on marketing and production tunnel down to the subsidiaries, so that the latter have little discretion to adapt to local circumstances. Global companies possess firm-specific advantages, mostly characterized by home country specificities that do not need to be complemented by the exploration of the host country advantages. These firm specific advantages are therefore not bound to a particular host location and artificially transferable to foreign locations, thus overcoming any natural or unnatural market imperfections in foreign markets. In short, the global MNC sees the world as a single market with little need to differentiate, wherever it operates. The focus is on integration as opposed to differentiation.

- **Multidomestic organizations**, by contrast, develop strategies for national responsiveness. Due to significant competitive differences between countries, the multidomestic strategy is determined by cultural, political and social national characteristics. The primary objective is the adapting of marketing and production strategies to specific local customer needs and government requirements. Products and policies conform to different local demands and the investor activities are usually tied to the buyer's location, which create incentives for the development of competitive advantages that are bound to a particular location. Responsiveness to different national markets requires the relation of a local country specific knowledge and the latter's efficient integration into local business networks. Whereas the global MNC is logically a single entity, the multidomestic is a collection of 'companies' each focused on the specific needs of the country within which they operate.

- **Transnational enterprises (TNE)** operate a balanced combination of the multidomestic and global strategies. Although activities and resources may differ from country to country (decentralization), particular activities are coordinated and executed globally (centralization). For example, a transnational enterprise might decide to carry out research and development centrally to make economies of scale and scope, but to organize local tailor-made advertising campaigns to guarantee a fit with national circumstances.

Multinational organizations have the opportunity to benefit from the comparative advantage of different countries, be they technology driven or factor abundance driven, to reduce the total costs of production, particularly through the ever more popular method of fragmentation (slicing up the value chain) in which different parts (activities) of the production process are located in different countries.

Supply chain management

The supply chain is a network of manufacturers and service providers who work together to convert and move goods from the raw materials stage through to the end user. These manufacturers and service providers are linked together through physical, information and monetary flows. Supply chain management (SCM) involves the active management of supply chain activities and relationships in order to maximize customer value and achieve a sustainable competitive advantage. It represents a conscious effort by an organization or group of organizations to develop and run supply chains in the most effective and efficient way possible. Internationalization, globalization and increasing competition has amplified the importance of SCM to managers working within international organizations. Major SCM activities include: running overseas plants or coordinating international activities, selection of transformation processes; forecasting; capacity planning; inventory management; planning and control, purchasing and logistics. From a practical standpoint, one of the attractions of developing international operations is the low labour cost available in many of the less developed nations. However, the low labour cost is not enough to offset the low labour productivity in some of these nations. Extremely low wages do not offset the differences in labour productivity in some of the reforming economies. This would suggest that to be an effective international operations manager, a sophisticated understanding of international differences is essential. The objectives of supply chain management (SCM) include (1) maximize efficiency and effectiveness of the total supply chain for all players and (2) maximize the opportunity for customer purchase by ensuring adequate stock levels at all stages of the process. Internet and associated technologies are vital to SCM since managing relationships with customers, suppliers and intermediaries is based on the flow of information and the transactions between these parties. Organizations seek to enhance the supply chain in order to provide a superior value proposition (quality, service, price and fulfilment times), which they do by emphasizing cost reduction, increased efficiency and consequently increased profitability. Not only can we conceive of the supply chain as an opportunity to increase profits, it may also be viewed as a sequence of events intended to satisfy customers. Typically, it will involve procurement, manufacture, and distribution, together with associated transport, storage and information technology.

Technology: Global Digital Business

International businesses today compete in two worlds: a physical world of resources (marketplace) and a virtual world of information (marketspace). The latter has given rise to the world of electronic commerce (EC) and e-business (EB), a new locus of value creation. Managers must now focus upon how their companies create value and wealth in both the physical and virtual worlds. International organizations may buy raw materials from one country, use finances from another country, procure human resources from yet another country, and sell the finished products in whichever location is possible in order to achieve or sustain competitive advantage; such activities may be accomplished in either worlds. However, the processes for creating value are not the same in both the physical and electronic world. In thinking about economic value, it is useful to draw a distinction between the uses of the Internet (such as buying and selling) and Internet technologies (such as communication networks and platforms which support interoperability), which can be deployed across many uses and in support of several key business activities. Those who understand how to master both worlds can create and extract value in the most efficient and effective manner. Internet and digital technologies have created new opportunities for value creation. The Internet and internet technologies enable EC and EB. To understand the nature and scope of opportunities afforded by EC/EB it is helpful to unpack the various aspects underlying the broad phenomenon of the Internet. The main business uses of the Internet include: enabling internationalization; enabling communications; achieving competitive advantage; inter firm collaboration; as an information search and retrieval tool; for marketing and sales promotion; and the transmission of any type of data. Broadly speaking, the Internet presents three distinct types of opportunity. Firstly, it links companies directly to customers, suppliers, and other interested parties wherever they are in the world. Secondly, it lets companies bypass other players in an industry's value chain. Thirdly, it is a tool for developing and delivering new products and services to new customers.

The WWW makes it easier for small companies to compete on a world-wide basis. Global advertising costs, a traditional barrier to entry, are significantly reduced as the Web provides relatively cheap access to a global audience. Small companies offering specialized niche products can find the customers necessary to succeed through the worldwide reach of the Internet. Overall, the Internet's low cost communication permits organizations with limited capital to become global marketers at an early stage in their development. Further international marketing implications of the Internet include: the increasing standardization of prices across borders, or at least, the narrowing of price differentials as consumer awareness of prices in different countries grows; connecting end-users and producers directly will reduce the importance of traditional intermediaries in international marketing (i.e. agents and distributors); the Internet is a powerful tool for supporting networks, both internal and external to the organization; the 'Net' is an efficient medium for conducting worldwide market research, e.g. gaining feedback from customers; establishing on-line consumer panels; tracking individual customer behaviour, etc. E-marketing strategy leverages new technology to allow more effective ways of selling a business product to existing or new customers. Opportunities presented for marketing include: enhancing the selling process (making the sales effort more effective through better product and market targeting or by more successfully expressing the characteristics and benefits of the product); enhancing the customer's buying experience (providing support services that make the product easier to buy or better matched to the customer's needs); and enhancing the customer's usage experience (providing support services that increase customer satisfaction over the life cycle of product use). The major advantage of EC is the ability to undertake business at any time, from anywhere and at low cost. Throughout this section we have explored how globalization has opened up opportunity from which the firm may benefit. However, it is widely recognized that there are many winners and losers from the changes globalization brings. These are discussed in our final section.

EVALUATING GLOBALIZATION: 'WINNERS' AND 'LOSERS'

Throughout this chapter we have provided a number of perspectives on what globalization means. We conclude the chapter with a brief review of two further perspectives (anti globalist and globalist) that seek to evaluate globalization: who does it benefit: the world, or select parts of it? A multiple stakeholder perspective is required when evaluating the winners and losers. Stakeholders include consumers, producers, employees, individuals from developed, developing and less developed countries.

Anti-globalist perspective

Anti-globalization is a term most commonly ascribed to the political stance of people and groups who oppose certain aspects of globalization. Participants are united in opposition to the political power of large corporations, as exercised in trade agreements and elsewhere, which they say undermines democracy, the environment, labour rights, national sovereignty and the third world. Opponents to globalization may include trade unions, concerned with jobs at home and labour standards abroad; and farm lobby and other producer groups, determined to protect their vulnerable economic positions. In addition there are conservationists and environmentalists, fearful the liberal world economy will exacerbate perceived global environmental damage. There are consumer groups who worry about product safety; human rights groups, troubled by exploitation and church groups and campaigners for indigenous groups seeking to protect traditional ways of life. Finally, there are the nationalists – those with strong patriotic feelings, possibly believing in the superiority of their country over others. Such groups are typically self-interested, pursuing narrow goals, (Wolf 2005). The protest movement is fractured into many different and often conflicting communities of ideas. What they share is only what they are against argues Wolf. As the British journalist John Lloyd argues, many in the movement share 'the belief that globalization is essentially Western/American capitalism, which is an oppressive and impoverishing force'. According to Wolf the critics make the following objections to market-driven globalization:

- destroys the ability of states to regulate their economies, fiscal and monetary policy,
- undermines democracy,
- causes mass destitution and increased inequality within and between nations,

* creates an uneven distribution of wealth,
* is destroying the livelihood of peasant farmers,
* is depriving the poor of affordable medicines,
* is lowering real wages and labour standards and increasing economic insecurity everywhere,
* is destroying the environment,
* is permitting global financial markets to generate crises, and
* is destroying the variety of human cultures.

Others have additionally argued the gap between rich and poor nations has widened, and globalization leads to a proliferation of international crime. The International Forum on Globalization state that 'Globalization is the present worldwide drive toward a globalized economic system dominated by supranational corporate trade and banking institutions that are not accountable to democratic processes or national governments'.

BUSINESS IN DEBATE

Occupy Wall Street (OWS)

Occupy Wall Street is a people-powered movement started on September 17, 2011 in Liberty Square in Manhattan's Financial District, and has spread to over 100 cities in the United States and actions in over 1500 cities globally. 'OWS is fighting back against the corrosive power of major banks and multinational corporations over the democratic process and the role of Wall Street in creating an economic collapse that has caused the greatest recession in generations.' The movement aims to fight back against the richest 1 per cent of people 'that are writing the rules of an unfair global economy that is foreclosing on our future' (http://occupywallst.org/about/).

Occupy London

In London, Occupy London occupied the forecourt of St Paul's Cathedral, next to the London Stock Exchange. The group desire 'A future free from austerity, growing inequality, unemployment, tax injustice and a political elite who ignores its citizens' (http://occupylsx.org/). In October 2011, the group posted their initial statement that read, '...We want structural change towards authentic global equality. The world's resources must go towards caring for people and the planet, not the military, corporate profits or the rich. The present economic system pollutes land, sea and air, is causing massive loss of natural species and environments, and is accelerating humanity towards irreversible climate change... We stand in solidarity with the global oppressed.' In a further statement, 'United for Global Democracy', the organization states

that, 'united for global change, we demand global democracy: global governance by the people, for the people... Undemocratic international institutions are our global Mubarak, our global Assad, our global Gaddafi. These include: the IMF, the WTO, global markets, multinational banks, the G8/G20, the European Central Bank and the UN Security Council. Like Mubarak and Assad, these institutions must not be allowed to run people's lives without their consent. We are all born equal, rich or poor, woman or man. Every African and Asian is equal to every European and American. Our global institutions must reflect this, or be overturned. Today, more than ever before, global forces shape people's lives. Our jobs, health, housing, education and pensions are controlled by global banks, markets, tax-havens, corporations and financial crises. Our environment is being destroyed by pollution in other continents. Our safety is determined by international wars and international trade in arms, drugs and natural resources. We are losing control over our lives. This must stop. This will stop. The citizens of the world must get control over the decisions that influence them in all levels – from global to local. That is global democracy. That is what we demand today.' Finally, in their 'International Statement' they declare that 'Our global system is unsustainable. It is undemocratic and unjust, driven by profit in the interest of the few. An economic system based on infinite growth, but which relies on finite resources, is leading humanity and the environment to destruction. As long as this system remains in place, people of the world continue to suffer from an increasingly unfair share of income and wealth.'

Source: Reproduced with permission from Occupy Wall Street USA and Occupy London - http://occupylsx.org/

Opponents also question whether or not there is more security within the world, citing numerous local and regional conflicts. They also question health improvements, commenting on the rapid spread of diseases. Opponents to globalization believe that the beneficiaries are a minority. However, like many others, Wolf (2005:11) rejects the views of the critics because he believes the world would be worse if they had their way. In the next section we review the arguments in support of Globalization.

Globalist perspective

Globalization is the integration of economic activities, via markets (Wolf 2005); the driving forces are technological and policy changes, falling cost of transport and communications and greater reliance on market forces and there are cultural, social and political consequences. Rejecting the critics, Wolf (2005:3) asks why humanity would be better off if its economy was broken up into more than 200 entirely self-sufficient pieces. He develops this idea by asking us to imagine the welfare of Americans if their economy was fragmented among its 50 states, each with prohibitive barriers to movement of goods, services, capital and people. Wolf declares that, 'it cannot make sense to fragment the world economy' and that 'the failure of our world is not that there is too much globalization, but that there is too little'. According to Wolf, 'The potential for greater economic integration is barely tapped. We need more global markets, not fewer, if we want to raise the living standards of the poor of the world'; this is the central argument of his book. Globalism is an ideology based on the belief that people, goods and information ought to be able to cross national borders unrestricted; the attitude or policy of placing the interests of the entire world above those of individual nations. A Globalist is a person or organization advocating or practicing operations across national divisions. The globalist perspective recognizes a convergence of global products, markets, culture and economies. Under this perspective, consumers win as productive organizations can benefit from greater economies of scale and are thus able to reduce costs and price. Not only do consumers benefit but so too do workers in developing countries who may receive better wages from multinational companies than local firms can afford to pay. Hyperglobalization views the emergence of a global society and economy as inevitable, predicting the end of the nation state and the rise of global forms of political authority. Supporters of globalization list advantages such as:

* goods and people are transported with greater ease and speed
* the possibility of war between developed countries decreases
* free trade between countries increases
* cost and price reduction (see economies of scale and global production)
* increased access to knowledge, information and technology
* increased prosperity
* increased wages
* health improvements
* increased security
* greater choice
* the development of global initiatives (sharing and targeting resources worldwide)
* there is a propagation of democratic ideals

However, according to Global Economic Prospects 2007 (World Bank 2007) the benefits of globalization are likely to be uneven across regions and countries. The next wave of globalization will feature: the growing economic weight of developing countries, the potential for increased productivity by global production chains, and the accelerated diffusion of technology. Possible consequences of this globalization include: growing inequality, pressures in labour markets, and threats to the global commons (that which no one person or state may own or control and which is central to life – resources shared by all members of the international community, such as ocean

FIGURE 13.5
Evaluating globalization

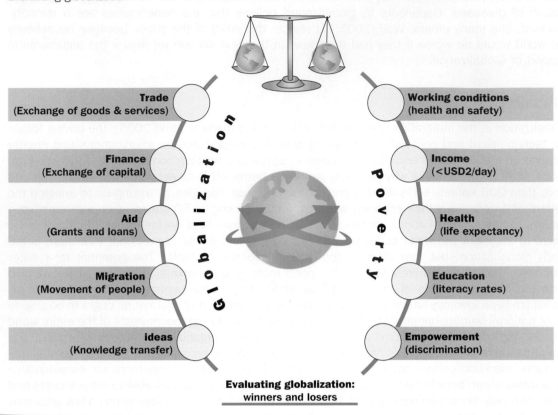

Trade
(Exchange of goods & services)

Finance
(Exchange of capital)

Aid
(Grants and loans)

Migration
(Movement of people)

ideas
(Knowledge transfer)

Working conditions
(health and safety)

Income
(<USD2/day)

Health
(life expectancy)

Education
(literacy rates)

Empowerment
(discrimination)

**Evaluating globalization:
winners and losers**

beds and the atmosphere). All of these developments, along with deepening economic interdependence, place a burden on the collective actions of the international community: to manage globalization or risk being overrun by it. Thus the uneven impact of globalization seems to create winners and losers. See Figure 13.5.

One key concern shared by many is the impact of globalization on poverty. The relationship between globalization and poverty is not well understood, (Goldin and Reinert 2012:1). For many, globalization may be a solution, for others it is seen as a cause of global poverty. The central message from Goldin and Reinert is that, with appropriate national and global policies, globalization can be important in alleviating global poverty. Goldin and Reinert evaluate the globalist and anti-globalist perspectives. They cite the globalist, Wolf (2004) who claimed that, 'a world integrated with the market should be highly beneficial to the vast majority of the world inhabitants'. In contrast, the International Forum on globalization claimed that 'while promoters of globalization proclaim that this model is the rising tide that will lift all boats, citizen movements find that it is instead lifting only yachts'. Goldin and Reinert also view globalization as a process and identify five economic dimensions: trade, finance, aid, migration and ideas (see Figure 13.5). Trade is the exchange of goods and services and finance involves the exchange of capital or money amongst countries. Aid is the transfer of loans and grants and migration takes place when persons move between countries, either temporarily or permanently, to seek education and employment or to escape adverse natural or political environments. Finally, ideas refer to the transmission of intellectual constructs (knowledge) in areas such as technology, management and governance. Similarly Goldin and Reinert consider poverty to be a multi-dimensional phenomenon and identify five dimensions: income, health, education, empowerment and working conditions. They believe that the most important measure of poverty is income poverty which prevents consumption of goods and services. Using World Bank terms, they define the poor as those living below US $2/day and the extremely poor living below US $1.25/day. Health deprivation can be assessed in terms of life expectancies; education can be assessed in terms of literacy rates, average years of schooling, or enrolment rates. A lack of empowerment limits an individual's ability to participate in society because of discrimination. Finally, many people spend half of their waking hours at work and as a consequence, the maintenance of safe and pleasant working conditions and the creation of jobs that contribute to individual and social well-being is highly important. Each of these policy dimensions can be assessed in absolute or in relative terms. See Figure 13.6.

Goldin and Reinert (2012) trace the relationship between globalization and poverty during the three stages of globalization (refer back to Figure 13.2) and conclude that, historically, globalization and global poverty can be either positively or negatively related to each other. Between stage one and two (a nationalist era), the decline in foreign trade was accompanied by a continued increase in global poverty. In the second half of the 20th century, trade as a percentage of GDP increased dramatically 'from approximately 6 to 23 per cent'. However, extreme poverty remained more or less the same over the period. Based on their analysis they concluded that simple statements about globalization and poverty are not helpful. Returning to the five primary economic dimensions of globalization (trade, finance, aid, migration and ideas) they suggest that increases in these dimensions, if managed in a way that supports development in all countries, can help to alleviate global poverty under certain conditions. Increased international trade can help to alleviate poverty through job creation; capital flows (for example in the form of FDI) support the generation of new employment and can provide education and training of host country workers whilst transferring new technology and knowledge. Foreign aid can be used to finance investment in infrastructure and services, supplement capabilities in health and education, and provide access to new ideas in the realm of policy. Historically migration has been the most important means for people to escape poverty (see Figure 13.6). In addition, migrants may also send part of their overseas earnings back home. However, migration is not without its downside in that it causes a 'brain drain', the loss of educated and highly skilled citizens to other countries. This has detrimental impacts, particularly in the case of what is known as 'medical brain drain'. Finally, ideas, in the form of knowledge transfer, have a powerful influence on development.

FIGURE 13.6
Net migration

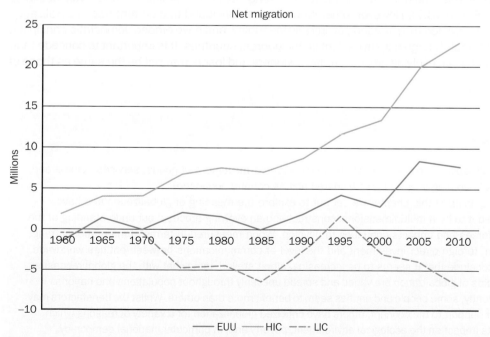

Source: The World Bank: Dataset name: (Aid Effectiveness) Data source (Net migration) 2012. With thanks to The World Bank.

FIGURE 13.7

Poverty headcount ratio at $2 a day (PPP) (% of population)

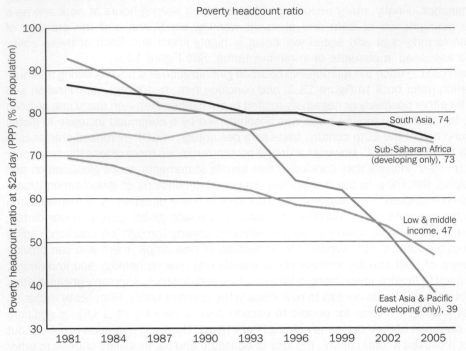

Source: The World Bank: Dataset name: (Poverty) Data source (Poverty headcount ratio) 2012. With thanks to The World Bank.

Such knowledge can impact upon production systems, education and health. Goldin and Reinert (2012:43) when commenting on globalization and poverty, recognize global poverty to be a widespread phenomenon that has finally shown some recent trend towards levelling off and even declining somewhat (see Figure 13.7). However, other studies have concluded that current trade liberalization rules and policies have led to increased poverty and inequality, and have eroded democratic principles, with a disproportionately large negative effect on the poorest countries. It is important to concede that, since globalization is an evolving process, today's winners and losers may not be the same as those of the future.

SUMMARY

- Businesses operate in a global context where the free movement of goods, services, capital and people is becoming less and less hindered across country boundaries.
- At the beginning of this chapter we set out to explore the meaning of globalization and have recognized it to be a multidimensional construct and an evolving process; our understanding of the drivers, forces and impacts continues to develop. When measured in terms of international trade, migration, foreign direct investment and the level of communications between entities worldwide, we can conclude that it seems to be increasing, albeit stalled somewhat with the global recession.
- The impacts of globalization are varied and spread unevenly throughout populations and nations. Consequently, some people and entities seem to benefit more than others. Whilst the benefactors may lend their support to the concept, others have criticized globalization for a variety of reasons which include its impact on the ecological environment, poverty and, in particular, national democracy.

- Globalization presents many challenges from a business perspective. Challenges, framed as threats or opportunities, exist in both home and 'foreign' country environments.
- Globalization and especially the continued fragmentation of production will increase the interconnectedness of the global economy. This will have many benefits, but may also increase the disruption that shocks can cause and will make it harder to interpret and explain the complexities of international trade and investment.
- A key challenge for global institutions and business generally will be to ensure that globalization brings a more even set of benefits, increasing prosperity for all.

REVISION QUESTIONS

1. Explain what is meant by globalization, discussing the globalization process, drivers and trends.
2. Discuss the changing nature of globalization: what is globalization, how new is it and what has led to its increase?
3. Evaluate the impact of globalization on markets, economies and national cultures highlighting implications for business.
4. Evaluate how globalization influences the national environment – debate the comment, 'there seems little doubt that governments have become less and less able fully to control events in their states in the face of globalization'.
5. Examine how organizations may respond (strategically) to the challenges and opportunities presented through globalization.
   – Discuss how organizations may gain cost/efficiency advantages through international strategies.
   – Evaluate the view that one day all organizations will think and act globally, standardizing operations, as if the world were one market without boundaries.
6. Evaluate globalization from a multiple stakeholder perspective, identifying the 'winners' and 'losers' – how do nation states benefit from globalization?
7. Explain what is meant by Internationalization, commenting on alternative market entry methods (contrast Internationalization with globalization).
8. Discuss the classification of multinationals, describing the multidomestic organization, global company and transnational enterprise (TNE).
9. Evaluate the contribution to society of the MNC.
10. 'Globalization is good for the world' – critically discuss.

DISCUSSION QUESTIONS

1. Read the Business in Action: Forbidden City: Starbucks 'tramples over Chinese culture' insert and then discuss it. This article attracted more than half a million readers and inspired more than 2700 commentaries, most of which were written in Chinese and sympathetic to Rui's cause. In July 2007, Starbucks closed its shop in the Forbidden City. Some bloggers suggested that the entry of Starbucks to the Forbidden City would ruin traditional Chinese culture. They believed that having a Starbucks within the Forbidden City made a mockery of Chinese traditional culture because an icon of a foreign mass-consumption fast food culture is discordant with a sacred symbol of Chinese civilization. There was strong support on preserving national cultural integrity in the age of global integration. Discuss the case. Can you list any similar stories? Do you think that this reflected nationalistic behaviour, a fear that global culture will contaminate local culture, or something else?
2. Read the World in Debate: Occupy Wall Street (OWS): Occupy London is part of the global movement for social and economic justice. The Occupy protests spread from Wall Street to

London to Bogota. Tens of thousands marched in New York, London, Frankfurt, Madrid, Rome, Sydney and Hong Kong as organizers aimed to 'initiate global change'. Some reports claimed there were protests in 951 cities in 82 countries. Is this an anti-globalist movement or the venting of frustration at the 2008 financial crisis and measures used for economic recovery – is it a genuine protest, suggesting a viable alternative or is it simply an attack on the current system?

3. Discuss the negative effects of globalization – how may they be lessened? Why do you think so many people oppose it? How should developed countries respond to the challenges presented by developing countries which have lower wage costs?

4. Critically discuss the roles of the IMF, WTO and World Bank in globalization: what changes might you argue for?

5. What might globalization look like in twenty years' time?

REFERENCES AND FURTHER READING

Abdelal, R. and Tedlow, R. S. (2003) 'Theodore Levitt's "The Globalization of Markets": An Evaluation after Two Decades', Harvard NOM Working Paper No. 03-20; Harvard Business School Working Paper No. 03-082

Bartlett, C. and Ghoshal, S. (1987) 'Managing across Borders: New Strategic Requirements', *Sloan Management Review*, Summer 87, Vol. 28 Issue 4, 7–17

Chiu, C., Gries, P., Torelli, C. and Cheng, S. (2011) 'Toward a Social Psychology of Globalization', *Journal of Social Issues*, 67 (4), 663–676

Department for Business, Innovation and Skills (2011) 'Global Context – How Has World Trade and Investment Developed, What's Next?', Trade and Investment Analytical Papers Topic 1 of 18, URN 11/722 © Crown copyright

European Commission,(2009) 'EU action against climate change – Leading global action to 2020 and beyond', European Commission: Luxembourg: Office for Official Publications of the European Communities

Goldin, I. and Reinert, K. (2012) *Globalization for Development – Meeting New Challenges*, Oxford University Press

Haynes, J., Hough, P., Malik, S. and Pettiford, L. (2010) *World Politics*, Longman

Hofstede, G. (1984) *Cultures Consequences – abridged*, Sage

Kelly, P. P. (2009) *International Business and Management*, Cengage Learning EMEA

Levitt, T. (1983) 'The globalization of markets', *Harvard Business Review*, May/Jun83, Vol. 61 Issue 3, 92–102

UNESCO (2010) 'UNESCO Science Report 2010', *United Nations Educational*, Paris Scientific and Cultural Organization, Paris

Wolf, D. (2005) *Why globalization works*, Yale University Press

World Bank (2011) 'Global Development Horizons 2011- Multipolarity: The New Global Economy', The International Bank for Reconstruction and Development / The World Bank

World Bank (2007) 'Global Economic Prospects: Overview and Global Outlook 2007', The International Bank for Reconstruction and Development / The World Bank

GLOSSARY

Anti-globalization A term most commonly ascribed to the political stance of people and groups who oppose certain aspects of globalization. Participants are united in opposition to the political power of large corporations, as exercised in trade agreements and elsewhere, which they say undermines democracy, the environment, labour rights, national sovereignty, the third world, and other concerns

Economic Integration The elimination of tariff and nontariff barriers to the flow of goods, services, and factors of production between a group of nations, or different parts of the same nation

Exporting Sale of products produced in one country to residents of another country

Foreign Direct Investment (FDI) A long-term commitment to marketing in a foreign nation through direct ownership of a foreign subsidiary or division

Franchizing A form of licensing granting the right to use certain intellectual property rights, such as trade names, brand names, designs, patents and copyrights

Geographic Scope Choice of countries in which to do business

Global an approach or philosophy that views the world as a single market

Globalist A Globalist is a person or organization advocating or practicing operations across national divisions

Globalization Growth and integration to a global or worldwide scale

Global Culture One world culture; the loss of national cultural diversity and the development of one culture to be experienced by all people

Global Strategy Assumes a single market and offers a standard product(s) to meet customer needs wherever they are located

Hyperglobalization Views the emergence of a global society and economy as inevitable, predicting the end of the nation state and the rise of global forms of political authority

Interconnectedness The state of being interconnected – connected reciprocally; a worldview which sees a oneness in all things (brought about by Improved communications across national borders)

Interdependence The extent to which the behaviour of one country depends upon others

Internationaliaation The process by which a company enters a foreign market

International Trade The purchase, sale, or exchange of goods and services across national borders

Licensing Occurs when a firm (the licensor) licenses the right to produce its product, use its production processes, or use its brand name or trademark to another firm (the licensee) In return for giving the licensee these rights, the licensor collects a royalty fee on every unit the licensee sells

Multidomestic Organization An organization that trades internationally as if the world were a collection of many different (country) entities

National Culture Culture, including a sense of identity and belonging, which distinguishes and unites people, linking them to a territorial homeland, usually a nation state

Transnational Corporation A firm that tries to simultaneously realize gains from experience curve economies, location economies, and global learning, while remaining locally responsive

CHAPTER CASE STUDY

The BRIC economies (the 'Big Four') – away from the developed economies towards the developing world

FIGURE 13.8

Trends in world influence – a focus on emerging markets: Fast-growing developing countries – the economies of China and India are considered to be the largest

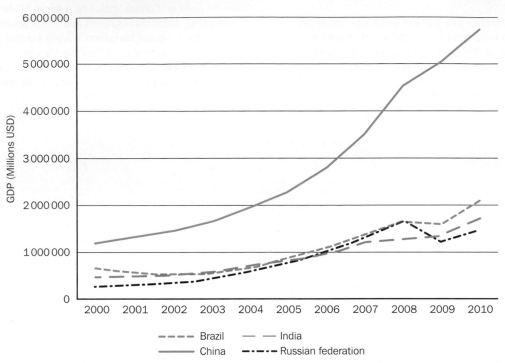

Source: With acknowledgment of United Nations Conferrence of Trade and Development (UNCTAD 2012)

Goldman Sach's Chief Economist Jim O'Neill (2001) argued that 'over the next 10 years, the weight of the Brics and especially China in world GDP will grow' and as a result 'world policy-making forums should be reorganized' in favour of the BRIC countries.[1] Since then this economic grouping has taken on greater significance. By 2008, the phenomenon was emerging as Russia hosted the first formal BRIC summit, a meeting of BRIC foreign ministers in Yekaterinburg. In July 2009, it followed this with a formal gathering of all four BRIC heads of state. The four countries discussed how they could better co-ordinate their affairs to gain greater influence. See Figure 13.8.

The chart above compares GDP (nominal) trends for BRIC economies. China is now ranked 2nd, Brazil 7th, India 9th and Russia 11th in terms of countries worldwide. In terms of world population, area, labour force, number of Internet users, and number of mobile phones, the four countries occupy a top 10 position. It is estimated that BRIC economies will overtake G7 economies by 2027[2].

BRIC is a grouping acronym that refers to the countries of Brazil, Russia, India and China, which are all deemed to be at a similar stage of newly advanced economic development.

Emerging giants like China are stronger, more economically competent and vastly richer argues Rana Foroohar. Whereas (2009) the richest economies (such as the US, Europe and Japan) are shrinking, others like China and India, are expanding. This growth gap is destined to reshape the economic future of the world. Rana further argues, as do many, that power is shifting toward the BRICs.

In April 2010, there was a call from the increasingly influential BRIC countries for more say in global financial institutions such as the World Bank and the International Monetary Fund.[3] 'Brazil, Russia, India and China have a fundamental role in creating a new international order that is more just, representative and safe', Brazilian President Luiz Inacio Lula da Silva said after holding talks with his counterparts. The group has campaigned for reforms since the global financial crisis of 2008, arguing the current system is unfairly dominated by advanced economies such as the United States, Japan and Europe.

BRIC has become a near ubiquitous financial term,[4] shaping how a generation of investors, financiers and policymakers view the emerging markets: companies have developed Brics business strategies; financial institutions now run Brics funds; business schools have Brics courses and authors of business text books frequently discuss the concept! 'The Brics concept ... that O'Neill created ... has become a strong brand'.

Ilyashenko[5] (2012) reported that 'China, Russia, India, Brazil and South Africa are gaining strength by the year, and their ability to influence global matters is growing'. At the New Delhi summit, the Brics countries also made a move towards unity on foreign policy issues. Following the summit, Radhika Desai, in the UK's *Guardian*, wrote, 'The west must wake up to the growing power of the Brics'. Desai[6] wrote, the Brics' political clout has grown with their importance to the world economy and the latest summit declared its intention to set up a development bank to mobilize 'resources for infrastructure and sustainable development projects in Brics and other emerging economies and developing countries, to supplement the existing efforts of multilateral and regional financial institutions for global growth and development.'

Source: (1) Rozhnov, K. (2010), 'Bric countries try to shift global balance of power', BBC News (Online) available from http://news.bbc.co.uk/1/hi/8620178.stm; (2) Foroohar, R. (2009), 'Power Up', The Newsweek/Daily Beast Mar 20, 2009 – available online at www.thedailybeast.com/newsweek/2009/03/20/power-up.html ; (3) FT (2010), 'Bric countries call for greater clout', April 16, 2010 available online www.ft.com/cms/s/0/01ee9300-4907-11df-8af4-00144feab49a.html; (4) Tett, G. (2010), 'The story of the Brics' *FT Magazine* January 15, 2010 available online atwww.ft.com/cms/s/0/112ca932-00ab-11df-ae8d-00144feabdc0.html; (5) Ilyashenko, A. (2012), 'BRICS moves towards greater unity', Russia and India report available from /indrus.in/articles/2012/04/10/brics_anticipates_new_ challenges_15293.html (6) Desai, R. (2012), 'The west must wake up to the growing power of the Brics', *The Guardian* 2 April 2012 available from www.guardian.co.uk/commentisfree/2012/apr/02/west-powerbrics-world-bank

Questions

- Compare the BRIC's contribution to world GDP with that of other major global economies.
- How do the BRIC economies differ? In what ways are they similar? What unites them?
- To some critics, the fuss about BRICs is overblown. Discuss.
- There are and have been numerous forecasts about the BRIC economies. Some economists have suggested it is ridiculous to make far out forecasts (such as 30 or 40 years ahead) – what do you think?
- Why do you think most of the BRICs emerged from the crisis well, relative to the economies of the western world?
- Is there much evidence that the BRICs countries are collaborating today in practical terms? How might they influence worldwide business?

INDEX